Catherine de Medici

Catherine de Medici

RENAISSANCE QUEEN
OF FRANCE

Leonie Frieda

Fourth Estate
An Imprint of HarperCollins*Publishers*

First published in Great Britain in 2003 by Weidenfeld & Nicolson

CATHERINE DE MEDICI. Copyright © 2003 by Leonie Frieda. All rights reserved.
Printed in the United States of America. No part of this book may be used or
reproduced in any manner whatsoever without written permission except in the case
of brief quotations embodied in critical articles and reviews. For information, address
HarperCollins Publishers Inc., 10 East 53rd Street, New York, NY 10022.

HarperCollins books may be purchased for educational, business, or sales
promotional use. For information, please write: Special Markets Department,
HarperCollins Publishers Inc., 10 East 53rd Street, New York, NY 10022.

FIRST U.S. EDITION

Printed on acid-free paper

Library of Congress Cataloging-in-Publication Data is available upon request.

ISBN 0-06-074492-8

For Lil' and Jake
with love

Contents

Illustrations

A 'magnificence' in Paris in 1573 in honour of the Polish ambassadors, celebrating Catherine's son Henri III's election as King of Poland. (Uffizi, Florence)[3]

Charles IX as King. (School of Clouet, c. 1572, Musée Condé, Chantilly)[2]

Hercules, later Francis, Duke of Alençon; the runt of Catherine's litter. By Clouet, 1561.[2]

King Philip II of Spain and his wife Elisabeth, Catherine's eldest daughter.[1]

Catherine's favourite son, the Duke of Anjou, shortly before his accession as Henri III. By François Ovesnel (Louvre, Paris)[2]

The rival factions: Anne de Montmorency, Constable of France, and Henry II's mentor. By Corneille de Lyon. (Musée Condé, Chantilly)[2]

François, 2nd Duke of Guise: soldier-statesman who masterminded the 1559 coup. By Clouet (Louvre, Paris)[4]

The Catholic Paladin: Henri, 3rd Duke of Guise, '*le balafré*', later known as 'The King of Paris'. (Musée de la Ville de Paris, Musée Carnavalet, Paris)[2]

Between pages 296 and 297:

Admiral Gaspard de Coligny, leader of the Huguenots. School of Clouet, c. 1550. (Musée Condé, Chantilly)[2]

The exquisite Château of Chenonceau.[2]

A romanticised portrayal of the 1561 Colloquy of Poissy. (Bibliothèque de l'Histoire du Protestantisme, Paris)[2]

Catherine as Queen of France, the image of majesty. (Palazzo Pitti, Florence)[2]

A nineteenth-century depiction of the wedding celebrations of Henri de Bourbon, King of Navarre (later Henri IV) and Margot, some days before the Massacre of St Bartholemew.[2]

Catherine standing over corpses after the massacre of St Bartholemew. By François Dubois. (Musée des Beaux Arts, Paris)[4]

The Valois dynasty ended with the assassination of Henri III in 1589, depicted in this contemporary engraving.[2]

The future: Henry IV, King of France and Navarre. (Musée de la Ville de Paris, Musée Carnavalet, Paris)[2]

The 'gisants' of Henry II and Catherine at the Cathedral of St Denis.[2]

The author and the publishers offer their thanks to the following for their kind permission to reproduce images:

1   Bibliothèque Nationale, Paris
2   Giraudon/Bridgeman Art Library
3   Scala
4   AKG Images, London

The Italian peninsula during the latter half of the sixteenth century

Abbreviations:

Monf. **Monferrato** (to Mantua)
G. **Genoa**
L. **Lunigiana** (Imperial fief)
Ist. **Istria** (to Venice)
C. **Crema** (to Venice)
Lan. **Langhe** (Imperial fiefs)
Gar. **Garfagnana** (to Lucca)
Sal. **Saluzzo** (to France)
Cas. **Castro** (to Parma)

PIEDMONT

Trento (Austria)

HOLY ROMAN EMPIRE

DUCHY OF MILAN (Spain)

REPUBLIC OF VENICE

Monf.

Ist.

MANTUA

Sal.

Monf.
Lan.

PARMA

Modena (Ferrara)

FERRARA

REPUBLIC OF GENOA (Spain)

Gar.

Papal States

G. G.

Finale (Spain)

MASSA

LUCCA

TUSCANY

URBINO

Piombino (Spain)

Siena (Tuscany)

PAPAL STATES

Corsica (Spain)

Presidial State (Spain)

Cas.

Adriatic Sea

KINGDOM OF NAPLES (Spain)

SARDINIA (Spain)

Tyrrhenian Sea

N
W   E
S

SICILY

0   50   100   150 miles
0   50   100   150   200 km

Mediterranean Sea

France during the latter half of the sixteenth century

N
W — E
S

Calais
Boulogne
FLANDERS
Antwer
BRUSSELS
NET
Cambrai
Cateau-
Cambrési
PICARDY
Guise

La Havre
Rouen
Chantilly
Rheims
St-Denis
ILE-DE
Dormans
Poissy
Meaux
Chalon
St-Germain
St-Maur-les-Fossés
Anet
PARIS
Montceaux
Dreux
FRANCE
Chartres
Fontainebleau
Troye

NORMANDY
ALENÇON
MAINE

BRITTANY

Orléans
R. Loire
Auxerre

Angers
Amboise
Blois
Tours
Chenonceaux
NIVERNAIS
Nantes
ANJOU
TOURAINE
BERRY
Bourges
Nevers
Moncontour
Moulins

POITOU
BOURBON

La Rochelle
St-Jean-d'Angély
Jarnac
LEME
Cognac
Angoulême
ANGOU
LIMOUSIN
AUVERGNE
SAINTONGE

Bay of Biscay

Coutras
PERIGORD
Bordeaux
Bergerac
GUYENNE

Nérac

LANGUEDO
Bayonne
Principality of
Béarn and
Kingdom of
Navarre
Toulouse
Montpellier
BASSE-
NAVARRE
HAUTE
NAVARRE
GASCONY

SPAIN

0   50   100   150   200 miles

0   100   200   300 km

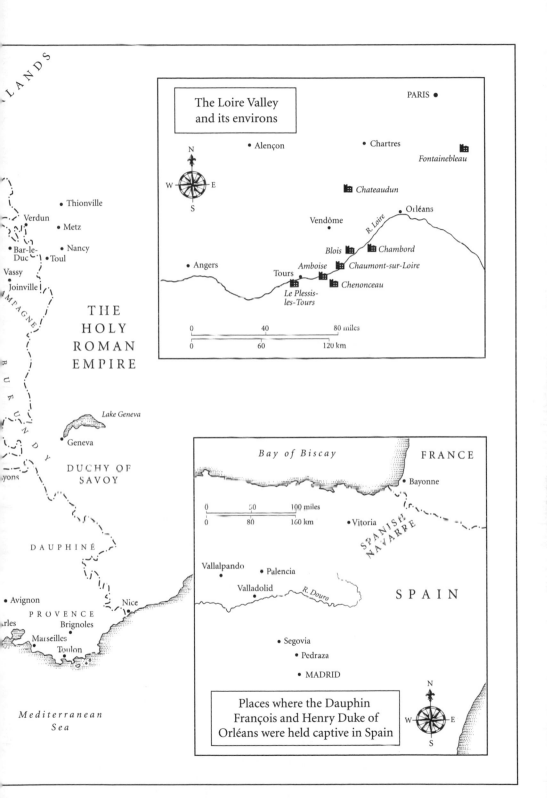

LANDS

• Thionville

Verdun
• Metz

• Bar-le-
Duc   • Nancy
        • Toul

Vassy

Joinville

CHAMPAGNE

BURGUNDY

THE
HOLY
ROMAN
EMPIRE

Lake Geneva

• Geneva

DUCHY OF
SAVOY

Lyons

DAUPHINÉ

• Avignon

PROVENCE
Arles   Brignoles

• Marseilles
  Toulon

Nice

Mediterranean
Sea

The Loire Valley and its environs

PARIS •

• Alençon   • Chartres

                                          Fontainebleau

N
W — E
S

                              Chateaudun

                                          • Orléans
            Vendôme   R. Loire
                      Blois   Chambord
• Angers   Amboise   Chaumont-sur-Loire
            Tours
                              Chenonceau
         Le Plessis-
         les-Tours

0   40   80 miles
0   60   120 km

Places where the Dauphin François and Henry Duke of Orléans were held captive in Spain

Bay of Biscay   FRANCE

                                          • Bayonne

0   50   100 miles
0   80   160 km

                        • Vitoria   SPANISH
                                          NAVARRE

Vallalpando   • Palencia

        Valladolid   R. Douro   SPAIN

                • Segovia
                • Pedraza

                • MADRID

                                    N
                                W — E
                                    S

THE HOUSE OF FRANCE

*appear more than once

Louis IX (Saint Louis)
1214–70

Philippe III

(branch of Valois)

Charles V
1336–80

Charles VI
1368–1422

Louis of Orléans
1336–80

Charles VII
1403–61

Charles of Orléans

Jean of Angoulême
1336–80

Louis XI
1423–83

Louis XII
1462–1525

Louis of Angoulême

Charles VIII
1470–96

Charles of Angoulême
= Louise of Savoy

Claude of France
1499–1524
= Francis I
1494–1547

Marguerite of Angouléme
= Henri d'Albret
King of Navarre

Jeanne d'Albret
Queen of Navarre
= Antoine de Bourbon

Henry IV*
King of Navarre
1553–1610
=(1) Marguerite (Margot)*
(2) Maria de Medici

Catherine

Louis XIII

Robert de Clermont (6th son)
=Beatrice de Bourbon

branch of Bourbon-Vendôme

Jean Comte de Vendôme

Francis de
Bourbon-Vendôme

Jeanne de Bourbon-Vendôme
= Jean de La Tour

Madeleine
= Lorenzo II de Medici
(Duke of Urbino)

Antoinette
de Bourbon
Duchess of Guise

Charles de
Bourbon-Vendôme

Louis I
Prince de Condé
d. 1569

Charles
Cardinal de Bourbon
'Charles X' *d.* 1590

Charles
Comte de Soissons

Henri I
Prince de Condé
d. 1569
= (1) Marie of Clèves

Henry II =
1519–59

**CATHERINE DE MEDICI
1519–89**

Francis II (1544–1560) = Mary Stuart Queen of Scots	Claude (1547–75) = Charles Duke of Lorraine	Charles IX (1550–74) = Elizabeth of Austria	Marguerite* (Margot) (1553–1615) = Henry of Navarre *	Victoire 1556

Elisabeth
(1545–68)
= Philip II
King of Spain

Christina
(1565–1636)
= Ferdinand I

Louis
1549

Henri III
(1551–89)
= Louise de
Vaudémont-
Lorraine

François-Hercules
Duke of Alençon
(1555–84)

Jeanne
1556

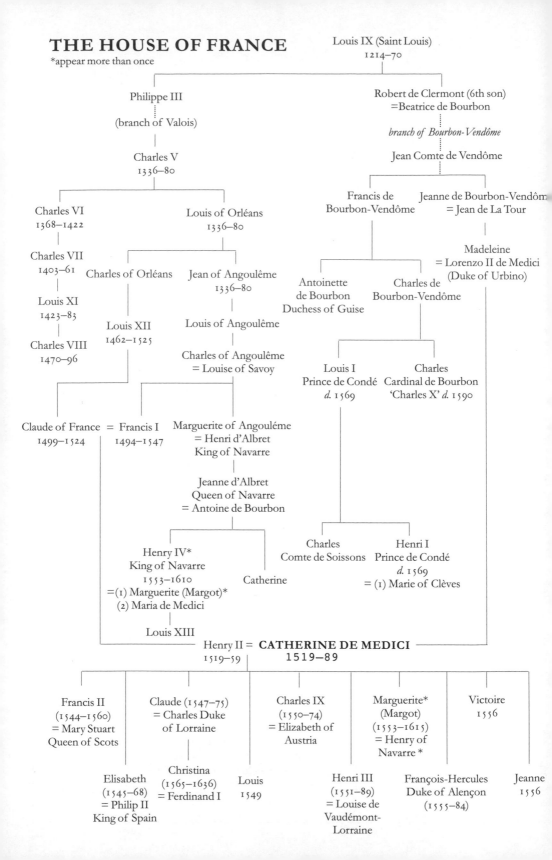

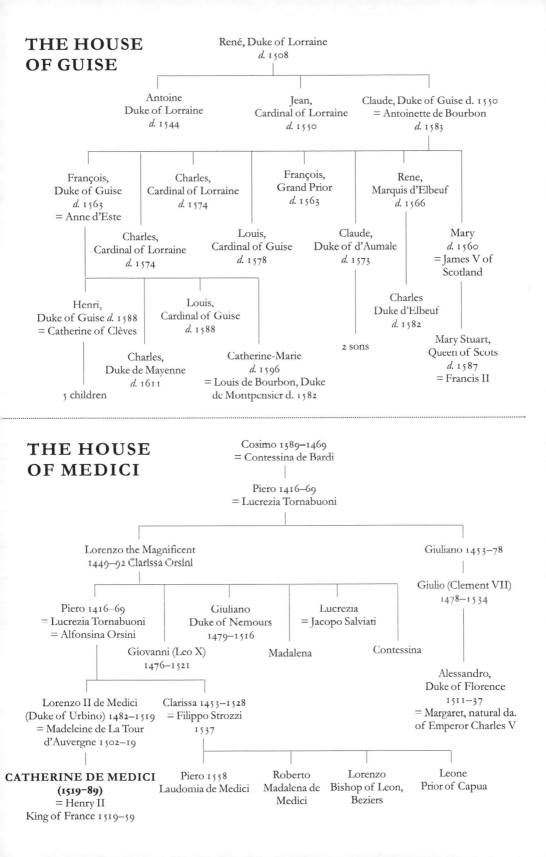

THE HOUSE OF GUISE

René, Duke of Lorraine
d. 1508

- Antoine, Duke of Lorraine d. 1544
- Jean, Cardinal of Lorraine d. 1550
- Claude, Duke of Guise d. 1550 = Antoinette de Bourbon d. 1583
  - François, Duke of Guise d. 1563 = Anne d'Este
  - Charles, Cardinal of Lorraine d. 1574
  - François, Grand Prior d. 1563
  - Rene, Marquis d'Elbeuf d. 1566
  - Charles, Cardinal of Lorraine d. 1574
  - Louis, Cardinal of Guise d. 1578
  - Claude, Duke of d'Aumale d. 1573
  - Mary d. 1560 = James V of Scotland
    - Henri, Duke of Guise d. 1588 = Catherine of Clèves
    - Louis, Cardinal of Guise d. 1588
    - Charles Duke d'Elbeuf d. 1582
    - 2 sons
    - Mary Stuart, Queen of Scots d. 1587 = Francis II
      - Charles, Duke de Mayenne d. 1611
      - Catherine-Marie d. 1596 = Louis de Bourbon, Duke de Montpensier d. 1582
      - 5 children

THE HOUSE OF MEDICI

Cosimo 1389–1469 = Contessina de Bardi

Piero 1416–69 = Lucrezia Tornabuoni

- Lorenzo the Magnificent 1449–92 Clarissa Orsini
  - Piero 1416–69 = Lucrezia Tornabuoni = Alfonsina Orsini
  - Giuliano Duke of Nemours 1479–1516
  - Lucrezia = Jacopo Salviati
  - Giovanni (Leo X) 1476–1521
  - Madalena
  - Contessina
    - Lorenzo II de Medici (Duke of Urbino) 1482–1519 = Madeleine de La Tour d'Auvergne 1502–19
    - Clarissa 1453–1528 = Filippo Strozzi 1537
- Giuliano 1453–78
  - Giulio (Clement VII) 1478–1534
  - Alessandro, Duke of Florence 1511–37 = Margaret, natural da. of Emperor Charles V

- **CATHERINE DE MEDICI (1519–89)** = Henry II King of France 1519–59
- Piero 1558 Laudomia de Medici
- Roberto Madalena de Medici
- Lorenzo Bishop of Leon, Beziers
- Leone Prior of Capua

Principal Characters

House of Valois

Francis I, King of France, father-in-law to Catherine de Medici

Marguerite of Angoulême, sister of Francis I, wife of Henri d'Albret, King of Navarre

Dauphin Francis, eldest son of Francis I

Henry II, King of France, second son of Francis I, formerly Duke of Orléans, husband of Catherine de Medici

Marguerite of Valois, sister of Henry II, wife of Emanuel-Philibert, Duke of Savoy

Francis II, King of France, eldest son of Henry II and Catherine de Medici

Charles IX, King of France, third son of Henry II and Catherine de Medici

Henri III, King of France, Duke of Anjou, fourth son of Henry II and Catherine de Medici

Duke of Alençon, youngest son of Henry II and Catherine de Medici

Elisabeth of Valois, daughter of Henry II and Catherine de Medici, wife of Philip II of Spain

Claude of Valois, daughter of Henry II and Catherine de Medici, wife of Charles, Duke of Lorraine

Marguerite of Valois (Margot), daughter of Henry II and Catherine de Medici, wife of Henry IV, King of France

House of Medici

Cosimo the Elder

Lorenzo The Magnificent, grandson of Cosimo the Elder

Guiliano de Medici, brother of Lorenzo the Magnificent

Lorenzo II de Medici, Duke of Urbino, grandson of Lorenzo The Magnificent, Catherine de Medici's father

Madeleine de La Tour d'Auvergne, wife of Lorenzo II, Catherine de Medici's mother

Pope Leo X, son of Lorenzo The Magnificent

Pope Clement VII, Giulio de Medici, illegitimate son of Giuliano de Medici, cousin of Pope Leo X

Alessandro de Medici, Duke of Florence, illegitimate son of Pope Clement VII

Ippolito de Medici, illegitimate nephew of Pope Leo X

Cosimo I, Grand Duke of Tuscany, distant kinsman of Catherine de
Medici

Maria de Medici, granddaughter of Cosimo I, second wife of Henry IV,
King of France

Piero Strozzi, nephew of Lorenzo II

Leone Strozzi, younger brother of Piero Strozzi

House of Bourbon

Antoine de Bourbon, King of Navarre, First Prince of the Blood, father
of Henry IV, King of France, husband of Jeanne d'Albret

Jeanne d'Albret, Queen of Navarre, wife of Antoine de Bourbon,
daughter of Marguerite of Angoulême

Louis de Condé, Prince of the Blood, younger brother of Antoine de
Bourbon

Charles, Cardinal de Bourbon, Prince of the Blood, became the pretender
Charles X and younger brother of Antoine de Bourbon

Henry IV, King of France, son of Antoine de Bourbon and Jeanne
d'Albret, husband of (1) Marguerite de Valois (Margot) and (2) Maria
de Medici

Henri de Condé, Prince of the Blood, son of Louis de Condé

House of Habsburg

Charles V, Holy Roman Emperor, formerly Charles I of Spain

Ferdinand I of Austria, Holy Roman Emperor, brother of Charles V

Philip II of Spain, son of Charles V, whose wives included Mary I of
England and Elisabeth of Valois

Maximilian II of Austria, Holy Roman Emperor, son of Ferdinand I

Elisabeth of Austria, daughter of Maximilian II, wife of Charles IX

House of Tudor

Henry VIII, King of England

Edward VI, King of England, son of Henry VIII

Mary I, Queen of England, daughter of Henry VIII, wife of Philip II of
Spain

Elizabeth I, Queen of England, daughter of Henry VIII

House of Guise

Claude, 1st Duke of Guise, son of René, Duke of Lorraine

François, 2nd Duke of Guise, eldest son of Claude, 1st Duke of Guise

Anna d'Este, (1) wife of François, 2nd Duke of Guise, (2) of the Duke
of Nemours

Charles, Cardinal of Lorraine, second son of Claude, 1st Duke of Guise

Claude, Duke d'Aumale, fifth son of Claude, 1st Duke of Guise
Mary of Guise, daughter of Claude, 1st Duke of Guise, wife of James V of Scotland
Mary, Queen of Scots, daughter of Mary of Guise and James V of Scotland, wife of Francis II of France
Henri, 3rd Duke of Guise, son of François, 2nd Duke of Guise
Louis, Cardinal of Guise, brother of Henri, 3rd Duke of Guise
Louise de Vaudémont, great-niece of Claude, 1st Duke of Guise, wife of Henri III, King of France

House of Montmorency
Anne de Montmorency, Constable of France
Gaspard de Coligny, nephew of Anne de Montmorency
Ôdet, Cardinal de Châtillon, elder brother of Gaspard de Coligny
François d'Andelot, youngest brother of Gaspard de Coligny
François de Montmorency, eldest son of Anne de Montmorency
Henri Damville de Montmorency, second son of Anne de Montmorency

Other
Duchess d'Étampes, mistress of Francis I
Diane de Poitiers, Duchess of Valentinois, mistress of Henry II
Count Gabriel de Montgomery, accidental killer of Henry II
Cosimo Ruggieri, necromancer to Catherine de Medici
Ambroise Paré, court surgeon
Michel de L'Hôpital, Catherine de Medici's Chancellor
Marie-Catherine de Gondi, Catherine de Medici's closest friend, lady-in-waiting, Treasurer and Administrator of Catherine's buildings
Michel de Nostradamus, seer to Catherine de Medici

Introduction and Acknowledgements

Catherine de Medici has variously been called 'The Maggot from Italy's Tomb', 'The Black Queen' and 'Madame La Serpente'. To many she is the very incarnation of evil. It is, I believe, as mistaken a judgement as it is bigoted. Yet it is not far removed from the overall verdict of history on one of the most remarkable women of the sixteenth century.

To the extent that Catherine's name evokes any response today, it is as a Florentine, a patron of the Renaissance, and as a poisoner and intriguer of the stamp of Lucrezia Borgia, with whom she is often confused. Throughout her life her enemies condemned her for her country of origin, described by Thomas Nashe as 'The Academie of man-slaughter, the sporting place of murther, the Apothecary-shop of poison for all Nations'. Insofar as she is connected to any historical event in the public imagination, it is the Saint Bartholomew's Day Massacre in Paris, that infamous act of violence that so stained the name of the House of Valois and of Catherine in particular. When the admittedly terrible events of 24 August 1572 in Paris are placed in their proper historical context, however, I believe they can be explained in terms of a surgical operation that went wrong rather than an act of premeditated genocide.

During the course of her life, this indomitable woman faced a series of personal tragedies and setbacks, and when not being condemned as evil, she is pitied for the seemingly endless series of blows she suffered. Orphaned at birth and imprisoned during childhood, her marriage to Henry of Orléans (later King Henry II of France), whom she loved passionately, caused her years of unhappiness as she was ignored by him in favour of his mistress, the mesmerising Diane de Poitiers. After a decade of childlessness and near-repudiation, Catherine finally produced ten children – who were almost without exception rotten, sickly and corrupt. The sudden death of her husband brought this forty-year-old political neophyte to the centre of power and, forced by necessity, she became the skilful and doughty defender of her dynasty and adopted country.

Rather than deeming her evil, it would be equally mistaken to label Catherine as a victim of her terrible circumstances. She was, above all, a courageous survivor and a true product of her times. The life, the character, the personal details, the contradictions, the passions, the strengths, the weaknesses and the sheer guts of this incomparable woman constitute the main thread of my story. Catherine was not guided by religious beliefs, nor by ideological conviction. A sceptic at heart and a pragmatist by nature, neither morals nor remorse encumbered her fight for the survival of her children, her dynasty and France. To understand this complex woman one must recognise that to Catherine these three represented the same thing. After her husband's death, and based on her hitherto silent observation of the political and religious struggles in France, she tried to steer a middle course between the opposing parties. Yet if reason and conciliation failed, she did not hesitate to avail herself of the 'regalian right of summary execution' to preserve the kingdom.

I am, of course, not the first person to attempt to tell Catherine's story objectively. I would like to take this opportunity fully to acknowledge the invaluable recent contributions made by M. Ivan Cloulas and Professor Robert Knecht to the canon of Catherine de Medici scholarship. It is only by standing on the shoulders of great historians such as they that biographers can discern the landscape and, in my case, the genetic imperative that led Catherine to advance the interests of her husband and progeny.

In her biography of William the Silent, the historian C. V. Wedgwood wrote, 'History is lived forwards but is written in retrospect. We know the end before we consider the beginning and we can never wholly recapture what it was to know the beginning only.' This book has been written with that seminal historiographical fact in mind: the reader will be presented with Catherine's often limited political and personal options. How would we, or could we, have acted otherwise?

There is much that is absurdly ultra-nationalist about the contempt that many French writers have, until recently, expressed for the Italian-born Queen of France. That she was a woman who wielded power in the name of her feeble sons, was foreign-born but ruled France, and of non-royal blood but nonetheless became Queen, has been enough to condemn her in the eyes of many eighteenth and nineteenth-century French historians. Her constant struggle first to accommodate the Huguenots and later to contain their threat, culminating in the Massacre of Saint Bartholomew, has damned her in the eyes of both Catholic and Protestant writers and propagandists. There is also much that is factually inaccurate in their melodramatic accounts of Catherine's alleged wickedness, her appetite for vengeance, the quaint tales of her cabinet of poisons and above all a simple but lethal lust for power.

I have endeavoured to write a biography that redresses history's almost entirely anti-Catherine bias and objectively sees her for what she was: a woman of intelligence, courage and indefatigable spirit who did her best for her beloved if adopted country when it was – through no fault of hers – beset by a long series of dangers rarely experienced by any nation state before or since.

Catherine was a woman of fascinating contradictions, both a pragmatist and an idealist. Despite her own adherence to the Roman Church she approached the differences between Catholic and Protestant as though they could be resolved by sensible discussion. Her surprising capacity for sentimentality was matched by an ability to detach herself ruthlessly when required. Though usually a practical and enlightened woman, she sought solace and guidance from her soothsayers, astrologers and the occult. Her love of the arts, sumptuous grandeur and exploration of new ideas lay alongside her knowledge that behind the curtain of the glorious Court displays that she created, there was also a place for judicious bloodlettings, vendettas and the assassin's dagger.

After the death of her adored husband, Henry II, Catherine wore her widow's weeds with pride. As the famous beauties of her 'flying squadron' seduced information from their admirers at Court, Catherine stood, majestic and veiled, her perpetually black-clad figure a stark counterpoint to the nymphs in white. Mysterious and enigmatic when she wanted to be, the Queen Mother exasperated many of her political opponents.

The sixteenth century is notable for many reasons, but in particular the number of powerful women who dominated it. Of John Knox's 'monstrous regiment' the most obvious and familiar examples to English readers are Elizabeth I, Mary Tudor and Mary, Queen of Scots. Less well known to us are Marie of Guise, regent of Scotland, Margaret of Austria, regent of the Spanish Netherlands, Margaret of Parma – who also ruled there from 1559 to 1567 – and Juana 'La Loca' (the mad), daughter of Ferdinand and Isabella of Spain, who inherited the throne of Castile from her mother in 1504. Italy also produced fascinating women such as Isabella d'Este, the beautiful Duchess of Mantua, who played a central cultural role not only in her husband's duchy, but far beyond it too. There is no doubt, however, that by far the most important, notorious and influential Italian woman of this period was Catherine de Medici, daughter of Florence and Queen of France.

This book could not have been written without the help and active collaboration of a large number of people who have generously given of their expertise and time with no thought to recompense or reward. I am tremendously grateful to them. Foremost among them is M. Ivan Cloulas, Conservateur Général Honoraire at the Archives Nationales in Paris and his staff. M. Cloulas encouraged me to undertake this project. He and his staff have been unfailingly efficient and courteous. Professor Robert Knecht's superb scholarship and works on Catherine de Medici, King

Francis I and sixteenth-century France have proved a huge source of inspiration to me.

Along with M. Cloulas and Professor Knecht I would like to thank my friend of many years Mr Paul Johnson, particularly for his invaluable help both on the Renaissance and on the religious questions prevalent in sixteenth-century France. The Earl of Oxford and Asquith has also guided me through the theological minefields of the day and has helped and encouraged me in countless other ways. Similarly, Count Dr Niccolò Capponi has been instrumental in the research for this book, both through making available his peerless contacts in Florence and for the many conversations I have had with him and providing access to his private family archive.

I should like to take this opportunity to thank the following for their help by answering questions, directing my research and providing fascinating insights into Catherine de Medici, her life and times: Dr Franca Arduini, Director of the Biblioteca Medicea Laurenziana; Countess Brooke Capponi; Dr Alessandra Contini, Archivio di Stato di Firenze; Mr Robin Harcourt Williams, Librarian and Archivist, Hatfield House; Dr Giovanna Lazzi, Biblioteca Riccardiarna; Dr Sabina Magrini, the Public Relations Office, Biblioteca Medicea Laurenziana; Ms Rebecca Milner, Curator, Victoria and Albert Museum; Countess Dr Beatrice Paolozzi Strozzi, Director, Bargello Museum; Ms Helen Pearson, Assistant Curator, Department of Furniture, Textiles and Fashion, Victoria and Albert Museum; Dr Paola Pirolo, Biblioteca Nazionale Centrale di Firenze; Dr Renato Scapecchi, Biblioteca Nazionale Centrale di Firenze; Dr Margaret Scott, History of Dress, Courtauld Institute; Dr Marilena Tamassia, Gabinetto Fotografico, Uffizi Museum.

One of the most enjoyable aspects of writing this book was my visits to the châteaux built or used by Catherine. For their kindness during these visits – where I was often shown rooms that are not on general public display – I would very much like to thank Mme Gun Nihlèn Patou, Conferencière de la RMN at Fontainebleau; M. Eric Thierry Crepin Leblond, Conservateur Général du Château de Blois and his staff; M. Voison, Conservateur du Château de Chenonceau and his staff; M. Sueau, Secrétaire Général du Château d'Amboise and his staff; and Mme de Gourcuff, Administrateur du Château de Chambord and her staff.

A large number of friends have lent me books from their private collections, discussed different aspects of Catherine's life from their expert viewpoints, and have generally made an invaluable input to my work in a host of different ways, and I would like to thank: H.E. The French Ambassador M. Daniel Bernard, Marchesa Ginevra di Bruti Liberati, The Marquis and Marquise Pierre d'Angosse, H.E. The Portuguese Ambassador M. José Gregorio Faria, Lady Antonia Fraser, Mr Mark

Getty, Sir John Guinness, HRH Princess Michael of Kent, Viscount Lambton, Mrs Robert Nadler, Dr Guy O'Keeffe, Mr Andrew Ponton, H.E. the Spanish Ambassador the Marques de Tamarón, Lord Thomas of Swynnerton, Lady Anne Somerset, Professor Norman Stone, The Hon. Mrs Claire Ward, Lord Weidenfeld and Count Adam Zamoyski.

My editor at Weidenfeld and Nicolson, Ion Trewin's kindness and loyalty throughout this project have been heroic. My gratitude also goes to my publisher, Anthony Cheetham, and to my agent, Georgina Capel, whose belief in 'Catherine' never wavered. I salute Mrs Ilsa Yardley for her superb copy-editing, and the indispensable Victoria Webb, my assistant editor. I must also thank Tom Graves for his inspired picture research.

Finally, my love and thanks go to Andrew Roberts for his unfailing tenderness, punctuation, good advice, and for keeping me going when I wanted to give back the money and run; and to my parents and family, especially Lil' and Jake, God bless you for everything you have given me.

Leonie Frieda
October 2003

www.leoniefrieda.com

Author's Note

In Italian an apostrophe appears after the 'de' in de' Medici. For ease of reading I have excised it.

In this book there is a myriad of Henrys: for ease of reference I have designated Henry II of France with a 'y', the others are spelt in the French manner – Henri.

PROLOGUE

Death of a King

Cursed be the magician who predicted
so evilly and so well

June–July 1559

On the late afternoon of Friday, 30 June 1559 a long splinter of wood from a jousting lance pierced the eye and brain of King Henry II of France. The poisonous wound bloated his face, slowly robbing him of sight, speech and reason, and after ten days of suffering he died at the Château des Tournelles in Paris. His death was not only tragic – it would prove calamitous.

The jousting had been part of celebrations to mark the signing in April of the Treaty of Cateau-Cambrésis, which brought to an end France's and Spain's ruinous series of wars over Italy. Many dismayed Frenchmen believed Italy had been given away through the mere stroke of a pen and no one felt this more keenly than Henry's Florentine wife, Catherine de Medici, whose hopes of recovering her lost patrimony vanished with the peace. Yet she took one consolation from the treaty: that her eldest daughter Elisabeth would marry the most eligible *parti* in Europe, King Philip II of Spain. A further sweetener provided a husband for Henry's spinster sister and Catherine's closest friend, Marguerite, who at the age of thirty-six had been considered practically unmarriageable. She was to wed Philip's ally, Emmanuel-Philibert, Duke of Savoy, a hearty soldier with the unpromising nickname of 'Iron-head'.

No time was lost in arranging the weddings. Determined to show Philip that France remained undiminished despite her Italian sacrifice, Henry – although choked with war debts – had borrowed over 1 million écus 'to defray the setting out of these triumphs'.* A vigorous and robust man, he excelled at the joust and had arranged the five-day contest largely to show off his own skill. Both Henry and Catherine were, not surprisingly, disappointed when Philip – a widower since the recent death of the English Queen, Mary Tudor, the previous year – announced that he

---

* The French monetary system in the sixteenth century was complex. The most important coin was the écu d'or (crown). Depending on the exact date, this was made up of approximately 2 livres tournais. The livre was divided into 20 sous, which in turn was divided into 12 derniers.

would not be coming to Paris himself. Characteristically, the punctilious monarch offered tradition as his explanation, saying, 'Custom demands that the Kings of Spain should not go to fetch their wives but that their wives should be brought to them.'[1] Instead, the groom sent a dismal proxy – the severe soldier-statesman Fernando Alvarez de Toledo, Duke of Alba.

With the rise of Protestantism in France gravely threatening both the King's authority and the country's unity, Henry had been compelled to make peace with Philip. Early in June, Henry had issued an edict announcing a crusade to rid his realm of 'the Lutheran scum' and while nothing much could be done until the departure of his august guests, he ordered the arrest of several prominent Protestants in Paris. Quickly tried and sentenced to burn at the stake for heresy, their seizure caused a considerable outcry and a stay of execution was given until after the celebrations. The condemned men awaited their fate in the dungeons of Le Châtelet prison in Paris, while nearby in the wide rue Saint-Antoine next to the Château des Tournelles, they could hear the paving stones being pulled up to make way for the jousting lists, and the building of stands for the spectators and triumphal arches emblazoned with the arms of Spain, France and Savoy.

Heralds issued the King's challenge that His Majesty the King of France, his eldest son Francis, the Dauphin, the Duke of Guise and other princes at the French Court were to take on all comers. Sir Nicholas Throckmorton, the English ambassador, reported, 'The King himself, the Dauphin and the nobles ... do daily assay themselves at the tilt which is like to be very grand and sumptuous.'[2] The Parisians loved a spectacle, but their expectations were confounded when Alba and his suite arrived on 15 June. Spanish fashions had always been austere, but their dark and mean-looking clothes left the French wondering whether a deliberate affront had been intended. A few days later all this was forgotten when Henry welcomed his enemy of yesterday to the Louvre Palace. Emmanuel-Philibert of Savoy came escorted by 150 men gorgeously dressed in crimson doublets, matching shoes and black velvet cloaks embroidered with gold lace.

On Thursday, 22 June, the thirteen-year-old Elisabeth of France married Philip of Spain, aged thirty-two, by proxy at Notre-Dame Cathedral. After the wedding a primitive ritual took place. Elisabeth and Alba climbed into the huge state bed – each with one leg naked. As their bare limbs touched and they rubbed their feet together, the marriage was declared consummated. Six days later, on Wednesday 28 June, the jousts began.

By Friday, the third day of the tournament, the weather turned hot and heavy. The rue Saint-Antoine enjoyed little shade and a large number of peasants had climbed on to the roofs of the houses to watch the King enter the lists. For weeks the ladies and gentlemen of the Court had been preparing 'their handsome and costly apparel', some wearing the entire value of their estates on their backs.[3] In an attempt to dazzle at the celebrations Catherine had ordered 300 lengths of gold and silver cloth from Italy for her gowns; extravagant by nature, she delighted in wearing regal confections. One observer noted that it was hard to say whether the sun or the jewels shone more brightly. The King had never seemed happier.

The same cannot be said for his wife. Seated with her son the Dauphin and the lofty figure of her daughter-in-law, Mary, Queen of Scots, Catherine was noticeably anxious.* The night before she had dreamt that her husband lay stricken on the ground, his face covered in blood.[4] The Queen's unshakeable belief in seers and astrologers gave her every reason to be fearful. In 1552 Luca Guorico, the Italian astrologer of the Medici family, had warned Henry that he must take particular care around his fortieth year to 'avoid all single combat in an enclosed space', lest he risk a wound that could blind or even kill him. Henry was now forty years and four months old. Furthermore, in 1555 Nostradamus had published this prophecy in *Centuries*, quatrain no. I.XXXV:

> The young lion will overcome the old, in
> A field of combat in a single fight. He will
> Pierce his eyes in a golden cage, two
> Wounds in one, he then dies a cruel death.

Citing these evil omens, for the old lion could be interpreted as the King and the cage of gold his visor, Catherine had implored her husband not to joust that day. He is even supposed to have remarked to the same man who was accidentally to strike him down, 'I care not if my death be in that manner ... I would even prefer it, to die by the hand of whoever he might be, so long as he was brave and valiant and that I kept my honour.'

Henry's mistress was conspicuously seated surrounded by ladies of the Court. The superb Diane de Poitiers, Duchess of Valentinois, had held the heart of the King since he was a teenager. Now almost sixty years old, 'Madame' as she was known by all – including the Queen – had lost none of her charms, in his eyes at least, being still 'the lady that I serve'. Cold, remote and elegant, Diane had been widowed in 1531. Since the death of her husband she wore only black and white mourning, knowing how well it became her, particularly beside the dandified courtiers.

---

* At 5ft 10ins, Mary, Queen of Scots was an exceptionally tall woman by sixteenth-century standards.

Catherine, forty years old, plump and dumpy after giving birth to ten children, had long since mastered the 'art of opportune pretending' and, with a few rare exceptions, she had spent the last twenty-six years gracefully not noticing 'Madame's' total enslavement of the husband she pathetically adored.

Henry began the day by jousting well. Wearing Diane's colours of black and white, he saw off challenges from the Dukes of Guise and Nemours. Pleased with the horse given to him by Emmanuel-Philibert of Savoy, Henry graciously shouted up to him, 'It is your horse that has helped me tilt well today!' By now the King was tired, but insisted on riding a further course. Catherine sent word asking him not to continue. Irritated, Henry nevertheless replied courteously, 'It is precisely for you that I fight.' Once more he mounted his horse – prophetically named Malheureux – and prepared to tilt against the valiant young captain of his Scottish guard, Gabriel Count de Montgomery.* As he did so, it is said that a boy in the crowd broke the expectant silence with the cry: 'The King will die!'

A few moments later the two men clashed and Montgomery almost knocked Henry from the saddle. It was five o'clock and some spectators rose to leave. The King was good-humoured but wanted his revenge. Although Montgomery had become afraid and begged to be allowed to retire, Henry insisted with the shout: 'It's an order!' Catherine once again asked the King to stop. Ignoring her, he demanded his helmet from the Marshal de Vieilleville, who said, 'Sire, I swear before God that for the last three nights I have dreamt that today, this last day of June, will be fatal for you.'[5] Henry could barely have heard these words because he did not wait for the customary trumpet call that signalled the opening of the course. The two riders thundered towards each other. As they met with a crack of splintering wood, Henry, his arms clinging to the horse's neck, 'had great ado (reling to and fro) to kepe himself on horseback'.[6] The Queen shrieked and with a loud cry the crowd rose to their feet.

The two most powerful men in France after the King himself – the Duke de Montmorency and the Duke of Guise – rushed forward to stop Henry from falling out of the saddle. Lowering him to the ground, they removed his armour. They found the visor half open and his face soaked in blood with wooden splinters 'of a good bigness' protruding from his eye and temple. The King was 'very weak ... almost benumbed ... he moved neither hand nor fote, but laye as one amazed'.[7] Seeing this, his young opponent begged his sovereign that his head and his hands be cut off, but: 'The good natured King who for his kindness had no equal in

---

* Some historians argue that it is unlikely that any horse presented to a king would be given a name such as Malheureux and that it was given the name only after the accident.

his time answered that he was not angry ... and that he had nothing to pardon, since he had obeyed his King and carried himself like a brave knight.[8] The crowd pressed round to catch a glimpse of Henry, who was carried away to the Château des Tournelles. Once there, the gates were locked and he insisted on mounting the grand staircase on his feet, but having his head and shoulders supported. It was a miserable procession. The Dauphin, who predictably had fainted, was carried up after the King, followed by Catherine and the most senior nobles. Collapsing on to his bed, Henry immediately tried to clasp his hands in prayer and strike his chest in contrition for his sins. It was as if he were already preparing for death.

'There was marvellous great lamentation and weeping for him from both men and women,' wrote Throckmorton, and it was feared that the King would not live for many moments longer. The royal surgeons were summoned. Henry's bravery was singular as the doctors tried to remove the splinters. Retching with pain, only once was the unfortunate patient heard to cry out. The usual appalling (by modern standards) remedies were prescribed: he was bled, purged and given an ounce of barley gruel which he promptly vomited, 'refrigeratives applied', the wound was dressed with egg white. After this he sank into a state of feverish semi-consciousness and was attended that night by his wife, the Duke of Savoy and the Duke of Guise's brother, the Cardinal of Lorraine. The King had a 'very evil rest' and at three o'clock in the morning the vigil changed. Taken away to lie down, Catherine seemed in a trance of shock.

Savoy had meanwhile summoned Philip II's own surgeon, André Vesalius. The decapitated heads of several criminals who had been executed the day before were brought to the celebrated physician. He and Ambroise Paré (his French counterpart) tried with jagged shards of wood to reproduce the wound on the skulls of the corpses. As they discussed the inconclusive results of their grisly experiments, Henry continued his decline. In brief periods of lucidity he asked for music and dictated a letter to the French ambassador in Rome expressing the hope that the fight so recently begun against the heretics would continue if he recovered. The notable absence of Diane de Poitiers reflected Henry's hopeless condition. 'Madame ... has not entered the bedchamber since the day of the wound, for fear of being expelled by the Queen,' noted one chronicler.[9] Catherine had shared her entire married life with Diane, but these last moments belonged to her alone. In another part of the château, Diane anxiously waited for news of her lover. Two nights before Henry died an officer came from the Queen, demanding the return of the many jewels belonging to the Crown that Henry had given to his greedy mistress. 'What! Is he dead?' she is said to have asked. 'Not yet, Madame,' he answered, 'but he cannot last long.'[10] Diane replied that as long as there was breath in the King's body she would not lose heart and would obey 'none but him'.

On the evening of 4 July the King's temperature rose sharply. Septicæmia had set in. There was talk of trepanning the wound to relieve the pressure and ease his pain, but removal of the bandages revealed such large quantities of pus that the idea was abandoned. Henry was doomed and nothing further could be done but to await his death. This was the event Catherine had dreaded ever since she had married Henry as a fourteen-year-old girl. She had been a passionately devoted, adoring wife. Always fearful of losing him, she and her ladies had worn mourning whenever he had gone off to war. During his martial expeditions, when not constantly writing asking for news of him, she had been at prayer making extravagant offerings, clasping her many amulets and charms to ensure his safe return. Though she had always feared the doom-laden prophecies, she had not prepared herself for this.

Alternating between prayers and tears, Catherine hurried from her dying husband to the Dauphin, who lay in bed rocking to and fro, moaning and crying as if unhinged as he knocked his head against the wall. She was finally unable to watch as Henry lost his power of sight and speech. During his last lucid moments he had told his son to write to Philip of Spain commending his family and his kingdom to his protection. Taking his hands, he said, 'My son, you are going to be without your father but not without his blessing. I pray that you will be more fortunate than I have been.' 'My God! How can I live if my father dies?' cried the Dauphin and promptly fainted again.

Some say the King called for Catherine on 8 July and, after urging the Queen to ensure that his sister Marguerite's marriage went ahead, 'he commended to her his kingdom and his children'.[11] The following night the cheerless wedding of Marguerite and the Duke of Savoy duly took place in Elisabeth's room, the Mass said hurriedly in case news of the King's death arrived before it was completed. Catherine was too tormented to attend. The following morning at dawn Henry received extreme unction and at one o'clock that afternoon he died.[12] Years later his daughter, Margot, recalled her father's death as 'the vile blow which deprived our House of happiness and our country of peace'.[13]

During the King's last days the most powerful men in the country gathered around their master's bed. They were not, however, united. The Duke de Montmorency, Grand Master and Constable of France, had been Henry's mentor, friend and surrogate father. A military man and a conservative, he was, aside from the Crown and Church, the largest landowner in France, enjoying unquestioned support from his fiefdoms. Although he was a Catholic himself, some of his family had recently become Protestants or Protestant-sympathisers. During the last year of

Henry's life the Constable had joined with Diane, the King's mistress, to keep their rivals, the Guise brothers, from power.

The two elder Guise brothers, from a cadet branch of the House of Lorraine (a duchy on France's north-eastern border), could also call upon the assistance of many client vassals. The elder – Duke François – was a popular war hero. A brave and distinguished soldier, he had been a favourite of the late King. His brother Charles, Cardinal of Lorraine, a masterly politician and a supreme courtier, was also France's Chief Inquisitor. The pair, both ultra-Catholics and with complementary talents, made a formidable team. Latterly they had fallen out of favour for not supporting the return of France's Italian possessions in the recent treaty. This in turn had brought them more into sympathy with Catherine. Now they expected a central role in the government of the country, not least because they were the uncles of Mary, the sixteen-year-old Queen of Scots, wife of Catherine's feeble eldest son, the Dauphin, and since Henry's death the new Queen of France. To Catherine's intense irritation, Mary had enormous influence over her husband, still a teenager but now King Francis II, and she in turn relied upon her uncles for guidance in matters large and small.

Since the accident, Paris had turned from a crowded festive city to a silent place where the overwhelming majority of people were stunned and sorrowful at losing their King. They also rightly feared the political uncertainties that lay before the kingdom. 'The palace has passed from marriage to a morgue,' wrote one observer, and in the streets the common people genuinely mourned their sovereign's passing. The proclamation of King Francis II gave them little reason to feel encouraged.

Montmorency and other senior noblemen of the non-Guisard faction stayed with the corpse of the late King as the surgeons removed his heart and entrails for separate burial, and then embalmed his body. All over the Château des Tournelles altars were set up, and rooms and passages were draped in black. Around the now embalmed body of the King came relays of bishops and other churchmen. The clerics, surrounded by tall candles, knelt and sang psalms for the dead as Henry's room became transformed into a richly decorated chapel with an altar at each end of his bed. On benches covered in silver cloth sat subjects high and low who attended one of six Requiem Masses held daily for the King's soul. Catherine also went to pay reverence to her late husband of nearly twenty-six years. Kneeling before him she bade his body farewell as those remaining at the château began the elaborate forty-day vigil.

During this critical period, Constable Montmorency and his party were sidelined as the Guises took over the major offices of state. While Montmorency – whom Francis II loathed – had probably anticipated some loss of power, he could scarcely have imagined the extent to which he would find himself politically marginalised. Indeed, the bickering had already begun before the King was dead; the Guises spoke of impeaching the Constable for not ensuring the King's safety during the jousting, while the old man wandered the corridors, inconsolable at the prospect of losing his master, friend and comrade in arms.

Leaving the body of the late King with Montmorency and his allies, the Guises knew they must establish themselves in power before the country had time to react to the tragedy. A serious threat to their hegemony could be anticipated from the First Prince of the Blood, Antoine de Bourbon, and his brothers. The Bourbons, like the Valois, were both descended from the Capet dynasty that had ruled France since the year 987. In 1328 Charles IV 'Le Bel' died without a male heir and the main branch of the Capetians died out, passing the Crown to the Valois, a junior branch of the dynasty. Should Henry's and Catherine's four surviving sons die without male issue the Bourbon family were next in line to the throne. Legally, as the only Princes of the Blood apart from these four Valois princes, the Bourbons would dominate any ruling council. Though Antoine de Bourbon was lazy, selfish and weak-willed, the Guises did not want to take unnecessary risks and decided that the new King should be removed to the Louvre, away from their rivals. Accordingly, Francis and his wife, as well as Catherine's younger children, were gathered together to make the short journey across Paris. The bleak figure, clad in black, of the stricken Dowager Queen then unexpectedly joined the party. She spurned not only the usual white mourning of French queens but the tradition that demanded she remain in seclusion for forty days where her husband had died. Catherine knew that she must now break with custom. Though devastated by her loss, she was essential to the Guises' *coup d'état*.

During her husband's reign Catherine had skilfully kept from openly siding with either the Guise or the Montmorency faction. Maintaining a sweet disposition and good relations with both, she frequently sought their advice and help, disarming them with her appearance of humility. Though they were unaware of it, she detested both parties in almost equal measure. She would not forget their past wrongs, their toadying to Diane de Poitiers and their immense hold over her late husband. They in turn had generally ignored the Queen, badly underestimating her intelligence and hidden pride. Meanwhile, although King Francis II was technically old enough to rule, his obvious weaknesses both physical and mental required a council to administer the country. To protect her son, her small children and herself, Catherine had to join the Guise brothers' cabal.

The Guises did not lack enemies: some were jealous of their wealth and power, some did not share their ultra-Catholicism and some regarded them as foreign usurpers. The brothers needed Catherine to legitimise their position; her presence lent them her implicit sanction. Thus an unspoken compact seems to have been made between the widow and the Guises. The gates of the Château des Tournelles were opened in order to allow the royal carriages to depart for the Louvre and so that the large crowd outside could witness the royal family leaving. Various observers recalled the Duke of Guise carrying one of Catherine's youngest children in his arms, presenting a potent image of fatherly protection for the onlookers. Mary was seen to hang back for a moment to let her mother-in-law enter the coach first but Catherine understood her new place and seemed even to relish it, publicly insisting that the new Queen take precedence.

For the first time Catherine was to have a role that belonged exclusively to her. She had had to share her husband with Diane de Poitiers. She had to a large extent shared being Queen of France with Diane; she had even been forced to share the upbringing of her young children with the favourite. Yet her widowhood would be hers alone. For the rest of her days she was to guard it with jealousy. Her life would be dedicated to the memory of Henry and their children, for they were his legacy to France. She would be the guardian of the monarchy and his legend, learning to fashion history according to her needs. After a lifetime obscured behind her mask of supple self-effacement, the forty-year-old Queen Mother shrouded in widow's weeds was taking her first cautious steps towards becoming mistress of France.

PART ONE

ONE

Orphan of Florence

She comes bearing the
calamities of the Greeks

1519–33

Caterina Maria Romula de Medici was born at around eleven o'clock on
the morning of Wednesday, 13 April 1519. Her father, Lorenzo II de
Medici, Duke of Urbino, scion of the ruling House of Florence, had
married her mother, Madeleine de la Tour d'Auvergne, the previous year.
This royal-blooded French countess and great heiress made a brilliant
catch for the Medici, who were considered by many in France to be
merely nouveaux riches merchants. Since their magnificent wedding,
hosted by the bride's kinsman, King Francis I of France, and the couple's
glorious return to Florence, there had been little cause for celebration.
Madeleine's pregnancy, which had been announced in June, progressed
well but the young duke, whose health had been poor for some time,
had fallen ill in the autumn of 1518. Intermittent high fevers and fears
over his condition led to him leaving Florence where the newlyweds had
been living in princely state. The duke, probably suffering from syphilis
and possibly tuberculosis, moved to the cleaner air of the surrounding
countryside to await the birth of his child. By the time he returned to
the city for his wife's confinement, he was dying.*

Immediately after her birth, attendants carried the baby to her bedridden
father for inspection. The news that her mother had by now also become
very ill was kept from the duke for fear of hastening his decline. The
fact that she had borne him a daughter cannot have cheered him much
since there would clearly be no further issue from this illustrious couple.
In an attempt to brighten the gloomy reality of the baby's sex, a
contemporary chronicler applied a sycophantic gloss to the ducal disappointment: he declared that the couple 'have both been as pleased as
if it had been a boy'.[1] Due to the illness of both parents, the child's
hurriedly organised baptism took place on Saturday, 16 April at the family
church of San Lorenzo. With four senior clerics and two noble relations

---

* It was claimed by Florange, the French memoirist, that Lorenzo had syphilis and had
infected his bride.

in attendance, the baby received the names Caterina, a Medici family name, Maria, since it was the day of the Holy Virgin, and Romula, after the founder of Fiesole – although I shall henceforth refer to her throughout as Catherine. On 28 April the duchess breathed her last followed by the duke only six days later on 4 May. The entombment of the couple in the splendid family vault at the church where their baby had so recently been baptised provided a dismal conclusion to their brief marriage.

On the day the duke died his friend the poet Ariosto had arrived to condole with him over the death of the duchess. When he discovered that only an orphan child remained of the marriage that had promised a revival of the Medici fortunes he wrote a short ode: 'Verdeggia un solo ramo', dedicating it to the last hope of this pre-eminent merchant dynasty:

> A single branch, buds and lo,
> I am distraught with hope and fear,
> Whether winter will let it blow,
> Or blight it on the growing bier.

Catherine owed her existence to the obsessive Italian territorial ambitions of Francis I of France. Between the fall of the western Roman Empire and its late-nineteenth-century unification, Italy was a patchwork of principalities, duchies, and city-states. Most of these showed a precocious vigour in the arts, technology and trade, making them tempting acquisitions for outsiders. Unlike Florence, they were usually ruled by families descended from famous warriors (known as *condottieri*); names like the Sforza of Milan and the Gonzaga of Mantua evoke the mercenary soldiers who carved their fortunes from battle. While a small number of states such as Venice, Genoa and Florence were – for a time at least – independent, by the mid-sixteenth century the majority were ruled either directly or indirectly by Spain. From 1490 until 1559, when Spanish supremacy was established, Italy became the bloody arena where the two Continental superpowers played out their bitter struggle to dominate Europe.

Francis I, descended through his great-grandmother from the Visconti of Milan, required a sturdy ally in the peninsula to press his claim for the duchy. Accordingly, he forged an alliance with Pope Leo X, Giovanni de Medici. Unlike popes today, His Holiness was not only Christ's representative on earth, but he also exercised the temporal powers of a monarch as ruler of the Papal States, most of which were in central Italy. The papal tiara was a triple crown that placed the popes above kings and emperors; not only did the papacy hold claim to a huge amount of property throughout the Catholic world (in pre-Reformation England one fifth of the land was held by Rome) but the pope also had the right to legal jurisdiction in Catholic countries and many types of legal cases were referred to the Ecclesiastical Court. To strengthen his agreement with the Medici Pope, Francis decided to arrange the marriage of an orphaned Bourbon heiress, Madeleine de la Tour d'Auvergne, to Leo's nephew, Lorenzo de Medici. At Leo's instigation Lorenzo had recently snatched the duchy of Urbino from the della Rovere family.* For this enterprise the Pope had provided prodigious financial support with monies gained from the creation of thirty new cardinals. In private, Francis felt snobbishly sceptical about Lorenzo's ability to keep the newly acquired fief of Urbino, commenting that he was after all 'only a tradesman'.

It is true that by early-modern standards the Medici of Florence could not claim any blue-blooded descent, but wise husbandry and steady expansion of the family banking business by the founder Giovanni di Bicci de Medici (1360–1429) had ensured that they were the most prosperous and powerful family in the important city-state of Florence. The Medici originally came from the Mugello, ten miles north of Florence. Although their name and the red balls or *palle* – varying in number from twelve to six – on a field of gold on their emblem suggested medicine, and they appropriated the martyred physicians Sts Cosmas and Damian as their patron saints, they had always been in commerce, specialising in wool, silk, precious metals, spices and banking.† They rose to become papal bankers and with the economic opportunities after the decimation of the Black Death in 1348–49 there was much demand for their services. Like his father Giovanni, Cosimo de Medici (1389–1464) was a quiet, unassuming man who did not favour the grandiose way of life of his later descendants, though he did build the most impressive palace yet seen in the city – the Palazzo Medici. Today, although much changed since Cosimo's time, one can still see the formidable defensive walls that once protected Catherine as a young child from a rebellious mob; the solid outer walls reflect the need for protection against the political uncertainties of that age and hide the building's exquisite interiors.

Cosimo was learned and philanthropic, and the most significant private patron of the arts of his day, employing Michelozzo, Donatello, Brunelleschi, Paolo Uccello, Filippo Lippi and other leading figures of the early Renaissance. Underlining their importance by patronising the arts, which, from the thirteenth century onwards, became the most visible

---

* Leo X had originally planned to take Urbino for his brother Giuliano. The ambitious Pope had focused upon the relatively minor and unsupported duchy as an easy prey to extend to his family's territory. On Giuliano's death Lorenzo succeeded his uncle in the Pope's plan.
† There is continued controversy about the origins of the family emblem, the balls, or *palle*, were the symbol for cupping glasses or pills. Some argue that they may also represent pawnbroking.

symbol of Italian wealth and dynamism, the Medici played an indispensable role in the process which produced the Italian Renaissance.

Cosimo took the family bank to new heights, opening branches all over Europe, including ones in London, Geneva and Lyons. After a brief period of banishment by rival Florentine factions, who tried but failed to take control of the executive council of the Florentine Republic, the Signoria, Cosimo returned at the people's invitation to become Gonfaloniere (head of the Signoria), a citizen of Florence but in effect the uncrowned ruler of the city-state. He understood the need, in order for commerce to flourish, for political harmony both internally and externally, and used his huge resources to influence matters in favour of his family and Florence. A benevolent dictator with a quiet manner, Cosimo assumed the air of a private citizen but in fact nearly all major decisions were made by him or with his consent. Pope Pius II described him as 'the arbiter of peace and war and the moderator of the laws, not so much a private citizen as the lord of the country ... he it is who gives commands to the magistrates'.[2] Cosimo was looked upon as a father by many of the Florentines who, after his death, awarded him the affectionate title 'Pater Patriae'. One contemporary called him 'King in everything but name.'

Cosimo's grandson Lorenzo (1449–92), known as 'The Magnificent' (the title was given to persons of note who were not of princely blood), was to prove himself truly worthy of the sobriquet. He is perhaps the most famous of the Medici, although it was paradoxically under his charge that the family's commercial fortunes began to decline. He was a poor banker but a superb scholar, poet and collector. History recalls Lorenzo as the extraordinary patron of such great artists as Botticelli, Perugino, Filippino Lippi, the Ghirlandaios and Verrocchio. His patronage also touched future masters such as Leonardo da Vinci. In his garden at the Palazzo Medici, Lorenzo set up a workshop for sculptors, and it was there that Michelangelo first came to the attention of buyers and artists alike. Lorenzo was a gifted diplomat, a wise politician devoted to the welfare of Florence and above all zealous in his promotion of the Medici family and its supporters. When Pope Innocent VIII heard of Lorenzo's death he is said to have cried out, 'The peace of Italy is at an end!'

Lorenzo had three sons; it is said that he called one good, one wise and one a fool. Unfortunately it was the 'fool', Piero the Fatuous (1472–1503), who was the eldest. Ill suited to rule, Piero found himself and his family quickly ejected from the republic and he later died in exile. His brother Giuliano – 'the good' – worked with Giovanni – 'the wise' – who had become a cardinal at thirteen thanks to his father's intervention, for the only thing that mattered – their eventual return to Florence. They had to plot in penury for they were virtually bankrupt, their fortune taken by usurpers and their properties confiscated by the republic. Giovanni had a good head for intrigue but required patience; it was to be a long wait before events turned in the Medici favour again. Perhaps the family motto, *Le Temps Revient* (Our time will return), gave them courage. It was certainly the moral by which Catherine was later to live her life.

In 1512 a league of small Italian states managed temporarily to expel the French from Italy. Unwisely the Gonfaloniere, Piero Soderini, an unremarkable but honest man, had denied the league Florentine support. The league turned upon Florence in revenge for not joining them against the French and Soderini fled with his government. The Medici seized the moment and manoeuvred to regain their lost citizenship as a new regime took power in the Arno city.

Soderini was not alone in exile following the return of the Medici. Among the friends and advisers stripped of office in the political purge was a minor official of the Second Chancery, Niccolò Machiavelli. Among other things, Machiavelli travelled on diplomatic missions to leading figures such as the Holy Roman Emperor and Cesare Borgia; he also created a Florentine militia for Soderini and was charged with matters relating to the defence of the republic. But in 1513, languishing in exile and eager to return to power, Machiavelli wrote *The Prince*, dedicating it to Catherine's father* in an effort to ingratiate himself with the family. This, Machiavelli's most celebrated work, is a brilliant study on statecraft. The author radically discarded cherished and traditionally held tenets of the virtues that defined a good ruler; instead he boldly and emphatically embraced *Realpolitik* and argued that to be an effective 'Prince' all means were justifiable for the good of the state. The pragmatism and the ability, when necessary, to step outside normal bounds of morality were not based on Christian or Classical ideals. The goodwill of the people was a necessity, but a ruler must be prepared to earn their respect by using exemplary punishment, or eliminating those who endangered the nation's health. It took some time for the work to surface and make an impact outside Florence but the 'little book' was to bedevil Catherine during the wars of religion and long afterwards as this work, advocating a steely adherence to practical solutions for the good of the state, was quoted (often purposely out of context) by her enemies. They called it Catherine's bible, and it eventually acquired the reputation as a manual for cruel autocrats while the name Machiavelli became synonymous with scheming, evil and tyranny.

On 1 September 1512, after eighteen years of exile, Lorenzo the Magnificent's two surviving sons, Giovanni and Giuliano, made their triumphant return to Florence. With them came Lorenzo's grandson and

---

* It is thought that Machiavelli had originally intended to dedicate *The Prince* to Giuliano de Medici, but when he died the letter of dedication was made to Lorenzo II.

eventual heir, also called Lorenzo. Unfortunately he had none of the qualities of his grandfather. Spoiled by his doting mother, Alfonsina, he grew into an arrogant, selfish and lazy young man. This pair were not only grasping, but once the Medici returned to power in Florence, the young Lorenzo lived extravagantly and with such strutting grandiosity that he risked losing the affection people still held for his family.

Almost immediately after the joyful reinstatement of the Medici in Florence, Julius II died and Giovanni was elected Pope Leo X. He was thirty-seven years of age, overweight, troubled by a stomach ulcer and an agonising anal fistula. His formal entry on horseback into the Vatican was thus not quite the unalloyed pleasure it might have been. Although sitting side-saddle to avoid some of the discomfort, he suffered terribly from the heat and the pain of riding in his condition. Those who stood nearby suffered almost as much from the overpowering and noxious smell emanating from his ulcerous stomach and the infected fistula on his enormous backside.[3] Nevertheless Leo's joy was evident to all and the crowd responded with an enthusiastic welcome. While the words he is supposed to have uttered upon his election – 'Now God has given us the papacy. Let us enjoy it!' – are almost certainly apocryphal, enjoy it he did. The glorious painting by Raphael of Leo seated flanked by two cardinals shows us a Renaissance voluptuary. His face is plump, his body plumper, the large pendulous cheeks, bulbous eyes and sensuous lips were strong family traits; unfortunately, some of these were later to be inherited by his great-niece Catherine. Though nepotistic, Leo was far less prey to some of his predecessors' vices, and this enlightened man brought the fruits of his learning to the papacy. He lived in splendour with a huge household; naturally generous, after his years of exile and poverty he now possessed the means to patronise the arts, commission building projects and above all to indulge himself and others. He gave lavish and frequent banquets at which he entertained his guests with novelties, such as tiny birds flying out of pies. He loved comedies and practical jokes.

Leo's most serious flaw as Pope was his failure to grasp the critical need for reform of the Church. While this need had existed for some time, it had become acute since the rise of an obscure German monk named Martin Luther. Luther had spoken out against the sale of indulgences, appealing to the Church to rid itself of corruption and criticising the worldliness of the papal court. He believed in 'sola fide' (faith alone) and that man could reach God without the intervention of 'cleric or sacrament'. Leo called the controversy 'a monkish squabble', not realising that the touchpaper had been lit for a conflagration that would one day split the Church, tear nations apart and shake the thrones of his great-niece Catherine and her sons.

As head of the family and due to his removal to Rome, Leo needed to select a successor to protect the family's position in Florence. It was decided that Giuliano 'the good' (whom Leo thought far too soft) should help the new Pope in Rome and that their nephew Lorenzo could be left in charge of Florentine affairs, though he had no patience for them and was often in Rome with his uncle, leaving Florentines to feel like a subject state. This was hardly in the tradition of even the nominal Florentine republic but with a Medici wearing the papal tiara, Leo wisely made it seem that there would be plenty of advantages for the people. In 1515 Giuliano travelled as Leo's emissary to France to congratulate Francis I on his accession to the throne. The King was in a hurry to conquer Milan and take Naples, of which the Pope was suzerain. The two met later the same year at the papal town of Bologna where they signed an agreement that restored relations between the French Church and the papacy.

To flatter Leo, the King offered Giuliano the dukedom of Nemours in France and his Aunt Philiberta of Savoy's hand in marriage. In exchange Francis was to have the Italian states of Parma and Piacenza, and the support of the Pontiff regarding his ambitions for Milan and Naples. The marital alliance between the ruling House of France and the merchant Medici was as thrilling to the latter as it was to prove short-lived. Giuliano, Duke of Nemours, died within a year of his marriage, leaving no legitimate heir but only a bastard son named Ippolito. Now all Leo's hopes rested with his nephew Lorenzo.

Leo and Francis both wished to continue their alliance despite Giuliano's death, so Lorenzo, by then the Duke of Urbino, became His Holiness's emissary representing the pope at the christening of Francis's first-born son the Dauphin. Leo had been asked to stand godfather to the baby. Some time before the christening, Francis had written to Lorenzo to congratulate him on becoming Duke of Urbino, adding, 'I intend to help you with all my power. I also wish to marry you off to some beautiful and good lady of noble birth and of my kind, so that the love which I bear you may grow and be strengthened.'[4] Once the bride, Madeleine de la Tour d'Auvergne, had been selected, it was decided that the marriage should take place soon after the baptism of the Dauphin. The other important matter was the bride's enormous inheritance. Both her mother, Jeanne de Bourbon-Vendôme, a royal princess, and her father, Jean III de la Tour, were dead and she shared their extensive properties in Auvergne, Clermont, Berry, Castres and Louraguais with her sister, the wife of the Scottish Duke of Albany. The Medici needed cash to re-establish themselves firmly in control of Florence, and Madeleine's double dowry of blue blood and gold was gleefully anticipated by the older generation. The good times were back.

Lorenzo's appearance in France was so sumptuous, his crimson-clad train so large, his gifts so extravagant, including a vast bed made of tortoiseshell decorated with gems and mother-of pearl, that it seemed as though an eastern potentate had arrived.⁵ Lorenzo and his bride-to-be immediately liked the look of each other and matters progressed better than anyone could have hoped. The duke was given the honour of holding the infant heir to France at the baptism at the Château of Amboise on 25 April 1518, and it was there that the wedding took place three days later. The groom was twenty-six years old and the bride just sixteen. At Amboise the inner courtyard was covered with fabulous silk awnings and gorgeous tapestries clothed the walls over the ten days of feasts, banquets, masked balls and ballets. During the day there were tournaments and a mock battle, which must have been fairly realistic since at least two people were killed. Francis knew how to dazzle with his entertainments and seemed particularly anxious to show the Italians, whose culture he so admired, that the French did not lack polish.

By the time the couple set off for Florence, where they arrived in September 1518, Francis had taken Lorenzo on a tour of Brittany and behaved very agreeably towards him. He also awarded the duke the Order of Saint-Michel, the highest order of French chivalry, and a company of *gens d'armes* (heavy cavalry). There was much to celebrate, especially upon the announcement of the young duchess's pregnancy. The news sent Francis and Leo into raptures of delight.

It is not hard to imagine the dismay of both the Pope and the King of France when Lorenzo and Madeleine de Medici, Duke and Duchess of Urbino, both died months later, leaving only a daughter as the living token of their great schemes. To make matters worse, Catherine fell ill in August 1519 when only three months old and for several weeks her life hung in the balance. Yet she survived and by October Leo insisted that the 'duchessina', as the Florentine people fondly called her, could be moved to Rome without risk to her health. Leo had already emphatically refused Francis's request that the child be brought up at the French Court. He sensibly declined to offer up his great-niece as a hostage against the promises he had recently made to Francis, for he was already planning to break them. The circumstances had completely changed, so now must his policies. After wiping away his seemly tears at the death of his nephew and niece, Leo lost no time in opening secret talks with King Charles of Spain, now Charles V the new Holy Roman Emperor and Francis's mortal enemy.* By May 1521 Leo was openly allied to Charles, whom he had promised to crown as Emperor and to invest with Naples. When

* Charles I of Spain, a Habsburg, was elected Holy Roman Emperor in June 1519. He took the title Charles V.

he heard the news, Francis fell into a furious rage at the Pope's betrayal and before long France and the Empire were once again at war.

When Catherine was brought to her uncle in Rome, he is said to have greeted the baby with the words: 'She comes bearing the calamities of the Greeks!' After a long and careful look at the baby, however, he declared with satisfaction that she was 'fine and fat'. Leo's first reaction to the disastrous death of Lorenzo and his wife had been to take a resigned and pious stance, saying, 'God has given. God has taken away.' He now faced a dilemma over whether to hand the family inheritance to the collateral branch of the Medici, whom he had hitherto studiously snubbed and ignored, regarding them as a possible threat to his dynasty, or have the illegitimate members of the senior branch made his heirs. He decided on the latter. He created Catherine Duchess of Urbino and as soon as she was old enough, Leo intended to marry her off to Ippolito, the Duke of Nemours's son, whom he would legitimise. The pair would then become the ruling couple of Florence.

There existed another illegitimate boy, Alessandro de Medici, born in 1512, who had been loosely acknowledged as the child of Lorenzo and therefore Catherine's half-brother. It is certain that Alessandro was in fact Cardinal Giulio de Medici's son, though for the sake of expediency he had been attributed to Lorenzo, not least because Giulio himself was not only illegitimate, the son of Lorenzo the Magnificent's brother, but a cardinal to boot. Meanwhile Catherine remained in the hands of her grandmother, Alfonsina Orsini. After Orsini's death in 1520 Catherine moved into the care of Lorenzo the Magnificent's daughter, Lucrezia Salviati, and her aunt Clarice Strozzi, the woman who was to become her surrogate mother for the next few years. Both women had married extremely rich bankers and Clarice, a strict and exigent guardian, had young children with whom the little girl could play. The Strozzi cousins became the brothers and sisters the child never had, and she loved them prodigiously for the rest of their lives.

Leo did not live long enough to see his plans for Catherine and Florence come to fruition. Having had an operation on his persistent and troublesome anal fistula in late November 1521, he had decided nevertheless to go out hunting. He caught a chill, weakened quickly and died a few days later on 1 December. Catherine's future now depended upon the Medici maintaining power in Florence without papal prestige and influence to back them. Leo's illegitimate cousin, Cardinal Giulio de Medici, until recently his highly efficient assistant, had hoped to succeed him, but now retreated to Florence with Catherine and the two bastard boys Ippolito and Alessandro. The new Pope was Hadrian VI, formerly Adrian of Utrecht, previously Grand Inquisitor of Spain and Charles V's boyhood tutor (he was nicknamed 'the Emperor's schoolmaster'). The election of such a severe and pious man from what the Italians considered barbarian northern Europe was a horrid surprise to them. They tried to comfort themselves that at sixty-three years old he might die soon.

The French were appalled that someone so close to the Emperor now sat upon the papal throne. Nor was there to be much cheer for the Medici, as Hadrian promptly handed the duchy of Urbino back to its rightful owners, the della Rovere family.* The Medici even experienced difficulties paying for some of Leo's funeral expenses and a syndicate of leading Florentine families including the Strozzi and the Capponi contributed 27,000 ducats to help meet the costs (the monthly wage for a foot soldier at the time was 2 ducats). As security Giulio used Leo's jewel-encrusted cross worth 18,000 ducats. A document survives describing the most precious stones that adorned it: 'There is a central diamond, four emeralds, two large sapphires and three rubies.' The cross was given for safe keeping to the nuns of a Roman abbey until the eventual discharge of the debt.[6] Although it was not a particularly prosperous time for the Medici, Catherine spent the next two years in comparative peace in Florence living with the two boys, Ippolito and Alessandro, under Cardinal Giulio's careful supervision.

In September 1523 Hadrian VI obliged everyone except the Emperor and himself by dying, some said through poison – 450 years were to pass before a non-Italian was elected pope again. On 19 November, having used every blandishment, bribe and promise at his disposal, Leo X's 'ecclesiastical flunkey', Cardinal Giulio de Medici, managed to get himself elected Pope, becoming Clement VII. This half-caste Medici set off for Rome, leaving his stooge, Cardinal Passerini, in charge of Florence nominally on behalf of the minor Ippolito. With Clement as Pope, Catherine became a valuable marriage pawn once more. Even without the Duchy of Urbino, her inheritance still meant she was an important heiress, the properties from her mother alone made her one of the richest young women in Europe.† To present her in the correct setting, Clement ensured that she lived in state with a princely retinue at the Palazzo Medici.

Yet the Florentines grew restless. Despite embezzling huge sums from Florence to pay for his Court and brilliant lifestyle, Leo X had deftly managed the papacy and Florence. Clement VII, who lacked his cousin's dexterous flair, inherited the bitterness that now emerged over Leo's financial misdealings. People also felt unhappy with the all but direct rule from Rome barely and ineptly disguised by Passerini. To complicate

---

* Leo had created Catherine Duchess of Urbino but annexed the duchy to the Papal States, allowing Florence to keep the fortress of San Leo.
† Catherine continued to carry the title Duchess of Urbino by pro-Mediceans even after the della Rovere were reinstated to the duchy.

matters further, it became clear that Clement did not favour Ippolito as eventual ruler of Florence, but pushed the candidacy of his own son Alessandro. Nicknamed 'Il Moro' because of his thick lips, dark skin and curly hair – his mother may have been a Moorish slave woman – Alessandro was growing up to be as vicious and nasty as he was ugly. Meanwhile, as time passed Ippolito had grown into a dashing, handsome and charming young man.

Clement VII had been an energetic second-in-command to Leo X and as long as life proceeded along the same lines as before, he had the ability to keep matters under control. This critical period of religious unrest and war, however, required creative initiative and Clement was lost. For much of the 1520s, Francis and Charles were either at war with each other or threatening to fight, while a clamour for Church reforms grew and Lutheranism took hold in many German states within Imperial borders. The Pope lacked the courage to deal decisively with these problems. His half-measures, secret agreements and slippery shifts in policy were to prove disastrous. Clashes between France and the Empire overflowed into Italy once more, with catastrophic results for the benighted peninsula.

In 1526 Clement formed part of a league with France, England, Florence and Venice – known as the League of Cognac – to expel the Empire from Italy. Charles V was preoccupied with the Turks who had invaded his eastern borders and had Francis acted vigorously and promptly the league could well have trounced him. Yet the French King, who had just been returned from captivity by Charles after his disastrous defeat at the battle of Pavia in 1525, seemed to have lost his touch. He failed to give the league the support it needed, which led to its defeat by the Emperor. This left Clement, Rome, Florence and eventually Catherine at Charles's mercy. At the Emperor's instigation a Roman faction, hostile to Clement, rose up against him and he took refuge in the fortress of Castel Sant' Angelo on the banks of the Tiber, from where he quickly renounced the league. Once freed, he soon found himself under even greater threat.

On 6 May 1527 the Imperial troops in northern Italy had marched south and now stood before Rome: unfed, unpaid and in an ugly mood. As Charles did not pay their wages he proved powerless to stop his troops, many of them Lutherans from his own dominions, rampaging through the Eternal City. While Rome was being sacked and pillaged, her craven and luckless Pope fled once again to his redoubt at the Castel Sant' Angelo. He rushed along a passage which led directly to the fortress with his skirts held up for him by the Bishop of Nocera to prevent him from tripping. Once in the formidable circular stronghold he sat besieged.

From his bolt-hole Clement could hear the cries of his flock begging for mercy as the Imperial troops ran amok. The soldiers taunted His Holiness from beneath the solid castle walls, promising that they would eat him when finally they breached its defences. They ran in packs, desecrating sacred relics, raping and murdering citizens, lopping off bejewelled arms and fingers, destroying ancient monuments and treasures. Some soldiers even dressed themselves in the scarlet robes of murdered cardinals. Clerics, even the most insignificant of them, who did not escape the rabble were held to ransom and in many cases recaptured and ransomed again.

Clement's own ransom was set at nearly half a million ducats, a sum greater than his annual income. To raise the money he ordered his goldsmith, Benvenuto Cellini – also besieged with him – to improvise a furnace for melting down the papal tiaras he had managed to take with him. Horses were stabled in St Peter's itself, grotesque mock services were held and the leader of the many Lutheran despoilers carried a silken cord intended as a noose from which to hang Clement. The iconoclastic plunder of the Holy City outraged the civilised world. It was to take over seven months before the occupying mob were driven from the foetid ruins by hunger and a plague epidemic. As Rome was sacked, an insurrection was mounted in Florence. Aided by the arrival of the Emperor's army, the overthrow of Passerini and the Medicean regime proved easy.

Catherine's position now became fraught with uncertainty. By 11 May 1527 news had filtered back to Florence about the horrors taking place in Rome. In the Medici Palace on the via Larga, the eight-year-old girl would have grasped that this was a calamity. Clarice Strozzi, considered by many as 'the man of the family', proceeded to rave at Passerini, whom she thought incompetent and an unmitigated fool; she also rounded upon Alessandro and Ippolito, calling them unworthy of the Medici name to which they aspired. All the while, a menacing crowd pushed at the palace gates. Passerini and the two boys managed to escape thanks to Clarice's contacts with the new regime, with whom she struck a deal that was promptly reneged on by Passerini. They fled Florence on 17 May. This left Catherine and her aunt to face the mob. The new rulers of Florence boiled with fury when they realised that Alessandro and Ippolito had managed to flee without fulfilling the bargain. Catherine, their remaining hostage, would not be allowed to slip through their hands.

It was decided that the child should be taken to the Santa Lucia convent in the via San Gallo, a place known for its antipathy to the Medici family. Clarice stormed in protest at Bernardo Rinuccini leading the large troop escort that had come to take her niece. They were at Poggio a Caiano (a splendid Medici country villa) where she and Catherine had managed to escape from the angry citizens, but Clarice's exhortations availed her little and did not prevent the child from being bundled off for what were to be three hazardous years of semi-incarceration during which her life was under different degrees of threat, depending upon the tergiversations of the political scene. The little girl lived miserably in the Santa Lucia convent, but in December 1527 orders came that she be moved to the convent of Santa-Caterina of Siena, also in Florence. When the French ambassador visited her there he found the place a disease-ridden hovel and insisted that Catherine must be relocated immediately. With the permission of the Signoria (the executive council), the ambassador arranged for the child's transfer to a far more agreeable place, the convent of the Santa-Maria Annunziata delle Murate (literally 'the walled-in-ones'). The journey of a heavily veiled Catherine to the Murate took place at dead of night on 7 December 1527. The walls deprived her of her liberty but they also protected her from the hostile world outside. Hatred now fuelled the Florentine people's mood as they desecrated and damaged all reminders of the Medici. During an angry outburst early in this rebellion Michelangelo's masterpiece, the statue of David, lost its left arm when a stone was thrown at it. If Catherine were to remain a valuable negotiating tool for the Signoria, however, they must see to her well being.

Generally regarded as pro-Medicean, the Murate was a convent which undertook the education of aristocratic young women but also allowed elderly noblewomen to withdraw from the world in some comfort. It appears from records and receipts for alms dating from between 1524 to 1527 and overseen by Cardinal Armellino, Apostolic Chamberlain for Leo X and then Clement VII, that the convent had been given substantial support by the Medici.[7] One of the nuns recalled Catherine's arrival: 'The magistrates gave her to us and we received her very happily and graciously for the obligation we have to her family. Notwithstanding that she may have been infected by the plague we received her. ... One evening at two at night the band took her to the gates of the monastery and all the nuns without fear gathered around her, protected by God and Our Lady we received no wound. The Duchessina stayed for three years.'[8] She continued, 'With how much humanity and refined conversation she would talk, [all] could not be said because she had two women who looked after her.'[9]

The abbess was Catherine's godmother and she arranged for her to have the spacious and comfortable cell once occupied by a widowed relation and namesake, Caterina Riario de Medici. Spoiled by the nuns, many of whom were themselves of high birth, Catherine had found a corner of calm from the raging world outside and she learned much from these good women. Her graceful deportment, her enchanting manners – later to become such formidable weapons – the ability to charm in conversation and the strength of mind to keep her own counsel can be attributed to this time. One historian wrote, 'At the Murate the Catherine of the wars of religion was formed.' Here too she would have learned all the traditions and ceremonies of the Church for which she always showed reverence. Yet a truly spiritual education seems to have been omitted.

One of the nuns, Sister Niccolini, wrote of the 'dear little child ... with such gracious manners ... that she made herself loved by all' adding that she was 'so gentle and pleasant that the sisters did all they could to ease her sorrows and difficulties'.[10] Another wrote of the little girl's 'good disposition'.[11] No wonder they felt protective of the 'duchessina'. Death continued to take Catherine's loved ones when her protector and mother figure, Clarice Strozzi, died on 3 May 1528. The French ambassador now became her mainstay and he did what he could to see to her well-being. After a visit he wrote to her uncle, the Duke of Albany, who had been married to Catherine's maternal aunt, 'Madame, your niece is still in a convent leading a good life, but rarely visited and little regarded by these Florentine signori who would gladly see her in Kingdom Come. She expects you to send her some presents from France for the Seigneur de Ferraris. I can assure you that I have never seen anyone of her age so quick to feel the good and the ill that are done her.'[12]

By 1528 the French forces left in Italy had been soundly beaten and Clement decided to make overtures to Charles, saying, 'I have quite made up my mind to become an Imperialist, and to live and die as such.' On 29 June 1529 the Treaty of Barcelona was signed between Clement and Charles. In it, Clement promised to crown Charles Holy Roman Emperor; in return Charles would support the restoration of the Medici to Florence. The coronation did indeed take place at Bologna on 24 February 1530, though Charles V was the last Holy Roman Emperor to be crowned by a pope. The agreement also provided for a marriage between Clement's bastard son Alessandro and Charles V's illegitimate daughter Margaret of Austria. At Cambrai on 3 August 1529 the French signed their own peace with the Empire, known as 'La Paix des Dames' as it was concluded by Francis's mother, Louise of Savoy, and the Emperor's aunt, Margaret, regent of the Netherlands. As events began to turn in Clement's favour, the extremist People's Party that had replaced the moderates ruling Florence early in the revolt began to wonder if 'Kingdom Come' might not be the best place for Catherine after all. Her murder would finally deprive the Pope of his marital jewel.

In October 1529 Imperial troops led by the Prince of Orange laid harsh and effective siege to the city of Florence. Among others, Michelangelo was drafted by the citizens to protect the city as a military engineer. Plague and famine exacerbated the people's terror and hatred of the Medici, and their efforts to withstand the siege were not helped by traitors from within. It was now that Catherine, who had remained tucked away in the convent, became the focus of attention for the increasingly desperate rebel rulers of the city. One suggestion was that she be lowered naked in a basket, in front of the city walls and thus possibly killed by her own allies' gunfire. There was also talk of leaving the eleven-year-old girl in a military brothel so that any valuable marriage plans by the pontiff would be spoiled for ever. Without making a decision about Catherine's ultimate fate, the council determined that she be removed immediately from the friendly Murate convent, from which they feared she might be liberated without too much difficulty. Thus it was that the Signoria sent Silvestro Aldobrandini with an escort of troops to fetch Catherine late on the evening of 20 July 1530. In the words of one of the nuns: 'They decided to remove her at night and this happened with such tribulation and effort ... but such force was used by the eight that we had to give her up.'[13]*

Catherine, certain that she had been condemned to death and that Aldobrandini had come to fetch her for execution, put up a struggle. In preparation the eleven-year-old girl had shorn her hair and donned a nun's habit. Announcing that as a bride of Christ she refused to go quietly, Catherine cried out, 'Holy Mother, I am yours! Let us now see what excommunicated wretch will dare to drag a spouse of Christ from her monastery.'[14] She refused to change out of her nun's clothing, and Aldobrandini brought her through the small streets riding on a donkey, braving a starving and menacing crowd voicing threats and open hatred. The perilous journey proved a formative experience for the young woman as Aldobrandini kept Catherine safe and surrounded by his soldiers until he delivered her to the St Lucia convent. It was here that she had first started life as a captive nearly three years earlier. She never forgot Aldobrandini's goodness to her and when, on 12 August 1530, the siege was lifted and Clement took possession of his native city once more, she interceded for him and succeeded in having his death sentence commuted to exile. Upon her release, Catherine visited the sisters of the Murate and together they celebrated her good fortune. She remained in contact with the order for the rest of her life and wrote to them regularly, sending them money annually and gave them the revenues from one of her properties. Catherine never forgot a kindness any more than she forgave a disservice.

All too soon the girl found herself a central feature in Clement's international policy and she moved to Rome where her 'uncle', as he called himself, greeted her with such warmth that the old hypocrite managed to convince one onlooker 'she is what he loves best in the

* The 'Eight of Watch' were in charge of internal security in the Florentine state.

world'. Another noticed that Catherine seemed emotionally marked by her dreadful time in the hands of her family's enemies: 'She cannot forget the maltreatment she suffered, and is only too willing to speak of it.' Clement installed Catherine with Ippolito and Alessandro at Rome's exquisite Palazzo Medici (today the Palazzo Madama and used as the Italian Senate). He wanted her to acquire the veneer and accomplishments necessary for a glorious marriage. Antonio Soriano, the Venetian ambassador, described her physical appearance at the time of her arrival in Rome, writing that she was small of stature, and thin, and without delicate features, but having the protruding eyes peculiar to the Medici family'.[15] Nobody called her beautiful because she was not, but her manners lent her an elegance that her physique lacked. One observer from Milan called her heavy-looking, although he was probably describing her face, adding that she seemed a sensitive child who 'for her age, shows great spirit and intelligence'. The same man noted that 'altogether this little girl does not look like she will become a woman for a year and a half yet'.

Catherine lived under the care of her great-aunt Lucrezia Salviati (Leo X's sister) and her husband. It is not known how she spent her days but perhaps it was in Rome, a city being rebuilt after the ravages it had endured, that she acquired her love for art in general and architecture in particular. She had the opportunity of watching the greatest artists of the day not only restoring the damaged city but creating new masterpieces to adorn it. She certainly enjoyed access to one of the finest libraries in the world and lived surrounded by the treasures both of antiquity and the Renaissance. In Rome at Clement's Court, too, Catherine became accustomed to the attendant rituals and particular formalities of this way of life.

Also during her time in the Eternal City, much to Clement's alarm, Catherine fell under the enchanting spell of Ippolito de Medici. By the spring of 1531 rumours were circulating about the couple and the young man might well have nurtured ambitions of marriage. He cut a tremendous figure. According to contemporary descriptions, spectacularly supported by the famous Titian portrait of him in the dress of an Hungarian horseman, now at the Pitti Gallery in Florence, he was slim and tall with dark good looks. He had a penchant for theatrical adornments, dressing with diamond aigrettes and jewelled scimitars. Ippolito provided the perfect antidote to Catherine's years of loss and suffering. Older than Alessandro, he should by rights have been groomed as the ruler of Florence: the peace Treaty of Barcelona, however, indicated that Clement had other plans.

The marriage was agreed between Alessandro and Margaret of Austria, the Emperor's illegitimate daughter, and a new constitution had been drafted by a group of Florentines known as 'the thirteen reformers of the republic' making the Medici hereditary rulers of the city and finally settling 25 years of political revolutions and instability. With the Emperor's backing, therefore, Ippolito had been bypassed in the succession. He had unwillingly been created a cardinal at the age of twenty but would happily have put his red hat aside, left the Church and married Catherine, taking what he felt was his rightful place as Florence's ruler. After a failed attempt to raise support in the Tuscan capital – where people now rejected further strife and yearned for a return to calm and prosperity – Ippolito, bribed by His Holiness with rich benefices and other gifts in exchange for a promise to agitate no further, found himself packed off to Hungary as Clement's legate in June 1532.

Pressing family matters crowded the Pope's agenda. He wished to expedite the implementation of the Treaty of Barcelona; and to see his son Alessandro properly invested as Duke of Florence and married off to Margaret of Austria. The Signoria was abolished under the new constitution and on 27 April 1532 the Pope's illegitimate son was officially created Duke of Florence. Catherine had been sent to the city to lend legitimacy to the proceedings and for the first time in her life undertook official public duties at Alessandro's side. Observers noted that the thirteen-year-old girl carried herself with admirable dignity and grace. She continued her public role in Florence while awaiting the arrival of Alessandro's bride in April 1533. Apart from enjoying the many and lavish celebrations marking the new duke's confirmation, Catherine also pursued her studies. We know little about her formal education except that she learned Greek, Latin and French; she was also a keen mathematician, an interest that would have coincided well with her later love of astrology. Clement kept her in Florence while he proceeded carefully with marriage talks on her behalf in Rome.

Since her birth, Catherine had inevitably been the object of much matrimonial discussion. Even before the revolt in Florence, Clement had been approached by various potential suitors, mainly Italian potentates from families such as the Gonzaga of Mantua, the Este of Ferrara and the della Rovere of Urbino. Now that the Pope enjoyed a far stronger position than formerly he looked for more illustrious offers. Among the earlier candidates was Henry VIII's illegitimate son the Duke of Richmond. Although Sir John Russell, the English ambassador to the Vatican, reported that His Holiness was 'very wel contentyd to have suche alliaunce' nothing came of the talks and the duke died a few years later, quite possibly from poisoning. When the Duke of Albany, Catherine's uncle, proposed the candidacy of King James V of Scotland, Clement did not think this offered him any real advantages and worried that the courier service between the two countries might be too costly. The Prince of Orange had briefly been considered as a possible husband until his death while campaigning to retake Florence.

The one candidate Clement could not afford to ignore, however, was the Holy Roman Emperor's own preference. Charles backed a marriage between Catherine and Francesco II Sforza, Duke of Milan. Unfortunately for Catherine the duke, a somewhat dim-witted man, prematurely aged at thirty-seven, sick and broken, mainly by the huge sums of money demanded by the Emperor in order to retain his duchy, was not a particularly gleaming matrimonial prospect. In addition Clement feared that by marrying Catherine to Charles's client he would find himself too deep in the Emperor's pocket to be able to free himself if necessary. Another worry for Clement was Charles's request for a general Church Council. The Pontiff feared that this might provoke a schism in the Church. Besides, Clement had never been ordained into the priesthood, thus making him technically ineligible for the papal throne. At this point a giddying proposal arrived from Francis I of France. His ambitions for territories in Italy stirred anew and he required a friendly pope to back them. In 1531, with this in mind, Francis offered Clement his second son, Henry, Duke of Orléans, as a potential husband for Catherine.

Early in 1531 Gabriel de Gramont, Bishop of Tarbes, was sent as Francis's envoy to discuss such a marriage. By April a preliminary agreement had been signed by Francis at the Château of Anet (ironically enough the home of Henry's future lover Diane de Poitiers). It stipulated that Catherine would live at the French Court until of an age to consummate the marriage and secret clauses in the agreement stated that her dowry would include Pisa, Parma, Piacenza, Reggio, Modena and Leghorn. Clement also committed himself to backing French efforts to take Genoa and Milan, and to making a joint attempt to annex Urbino for the young couple. In June 1531 word came back to France that Clement would not after all send Catherine to live at the French Court before her marriage. He was both wary of the wrath he knew this alliance would incur in the Emperor and fearful of a change in French policy once Catherine was already in Francis's hands. His matrimonial ace would thus remain in his own care until the wedding. Clement also stipulated that Catherine's dowry of 100,000 gold écus would include an extra 30,000 écus in exchange for the revenues from her Florentine inheritance. Francis agreed to give Catherine a further 10,000 livres per annum, and she would also enjoy the substantial income that came from her mother's inheritance.

As the second son of the mighty King of France, Henry, Duke of Orléans had no shortage of possible brides. The most important of these was Mary Tudor. The possibility of a marriage with Henry VIII's eldest daughter had been marred when the English King tried to have the marriage to her mother, Catherine of Aragon, annulled. Meanwhile Francis concentrated his attentions on Catherine, who could best further his

Italian ambitions. Henry of Orléans had been born on 31 March 1519 and, while not expected to inherit the French throne, represented a substantial catch for any royal princess, let alone an Italian duchess without a duchy. Catherine might have been rich but she was emphatically not of royal blood. In January 1533 at Bologna, secret talks were held between Clement and Francis's emissaries. The Pope, terrified that the Emperor would put a stop to the French alliance if he caught wind of it, decided to continue the negotiations regarding a marriage to Francesco II Sforza, Duke of Milan, as a feint. In fact Charles, certain that Francis would never stoop to marrying his son to a 'merchant's' daughter, generally laughed off the rumours he did hear as preposterous. When he eventually taxed Clement on the matter, the Pope hedged and promised the Emperor that if Francis did prove serious about the marriage then he would contrive to sabotage the talks: 'I know his nature, he [Francis] will want the honour of breaking with me, and this is what I desire.'[16] By the time the marriage was announced later on that same month, Charles could do nothing about it other than be amazed.

Clement's finest hour had arrived. He had defied adversity against monstrous odds. He had survived the sack of Rome and was restoring the city. His family had been thrown out of Florence; now they were reinstated in glory. He had, through an alliance with the Holy Roman Emperor, not only re-established his family as rulers of Florence, but managed to place the republic under the rule of his son as its hereditary duke.* His illegitimate son Alessandro had been created Duke of Florence with the Habsburg potentate's daughter for his duchess. By playing the Emperor off against the King of France, and dazzling the latter with over-optimistic promises of vast territorial gains in the peninsula, he had managed the match between Catherine and Henry of Orléans. He had reconciled the irreconcilable. Albany wrote to Francis that 'His Holiness marvellously desired this marriage.' Clement's simpering evidently amused de Gramont, the French envoy to Rome, who recorded the discussions during which Clement 'kept repeating over and over that his niece was not worthy of so lofty an alliance but ready nevertheless, for every sacrifice and any concession to secure it'.[17] Clement could not have foreseen that concession and sacrifice were indeed to become the young bride-to-be's most constant companions for what he rightly called 'the greatest match in the world'.

---

* Florence is sometimes referred to as a hereditary duchy, though technically it remained a republic until the 1700s. Although the republic was ruled by Duke Alessandro, the title of duke was a purely honorific one and conferred by the thirteen 'reformers' of the republic and it was hereditary. The matter had the Emperor's blessing but the title was not actually conferred by him. The Florentines believed that this would help keep them as independent as possible and not legally his vassals or clients.

TWO

'The Greatest Match in the World'

J'ai reçu la fille toute nue

1515–34

Henry, Duke of Orléans, Catherine de Medici's future husband, was born on 31 March 1519, a fortnight before his intended bride. The second son of 'Le Roi Chevalier', King Francis I, Henry suffered a childhood at least as traumatic as that of his wife-to-be. He lost his mother, the pious and sweet-tempered Queen Claude, who suffered from chronic ill health, at the age of five.* Not long afterwards he and his elder brother became the innocent victims of their father's worst political and military disaster, his catastrophic defeat at the hands of the Habsburg Empire at the Battle of Pavia in 1525. To understand Henry as a man, as a king and a husband, it is necessary briefly to examine this early drama of Francis's reign.

When Francis of Valois-Angoulême, twenty years old and ambitious, became King in 1515 he immediately directed his energies towards conquests in Italy. Showing both courage and resourcefulness, he claimed and won Milan from the Sforza family who were backed by the Empire.† Francis had ingeniously brought his army, guns and horses across a dangerous and little-used alpine pass into Italy, thereby entirely wrong-footing his enemy. Initial skirmishes and manoeuvres resulted in the decisive battle over Milan at Marignano, on 13–14 September 1515. After his dazzling victory Francis installed himself as Duke of Milan. He had only been King of France for nine months but Marignano, even though he could not know it, was to be the high point of his entire military career. As his predecessors had already discovered, French conquests in Italy were hard to preserve and proved a constant drain in blood and treasure. Francis's success at Marignano also triggered an enduring hostility between himself and the Habsburg King Charles I of Spain. The French

---

* King Francis I and Queen Claude had seven children: Louise (1515–17), Charlotte (1516–24), François (1518–34), Henry (1519–59), Madeleine (1520–37), Charles (1522–45), Marguerite (1523–74).
† Charles's interest in Milan was based on the fact that the duchy was a fief of the Empire. Francis's claim was based on his descent from the Visconti family who preceded the Sforza dynasty as rulers of Milan.

King's quests for Italian territory and his enmity against the Habsburg Emperor were the two themes that were to characterise, and to an extent bedevil, his entire reign.

After Marignano, Francis became for a while the cynosure of European monarchs; success, it seemed, was his constant companion. In 1515 he allied himself with the Medici Pope Leo X for his support in Italy and unwittingly set in motion the course of events that would bring Catherine to France as his daughter-in-law almost twenty years later. In 1519 King Charles of Spain was unanimously elected Holy Roman Emperor, becoming Charles V. Francis had also put himself forward as a candidate and felt bitter at the humiliating outcome.

In 1521 Francis overreached himself and the city of Milan fell to the Emperor's troops the same year. By 1523 France stood virtually alone, England having joined forces with the Empire in a general league against the French. Treason, a failed rebellion against Francis from within his own kingdom, and invasion in both the north and the south of France forced him to act decisively. His army pursued the Imperial invaders southwards into Italy and after a harsh winter in the open laying siege to the city of Pavia where the Imperial troops had holed up, the two sides finally met in battle on 24 February 1525.

Numerically the armies were evenly matched and at first the fighting proved inconclusive. For reasons that are still not clear, Francis, probably believing the Imperialists to be in flight, charged out into the open at the head of his elite bodyguard and cavalry in pursuit of the enemy. It proved a critical error. By pushing forward into exposed terrain he found himself not only between his own guns and the enemy but also at the mercy of over 1000 hidden Imperial arquebusiers, well placed to pick off the distinctive French knights with relative ease. Gradually Francis and his men – who had cut a fantastic swathe through the enemy – found themselves stranded from the rest of their troops and encircled by Imperial soldiers. When his horse was killed beneath him, Francis showed immense personal valour as he continued the now hopeless fight on his feet. Burdened by his heavy armour he managed to hack men down with his sword, as the elite of the French nobility, though inspired by their King's courage, were being decimated around him. Eventually Francis and his surviving nobles were taken prisoner. Not since Agincourt had France lost so many gallant and high-born warriors on the field of battle. Pavia was an unmitigated disaster for her and her King.

Orders came to bring Francis to Spain where he would eventually meet his adversary Charles V. He believed strongly in the chivalric code and hoped that by appealing directly to his captor as one regal knight to another he might soften the extreme terms that the Emperor now demanded. The most important item, the Duchy of Burgundy, stood at the head of the list. The duchy had been seized by the French in 1477 at the death of the last duke, Charles the Bold, without leaving a male heir. Although Charles V claimed descent from the Burgundian duke on the female side, his political sense, not his dynastic pride, spurred his claim to Burgundy. The incorporation into the Empire of this rich and fertile duchy that stretched down his western borders with France creating a strategic foothold, would pose an alarming threat to the French. Francis received a royal reception in Barcelona on 19 June, and the crowds roared with excitement as he came out of the cathedral after celebrating mass. People clamoured around the King, begging him to use monarchical healing powers to touch the sick wherever he went. It is hardly surprising that a Venetian observer commented, 'He bears his prison admirably,' adding, 'he is well nigh adored in this country.'[1] After much fêting and excitement Francis arrived in Madrid in the late summer of 1525.

Before too long, however, the reality of his situation began to tell. Used to an active outdoor existence, the company of women and all the other essentials that made his life agreeable, Francis proved to be a terrible prisoner after all. He became too depressed to eat, which in turn caused him to fall dangerously ill from an abscess in the nose. Even the Emperor, who had so far avoided meeting the royal hostage, hurried to Francis's sickbed and looked anxiously at his most valuable asset, whose life seemed to be dwindling away. He granted permission for the King's sister Marguerite to come from France to minister to him. After several weeks of serious illness the abscess burst and the King rallied. A Frenchman at Francis's bedside reported back to Paris on 1 October 1525 that 'he has improved steadily ... Nature has performed all its functions, as much by evacuation above and below as by sleeping, drinking and eating, so that he is now out of danger.'[2] With Francis recovering, peace terms could be worked out.

On 14 January 1526, in the Treaty of Madrid, Francis renounced his claim to Milan and various other territories that the Empire had hitherto regarded as its own. To seal their accord the King betrothed himself to marry Charles's widowed sister, Queen Eleanor of Portugal, who had been waiting at the gloomy Spanish Court for her brother to find her a new husband. Physically, Eleanor had too many of the unfortunate Habsburg traits to be considered anything other than tolerable-looking. Francis – with a few casual gallantries – had charmed the dull, devout and kind-hearted Queen, who had by now completely fallen for him and could hardly believe her good luck when the treaty was agreed.

As for Burgundy, Charles would allow no discussion over the duchy. Francis finally consented to relinquish the territory to the Empire, but declared that he must supervise the handover himself. Charles knew that the transfer would be difficult. Realising that the French King's presence would help to smooth the process, he therefore decreed, with justifiably enormous misgivings, that Francis could return home provided he offered sufficient security in his stead. The King's mother and official regent during his captivity, Louise of Savoy, decided that her two eldest grandsons should take their father's place.

Thus, out of political necessity, Henry, Duke of Orléans and his elder brother the Dauphin François were doomed to be held hostage in Spain until their father redeemed them by fulfilling the obligations of the treaty. Henry VIII's ambassador John Taylor had been ordered to accompany the party on the long voyage to the rendezvous. Before their departure he saw the two boys and reported to Cardinal Wolsey, 'After dinner I was brought to see the Dauphin, and his brother Harry; both did embrace me, and took me by the hand, and asked me of the welfare of the King's highness. ... The King's godson [Henry] is the quicker spirit and the bolder, as seemeth by his behaviour.' The two brothers were aged eight and six when they exchanged their beautiful châteaux of Blois and Amboise for a series of increasingly forbidding fortresses in Spain.

Accompanied by their grandmother, Louise of Savoy, the two 'goodly children' made the journey southwards in appalling weather to the border between France and Spain. The exchange, for which a strict convention had been agreed, was scheduled to take place at seven o'clock in the morning on 17 March 1526. A ten-mile area had been sealed off around the Bidassoa river which marked the frontier. In the middle of the river floated a large raft, where the royal prisoners must be delivered. At the appointed hour two boats left, each from its respective side. The vessels measured the same size and contained the same number of men, all similarly armed. Outside the sealed-off sector the two boys had embraced members of their family and their household before leaving.

One of the noblewomen in their entourage, who were all deeply affected by the departure of the little boys, seemed to show particular concern and tenderness for Henry. Later to become the central figure in his life, it transpired that the kind lady of the court was the 25-year-old Diane de Poitiers. Obviously moved by the children's plight, she kissed the little boy on his forehead, bidding him farewell.

As the two boats arrived at the raft and the prisoners awaited the exchange, Charles de Lannoy, the Emperor's viceroy at Naples, declared to Francis, 'Sire, your highness is now free; let him execute what he has promised!' 'All shall be done,' replied the King who turned to his forlorn sons, tearfully embracing them and briefly making the sign of the cross over their heads. Henry and his brother kissed their father's hand, and he climbed into his boat with a promise that he would soon be sending for them. He then set off for the French side of the river. As he arrived on French soil Francis cried, 'I am King! I am King once again!'

At first Henry and his brother the Dauphin were held in 'honourable captivity' at Vitoria in Castile. Waiting for their release, they stayed with Queen Eleanor, who expected to become their stepmother shortly. A good-hearted woman, she took a kindly interest in their welfare. The boys also enjoyed the attentive care of a large French household including their governor, tutor, maître d'hôtel and seventy attendants and servants.[4] Yet it quickly became clear that their father had no intention of honouring the Treaty of Madrid and the boys soon felt the effect of his broken pledges. Before signing the treaty, the King had taken the precaution of telling his emissaries from France that the promises he signed as a captive must be regarded as void since they had been extracted under duress.

To modern readers it may appear ruthless that Francis could send his sons away into what he must have known would be a long captivity while he defied the Emperor, but in fact he had very little option. In order to liberate his kingdom from the aftermath of Pavia he had to be able to act as a free man. His mother Louise, suffering from failing health, lacked the authority to deal with matters effectively as regent, surrounding herself with notoriously corrupt advisers only interested in extracting what they could for themselves. Throughout her adult life Louise's abiding passion was her son. She called Francis 'my lord, my King, my son, my Caesar' and had struggled to keep his kingdom intact for him during his imprisonment, braving the people's hostility at his military failures and the unwelcome attentions of foreign predators.

Now Charles V found himself facing serious difficulties too. Thwarted by Francis's breach of their agreement, his careful plans had been shattered. Not only was the Treaty of Madrid in tatters, but the impecunious Emperor lacked the money to pay his armies; his German territories were torn with religious strife while the Turks attacked Hungary. No wonder a report from an English envoy at the time described him as being 'full of dumps'.[5]

Immediately after his release, Francis tried to stir up support for himself and trouble for the Emperor by creating the League of Cognac on 22 May 1526. Ostensibly the league had been formed 'to ensure the security of Christendom and the establishment of a true and lasting peace', though in reality it was composed of states that feared Imperial domination. It included France, Venice, Florence, the Papacy and the Sforza of Milan. Henry VIII of England also took a place as the league's 'protector'. As a direct response to Francis's actions, the children's 'honourable captivity' now changed abruptly for a cruder confinement. Charged with responsibility for the princes, the Constable of Castile, Don Iñigo Hernandez de Velasco, received orders to move them deeper into

Spain.* They were first moved to a castle near Valladolid. Then, in February 1527, a supposed plot to free the boys and bring them back to France prompted their transfer still further south.

Charles ordered the return of some of the children's attendants to France and took his hostages to a castle near Palencia about one hundred miles north of Madrid. By October – with Rome now sacked, Italy engulfed by war and Catherine herself a prisoner at the Murate – Charles gave permission for a brief visit by English emissaries to Henry and his brother. They spoke to the princes' tutor, Benedetto Taglicarno, and reported that he 'could not enough praise the Duke of Orléans of wit, capacity and great will to learn, and of a prudence and gravity passing his age, besides treatable gentleness and nobleness of mind, whereof daily he avoweth to see great sparks'.[6]

In 1529 the Spanish captured and executed a French spy found near Palencia, not far from the princes' castle. Fearing another escape attempt, the Emperor ordered that the boys be moved once again. Their new home, the grim mountain fortress of Pedraza, lay between Madrid and Segovia. Their French suite and attendants had been taken from them some months before their move. Put to work as galley slaves, the unfortunate servants were, according to one account, shipwrecked, captured by pirates and finally sold as white slaves in Tunis where, ironically enough, ten of the forty-one were later liberated by Charles V when he captured the city in 1535. The boys had been left with a sole companion, a French dwarf, to entertain them. Their gaolers, coarse Spanish soldiers, kept them under close watch and cared little for their charges.

Reports from a French agent near Pedraza described his two sightings of the boys in July 1529. On the first occasion he saw them led by a Spanish prince to Mass heavily escorted by eighty foot soldiers. He next sighted them surrounded by fifty mounted men on their way out to play. The spy reported that whenever Henry came out he rode a donkey held by two men because of his constant attempts to flee; he also noted that the prince insolently cursed the Spaniards at every opportunity.

Meanwhile the international situation began to look promising for the princes' eventual return home. While Francis and the Emperor busied themselves absurdly challenging each other to duels, still locked in their mutual antagonism, both sides, exhausted by war, nonetheless urgently needed to conclude a settlement. To break the impasse, Francis's mother Louise and Charles's aunt Margaret of Austria, regent of the Netherlands, were authorised to carry out talks on behalf of the two rulers, neatly providing the men with a face-saving solution at the same time. 'La Paix

* Don Iñigo Hernandez de Velasco died in October 1528. Upon his death his son Don Pedro became both the new Constable of Castile and the princes' gaoler.

des Dames' (the Peace of the Ladies), properly called the Treaty of Cambrai where it was concluded and signed by Louise of Savoy and Margaret of Austria in August 1529, would eventually set the princes free. Its most significant article involved part of Burgundy being yielded to Charles in exchange for the princes; instead they would be released for a ransom of 2 million écus. Charles's sister Eleanor, who had been languishing in despair believing that matters would not be resolved, was still to marry Francis and when 1.2 million écus, the first part of the ransom had been paid to the Emperor, the children and the Queen would be allowed to travel to France.

The regent Louise asked for permission to send her usher, M. Bodin, to visit the boys at Pedraza to give them the good tidings of their imminent homecoming. Under heavy guard the man travelled to Castile where, after many delaying tactics by the Spanish, he arrived in September 1529. Bodin's moving account of the meeting describes the hardship and the solitude Henry and his brother the Dauphin Francis had had to endure. After being kept waiting at Pedraza, the usher finally received authorisation to enter the fortress itself where he saw the princes in their small dark cell with walls ten feet thick and iron bars to prevent escape. A small shaft of light came from a window too high to reach and the only furnishings were straw mattresses. When Bodin set eyes upon the two pathetic and shabby boys, he wept. After bowing to them he explained he had come on behalf of the King and to say that they would soon be returning home. The Dauphin turned to his gaoler saying that he had not understood a word the man had said and wanted him to 'use the language of the country'. The Marquis of Berlanga, entrusted with the princes' security and well-being at Pedraza, retired leaving Bodin with the boys, who then repeated his message in Spanish. Astonished, the usher asked if the Dauphin had forgotten his native tongue. The prince retorted that since his suite had been removed from him he no longer spoke French. At that moment Henry interjected, saying, 'Brother, this is the usher Bodin.' The Dauphin acknowledged that he knew the man and had been feigning his ignorance for the benefit of Berlanga.

The two boys then fired excited questions at their visitor, asking about everything at home, their family, the King and their friends. Allowed to withdraw to an adjoining room, the princes rushed to the window for fresh air. Bodin also noticed two small dogs. One of the guards remarked, 'That is the only pleasure which the princes have,' another added, 'You see how the sons of the King your master are treated, with no company but that of the soldiers ... and neither exercise nor education.' Presumably even the entertaining dwarf had been sent away by this time. The Spaniards, fearful that Bodin might use some sophisticated French sorcery to remove the boys, refused to allow him to measure them (he wished to report their growth to the King), nor was he permitted to give them new clothes in case they possessed magic powers. Bodin shed further tears when he bade farewell to the princes and returned home to report their miserable plight.[7]

After many difficulties and postponements, at last the time arrived for Henry and the Dauphin to be exchanged for the gold. One of the principal impediments to the transfer had been Francis's problem in raising the money for his sons' freedom. Extravagant promises to contribute to the ransom had been made by the King's richer subjects, though in the event they only grudgingly produced the money after much prodding. Francis's blunders had been expensive for the kingdom. When the correct amount of écus had finally been collected, inspected and weighed, it was discovered that unscrupulous officials had clipped some of the coinage, so further appeals for funds had to be made. Eventually the gold was ready and once again a strict protocol agreed, noting all the details of how the exchange should take place.

The King charged the Grand Master of France and renowned soldier, Anne (pronounced Annay) Baron de Montmorency, with the safety of the gold and its exchange for the prisoners. The Constable of Castile brought his charges to the Bidassoa river accompanied by the Emperor's sister, Eleanor, who had been languishing in a convent waiting in despair for her marriage to Francis.* The exchange, which had originally been fixed for March 1530, was now to begin on 1 July, almost a year after the peace treaty had been signed at Cambrai.

The day before the transfer the Constable of Castile accused Montmorency and the French of a slight to his honour over some trifle. Without a full apology from the French government, he declared that the arrangements for the exchange would be halted. For months Montmorency had been painstakingly fulfilling even the most petty obligations laid down in the agreement; now some self-important Spanish windbag threatened to prolong the business indefinitely. Exasperated, Montmorency offered to give satisfaction in person. Fortunately the Grand Master's reputation as a fierce soldier had the Spaniard offering to set aside his grievance with sudden grace. All was set for the following day.

Just before the prisoners left his care, the Constable of Castile presented Henry and his brother with a pair of horses each, asking them to forgive any wrongs that he might have done them. The Dauphin appeared good-natured, but Henry merely turned his back on his despised erstwhile gaoler and farted. Queen Eleanor and the two boys arrived in France by torchlight on the night of 1 July to be reunited with their father and his

---

* Eleanor and Francis had already been married by proxy, although a proper wedding ceremony with both parties present was considered desirable.

Court two days later. Henry, now eleven years old, and the twelve-year-old Dauphin had been prisoners for almost four and a half years.

At first sight the boys looked well and they had grown considerably, though soon it became obvious that both children had been deeply affected by their ordeal. Quiet and reserved, their insistence on points of etiquette, their clothes and other details made them seem more Spanish than French. Henry, who had once been described as a lively intelligent boy, had changed into a withdrawn and quiet youth. Their incarceration and all its attendant deprivations had marked both children for life. After the celebrations and receptions were over, Francis soon became impatient with his gloomy sons. He declared, 'The mark of a Frenchman was to be always gay and lively,' adding that he had no time for 'dreamy, sullen, sleepy children'. To add to this, the King now tactlessly showed a marked preference for the princes' younger brother, Charles, Duke of Angoulême. Younger than Henry by one year, Charles greatly resembled his father in looks and his outgoing manner.

Henry vented the frustration and anger he felt in a mania for sport, finding relief in hunting, tilting, wrestling and other rough exercise. He also became an accomplished tennis player and surrounded himself with a tight-knit band of friends, most of them noble youths who were his 'enfants d'honneur'. He became particularly attached to Jacques d'Albon de Saint-André, son of his governor. Although Saint-André was eighteen when Henry returned from Spain, he took a great shine to this clever and amusing companion, the boy idolized his flamboyant and worldly friend, remaining loyal to him for the rest of his life. At the same time he quickly developed an affection for François of Guise, the eldest son of the great soldier Claude, first duke of Guise, who bore the courtesy title of Comte d'Aumale. They were the same age and both admired military achievements, thriving on stories of valour and warfare.

Henry also found his mentor during this period, as his devotion to Anne de Montmorency grew. The Grand Master had charge of the royal children's household, and Henry's failure to find intimacy with his father encouraged a growing dependence on Montmorency. The soldier and courtier embodied all that Henry aspired to be; a great warrior, as well as a chivalrous and learned man. He appreciated Montmorency's solid conservative values, and sought the older man's advice and guidance whenever he could. Henry's loathing of the Emperor was understandable and obvious; Charles V was now his sworn enemy and would remain so for the rest of his life. Just like his future wife Catherine – who, coincidentally, emerged from captivity at the same time – Henry never forgot a wrong, nor a loyal friend.

After a happy reunion with his siblings at Amboise, Henry and his brothers and sisters attended and assisted at Queen Eleanor's coronation at Saint-Denis in March 1531. Already bored by his wife, Francis made not the slightest effort to hide his feelings. Making her official entry into Paris, Eleanor passed by where he stood at a prominent window. Immediately in front of him stood his mistress, Anne d'Heilly, Duchess d'Étampes, with whom he was shamelessly engaged in some kind of sexual activity. An observer wrote that Francis was 'devising with her for two long hours in the sight and face of all the people'. To say that they 'marvelled' at the Most Christian King's behaviour is hard to dispute. To make matters worse the King's sister Marguerite commented to the Duke of Norfolk that the new Queen was 'very hot in bed and desireth too much to be embraced'. The King found poor Eleanor 'so unpleasant to his appetite that he had neither lain with her nor yet meddled with her'.

In the autumn of the same year, Francis and the royal family embarked upon a grand progress through France. The King wished to make this a gigantic national celebration to thank his loyal subjects for their sacrifices to help free the royal children. The magnificent official entries under ornate triumphal arches into important cities throughout the kingdom made a deep impression on Henry, and while the dignitaries listened to speeches and attended banquets, the people danced in the streets and drank wine flowing from the water fountains. Later, during Henry's reign, royal entries (*les entrées joyeuses*) reached new heights for splendour, expense and creative genius. Both Francis and Henry understood the importance of making dazzling royal visits to the provinces.

Since his return to France, Henry had increasingly become the object of his father's matrimonial plans. After the marriage talks with Henry VIII over his daughter Mary Tudor had collapsed, Francis turned to Pope Clement VII to discuss a proposed match with Catherine de Medici. Francis believed this to be a sure route back to conquests in Italy, an opinion Clement did nothing to discourage. It was decided that the marriage, set for the summer of 1533, should take place at Nice, in what promised to be one of the grandest celebrations of the century. The Pope had decided to accompany his niece, and Francis, ever anxious to show the French monarchy at its most brilliant, could be counted upon to make the occasion unforgettable.

The marriage contract stated that Clement should 'at his own discretion, furnish his illustrious relative with clothing, ornaments, and jewels'. The Pontiff, determined that Catherine's trousseau should befit her new status, enlisted the help of Isabella d'Este, one of the most brilliant women of the Italian Renaissance, renowned for her beauty, good taste and setting the latest fashions. From Mantua she sent 'three pounds of gold, two pounds of silver and two pounds of silk' for embroidering the glittering gowns being made up by the most talented seamstresses in Florence. The bed hangings and black-and-crimson silk sheets were of the finest quality and Catherine's lingerie was as exquisite as her gowns. Such quantities of lace, gold and silver cloth, brocade and damask were ordered that Alessandro, Duke of Florence, levied a tax of 35,000 écus on the Florentine people ostensibly for the reinforcement of the city's defences but actually to pay for Catherine's bridal bottom drawer.

The jewellery that Catherine brought with her to France was considered without parallel: comprising ropes of pearls, rings, golden belts – one encrusted with rubies – and many other fabulous gems, it added significantly to the collection of French Crown jewels. The most famous of this collection were the vast pear-shaped pearls, said to be worth 'a kingdom'.* Catherine later gave the pearls to Mary, Queen of Scots, who would eventually return with them to Scotland as a widow. After Mary's beheading they were appropriated by Queen Elizabeth I who wore them 'without a blush'.

Clement also presented his niece with parures of emeralds, rubies with a gigantic pendant pearl, and two enormous diamonds. By far the most valuable and significant *objet* that Catherine brought with her was the casket of rock crystal created by the master of precious stone cutting, Valerio Belli Vincentino. The casket's twenty-four panels depict religious scenes from the life of Christ with figures of the four Evangelists at each comer, and is set in silver-gilt. (It can be seen today at the Uffizi Gallery in Florence.) Clement, unable to fund Catherine's cash dowry, borrowed from her uncle by marriage, the banker Filippo Strozzi. He pawned papal jewels as security to the banker against a loan for the first sum of 50,000 écus due at the time of the marriage. The agreement stated that the balance be paid in two instalments six months apart, but before long Strozzi came to regret what must have looked like a sound investment at the time.

The traditional portraits had been exchanged between the two parties. They seem to have been relatively faithful to their subjects, though portrait painting, particularly in this context, was a medium notorious for flattery. Commissioned by Duke Alessandro de Medici, Giorgio Vasari painted Catherine's life-size portrait for Francis and found his subject's personality, if not her looks, quite beguiling. When Vasari left the room to take a short break during a sitting, Catherine is said to have picked up the brushes and remodelled her features to resemble those of a Moorish woman. Vasari rather breathlessly recalled the incident, saying, 'I am so devoted to her on account of her special qualities and of the affection she bears not only me but my whole nation, that I adore her, if I may say so, as one adores the saints in heaven.'

---

* In fact the pearls, though of a rare shape and size, were bought from a Lyons merchant for 900 écus.

On the afternoon of 1 September 1533, after a lavish farewell banquet given by Catherine for the noble ladies of Florence, the bride-to-be set off on her journey to the coast. Accompanied part of the way by Alessandro de Medici, she travelled with a huge retinue consisting not only of various noble relations but seventy gentlemen sent by Francis. Their schedule allowed for various overnight stops en route to La Spezia; from there she and her entourage would make the short sea crossing to Villefranche and await the Pontiff. From Villefranche the two parties would complete the journey together.

Plans for the wedding to take place at Nice had been thwarted by its ruler, the Duke of Savoy – a vassal of the Emperor – and Marseilles was substituted. Shortly after Catherine's departure from Florence an emissary of the King of France arrived bringing her jewellery as a welcoming gift; among these were a superb diamond and a sapphire. Finding Catherine had already left on her journey towards the coast, the Frenchman galloped after the party and presented the delighted girl with the jewels.

On 6 September Catherine arrived at La Spezia where her uncle, the Duke of Albany, awaited his niece with eighteen galleys, three sailing ships and six brigantines, for what proved to be a calm crossing to Villefranche where Catherine remained as the Duke returned to fetch the Pope. Exactly a month later Clement embarked with his glittering suite, including thirteen cardinals, a large number of bishops and other senior members of the curia and nobility. Albany now supplemented the naval escort with at least forty further vessels, some Spanish, some Genoese. Forming a line, the vessels fired cannon salvoes to honour His Holiness as he departed. The flotilla then set off to collect Catherine, a galley named *La Duchessina* carrying the Host (as was the custom) led the fleet and the Pope sailed in a vessel covered with gold brocade, like an emperor of antiquity.

Catherine came aboard on 9 October and the party set sail for Marseilles where extravagant preparations for their arrival had been under way. Montmorency had already been in the city for some time making ready for the reception of the royal family, the Pope and his niece. He had blown up a whole *quartier* in order to make way for a temporary palace of wood fitting for the city's exalted visitors. The flotilla hoved into view on Saturday, 11 October and immediately small craft loaded with musicians and cheering people came out to welcome the visitors and surrounded the Medici armada.

The ships dropped anchor to a deafening greeting: the sound of 300 cannon firing off their welcoming salvoes to the accompaniment of 'hautbois, clarion and trumpets', as well as pealing church bells throughout the city. Montmorency went to collect the Pope and his niece in a frigate decorated in precious damask and they were brought ashore. The excited crowds were giddy with anticipation. Meanwhile Clement and Catherine spent the night just outside Marseilles preparing for the Pope's solemn entry into the city.

The next morning, a Sunday, Clement, accompanied by Catherine informally as her own official entry was yet to come, made his state procession into the town. He sat enthroned upon the *sedia gestatoria*, behind the Holy Sacrament carried on a sumptuously caparisoned grey horse. Behind His Holiness came the cardinals riding in pairs, followed by Catherine and the gorgeously dressed ladies and gentlemen of her suite. Among the cardinals was her beloved Ippolito, recently returned from Hungary. His spell abroad had blunted none of his dramatic sartorial inclinations, and he drew admiring looks as he rode accompanied by an escort of Magyars and pages dressed as Turks, their costumes of green velvet embroidered with gold. They wore turbans and were armed with scimitars and bows. At last the party arrived at their specially constructed residence opposite the King's own lodgings at the palace of the Comtes de Provence on the Place-Neuve.

By closing off the Place-Neuve a vast chamber had been built between the two buildings to serve as both a magnificent reception room and audience chamber for the coming feasts, ceremonies and interviews. Above this ran an enormous passage so that meetings could be held between the King and the Pope, each crossing to visit the other when the need arose, without having to be observed by outsiders. Montmorency had ensured that the two parties were housed in splendour, bringing the finest tapestries, furniture and works of art from the Louvre and other royal palaces.

On Monday, 13 October Francis, his family and the Court made their entry into Marseilles accompanied by 200 soldiers, 300 archers and his velvet-clad Swiss bodyguard. As soon as the King and his entourage arrived at the Place-Neuve, he went to pay homage to Clement and then the two set about finalising their agreement – which had to be done before the marriage could take place. A handwritten note thought to have been made by Francis survives. According to the main points the papacy and the French were to reconquer Milan, which would then be ruled by Henry. Parma and Piacenza would be rendered to Francis by the Pope and Urbino retaken. Power politics having been taken care of, the time had come for the bride-elect to make her state entry into the city.

On 23 October 1533 Catherine officially entered Marseilles, riding a roan horse decked out in gold brocade. She was preceded by six horses, five caparisoned in scarlet and gold, and one grey charger in silver cloth led by her cousin Ippolito's pages. Wearing an outfit of gold and silver silk, Catherine's appearance did not disappoint the crowd. A fine horsewoman and brilliantly dressed, she made a striking impression. Among her train rode twelve 'demoiselles' with a royal and papal guard.

A coach draped in black velvet with two pages on horseback also followed. Making up part of her entourage were three women, Marie the Moor and Agnes and Margaret the Turks, all captured 'in expeditions against Barbary, the people marvelled at the spectacle'. In the audience chamber at the Pontiff's temporary palace, Francis stood nearby with Henry and his younger brother Charles as Catherine made a deep curtsy to Clement and knelt to kiss the Pontiff's feet. This humble gesture pleased the French King who lifted the young girl to her feet, kissed her and bade both his sons do likewise.

Catherine then received a warm greeting from Queen Eleanor, after which a great banquet was held. The Pope and Francis sat at a high table alone together. After the dinner a concert and other entertainments had been arranged. The two Courts spent the days preceding the wedding enjoying themselves. In the warm weather it became the fashion to take boats borrowed from fishermen and draped in brocade and other luxuries out on to the sea and spend the days picnicking in hidden bays on sandy beaches. According to some chroniclers the Mediterranean air relaxed the manners and morals of a number of courtiers when out of royal view.

It would seem that Catherine did not appear disappointed by her fiancé's appearance even if the taciturn and awkward prince could not be described as particularly forthcoming. But pushed on by his father to make a good impression, the boy danced and jousted and participated in the celebrations during the days that followed. Henry was tall for his age and muscular, he had almond-shaped brown eyes, a straight nose, dark-brown hair and a clear complexion – although Pierre de Brantôme, the famous Court chronicler, called him 'a little swarthy' – altogether the groom was not ill-looking.* Catherine still had the advantage of youth, which to some extent would have masked her lack of beauty. She understood that wearing superb and luxurious clothes helped the overall impression she created, as did her lively intelligence, wit and fine manners. One historian described an unnamed portrait of Catherine at around this time: 'The face is at least agreeable, with features, which, though strongly marked, are not irregular.'

On 27 October the signing of the marriage contract took place and the Cardinal de Bourbon blessed the couple who were then taken into a hall erected for the celebrations. Clement led Henry in by the hand and Montmorency, who represented the King, brought in Catherine. Here the groom kissed the bride before the assembled company. Their embrace gave the signal for a fanfare of trumpets and the start of a great ball. Afterwards Henry and Catherine went to their separate lodgings. The religious ceremony was scheduled for the next day.

* Brantôme would have been relying on hearsay as he was not born until 1540.

Next morning, Francis collected the bride from her chamber. The King looked more like the bridegroom than the prospective father-in-law, wearing white satin embroidered with the fleur-de-lys and a cloak of gold cloth covered with pearls and precious stones. Catherine wore ducal robes of golden brocade with a violet corsage of velvet encrusted with gems and edged with ermine. Her hair had been neatly dressed with precious stones and upon her head sat a ducal crown of gold given her by Francis. The nuptial Mass took place in the chapel of the Pope's palace; the bride and groom exchanged rings and vows. Catherine was now a royal duchess of France.

That night Clement gave a wedding banquet during which the new Duchess of Orléans sat between her husband and his brother the Dauphin. After the banquet came a masked ball. Though they wore thin disguises, Francis took part energetically, as did Ippolito, clearly not in the least heartbroken at the marriage of his little cousin. At around midnight, after the bridal couple had left, the masque descended into a raucous orgy. A Marseillaise courtesan had been brought to the proceedings and as the night wore on her clothes slipped off. Finally she dipped her breasts into goblets of wine placed on the long tables, and offered them to the eager gentlemen surrounding her. Not to be outdone, some of the ladies of the Court followed suit and one observer wrote that 'their honour was wounded'.

Meanwhile, with all decorum, Catherine, led by Queen Eleanor and followed by a select group of women, made her way to the nuptial bedchamber. Soon afterwards Henry entered the room. The richly decorated bed alone was said to have cost 60,000 écus. The newlyweds – each fourteen years old – were attended with great ceremony at their 'coucher'. Both the King and the Pope wanted to be sure that the marriage was consummated that night and Francis is supposed to have remained in the couple's room until he announced himself satisfied that 'each had shown valour in the joust'. Clement waited until the morning to bless the ducal couple and beamed with contentment to find Henry and Catherine still in bed.

Before the two Courts started on their long journeys home the ritual exchange of gifts took place. Among the endless items given and received was a superb Brussels tapestry depicting the Last Supper presented to Clement by Francis. In addition to the crystal casket, the Pope gave the King a gold-mounted unicorn's horn (probably a narwhal's tusk) reputed to ward off poison.[8] Adding to his exotic menagerie, Ippolito accepted a rather daunting lion from the French King, which the infidel pirate Barbarossa had given to Francis only a few months earlier. In fact, Ippolito would have done better to ask for a unicorn's horn for himself, since he died soon afterwards, poisoned by his cousin and lifelong rival

Alessandro de Medici. Alessandro was himself murdered in 1537 by his cousin Lorenzino and the dukedom of Florence passed – with the Emperor's backing – to a distant relative named Cosimo de Medici, son of the famous *condottieri*, Giovanni de Medici, known as 'Giovanni delle bande nere'. Catherine despised Cosimo, considering him a nonentity and a creature of the Emperor's; it is also worth noting that none of this 'Italian' behaviour was to enhance Catherine's reputation later on.

On 7 November Clement created four new French cardinals. One of their number was Montmorency's nephew Ôdet de Châtillon, later to prove a source of great embarrassment after he joined the Protestant reformers. Francis reciprocated by investing four of the Pope's entourage with the Order of Saint-Michel. The King and members of his suite took their leave of Clement on 13 November, but the Pope's journey had been delayed by rough seas. Catherine, Queen Eleanor and the ladies remained behind until the weather cleared for the Pontiff's departure a week later; he arrived back in Rome in mid-December. Just before embarking, Clement is said to have whispered this advice to his niece: 'A spirited girl will always conceive children.' That was her duty now, to bear children would seal the Franco–Papal alliance beyond doubt.

By mid-winter Catherine and the royal women joined the King and his Court in Burgundy, where Francis immediately announced details of the agreement he had made with Clement. First he proclaimed the Duchy of Urbino to be the rightful territory of his son Henry through his marriage to Catherine, and by July 1534 he was building an army ready to reconquer Urbino, Milan and other Italian territories with his new papal ally. Meanwhile Catherine spent little time with her husband and more with his sisters Marguerite and Madeleine, whose household she shared. Travelling back through France to Paris with her father in-law's huge itinerant Court, Catherine, amiable and eager to please, made great efforts to be liked. Gradually she became part of her new family and won over some of the more snobbish courtiers, though there were those among them who muttered that they would rather have their knees broken than bend them to the Italian merchant's daughter. Then disaster struck.

On 25 September 1534, less than a year after Catherine's marriage, Pope Clement VII died in Rome, his territorial promises to Francis unfulfilled and Catherine's dowry only partly paid. Francis was apoplectic and the French people soon decried the union as a *mésalliance*. The child who thought she had found a family, peace and security was left to reap the bitter harvest of her uncle's untimely death. The new Pope, Alexander Farnese who took the title Paul III, was neutral but firmly refused to honour either Clement's dowry obligations or the alliance with Francis. Catherine was now of no value to the King politically, and he declared

'*J'ai reçu la fille toute nue*' (The girl has come to me stark naked). In contrast to her triumphant arrival in France, Catherine now faced a thousand pinpricks of humiliation as her prestige vanished along with Clement's now worthless promises.

THREE

A Barren Wife

Her role was not to have one unless it were
to sue for the King's favour

1533–47

Catherine was only fifteen when Clement's unexpected death entirely destroyed her political *raison d'être*. Knowing she was regarded as a poor excuse for a princess by the caste-conscious French, lacking any foreign dynastic support and without powerful French connections of her own, she must have felt vulnerability bordering on fear. If she had been beautiful, perhaps she could have evoked the love of the common people, but her heavy cheeks and bulging eyes were stubborn features that could not be coaxed away by paint. Her Italian fashions and other hints of her origins served only to remind people of past military failures in Italy and a lost opportunity of allying France with a superior bride. Besides, when the French were not busy imitating the Italians in art and culture or occupying their country, they despised them as money-grabbing opportunists who would slip a knife between a man's shoulder blades as soon as his back was turned. It is unlikely that the Venetian ambassador exaggerated excessively when he wrote that the marriage 'displeases the entire nation'. Catherine, above all a practical girl, knew that she could change neither her birth nor her face but she could use her formidable will-power and intelligence to overcome her present misfortunes. Recognising her unpopularity, she decided to cultivate the most important people at Court. The first and most obvious conquest must be the King himself. Fortunately, Catherine seems from the start to have evoked protective feelings in her father-in-law.

Ever quick to see what pleased people, she had no trouble identifying the monarch's weaknesses. The King put pleasure before almost anything else. One of his ministers remarked that 'Alexander [the Great] attended to women when there was no more business to attend to; His Majesty attends to business when there are no more women to attend to.' Driven by strong appetites, Francis could not live without beauty, whether it be artistic, architectural, female or literary. He could most frequently be found in the company of a striking group of courtly ladies called 'La Petite Bande'. Membership of the King's clique required good looks, wit, courage on horseback and a stomach for bawdy jokes. Entry, though strictly vetted by the King's mistress, Anne d'Heilly, Duchess d'Étampes, proved no problem and she welcomed Catherine in. Since her looks could not gain her a place, the young duchess became a member valued above all for her spirit. She sensed how to amuse the King whatever his mood; quick, clever and physically tough, she did all she could to keep up with him. Catherine enjoyed 'honest exercise like the dance at which she showed great skill and majesty' and could quickly pick up the latest steps from Italy that Francis admired so much.[1]

Catherine also loved to hunt and proved ready to take any fence or hedge to stay alongside His Majesty. She took her falls gracefully and bravely, always game for further challenges. Among several innovations that have been attributed to her, Catherine is credited with having brought the side-saddle to France. Hitherto Frenchwomen had been stuck on a cumbersome apparatus that resembled a sideways armchair (called the *sambue*) perched on the horse's back, which permitted only the most decorous amble. The side-saddle allowed women both to keep pace with men on horseback and to show off their legs. Catherine's own calves were well shaped and she enjoyed any opportunity to display one of her few physical strong points. With the side-saddle, the Duchess of Orléans had also brought another innovation, a primitive form of drawers, or pantaloons. Hitherto the lack of undergarments as we know them today meant that a well-placed gallant offering to help a lady down off her mount might also glimpse 'the sights of heaven', if only for a moment.

The young duchess showed her canniness by allowing herself to be taken up by the Duchess d'Étampes who was actually part of the royal princess's household, and it pleased the King that the favourite received his daughter-in-law's endorsement. Catherine spent as much time as she could with Francis – listening, learning and watching. Despite his many shortcomings he was every inch a king. The soldier and courtier turned historian and raconteur, Pierre, Abbé de Brantôme, said of Catherine at this time, 'Her role was not to have one unless it were to sue for the King's favour.' Her conversation, more learned than most girls of her age, amused Francis who appreciated her bold wit and quick intelligence. Listening to and appearing entertained by the bawdy talk of the King's entourage also proved that Catherine had an abundance of patience.

A glimpse of how homesick the young duchess must have been is shown in a letter written some time in 1534 to Maria Salviati (the mother of Cosimo de Medici later to become Duke Cosimo I) who had been one of Catherine's surrogate mothers. The handwriting is clear but childish: 'I am surprised because I have written to you a number of letters and have never had any answer which surprises me even more.' She then goes on to ask for progress on a number of commissions:

'Have you done all that I asked when I left – if so please send them through somebody trustworthy and the inventory of what they cost.' Conscious of living up to Francis's fashion standards, she ordered 'large white sleeves all covered in embroidery work in black silk and gold and send me the bill for the work'.[2]

Catherine also appealed to the King's sister, Marguerite – now Queen of Navarre – for her friendship and guidance.* One of the cleverest and most amusing women at Court, she also supported the reform religion. Marguerite enjoyed great influence with her brother and took the little Duchess of Orléans under her wing.† Henry's own sisters, Marguerite and Madeleine, became close companions as the Court made its way from one château to another, usually around the axis of the Loire river. The King particularly enjoyed visiting the building works at his royal palaces and discussing their progress and problems. One of the greatest builders of his day, he employed master craftsmen mainly from Italy, and was an innovative, lavish and talented patron, his building embodying the French Renaissance as 'Italianate models met with French taste'. Francis started the modernisation of the Louvre and commissioned the building of the Château of Madrid in the Bois de Boulogne. Unfinished at his death, the work was later completed by Catherine, who used the place occasionally. The King also made additions to Blois, Saint Germain-en-Laye and Villers-Cotterêts, though the rebuilding of the Château of Fontainebleau is probably considered his greatest undertaking. He decided to turn the former hunting lodge into a splendid palace, and it was the only place he called '*chez moi*' and he spent as much time there as he could.

Chambord, one of the most beautiful châteaux north of the Alps, is a haunting masterpiece set in woodland close to Blois near the Loire river. Alfred de Vigny wrote of the palace that Francis created from scratch in 1519, 'Far from any road, you suddenly come upon a royal or rather a magical château ... [stolen] from some country of the sun to conceal it in mistier lands. The palace is hidden away like buried treasure but its blue domes and elegant minarets rounded where they stand might suggest you were in the realms of Baghdad or Kashmir.'[3] The major works on the vast château were completed by 1540, though it was little used by Francis or his successors. 'If Chambord were ever destroyed, no record

---

* Marguerite of France was first married to the Duc d'Alençon. Her second marriage (in 1527) was to Henri d'Albret, King of Navarre. Navarre was a small Pyrenean mountain kingdom on the border between France and Spain.
† Marguerite, Queen of Navarre, enjoyed the spiritual and philosophical debates that had been sparked by Luther and Erasmus. In the early 1530s Jean Calvin, the French theologian and reformer, spent time in Paris until he went to live at Marguerite's Court at Nérac. Eventually the persecution of reformers forced him to live in Switzerland from where he would mastermind the dissemination of his doctrine that became known as Calvinisim.

of the pure early style of the Renaissance would be left anywhere ... [its] beauty was restored by its abandonment.'⁴ If the palace was not much used, it certainly provided an effective showpiece when required, and Catherine well understood the vital prestige that buildings on such a scale could lend to the monarch. She accompanied Francis on his visits to the châteaux and almost certainly absorbed the King's love for Italian workmanship and witnessed his prodigious spending on collections of sculpture, paintings and rare books to adorn his great palaces, most of which came from her mother country.

Unfortunately, while her charm and vivacity won over her father-in-law and his cronies, the one person to whom Catherine did not seem to grow any closer was her own husband. Although he treated his wife with civility, his indifference to her was obvious for all to see. He probably resented his father's choice of bride for him, and he had reason enough since she did not attract him sexually, was not of royal birth and had failed to bring the dowry that had been promised. Catherine's friendship with the King's favourite, the Duchess d'Étampes, displeased Henry, for there was a growing rivalry between the duchess and the woman who had become his favourite – Diane de Poitiers.

Born in 1500, Diane de Poitiers, widow of the Grand-Sénéschal of Normandy, Louis de Brézé, was the daughter of Jean de Poitiers, Seigneur de Saint-Vallier. His mother, like Catherine's, was a De La Tour d'Auvergne, making Catherine and Diane second cousins, sharing a great-grandfather. Jean de Poitiers's maternal uncle married into the Bourbon clan, a royal connection of which he was inordinately proud. Unfortunately de Poitiers' judgement did not match his breeding and in 1523 he allowed himself to be seduced into complicity with the planned uprising that same year against Francis by the King's most powerful noble, his kinsman the Constable de Bourbon.* Sentenced to death for his part in the plot, Jean de Poitiers's reprieve arrived with the King's messenger just as he placed his head on the executioner's block. No doubt Francis had contrived this dramatic last-minute intervention to make an enduring impression on the one-time conspirator. At the time of her father's ill-

---

* Charles de Montpensier, Duke de Bourbon (1490–1527), better known as the Constable de Bourbon, was related to Francis I through both the King's parents. Some rivalry existed between the two men but Francis depended greatly upon his best military commander's brilliance and was mindful of the duke's large number of supporters and fiefdoms, particularly those in the Bourbonnais at the centre of France. The rivalry became an open rift when Francis and his mother tried to snatch the inheritance of Bourbon's wife and cousin Suzanne (a descendant of Louis XI). Louise even tried to marry Bourbon as she not only wanted his money but found him physically attractive as well. Unable to reason with Francis, the utterly frustrated Bourbon allied himself to Charles V. In 1523 his uprising failed due to indiscretion, poor communication and insufficient external support. Bourbon was killed fighting for the Emperor in 1527 as his troops breached the walls of Rome.

advised treason Diane had already been married for eight years to Louis de Brézé, forty years her senior and reputedly the ugliest man in France. It was largely thanks to his timely intervention that Jean de Poitiers had his death sentence commuted to life imprisonment and by 1526 he was a free man.

Diane, a creature of natural taste and elegance, had come to Court aged fourteen and been married off to the rich and powerful widower de Brézé the following year. From the start she acquired a deserved reputation for her virtuous and graceful behaviour. A conscientious Catholic, she strictly disapproved of the reform movement. While not the brilliant beauty described by later fawning poets and painters, she was certainly an attractive young woman whose natural elegance and slight aloofness lent her the air of a superior being. Fanatically careful of her looks, Diane never painted her face and her 'secret elixir of youth' was, in fact, just large quantities of very cold water on her face and body. An early proponent of personal and feminine hygiene, she even had a book dedicated to her on the subject. Diane went to bed early, took frequent rests and regular gentle outdoor exercise. Her formula for guarding her looks so well against age was simple; she avoided excesses of any sort. This proved less difficult than for some because her pragmatism, essentially cold nature and inherent sense of dignity left her devoid of passion.

By the time she first became close to Henry, many still considered Diane a beauty. Nineteen years his senior, she had placed the young prince under her tutelage since his return from Spain. She formed part of Queen Eleanor's household and had been asked by Francis himself to try to tame the unpolished and silent boy. Without compromising her spotless reputation, Diane, who had been widowed in 1531, had easily beguiled the awkward young prince. He not only became her willing pupil but also her devoted admirer. Catherine, far too clever not to notice this, observed her rival quietly and with outward serenity – biding her time. Ever cautious, she made sure that she treated both Diane and Madame d'Étampes with the same courtesy. At this stage, however, it is almost certain that Diane and Henry had not become lovers, although events were soon to encourage the ambitious but so far decorous Diane to make Henry hers completely, thus earning her Catherine's undying enmity.

In 1536 Francis unleashed a war against the Emperor and took his sons with him on the campaign. In August the royal family were at Lyons staying well behind the army lines and the fighting. The King, who had originally expressed a desire to lead the troops in person, nonetheless stayed away from the front. His absence was not entirely unwelcome to some soldiers, who feared that since his defeat at Pavia the King had become the harbinger of bad luck on the battlefield. On 2 August, despite intensely hot and oppressive weather, the Dauphin played a vigorous game of tennis with one of his gentlemen. After the game he felt hot and breathless. Sending his secretary, an Italian count named Sebastian de Montecuculli, for a glass of freezing water to cool himself, he collapsed immediately after drinking it. Not long afterwards the prince developed a high fever and experienced difficulty breathing. He died in the early hours of Thursday, 10 August at Tournon.

The King, then at Valence, had only been told that the Dauphin was unwell and did not seem particularly anxious. The Cardinal of Lorraine had been given the task of telling Francis what had happened.* At first Lorraine, unable to break the dreadful tidings to the King, said only that the Dauphin's condition had worsened. Francis, not taken in by this, said, 'I understand perfectly, you dare not tell me that he is dead, but only that he will soon die!' Lorraine admitted the truth and the King took himself off to a window seat, turned his back and, bent double by the shock, tried to contain his grief. At last he cried out, 'My God, I know I must accept with patience whatever it be Thy will to send me, but from whom, if not from Thee, ought I to hope for strength and resignation?' Probably Francis felt guilt at his impatience with the Dauphin when, years before, he had returned from captivity in Spain; since then he had been a distant father who criticised too much and made too few allowances. Lately, though, the young man had shown much improvement and many thought he had the makings of a fine monarch in him.

With the sudden and quite unforeseen death of the heir to the throne, Henry and Catherine automatically became Dauphin and Dauphine, the future King and Queen of France. They were both seventeen years old. Francis called Henry to his side after hearing the news. He wept and grieved with his least favourite son and then gave him a stern lecture, saying, 'Do all that you can to be like he was, surpass him in virtue so that those who now mourn and regret his passing will have their sorrow eased. I command you to make this your aim with all your heart and soul.' These were hardly encouraging words from a father who had almost made a practice of ignoring Henry's existence. While unexpected death was a common occurrence in the sixteenth century, when it struck a royal prince suspicions of foul play could not be ignored and in many cases for good reason. Francis employed seven eminent surgeons to carry out the autopsy on the prince's corpse, but nothing suspicious could be found. Modern medical opinion has it that the young man probably died of pleurisy.

---

* Cardinal Jean of Lorraine (1498–1550), brother of Claude, first Duke of Guise. Not to be confused with the famous Cardinal Charles of Lorraine (brother of François, second Duke of Guise) who was Jean's nephew and later played an enormous role during Catherine's struggle to rule France for her sons.

Francis hunted about for a scapegoat and the late Dauphin's unfortunate and devoted Page of the Sewer, Montecuculli, found himself incriminated on three counts. First, his nationality made him an automatic suspect as Italians were known for their frequent use of poison to rid themselves of their enemies. Second, the page had originally been in the employ of the Emperor but had left to come to France along with the Italians accompanying Catherine. Most damning of all was the wretched man's apparent interest in toxicology, as evidenced by a book on the subject found among his possessions. Taken away for 'questioning', the terrified Montecuculli, keen to keep the agony as brief as possible under torture, gave a less than reliable confession, which he later retracted. Spilling forth all that he thought the King wanted to hear and more, Montecuculli accused the Emperor's agents of having hired him to poison the Dauphin and even the King himself. Satisfied with the result, Francis announced the findings of the investigation to ambassadors and representatives of the foreign powers at his Court. Cries of indignation came from the Emperor's representatives, and letters of protest were exchanged. Nothing further remained to be done but for the poor man to be executed by *écartelage*, the cruellest death but customary for those convicted of regicide. Before the whole Court, including Catherine, Eleanor and the other ladies, the probably entirely guiltless fellow was lashed by his arms and legs to four horses and torn to shreds as they galloped off in different directions out of the Place de la Grenette in Lyons on 7 October 1536.

Catherine, now the first lady in France after the Queen, almost immediately found her new position under threat. The initial unpleasant shock came with the accusation from the Emperor's agents who, protesting their master's innocence, pointed the finger at the royal couple, explaining that they were the only true beneficiaries of the Dauphin's death. Fortunately the King gave no credence whatever to the Imperialists' rumours, though the new Dauphine, whose supposed expertise as a poisoner was practically considered an Italian birthright, found the whispering campaign inevitably damaging. In fact, becoming Dauphine held desperate potential hazards for her. The only vital function of the heir to the throne's wife was childbearing and after three years of marriage Catherine had not showed the slightest sign of becoming pregnant. Now she must produce children or face possible repudiation.

Physical intimacy with her husband became harder than usual for Catherine as Henry now urgently pressed the King to allow him to participate in the campaign against the Emperor. Francis, reluctant to lose his second son so quickly after the death of his eldest, refused. Henry insisted, claiming his right as Dauphin to serve in the field. Eventually the King permitted him to join the army in Provence, which had been invaded by Imperial troops on 13 July. The next day the French commander, Montmorency, received his appointment as Lieutenant-General with sweeping powers over the entire military operation. While Henry's royal blood meant that he was nominally the supreme commander, it was to Montmorency that he turned for all military decisions. An outstanding defensive tactician, the soldier employed a systematic scorched-earth policy on the Provençal countryside – filling in every well, reducing whole towns to rubble, burning and destroying anything that might be of the slightest use to the enemy – and succeeded in driving out the Imperial troops. Many miserable inhabitants of the despoiled area died of starvation and lack of shelter, but the ends had justified the means in the view of both the King and his commander. The Grand Master's stock rose greatly with Francis after this success. The campaigning sealed the friendship between Henry and Montmorency for life and the Dauphin wrote to him afterwards, 'Be sure that whatever happens, I am and shall be for my life as much your friend as anyone in the world.'⁵ He was to remain true to his word.

In 1537 there came a further blow for Catherine. Henry fathered a child with Filippa Duci, the hitherto virgin sister of one of his Piedmontese grooms, while campaigning in Italy. Henry exulted at the news of the girl's pregnancy, claiming he had spent only one night with her. This proved conclusively that it must be Catherine, not he, who was physically at fault for their so far childless union. The mother-to-be enjoyed all the care and attention she could want until she gave birth to a daughter in 1538. This baby, subsequently legitimised by Henry, received the name Diane de France, presumably in honour of Diane de Poitiers. The child's natural mother spent the rest of her days in a convent, generously pensioned off. Diane undertook responsibility for the baby's upbringing as she had two grown-up daughters of her own and was considered a perfect replacement mother. The honour and attention that the child received caused unfounded rumours to abound that she was in fact Diane's and Henry's natural offspring. By having the baby named after her and taking care of it, the favourite sent a clear signal to all at Court that the Dauphin belonged to her.

Catherine's endurance faced further tests as Diane de Poitiers became more assiduous in her attentions to her husband. In 1538 a truce was declared between France and the Empire, encouraged by Pope Paul III, who wanted Francis and Charles to unite in a campaign against the ever-threatening Turks. When Henry returned from the war Diane, now thirty-eight years old, found him grown in confidence and no longer the timid boy she had been coaching from truculent adolescence into manhood. She showered the Dauphin with compliments on his military prowess, knowing that the moment had arrived for her to take possession of him completely. Casting aside the platonic ideals with which she had fended him off for so long, she traded her much-guarded virtue for a far more coveted position as mistress to the future king. Aided by Montmorency, who offered the couple the use of his castle at Écouen for their trysts, Diane allowed Henry to become her lover. It is not known exactly when the *amitié sage* became a full-blown love affair, but a poem of the favourite's where she writes opaquely of having 'submitted' suggests that Henry's ardour and Diane's ambition blew away any remaining boundaries between them.

While a screen of respectability was relentlessly held up to the world by the older woman, certain indications of the true state of their relations were there for all to see. Henceforth Henry dressed only in black and white, the mourning colours that Diane had worn exclusively since the death of her husband. He adopted the crescent moon as his emblem, which also belonged to the mythological Diana, goddess of hunting. The motto 'Until it fills the whole world', beneath the crescent moon, could have been an allusion to the power that would one day be his as King of France or possibly to take the Imperial mantle from Charles V. Perhaps the most obvious sign of the love affair between them was an ingenious monogram interlacing the H and D of their names. There existed several versions of this though looking at the one most commonly used it is possible to discern two Cs back to back, within an H throwing a sop to Catherine's hidden but burning pride. From now on until the end of his life, Henry had the monogram placed everywhere he could. Today it can clearly be seen on the châteaux and buildings that he had constructed or rebuilt during his reign. Catherine's own resolutely cheerful device of a rainbow with the motto 'I bring light and serenity' beneath it rang hollow. If only she had had someone to whom she could bring either.

Stubbornly childless, the Dauphine knew that she would not last long as Henry's wife if she could not produce a baby. A secret campaign to have Catherine repudiated had been set in motion. The plan was heavily backed by Madame d'Étampes who wished to see her rival Diane's position destabilised by the arrival of a new bride for Henry. The movement gathered momentum. Brantôme wrote, 'There were a large number of people who tried to persuade the King and Monsieur le Dauphin to repudiate her, since it was necessary to continue the line of France.' The Venetian ambassador, Lorenzo Contarini, wrote over a decade later that the King and the Dauphin had definitely decided upon divorce. The Guise family, sensing an opportunity for their own advancement, promoted a union between Henry and Louise of Guise, sister of François and the beautiful younger daughter of Claude, who had been created first duke by the King.

The Guise, a junior branch of the House of Lorraine claiming descent from Charlemagne, had come to France to seek their fortune at the very beginning of the 1500s and to run their family's estates in northern France. Though naturalised as French subjects, these minor foreign princes provided a constant irritation to many of the nobles as they managed to enjoy both the benefits as French subjects close to the King and their position as princes of Lorraine. They were supremely successful at raising their status by marriage and the first duke (himself wed to a Bourbon) had just married off his daughter Marie to King James V of Scotland.* Catherine now found an unexpected and invaluable ally in Diane. Tame and pliable, she made a perfect foil for the older woman desperate to prevent the arrival of some eligible lovely young bride, who might not view her relationship with Henry with quite the same resignation as Catherine at least seemed to. Thus the favourite threw her weight behind those who supported the Dauphine and brought to bear her enormous influence over Henry. She underscored to him his wife's many qualities – her gentleness, her good nature, and the fact the she was still young and had many years of possible childbearing ahead of her. Above all, Diane cleverly argued that the talk of divorce bore the mark of Henry's (in other words her own) enemies, particularly Madame d'Étampes and those who fawned upon her. Any suggestion that either his father or his father's favourite might be trying to manipulate him always sparked the most furious indignation in the Dauphin and for the moment he let the matter drop.

The final decision rested with the King and knowing that he was, however unwillingly, having to consider a new wife for his son, Catherine gambled everything on a peerless show of feminine submission to the man who liked to call himself 'the first gentleman of France'. Throwing herself at his feet sobbing, the Dauphine told Francis that she accepted that she must stand aside for a bride who would bear Henry children, begging only to be allowed to remain in France and serve the fortunate lady who would replace her in whatever lowly capacity the King might permit. Her sorrow and humility were so touching that the King found himself her champion against his own better judgement. Unable to stand the sight of any woman in tears, Francis, profoundly moved, declared, 'My child, it is God's will that you should be my daughter and the wife of the Dauphin. So be it.' It was a reprieve. Yet any such reprieve could only be temporary and she now employed all means at her disposal to overcome her barrenness. In her increasingly frantic attempts to become a mother, Catherine's unbending determination emerged, usually so nicely

*James V of Scotland had first married Henry's sister, Princess Madeleine of France, in 1537; after her death only a few months later he married Marie of Guise in 1538 and their daughter later became the famous Mary, Queen of Scots.

disguised. She was prepared to go to extraordinary lengths to preserve her place as Henry's wife and the future Queen of France.

After the King had, for the moment, abandoned the idea of repudiation, Catherine found herself given encouragement by those not normally interested in her. The King had spoken; if he wished her to remain Dauphine, so too did the flatterers. Matteo Dandolo, the Venetion ambassador, wrote, 'There is no one who would not willingly give their own blood to give her a son.'[6] He also noted that even the Dauphin now treated his wife with some affection. Marguerite of Navarre, Francis's sister, remained a solid supporter and constantly reminded him of Catherine's merits. She wrote to her, 'My brother will never allow this repudiation, as evil tongues pretend. But God will give a royal line to Madame la Dauphine when she has reached the age at which women of the House of the Medici are wont to have children. The King and I will rejoice with you then in spite of these wretched backbiters.'[7]

Her enemies silenced for a moment, Catherine turned first to traditional medicine with little success. Prayers and offerings to the Almighty were constantly on her lips. Diane gave advice, philtres and potions, and sent the Dauphin off to do his duty conscientiously and regularly by sleeping with his wife. He followed Diane's orders, but with little enthusiasm. The Dauphine pored over old texts by Photius and Isodore le Physicien that contained ancient magic and pagan remedies. Some of these 'remedies' were of the kill-or-cure variety. Showing she possessed a stomach as strong as her will, Catherine drank large draughts of mule's urine, the current wisdom being that it would provide a primitive form of inoculation against sterility. She was given clear instructions, though, not to go near the mule itself. Alchemists provided poultices that were so revolting it seems incredible that the Dauphin could make love to his wife at all. The soft, warm, stinking dressings were made up of ground stag's antlers and cow dung. To mask the smell a dash of crushed periwinkle was blended in with mare's milk. The poultices were then placed upon Catherine's 'source of life' and left to do their work, but these 'fullproof methods' yielded nothing, except, perhaps, an increased desire on the Dauphin's part not to get too close to his wife, much less sleep with her. The astrologers were also consulted, and she faithfully followed their every instruction, but still no child appeared.

Finally Catherine became convinced that she was sexually incompetent and committing a fundamental error of some sort. Whatever Diane was doing with her husband she must try to do the same herself. It is said that the stout-hearted young woman ordered that holes be bored through her floor (probably at Fontainebleau) so that she could look down into the bedchamber where her husband and Diane spent their passionate nights together. Catherine's ladies begged her not to go to these agonising lengths, but she would hear no argument and steeled herself to watch Henry make love to his mistress. When the time came her sorrow at the sight of the lovers' complete abandon in each other was so great that she actually saw very little; her eyes were filled with tears before she finally turned away. What she had seen, however, suggested to her that she and her husband did something very different when they lay together.[8]

At last a doctor named Jean Fernel was called. He examined the Dauphin and Dauphine, and found that their reproductive organs both carried slight physical abnormalities. The sensible doctor counselled a method that might overcome the problem although, irritatingly, we can only speculate as to what it was. The couple were told what to do, and Henry performed his duty. Their joy was obvious to all when in the early summer of 1543 Catherine became pregnant. In one of the letters that survive from her during this time, she wrote to Montmorency – who had by now been created Constable of France and had himself given her advice on how to start a family – 'Mon Compère, as I know well that you desire children for me as much as I do, I wished to write to tell you of my great hopes that I am with child.'[9] On 19 January 1544, at Fontainebleau, the Dauphine went into labour and in the late afternoon, to the great relief of all concerned, she gave birth to a son. For the first time since she had arrived in France as Henry's unwished-for wife ten years earlier, Catherine at last felt secure in her position.

The child was named Francis after the King, who had been present at the delivery. He had assiduously noted the details of the actual birth and even insisted upon examining 'all that came out with the baby'.[10] French and Roman astrologers were consulted, and a most detailed account of the birth was given to the papal nuncio. The savants announced that the infant would grow to be a strong, fit man, that he would take the Church under his protection and would have a large number of brothers and sisters. Unfortunately this last was the only prediction to come true. A brilliant christening was held at Fontainebleau at five o'clock in the evening of 10 February 1544 in the Saint-Saturnin Chapel. Under the blaze of torches held up by 300 of the King's guard the 'lights made everything so plainly visible that it seemed as though it were the middle of the day'. There came a procession of the King's household, consisting of the Chevaliers of the Order of Saint-Michel, Princes of the Blood and senior nobles, and then cardinals, prelates and ambassadors.[11] Queen Eleanor and the royal princesses came next, followed by the great ladies of the Court 'all very sumptuously attired in cloth of gold and silver with an infinitude of precious stones ... and in the midst of this crowd was the child being carried to be baptised'. The baby's godparents were Francis himself, his sister Marguerite of Navarre and the baby's uncle, Charles Duke of Orléans.

Whatever cure Dr Fernel had prescribed for the Dauphin and his wife, it clearly worked spectacularly, because over the following twelve years Catherine gave birth to a further nine children, seven of whom survived childhood. In defiance of her enemies and her ten years of perilous sterility she now produced an almost annual offering to her husband and the nation. The couple's first daughter was born on 2 April 1545 and named Elisabeth, followed by Claude on 12 November 1547; Louis on 3 February 1549 (died 24 October 1549); Charles-Maximilien on 27 June 1550, later to become Charles IX; Edouard-Alexandre on 20 July 1551, later Henri III; Marguerite on 14 May 1553, known as Margot; Hercules on 18 March 1555; and finally twin girls, Victoire and Jeanne who were born on 24 June 1556. Jeanne died during the birth itself, nearly killing Catherine in the process, and Victoire lived only for a few weeks.

It is a tribute to Catherine's magnificent constitution that she survived giving birth nine times in an age where high-born women had the dubious privilege of being attended to by physicians and midwives. The midwives' eager experienced fingers tearing at the mother's genital flesh to dilate her vagina sufficiently if a baby were slow in coming was the accepted practice of the day. This ripping and internal rummaging (often pulling out the placenta with the infant) caused blood poisoning, severe bleeding and other damage that all too frequently led to the mother's death. If she survived the birth, the very treatments recommended by the experts would weaken an already enfeebled constitution. It was generally prescribed that once the child had been delivered the patient should lie in a heated and darkened room. Her only sustenance was given in liquid form and no solids were allowed for some considerable time.[12]

Catherine's sturdy constitution was not, however, inherited by her children. With the notable exception of Margot, who enjoyed rude health, her siblings were a sickly lot. Of the seven children who survived infancy, six suffered from weak lungs and most likely tuberculosis. François, Charles-Maximilien and Edouard-Alexandre were also prone to septic sores, infections and, as they grew older, fits of dementia that imply genetically inherited syphilis from their grandfather, Lorenzo II de Medici. In many ways the dreadful health of the royal children, especially the boys, was one of the major factors that forced Catherine to maintain her central role in governing France even when her sons were mature.

At the birth of her first son Catherine immediately went from being barely tolerated to being widely celebrated. She received recognition even from the most stiff-necked French courtiers for finally ensuring the succession to the throne. While she rejoiced at her son's arrival and the pressures that it banished, she soon discovered that Diane, who had assisted at the birth, proceeded to take charge over the welfare of her firstborn and the children who were to follow. This galling mark of

Diane's continuing ascendancy over Henry was a bitter pill as Catherine watched the mistress usurp her place yet again. Her hope that by giving him a son she would perhaps win her husband back soon died as the same old pattern asserted itself. Indeed, if anything Diane's role in Henry's life grew stronger at the arrival of his children. Catherine had no choice but to accept that there were three people in her marriage. Diane had her cousin Jean d'Humières awarded with the governorship of the royal nursery and she proceeded to supervise and instruct, albeit with admirable efficiency, the raising of the babies of France. This did not, however, prevent their mother from sending a constant stream of letters enquiring about the children and handing out her own orders. For example, just before the birth of Claude in 1547 she wrote, 'Monsieur de Humyères [sic], you have given me great joy by sending news of my children. ... I ask that you write as often as possible to me about their health.'[13] Catherine had every reason to be concerned.

Since his elder brother's death, Henry had enjoyed the perquisites that came with his new position as Dauphin. Not only had Diane become his attentive lover, but a party of supporters began to form around the young prince from the late 1530s, hitching their fortunes to the coming man. In 1538 the Dauphin had the great personal satisfaction of seeing his friend Anne de Montmorency invested with the office of Constable of France. This was the most senior rank in the French military hierarchy. The post had been created in the time of the Frankish kings; the word constable deriving from 'count of the stables. ... The Constable in the field ranked over even the Princes of the Blood ... and was regarded as one of the major councillors of the king.' He led the army in the monarch's absence and received an annual pension of 24,000 livres.[14] The position was for life and had been left vacant since the treachery of the previous incumbent, the Constable de Bourbon. A patriotic servant of the Crown, Montmorency also devoted himself to the young Dauphin, who now hoped to wield more influence since his friend's advancement. Catherine disliked the Constable for his complicity in Diane's and Henry's relationship, although she buried her resentment and appeared, as always, cordial and charming. She also understood that this man, unlike so many of the other courtiers whose motives were fuelled by simple ambition, could truthfully claim to be a faithful supporter of Henry's and a true patriot. One day she would call upon his services herself.

Catherine now had a difficult path to navigate between the two favourites, Diane and Madame d'Étampes, whose rivalry had blown up into open hostility. At first their antipathy was based on little more than a mutual dislike, but their behaviour, beliefs and ambitions clashed in almost every area. The dislike grew into a conflict as d'Étampes, whose cupidity and influence over Francis can only be described as phenomenal, began to fear the day when she would be displaced by Diane. By 1540, as Francis began to weaken from excesses that stemmed from his youth, taunts from d'Étampes about 'the old lady', as she called Henry's mistress, grew louder and more scurrilous. She claimed to have been born on her rival's wedding day, though she was actually only nine years younger than Diane. Rumours about Henry's favourite were enlarged, and any differences between them was eagerly seized upon. She took an active interest in the new religion, while Diane detested the reform movement. Careless of her reputation, d'Étampes had other lovers besides the King. One day, returning early from the hunt, it is said that he found his mistress in bed with a young nobleman. Francis, ever the gentleman, is supposed to have feigned ignorance as to the lady's identity, taking her for one of his mistress's serving girls, and had the man arrested for molesting the maiden. This incident had no effect on the couple's relationship, and the King remained as devoted to the duchess as ever.

Such behaviour was anathema to Diane who had remained true to her husband while he lived and when, as a widow, she eventually did become Henry's lover she cloaked their relationship with endless respectable images of the chaste deity Diana, goddess of the hunt. In short, the younger woman was passionate, fiery, greedy and sensual, while Diane was cool, careful, imperious and remote. They loathed one another. Catherine floated ambiguously between the two, never becoming intimate with either and yet maintaining a civil relationship with both. Francis found himself unable to refuse his mistress anything; she tickled his tired tastes as he enriched her enormous family while scandalously submitting to her every desire.

The positions between the two parties at Court polarised progressively. Madame d'Étampes championed the King's favourite son, Charles. She planned to make him powerful enough to protect her when the King died. After the Emperor and Francis had met at Nice in 1538 and settled a ten-year truce the King, egged on by his favourite, entered into talks with his erstwhile enemy about a marriage between Charles and the Emperor's daughter Mary. Francis was led to believe that Milan would be her dowry, which infuriated Henry who considered that the duchy was rightfully his. Montmorency, who had promoted peace between the two rulers, found himself in disgrace and banished from Court when the Emperor proceeded to go back on his earlier promises by installing his son, later Philip II of Spain, as the Duke of Milan in 1540. The relationship between the two royal brothers, which could never have been described as cosy, now became a dangerous feud; each party, led by the two rivals Diane de Poitiers and the Duchess d'Étampes, enjoyed considerable backing by the princes' respective followers. Henry felt jealous of his father's evident love for his younger brother; he might also have resented the fact that the prince had not had to endure the appalling years of captivity in Spain. Now he was to witness quite blatant efforts by Charles to carve a strong base for himself as a feudal lord so powerful that he would represent a grave threat to Henry when he became king.

After the Emperor had made a fool of Francis with his promises of marriage and Milan for Prince Charles, the King had no choice but to go to war with his old enemy. The brothers now competed with each other for military glory. In 1542 Charles took Luxembourg with little effort, but when he heard that Henry was preparing to attack Perpignan he hastened to join him and share in any military success. Perpignan proved impossible to take and during Charles's absence the Imperialists recaptured Luxembourg. France suffered, running out of allies.* Henry begged his father to allow the Constable to return and with his undoubted military skills help France to recover the initiative. But the King denied his son's request. Nevertheless, despite his father, Henry fought with notable valour and distinction but could do nothing to prevent further Imperial successes. The Emperor's troops invaded the Champagne region and directly threatened Paris, but as so often happened in his reign, just as Charles V was about to destroy his old enemy his troops deserted for lack of payment. Both parties, now exhausted, negotiated a settlement and the Peace Treaty of Crépy was signed on 18 September 1544.

This treaty could possibly be described as the most foolhardy act of Francis's reign because it incorporated a marriage between Charles of France and either a daughter of the Emperor, or one of his brother's daughters. If it were the Emperor's own daughter then he would bestow the Netherlands upon her as her dowry; if it were his niece then she would receive Milan as her wedding gift. In return Francis agreed to give his son several of France's most important duchies: Angoulême, Châtelleraut, Bourbon and Orléans. Henry was apoplectic when he heard the details, for though the succession had been assured thanks to the birth of his son, his younger brother would become as powerful as a monarch in his own right and, worse still, receive backing from the Emperor. The House of Valois would be split by its enemies. Doubtless this is precisely what France's wily old adversary had intended. The country was only just emerging as a national entity, leaving behind the feudal factionalism that had bedevilled her for so long. Henry understood,

---

* Perhaps the most curious French allies in this war were the Turks led by the infidel corsair Barbarossa, who had become admiral-in-chief of the Turkish navy. The Turks brought their fleet to help the French take Nice. Unsuccessful, the fleet wintered at Toulon where they availed themselves of the locals when they ran short of slaves to man their galleys. It was not the first, nor the last, time that the Crescent of Islam flew alongside the Most Christian King's own banner, and the frequent Franco–Turkish alliances scandalised much of Europe over the years.

as did many other outraged members of the nobility, that the Treaty of Crépy contained all the ingredients to revive this dangerous situation. Having been obliged to sign the odious treaty out of 'fear and reverence for my father', Henry proceeded to write a secret denunciation of the pact which gave away inalienable Crown properties; three members of his closest coterie – François of Guise, Antoine de Bourbon and Bourbon's brother, the Comte d'Enghien – witnessed the document.

The triumphant mood of the Duchess d'Étampes is not hard to imagine; her manipulation of the increasingly decrepit King, possible treachery, and skilful undermining of the Dauphin and his party gave her every reason to hope that she might be secure after Francis's death after all. Although there is no direct evidence against her, it is thought that the duchess was passing secrets to the Emperor and therefore guilty of treason. She left for Brussels with Queen Eleanor and Charles to celebrate the signing of the treaty. The cool relationship between Francis and the Dauphin worsened to a chill. Henry rarely saw his father and absented himself from Court as much as he could. In revenge Francis ostentatiously lavished love, gifts and pride upon his youngest son.

Henry began, not always discreetly, to prepare for the day when he would at last wear the crown himself. One night after dinner he sat with his cronies having drunk a considerable amount of wine. Believing himself to be alone and among friends, the Dauphin noted 'that when he was King, he should name such and such persons marshals or grand-masters ... [adding] that he should recall the Constable'.[15] François de Vieilleville (one of the Dauphin's confidants and later made a Marshal of France), who recalled the event in his memoirs, worried that this talk might be overheard, told Henry that 'he was selling the skin before the bear was killed' and hastened to absent himself. His instincts proved correct, as unbeknown to the Dauphin the King's fool, Briandas, had been sitting in an alcove by a window in the dining room. Briandas rushed to his master. To impress upon him that another man threatened to usurp his position as King he addressed Francis as simply 'François de Valois' and proceeded to inform on Henry. Francis despatched armed men to his son's apartments, but the prince and his friends had received warning of their approach and made a quick escape before the guards' arrival. The King, infuriated by their flight, vented his temper on the remains of the hastily abandoned dinner. Pages and gentlemen took refuge by jumping out of the window as Francis hurled knives, plates, furniture and tapestries against the walls and at the courtiers and servants, who dived and leapt out of the way. Henry did not reappear at Court for over a month for fear of his father's wrath and many of his friends were not allowed back at all.

To make matter worse, in the autumn of 1544 the King banished

Diane from Court because the Dauphin had replaced one of d'Étampes's toadies while campaigning against the English in Picardy. Francis, unable to resist either the endless nagging of his favourite or her physical attractions, let his mistress have her way. Diane went to her château at Anet, closely followed by the Dauphin, who spent much of his time there in a grumpy protest against his father. Henry's favourite did not receive permission to return until the following year. Catherine enjoyed the secret satisfaction of seeing her rival disgraced, while the Dauphin forbade his wife to speak to his father's mistress.

Free of the older woman's presence, Catherine blossomed and enjoyed the attention given to her by the King. It was obvious that despite his dimmed powers he saw great qualities in his daughter-in-law and all that she could bring to Henry when she became Queen. He also showed that he understood all too well that much of the praise and attention that so often went to Diane rightfully belonged to Catherine. After so many scenes between the two warring favourites, it must have been a great boon to have a bright and loyal woman beside him who never publicly displayed her pain or anger. At Christmas that year, she was showered with presents by Francis as a mark of special favour, the most notable of which were a ruby and a diamond worth 10,000 écus. Catherine, by now heavily pregnant with her daughter Elisabeth, savoured the luxury of not having to listen to Diane's endless and dreary counselling on her health or that of her infant son. It was a happy time for her; usually starved of recognition, she basked in the King's approval and his delight was evident for all to see when she presented him with a granddaughter on 2 April 1545.

As Charles and Henry went off campaigning in the Boulogne area together, trying to evict the English who had captured the town in 1544, a gradual rapprochement could be discerned between the two brothers. Francis, anxious to keep busy in order to avoid dwelling on his dwindling health, accompanied his sons. Henry and his brother had hardly addressed one word to each other since the Peace of Crépy had been signed, but gradually a fraternal spirit began to emerge during the military operations. In the month of August 1545 plague broke out in the vicinity. On 6 September Charles and some of his young nobles came upon a house where all the inhabitants had recently died of the disease. In an excess of youthful confidence he decided to look inside, but was urged not to enter for fear of contamination. Laughing, the young prince proclaimed, 'Never yet has a son of France died of the plague', and with that he and his friends went in and started to tear the place apart, pillow-fighting and ripping up mattresses. His faith in royal immunity from the vulgar disease was evidently misplaced. By evening he began to feel sick and three days later he was dead.

During his brief illness the twenty-four-year-old prince suffered a high fever, pain and vomiting. As soon as he heard of his brother's illness, Henry had rushed to his sickroom but found his entry barred. Three times he had to be physically prevented from going to his brother's side, and when Charles died Francis and Henry grieved with heartfelt sorrow at his passing. The Peace of Crépy was now obsolete and the menace of a country split by Francis's foolishness finally removed. The old King crumpled with a melancholy that remained with him for the rest of his days. It now became essential to teach the Dauphin – whom he had kept at arm's length for so long – the art of statecraft, but Henry witnessed with frustration that his father was still being deeply influenced by Madame d'Étampes and her clique as attempts to shore up their position grew increasingly frantic. Henry merely refused to attend the council meetings, saying he did not wish to be tarnished by the misguided policies of his father when he finally ascended the throne.

On 7 June 1546 a peace was signed in which England agreed to hand back Boulogne after eight years, for 2 million écus with payments made in eight instalments.* With a natural sense of relief at the respite from war, that autumn Catherine and Henry went on their first official royal progress together to inspect the defences of the eastern borders of France. In the cold autumn weather the strain of giving birth to two children just fourteen months apart and all the political manoeuvring at Court told on the Dauphine, and she fell seriously ill. Henry halted the progress, and the couple stayed at Saint-Marc in order that his wife might recover. For Catherine it was almost worth being so ill just to have her husband present, caring for her with some tenderness, while she suffered. Her sturdy constitution soon had her on her feet again.

In February 1547 word arrived at the French Court that King Henry VIII of England had died on 27 January. Madame d'Étampes flew into Queen Eleanor's chamber crying, 'News! News! We have lost our chief enemy!' The wretched Queen, thinking it must be her brother the Emperor who had died, was on the point of collapse before she heard that he was quite well, though everyone else would have infinitely preferred the Emperor's demise to Henry's.[16] It had been a dismal Christmas and New Year due to Francis's poor health, but to hear that his contemporary and sometime ally had expired left the King 'more pensive than before' and 'he feared that he might soon follow him'. This was not helped by a message he is supposed to have received from Henry VIII given from his deathbed, reminding the French King that he too was mortal.

To increase the air of morbidity yet further, one of the monarch's young kinsman, the Comte d'Enghien, a Bourbon and part of Henry's

* Some historians put the figure at 800,000 écus.

circle of close friends, was killed in a snowball fight at a château near Mantes where the Court was staying. Francis had ordered the fight between two sides, one led by Henry and François of Guise, the other by d'Enghien of whom he was fond. In the horseplay that followed in which no quarter was given by either side, d'Enghien paused for breath and sat down beneath an upstairs window. A contemporary writes of how 'some ill-advised person threw a linen-chest out of the window, which fell on the Sieur d'Enghien's head and ... he died a few days later'.[17] Some suspected foul play, but there is no evidence to support this. Such high-spirited games in those days frequently caused serious injuries and fatalities, but the unfortunate young man's demise brought Francis further pain and grief. As the shadows lengthened on his reign, the King was possessed by a fitfulness that prompted him to travel from one beloved château to another, ostensibly to hunt, though he often had to be carried in a litter and could only follow the chase at a distance.

At last at Rambouillet the fifty-two-year-old Francis could continue no longer; feverish, he took to his bed. The abscess 'in his lower parts' that had been troubling him for many years and was cauterised in 1545, releasing great quantities of pus, had never quite healed satisfactorily. The wound kept reopening, particularly since he had not ceased his womanising. The King was treated with 'Chinese wood', and his old ally the infidel Barbarossa had recommended quicksilver pills (untreated mercury), believed at the time to be effective in treating syphilis.[18] In fact, modern medical opinion considers it unlikely that Francis suffered from syphilis as he appeared quite lucid up to his death. The most probable cause of his illness was gonorrhoea which, left untreated, would have led to infections of the bladder and urinary tract. At the time of his death he also suffered from serious infections in his stomach, one lung, kidneys and throat. One thing none of the so-called experts disagreed upon was that the King's 'insides were rotten'.[19] After surviving several health crises over the previous five years, Francis now appeared to accept that he was about to die and sent for the Dauphin, who had left Catherine to care for his father as he went to Anet to visit Diane.

Catherine felt sore of heart to see her protector and benefactor in such a pitiful condition and watched over him tenderly until the Dauphin arrived on 20 March. After Francis had made his confession, heard Mass and taken Communion, he began to speak earnestly to Henry about how many wrongs he had committed during his reign, urging his son to avoid the same pitfalls. He particularly warned the Dauphin against being influenced by a woman, such as he himself had been. The King spent the next few days talking to his son about his past errors and advising him how to act when king. He urged him not to recall Montmorency and above all to beware of the Guise family, 'whose aim was to strip him and his children to their doublets and his people to their shirts'.[20] He asked that the Dauphin take care of Queen Eleanor, admitting that he had been a poor husband to this good woman and then commended the Duchess d'Étampes to his protection, saying, 'She is a lady ... do not submit yourself to the will of others, as I have to her.'[21]

The favourite, who had been waiting in a room next to the King's and had been denied access to her lover since 29 March, was heard to shout 'Let the earth swallow me up!' and when it failed to oblige her she took off to her château at Limours in some haste. Hearing of a slight improvement the following day she returned, hoping for a miraculous recovery, but there was none and the Dauphin turned her away angrily. François of Guise was pacing about, anxious for the new reign to begin, muttering, '*Il s'en va le vieux galant*' (The old gentleman is leaving). The King asked for extreme unction and spent his last hours listening to the scriptures. When able, he talked to Henry who, overcome with emotion, asked for his father's blessing and held him in a tight embrace from which he would not let him go until the Dauphin 'fell into a swoon'. Some time between two and three o'clock in the afternoon of 31 March 1547 Francis I of France, Le Roi Chevalier, the Renaissance King north of the Alps who had started his reign so gloriously but brought much trouble upon his kingdom in his later years, finally breathed his last. It was considered by all to have been an exemplary death.

Catherine, who had been Francis's close companion during his declining years and last illness, spent most of his final days in an ante-room, sometimes seated on the floor with her back against the wall, her head in her hands, weeping. Not only was she losing her bulwark against Diane but she also genuinely grieved for the man who had brought her to France thirteen years earlier and had supported her when others would have sent her away. Catherine had learned much from Francis about projecting the grandeur of the monarchy; she had witnessed his courage, optimism and patience; she had seen him deal with Court politics and international relations. The Dauphine had also been inspired by her father-in-law's passion for the arts and his great building projects. For all Francis's mistakes, his young apprentice had learned her lessons well and in later years when she alone was left to protect France and the monarchy, she invoked the name and example of Francis I. She was determined to honour the man who had raised her from the daughter of a rich merchant family to become Queen of France.

FOUR

The Eclipsed Consort

For never did a woman who loved her husband
succeed in loving his whore

1547–49

Catherine was twenty-eight years old when she became Queen of France. 'The foreign woman' still spoke French with an indelible Italian accent but the people had, over the years, warmed to her, partly out of gratitude that she had borne an heir to the throne, but their feelings were also tinged with an element of pity for the ignored Queen and never more so than now. From the first days of Henry's reign Diane ensured that she availed herself of all the benefits that came with her position as the King's mistress. Formerly devoid of passion, but full of dignity and hauteur, the favourite now found something that inflamed her senses: greed. Diane's obsession with the accumulation of riches and honours consumed her. To satisfy her needs she had to keep the new King tightly in her thrall. Although she was now Queen, Catherine found herself as powerless as ever to come between Henry and Diane. Her role and influence during her husband's short reign were on the whole confined to motherhood and those of an eclipsed consort. Whenever possible, Diane took centre stage and pushed Catherine into a twilight area as she gave birth to a further eight children after Henry ascended the throne. As his reign progressed he gradually learned to rely on his wife's loyalty and sound judgement but he still excluded her from his confidences, especially in the early years. One historian wrote, 'Movement went on about her; [but] she was becalmed. Politics died at her doorstep, her life remained purely domestic except in the Italian matters.'[1]

To understand France and the internal and external forces driving the country that Catherine had to face when her husband died twelve years later it is essential to grasp the main features of Henry II's reign, in particular the band of nobles whom he favoured, enriched and empowered. While Henry lived these men gave their complete loyalty to the King, but by making his friends so strong he had unknowingly created an extremely hazardous situation for Catherine when she eventually became ruler of France.

The French people welcomed the start of Henry's reign. Most of them had grown heartily sick of the increasingly muddle-headed policies of Francis as his grasping favourite pulled him this way and that, his strength and judgement failing him at essential moments, particularly during his latter struggles against the Emperor. The new King's bearing and demeanour promised much. The people knew little about Henry except that he was a brave soldier, a robust sportsman and loved the hunt; he also seemed to eschew the showiness and extravagance of his father. So far the mask of respectability had not slipped publicly to reveal the true nature of his relationship with Diane.

The Venetian ambassador summed up Henry shortly before his accession, writing that the affection he held for his favourite resembled 'that between mother and son; and ... that the lady has taken it upon herself to instruct, correct and counsel ... him'.[2] Certainly, compared with the champing sexual urges of his father, people considered the former Dauphin 'little addicted to women'.[3] The ambassador also examined the essence of his personality and intellect, considering him

> not very ready with his answers when addressed, but very decided and very firm in his opinions, and what he has once said he adheres to with great tenacity. His is not a very keen intellect, but men of that stamp are often the most successful; they are like autumn fruits, which ripen late, but which are, for that reason, better and more durable ... he is in favour of maintaining a footing in Italy ... to which end he supports Italians who are discontented with the affairs of their country. He spends his money in a manner at once prudent and honourable.[4]

Only hours after Francis's death and during the traditional quarantine period between the passing of the old monarch and the public appearance of the new, Henry, recovering his spirits somewhat at becoming absolute ruler of France, began sacking ministers of the old regime and distributing favours to his friends and supporters. The first to be recalled to favour and high office was Anne de Montmorency, 'le premier baron de France'. The Constable had been languishing at his huge estates for six years since Francis had exiled him from Court in disgrace. On 24 April Henry and the Constable sat closeted alone for over two hours at Saint-Germain-en-Laye and by the time they emerged Montmorency had been created President of the King's Privy Council and put in charge of all government matters. He was now the most senior man in the kingdom after Henry, both in military matters and civilian affairs. He quickly installed himself in the recently vacated apartments of Madame d'Étampes, which adjoined those of the late King. This was quite an achievement for a man who despite being a solid defensive military tactician and an ultra-conservative had not particularly demonstrated any great genius or flair.

As well as his new honours, Montmorency received compensation for the loss of income he had suffered during his years of disgrace. A sum amounting to over 100,000 écus was paid to him and he also resumed his governorship of Languedoc. This had not been officially taken from him by Francis but had been run by others during the Constable's banishment. Montmorency held the King's signet and generally made sure that no business passed to His Majesty without his prior sanction. Henry permitted the old man to deal with much in his name, and it seemed to many that the Constable tried to keep the King away from administrative work by doing a good deal of it for him. Like most pedants, he had a close eye for detail and little escaped his notice. His famous arrogance convinced him he knew best on just about every matter. At council meetings he constantly interrupted anyone who happened to be speaking and gave his opinion on how the business should be handled. His autocratic behaviour and zealous guard over the King soon annoyed almost everyone. 'He is more insolent than ever before and provokes the hatred of men and women, and everyone in general,' commented the ambassador of the Italian Duchy of Ferrara. Foreign envoys soon began to complain that this impossible martinet prevented or slowed down business with his obsession for minutiae. Nevertheless Henry seemed grateful not to have to bother with the exhaustive details of government matters, which was doubtless precisely what the Constable had intended.

Despite Montmorency's quarrelsome nature and tyrannical ways, he possessed, at least in Catherine's eyes, one endearing feature. The man did not seek to fill his pockets and appeared less thrusting about the promotion of his family than others of Henry's close entourage. Instead, he primarily dedicated his existence to two things: the well-being of the King and the security and protection of France. Although the Constable had encouraged the earliest romance and union between Diane and Henry, Catherine was acute enough to see that for all his pompous and ridiculous posturing he stood apart as easily the truest of all Henry's senior nobles. The papal nuncio wrote of Montmorency at the time, 'This man is the most French, in word and act, of any that has ever been known. ... Do not suppose that he will ever resign himself ... to any course which is not the most advantageous to his King.'

The members of Montmorency's family who benefited most at Henry's accession were his three Châtillon nephews, one of whom, Gaspard de Coligny, was many years later to be the prime cause of the terrible massacre for which Catherine is chiefly remembered in France today. Of the nephews, sons of Montmorency's sister, Gaspard was by far the cleverest and most able of the brothers; an inspired military man of high integrity, he was made Colonel-General of the infantry. His brother Ôdet, Cardinal de Châtillon, the eldest, was given more benefices and moved into his uncle's apartment at Saint-Germain. François d'Andelot, the third brother, also received favours from the King.

Diane did not view the recall of the one person who rivalled her in the King's affections with unalloyed pleasure, but there existed an implicit understanding between them that they must work in harness for Henry's good. Diane and Queen Eleanor had the great satisfaction of seeing their nemesis, Madame d'Étampes, banished from Court. At her castle of Limours she stayed fearful that she might be prosecuted for the many crimes her cupidity had occasioned. Eventually, after handing back jewels and a large part of Francis's gifts, many the inalienable property of the Crown, she realised to her relief that she would not be secretly done away with or put on trial for treason. Henry, perhaps out of respect for his father's dying wish, did not ruin the duchess. Though her properties were much diminished it was generally acknowledged that she had escaped lightly. Gratefully, she spent the rest of her days in obscurity. The property and jewels recovered from Madame d'Étampes Henry promptly gave to his lover, Diane, who saw no point in pursuing her former rival further; she had better things to do.

Catherine, pregnant once again, spent the earliest days of her husband's reign watching him reward his friends for their loyalty to him during his father's rule. Apart from the Constable, the main beneficiaries were his trusted companions of old. The Guise family immediately felt the advantages of having Henry on the throne. François, Comte d'Aumale, the eldest son of Claude, first Duke of Guise, was one of Henry's closest friends. Known as 'Le Balafré' (Scarface) for the horrific wound that he had received outside Boulogne during the campaign against the English, he enjoyed constant access to the King and on most days they played tennis, Henry's favourite sport. François was admitted to the Privy Council, made Master of the Royal Hunt and a little afterwards the King created him Duke d'Aumale. The new dukedom was equal in rank to the most senior Prince of the Blood, Antoine de Bourbon, a measure that would cause endless protocol scuffles with the Bourbons over precedence. François's brother, Charles, who had been Archbishop of Rheims since the age of nine, also received a place on the council and a cardinal's red hat in time for the new King's coronation.

The brothers made a brilliant team and Charles, a man of extraordinary intelligence, received universal acclaim for his acute political sense and deft diplomacy, even from his enemies. Their uncle Jean, also a cardinal, sat on the council along with his nephews. Their sister, Marie of Guise, who had married King James V of Scotland, had been widowed in 1542 and ruled the kingdom as regent for her baby daughter Mary, Queen of Scots. Diane, anxious to forge a closer connection with the Guise family whose rising fortunes seemed unstoppable, married Louise, one of her two daughters, to another of François's brothers named Claude, Marquis de Mayenne. By patronising the Guises in this way she was ensuring that they would provide a counterbalance to the Constable. Thus, from the very beginning it was clear that the junior princes of Lorraine were to wield great influence during Henry's reign.

The King did not omit the Saint-Andrés, *père et fils*, when he distributed powerful posts and positions to his friends, and gave both of them seats on the council. Jaques de Saint-André, the boon companion of Henry's youth, was made a Marshal of France and given the office of Grand Chamberlain, which meant that he slept in the King's chamber. This unparalleled access to His Majesty's person gave Saint-André much power and prestige as people clamoured for him to promote their interests or obtain an audience for them with the King. In addition he received the governorship of Lyons, Bourbonnais and Auvergne. Henry meanwhile awarded the father with the governorship of Bresse. The younger Saint-André had grown greedy, dissolute and selfish over the years since he had first formed a bond with Henry as Duke of Orléans, and occupied his thoughts primarily with how to enrich himself, hardly bothering to promote his family. The Bourbons, most senior Princes of the Blood apart from Henry's own son, watched their position being usurped. They were not excluded altogether from the distribution of favours, but their seats on the council were crumbs in comparison with the riches and honours being harvested by Henry's coterie.

Without doubt the person to benefit most from Henry's accession was his mistress, Diane de Poitiers. As Diane's power waxed, so did her reputation wane. 'Her fair name [was tarnished] at last, not with looseness but with avarice ... it was her identity ... when her name was mentioned, it connoted nothing but the fortune she had acquired.'[6] The way Henry shamelessly showered his mistress with jewels, honours, estates and offices could not fail to be noticed by all. Although she had received most of the properties and jewels that belonged to Madame d'Étampes, his most sumptuous gift was still to come. Henry now entitled her to receive a tax levied on all office holders throughout the country whenever a new king ascended the throne. In addition to this, he allowed her the right to all properties in France known as '*les terres vagues*', properties to which there was no clear title or where the owners had died without leaving an heir (this included properties confiscated from heretics). Henry had made Diane rich beyond even her expectations, but still he deluged her with gifts. He presented her with the Château of Chenonceau, quite ignoring the fact that it was an inalienable property of the Crown. This beautiful castle in the Loire valley was considered a jewel, and Catherine, who had thought that she might receive it, could not restrain herself from protesting vehemently to Henry but with no result. An old law was dug up about a tax payable on all the church bells in the kingdom and this too was grasped by the insatiable mistress.

Having received these and many more presents and privileges from her lover, Diane kept a close eye on the progress of her fortunes. Every day her comptroller would come and report to her about rents received, rents due, repairs, vacant properties and so on. Henry appeared so spellbound by his lover that he seemed unaware of the envy and odium with which the people viewed her as a result of his largesse. For the rest of his reign he continued to heap riches, offices and honours upon her, and her family and supporters. One contemporary wrote of Diane and the others of the King's inner circle, 'Nothing escaped their greedy appetites as little as a fly escapes a swallow. Positions, dignities, bishoprics, every good morsel were all greedily snatched.'[7]

As for the queen herself, Henry had not forgotten her, but she received a meagre portion compared with that allotted to Madame, as Diane now preferred to be addressed. Henry gave her an allowance of 200,000 livres and the right to appoint a master in every guild, something she had already enjoyed under King Francis. As Diane spent huge amounts on improving her châteaux at Anet and Chenonceau, Henry allowed Catherine to refurbish the Château des Tournelles where she liked to stay when she was in Paris. The Louvre was intended to become the royal couple's Parisian residence, but the building work in progress transforming the old medieval fortress into a Renaissance palace made it as yet impossible to use. Complaining that she had no suitable country estate where she could receive her husband, Catherine was also given the Château of Montceaux-en-Brie near Meaux.

The most pleasing accession gift that Catherine received from the King was to see her dear cousins, the Strozzi, elevated to positions of importance. Exiled from Florence under the regime of the authoritarian Duke Alessandro de Medici, the Strozzi lived as *fuoriusciti* – the name given to Italian exiles – at the Court of France.*

The four brothers now found themselves rewarded by Henry, who wished to do something to please his wife. They longed to return home and throw out the upstart ruler of Florence, thus removing his stranglehold on the magistracies of the republic, and Henry decided to advance the two elder brothers' military positions. He elevated Piero, the eldest, to Captain-General of the Italian infantry. And Leone, the second brother, was made Captain-General of the Galleys of the Levant. This would, when the time came, give the two eldest Strozzi leading roles in any future campaign for Florence. The third brother, Lorenzo, became Bishop

---

* Although most of the Strozzi left during Alessandro's tenure, Cosimo de Medici exiled and killed other members of the family.

of Béziers and the youngest, Roberto, remained a banker, though he was now placed in charge of negotiating loans and raising funds for the Crown when necessary, a potentially very lucrative position.

Catherine loved Piero best of all the brothers, and Henry bore a deep fondness for him too, even making him '*gentilhomme ordinaire de la chambre*'. Piero cut a somewhat preposterous but colourful figure at Court. He combined a rare intelligence and learning with physical courage and a determination never to be beaten at anything. A man of contrasts, he wrote delicate poetry and enjoyed playing rather savage and dangerous practical jokes, just the sort that Henry always appreciated. He was short and fantastically vain about his appearance. To disguise his lack of height he wore extremely high heels and, hoping to hide the fact that his head was too small for his body, he sported towering, ornate and over-decorated hats. Piero translated Caesar from Latin into Greek and enthralled his listeners by his storytelling, but if crossed he was known to avenge himself to the death. Even Diane, the Guises and Saint-André found his company irresistible.

Catherine had always had an Italian entourage with her since the time of her marriage, but now that she had become Queen, her group of followers – Florentines and others – swelled. She found herself the rallying point for her exiled compatriots who pinned their political hopes on her, calling her their Italian Queen of France. At first the new reign saw little in the way of pickings for them. The Imperial ambassador reported to his master, 'An infinite stream of Italians came to the new Court to offer their services but they are not being placed on the pension list.'[8] Catherine, proud of her country of origin, imported her gowns from Italy, promoted Italian artists and craftsmen, and little by little her influence and sense of style and grandeur could be seen at Court. Her maître d'hôtel, the Florentine poet Luigi Alamanni, was also a leader of the *fuoriusciti*. Not all the exiles were artists, soldiers, merchants or political refugees; their community also comprised a considerable number of bankers. They were to become the strong arm of Catherine's supporters as the reign went on, especially once the King needed loans for his military expeditions into the peninsula. For it soon became obvious that Henry, just like his father before him, found the siren song of Italy and her rich territories irresistible.

The Queen forged one of her closest female friendships with Marie-Catherine Gondi, the French wife of Antonio Gondi, a Florentine merchant, who lived in exile in France. They first met in Lyons just after her marriage to Henry as the royal family were making their way back up to Paris from Marseilles. Madame Gondi was extremely practical and advised Catherine on everything from pregnancy and childcare to money matters. Later the Queen rewarded this remarkable woman and her family by giving her responsibility for her personal finances and she was made general administrator of her projects and building works, among other matters. In effect, Catherine chose Madame Gondi to be her treasurer, a highly unusual position for a woman in the sixteenth century. Most important of all, theirs was probably one of the few truly intimate friendships that Catherine ever enjoyed. To survive the intrigues of the previous reign and to keep a sliver of dignity as Queen in the face of Diane's countless triumphs, Catherine had to appear unaffected, aloof and silent. Marie-Catherine Gondi could probably be counted among one of the very few people ever to hear the Queen reveal her true anguish.

Another notable supporter of the Queen's was Gaspard de Saulx, Seigneur de Tavannes, a fearsome soldier as ugly as he was brave. A veteran of the Italian wars, Tavannes despised Diane and her toadies, and admired Catherine's patience and dignity in the face of the endless humiliations she had to endure. One day, after some particularly stinging slight from Madame to Catherine, the enraged Tavannes determined to take action and announced to the Queen that he would slice off Diane's nose. He hoped that by permanently disfiguring her, he would make the King lose interest in his paramour. Fortunately, Catherine dissuaded Tavannes from such a primitive and extreme act. Equally, the Queen's relative and great friend, the Duke of Nemours, approached her, offering to throw acid in Diane's face. This project too was abandoned when the Queen said she preferred a more 'patient' approach. Both these men and others of her entourage spotted the qualities in Catherine that others had so manifestly failed to identify.

On 23 May 1547 Francis was buried at Saint-Denis. Henry had decided upon a triple entombment and brought the bodies of his two brothers – who had not been given state burials – to accompany that of his father. He organised an epic funeral for the late King and the two princes, which cost over half a million écus. While the splendid and solemn procession passed through Paris to Saint-Denis he had arranged to watch the cortège from a window in the rue Saint-Jacques overlooking part of the route. Henry had to remain incognito until after the burials, when he would be officially proclaimed King. As the splendid coffins, surmounted by the traditional effigies, passed before his window, Henry became 'very troubled and deeply aggrieved, even to the point of tears'. M. de Vieilleville, one of the King's companions that day, tried to cheer His Majesty by telling him instead of mourning his father he should try to imitate the late King's virtues and strengths. This seemed to have little effect. Deciding upon a different tack, he announced that not for 300 years had there been a more pernicious prince of France than Henry's brother Charles. Adding for good measure, 'He never loved or esteemed you.'[9] Stubbornly Henry continued to cry until finally Vieilleville, by now thoroughly warming to his theme, recounted how years before, after a boating accident in which it was feared Henry and his elder brother had drowned, Prince Charles had been overcome by joy. His jubilation was cut short when news finally came that the two elder boys had survived, at which point he had remarked bitterly to a friend, 'I renounce God; I shall never be anything but a nonentity.'[10] At last after more stories in this vein the King seemed to cheer up and watched the rest of the procession with a passive countenance, even remarking as Charles's coffin filed past, 'See, there is the nonentity who leads the advance-guard of my felicity!'[11]

With the old King now buried, and before his own *sacre* at Rheims, Henry, urged on by Diane, had made up his mind to settle a quarrel which had its origins in the old rivalries of Francis's Court. A young nobleman, Guy Chabot, Baron de Jarnac, related to the Duchess d'Ét-ampes, had been cruelly slandered by Henry and his friends in the last years of Francis's reign. When Jarnac was forced for the sake of his dignity to demand satisfaction, the Dauphin had been prevented from fighting a duel because of his rank. To settle matters one of Henry's friends, François de Vivonne, Seigneur de La Châtaigneraie, an experienced soldier who had fought alongside the King and was also a virtuoso swordsman, stepped in to fight on the Dauphin's behalf. The duel was to be to the death, but Francis had refused to allow it to take place and the matter had been left unresolved, not least because Jarnac's obvious physical inferiority meant that he would prove no match for La Châtaigneraie. The latter was well-built, as well as a renowned wrestler and athlete; he had received his martial training under a great master in Rome and had already been victorious in previous duels. One of the secrets of his accomplishments was, he claimed, that he had been fed powdered gold, steel and iron with his food as an infant. Jarnac, on the other hand, was a tall but slightly built pleasant young man of a gentle nature, unlike that of the swaggering braggard La Châtaigneraie.

At the beginning of the new reign, La Châtaigneraie now asked permission to fight the duel; again it was to be to the death. Jarnac wrote to the King and supported the suggestion. Henry, who revered the code of honour of medieval knights, was delighted to allow the request. The duel soon became perceived as a symbolic fight between the two old parties; La Châtaigneraie representing Diane and the new King, Jarnac standing for d'Étampes and Francis. Several other matters had arisen since the quarrel first started, and while most of the Court, who wished to please the King, championed La Châtaigneraie, there were some, mainly those already sickened by Diane's influence, who supported Jarnac.

The whole Court was abuzz with excitement, wagers were taken and the two principals prepared for the coming challenge. Few people were prepared to wager on Jarnac surviving – the odds against him were monumental. Rumours also circulated that Catherine's cousin, Piero Strozzi, who so enjoyed protecting his own honour that he would fight over the tiniest of imagined slights, had decided to aid the stripling Jarnac by secretly giving him some tips that were ingeniously and specifically designed to destroy La Châtaigneraie. With the help of the great Italian duelling master Caize, Jarnac worked hard to prepare himself, and though Catherine would have enjoyed seeing Diane embarrassed she could not appear to support her rival's enemy. More than likely Strozzi had decided to take matters into his own hands to prepare Jarnac, without involving the Queen.

On the day of the duel, 10 July 1547, a meadow at Saint-Germain-en-Laye had been prepared with an arena and tribunes for the spectators. Colourful standards flew, and there were tents erected for the duellists. All the touches to this medieval tradition were in evidence. La Châtaigneraie, so sure of his success, had ordered a tremendous banquet on long tables to which he had invited the whole Court to celebrate after his victory. In marked contrast, Jarnac's own preparation had been to spend the weeks beforehand training assiduously and making pilgrimages to churches and abbeys, praying and contemplating on what lay ahead. The two contestants attended Mass before the duel began, and Jarnac's pious attitude received much favourable comment. La Châtaigneraie had merely looked around impatiently with a bored expression, making it obvious that he 'feared his enemy no more than a lion does a dog'.[12]

As the two contestants made their entrance into the arena, watched intently by an enormous crowd, the King took his place seated between Catherine and his mistress. A mob of rowdy Parisians had arrived for the spectacle, as well as some of the minor country gentry who saw Jarnac as a victim of Diane's undue influence; they hoped he would strike a blow for their class. At seven o'clock in the evening, after the endless ceremonies which accompanied this medieval tradition, the two men strode towards each other. Châtaigneraie struck a terrific blow at Jarnac, who instead of parrying with his sword, held up his giant and outmoded shield and lunged at his aggressor with a small dagger, striking him behind the knee twice, severing his tendons. La Châtaigneraie fell to the ground, blood pouring from his disabling wound. He was beaten. A huge cry came from the crowd as Jarnac had defeated arguably the greatest *bretteur* in the kingdom in a matter of seconds.

Jarnac, who was as astonished as his opponent at the outcome of events, approached La Châtaigneraie and, though he had the right to kill him, asked only for his honour to be restored. La Châtaigneraie refused, struggling to get to his feet and fight on but he collapsed. At this Jarnac strode to where Henry sat and offered his opponent to the King, who was so stunned at the upshot of the match that he hardly seemed to hear

Jarnac's request – phrased with noble humility – for his honour to be restored and to 'accept' La Châtaigneraie. Henry continued to sit in silence though Jarnac, fearing that his vanquished foe would die before the matter was settled, grew ever more persistent. Finally, after going once again to examine his opponent, Jarnac cried out before the assembled crowd, 'Sire, see! He is dying! For the love of God, accept his life at my hands.'[13] After further delays Henry was jolted into action by Montmorency, who saw the King risked obloquy for himself by behaving with such appalling grace, at which he formally restored Jarnac's honour. For hundreds of years afterwards the famous and quite legitimate thrust that had won the day for the underdog was known as 'Le coup de Jarnac'.

The King and Diane were furious at their public humiliation, for they had identified themselves completely with La Châtaigneraie, and they took themselves off as quickly as possible. The mob from Paris threw themselves upon the banquet that the King's champion had so prematurely prepared. 'The soups and entrées were devoured by an infinity of harpies, the silver plate and the handsome sideboards ... were broken or carried off, amid indescribable disorder ... and the dessert consisted of a hundred thousand blows [from] the captains and archers of the Guard.'[14] The day ended in complete chaos.

As for La Châtaigneraie, he had his wound bound and was told he would survive, but he did not care to do so having lost his honour and, tearing off the bandages, proceeded to bleed to death in a huff. Afterwards there was much talk about La Châtaigneraie's defeat being an ill omen for the King at the start of his reign. Personally, Henry came out of it badly for having behaved like a petulant child rather than a gracious monarch. For Catherine the fiasco was a source of secret satisfaction at seeing her rival so publicly humiliated. As a postscript to this drama, Henry decided to outlaw judicial combat as a method of settling quarrels.

There was little time to reflect upon the outcome of the duel because the King's coronation was to take place on 26 July and by ancient tradition at the cathedral of Rheims. Henry made his official entry into the city the day before. At ruinous expense the town had been transformed. Enchanting spectacles such as naked nymphs and men dressed as satyrs greeted the King in the brilliantly decorated streets. Catherine, only a few months away from giving birth and seated at a sumptuously decorated window, watched her husband pass by. As he did so he greeted her '*fort honorablement*' and when he approached the place where Diane sat with some other ladies he saluted them with notable enthusiasm. On the day of the coronation Catherine, by now very large, had been given a place on a tribune from which to view the sacred union between God, the King and France. While she had no proper role that day, the Queen must have felt hurt upon seeing Henry's tunic as he entered the cathedral:

it was covered with the interlaced embroidered letters H and D. Despite this Catherine watched with pride as her husband performed his part of the ancient ritual with distinction, devotion and nobility. Indeed, he prayed so long and devoutly that Diane questioned him afterwards, asking what he had been praying about. He replied that he had asked God to make his reign long if it were good for France and short if he made a bad king.

Much of the coronation oath was dedicated to explicit promises relating to upholding the Christian Church, its laws and privileges. He promised to protect the 'Christian populace subject to me' and later in the oath to 'expel all heretics'. The sacerdotal qualities of the French monarch's kingship were so vital that elements of the *sacre*, as the coronation was called, made him 'more priest than layman'.[15] Though political expedient had altered much of the ceremony's content as needs had changed over the centuries, 'one historical constant at least was clear: the enfolding together of the French monarch and the Catholic Church. The language and symbols of the French coronation service went far beyond the usual ecclesiastical overtones surrounding other monarchs of western Christendom.'[16] Henry VIII enjoyed the title 'Defender of the Faith', the Spanish King had the appellation 'Catholic Monarch', but the French King enjoyed the far more distinguished 'much older and more redoubtable title: *Rex christianisimus*, the "most Christian King"'.[17] When Henry found his hallowed role later challenged by the reformers, the ritual marriage between God, King and country made him first among the soldiers whose sacred duty it was to expunge the heretics from his lands. As soon as the crown of Charlemagne had been placed upon the King's head the cry of *Vivat rex in æternum!* was taken up by all the peers and dignitaries in attendance. Huge amounts of gold and silver coins for the common people, specially minted for the occasion, were then thrown up into the air to cries of *'largesse'* amid the clamour of trumpets and deafening cheers.

Henry had become a man transformed since the days when one ambassador wrote five years before that he had never seen him laugh. Although his personality remained essentially unchanged, the melancholy emotional restrictions from his Spanish sojourn seemed at last banished. The same ambassador, Matteo Dandolo, who had come to represent Venice at the coronation, now reported, 'I ought to assure you that he has become gay, that he has a ruddy complexion, and that he is in perfect health ... his body is well proportioned, rather tall than otherwise.' He went on to report that Henry was 'much addicted to tennis' and stag hunting. Dandolo added, 'Personally, he is all full of valour, very courageous and enterprising.'[18]

On 12 November 1547 Catherine gave birth to her daughter Claude at Fontainebleau. Enraged by the nickname 'Mademoiselle d'Anet' given to Claude, since she had been conceived at Diane's splendid palace, it sickened the Queen that the world knew of her reliance on the favourite 'who at night urges [the King] to that couch to which no desire draws him'. It was reported in the first months of the reign that the King's total dependence on Diane was such that he came to her after his midday meal and discussed all the state business of the morning. Jean de Saint-Mauris, the Imperial envoy, wrote this report about the King's behaviour and need for her: 'The King allows himself to be led and approves everything that [Diane] and his nobles advise. ... He continues to yield himself more and more to her yoke and has become entirely her subject and slave.'[19] On one occasion Henry actually wrote to his mistress, 'I entreat thee to keep in thy remembrance him who has only known one God and one friend, and to rest assured that thou shalt never feel ashamed of giving me the name of thy Servant. Let this be my name for ever.'[20]

Much has been written about Diane's influence, yet there is not much real evidence of it. Only on a few specific occasions did she involve herself with royal policy in foreign or internal affairs, though these were almost without exception fuelled by self-interest. Her real strength lay in matters of patronage and keeping the balance of power between the King's favourites. The same Saint-Mauris also reported that the King's behaviour had become far more careless with respect to Diane's reputation. Using the code name he had given her of Silvius, he recounted how 'After dinner he visits the said Silvius ... and whether with the ambassadors or other persons of importance, he seats himself upon her lap, a guitar in his hand, upon which he plays and enquires often of the Constable or of Aumale if the said Silvius "has not preserved her beauty" touching from time to time her bosom and regarding her attentively, like a man who is ensnared by his love. And the said Silvius declares that hereafter she will be wrinkled, in which she is not mistaken.'[21] Lorenzo Contarini, the Venetian ambassador, wrote of Catherine's increasing exasperation, 'Since the beginning of the new reign, the Queen could no longer bear to see such love and favour being bestowed by the King on the duchess [as Diane was shortly to become] but upon the King's urgent entreaties she resigned herself to endure the situation with patience. The Queen even frequents the duchess, who, for her part, serves the Queen well, and often it is she who exhorts him to sleep with his wife.'[22]

Many years later, as an old woman, Catherine wrote to one of her envoys, M. de Bellièvre, who was trying to untangle her daughter Margot's marital problems with Henry of Navarre. It is one of the very few surviving documents in which she mentions the trials of her life as part of the conjugal triangle. 'If I made good cheer for Madame de Valentinois

[Diane] it was the King that I was really entertaining, and besides I always let him know that I was acting sorely against the grain; for never did a woman who loved her husband succeed in loving his whore. For one cannot call her otherwise, although the word is a horrid one to us.'[23] In a more pathetic vein she admitted her feelings, after she had been widowed, in a letter to her daughter Elisabeth, then Queen of Spain. Writing about Diane and how she had tolerated the situation she explained, 'I loved him so much, I was always afraid.' Fear primarily motivated Catherine to keep quiet. So truly did she love her husband that his terms, however harsh, had to be endured just to be near him; realistically she knew she had no other alternative. Like a faithful dog, the Queen accompanied her husband everywhere. 'She follows him as much as she can, without a thought of fatigue,' noted Soranzo, the Venetian ambassador.

One source of solace for Catherine was the comfort she found in her fascination for astrology. She somehow managed to find a formula for an easy coexistence between both her religion and her belief in the power of the stars. The Queen also had a genuine talent for astronomy, science, physics and mathematics, all of which complemented her fascination for the heavens and their supposed influence upon the lives of human beings. She owned books with bronze pages and revolving discs to facilitate a quick analysis of her celestial readings. Indeed, a great deal of celestial activity occurred during Catherine's life, often at times of trouble. Comets, eclipses and other unusual sights were seen as indications of momentous events about to occur. Two notable Italian members of her suite were the Ruggieri brothers, Tommaso and, more important, Cosimo, who was known as a Florentine magician. The Ruggieri, renowned astrologers, also practised necromancy and the black arts. The family had long been patronised by the Medici, and Catherine's ancestors Lorenzo and Cosimo de Medici had been godfathers to the children of 'Ruggieri l'Ancien'.

Cosimo was undoubtedly the more sinister of the two brothers, and over the years Catherine would have much recourse to his talents. She both admired and feared him, always taking care in their dealings not to upset him. Among the many rumours about his frightful practices was that he had stolen a Jewish baby, decapitated it and, by employing his dark powers, interrogated the severed head for secrets that would enhance his strength. While the use of talismans and sacred relics was still commonplace to people in the superstitious sixteenth century, the Queen was rumoured to have one talisman (among her huge collection) made of human blood, the blood of a goat and the metals that corresponded with her birth chart.

The Queen's enduring fascination for astrology and the black arts were exceptional even for the time, and later did much to earn her the evil reputation that history and many of her contemporaries have accorded her. Her image was not helped by her *parfumier*, the Italian Maître René, who became greatly feared for his potions and powders, legendary poisoned gloves and rouge with which he is supposed to have hurried people to their deaths when he served Catherine in her widowhood. Passionately interested in people with prophetic talents, the Queen was said to have 'second sight' herself. A number of those close to her claimed that in the years to come she would awake from her sleep screaming and prophesying the untimely death of a loved one, even her daughter Margot witnessed her mother accurately foretell a death from her dreams.[24]

In April 1548, after spending eight months at Fontainebleau, Henry, Catherine and the Court left the château. The King now had important matters to deal with in order to keep his foothold in Italy and maintain good relations with the Farnese Pope Paul III. The Farnese had fallen out with the Emperor, and Henry decided to make the most of this breach by appearing to support that family's interests. The Pope's grandson, Orazio Farnese, had been brought up at the French Court and, to tie the two dynasties together, Henry promised his illegitimate daughter Diane de France in marriage to him. Earlier, in 1545, the Pope's son, Pier Luigi Farnese, had been awarded the Duchies of Parma and Piacenza by his father. The Emperor was greatly provoked as he considered Parma and Piacenza as part of the Duchy of Milan and therefore Imperial territory. Besides, the Emperor ensured that he had a strong military presence to protect his interests in northern Italy.* Shortly after Henry's coronation, news arrived that Imperial agents had murdered Pier Luigi. Henry received urgent entreaties from the Pope asking for help to avenge the killing of his son. Henry was keen for war, but Montmorency, full of gloom and foreboding at the prospect, counselled caution. When Henry could summon neither the Venetians nor the Turks as allies for the proposed military venture, he decided to take this opportunity to show his solidarity for the Farnese by making the journey to Piedmont, most of which was controlled by France. He travelled with a brilliant escort of his most important and glamorous nobles, and was determined to make a fine impression upon the Italians.

During his absence Henry created a council of five and made Catherine his nominal regent before he took his leave of her at Mâcon. This was the first important sign of his respect for her loyalty and ability, though

---

* In addition to the Milanese question the Emperor had other interests at stake in the Farnese issue. His illegitimate daughter, widow of Duke Alessandro de Medici, Catherine's murdered 'half-brother', had married Orazio Farnese's brother Ottavio and the Emperor had promised him Parma.

her actual political powers were limited. Taking Montmorency's advice that he should be lavish in all his dealings in Italy, Henry made a splendid show to the Piedmontese. He paid off old French debts, repatriated disabled French soldiers and gave them a pension known as '*ung donne*'.[25] He was the first monarch formally to recompense soldiers who had been wounded fighting for their country and his successors continued his tradition. He held an enlightened point of view with regard to the care of old soldiers and one of his commanders, Blaise de Monluc, called him the best king the soldiers had ever had.

Henry did make one tiny but important territorial acquisition while on his Italian journey, and that was the Marquisate of Saluzzo. This minute stretch of land gave the French essential direct access to the Italian peninsula. There was one additional event of importance which took place during Henry's visit to Piedmont and it further enhanced the standing of the Guise family. While Henry and his men were at Turin many personages of importance arrived to pay homage to the new French King. Among them came Ercole d'Este, Duke of Ferrara. His duchess was Renée de France, daughter of King Louis XII, Francis I's predecessor. The couple had a daughter named Anne whom they wished to marry to François of Guise, Duke d'Aumale. The King gave his consent, and the Guises were exultant; as they had often done in the past, they were increasing their standing by a prestigious marriage and were now more closely bound up with the French royal family than ever.

Catherine (who was, once again, pregnant) and her council suddenly found themselves faced with serious difficulties during Henry's absence when revolts and uprisings started over the salt tax, '*la gabelle*'. Henry received word of the trouble and arrived back in France on 7 September 1548, ending Catherine's short regency. Harsh measures were required to put down the rebels, and the King sent Montmorency to Guyenne and François d'Aumale to the Loire valley to take charge of operations. Naturally, d'Aumale's wedding to Anne d'Este had to be postponed until the rebellion had been extinguished.

When he reached Toulouse, Montmorency was merciless in his brutal reprisals against the rebels, who had returned to order by the time he arrived and pleaded for clemency. He tortured and executed over 150 people in the process. The condemned men, mainly the ringleaders, were broken at the wheel, hanged, impaled and dismembered. He even wanted to make an example of the local populace in the troublesome Bordeaux area where there had been a similar problem a few years earlier. He suggested removing or exterminating the inhabitants of the city of Bordeaux and replacing them with a more compliant populace transplanted from another part of France. To Henry's credit he refused to countenance this idea, but the Constable's abhorrent methods of punishment could not fail to taint the King in this, the only serious uprising of his brief reign.

Shortly after his return from Italy, Henry made his triumphant entry (*joyeuse entrée*) as the new monarch into the city of Lyons. This ancient and important tradition had developed over the years into a way for a new king to establish his relationship with a powerful town. The monarch would appoint new office holders and ecclesiastics to vacant positions; the visit also provided an opportunity to pardon criminals, listen to the people's grievances and review the taxation of a particular community. The most significant element of the *joyeuse entrée* was that the King received the city's formal act of fealty. In return he would recognise the town's rights and those of its officers. The lavish and extraordinary display given to welcome the monarch paid for by the town gave rise to intense competition between the larger cities. Henry's friend Saint-André, governor of Lyons – which after Paris was the foremost city in the land – could be counted on to make every effort to impress His Majesty with a brilliant welcome and celebrations. Lyons's prominence was due not least to the fact that it was the financial powerhouse of France, and many of its most important citizens were Italian financiers, exiles who had made this their new centre for business.

Catherine, Henry and Diane travelled by an enormous gondola down the Rhône to La Vaise, where the royal party stopped before their entry into Lyons. A superb pavilion had been erected for them, which resembled a small château. On 23 September 1548 Henry made his official entry into the city accompanied by his mistress; Catherine's official entry was not until the next day. Desiring to please their King by honouring Diane, the citizens and their governor treated the royal mistress as though she were Queen of France that day. Magnificent allusions to Henry and his lover could be seen everywhere. The goddess Diana was the predominant theme played upon by the grovelling burghers to honour the mistress. Allusions to the glories of the roman emperors of antiquity, so admired by Henry, were their offering to him. Upon entering the city, which had been transformed to resemble Ancient Rome, the king was greeted by 160 men dressed as Roman legionnaires. The party then came into an artificial forest from which emerged a group of nymphs led by a young beauty carrying a silver bow and quiver, representing the goddess of the hunt. The lovely girl approached the King leading a mechanical lion on a chain of silver and black silk, symbolising the city of Lyons. Saluting the King in verse on behalf of the city, she symbolically offered him its keys.

Among the other marvels and spectacles there was a mock battle between twelve men dressed as gladiators who fought with heavy two-handed swords, which Henry enjoyed so much he asked to see it again

a week later. As the party progressed through the town, every window
and triumphal archway and obelisk seemed decorated with the monogram
that Henry and Diane had created for themselves. Every possible allusion
was made to Henry's wisdom and greatness being comparable to that of
a Roman emperor and to Diane as a chaste goddess, her benign influence
represented in the various allegorical poses in which she was placed. The
colours dominating the decor were the black and white of the two lovers.
Once, these had been the emblem of Diane's mourning; now the colours
had become the symbol of her triumph.

Catherine made her entry the following day. It was late and growing
dark when the Queen and her retinue made their way into the city. Ill
wishers said that the King wanted the Queen to arrive in darkness 'so
that her ugliness should pass unnoticed'. Whatever the reason for the
delay, when she arrived she did so in majesty. Seated in an open litter
beside her sister-in-law Marguerite, Catherine dressed to ensure that she
left a lasting impression on the townspeople, so many of them from her
home country. From her head to her shoes, her dress was covered with
brilliant diamonds. Behind her, modestly retiring in contrast to the
previous day, rode Diane on a palfrey. The townsfolk flexibly altered
whatever they were able to in honour of the Queen. The lion duly arrived
as it had the day before, but for Catherine its mechanical breast opened
to reveal a heart decorated with her coat of arms. The black-and-white
decor had, where possible, been changed to Catherine's own colour,
green. To the astonishment of many and the mortification of the Queen,
the town dignitaries when paying homage to the King kissed his hand
first, and then in the most flagrant outrage against the Queen kissed
Diane's hand before her own. Saint-André had performed his duty well
in persuading his toadies at Lyons to please the King by so honouring
his mistress.

Catherine had at least been able to console herself that Diane's rank
ensured a certain distance between the two women in the placement at
official festivals and public ceremonies. Yet even this meagre comfort
was removed when Diane decided she was no longer satisfied with being
just the nobly born widow of a senior official. She now felt she required
a position that reflected her true status at Court more accurately. At
Lyons, therefore, on 8 October Diane de Poitiers was created the Duchess
of Valentinois, a duchy with which her family had ancient ties but which
had been awarded to Cesare Borgia by King Louis XII. Henry ensured
that Diane received enough property to maintain her title with dignity by
adding further to it. The elevation also meant that Diane had the right
to walk directly behind the Princesses of the Blood. The duchess changed
her coat of arms to illustrate her new rank, and the King announced that
henceforth Diane was to be one of the Queen's ladies-in-waiting.

The Court moved north to Moulins, for the wedding on 21 October 1548 between Henry's cousin Jeanne de Navarre, daughter of his Aunt Marguerite (married to the King of Navarre), and the most senior Prince of the Blood after Henry's own sons, Antoine de Bourbon. From her mountain kingdom of Navarre, Marguerite had remained aloof from Henry's Court since the death of her adored brother Francis. She and her husband had stubbornly tried to resist the marriage Henry proposed for their daughter Jeanne. Preferring instead a far grander catch for her, they had hoped that she might marry King Philip of Spain. But Henry could not allow Navarre to fall into Habsburg hands and insisted upon the Bourbon match taking place.

Jeanne, an independent and spirited young woman, was jubilant that the issue had been forced, since she found Antoine de Bourbon highly attractive. Earlier, when prospective husbands were being discussed for the princess, Henry had suggested François of Guise, Duke d'Aumale, as a possibility. Jeanne had retorted that she would not marry him for then Diane de Poitiers's daughter would have become her sister-in-law.* Enraged by this insult, Henry made it quite clear where his favour lay and the wedding between Jeanne d'Albret and Antoine de Bourbon took place without frills. For his friend François, Duke d'Aumale's wedding to Anne d'Este, which took place on 4 December at Saint-Germain-en-Laye, Henry ordered that the event be sumptuous and was heedless of the enormous expense.

Five days later, not to be outdone, Montmorency married off his nephew, François d'Andelot, to one of the richest girls in the kingdom – Claude de Rieux – in the same splendour. The only other event of note that autumn was Queen Eleanor's return to the Netherlands to live under the care of her brother the Emperor. Henry had always treated his stepmother kindly, but she was not sorry to leave France now that her husband was dead. She lived a further ten years, to die in Spain in 1558.

As the Court moved from château to château, hunting and feasting over Christmas and the New Year, Catherine remained behind at Saint-Germain waiting out the last phase of her fourth pregnancy. On 3 February at four o'clock in the morning, with the King beside her, Catherine gave birth to a boy. The baby was named Louis and, as tradition demanded for the second son of a King of France, given the title Duke of Orléans. Louis's baptism took place in May, and on 8 June Catherine and Henry arrived at Saint-Denis to prepare for her coronation two days later.

---

* Diane de Poitiers' daughter Louise was married to François of Guise's brother, the Marquis de Mayenne, and Jeanne wanted no family connection between herself and the King's mistress.

The night before the ceremony the royal couple visited the cathedral together. They were met by the Cardinal de Bourbon, Antoine's brother, and inspected the arrangements for the following day. The abbey was sumptuously prepared and a small loge had been built for the King, whence he could watch the proceedings hidden away from the congregation. The Queen's throne, elevated on a platform covered in gold cloth, was richly decorated with her gold-embroidered initials on a background of blue velvet; blue velvet also covered the steps with balustrades either side leading up to the dais. Tribunes nineteen rows high had been erected in the chancel. The princes were to sit on the right and Chevaliers of the Order of Saint-Michel on the left. Below the princes' seats were those for the captains of the guard and opposite them places had been reserved for the ladies and gentlemen taking part in the actual ceremony. Last of all came the seats for other guests and those courtiers not taking part.

On 10 June, the morning of her coronation, Catherine rose at dawn; dressing and preparation were a time-consuming process. Shortly before eleven o'clock she was ready and, as the hour struck, the two young Cardinals of Vendôme and Guise led a huge procession of princes and princesses to fetch her. Her bodice glimmered with vast diamonds, rubies, emeralds and pearls. Her robe of green blue velvet, the colour seeming to change slightly according to the light, was embroidered with fleur-de-lys in gold thread, as was her royal mantle, edged with ermine. Her robes were cut to give them fullness and length, adding to their already magnificent effect. Led by 200 gentlemen of the King's Household, all dressed in their richest ceremonial costume, the retinue made its way into the abbey, followed by the chevaliers of the royal order. Heralds at arms carried heavy gold maces; behind them walked the Constable holding his gold Grand Master's baton. After the Constable came the Queen flanked by the two cardinals. The two most senior Princes of the Blood carried her mantle at the sides, and the end of her long train was held by the elder and younger Duchesses de Montpensier and the Princess de la Roche sur Yon.[26] Trumpets announced the Queen's arrival. The long cortège of ladies following the Queen was led by Marguerite, Henry's sister. Diane was in the third row among the most senior princesses and her train was held by the Constable's son, Henri de Montmorency-Damville. She was followed by her namesake, Henry's eleven-year-old daughter Diane de France, known as 'Madame la Bâtarde'. The women of the procession were dressed in jewel-encrusted velvet and ermine robes to match the Queen's own, wearing diadems that signalled their rank. Diane and the other high-ranking dowagers were distinguishable, for they alone wore no rich trappings. The most senior of the Queen's ladies brought up the rear. Superbly adorned, for as *dame d'honneur* she had a great role in the day's ceremonial, came Diane's eldest daughter Françoise, wife of Robert IV de la Marck, the Prince of Sedan. Robert de la Marck had been created a Marshal of France at Henry's accession and was given a seat on the King's Council.*

After kneeling before the high altar and kissing a reliquary, the Queen sat upon her throne and the princesses and other ladies moved to their prearranged places. On the highest tribune to the right of the Queen sat Diane and her daughter Louise de Mayenne, who was married to the brother of François, Duke d'Aumale. To Catherine's left sat Diane de France and nearest to her sat Françoise de la Marck. After the opening prayers were said, Catherine descended from her throne and knelt at the altar for the anointing, which was performed by the Cardinal de Bourbon. He smudged the holy oil upon Catherine's forehead and her chest, then placed the ring on her finger which signified her marriage to the kingdom of France, and placed the sceptre in one hand and the '*main de justice*' in the other. Finally the great crown, supported by Antoine de Bourbon (the Duke of Vendôme) and the Comte d'Enghien, was placed on her head. It was so heavy that a lighter crown replaced it almost immediately. This was 'small and completely encrusted in diamonds, rubies, pearls, of great excellence and value'.[27] It was a most magnificent spectacle.

After her actual coronation the Queen, accompanied by the Princes of the Blood, proceeded to her throne. Louis, Prince de Condé, younger brother of Antoine de Bourbon, then placed the heavy state crown on a small stool, which was rather unfortunately positioned, as though it were an offering, at the feet of Diane's eldest daughter, Françoise. Mass was heard, after which Françoise de la Marck supervised the ceremonial of the offerings which were placed upon the altar. Catherine led the procession of four princesses carrying the sacred gifts. Diane, as part of this procession, walked to the altar with a serene, almost saintly demeanour, lingering with slow and stately steps before the King's loge as she did so. Her 'feigned modesty' did not go unnoticed.

Catherine had gone through the long ceremony with perfect grace and majesty, but Diane had triumphed too. By her elevation to the rank of duchess the King had given her a position which allowed her to sit with the very grandest princesses and watch her two daughters perform central roles in the proceedings. He must have felt pleased with himself that he had been able to honour his mistress so markedly at his wife's coronation. The ceremony drew to a close and the cry of '*largesse!*' rang out after the procession walked out of the abbey and the Queen's treasurer threw up gold and silver for the crowd.

Despite Diane's prominence that day, Catherine had the deep sat-

* In 1552 Robert de la Marck was awarded the Duchy of Bouillon.

isfaction of knowing that she was now the rightful and anointed Queen of France. No longer a Florentine nobody, Catherine was wedded, just as the King had been, to the kingdom of France and had been ordained by God to lead the French people if the sovereign were indisposed. For all Diane's elegance and false humility, Catherine wore the crown. Her 'sense of honour and reverence' at being Henry's Queen transformed the matronly, unimposing figure so dramatically that the usually censorious courtiers agreed: 'In public she was completely mistress of her dignity and performed her ceremonial and social functions with an authority as easy as it was unassuming.' They 'could not recall a queen, since Anne de Bretagne, so completely equal to her position'.[28]

On 16 June Henry made his official entry into Paris. The capital had spent enormous sums, employing the most famous artists of the day: Jean Goujon, Philibert de l'Orme and Jean Cousin were among those charged with the decoration of the city. The emphasis played mainly upon both a Gallic and classical theme in which they hailed Hercules as the original Gaul with Henry 'designated as Hercules'. Ronsard celebrated the entrée with verse as the citizens presented their sovereign with a series of gorgeous spectacles that, it was generally agreed, even outshone those of Lyons.[29] To Catherine's great satisfaction there was little allusion to Diane in the decorations and tableaux presented to their majesties. Her own entry took place on 18 June. The banquets and festivities continued for almost a full month. The Court stayed at the Château des Tournelles as the capital celebrated. For the King's pleasure a tournament and a mock battle were held upon the River Seine. The only upset was the usual squabble between the grandees over seating at the banquet given on the night of Henry's entrée.

The sombre spectre of religious disunity, however, cast a shadow on the festivities in Paris that month. The King had requested that one of the heretics being held in the city be brought before him so that he could question the man himself. A humble tailor was specially selected for the reason that he was so dismal and inconsequential-looking that the authorities hoped he would be struck dumb when he found himself in the presence of his King. This reduced the risk of Henry's essential kindness being awakened by any eloquence that might move him to clemency. The wretched man was duly presented and, when he spoke of his faith and his beliefs, produced a great effect upon those gathered with the King. Diane, whose loathing for the Protestants mirrored their abhorrence for her and her position as the King's mistress, tried to bait the piteous prisoner with her own questions. Surprisingly, this served to embolden the man's sincere and inspired response: 'Madame, rest satisfied with having corrupted France, and do not mingle your filth with a thing so sacred as the Truth of God.'[30] Henry, enraged at this spirited sally, demanded that he personally be present to watch the man burn. Three other men condemned for heresy were also selected to die with him.

Thus, on 4 July on the rue Saint-Antoine, Henry watched from the window as the faggots beneath the prisoners were lit. Often it could take as long as forty-five minutes for a fire to burn a man at the stake, and slowly the flames began to rise up around the tailor and his co-religionists. Instead of screaming in agony, the dying man fixed Henry with his eyes and did not stop staring at the King until he lost consciousness. Henry vowed never to watch a burning again and found he had difficulty sleeping over the next few weeks as the images of the dying tailor kept returning to him. Yet he continued his single-minded policy towards heresy and its proponents, for they were anathema to him and his straightforward approach to religion. By the time Catherine was charged with running the country such methods of repressing the new religion would no longer be effective.

FIVE

Catherine's Growing Importance

The King honours her and
confides in her

1548–59

Almost a year before Catherine's coronation a very important young personage had arrived in France seeking refuge. In August 1548, during Henry's short absence in Italy, the five-year-old Mary, Queen of Scots had fled her troubled kingdom. The young Queen had come at Henry's invitation following the urgent entreaties of her Guise uncles. Their sister, the widowed Queen Mother, Marie of Guise, finding herself increasingly embattled by English invaders, had sent her daughter to safety at the French Court.

Since her birth Mary had been the object of a planned marriage alliance with Henry VIII's son, now King Edward VI of England, but the French had no wish to see England and Scotland united. The Scots, always fearful of what they called the 'English bear-hug', decided instead to ally their child Queen by marriage to Henry's and Catherine's eldest son, the Dauphin Francis. Henry agreed to bring up Mary at the French Court and, if necessary, to fight for her inheritance. The project did not delight everyone; in particular, Diane and the Constable felt uncomfortable about the added prestige that Mary's presence would afford the Guise family. French opponents of the match kept quiet, however, and as the English threatened to overwhelm the Scots militarily, Henry sent Catherine's cousin, Leone Strozzi, with fifteen galleys carrying an armed force to her aid. He succeeded in capturing the Castle of Saint Andrews and among his prisoners was the Scots fiery protestant reformer John Knox, condemned to the galleys, something that may have added grist to his furious hatred of the Queen later on.

By September 1547 the Queen's and her mother's lives were in danger as the kingdom came within a whisker of being 'utterly lost and totally ruined'. Henry, anxious to avoid 'such a wound at the beginning of his reign', began earnest talks about evacuating Mary to France.[1] According to Knox, Mary was 'thus sold to the devil' and dispatched to France 'to the end that in her youth she should drink of that liquor, that should remain with her all her lifetime, for a plague to this realm, and for her final destruction'.[2]

The formalities settled, Mary arrived off Roscoff in Brittany on 13 August 1548, having survived several narrow escapes from English ships and dreadful storms. Aside from the four young attendants she brought with her who shared their Queen's name and were known as the four 'Maries', among her retinue came her governess, Janet Fleming, a bastard daughter of King James IV of Scotland.* Lady Fleming was a highly attractive blonde widow in her early thirties with a flawless white complexion. While the French rhapsodised about Mary's appearance and behaviour, they found the rest of her suite (apart from Lady Fleming) vile-smelling, dirty and barbarous. The Scots, largely unused to the refinements of Renaissance France, looked totally out of place and viewed the frills and sophistication surrounding them with the greatest mistrust. As though expecting an ambush or attack at any moment, the men kept their hands close to their weapons at all times. Most of Mary's attendants did not remain on French soil for long, however. Her grandmother, Antoinette of Guise, though delighted with her granddaughter from the first, determined she must erase all traces of the primitive kingdom from its young Queen so that she might adopt the ways of her new country. After a leisurely journey through northern France, Mary arrived at Saint-Germain in mid-October 1548, there to join her princely 'brothers and sisters'.

When Henry first saw the young Queen of Scots he declared her 'the most perfect child I have ever seen', and henceforth Mary was to enjoy a share in the huge fuss and attention lavished upon the royal children. Catherine and Henry were devoted parents by the standards of the day. Not only did Catherine spend hours writing letters to the children's *gouverneur* giving detailed orders and asking for news, but Henry involved himself quite as much as his wife. There also came a steady flow of instructions from Diane to d'Humières, who must, at times, have dreaded the sight of yet another royal *laquey* (footman or courier) and his heavy postbag. A typical example of the triplicated instructions from Catherine, Henry and Diane came nine months after the birth of Charles-Maximilien. On 15 May 1551 Catherine wrote to Madame d'Humières about her son's wet-nurse saying 'her milk is not good enough'.[3] Five days later Diane wrote about the same wet-nurse, 'I hear that her milk is not good and the milk makes the baby emotional.'[4] Three days after that Henry wrote, again about the wet-nurse, saying, 'You must make sure that she has fed more than one other child before, so that we can be certain that her milk is of good quality.'[5]

---

* The four Maries were Mary Seton, Mary Livingstone, Mary Beaton and Mary Fleming.

Though Catherine had amply demonstrated her ability to have children, none but Margot had inherited their mother's rude health. The Dauphin had been sickly from birth and the two girls, Elisabeth and Claude, constantly suffered from childhood ailments. The King and Queen feared plague and other contagious diseases, and the children were often moved further from any chance of infection during the summer months when outbreaks of plague were common. For example, in 1546 Catherine arranged for the children to be moved 'to a pavilion by the water where they will be better lodged'.[6] After the Dauphin had suffered from smallpox and was not quite '*bien guary*' (restored to health), the King ordered d'Humières, 'Keep your eye upon him for anything that he requires and keep me constantly informed about the health of my daughter.'[7] Catherine loved to receive pictures of her children, always asking for new ones to be painted. 'I would like', she wrote to M. d'Humières, 'to have paintings of all the children done ... and sent to me, without delay, as soon as they are finished.'[8]

Mary could not have come to a more welcoming place. As well as the kindness of the King and Queen towards the royal children, of whom she was now counted as one, she enjoyed the zealous protection of her Guise family. After all, she would bring them and their House a glorious future when she eventually became Queen of France. Mary enjoyed a particularly close relationship with François, Duke d'Aumale and his brother Charles, soon to become Cardinal of Lorraine. Her grandmother Antoinette continued to keep abreast of Mary's progress and soon received the gratifying news that the child's French, non-existent when she first arrived at Roscoff, now progressed well. The courtiers found Mary's native Scots tongue so hideous a noise they could hardly believe such ugly sounds were possible from her pretty mouth, and though it was not entirely forgotten, for the rest of her life Mary's first language became French, as did her habits.

Over the question of rank, Henry wrote the following instructions: 'In answer to your question as to the rank which I wish my daughter the Queen of Scotland to occupy ... it is my intention that she should take precedence over my daughters. For the marriage between her and my son is decided and settled; and apart from that, she is a crowned Queen. And as such it is my wish that she should be honoured and served.'[9] Diane wrote on Henry's behalf to d'Humières, 'The said Lord wishes Madame Ysabal [Elisabeth] and the Queen of Scotland should be lodged together; wherefore you will select the best chamber ... for it is the said Lord's wish that they get to know one another.'[10] Mary attended the marriage of her uncle François to Anne d'Este, which took place early in December of 1548 and Henry took great pleasure in writing to Marie of Guise describing how the three-year-old Dauphin and his intended bride aged five danced together at the wedding banquet. Henry often wrote to Marie giving 'tidings of our little household … so that you may experience yonder something of the pleasure which I enjoy constantly'. His letters, filled with touching details, resemble those of a sentimental Victorian patriarch more than a Renaissance king.

One man who viewed the little couple dancing at the Este–Guise wedding with scant comfort was the English ambassador. The pair incarnated the accord between England's two traditional enemies. Shortly after the Guise wedding in Paris, in the spring of 1549 the English were ejected from Scotland, and Henry decided that it was time to recapture Boulogne from England. Should there be a war against the Emperor, the town would prove a great strategic advantage and, besides, Henry did not relish the idea of paying the huge sum due in five years time when the English were supposed to surrender the town back to the French. During the early summer the Constable amassed a large army near Ardres, which lay inland between Calais and Boulogne. On 8 August 1549 Henry declared war on England and left Catherine at Compiègne, travelling north to lead the attack upon the heavily-fortified town. After disappointing skirmishes, fighting continued in a desultory fashion until early the following year when peace talks began. On 24 March 1550 peace was signed, and at the cost of 400,000 écus Boulogne, having been in English hands since 1544, was ceded back to France.

The peace-making policy largely led by the Constable resulted in an alliance between the two countries that would be sealed with the eventual marriage of King Edward VI of England to Henry's eldest daughter Elisabeth. Montmorency saw his efforts rewarded when Henry raised his barony to a duchy in 1551, the same year as the full treaty was signed. Boulogne hardly represented a tremendous military victory, but rather a sound move for Henry who needed peace with England in order to devote his full attention to problems looming with the Empire. The situation in Italy also remained unsettled. In November 1549 Pope Paul III, upon whom Henry had lavished such efforts, had died and was replaced by Julius III, a pacific man with no dynastic ambitions of his own. Naively believing he could put matters straight between the Habsburgs and France, practically his first act as Pope accidentally ignited a war involving both, this time over Parma.

Just before Paul III's death, Henry and Catherine suffered a personal tragedy. On 24 October 1549 their nine-month-old son Louis died suddenly at Mantes. Henry hastened to his wife in the Loire valley and most of the winter was spent at Blois. Just one month after losing her son Catherine announced that she was pregnant again. The following spring saw significant changes at Court after the death of Claude, first Duke of Guise, followed shortly afterwards by the demise of his brother

Cardinal Jean of Lorraine. This put the two brothers, François and Charles, at the head of the family. They became second Duke of Guise and the Cardinal of Lorraine respectively, and were to lead their dynasty to hitherto undreamt-of heights, and depths.

On 27 June 1550, at Saint-Germain, the Queen gave birth to her fifth child, a son, Charles-Maximilien (later Charles IX). Henry had arrived at Saint-Germain at the end of May and assisted at the birth as usual. Mercifully for the Queen, Diane was not present with her tiresome attentions, as she had taken a fall from her horse at Romorantin and fractured her leg. She decided to stay at her fabulous palace at Anet, where she could both recuperate and keep an eye on her business transactions, pressing for the titles to yet more properties and generally advancing her huge business interests.

At Saint-Germain Catherine lay recovering from the birth of her son while the King seemed, even by his standards, to be spending an unusual amount of time with his children in the royal nursery. During Henry's long stay there the Guise brothers, who kept their precious niece under close observation, heard rumours that Montmorency – their principal rival with the King – had been noticed paying lavish attention to Lady Fleming, Mary's governess. Told that he paid frequent visits to 'court' her, many believed that the Constable 'was going very much further with the lady'. The Guises quickly informed Diane, making the excuse that their niece risked being dishonoured by the Constable's affair with her governess. The favourite's instructions were clear; she sent the Duke of Guise and his brother, the Cardinal of Lorraine, a key with which they could enter the lady's apartment and catch the Constable *in flagrante*. To their consternation they discovered that it was not Montmorency who was making love to the Scots beauty, but the King himself. Montmorency, having seen Henry's eye alight upon Lady Fleming, had decided to encourage an affair, which he hoped might even topple Diane herself.

According to the Ferrarese ambassador, the Guises reported all this back to Diane who having barely recovered from her fall, made the journey to Saint-Germain and brazenly posted herself outside Lady Fleming's door that night. She told the brothers to stay away and to say nothing to anybody. After a short wait Diane saw the King and the Constable coming out of Fleming's apartment. Placing herself squarely before Henry she cried, 'Sire, from where do you come? How you betray your devoted friends and servants the Guises, their niece, the Queen and your son the Dauphin! He is to marry the child who has that woman for a governess! As for myself, I say nothing, for I love you honestly – as I always have done.' Henry, who thought Diane was still at Anet and was too overcome with shock to think clearly, mumbled only that he had been chatting to the governess 'and that there was nothing evil in it'. His

lame reply confirmed everything and Diane, scenting an opportunity to
disgrace her rival Montmorency, proceeded to cover him with abuse. She
accused him of betraying the Guises as well as the King by encouraging
a liaison that dishonoured them, for now 'their niece was being raised by
nothing better than a whore'. Finally she told the Constable – and how
she must have enjoyed it – that she wished neither to see him 'in her
path, nor should he address a single word to her in future'. Henry made
a pathetic attempt at appeasing his incandescent mistress but realising
that this only made her more furious implored her not to mention the
matter to the Guises. So this French farce continued, Diane promising
faithfully to keep the matter secret from the very men who had warned
her of it and the Constable in 'disgrace', which suited Diane perfectly,
since she wanted to share Henry with Montmorency as little as he did
with her.[11] Henceforth, until the very last months of Henry's reign, Diane
used all her influence with the King to aid the Guises.

As for Catherine, she played her role in the pantomime to
perfection. While acting the outraged wife, she enjoyed watching Diane
suffer a tiny soupçon of the humiliation she herself had had to endure
for nearly fifteen years. Nor did the matter rest there, for the King
continued his secret assignations with Lady Fleming who eventually
became pregnant; indeed, she and the Queen both found themselves
with child at around the same time. Fleming behaved outrageously,
announcing her condition in excruciatingly bad French to anyone who
would listen. Brantôme quotes her saying, 'God be thanked. I am
with child by the King, and I feel very honoured and very happy
about it,' adding that the royal 'liquor' must possess magic properties
for she had never felt so well.[12]

As in all things at the French Court, royal love affairs had certain
unspoken rules attached to them. Fleming's barefaced and vulgar declaration that the King was her lover and the father of her child meant
the game of polite pretence had to be abandoned. For once Catherine
and Diane worked harmoniously together to make the King's life so
intolerable that in the end he sent Lady Fleming away. When her child,
a son, was born, the King recognised the boy as his own and gave him
the name of Henry, Chevalier of Angoulême. He was brought up with
the other royal children and eventually became Grand Prior of France.
Aside from an ability to write lyrical verse, he was noted for his extreme
cruelty, particularly during the Saint Bartholomew's Day Massacre, and
was finally killed in a duel in 1586. Henry had a further royal bastard,
born in 1558. The child's mother, Nicole de Savigny, was married, and
this is probably why the King did not legitimise the boy, who nonetheless
received the name Henry and took the title of Saint-Rémy, which was
that of the cuckolded husband. Many years later Henry III gave his half-

brother a payment of 30,000 écus and the right to wear three gold fleur-de-lys on his coat of arms.*

Years after the Fleming scandal, Catherine mentioned it in a letter to her son-in-law, Henri of Navarre, who was conducting a flagrant affair with one of his wife Margot's ladies. Margot had dismissed the woman for her shameless exhibition of the liaison, and Henri was furious. Catherine's letter is of particular interest because there are so few that survive in which she mentions Diane de Poitiers, Duchess of Valentinois. Rebuking Navarre, she wrote,

> You are not, I am aware, the first husband who is young and of little prudence in such matters but I believe that you are the first, and only one, who, after an affair of this nature, would venture on such language to his wife. I had the honour of marrying the King, my lord and your sovereign, but the thing which annoyed him the most in the world was to discover that I had heard news of this kind; and when Madame de Flamin [*sic*] was with child, he considered it very fitting that she should be sent away and never showed any temper, nor spoke an angry word, about it. As for Madame de Valentinois she, like Madame d'Étampes, behaved in a perfectly honourable manner; but when there were any who made a noise and a scandal he would have been very displeased had I kept them near me.[13]

The child Catherine was carrying at the same time as 'La Flamin' was born on 19 September 1551. The birth actually took place at twenty minutes past midnight on the 19th though his birthday was always celebrated on 18 September and this was henceforth given out as the birth date. This baby, named Edouard-Alexandre, later to be known as Henri, Duke of Anjou and then Henri III, was the child she was to love more than the others and for whom she nursed an obsessive devotion as he grew up. His birth coincided with France's renewed hostilities against Charles V and disgrace for Catherine's dear cousins, the Strozzi. Although Henry had been much preoccupied with his domestic life, the festering hatred he bore for his erstwhile captor, the Emperor, now found full opportunity for expression. Henry was also encouraged to act by the Guises and Catherine, the Queen's latent political and patriotic feelings aroused since the matter concerned her homeland.

Henry had started his reign by deliberately offending the Emperor. As Charles V was also Count of Flanders and in this capacity technically a vassal of the King of France, Henry demanded that Charles come and pay allegiance to him at his coronation. This impertinence infuriated the

---

* There is an interesting later connection with the French royal family, for it was the Comtesse de la Motte-Valois, a descendent of this bastard son of Henry II, who played a leading role in the scandal of Marie Antoinette's famous diamond necklace, the 'collier de la reine'.

Emperor who replied he would be delighted to attend, but only at the head of 50,000 men to teach Henry a lesson in manners. Shortly afterwards, when the King was preparing to take Boulogne, Charles sent him a message warning that if he proceeded he would come and 'treat him like a young man'. Henry replied by calling the Emperor 'an old dotard'. While trading insults with his enemy, the King set about organising the army and his defences. Upon the election of Julius III, the question of Parma re-emerged when the new Pope backed Charles's demand that Ottavio Farnese return Parma to him. The Farnese appealed to Henry who, encouraged by the Guises and Catherine, signed a treaty in May 1551 promising to help the family to hold on to their duchy.

Catherine saw military intervention in the peninsula as an opportunity to reclaim her rightful inheritance from Cosimo de Medici, Duke of Florence and vassal of the Emperor. The idea of capturing his wife's rightful patrimony inspired Henry, who hoped either to re-establish a nominal republic there supervised by the Strozzi and dependent upon France, or to put one of his own sons on the ducal throne. Some provision clearly had to be made for the ever-increasing number of Valois boys in the nursery. The Guises were always more interested in Italian conquests than those against England, for their ancestors 'fancied themselves as kings of Naples, Sicily and Jerusalem through their lineage of the Dukes of Anjou'.[14] Though it is fair to say that Henry's eyes were generally turned to the northern parts of Italy and his wife's 'possessions' in Tuscany, he was not unsympathetic to the interests of the Guises further south.

Julius III declared Ottavio Farnese a rebel and officially deprived him of the right to the Duchy of Parma, demanding it be returned to the Emperor. When war broke out between Parma and the Papal States in June 1551, both sides were backed by their superpower rivals. Among the soldiers sent out from France was Piero Strozzi. Military matters drifted without conclusion into the winter with both France and the Empire still not yet officially at war with one another. Technically they were only involved in the conflagration as allies of the two principal parties, the Papal States and the Farnese family. Only the slightest excuse was needed, however, for both parties to go to war openly.

As no conclusive successes were scored by the French and the Pope announced his desire for peace talks, military efforts in Italy grew unpopular. Montmorency, sensing his moment, denounced the Italians at Court who had encouraged Henry to become involved in a pointless struggle. This was a barely veiled attack on the Strozzi, the Guises, and of course Catherine herself. Two days before Catherine gave birth to the Duke of Anjou, a mysterious incident occurred involving her cousin Leone Strozzi. Stationed at Marseilles, he had fled to Malta taking two

French galleys with him, having had one of his subordinates – known as Il Corso – killed. The man had apparently been plotting against him. By fleeing his post, Strozzi left himself open to accusations of treason, murder, cowardice and desertion. The consequent odium threatened not only the rest of his family but also the Queen herself, who had promoted her cousins whenever she could. Little is known about what actually took place and what the motives of the protagonists were, but Catherine well understood that the whole family risked having its honour and standing at Court impugned by Leone's flight. Dragging herself from her maternity bed, she took swift action to limit the damage; throwing herself at the mercy of the King she also managed to coax the Constable into helping her by showing herself to be as outraged as he was.

In her terror she wrote to Montmorency that she was '*la plus, la plus ennuyée*' (most, most vexed) adding, 'I wish to God that he had drowned ... if only God had taken him from this world before he fled, but I believe that he will recognise his mistake and not linger in this world which would be the greatest news I could have, for I am certain he would not act in bad faith.'[15] Unfortunately Leone did not have the good manners either to drown or kill himself, but had, she soon learned, arrived safely in Malta. This prompted another emotional letter to Montmorency saying that her '*grant ennuye et deplesyr*' was daily increasing and asking that Leone should be allowed to explain himself to the King.[16] Catherine also wrote a nervous rant to her husband: 'I beg you to forgive me if I annoy you with so long a letter, and to excuse me, considering the grief I feel that the person of whom I have spoken to you so much, and who is what he is to me, should have wronged you at a time when I hoped that he would serve you so well, and the only thing that would console me would be to hear that God had drowned him.'[17] Her loud protests against her cousin and supplications to Henry and the Constable must have had good effect for Leone was allowed back to Court two years later and, thanks to Catherine, Piero's reputation remained unaffected by the scandal.

Apart from seeing her cousins extricated from a potentially disastrous situation, Catherine had another reason to feel more cheerful. Henry had for some time now been showing the Queen great tenderness and affection. The marked change in the King's behaviour was quickly noted by the Court. One observer wrote, 'The King visits the Queen and serves her with so much affection and attention that it is astounding.' It is likely that a combination of reasons caused Henry's growing esteem for his wife: she had borne him six children and had been as undemanding as she was loyal. Diane, now fifty-one years old, had probably never been very interested in sex and grew increasingly tired of the highly athletic King's frequent attentions. What better than to send him to his wife's side where the King might chafe, but where he would be fairly safe from other predators? Henry had also begun to seek Catherine's political counsel, particularly in the latter half of his reign as the international situation grew more fraught. She now entered her second regency as head of the ruling council when, once again, Henry went to war with the Emperor.

On 15 January 1552 Henry signed the Treaty of Chambord, supporting the German Lutheran princes straining against Charles's political and religious yoke. France had eagerly stepped in with promises of help and in February 1552 Henry declared war on the Emperor, announcing that he himself would lead his troops as the 'Defender of German Liberties'. In return he received the administration as 'Imperial Vicar' of Toul, Metz, Verdun (known as the three Bishoprics) and Cambrai. These strategically valuable French-speaking towns on France's north-eastern border were a key acquisition and the project was warmly received by the French people.

When Catherine heard of her second regency, she was in raptures to find that Henry had placed such confidence in her. Her joy turned to consternation and then disappointment, however, when she discovered that her powers were to be shared with one of Diane's cronies, Jean Bertrand, the Keeper of the Seals, with whom she was to sit as joint president of the ruling council. Upon reading the document promulgating the council she remarked, 'In some places I am given a great deal of authority but others very little, and if this power had been cast in the full form which it pleased the King to say that it would be framed, I should have been careful to use it soberly.'[18] When this polite protest evoked no response, Catherine – whose main responsibility would be, in effect, to act as quartermaster-general and raise troops in case of need – remonstrated with Montmorency. Unmoved, the Constable made the dour reply, 'You should not incur any expense nor order any additional disbursement of money without telling him [Henry] first and knowing his pleasure.'[19] Exasperated, Catherine insisted that the *brevet* describing her powers should not be published for it 'diminished rather than augmented the authority and esteem she was believed to enjoy, having the honour of being who she is to the King'.[20] Catherine had her way, and the King ordered that the document be modified.

A month after Henry had departed on his German expedition Catherine fell seriously ill with scarlet fever. Diane nursed her diligently at Joinville-en-Champagne, and as soon as she recovered Catherine put aside any chagrin over her circumscribed powers and set about her duties with such brio that she nearly drove her fellow councillors mad. She wrote proudly to the Constable in one of her many letters, 'If everyone does his part and what he promises, I shall soon be past mistress, for I study nothing else all day long, and I employ most of the time of ... the members of the council on this question, for fear there may be some slip, though it is difficult when matters are so hasty and precipitate to avoid some confusion and disorder, but I hope ... you will be satisfied; at least you may count on me to press and push.'[21] At last given an outlet for her talents, Catherine slaved to please Henry when, for once, he asked something of her. Ever vigilant, she heard of some preachers speaking seditiously in Paris. Writing immediately to warn the city's governor, she recommended that the preachers be quietly apprehended and replaced with men who spoke favourably of the King's policies. The preachers, she wrote, 'have nothing better to do than incite the people to mutiny ... their arrogance is so great in the face of the goodness, prudence and religion of their Prince ... that under colour of their zeal and devotion they can move the people to rebellion'.[22] The Cardinal of Lorraine warned that arresting the preachers would only have exacerbated a relatively minor problem, but Catherine had not yet the experience to know how to deal with critics of the regime.

Working hard on Henry's behalf, Catherine discovered that she enjoyed the power that came with her rank and the untapped resources she possessed in the exercise of it. By late June Henry and his armies returned home after successfully occupying the new territories with almost no loss of life. From now until just before the end of his reign Henry, Catherine and France were to enjoy only the briefest respites from consequences of the Habsburg–Valois enmity. The battlegrounds for their almost continuous feuding would be Italy and the north-eastern border between France and the Holy Roman Empire.

In November 1552 the Emperor, armed with a huge force and determined not to allow Henry to hold on to his prestigious gains in the north-east, laid siege to Metz. There followed a ferocious six week bombardment of the city, the defence of which was led by François of Guise. Though he had only 6000 men and a handful of guns, Guise, helped by Piero Strozzi and Jean de Saint-Rémy (a superb artillery officer and specialist in fortification) set about improving the city's lamentable defences. Guise's leadership was so inspiring, as he himself laboured with a shovel alongside his men rebuilding vital walls, that he even persuaded the citizens to lend a hand in the demolition of their own houses and churches to fortify the city. Vieilleville wrote of Guise's industry, 'He was not seen to waste a single hour' and his efforts were rewarded as the town held out until the bitter cold of winter decimated Charles's exposed troops. The Imperial soldiers died in scores every day; dysentery, typhus, hunger and cold were France's allies at Metz. When Charles called off the siege in January 1553, Guise showed humanity rare in sixteenth-century warfare when he ventured out from the city and organised humane treatment for the sick and dying enemy soldiers. His reputation for saving Metz with such puny defences was already that of a hero defying impossible odds; such charity to the defeated foe added further lustre to his name.[23]

While the Metz problem was being satisfactorily resolved, an opportunity arose for France when the Tuscan city-state of Siena rebelled against the Empire. In July 1552, shouting the war cry 'Francia! Francia!', the Sienese revolted against the Spanish garrison that had been stationed there for twelve long years. The rebels asked to be taken under Henry's protection, who needed little prompting to accept the offer. Siena provided a perfect springboard from which to launch attacks on both Florence – where they hoped a popular uprising from within would aid them – and the Papal States. Catherine felt overjoyed; the situation brimmed with promise for the overthrow of Cosimo and the 'liberation' of Florence. Without wasting any time Henry sent the Cardinal d'Este as his representative to Siena with a 'bodyguard' of nearly 5000 men, which really constituted a small army.

Catherine, passionately energetic in her support of the Italian venture, became fearful when Henry's bastard daughter Diane of France married Orazio Farnese in February 1553. She worried that his attention might once again favour Farnese projects at the expense of her Florentine ambitions. Angry and tearful, Catherine went before the King while he gave an audience to the Tuscan ambassador; she declared that no one had any regard for her or for Florence. She had no cause for concern; the King was more than alive to his matrimonial rights with respect to that city. The episode marks a further step in Catherine's increasing importance to Henry and her growing confidence; such an outburst from the Queen would have been unthinkable only a few years earlier. As for Diane of France, married shortly after the victory at Metz, she was widowed within a few months. Her husband Orazio died fighting for France against Imperial troops at Hesdin, a French stronghold near Boulogne which had fallen to the Empire. With Henry's natural daughter now widowed, she became a tempting prize for one of his ambitious circle.

Just before his daughter's short-lived marriage to Farnese, Henry replaced d'Este in Siena with Piero Strozzi, who arrived there on 2 January 1554. With the financial support of the *fuoriusciti* he was to lead an attack on Florence, bringing Tuscany under French control. Catherine busied herself raising money from the Italian financiers in France and even added 100,000 écus of her own by mortgaging properties in the Auvergne inherited from her mother. She also received the Constable's grudging backing for the campaign. This not inconsiderable achievement was due largely to Montmorency's jealousy of the military laurels being won by François of Guise and his desire to garner some for himself. As well as her activities on behalf of the campaign in Tuscany, at Rheims Catherine was accorded her third regency while Henry went off to fight against the Imperial troops now stationed in Picardy.

The arrival in May 1554 of Charles V's army to besiege Siena and Strozzi's invasion of Florentine territory spelt disaster for France. Strozzi suffered an overwhelming defeat at the battle of Marciano on 2 August 1554, but eventually managed to reach Siena despite being badly wounded. Catherine raved about the cowardice of the Italian soldiers and despatched Piero's valet to find his master and nurse him. There followed a long hard siege of Siena by Imperial and Florentine troops before the city fell in April 1555. By then Piero's brother, Leone, who had returned to favour after the Malta fiasco and been given command of the galleys in the Mediterranean, had been killed in action. The news of Leone's death was, on Henry's express orders, withheld from Catherine for a few days because of the imminent birth of their daughter Marguerite, known as Margot. The King initially felt sorry for Strozzi upon losing his brother and created him a Marshal of France, but when Siena fell Henry finally lost patience with Catherine's favourite cousin for his brave but ultimately ineffective action in Italy.[24] When Piero managed to escape and return to France he was received with such *froideur* by Henry that Catherine advised her cousin to stay out of the King's sight.

Even before Siena had fallen, Henry was putting out tentative peace feelers to Cosimo de Medici, at the same time as assuring Catherine that he would not abandon the campaign. The Queen wrote to the Italian exiles and allies urging them not to give up hope and promising that the King would not turn his back on them. Her relentless efforts proved futile as the constant fighting in the north and in Italy began to tell on both protagonists. Some dramatic changes on the international landscape now also took place. On 8 July 1553 Edward VI of England had died and was succeeded by his half-sister Mary Tudor. Charles V, now infirm and suffering from crippling gout and piles, had seen his dream (and France's nightmare) realised when his niece, the new Queen of England, married his son Philip of Spain. After failing to retake Metz in 1553, Charles had observed that it was clear he had 'no real men left and must take leave of the world and get him to a monastery'.[25] Accordingly, he started preparing to hand the mantle to his son. His unwieldy and almost bankrupt Empire had broken him, but he wanted accord with France before he withdrew from public affairs altogether. The French, too, were in a poor financial position and the people now rapidly grew disenchanted with the interminable warring. Both Montmorency and Diane de Poitiers had their own pressing reasons for an agreement to be reached since the Constable's son, François, and Diane's son-in-law, Robert de la Marck, had both been taken prisoner during the hostilities. They were waiting to be ransomed when informal peace talks opened at Marck, near Calais, in May 1555.

A glistening temptation now presented itself before Henry, which even distracted him from the peace talks. Following the death of Julius III on 23 March 1555, and that of his successor Marcellus II (who wore the tiara for just twenty-one days before dying), a pope openly hostile to the Empire was elected. Paul IV (Gianpietro Carafa) succeeded Marcellus II on 23 May; he hated the Emperor and nursed fantastic ambitions for his nephews. His favourite, Cardinal Carlo Carafa, was a particularly loathsome character. A vicious one-time soldier of fortune now masquerading as a prince of the Church, Carafa received the position of His Holiness's Secretary of State, the papacy's most senior minister. The new regime in Rome made seductive overtures to the French for an alliance in which each would support the other's claims.

Catherine urged Henry not to let this opportunity slip; with papal backing, she argued, their Italian ambitions could hardly fail. Most people at Court supported this view, especially the Guises. Naples formed a crucial part of Paul IV's tempting promises to Henry. It was agreed that the Pope would bestow Naples upon Charles-Maximilien, Henry's second son, and Milan was to go to Edouard-Alexandre, his third boy. Guise expected to become regent of Naples during Charles-Maximilien's minority. In addition the Pope pledged his support for the overthrow of Cosimo de Medici, ensuring Catherine's formidable assistance and her remobilisation of the *fuoriusciti*. The Venetian ambassador, Michele Soranzo, wrote confirming Catherine's growing importance, 'The Queen will have all the merit should Florence be liberated.'[26] Diane, too, had been promised a fine harvest for herself, so she also threw her weight behind the war party. Practically the only dissenting voice to be heard in this ambitious chorus was the Constable's. He argued that Paul IV was not in a position to fulfil his promises, that the papal treasury was empty and that the Pontiff lacked allies within Italy. Everyone who mattered ignored Montmorency's doom-laden muttering, however, and the Franco–Papal alliance was signed on 15 December 1555. A few months later the odious Cardinal Carafa arrived in France, ostensibly in 'the holy task of peace' but really with only the most bellicose of intentions.

The treaty frightened Philip of Spain, still inexperienced and ruling without his father to guide him. Charles had abdicated by January 1556 and broken up the Empire. Philip was now King of Spain, Duke of Milan, King of Naples and sovereign of the Low Countries; Charles's brother Ferdinand was elected Holy Roman Emperor later that year. After much blustering and brinkmanship, Henry and Philip signed the Treaty of Vaucelles, a five-year truce, in February 1556. Given that France had just allied with the papacy and Philip had recently been excommunicated for not awarding Cardinal Carafa the See of Naples, it is highly unlikely that either party really viewed the treaty as more than a chance to draw breath before the outbreak of further hostilities. Philip felt so unnerved by events, however, that he wrote asking his father to 'help and aid me', adding that his enemies 'would behave differently' if they knew Charles were there to counsel him. Despite this filial plea, Philip soon established that he was equal to the challenges Henry now threw at him in what proved to be the military climax of his reign.

Having given birth to a boy, Hercules, during the last days of the siege of Siena, in March 1555 Catherine made her final maternal oblation to France by giving birth to twin daughters, Jeanne and Victoire, on 24 June 1556. She had borne Henry ten children in twelve years, but the arrival of these twins nearly cost Catherine her life. After the first baby was born, the second failed to emerge and the Queen began to weaken. To save her life the unborn infant, already dead or dying, had to have its legs broken to remove it from the womb. The surviving child was optimistically called Victoire, a name that would soon ring hollow in the year that Henry suffered the worst military defeat of his reign. In any event she died only weeks after her birth.

On 15 September 1556 the Duke of Alba, Philip's viceroy in Naples, launched an attack on the Campania region, provoked by the Pope who wanted to spark off a war in order to commit France to support him without further delay. Yet the unexpected speed of Alba's approach towards Rome terrified Paul IV, and he appealed for help from Henry as Imperial troops once again threatened the Eternal City. Henry despatched François of Guise who, aside from rescuing the Pope, intended to take Naples. Catherine immediately set to work raising money and men from the Italian exiles to aid the Guise expedition. The duke's Italian allies, Este and Cardinal Carafa, argued about what his campaign goals should be when the three men met in February 1557, each resolutely promoting his own interests. Thwarted by his shambolic allies and checked in an attempt to take Florence, Guise marched south to Naples, but he still lacked support, funds and men. Hearing that the perfidious Pope was now seeking a separate peace with Alba, Piero Strozzi brought Carafa's two great-nephews back to France with him as hostages. When he arrived at Senlis, where Henry and Catherine were expecting him, the Queen, who was at dinner when she heard of his arrival, dropped all protocol and rushed to embrace her cousin. The King and Queen spent the rest of the evening poring over campaign plans with Strozzi, now rehabilitated in the King's eyes, before he returned to the mess in his homeland.

While Guise struggled with the maze of obstacles in Italy, Philip's ally Emmanuel-Philibert of Savoy invaded northern France. Montmorency and his army stood before him at Saint-Quentin in Picardy. This vital stronghold approximately eighty miles from Paris is situated near the end of the River Somme as it flows towards France's north-eastern border with the Empire. On 10 August 1557 battle was joined, and the Constable suffered a catastrophic defeat. Although Saint-Quentin itself had not fallen, it was completely surrounded and the French army routed. Montmorency had been taken prisoner and those nobles who were not killed went into captivity with him. Among them were some of the most important men in France, including many of Henry's coterie.

Forty-five miles away, alone at Compiègne, Henry received the news with calm. Catherine, who had been made regent again, was already in Paris, a city gripped with panic as people scrambled to escape from the enemy who now had nothing to bar their advance to the capital. The Queen, displaying exemplary composure and fortitude, helped quieten the terrified populace. Henry, separated from his usual circle of advisers and alone but for two remaining secretaries to write out the essential orders, issued two vital commands. Knowing his wife's ability for rallying support, he sent her word that she must get money out of the Parisians without which he could not hope to raise more troops. He also issued immediate orders to recall François of Guise, his finest soldier, from Italy.

Catherine and her sister-in-law Marguerite appeared at the Bureau de Ville (Paris Town Hall) on 13 August 1557. Both women and their attendants wore black mourning, Catherine ensuring that their appearance evoked sombre drama. In her first significant public address she played her hostile and frightened audience with consummate skill. She did not command them to help their King, she appealed for their support, flattering them with her humble speech. Speaking of the peril which threatened them all, she asked the people to 'aid their King'. Unused to such gentle tones from a sovereign, the 'good bourgeois' of Paris requested that the Queen withdraw while they debated the matter. She was kept waiting for only a moment before returning to a unanimous vote that they would raise men and money from the 'said city and faubourgs, with no exemptions, the sum of three hundred thousand livres'. Tearfully Catherine thanked them, her voice trembling with emotion.

On 29 August the town of Saint-Quentin fell despite the confident assurances of Montmorency's nephew Admiral Gaspard de Coligny that it would hold out for at least ten weeks (in France, 'Admiral' was a rank that originally applied to commanders at sea, but had long been used for army officers too). Henry had counted on Philip not daring to advance on Paris with the still-uncaptured garrison to his rear. This fresh blow caused further panic as the route to Paris now lay clear before the enemy. He issued commands that precious items and sacred relics in the capital should be taken away from the city to avoid being looted, and those people who could, fled.

The return of Guise from Italy put heart into all. At their first encounter the duke fell to his knees before the King. 'He was received by His Majesty so lovingly, and with so many embraces, that he seemed unable to detach himself from his neck.'[27] Guise came with some of France's best soldiers, including Monluc and Piero Strozzi. He was made Lieutenant-General of the kingdom, and his brother the Cardinal of Lorraine undertook many of the captured Montmorency's responsibilities. Philip, who had been unable to believe the success at Saint-Quentin, failed to push home his victory and drive on to Paris. He dallied, taking defenceless towns in the area, and started to release some of his troops, never imagining that the French would be able to recover as fast as they did. His father, the ex-Emperor, sat in retirement in Spain asking one question over and over again: 'Is he in Paris yet?' Perhaps Philip feared that he would overreach himself by pressing on to the capital and suffer the same fate as his father had once done: 'He might march into France eating pheasant and leave it eating only roots.'[28] The campaign season over and mistakenly expecting no serious trouble from the French for some considerable time, Philip returned to Brussels.

Henry then decided upon a course that would avenge the humiliation of Saint-Quentin and remove the last English thorn remaining in France from the Hundred Years War. He would recapture Calais, so long in enemy hands. This foreign foothold was especially dear to Philip's wife, Queen Mary of England, and as an added bonus its loss would thus also wound the Spanish King deeply. It was a bold and unexpected move. The town was considered impregnable and the weather unfavourable for such an expedition; even Guise felt sceptical about the plan. Strozzi was sent to examine the fortifications and after reporting his conclusions back to the King, Henry decided to press ahead; the element of surprise would be so great that he ignored the caution of his commanders. Guise was to lead the force against the town, whose banner above the city gate bore the unfortunate prediction, 'Then shall the Frenchmen Calais win; when iron and lead like cork shall swim.'[29] After a brilliant attack the garrison's commander surrendered on 8 January 1558. Henry and Catherine were in the midst of a wedding banquet at the Château des Tournelles in Paris when news arrived of the victory. The people's joy was unbounded. Henry departed for the front, taking the Dauphin with him, leaving Catherine in charge of government matters during his absence.

Piero Strozzi had particularly distinguished himself during the attack and fought with great courage. His valiant but often hopeless past failures were forgotten as he received honours and rewards from the King. Catherine was vindicated for the support she had always extended to her cousin. The hero of the hour, François of Guise, received the greatest reward of all: Henry agreed that the marriage between his niece, Mary, Queen of Scots and the Dauphin Francis should now take place. Catherine brought all the royal children to Paris for the lavish wedding on 24 April 1558. Montmorency, still in captivity, had tried to prevent this ultimate alliance between the House of Guise and the Crown. He suggested to Henry that Philip's sister become the Dauphin's bride and Elisabeth of France be engaged to marry Don Carlos, Philip's increasingly mad son. While it gave Henry something to reflect upon, he nonetheless decided to proceed with the original plan, not least because the Constable's proposal had received no encouragement from the Spanish and the victor of Calais must be rewarded.

Guise himself oversaw the details of the celebrations. Particular attention was given to ensuring that the common people could see the brilliant beauty of the fifteen-year-old bride and her fourteen-year-old groom. The puffy-faced, sickly-looking Dauphin, with a constantly running nose, standing beside his much taller lovely new wife, must have made an unprepossessing sight. It had been decreed that the couple should henceforth be known as the Queen-Dauphine and the King-Dauphin to remind people that the Dauphin Francis was also King of Scotland. Among the fantastic entertainments laid on for the wedding was a banquet at which twelve man-made horses covered in gold and silver cloth were led in to be ridden by the royal princes and the small Guise children. The shimmering horses pulled carriages carrying singers glittering with jewels, who entertained the guests with their music. These were followed by the arrival of six silver-sailed ships that appeared to float over the ballroom floor, on board sat the gentlemen who were allowed to bring a lady of their choice. Francis invited his mother to join him and Henry chose his new daughter-in-law.[30]

On 13 May 1558 a Protestant demonstration lasting several days presaged the religious trouble to come when 4000 reformers staged a march at the Pré-aux-clercs in Paris. To the outrage of the general population there were seen among the crowd a number of noblemen and the psalm-singing marchers were led by Antoine de Bourbon on horseback. On 18 May Henry responded by publishing a decree that prevented demonstrations by those singing and praying in public. Nine months earlier a furious mob had broken up a prayer meeting of Calvinists in the rue Saint-Jacques and 132 people had been arrested, among them a few noblewomen. Henry was disgusted at the contamination of the nobility by the reform movement; to him it was a gross perversion and utterly incomprehensible. Although he had issued the Edict of Compiègne in July 1557 against the Calvinist reformers – sparing the Lutherans because so many of his allies, mercenaries and bankers were German

Lutherans – he had been hampered from putting the edict into effect by resistance within the realm and by continued international hostilities.

Calvin operated from Geneva and had created a far more effective proselytising organisation than earlier Protestants; his agents were now slipping into France and spreading the new doctrine. Among the repressive measures were the death penalty with no right of appeal for preachers and those coming in from Geneva distributing Protestant literature. This also covered anyone fomenting religious unrest. At the same time Henry had asked the Pope's permission to create a French Inquisition. Three cardinals were chosen to lead this body; Lorraine, Bourbon (Antoine's brother) and Montmorency's nephew, Châtillon. The Cardinal of Lorraine was the de facto leader of the French Inquisition, but Henry had difficulty with the magistrates who balked at the Inquisitors' authority. Secular courts were given additional powers to act against the Calvinists, but progress was slowed by confusion as to which legal body had the jurisdiction to enforce the harsh new measures. One thing was quite clear, however: in order to stop the canker within his realm, Henry needed peace to implement the edict and wage his war against heresy.

At Thionville on 20 June, Guise recaptured the town which had been held by Philip, though the military triumph brought personal tragedy to Catherine. Her adored Piero Strozzi was killed by a shot from an arquebusier while launching an attack on the stronghold. He went to his death in a manner quite as unconventional as his life. When Guise saw his friend and comrade mortally wounded he held the dying Strozzi in his arms saying, 'Pray to Jesus that you will be received by him.' To which Strozzi replied, 'What Jesus? For God's sake don't try to convert me now. I renounce God, my joys are over [ma fête est finie].' The pious duke, appalled at this outburst, redoubled his efforts and begged Strozzi to ask God's forgiveness for he would stand before Him that very day, to which Strozzi answered, 'But for God's sake! I will be where all the others are who have died over the last six thousand years' and with that the Italian expired leaving Guise deeply afflicted.[31] Catherine and Henry were both devastated and took great pains over the welfare of Strozzi's widow and son.

Montmorency's continued imprisonment was a source of great distress to Henry. Diane also regretted the loss of the balance that he brought to counter the weight of the House of Guise. The Venetian ambassador wrote of the shift, 'At the present there is open rupture and enmity between her and the Cardinal of Lorraine, she being so united with the Constable that they are one and the same thing.'[32] A useful function that the Constable could perform from his captivity at Ghent was to hold informal peace discussions. After all, there was no one who knew his master's mind better than he who had helped form it. Philip was short of money and knew that Henry needed peace as badly as he did, and welcomed the use of Montmorency. The Constable fretted at the thought of what might be happening at Court without him, despite the fond handwritten letters he received from Henry full of love and assurances. Diane joined with Henry and added her own soothing words in a letter to the old man. Saint-André had also been taken prisoner, as was the Constable's nephew Coligny.

The King began to show his disaffection with the Guises who, now unchecked, were promoting their interests marvellously. He blamed the duke for talking him into the last war with Italy and openly declared himself exasperated with the family's limitless aspirations. This was largely irritation on Henry's part at the predicament in which he found himself and for which he was ultimately responsible, though the Guises were the obvious party to blame. Catherine remained, for her part, stout in her defence of the Guises and the Italian campaign. She was so overwrought at the concessions she feared would jeopardise French hopes in Italy for ever that for the first time in her marriage she chose to stay away from Henry for a full three months. She only rejoined her husband in October 1558 shortly before the return of the Constable, who had been paroled by Philip.

The reunion between Henry and his old mentor on 10 October 1558 was pathetic and moving. Henry had been restlessly kicking his heels all day looking out for the Constable; finally he decided to ride out in the hope of catching sight of him. At last Montmorency appeared alone on his horse. The two men embraced like father and son. Much to the relief of the Constable, they touched only briefly on the disaster of Saint-Quentin, his staggering military failure of Pavia-like proportions, before the two proceeded to denigrate the Guises, their greed, hawkishness and ambition. The Constable slept in the King's chamber, and Henry was inconsolable when Montmorency had to return to captivity two days later.

After tremendous haggling and changing his mind at least once, Henry agreed to a peace treaty, the merits of which have been hotly debated ever since. The most important terms of the Treaty of Cateau-Cambrésis were, broadly, that France retained Calais for eight years, after which an indemnity must be paid or Calais returned. She also kept the three bishoprics of Toul, Metz and Verdun. All French positions in Tuscany were ceded to the Duke of Mantua or the Duke of Florence, Cosimo de Medici. Spanish rights to Milan and Naples were recognised, and Bresse, Savoy and Piedmont were handed back to the Duke of Savoy. The only French possessions left in Italy were the Marquisate of Saluzzo and five strongholds in Piedmont, including Turin.[33] Two marriage alliances were brokered to shore up the treaty. Henry's and Catherine's eldest daughter

Elisabeth was to marry Philip of Spain, a widower since Mary Tudor had died on 17 November 1558. Meanwhile the Duke of Savoy agreed to take Henry's sister Marguerite as his bride. In short, Henry was surrendering gains and expensive possessions in Italy for territory and strength on the north-eastern border of his kingdom, although that is not at all how his subjects perceived the treaty at the time. Today the view that Cateau-Cambrésis 'was a strategic retrenchment that made France less vulnerable' is the one most widely held.[34]

Catherine was appalled when she first heard the terms of the treaty. Falling on her knees before her husband, she begged him not to ratify it. She denounced the Constable, saying, 'He has done us nothing but harm,' to which Henry retorted, 'All the harm has been done by those who advised me to break the Truce of Vaucelles.'[35] Guise announced to the King himself that he would rather have his head cut off than 'say it is honourable or advantageous to Your Majesty'. A few months later he repeated his convictions to Henry: 'I swear to you, Sire, that there is evil in taking this road. For if you do nothing but lose for the next thirty years you would not give up as much as now at a single stroke.'[36] The duke left the Court in disgust at Christmas 1558. Henry's most senior military commanders were incredulous at the treaty; their feelings were shared by many. Catherine felt much of the blame could be laid at Diane's door. When the latter walked into the Queen's presence and found Catherine reading, she asked politely what the book was. The Queen is said to have answered, 'I am reading the chronicles of France, and I find that from time to time, at every period, the affairs of Kings have been governed by whores.'

The Guises enjoyed a moment of glory when Henry's and Catherine's daughter Claude married the young Duke Charles of Lorraine. There was a splendid ceremony at Notre-Dame on 22 January 1559. A few days later Montmorency sealed his pact with Diane by marrying his son Henri to her granddaughter, Antoinette de la Marck. Catherine accompanied her husband for the celebrations at the Constable's château of Écouen. Earlier in 1558 the King had honoured the Constable by marrying his widowed illegitimate daughter Diane to the old man's eldest son François. Montmorency was quite overcome to be so closely allied to the royal family. Much loved by her royal half-brothers and sisters, the Constable's new daughter-in-law was not only beautiful and sweet-natured but of all his children she had inherited the most of her father's finest traits.

The unpopular Treaty of Cateau-Cambrésis was officially ratified on 3 April. Now Henry could concentrate on eliminating the 'Protestant vermin' from his realm. On 10 June, shortly before the two treaty weddings of his sister Marguerite and his daughter Elisabeth, Henry appeared without warning at a *mercuriale*, a quarterly examination of members of the judiciary, many of whom were suspected of heretical leanings. The magistrates could not hide their astonishment when they saw the King arrive, bringing with him the Cardinal of Lorraine, the Constable and other nobles. The King spoke first, saying that now that the country was at peace heretics must be brought to trial and punished according to the law. He then asked the assembled men to proceed with their meeting. What he heard left him dumbfounded. Some councillors, notably Anne du Bourg, were critical of the rich ecclesiastics who ignored their flock. The cardinal remained silent, but Montmorency sharply interrupted du Bourg's insolence. The magistrate, unheeding, went on to denounce the burning of heretics: 'It is no light thing to condemn those who from the midst of the flames call upon the name of Jesus Christ. What! Crimes worthy of death – blasphemy, adultery, horrible debaucheries ... are committed day by day with impunity ... while day by day new tortures are devised for men whose only crime is that by the light of the Scriptures they have discovered the corruptions of the Church of Rome.'[37] Furious, the King ordered the arrest of du Bourg and four other councillors as soon as the session was over. Although the others were released, du Bourg was put on trial and condemned to death. Henry had taken the tirade as a personal insult on his relationship with his mistress.

Although Diane still dominated his private life, Henry's sexual appetites were now more often met by discreet liaisons with courtesans whom he met in secret, disguising himself in a cloak and covering his face. His valet, Griffon, kept guard outside the bedchamber where His Majesty entertained these *belles inconnues*. His sixty-year-old mistress turned a blind eye to the King's romantic sorties, and Catherine minded them far less than she minded Diane's continued pre-eminence. The Venetian Giovanni Capello (also an envoy to the French Court) gives a picture of the Queen as she reached her fortieth year. Her dress was always magnificent and her manner regal, though he qualified this somewhat crushingly by saying she could not be considered good-looking except 'when her face is veiled'. He continues, 'Her mouth is too large and her eyes too prominent and colourless for beauty, but a very distinguished-looking woman, with a shapely figure, a beautiful skin and exquisitely shaped hands; her manners are charming, and she has a pleasant smile or a few well-chosen words for each of her guests.'[38] The Venetian ambassador, Michele Soranzo, described Catherine in a despatch during 1558. He wrote, 'Queen Catherine has an extremely large face though her body is well proportioned. She is extremely generous, particularly with the Italians. She is loved by all and more than anyone else she loves the King, for whom she overcomes all fatigue to follow. The King honours her, and confides in her ... the fact that she has borne him ten children counts very much for his attachment to her.'[39]

The children were Henry's joy and he was a kind and affectionate father. He played with them and watched their games, following their achievements with pride. Catherine, emotionally hampered by Diane's jurisdiction within the royal nursery, was a viscerally protective and devoted mother, concerned with health, education and upbringing, but she suffered from an inability to be intimate with her children in the same way as Henry. After he died, however, she was to lavish unrestrained love upon one child, her favourite, Edouard-Alexandre, later Duke of Anjou, whom she alone called her '*chers yeux*' (my precious eyes). To find that the many little treasures of motherhood such as the nicknames she and the King invented for their brood were also used by his mistress tarnished their magic for her. Nothing, it seemed, belonged to Catherine without Diane's corrupting inclusion. While the Queen instilled awe, respect and a desire to please in the children, it was their father to whom they turned for warmth.

The couple presided over a Court noted for its relative decorum. Unlike his father, Henry insisted upon courtiers keeping up a show of respectability, and should a young man attempt to take liberties with one of her *filles d'honneur* Catherine ferociously protected her ladies' virtue and reputation. Many an over-ardent suitor would have to cool his passion away from Court until the Queen's fury had abated. Equally, when Catherine discovered that any of her young women had abandoned their dignity, her wrath could be terrifying. One luckless girl, Mademoiselle de Rohan, was asleep with her lover when she awoke to hear people entering her chamber. She opened her eyes to find the Queen, Diane and the Constable's wife standing beside the bed. Outraged, the Queen exclaimed 'How you shame me!' and the indignant matrons marched the young woman before the King, the Constable and the Cardinal of Lorraine who backed up Catherine's demand to have the girl, who was pregnant, sent away from Court.[40] In later years the decorum the Queen expected from her *filles d'honneur* was to become far more elastic as she needed their seductive qualities to further her own political ends.

Catherine still loved to hunt and lavished a fortune on her horses and stables. Brantôme wrote of her, 'She was a very good and fearless horsewoman, sitting with ease, and being the first to put her leg around a pommel ... until she was over sixty she loved riding, and after her weakness prevented her, she pined for it. It was one of her greatest pleasures to ride far and fast, though she fell many times.'[41] When out riding she often carried a crossbow in case she came across any game, and used it with considerable skill. Perhaps the other reason she loved to hunt was that it afforded a rare opportunity to be with her husband without Diane. For all the allegorical connections that the favourite liked to make between herself and the goddess of the chase, Diane now only rode out in the morning for exercise and despite wearing a mask for protection (which was common practice at the time) did not want to risk acquiring the ruddy complexion of a huntswoman.

On hunting days the Queen held a *cercle* in her chambers, which Henry punctiliously attended. The Constable, Diane and the Guises also made a point of appearing at these rather staid gatherings during which no music was played nor any entertainment offered. The assemblies were Catherine's way of getting to know the courtiers. By three o'clock the *cercle* had usually finished and the courtiers often went to play games such as pell-mell or watch the King and his nobles tilt, or play tennis. In the evening after dinner the Queen frequently arranged another party, though these were made jollier by music and dancing. Henry had also begun to make a practice of spending an hour or so alone with his wife before he went to bed, which he did at ten o'clock most evenings.[42]

Now with tensions running high between the Guises and the Montmorencys, and between Diane and the Queen, the date for the wedding celebrations to seal the peace approached. Diane, allied by the marriages of her daughters and granddaughter into both rival factions, felt herself insured by these links. Most important of all, she still held Henry's complete devotion safely in her possession. Yet the divisions created by the new religion had permeated even this close circle around the King. Montmorency's nephew d'Andelot had embraced the new faith and it was rumoured that his brother Gaspard, Admiral de Coligny had also converted during his captivity, though he had not yet come out into the open with his beliefs. The King often chose to ignore these transgressions when they affected those so close to his heart, but it made for increased difficulties. The line between heresy and treacherous sedition was – as yet – a faint one.

Catherine had the great joy of watching her thirteen-year-old daughter Elisabeth – given the popular name of Isabel de la Paz – married, by proxy, to Philip of Spain. The merchant blood of the Medici was now to be mingled with the blue blood of the Habsburgs, the grandest dynasty in Europe. Catherine's matronly breast felt any stain of her origins erased by this glorious connection. But her unease at the coming jousts to celebrate the wedding was manifest. Henry had not felt well all summer, suffering from vertigo, and showed signs of the strain he had been under since the defeat of Saint-Quentin. The Queen's sleep was horribly disturbed on the night of 29 June, the day before Henry was to take part in the joust: she dreamt that he lay wounded, bleeding in the face. Her entreaties that he should not take part went unheeded and she watched as he fell, mortally wounded in his contest against Gabriel de Montgomery the following day. For the next ten days she kept vigil beside her dying husband, who finally expired on 10 July 1559. Her grief was penetrated only by the knowledge that she must now ensure the safety of their children's future and do all she could to keep Henry's memory and legacy alive. Although Henry had only nominally belonged to Catherine during his lifetime, she was now to make him her own for ever.

The power-hungry favourites of her late husband, already manoeuvring for position, would threaten her place if she allowed them the opportunity. The Guises, only months before in semi-disgrace for opposing the Peace of Cateau-Cambrésis, now saw that their time had come. They held the person of the new King, Francis II, with their niece, Mary, now Queen of France, and decided to remove them from the Château des Tournelles to avoid any intervention from their enemies. Montmorency, deprived of the powers he had enjoyed, could only watch as the de facto new rulers of France set out for the Louvre Palace leaving him and his party behind. Diane quit Paris, fearful of what was to become of her and her fortune.

Catherine, mastering her agony, decided not to risk remaining with the body of her late husband as tradition dictated. She would lend her tragic presence to the Guises in what has been called their 'elopement for power' and, as the mother of the fifteen-year-old King, make herself an indispensable element in their plans for him and the ruling council that France now required. It was clear to all that the sickly boy did not possess the maturity to reign alone. One wag called the death of Henry and accession of his son 'the eve of the three kings', alluding to Francis II, François of Guise and Charles, Cardinal of Lorraine. Yet France could not be ruled by such a triumvirate for long and Catherine was determined that, with her help, her son must be the ultimate victor in the power struggle that lay ahead.

PART TWO

SIX

An Uneasy Partnership

From this come my tears and my pain

1559–60

The sudden death of King Henry II of France brought with it the certainty of a new order. With a grieving passivity that masked her absolute determination to form a central part of the Guise's ruling clique, Catherine, despite her tragic loss, ensured she did not become separated from her eldest son, the new King Francis II. While many favourites of the old regime prepared themselves for an all too bracing change in status, Catherine knew she brought legitimacy to the Guise family that stood so close to her son's throne. Just how much influence she would be able to wield to protect him and his kingdom she had yet to find out.

The royal party moved into the Louvre Palace on 11 July 1559 and with this simple act the Guises accomplished their *coup d'état* without spilling a drop of blood. By installing themselves in the best apartments the new regime lost no time falling upon the initial spoils of their stunning victory. The Duke of Guise took Diane de Poitiers' rooms, and his brother the Cardinal those of Montmorency. Catherine had covered her walls and floors with black silk. With no daylight allowed to penetrate, the two flickering candles did little but add to the gloom. Wearing black, with only a tiny white ermine collar to highlight the effect, Catherine was described by observers as remaining virtually motionless in her anguish. She was exhausted by the strain of the past ten days and barely acknowledged the visiting foreign dignitaries who came to pay their doleful respects. Many confessed that they were moved to tears themselves at the sight of Catherine's utter desolation. Often the new Queen would stand behind her mother-in-law to help with these difficult interviews. Wearing her lily-white wedding dress (the traditional hue of royal mourning) Mary would reply on Catherine's behalf, thanking the visitors for their condolences and whenever possible managing to insert a flattering reference to her uncles and their ability to help the new King steer France safely forward.

Henry's legacy to his heirs and widow was pregnant with peril as they now had little more than his Valois name to sustain them. Medieval monarchs were judged according to the moral authority that they could project and the allegiance that they were able to command, and according to these lights Francis II could not have had a worse start to his reign. His father had acceded to the throne as a mature adult with the personal qualities required of a successful king. He had sought the advice of Montmorency and the Guises but had been controlled by neither. His death turned their competition for influence into a struggle for supremacy.

Henry's recent war had left France flayed by debt; strict financial retrenchment was now unavoidable if she were to recover economic prosperity. Such sacrifices would be bound to test to the utmost loyalty to the new young King. Pouring back into France from Italy were large numbers of troops who felt as angry at their arrears in pay as they were enraged by the treaty of Cateau-Cambrésis. They were to provide the foot soldiers for the coming wars of religion. Their primary reason to be loyal to the state – their love for Henry – had died with him.

Meanwhile what the state regarded as Protestant heresy was on the increase; the harsh Henrician policy of repression could not be imposed with the same degree of confidence by the incoming regime. In the international arena there were looming problems too, with a resurgent Spain under Philip II to the south and a newly unified England under her recently crowned Queen Elizabeth I across the Channel. More serious than any of France's economic, religious or diplomatic problems, however, was the potentially disastrous rivalry between the factions that had coalesced around the Guise and Montmorency families. Whereas in earlier years Henry II had provided a fulcrum between these vying groups ensuring they balanced each other, now there was the real danger of the monarch being identified with one party alone. With their niece Queen of France, the Guises were triumphant.

Montmorency arrived on the day after the family's move to the Louvre. He offered himself and his clan to the new King, who declined in a nervous speech carefully rehearsed by his uncles. Francis thanked the Constable for his long service, adding, 'We are anxious to solace thine old age, which is no longer fit to endure the toils and hardships of my service.'[1] The polite exchange finished, the seals of office were given up. Montmorency, effectively dismissed by his rivals, went to find Catherine to take his leave of her. After his short speech about the dangers she and her family faced at the hands of the Guises, the Queen Mother collapsed, tearfully promising that she would do all in her power to protect his estates and prerogatives. The Constable had never been fond of the Queen, and she had always been jealous of the power he had held over her late husband. She had not forgiven him for apparently advocating repudiation during her barren years, nor for the Peace of Cateau-Cambrésis, but Catherine knew she might need the services of the doughty old patriot one day and was determined not to alienate him. He would remain at a distance, ready to come to her assistance if the situation required it.

Montmorency remained Constable of France, though it was now an empty title with the Guises in effective control of the government and the army. Catherine hid her true feelings about the soldier by acting as an intermediary. In exchange for the Grand Mastership, which was to be given to François of Guise, she had his eldest son, François de Montmorency, who was married to Henry's natural daughter Diane, made a Marshal of France. She wrote to the Constable confirming that because of his prompt co-operation in handing back '*la grant mestrise*' she would '*fayst depeche la marichausye a votre fyls*' (ensure the prompt creation of your son as Marshal).[2] Catherine also guaranteed that the general kept the governorship of the Languedoc. This vast territory in southern France, firmly in the Montmorency family grip, would in any case have been practically impossible to wrest from the clan. His nephews, Coligny, an Admiral of France, François d'Andelot, Colonel-General of the Infantry, and Cardinal Ôdet de Châtillon, all retained their positions. Largely thanks to Catherine's diplomacy the old warrior left Paris peacefully 'with such a retinue that the King's train seemed small in comparison'. One potential source of strife had been removed, at least for the time being.

Trouble could be expected from the First Prince of the Blood, Antoine de Bourbon who, because of his status, should head any regency council. Catherine and the Guises managed to render Bourbon ineffective by a combination of flattering messages, assurances and the sheer indolence of the man himself. Despite being urged by both the departing Constable and his own brother, Louis de Condé, to get to Paris as quickly as he could to claim his rightful place, Bourbon – who had been in Guyenne in south-west France at the time of Henry's sudden death – made his way up through France to Paris slowly. The Guises had promised a warm welcome and a role in the government, but by the time he finally arrived he found only slights awaiting him. The King, who by custom should meet an exalted visitor on the road as though by chance, had gone out hunting and no rooms had been put aside at Saint-Germain, where the Court had moved in preparation for Bourbon's arrival. Both Catherine and the Guises feared him as a figurehead of legitimacy for those disaffected members of the nobility who saw no future for themselves under the new regime. Bourbon had paraded his allegiance to the Protestant cause, notably appearing at the Protestant rally at the Pré-aux-clercs in 1558, and this made him the natural, if as a cardinal's brother somewhat unlikely, leader of the reformers. The Bourbon family, though the most senior in France after the Valois, had long suffered from the treason of the Constable de Bourbon early in the reign of Francis I.

Antoine de Bourbon's inability to rub along with Henry's favourites had infuriated the late King, who treated him with scant regard, often pointedly ignoring his rank.

Bourbon's main interest in life was to restore the tiny kingdom of Navarre, which had been halved in size by the Spaniards in the early 1500s. Dithering and hopelessly self-indulgent, he became miraculously animated by the slightest hint of retrieving these lost territories, which were his by virtue of his marriage to Henry's cousin Jeanne d'Albret. Otherwise he proved an uninspiring leader, surrounded by bad advisers. Furthermore, he was a man incapable of making any decisions, especially good ones. When he arrived at Saint-Germain it had been placed under heavy guard by the Guises in case he came in force. There he was simply outfaced and outmanoeuvred by Catherine and the Guises; their public disdain for him, and his spineless acceptance of their treatment, emasculated him in front of his followers.

Catherine, who watched Bourbon accept the insults, commented that he was 'reduced to the position of a chambermaid'. He was offered a place on the essentially bogus council, where he was outnumbered by Guisards and others, including both Queens and Catherine's younger sons. Together they ensured Bourbon's voice would not be heard should he ever dare to speak up. When Catherine later offered him the job of accompanying her daughter Elisabeth to Spain to be united with King Philip, Bourbon accepted for it offered him the opportunity – or so he thought – of treating with Spain over Navarre. However, by agreeing to the regime's suggestion that he make the long journey away from the Court, Antoine de Bourbon effectively neutralised himself as a contender for power. Thus Catherine and the Guises relieved themselves, for the moment at least, of another potential opponent.

One who no longer posed any threat was Henry's favourite. Almost as soon as her lover had died and knowing that her reign was over, Diane de Poitiers promptly returned all the jewels that were inalienable Crown property to Catherine and the new King. Typical of her thoroughness and businesslike ways, a full inventory accompanied the gems that Henry had given his mistress. Fearful for her life, she also sent a letter begging forgiveness for any past wrongs she might have committed against the Queen, and theoretically offered the Queen Mother her life and her goods. Catherine, perhaps remembering Francis I's dictum that vengeance was the mark of a feeble king and magnanimity a sign of his strength, seemed curiously uninterested in pursuing Diane. But she was behind the letter written by her son, Francis, to Diane. According to the Venetian diplomat Giovanni Michiel in his report of 12 July 1559, 'The King has sent to inform Madame de Valentinois that, because of her evil influence with the King, his father, she merited a severe punishment; but that in his royal clemency, he did not wish to disquiet her further.'[3]

The Queen Mother contented herself with banishing Diane from Court and included her daughter Françoise de la Marck, Duchess of Bouillon, in the interdiction. Catherine could not extend the ban to Diane's other daughter for she was married to François of Guise's younger brother, now the Duke d'Aumale. So Diane's policy of marrying one of her daughters into the Guise family had paid off. This also meant that the fabulous estates and riches belonging to Diane de Poitiers remained more or less intact, since the Guises knew that half her goods would (via Louise d'Aumale) be incorporated into their fortune upon her death.

There was one of the mistress's properties that the Queen Mother coveted more than any other and that was the enchanting Château of Chenonceau. Diane had, by false means and the support of King Henry, bought the estate from the Crown; Catherine now saw that the simplest way to have it was to offer Diane her own castle at Chaumont in exchange for the less valuable but far lovelier Chenonceau. Diane was hardly in a position to refuse. She had spent a considerable amount of time and money embellishing and extending it. Now Catherine set about making it even more beautiful. She lavished money on the gardens, creating waterfalls, enclosures for exotic animals, aviaries for rare birds and planted mulberry trees for silkworms.[4] She added significantly to the building itself, which is set beside the River Cher, over which Diane had built a bridge to extend it. Catherine was determined to efface the memory of her rival and increase the castle's splendour, including adding two storeys of long galleries on to the bridge that straddles the river. The delicate palace still stands today, with the waters of the Cher rushing beneath the gracious rooms above.

Diane retired to her other estates, spending most of her remaining days at Anet doing good works and ensuring that her family would inherit her vast wealth at her death in 1566. With so much Crown money spent creating her Renaissance masterpiece, she was fortunate not to have had Anet confiscated. A Florentine gentleman travelling nearby in the late 1550s wrote 'that the golden house of Nero was not so costly or so beautiful'.[5] Catherine later employed many of the master craftsmen Diane and Henry had used at Anet when she came to her own building projects. She also got rid of Diane's lackeys who had tormented her during her early regencies. After Henry's death she and her late husband's favourite never met again.

Enjoyable though it would doubtless have been, Catherine had too much on her mind to bother with vengeance. The new King was far from strong, and while he showed his mother respect and filial love, she had carefully to protect him from being over-influenced by the Guises and his young wife, whom he worshipped. He showed little interest in governing the country and spent most of his time hunting frantically, or engaging in other sporting pursuits to which his puny physique was unequal. His health proved an ever-present worry. He was still subject to weakness and dizzy spells, his nose ran constantly and he had problems breathing due to a childhood respiratory infection.[6] More significantly for Mary and the Guises, Francis is believed to have suffered from a condition which meant that his testicles had not dropped at puberty, which might have made him incapable of fathering a child, or possibly (depending upon the cause) of even having sex.

Despite his obvious frailties Francis had, since childhood, behaved in a manner that did not allow anyone to forget his position. Perhaps his infirmities made him more determined to act with dignity, but instead he managed only to seem pompous. He had a weakness for display and dressed gorgeously in the finest costumes, but rather than enhancing his appearance his attempts at glamour made a pathetic sight. His body's weakness frustrated him and he was apt to fall into rages and tantrums when thwarted by ill-health. Physically timid except when he was out hunting, he seemed more than happy to leave the horrible difficulties of running the kingdom to others. The large official council only met in full on one occasion in the year 1560; the real power lay with the Guises and Catherine who conducted their secret meetings either in the King's chambers or those of his mother. François of Guise took charge of all military matters and his brother the Cardinal of Lorraine was given the domestic and foreign affairs portfolios.

The funeral of Henry II took place between 11 and 13 August 1559. The late King was buried with his predecessors at Saint-Denis, where Catherine had been crowned Queen only twelve years earlier. On 18 September the young King, wearing black velvet, was crowned at Rheims. The stormy wet weather did nothing to lift the occasion, which was by necessity kept muted due to Henry's untimely and violent death. Mary, already crowned Queen of Scotland, could not be crowned twice; however her pretensions to the English Crown were carefully noted by the English ambassador, Throckmorton, who reported that the French had displayed the 'arms of England, France and Scotland quartered brimly set out in show over the gate'.[7] This deliberately provocative gesture was duly registered by the English Queen. Mary based her claim to the throne of England on the questionable validity of Henry VIII's marriage to Anne Boleyn and Elizabeth's consequent bastardy in the eyes of the Catholic Church. If Elizabeth were illegitimate she could not rule and the throne therefore theoretically belonged to Mary.

Francis made sure that his mother was well provided for and on 15 August 1559 he issued letters patent which accorded Catherine 'the most opulent settlement that had ever been made to a queen dowager'. He set

her annual pension at 70,000 livres, and among other properties and
lands he gave her the chateaux of Villers-Cotterêts and Montceaux, in
addition to the Duchy of Alençon. The King also gave his mother the
right to half of the payments now due for the confirmation of offices,
fiefs and privileges sat the start of the new reign.[8] Underscoring Catherine's
importance, henceforth all the young King's official acts opened with the
words: 'This being the good pleasure of the Queen, my lady-mother, and
I also approving of every opinion that she holdeth, am content and
command that . . .' Mary commented in a letter to her mother in Scotland,
'I believe that if the King her son were not so obedient that he does
nothing but what she desires, she would soon die, which would be the
greatest misfortune that could happen to this poor country and to all of
us.'[9] In case anyone needed reminding of her loss, the Queen Mother
adopted a new personal device to replace her cheerful rainbow. Henceforth her emblem depicted a broken lance with the words '*Lacrymae hinc,
hinc dolor*' (From this come my tears and my pain). For the rest of her
life she also refused to do business on Fridays, the day of Henry's
accident.

Catherine meanwhile treated the new Queen with deference and
respect. She handed over the Crown jewels to Mary and among the
fabulous gems she added pieces that belonged to her personally. She was
studiously correct in her dealings with her daughter-in-law and never
treated her less than cordially. It is said that Mary felt unwisely snobbish
about Catherine's less exalted origins than her own and the notorious
comment that Catherine was just a Florentine shopkeeper's daughter has
been attributed to her, among other people. If Catherine heard these
remarks, she chose to ignore them. But she would not forget them.
Besides, the Queen Mother seemed more regal and remote than ever in
her severe black gowns and widow's dignity.

Much has been made of a rivalry between the two women, or at least
of jealousy on Catherine's part. Fantastic stories about her desire to rid
herself of Mary – there is even one suggestion that the Queen Mother
was planning to poison her own son to remove the young woman from
her powerful position – are romantic fiction. While Catherine might have
been keen to minimise her daughter-in-law's hold over the young King,
she always appeared kind and good-natured to Mary, at least while her
son lived. At Blois during the first winter since Henry's death the two
Queens could often be found in each other's company, sometimes
listening to their daily sermon together either in their shared dining room
or the chapel. They also received visitors jointly on many occasions. They
were frequently together when Francis left for one of his frantic hunting
expeditions. It is likely that Mary learned her love of intrigue from her
mother-in-law, though as her later career shows she was to prove herself

a keen but poor pupil in this art. Catherine's maternal considerations would also have played an important part in her relationship with Mary; while the girl made her son happy Mary's own contentment would have been of interest to her.

Forced to take an active role in affairs of state, the Queen Mother was also nursing her terrible loss. She replied conscientiously to the countless letters from foreign monarchs and princes who wrote to condole over the tragic death of her husband. In a letter to Elizabeth I of England, Catherine addressed her as 'The Most High and Excellent Princess, our true friend, good sister and cousin, the Queen of England'. Thanking Elizabeth for her 'wise and kind words of consolation', she wrote, 'The loss ... of the late King ... is so recent and so dreadful and brings such pain, regret and despair that we have need of God, who has visited us with this affliction, to give us the power to endure it.'[10] In the months just following Henry's death one visitor described Catherine's grief: 'The queen is so wept out, that she brings tears to our eyes.'[11] Mary wrote to her mother in Scotland, 'She is still so troubled and has suffered so much during the sickness of the late King that, with all the worry it has caused her, I fear a grave illness.'[12]

Not long after this letter was written there arose an intriguing legend about Catherine's use of the occult. Tradition has it that during the Queen Mother's final visit to the Château of Chaumont before handing it over to Diane de Poitiers, she wished to know the fate of her sons and the dynasty. Summoning Cosimo de Ruggieri, her astrologer and expert in the black arts, she asked him to use his craft to foretell the future. According to Marshal de Retz, son of Catherine Gondi, Catherine's close friend, Ruggieri produced a mirror in a darkened room of the castle. Apparently possessing powers similar to the looking-glass in the fairy tale *Snow White*, the mirror became a magic chamber, and each of Catherine's sons, except Hercules, appeared in turn. Ruggieri told the Queen that the number of times the faces circled the mirror would correspond to the number of years they would reign. First King Francis emerged: his face, only faintly discernible, circled the mirror once. He was followed by Charles-Maximilien (later Charles IX), who appeared to circle fourteen times, then Edouard-Alexandre (later Henri III) whose ghostly face made fifteen turns. After Edouard-Alexandre a flash is supposed to have appeared showing the Duke of Guise crossing the mirror's face, followed by the son of Antoine de Bourbon, Henri, Prince of Navarre. He would be the legal heir to the throne should the Valois line die out. His image orbited the mirror twenty-two times. Catherine who, since the accurate predictions of Henry's death, hardly needed persuading that the forecasts of her sorcerers and astrologers were sound, cannot have felt comforted by what she might have seen. There are many different contemporary accounts of Catherine and this bizarre episode with the enchanted mirror, but how successful it was is impossible to say. When Diane took possession of the castle she found a considerable number of items, including pentacles drawn on the floor and other sinister indications that the Queen Mother had used the place for her occult practices. The former favourite, who disliked Chaumont anyway, never returned there.

From the first days of her eldest son's reign, Catherine wisely left the political spotlight to fall on the Guise brothers, keeping for herself the pathos-laden image of a stricken woman with small fatherless children, and the mother figure of the kingdom. She knew that as the country gradually became engulfed in the crises left after Henry's death, the stringent measures required to deal with them would almost inevitably make the brothers deeply unpopular. Unwilling to be tainted by their methods and beliefs, she kept herself at a distance, leaving the others to wonder what her position on policy matters truly was. Even if the Guises were successful they would alienate certain vital elements of society with their extreme religious views, impetuous ambition and an ever-growing band of enemies. Catherine felt their ultimate success seemed unlikely. Had Henry survived, his most pressing problems were the near bankruptcy of his kingdom and the reform religion that threatened to split France. With Henry alive, the presence of a strong monarch ensured control over his rival nobles and kept the essential social hierarchy intact. With his disappearance, however, there no longer existed the quasi-mystical figurehead of a powerful anointed king behind whom they rallied and beneath whom their differences could be buried.

Catherine could only watch as the Cardinal of Lorraine struggled with France's stricken economy. At Francis II's accession the public debt was around 40 million livres, mainly a legacy of the wars in Italy and northern France. Royal revenue derived from taxes amounted to less than 10,000 livres per annum. To make matters worse, half the debt was due to be paid immediately. The Guises, who had begun the new reign with lavish gifts to their various client vassals and repayments of their own debts, none of which went unnoticed or enhanced their popularity, now had to find a solution. Rather than raise taxes, the Cardinal decided to cut expenditure drastically, which he did in a highly arbitrary fashion. Royal interest due on loans was simply reneged upon; pensions were frozen; magistrates and other officials had their salaries stopped. French soldiers, many of them still returning from Italy, were demobilised and left unpaid. They had every reason to feel betrayed by the politicians who had simply handed back hard-won territories. These disillusioned men, now receptive to ideas of rebellion, would form the ranks of the armies that were to fight each other in the civil wars to come. The regime was intolerant of criticism; protests at its measures were met with swift punishment.[13] The

Cardinal of Lorraine, until now schooled only in the cocooned world of silky diplomacy, could soon be heard lamenting, 'I know that I am hated.'

The religious problem was also growing as the regime enforced ever harsher measures against the Protestants. It was believed that Catherine held moderate views on the religious question; certainly she was extremely fond of her sister-in-law, Marguerite, the new Duchess of Savoy, and others in her close circle with Protestant sympathies but who were not active reformers. Many favoured a softer line in dealing with the heretics. The Queen Mother received appeals from senior Protestants to come to their aid; she told the Protestant Pastor François Morel that she would try to ease the persecution against the reformers provided they in return 'did not hold assemblies and that each lived secretly and without scandal'.[14] She was unable to help save Anne du Bourg, however, who had been sentenced to death just before Henry's demise. Du Bourg put up a spirited defence that he knew would prove fruitless but might highlight the Calvinist's plight and render him a martyr. On 23 December 1559 he was put to death by strangulation and then burned at the Place du Grève. Unwisely, Morel wrote an angry letter to Catherine saying that 'God would not allow such injustice to go unpunished ... and just as God had begun by punishing the late King, so she should realise that His arm was still raised to complete His revenge by striking her and her children'.[15] This was the very last way to win Catherine's support; she regarded such threats as treacherous insults; besides, she argued that her offer of help stemmed from a desire to avoid bloodshed and in no way related 'to the truth or falsehood of their doctrine'.[16]

The Guises continued to pursue their ruthless policy of persecution, which Catherine believed would merely ignite an avoidable conflagration. Even the Cardinal, who was the enforcer of the new draconian laws against heretics, declared to Throckmorton that 'No man hates extremes more than I do.' Despite being unable to save Anne du Bourg or noticeably ease the plight of the reformers, Catherine did maintain contact with certain Calvinists through her moderate or Protestant friends. For the moment, though, her hands were tied. If Catherine was unable to help, then the desperate Calvinists sought leadership and protection elsewhere. Antoine de Bourbon was proving to be nothing short of pathetic. His brother, Louis de Condé, offered a more inspiring figure, however, and began to attract attention as a natural rallying point. Condé was as frustrated by his brother as the other Calvinists had become and, driven by personal ambition, family pride, some religious conviction and the poverty arising from being a second son, he found that the religious cause could provide him with an excellent platform. Condé's main problem as the potential opposition leader was that he lacked the legitimacy his elder brother possessed as First Prince of the Blood, that gave him his claim to head what was effectively a regency council.

France's military involvement against the English in Scotland provided another reason for the Guises' growing unpopularity. When Francis became King of France he was already King of Scotland, by virtue of his marriage to Mary Stuart, and he claimed, with his wife, the throne of England. To the fury of Queen Elizabeth I the royal couple's coat of arms, incorporating those of Scotland, France and England, brazenly professed this assertion. In September 1559 Marie of Guise, the regent of Scotland, found herself once again facing rebellions, fuelled by religious dissension and political grievance. Elizabeth did all she could to support the rebels in the north. Marie was only saved from catastrophe by the arrival of French troops in what became known as 'The War of the Insignia', the name stemming from Mary's and Francis's incorporation of the English arms into their own.[17] Catherine, whose ambitions did not coincide with the Guises regarding Scotland, rightly feared that France could ill afford further foreign adventures and needed her troops at home. She considered the whole campaign a potential disaster.

Francis's health meanwhile gave continued cause for grave concern. By the autumn of 1559 his deeply frustrating dizzy spells had become worryingly frequent. When he felt himself lose consciousness he would frantically move his limbs in an attempt not to faint. His skin was blotchy and his face, more swollen than ever, now became covered in boils and pimples. Although he had grown considerably in height since becoming King, this seemed to have sapped his strength further. In an attempt somehow to defy his weakness, hunting became his increasing obsession. At last he fell ill with an abscess of the ear. The agonising pain almost drove him mad. Catherine called in physicians who advised her to remove the King to the Loire valley, where he might recover in the peaceful countryside. She decided to take him to Blois for the winter and early spring. Queen Mary was no stranger to ill health and fainting spells either. She suffered from often minor but debilitating ailments. Unsurprisingly, the Guise family felt unease about the future of the Valois–Guise dynasty, since prospects for a healthy baby – particularly in view of the deformity of Francis's 'secret parts' – did not look promising.

During the early autumn of 1559 Mary seems to have mistaken a usual bout of ill health and fainting fits for the first signs of being pregnant. She optimistically took to wearing a tunic, the customary dress for a woman with child, but quickly abandoned it when she realised it was only a phantom pregnancy. The royal couple's dismal health could not be kept a secret; apart from the glaringly obvious physical signs that they were not strong there was little or no privacy in sixteenth-century life, and rumours about their various problems circulated quickly and widely.

The higher up the social scale one was the less privacy one enjoyed; consequently a monarch almost never had a moment alone and it was quite usual to perform the most personal acts of hygiene in the presence of servants and privileged courtiers. Servants were often paid to spy on their royal masters and mistresses; reports on the state of the bed linen and other such intimate details could tell an ambassador or senior courtier much that was of value.

As well as apprehensions about her ailing son, Catherine had to face the wrench of parting with her two daughters, Elisabeth and Claude, and her sister-in-law, Marguerite, Duchess of Savoy, as they were now married. Claude, Duchess of Lorraine, left France first. During Henry II's reign her husband, Charles III of Lorraine, had been largely brought up at the French Court where he had been held as a guarantee of the duchy's good behaviour. Charles and Claude contracted a happy marriage and because their state lay on the eastern border between France and the Empire the couple were able to make frequent visits to Catherine, later bringing her grandchildren with them. Catherine made many visits to Lorraine and some of her happiest moments *en famille*, rare events in the Queen Mother's life, were spent there. Duke Charles was kind and attentive and genuinely fond of his mother-in-law.

On 18 November 1559 Marguerite of Savoy made her tearful departure from Blois. Catherine grieved to see Henry's sister leave. Not only would she miss her close companionship, but also her level-headed advice. During her time with Catherine after Henry's death she had provided much-needed comfort, and had, too, talked much about the Protestant reformers, and urged clemency and understanding for their plight. Marguerite was to have a considerable impact on Catherine's religious policies through the person of Michel de L'Hôpital, an erudite lawyer and humanist. Like Catherine, he believed strongly that a settlement between the state and the reformers could only be reached by peaceful means. Upon becoming Chancellor in May 1560, de L'Hôpital helped form the Queen Mother's attitude towards French Protestants in the early days of the coming religious strife.

On the same day that Marguerite of Savoy left for Nice to join her husband, Catherine and her retinue left Blois to accompany her daughter Elisabeth on the first stage of the journey to meet her husband Philip II. Despite great preparations, packing and other arrangements, Catherine delayed her daughter's departure as much as she could, but on 18 November 1559 the royal party and Elisabeth's vast baggage train set out from Blois. One week later they reached Châtellerault where the Queen Mother and the younger royal children bade their agonising farewells to their sister, the thirteen-year-old new Queen of Spain. Catherine's sobbing was so piteous that even the crustiest onlookers found it hard to remain unaffected. The final adieus said, Elisabeth, slim and dark-eyed, not yet nubile but wise beyond her years, set off with composure and presumably not a little excitement to meet her twice-widowed husband twenty years her senior. Catherine was to maintain an energetic correspondence with her eldest daughter. These letters, crammed with advice, instructions and snippets about goings on at Court, give a rare glimpse into the workings of the Queen Mother's heart and mind. Unable to show her affection with physical tenderness, she more than compensated with these letters. Many of them, written in her own near-indecipherable handwriting, are an outpouring of gossip mixed with news. Catherine's written French remained phonetic, her spelling entirely inconsistent, but they give the impression that the reader is almost listening to her speaking.

Philip declared his 'complete happiness' when he met his bride on 30 January 1560, at Guadalajara in Spain. Elisabeth soon wrote to her mother announcing herself to be the luckiest girl in the world to have such a husband. Although the young woman enjoyed a cheerful and good-natured disposition, it is difficult to imagine how Philip evoked quite such enthusiasm in his bride. Dour, desiccated and pedantic, the Spanish King was driven by duty and the cold conviction that his role was to save the world from heresy, someone for whom no detail could be considered too small to examine, ponder and deliberate upon. As the years went by, Catherine, whose life was fuelled by a tortuous combination of maternal and dynastic preoccupations, proved an incomprehensible anathema to Philip. For the moment however, in part thanks to Elisabeth of Spain's good offices, the relationship between France and Spain enjoyed a short phase of almost unprecedented warmth. Philip also kept the promise he had made to Henry II when he was dying, that he would take France under his protection. The Spanish King was loath to see his neighbour swamped with heretics that might infect his own kingdom and this furthered the cordial relations between the two countries.

In February 1560 rumours of a plot against the Guises and their regime had started to filter through from Paris to Blois. The swelling number of reformers and others hostile to the administration now looked to the vigorous figure of Louis de Condé to help take direct action against the Guises. They wanted to seize the brothers, put them on trial, and 'liberate' the King while making a pledge of loyalty to him. The twenty-nine-year-old Condé, who had become a Protestant through his wife, Eleanore du Roye, was a short, energetic man, with both courage and spirit. Unable to involve himself directly in the plot, the prince entrusted a minor Perigordian nobleman, the Seigneur de la Renaudie, with the preparation of the details. La Renaudie, once a client of the Guises, with a grudge against them and a dubious past, had had to flee to Geneva, where he converted to Calvinism. Calvin himself wanted nothing to do with him, but he did receive support from Theodore de Bèze, Calvin's most senior lieutenant. After a meeting which took place on 1 February 1560, at Nantes near the port of Hugues, the plotters agreed their aims, which were essentially to capture the Guises and to beg the King to try his ministers for corruption. After that they hoped it would be possible to redress the other wrongs in the kingdom by establishing a Bourbon regency. La Renaudie sent out 500 agents in secret to recruit mercenaries, without being given the name of their chief. Foreign soldiers were enlisted, and the plotter also approached Queen Elizabeth of England for help. Some sources say that the Queen supplied a little money, others that she gave only her moral support, an altogether cheaper commodity. The conspirators' meeting at Hugues was the origin for the name 'Huguenot', the term subsequently used for French Protestants. They initially agreed that the coup should take place on 10 March, although this was later changed to the 16th.

Unfortunately the essential element of surprise vanished as rumours of the plot spread. In the days of informers and agents provocateurs it proved almost impossible to keep an undertaking of this size secret, even with the greatest discretion being employed. In this case there came a profusion of leaks from nearly every quarter. English Catholics, who heard of it, warned the Cardinal of Lorraine; a German prince confirmed the story to the Bishop of Arras. As if to seal the fate of his own plot, la Renaudie recklessly boasted about his involvement and the imminent downfall of his enemies. He told a Parisian lawyer and Huguenot sympathiser with whom he was staying about his plans, down to the last detail. The lawyer, terrified that he himself would be charged with treason, reported all he knew to the Cardinal. As the rumours received confirmation from different quarters, the Guises and Catherine became alarmed. Convinced that Queen Elizabeth of England stood behind the plot in retaliation over French involvement in Scotland, and that the force of rebels might be much larger than reported, François of Guise set about planning how to thwart the uprising and defeat the enemy. Catherine wrote to the Duchess of Guise, 'We have been warned that from all directions men are marching towards Blois ... the King, my son, has been much annoyed by this and ordered that these men should return to their homes.'[18] She continued that it would be her policy to act as though there were nothing amiss, but François of Guise had other plans. Because Blois was deemed an easy target for attack, on 21 February 1560 the duke ordered the immediate removal of the King and Court to the nearby fortress of Amboise. This huge medieval stronghold would prove difficult to take particularly since the defenders had received such detailed forewarning about the plot.

Catherine argued with the Guises that far from being an English plot, it seemed more likely to stem from enemies of the regime within France. With the support of Coligny, brought in both as a possible hostage and for his military expertise, the Queen Mother urged that softening the brutal measures against the Protestants might even now prevent the uprising. Initially shaken by news of the planned insurrection and the regime's growing unpopularity, François of Guise resumed his usual sang-froid. Safe behind the walls of the fortress, he sent out frequent search parties for news or signs of rebel troops. Catherine meanwhile continued to press for a declaration to appease the Huguenots. The Queen Mother's urgent efforts resulted in the Edict of Amboise, offering an amnesty for all past religious crimes except to those who incited or took part in rebellion. It did not, however, permit freedom of worship. As a result, a few days later some religious prisoners were freed. Her identification with this pacific initiative encouraged the Protestants to believe that she would treat them with more leniency than the brothers from Lorraine. None of this, however, altered the fact that the surrounding countryside hid armed units of hostile soldiers preparing to attack the castle.

For the moment a strange calm reigned over the huge fortress. Court business continued but for the urgent whispered enquiries for news between courtiers. At the same time, La Renaudie was busy deploying his men around the town of Amboise, still confident of the success of his plan. The royal family and chief nobles awaited the first strike, though they hoped that their troops would find the rebels first. In the mounting atmosphere of tension with false alarms and mistaken sightings, the mood of suspicion increased. Word arrived from a foreign informant that the leader of the uprising was 'a great prince'. Wondering who might be involved of the most senior nobles at Court, Catherine made Condé, who had only just arrived and whose Protestant sympathies were no secret, chief of the King's bodyguard. This cunning move obliged the prince to remain at the castle by the King's side. While this post could ostensibly be taken as a great honour, it was also a subtle form of arrest, since he no longer enjoyed the freedom to move about. Condé, however, affected an air of complete calm.

On 6 March a small group of about fifteen men were captured in the woods surrounding Amboise. They seemed relieved to have been caught and appeared confused about the plot and their intended role. A captain of the guard came and confessed to the Queen Mother that he had intended to take part in the plot, and described a plan to seal off the King's apartments and there to separate him from the Guises. Where small groups of disorganised men were found they appeared to be simple people who merely wanted to speak directly to the King about the new religion. At last on 15 and 16 March the principal captains of the rebels were caught. La Renaudie himself was discovered in the woods on 19

March and killed by an arquebus shot. Larger forces from further afield turned back when they heard of the failure of the enterprise and those who did arrive were easily overcome. Locals and troops sent out by Guise not only repulsed the feeble effort of the remaining rebels but hunted them down in the countryside, either killing them on the spot or bringing them back to summary justice. The triumphant duke wanted the punishment of the rebels to send a message that would resound throughout the kingdom, deterring others from such action. The lowlier rebels were either sewed into sacks and dumped into the River Loire to drown, or hanged from a high balcony in clear view above the town. The battlements proved convenient gibbets and for the next ten days dangling clusters of decomposing bodies decorated the castle. Belying her later bloodthirsty reputation, Catherine tried to intercede for the life of at least one of the officers, but the Guises ignored her. Even Anne d'Este, François of Guise's wife, came crying to the Queen Mother about the 'cruelties and inhumanity' of the retribution.

The grand finale was the execution of the plot's ringleaders. Tribunes were erected for spectators in the large courtyard of Amboise. The crowd consisted of most of the Court and their distinguished visitors. The King, his mother and younger brother, Charles-Maximilien aged only ten years, watched together as fifty-two noble rebels lost their heads on the block. With the royal family sat Condé. No proof of his complicity had been found and he remained impassive as he watched the men die bravely, commenting only, 'If the French know how to mount a rebellion, they also know how to die.' Some say that the condemned men sang psalms as they awaited their turn on the block, the sound becoming ever fainter as the heads in the basket piled up. On horseback near the scaffold, François of Guise presided over the death of each of the traitors. Catherine remained erect and unflinching throughout the bloody spectacle, and anyone who did baulk at the sight drew a furious look from the Queen Mother. For her this brutal parade was no long-term solution, but it was the necessary outcome that must follow treason, especially when the monarch was her son. Even though the protestors had maintained that they were loyal to the King, they had put both him and the peace of his kingdom at risk. For her, therefore, the bloodletting was merely a necessary ritual. Now Catherine wanted to understand exactly what prompted men to risk their lives and her son's throne in this way.

As soon as the executions were over she sent out enquiries. The answers were clear: there were two types of Huguenots, those who genuinely followed the new religion and others who were unwilling to be ruled by the 'illegal' regime of the Guises. The latter would be appeased if the Lorrainers and their stooges were replaced by a proper council with the Bourbon Princes of the Blood at its head. Catherine sought direct talks with these Protestants but understandably received their views only in writing. A propaganda war was being fought throughout the kingdom and Catherine found herself as much a target as the Guises themselves. The pamphlets circulating France called her a whore who had borne a leper for a son. (Francis II was believed by some to have leprosy.) Unrest and open flouting of the religious laws spread throughout the country, with the main trouble spots in the Dauphiné, Guyenne and Provence regions. More worrying still was the fact that the reformers were becoming organised and armed. The Conspiracy of Amboise and the vicious reprisals that followed it had provided a propaganda weapon for the Huguenots, who appealed to Protestant foreign princes for help. It also stiffened the resolve of those who opposed the regime and won over new converts, many of them noblemen, who were able to train and organise the reformers into a fighting force.

Even Catherine's own initiative, the Edict of Romorantin of May 1560, which ordered that only ecclesiastical courts could hear religious cases, proved impossible to register or enforce. The Church no longer had the authority to order the death penalty and in general terms the edict was designed to circumvent Henry II's harsh religious laws. Coligny, the Constable's nephew, who had undertaken enquiries on behalf of the Queen Mother, advised that the only way to save the kingdom from chaos was to call a meeting of the full council. With Catherine's agreement it met at Fontainebleau on 21 August 1560. At the same time she insisted that peace be made with England and that France must withdraw from its active role in Scotland's problems, arguing that the kingdom could no longer afford either the men or the costs of the war in the north. Despite the eventual removal of French and English troops from Scotland, Mary and Francis refused to renounce their claims to Elizabeth's throne and continued to quarter their arms with those of England. Francis, under Mary's and her uncles' influence, refused to ratify the Treaty of Edinburgh (as the peace treaty was named), but Catherine had achieved her main objectives: peace with England and to put an end to the haemorrhaging of men and money to Scotland. She enjoyed the added satisfaction of seeing the Guise family's ambitions no longer supported at the expense of France.

Mary had endured a difficult few months; not only had she witnessed the withdrawal of French military support from her Scots kingdom, but her beloved mother, Marie of Guise, had died of dropsy on 11 June 1560 after a long illness. John Knox, gleeful at the Regent-Queen's demise and her dreadful suffering, wrote of how 'Her belly and loathsome legs [did] ... swell, and so continued till that God did execute his judgement upon her'.[19] He had written earlier that the crown upon the Queen's head was 'as seemly a sight ... as to put a saddle upon the back of an unruly cow'.[20] Mary collapsed when the Cardinal of Lorraine broke the news of her mother's death. The Queen, passing 'from one agony to another', was comforted by Catherine, so recently bereaved herself. Much pre-occupied with the forthcoming meeting at Fontainebleau, Catherine's energies were directed at preserving the peace within France now that the Scots matter was resolved.

Unfortunately two important members of the council – Antoine de Bourbon and his brother Louis de Condé – boycotted the proceedings at Fontainebleau. Condé, having escaped implication in the Conspiracy of Amboise, had, after his papers and possessions were searched, grown increasingly worried about his personal safety and fled south to join his brother out of reach of the Guises. Catherine by now had the support of Michel de L'Hôpital, who had become Chancellor in May 1560 and whose desire for a peaceful solution was coupled with the motto '*Un Roi, une Loi, une Foi*' (one king, one law, one faith). He considered it ultimately impossible for the two religions to coexist peacefully in France, but passionately opposed violent and oppressive measures that only ever seemed to stiffen the resolve of the Huguenots. This opinion was much more in sympathy with Catherine's own. She knew she must tread extremely carefully now, for while she tried to free herself from the iron grip of the Guises, she did not wish to be rid of them entirely. The Queen Mother wanted them brought to heel, thereby giving her more freedom to conduct her son's business in what she believed were his best interests. If she undermined the Lorrainers too much they might be ousted altogether, and both their military strength and their large following were too important for her to contemplate having in opposition. Replacement of the Guises by the Bourbon princes meant chaos, notwithstanding the fact that, as Princes of the Blood, their proximity to the French throne presented a possible danger to her own children. Catherine considered Montmorency's recall an even more repugnant option; not only did she dislike him personally but she also feared his strength.

The Queen Mother opened the proceedings at Fontainebleau on 21 August 1560 with a speech asking the councillors to pursue a policy by which the King could 'conserve his sceptre, his subjects find relief from their suffering and the malcontents find contentment, if it were possible'.[21] The new Chancellor took the floor after Catherine and spoke at length about the ailing kingdom and how to find a possible cure. The Guise brothers then proceeded to report on their areas of responsibility. After the discussion was opened to include the other councillors, Coligny presented two petitions, one to the Queen Mother and the other to the King, asking that the reformers might practise their faith in peace until a meeting of the general council to decide the final outcome of the religious issues. The document contained a request for Catherine to become a new Esther and lead God's people from oppression to salvation.[22] In one report of the assembly (which mentions only a single petition) Guise rejected it with contempt, saying that it was unsigned. Coligny replied he could easily furnish 10,000 signatures, to which the duke said he would respond with one of 100,000 signatures signed in blood and he would come riding at the head of the men whose names were upon it.

Jean de Monluc, a supporter of the Queen Mother's, then spoke. He reflected Catherine's own views when he asked how anyone could justify the brutality used attacking the reformers, 'who had such a fear of God and reverence for their King'. He went on to suggest that with a gentler approach the country might calm down and there would then be no need for any drastic changes in the government. After days of discussion, it was agreed that the Estates-General be called for a meeting at Fontainebleau on 10 December 1560, followed by a general meeting of the clergy a month later to consider the religious problems in France and to examine abuses within the French Church. Such a religious council outside of his control appalled Pope Pius IV, who worried that it might be a step down the path towards a schismatic Gallic Church. On the whole, members of the council praised Catherine for her moderation in dealing with the reformers, and while the Guises came away chastised, their powers were left intact. The reformers nursed hopes that they might eventually be allowed to worship in freedom, or at least without oppression. The meeting at Fontainebleau could be considered a political victory for Catherine and it greatly enhanced her standing with the councillors of both sides. It also demonstrated how she had matured politically.

There were those who viewed the proceedings with little hope, however, and still believed that direct action should be taken to remove the Guises and give the Bourbons their rightful place at the head of the council. Their notable absence sent a clear message to the country that there remained many who regarded the Guise regime as essentially illegal. Antoine de Bourbon called a meeting at Nérac for the same time as Catherine's assembly, and heated talks were held between him and the increasing number of disaffected nobles who now supported him. Montmorency was believed to be sympathetic to Bourbon's efforts, though he was careful not to be directly implicated in any treacherous behaviour. By November 1560 Huguenot preparations were under way for a military confrontation, and for all Catherine's hopes after the Fontainebleau assembly, the militant element of the reforming party were left unappeased by the present ambling rate of progress and schedules for further meetings. They believed that only by military force could they rid themselves of the foreign princes and free France's rightful King from their pernicious influence. Trouble erupted in the autumn of 1560 as Huguenot forces attacked major towns in southern and south-western France. Catherine called for help from both Philip of Spain and the Duke of Savoy. Civil war seemed imminent.

In a bold move in which she hoped to force Bourbon's hand, the Queen Mother sent a command from the King, summoning him to Court at Orléans. He was ordered to bring his brother Condé with him for an explanation regarding the latter's activities, particularly in the illegal levying of troops. Catherine made sure that the messenger sent to Bourbon subtly informed the brothers that it was the Constable himself who had exposed Condé's military preparations. This was, in fact, quite false but the ruse had the desired effect, rupturing the trust between Bourbon and the 'Connetabilists'. It also flushed the prince out to face a direct challenge. Unnerved, he feebly decided that rather than take up arms he would go with his younger brother to Court and explain himself. The pair duly journeyed to Orléans, and Condé was arrested the moment he arrived.

Arresting a Prince of the Blood was a risky undertaking, and Catherine certainly did not wish to see Condé suffer the death sentence for his crimes. She knew all too well that the Guises, ignoring Condé's right to be tried by his peers, would have their cronies on the special tribunal in order to dispose of the troublesome prince as quickly as possible, thus inciting his followers to immediate open rebellion. Condé's death would therefore also kill any hopes of a peaceful settlement. The trial opened on 13 November 1560, and on the 26th Condé was duly found guilty of the charge of *lèse-majesté* and condemned to be executed on 10 December. Catherine's two supporters on the tribunal, de L'Hôpital and du Mortier, refused to add their signatures to the document, delaying his death, but only for a short while.

Just as matters seemed at an impasse the King fell desperately ill. Already ailing since a fainting fit on 9 November, a week later – after hunting on an extremely cold day – he fainted again after complaining of pain in his left ear. The following day, however, he attended a service celebrating Saint-Aignan at Orléans where, as was the custom, he touched the scrofulous. The poor boy looked so ill himself that it is hard to think that the sick people he touched laid much store by his 'healing' powers; indeed, they could credibly have feared further infection. Leprosy rumours about the King were not helped by his patchy skin and the violent purple colour of his face. At vespers the same afternoon he fell into a faint for the second time in two days. Upon examination the doctors found a fistula in his left ear which was causing the King terrible pain. They were powerless to relieve his agony, and his face took on a terrible red and blotchy hue. Francis's body was collapsing; even his rotten breath betrayed the decay within.

Catherine and the Guises had access to the King sealed off from the Court, and for a time the gravity of his condition remained a closely guarded secret. To complicate matters further, members of the Estates-General summoned to meet on 10 December – the date set for Condé's execution – were even now arriving at Fontainebleau in preparation for the opening session. They had at all costs to be kept in ignorance of the King's desperate state. Meanwhile the infected ear caused swelling around it as the sepsis spread. The foul-smelling discharge from Francis's abscess seemed to do little but irritate his skin into further eruptions of violent colour and boils. As he lay in restless agony, the doctors warned the Queen Mother to expect the worst. Although she had always known her son was fragile, and had been told both by doctors and her soothsayers to expect him to die young – Nostradamus had predicted that Catherine's eldest son would die before he was eighteen – the Queen Mother watched helplessly as Francis suffered and was finally rendered incapable of speech. She wrote to her sister-in-law Marguerite, the new Duchess of Savoy,

> I do not know how to start this letter to you when I think of the terrible trouble and affliction that it has pleased God to visit upon us, after so many sorrows and such unhappiness, to see the terrible and extreme pain that the King, my son is suffering. Still I hope that Our Heavenly Father will not suffer me the agony of taking him from me. .... This kingdom cannot be saved unless God takes it into His hands.[23]

The concerned looks on the faces of the Guises and their followers could finally no longer be disguised, and rumours flew that the King was desperately ill. Condé's followers grasped at the hope that he might be reprieved if the King died. Catherine had meanwhile to consider the likely outcome should Francis not survive. With Charles-Maximilien, the heir, only ten years old, he would legally be declared a minor and a regency would be set in place to rule until he reached the age of fifteen. The Estates-General would be most likely to vote for a Bourbon regency, in which Catherine would have much less power than she had enjoyed in harness with the Guises. She knew that she must act swiftly to prevent a vote from taking place. Catherine now showed how consummate a political manipulator she had become. As the King recovered slightly, thanks to a lancing of the abscess which released a huge amount of pus through his mouth and nostrils, the Queen Mother decided on her move.

She summoned Condé's brother, Antoine de Bourbon, to her presence. There, in front of the Guises, Catherine bitterly accused Bourbon of plotting to incite rebellion and reproached him for his treacherous behaviour. Fearful of ending up condemned to die like his brother,

Bourbon completely lost his head and, while loudly protesting his innocence, he offered – as a sign of good faith – to give up his right to the regency to the Queen Mother. She made him sign a document to this effect and in return she promised that he would be made Lieutenant-General should Charles ascend the throne. The Guises – who now feared for their own safety for prosecuting Condé without due process of law – were paid off by Catherine when she made the dying King confirm the fiction that it was he, and not the Guises, who had ordered the arrest and trial of Condé. Catherine then asked the brothers and Bourbon to embrace each other as a sign of reconciliation. She employed this utterly meaningless gesture as part of a formula for 'reconciling' her enemies and it capped her triumph. By brilliantly playing her two rivals off against each other, Catherine had emerged supreme.

Francis's slight improvement proved to be a false dawn and Catherine, who had been almost constantly at his bedside with Mary except when making her necessary political manoeuvres, took her place by her son again. Vile remedies did little but exacerbate the boy's suffering. The popular cure-all, rhubarb, proved as incapable of stopping the abscess from spreading to the King's brain as the prayers led by the royal women and children in a procession to the churches of Orléans. On 5 December 1560, after a reign of only sixteen months, King Francis II of France breathed his last agonising breath and his fragile ruined body rendered up his soul.

With swift and decisive action, Catherine took over the running of the royal household. The day after Francis's death she demanded the crown jewels back from his widow and then left the bereft, grieving girl sitting in her black-draped room. None can deny the torment Catherine suffered at the loss of her son, but she now required her immediate concentration to secure her own position and that of her ten-year-old son, the new King. After ordering that access to the palace be barred, the Queen Mother called a Privy Council meeting at which she declared Charles-Maximilien King of France, henceforth to be known as Charles IX. She opened the meeting with the words: 'Since it has pleased God to deprive me of my elder son, I do not mean to abandon myself to despair, but to submit to the Divine Will and to assist and serve the King, my second son, in the feeble measure of my experience.' She then delivered her clear intention to rule until her son was of age: 'I have decided, therefore, to keep him beside me and to govern the state, as a devoted mother must do. Since I have assumed this duty, I wish all correspondence to be addressed in the first place to me; I shall open it in your presence and in particular in that of the King of Navarre, who will occupy the first place in the council as the nearest relative of the King ... such is my will. If any of you wish to speak, let him do so.' Antoine de Bourbon,

King of Navarre gave his assent, and the others formally added theirs, as she knew they would.

Earlier, on the day after Francis's death, the Duke of Guise and his men, who had spent the night in vigil over the late King's body, came to express their loyalty to the Queen Mother and her son. Also present were Queen Mary, the younger royal children, the Cardinal of Lorraine, Antoine de Bourbon, and a few other favoured courtiers. It was an important opportunity for both the Guises and Bourbon to load the blame for any past mistakes on to the dead King and thereby clear the way for the future. The Queen Mother listened to their speeches in which they admitted their errors but said that they had acted solely at the express orders of King Francis. Whenever the duke paused, Catherine nodded slowly and replied in a quiet, mournful voice, 'It is true, it is true, what you have done was by the command of my son.' Bourbon then proceeded to exculpate himself from past wrongs by saying he wished for nothing but the good of the kingdom. The Cardinal also promised to act in the best interests of the Queen Mother and her son, the new King. Not one of the protagonists departed from the script prearranged by Catherine in her intrigues over the past few days. It is hard to overestimate the satisfaction the Queen Mother must have derived from these professions of loyalty and humble offers of service, coming from those who had not only set themselves above her for so long, but had also frequently ignored her. She knew that their protestations were only that, but for the present they were all she needed while she consolidated her grip on power.

Pressed for time as the Estates-General – which did not know that Bourbon had handed his rights to the regency to Catherine – were gathering, Catherine called a *conseil privé* on 21 December. Having neutralised both the Guises and Bourbon, she had herself proclaimed Governor of the Kingdom, effectively enjoying all the powers of a monarch. Much as the Guises had done after Henry's death, she presented the people with a fait accompli. In a country where the monarch had changed three times in seventeen months, Catherine, the regal matriarch clad in mourning, had become a comforting familiar figure and had even come to represent continuity. Finally, at the age of forty-one, she had arrived at the pinnacle of natural power and pre-eminence. The dangers facing France had not diminished, but at last she could now try to deal with them in her own way.

SEVEN

'Gouvernante de France'

I am what I am in order to preserve
your brothers and their kingdom

1560–62

Due to a series of 'dynastic accidents' and dexterous manipulation of her opportunities, Catherine de Medici, the forty-one-year-old Italian Dowager Queen of France, now found herself de jure as well as de facto ruler of the kingdom. Her foremost desire was to bring back the glorious days of Francis I and Henry II. To do this she needed to heal a divided realm.

Catherine set about creating the national symbols of authority reflecting her new position. As for a new monarch, she had a huge seal specially created for her as 'Gouvernante de France'. It depicted Catherine standing, holding the sceptre in her right hand with her left hand raised and index finger pointing upwards in a gesture of command. Upon her head sat a crown with her widow's veils clearly visible. The following legend was inscribed around the edge: 'Catherine by the grace of God, Queen of France, Mother of the King'. The phrase 'Mother of the King' implied a different and more important status than queen mother and all previous regent queens of France. Catherine had begun carving out a new and unique role for herself, and her powers were far superior to those of a regent. She was effectively the absolute monarch of France.

Though he had been with her from the beginning of Charles IX's reign, Michel de L'Hôpital was officially confirmed as Catherine's Chancellor in March 1561. This educated man with his legal training helped Catherine develop intellectually some of the ideas which had hitherto been reached by her sometimes primitive, visceral instincts. Her half-formed solutions based on common sense now acquired a finished elegance. Though her innate ability to understand what a situation required had proved sound enough thus far, de L'Hôpital translated the Queen Mother's will into a form that could be converted into policy by the state apparatus. He also aided the Queen Mother's presentation of her agendas. Through de L'Hôpital she acquired a polish and gravitas that frequently left her listeners surprised and impressed.

Catherine accorded Bourbon the prize that had bought his quiescence, making him Lieutenant-General of France, and freed his brother Condé on 8 March 1561. But when Bourbon suggested, at an early Privy Council meeting, that if the Queen Mother fell ill he should be automatically placed in charge, Catherine's emphatic response crushed his aspirations: 'My brother, all that I can say is that I shall never be too ill to supervise whatever affects the service of the King my son. I shall ask you therefore to withdraw your request. The case you foresee shall never arise.' Perhaps she also feared that some 'Florentine malady' – the popular sobriquet for poison – might one day afflict her if this road were left available to him. Catherine now opened all despatches before the King, who signed nothing until she had read and approved it first, and a letter from her would always accompany any order or letter from Charles. Presiding over the King's Council, all policy decisions, whether domestic or foreign, were hers, and she could dispose of the rewards and benefices that were in the monarch's gift as she wished. As Charles was only ten and would technically be a minor for another four years, the Queen Mother's plans were designed for a long stay in power.

Catherine, despite her unpromising physique that might at first glance suggest a woman of country origins, still managed to convey the dignity her position required. Her face had grown heavier, the large nose and bulbous eyes seemed more pronounced. Her pale-brown hair could only just be seen from under her veils and her olive skin was still smooth. Though her waist had thickened, her legs remained well shaped and, as usual, her hands were singled out for their supposed loveliness. She was capable of the most elegant deportment, yet, when inspired and hard at work she seemed equally able to leave aside her feminine and regal bearing to become robust and energetic. 'While she walks or eats she talks always of business with this one or that,' the Venetian ambassador wrote. 'Nor does she confine herself to politics but thinks about other subjects so numerous that I do not know how she is able to keep an interest in such diverse matters.' Catherine loved to walk fast while talking to her ministers. She was also extremely greedy. 'Her appetite is enormous,' the ambassador noted, 'she is already a stout woman.' Indigestion as a result of overeating dogged Catherine's otherwise remarkable constitution.

Regal and serious when the situation required, with her keen sense of the ridiculous Catherine was generally the first to burst into gales of laughter when it did not. She also enjoyed comedies and clowns, but could just as easily shed tears when presented with anything sentimental. She continued to take the greatest pleasure in the hunt. 'She loves exercise, walking a great deal and riding too, very active, she hunts with the King her son, and follows the chase deep into the bush with rare courage.'[1] This woman of passionate and extreme contradictions managed an extraordinary feat of combining the looks of an Italian matron with the manners and bearing of a French queen.

In the first days after Francis's death, Catherine wrote to her daughter, Queen Elisabeth of Spain. The magnitude of the crisis in France was not lost on the Queen Mother:

> Madame ma fille, the bearer will tell you many things, which dispenses me from writing a long letter, all I shall say is that you need not trouble your mind about anything, and may rest certain that I shall govern myself in such a manner that God and the world will have cause to be pleased with me, since my principal aim is to honour God in everything and to preserve my authority, not for myself but for the conservation of this kingdom and welfare of all your brothers, whom I love as springing from the same source whence you all came.

She then added a tiny glimpse into her past unhappiness, and her present fears and isolation:

> Ma fille, m'amie, commend yourself to God, for you have seen me as happy as you are now, never knowing any sorrow but that I was not loved as much as I wished to be by the King your father, who honoured me more than I deserved, but I loved him so much that I was always in fear, as you know; and God has taken him from me and, not content with that, has deprived me of your brother whom you know how I loved, and has left me with three little children and a divided kingdom, where there is not one man whom I can trust, who is not governed by private passion of his own. So, m'amie, think of me and take me as an example, not to trust so much to the love your husband feels for you, and to the honour and ease you enjoy, as to neglect to pray to Him who can continue your blessing, or if He please, can place you in my position; I had rather die than see you in it, for fear you could not bear so many ordeals as I have had, and still have, which without His aid, I am sure I could not endure.

This letter is exceptional in the way that Catherine opened her heart to her young daughter. It has been argued that it proves Catherine did not wish for the power she now possessed. Whatever the truth, she certainly protected the power jealously from anyone who threatened it and in time she came to guard her position with increasing vigour, though her motives were – at least initially – born out of necessity. As she pointed out, whom else could she trust with the monumental task of governing France? This emerging part of Catherine came from a woman who had lived in the background for too long. She had been born into mercantile splendour, acquiring from birth lavish tastes and expensive habits. She considered the glory that came with her position a perquisite for her to enjoy, though now was clearly not a time for spending but for major retrenchment. To set the tone she made instant, even though largely symbolic, economies in the running of the royal household.

Due to the pressing financial nightmare that continued to bedevil France, Catherine needed the Estates-General's endorsement of her position and to support her desperate need to raise money. Despite the death of Francis II, it had been agreed that the meeting of the assembly should proceed, and Catherine had spent the days immediately beforehand reinforcing her powers. Guise was still at hand with his small army; Bourbon continued to be docile; letters were sent out to the provinces and to foreign powers announcing Catherine's new powers and the subordinate role accorded to Bourbon. The arrival of the Constable with 400 armed men suggested he might cause difficulties, especially when Catherine confirmed that Guise remain in command of the army, but Montmorency well understood that with the change of regime he and his family could expect to prosper more than they had under Francis II and the Guises. Nothing would be gained from agitating now; he needed the transition of power to be confirmed first. Thus Catherine managed to present an at least superficially united front to the Estates-General when they finally convened.

The historic purpose of the Estates-General was to 'present grievances to the King and the voting of money', but it was only rarely and reluctantly called.* To present the factions of Guise, Bourbon and Montmorency as both loyal and harmonious – however incredible a picture that projected – was essential to the Queen Mother. Seated together at the opening ceremony with Catherine and her children, their albeit incongruous unity strengthened her image as an effective ruler and sent a message to the Estates' potentially troublesome representatives that she had the backing of the country's most powerful nobles. In his address to the deputies, de L'Hôpital made it quite clear that the Queen Mother viewed decisions by the Crown to be above debate and final. Nor would she hear any claims made arising from the past.

It rapidly dawned on the deputies that they had been called not for genuine consultation but in order to ease the plight of the exchequer. If Henry's wars and gifts had depleted King Francis II's patrimony, his son's short reign left Catherine staring at an empty treasury. Even the usual means of raising money by the sale of offices – however corrupt – had been so diluted that they could no longer contribute anything of substance. Squeezing money from the peasantry during the wars of Henry II had left them so impoverished that the Estates were now being called upon to replenish the treasury. This invoked the phantom of partnership between the Estates and the Crown, for when the monarchy ceased to be able to finance its government it ceased to be independent. The

---

* It is worth noting that Francis I never once called a meeting of the Estates-General during his reign.

Chancellor proceeded to ask that the Estates help buy back alienated Crown properties, offices and other usual sources of royal revenue that had been squandered. Of the three Estates that made up the Estates-General (the nobility, the clergy and commoners), only the clergy felt itself really vulnerable, since its riches were still relatively intact. It was certainly the most contentious Estate to pillage. In effect, the Chancellor was asking the Estates-General to raise the funds and the means to give the Crown back its independence from themselves. Once the flowery legal and loyal language had been removed, the bare fact remained that this was an audacious proposal.

Since none of the three Estates offered to produce a solution, de L'Hôpital asked them to consider the proposal he now put to them. His prescription was to raise the *tailles* (the Crown's only direct tax, the burden of which fell upon the peasantry as the nobles and clergy were exempt) for six years, and that the clergy should buy back the rents and revenues that the Crown had been forced to sell. The only suggestion that emerged from the Estates themselves could best be described as unimaginative: the Crown must prune its expenditure. Catherine diligently cut down the number of servants and offices, lowered pensions and salaries, and triumphantly announced a saving of 2.3 million livres. Instead of congratulating the Queen Mother on her endeavours, however, the deputies merely observed that if such a sum could be saved with ease, could not more telling cuts be made?

One contemporary wrote of Catherine's efforts, 'The greatest of subsidies is the drastic economy which the Court imposes on itself in all things.' De L'Hôpital received instructions from the Queen Mother to send the deputies away and to return with an answer in May. Although the financial question had been left without solution, Catherine and de L'Hôpital congratulated themselves upon the reforms of the judicial system that they had pushed through. In an attempt to alleviate the terrible abuses taking place within the judiciary, magistrates must henceforth be elected, and several other measures were agreed which would protect the peasantry and prevent abuses mainly by the nobility and the Church. A unification of weights and measures was adopted and the taxes levied on moving goods from one area within France to another abolished. The further notable decision taken decreed that the Estates-General should meet at least once every five years.

As to religion, the Chancellor pronounced that he considered it impossible to expect accord between people of different faiths, confirming his axiom: 'One faith, one law, one king!' He added, 'Let us not innovate lightly. Let us deliberate long and previously instruct ourselves ... if a man may be allowed to adopt a new religion as he chooses beware lest there be as many religions as there are families and heads of men. You may say that your religion is better, I defend mine; which is more reasonable, that I should follow yours, or you mine?'[2] For all its orthodoxy, de L'Hôpital's speech nonetheless outlined Catherine's clear break with the Guises' methods of violent persecution. 'The knife is of no avail against the spirit, save to lose both body and soul,' he said. 'Gentleness will accomplish more than rigour.'[3] He spoke of the need for a general assembly of the Church Council to get to the root of the religious troubles and made it clear that a council would be convoked for this purpose in the near future.

Once again the Protestants misunderstood this measure of toleration as a gesture of support from the Queen Mother. Unfortunately, as a consequence they grew ever more brazen in their open practice of the new religion and magnified Catholic fears by damaging Church property, smashing sacred statues and committing other sacrilegious acts. None of this gave any comfort to Catherine. While eager to understand and reach an accommodation with the more moderate reformers, and to prevent the worst abuses of the Church, their beliefs per se did not concern her; she merely wanted to find a way around the many entrenched difficulties that separated the two religious parties. Catherine would only remain a religious moderate if she believed it would preserve her son's crown and the kingdom's unity. Her moderation was directly proportionate to what she believed to be politically expedient, beyond that it simply did not interest her. Sadly, the Protestants seemed blind to this essential fact.

There then occurred a brief and dangerous moment as Antoine de Bourbon, fired by his supporters from the Estates-General, made a pathetic lunge for the regency he had earlier so feebly relinquished. First he demanded that François of Guise be sent away from Court. Catherine furiously demanded an explanation. Montmorency and his nephews declared that they would leave with Bourbon if she did not expel Guise, which she had no intention of doing, not least because he was still commander-in-chief of the army. Catherine called upon the Constable to visit the King. The little boy, rehearsed by his mother, asked the Constable to remain at Court. Loyalty to the Crown had been so bred into the old man that he declined to leave the boy. Bourbon, faced with departure alone, lost his nerve as usual. Finally giving up his claims to the regency, he was officially confirmed as Lieutenant-General of the Kingdom, Condé received a full pardon and promised 'all that will conserve the honour of a Prince of the Blood' including a seat on the King's Council.[4] With this the bottom fell out of any further opposition to Catherine's supremacy. As the meeting of the Estates broke up, Catherine had her position as 'Gouvernante' ratified, although she had been voted no money. For all the glory of her position it was empty without funds.

Catherine had weathered the meeting of the Estates-General but she still knew the unity of the kingdom as guaranteed by her most powerful nobles to be far from assured. From Fontainebleau, where she and the Court had moved for Easter, she wrote of the assembly in a garbled letter to her ambassador in Spain:

> Considering how difficult it is that this farce should be performed with so many characters without someone looking black, and that the diversity of men's minds, moved by so many passions, of which this world is so full, is much to be feared, especially since so sudden and unforeseen a change cannot, I fear, be accepted at once by everyone, and above all by those who lately held the first place here...[5]

She went on to congratulate herself about her handling of Antoine de Bourbon: 'The position which the King of Navarre [Bourbon] holds here is beneath mine and under my authority, and I have done nothing for him or for the other Princes of the Blood ... except by force or necessity, but I have so won him that I dispose of him and do with him what I please.' But could Catherine count upon a man who, one observer noted, 'is frivolous enough to wear rings on his fingers and earrings like a woman, in spite of his age and his white hair?' adding, 'In an important matter he follows the advice of his sycophants and of light persons ... and I can attest that concerning religion he has shown neither firmness nor wisdom.'[6]

Montmorency, though jubilant at power being wrested from his enemies the Guises, was as much a traditional Catholic as they and feared that Catherine's overtures to the new religion were merely the first steps towards according them full religious liberty. Nor did he find comfort in the Edict of Romarantin (registered on 28 January 1561), which Catherine had tried to enforce the previous year and which had been modified to alleviate the Protestants' situation further. Under its terms religious prisoners were released and, apart from surviving ringleaders, even those who had taken part in the Conspiracy of Amboise received a pardon. This displeased her son-in-law, Philip of Spain, who had written earlier in January instructing his emissary to impart the following message to Catherine:

> Respecting the affairs of religion, you are to speak to Queen Catherine very clearly and frankly, exhorting her on our part to the greatest care and vigilance: she must never permit the innovations which have sprung up in her kingdom to make further progress; and she must not favour in any manner whatsoever or admit to her intimacy any of those who are not as firm in their faith as they should be.[7]

Catherine countered with an argument that she believed would appease the anxious Philip. 'As for the fact of religion, the examples which we have seen for several years have taught us that to cure an evil of such long standing one remedy alone will not suffice ... we must vary our medicaments. For twenty or thirty years now we have tried ... to tear out this infection by the roots, and we have learned that violence only serves to increase and multiply it, since by the harsh penalties which have been constantly enforced in this kingdom, an infinite number of poor people have been confirmed in this belief ... for it has been proved that this fortifies them.' She continued disingenuously, 'I have been advised by all the Princes of the Blood and the other princes and lords of the council to consider the season in which we live, and in which we are sometimes obliged to dissimulate many things which in other times we should not endure, and for this reason to pursue a course of gentleness in this question ... [this] may preserve us from the troubles from which we are only just beginning to emerge.' She asked her ambassador to Spain, Sebastien de l'Aubespine, to explain all this to the King 'so that he may not conceive a worse opinion of my actions until he has sifted them as he should; for he must consider that the situation is not the same here as in Spain'.[8] Philip, a man unable to comprehend words that implied half-measures, or proceeding with caution when it concerned others (he could be pragmatic when it suited Spanish interests),* remained deeply troubled. He believed that Catherine would be unable to pursue religious matters as methodically, and if necessary brutally, as he.

As Catherine's moderate religious policy began to take effect, an unlikely alliance arose between former enemies. Montmorency and the Guises came together with the Marshal de Saint-André and on 7 April 1561 formed what became known as the Triumvirate. Their stated aim was to preserve the Catholic faith in France and, once that was secure, to take the holy struggle against Protestantism to the rest of Europe. More than likely they also held a covert aim: to dislodge Catherine from her position of political hegemony. Not only did they enjoy the support of Philip of Spain but that of the papacy and the Empire too. The Triumvirs deemed Antoine de Bourbon essential to their success in France and a battle to win him over from his lukewarm Protestantism ensued as Catherine also tried to entice him down her own political path. She even suggested that Philip might restore Spanish Navarre to Bourbon's kingdom, something Philip had no intention of doing. This bird-brained man, largely ignored and overlooked all his life, felt quite overcome with all the attention he now received from the greatest powers in France and abroad. Much in the same way that the Huguenots were causing trouble in various parts of the kingdom, now supporters of the

---

* For 12 years Philip helped prevent the excommunication of Elizabeth I as it was in his interests to do so.

Triumvirate came out and spread disorder by openly attacking Protestants.

After Easter, during which the Duke of Guise and Saint-André dined conspicuously with Montmorency to celebrate the inauguration of their Triumvirate, the three men left Court without permission and announced they would not return. Catherine wrote an excoriating letter about the Guises to her daughter in Spain. Had they not stolen her husband from her? Had they not turned her son against her? Despite these crimes, she wrote, 'I decided I would preserve them from harm, but I would ... no longer mingle their quarrels with mine, knowing that they would have appointed themselves, if they could have, and would have left me out, as they always do whenever there is ... greatness and profit; for they have nothing else in their hearts.'[9] Her bitterness grew as she described how they misrepresented her to Philip 'and to the country as a whole ... giving out that I was not a good Christian, to make everyone suspect me and to force me to trust no one but them, telling me that everyone is my enemy. ... I have discovered just the contrary that I was hated only for favouring them ... Therefore ma fille, m'amie, do not let your husband the King believe an untruth. I do not mean to change my life or my religion or anything. I am what I am in order to preserve your brothers and their kingdom.'[10] For all her ranting, Catherine knew she was ultimately doomed without the support of either the Guises or the Constable.

Furious that the Triumvirs backed by Philip were agitating against her, Catherine determined to tie the Spanish King in closer to the Valois family. She already blamed the Guises for causing strife with their violence and refusal to follow her policy of clemency, so when she subsequently heard rumours of marriage talks between Philip and the Guises, proposing a union between Mary, Queen of Scots and Philip's son and heir, Don Carlos, she was livid. The attentions paid by the Spanish ambassador, Chantonnay, to the mourning Queen of Scots were noted by all. Throckmorton reported to Elizabeth of England, 'The House of Guise use all means to bring to pass the marriage between the Prince of Spain and the Queen of Scotland.'[11]

Catherine, who had not been officially informed of these marriage talks, maintained a show of kindness towards her daughter-in-law, but wrote in code to Elisabeth in Spain that any influence she had must be used to prevent a match between 'the gentleman' (Catherine's code name for Mary) and Don Carlos. Mary, once the embodiment of Guise hopes in France, now threatened, in Catherine's fevered imagination, her own daughter. If Mary became the Spanish Infante's wife and Philip were to die young, Elisabeth would suffer the same fate as Catherine had herself and be swept to one side by the Scots Queen.[12] The further threat Catherine saw before her, if the union were to materialise, was the massive Spanish support the Guises would receive, perhaps endangering her and her sons' futures and France itself. Philip, however, daunted by the international complications – Elizabeth of England wanted the match as little as Catherine did – decided not to press ahead and by April 1561 the project was dead.

The prospect of a grand marriage for one of her children always guaranteed Catherine's wholehearted attention and energy. She immediately put forward her own solution, proposing that Margot, her youngest daughter, be promised to Don Carlos instead of the Queen of Scots. Don Carlos, a short, frail epileptic who weighed less than six stone, had a hunched back and twisted shoulders. He was severely brain-damaged since tumbling head first down a stone staircase in pursuit of a servant girl whom he particularly enjoyed flagellating. The fall had almost killed him. Philip's doctors operated to save his life and drilled a hole in Don Carlos's skull to relieve the pressure that had built up on his brain. The operation seemed a success, but for good measure Philip put the shrivelled corpse of a pious Franciscan monk into his son's bed, and insisted that it was this 'odour of sanctity' and not the doctors that had saved the Infante's life. Though he made a partial physical recovery, the accident left Don Carlos prone to periods of sadism that progressed to homicidal mania. Prevented from embracing opportunities to murder human beings, he sought light relief in roasting live rabbits and torturing horses for the pleasure of hearing them scream. There was thus little to commend him as a husband, apart from the huge inheritance he stood to receive when his father died.

Perhaps luckily for Margot, Philip, who probably already felt the strain of having Catherine as a mother-in-law, did nothing to encourage her plans to become his mad son's mother in-law as well. At the same time another marriage rumour reached Catherine. Mary's uncles were in talks with the Emperor Ferdinand of Austria about a possible alliance with his son Archduke Charles. The Queen Mother wrote urgently to her ambassador in Vienna, 'The King wishes you to use all your skill to discover what you can about what is being said and done about the proposed marriage between the Queen of Scotland, my daughter, and Prince Charles. Use all the means at your disposal to find out what the true state of affairs is.'[13] She instructed him to forward any news on the matter to her in code so that she could assess the situation and 'being warned, as I shall be, it will aid me in whatever remedy I feel to be necessary'.[14]

Catherine was impatient to be rid of the attractive but troublesome young woman who, as another Dowager Queen, would have been a political nuisance as well as an expense for France. According to her original marriage contract, Mary had the right to choose whether she remain in France or return to Scotland. She had enough properties in

France to maintain her in some style and being Francis's widow entitled her to live befitting her high rank. Having the charming and beautiful young Dowager at Court provided a general irritant that Catherine preferred to be without. Mary, who had ended her official period of mourning in March, seemed accommodatingly anxious to make a courageous return to her country of origin; how welcome she would be there only time would tell. She made a farewell tour of her relatives in preparation for her departure. Ill health prevented her from attending the coronation of her brother-in-law but on 14 August she left France, the home of her happy youth, for ever. As she sailed away from French shores she was heard to murmur the prophetic words: 'Adieu France, adieu France adieu donc, ma chere France ... Je pense ne vous revoir jamais plus.' (Adieu France, Adieu France, my beloved France, I do not think I shall ever see you again.)[15]

On 15 May 1561 the coronation of Charles IX took place at Rheims. There was little pomp or splendour; economic realities forced themselves even upon this noticeably mean event, usually a monument to regal grandeur. In fact, had it not been for the Pope urging the Duke of Guise and his co-Triumvirs to attend, on the basis that the King would automatically fall under Protestant sway if they continued to absent themselves, the most powerful men in France would have stayed away altogether. Their surly presence strongly suggested their loyalty to the throne itself, if not its present incumbent. Although Catherine had asked the Constable if her favourite son, Edouard-Alexandre, or Monsieur – as the eldest brother of the King was known – could take his place as leader of the peers and Montmorency refused, nevertheless Catherine placed her second son next to the King throughout the ceremony. The Cardinal of Lorraine spoke stern words as he crowned the little boy, though Monsieur actually placed the crown on his brother's head. Lorraine reminded Charles and those participating in the ceremony who were of the reform faith that 'anyone who advised the King to change his religion would at the same time tear the crown from his head'.

The little boy cried with fatigue under the weight of the crown. He presented a pathetic image, a physical incarnation of the monarchy's present weaknesses. Open criticism of Catherine could also be heard; the Duke of Guise had loudly accused her of 'drinking at two wells' with her tolerant attitude towards the reformers. The duke and his fellow Triumvirs, Montmorency and Saint-André, posed a serious threat to Catherine, for between them they controlled the French army. Since the creation of the supposedly secret Triumvirate, its leaders had behaved with open hostility towards the Queen Mother. The bullying and impertinence of 'those who were used to playing king' were nonetheless unable to deter Catherine from her course. She still believed that religious moderation would heal

France and she certainly had the stomach pointedly to ignore the increasingly menacing attitudes of her son's 'overmighty subjects'.

Immediately after the coronation Catherine attempted to bring the Constable and the Guises back to the King's side. First she paid a visit to the cardinal at Rheims, then she announced to the Constable that she would spend one night with him at Chantilly, making a bitter but mocking comment that if she stayed longer 'you would drive us from your door'. She then insisted that François of Guise come to Paris to lead the great Fête-Dieu procession and thus 'to defend the honour of God'. It was the only reason he would attend and she well knew it. He replied, 'Since it is a matter of the honour of God I go, and whatever befalls, I shall die, for I could not die better.' He duly led the procession through the streets of Paris crowded with throngs of cheering people alongside the King and Bourbon. Paris, that most Catholic of French cities, had been presented with a united front; the Queen Mother had once again applied a cosmetic and temporary cover to disguise the festering sore beneath.

Catherine knew that Philip backed the Triumvirs and in an extraordinary scene even found herself being threatened by his ambassador Chantonnay. As a punishment for her clemency towards the Protestants, he said she would be banished to her Château of Chenonceau. Seeking a meeting with her son-in-law, she wrote to her ambassador in Spain saying their encounter 'was the thing I desire most in the world, for the fruit it will bear'.[6] She wanted to be able to show the world 'that the said Catholic King has taken my son under his tutelage and protection'.[7] For all her efforts to win Philip over, Catherine behaved with remarkable tolerance regarding her children's access to Protestant literature, and it was even said that her son Edouard-Alexandre had stopped going to Mass and sang Protestant psalms to his sister Margot, while snatching the prayer book from her hand. This hardly presented the image of a strict Catholic mother that she should be showing Philip. Rumours also abounded that Edouard-Alexandre already showed signs of being a Huguenot. According to gossip, he even called himself 'un petit Huguenot'. Mocking the statues of saints – he was nine years old – and on one occasion biting the nose off a statue of Saint Paul, he also exhorted his sister Margot to 'change my religion and he would throw my book of hours into the fire'. One day, while Catherine was giving an audience to the papal nuncio, the King, his cousin Henri of Navarre and a group of friends dressed up as cardinals, bishops and abbots, and burst into the Queen Mother's chamber riding a donkey. The hoots of laughter from Catherine could not be disguised and she excused the children's behaviour as childish antics. The horrified nuncio reported everything back to Rome.

Margot recalled that the Court was 'infested with heretics' after her brother's coronation. She states in her memoirs that Catherine finally reacted to protect her children in their Catholic faith and forbade them to read Protestant literature and had them instructed again 'in the true, holy and ancient religion, from which she herself had never wavered'.[18] The reckless latitude with which the royal children were apparently allowed to conduct themselves, at least superficially, had sent quite the wrong message to the Calvinists in Geneva, whose hopes grew daily of a royal conversion. Theodore de Bèze, Calvin's closest lieutenant, wrote to his master, 'This Queen, our Queen, is better disposed towards us than she has ever been. If only it would please God to allow me a way to write secretly about her three sons of whom so much has been told me by reliable sources. They are so advanced for their age that you could not hope for better.'[19] Catherine would never have considered their childish flirtations with Protestantism anything other than youthful curiosity; she found it inconceivable that any of her own children would ever convert. She began to understand, however, that appearances had to be strictly kept and that she must remain above suspicion of heresy herself as the various factions circled menacingly around her and the royal children. Working long hours, sending despatches all over France, her courage and endurance were evident in these early days of simmering revolt and hostility. 'As a mother she keeps the King close to her, she does not allow anyone but herself to sleep in his chamber, and she never leaves him,' reported the Venetian ambassador.[20]

The kingdom grew unsettled by the religious issues and Catherine's conciliatory policies appeared to achieve nothing but make her look weak to both Protestants, who demanded more and more concessions, and Catholics, who grew increasingly belligerent towards her and the reformers. De L'Hôpital, after a series of meetings with experts both legal and religious, could offer no solution. The *Cour des Pairs* was summoned, which included the princes, all chambers of Parlement and the King's Council. The word 'Parlement' in sixteenth-century France could mean 'the entire judicial complex that included the Parlement of Paris and the six provincial courts at Rouen, Bordeaux, Toulouse, Aix, Grenoble and Dijon ... or it could refer only to the Parlement of Paris' which considered itself the 'sovereign court of the entire realm and looked on the provincial Parlements as mere branches of their own court'.[21] For two weeks they met and this resulted in a ban on 'conventicles and assemblies', meaning all Protestant religious meetings and gatherings. Catherine and her Chancellor ignored these findings and once again walked the middle ground.

On 30 July an edict was announced that offered amnesty for all religious offences since Henry II's death, with the proviso that in future those persons led 'peaceful and Catholic lives'.[22] It was yet another stopgap. With the meeting of the Church Council that had been promised at the Estates-General only a month away, Catherine felt more optimistic than most that a reasonable solution could be found. To her, God Almighty should be invoked as a protector, not as an avenger. In religious matters she was no fanatic except when her sons and their birthright were concerned. The Catholic Mass suited her, a lifelong habit that she found comforting, almost as though it were another talisman to ward off evil. Unfortunately, she signally failed to grasp that the burning issues were not niggling doctrinal differences between Christians, but a profound rejection by the reformers of two fundamental truths upon which the Catholic Church was built, the Eucharist and doctrinal authority of the papacy.

Pope Pius IV expressed extreme alarm at the idea of the conference scheduled to take place at Poissy at the end of August; at the very least it undermined his authority and it gave an almost formal recognition to the French Protestants by their inclusion. The Council of Trent – the Catholic Church's general assembly originally created to fight the Reformation and bring about the Counter-Reformation – had been recalled and this, he stated, should be the only official venue for discussions about the Church. Catherine, afraid that Trent would come too late and anyway prove ineffective for her purposes, pressed on with her own agenda. While it has been argued that the initiative for the forthcoming conference did not belong to her since it had been officially ordered by the Estates-General at the beginning of the new reign, the Queen Mother put her formidable energy into ensuring that the Colloquy of Poissy went ahead. The Pope, unable to prevent the meeting from taking place, sent the Cardinal of Ferrara to attend as his special legate. His instructions were clear; to curb the agenda as far as possible and prevent further concessions to the Protestants. Meanwhile Catherine let it be known that all her subjects would be welcome to present their views.

Shortly before the church conference, the Estates-General met on 27 August. The meeting set for May had been postponed due to the coronation. The outcome of the meeting, which had been called to deal with the Crown's financial predicament, resulted in money being voted to curb the King's financial problems. Most of the funds came from the Church which, fearing even harsher demands being made upon it, offered $1\frac{1}{2}$ million livres over six years 'for the redemption of royal domains and of indirect taxes which had been alienated'.[23] A further $7\frac{1}{2}$ million livres would be paid to settle the King's debts. The financial aid promised came as a huge relief for the Queen Mother. With one problem solved, she moved on to the next.

Theodore de Bèze, who had been invited to attend the conference at Poissy to represent the Calvinists, had arrived on 23 August at Saint-Germain, where he was welcomed by Catherine in Antoine de Bourbon's apartments. De Bèze, a cultivated nobleman, was reckoned to be the least provocative of the Calvinists. Intelligent and sophisticated, he understood the importance of appearing reasonable though devoted to his cause. Fanaticism would not further his aims at Poissy. The Cardinal of Lorraine was also present and the two men had a courteous and brief discussion about the Eucharist. Lorraine asked de Bèze what he understood by the words 'This is my body'. De Bèze replied he 'held for a real but sacramental presence'.[24] Lorraine then asked if he believed 'that we communicate truly and substantially the body and blood of Jesus'. He received de Bèze's careful and qualified reply that he believed it 'spiritually and by faith'.[25] The encounter broke up with the most cordial professions on both sides, the cardinal saying, 'I am very happy to have seen and heard you, and I adjure you in the name of God to confer with me, in order that I might understand your reasons and you mine, and you will find out I am not as black as they make me out to be.'[26] Catherine's triumphant remark to Lorraine that the reformers 'have no other opinion than this with which you agree' was a touch premature, as the following days would soon bear out.

The Colloquy of Poissy – as it came to be called – opened in a refectory of the Dominican Convent there, not far from Paris. Seated on a raised dais were Catherine and her children, the Princes of the Blood and the King's Council. Along each side of the long room sat the prelates, doctors of theology, cardinals and ministers who were to participate in the debate and hear the arguments. The Duke of Guise brought in the meagre number of Protestant representatives under guard and placed them behind a low barrier, as if to prevent them from contaminating the rest of those present. As seating arrangements go, it was neither tactful nor auspicious. De Bèze opened with a graceful speech and then proceeded to go straight to the heart of the matter before them. Lulled by his eloquence, his listeners heard him move on to the subject of the Eucharist. He then spoke the fatal words about the Host: 'His body is as far removed from the bread and wine as heaven is from the earth.' A horrified silence was followed by uproar, then shouts of 'Blasphemy!' and 'Scandal!'. The Cardinal de Tournon rounded upon the Queen Mother on her raised platform crying, 'How can you tolerate such horrors and blasphemy to be spoken before your children who are still of such a tender age?' Catherine replied that she and her sons would 'live and die as Catholics'. The Jesuit General, Diego Lainez, warned the Queen Mother that the kingdom was doomed if she did not banish the heretics. With de Bèze's words Catherine's hopes for doctrinal compromise collapsed. After a few more days that produced nothing but deeper division and hatred, the Colloquy of Poissy closed on 13 October 1561.

Despite the acrimony at Poissy, Catherine continued to show favour to the Protestants. One explanation, apart from her pragmatism and hopes of unity based on reason, could be put down to the conduct of the Huguenot hierarchy. While the Triumvirs and Spain bullied and threatened her, the Protestant leaders and noblemen treated the Queen Mother with the greatest respect, calling her 'our Queen' and making endless loyal professions as French subjects to the King, the Crown and Catherine herself. Their clever policy of appealing to her as their ruler and protector, lauding her wisdom and foresight, gained them much ground. This was particularly true since the Catholic chiefs were frequently absent from Court sulking on their estates, and if they did deign to appear at Court at all they were often insufferably rude to the Queen Mother. In the absence of the war hero Guise and other Catholic icons, the most brilliant Huguenot leaders such as the charismatic Admiral Gaspard de Coligny, who had been publicly disowned by his uncle Montmorency for his change of religion, his brother d'Andelot and Louis de Condé had the stage to themselves. They proved irresistible to many, and de Bèze received a gracious invitation to remain at Court; indeed, Catherine allowed him to preach to the increasing number of Protestant converts there, among them some of the most important noblemen and women in the country.

Again the Guises withdrew in protest. As they did so, they made an attempt to kidnap Catherine's adored son, Edouard-Alexandre. The boy had been approached by various members of the Guise clan to come with them and stay with his sister, Claude, Duchess of Lorraine, or to be taken to his aunt, Marguerite of Savoy. The prince listened to their proposals and promptly went to tell his mother. He reported that the Duke of Nemours, a one-time friend of Catherine's but now a supporter of the Guises, had visited his bedroom and demanded, 'What religion are you? Are you a Huguenot? Yes or no?' The frightened boy answered, 'I am of the same religion as my mother.' Nemours had insisted that the prince, as heir presumptive, would be much better off out of France in the safety of Lorraine or Savoy, since Condé and Bourbon were plotting to take the throne. Nemours finished by warning the prince, 'Mind well not to speak to your mother of this, and if anyone asks you of what I have spoken, tell them I was merely entertaining you with comedies.'[27] Catherine also heard that the Duke of Guise's eldest son Henri had on several occasions tried to tempt Edouard-Alexandre to come with them saying, 'You will be so happy. You will have so much freedom ... you cannot imagine the pleasures we shall share.' Henri of Guise went on to tell the prince that they would fetch him in the middle of the night and he would have to climb from a window into a coach. And before anyone had had time to discover his absence, Edouard-Alexandre would be in Lorraine.

This threat to Catherine's children, and most of all her beloved second son, struck at her heart. Handsome and tall for his age, Edouard-Alexandre seemed to have inherited more Italian than French looks and interested himself less in physical exercise and more in reading and the arts than was the Valois habit. With long and beautiful hands like his mother, he had a handsome face and well-proportioned body. He was more precious to her than anyone or anything. Catherine decided for the moment to pretend that she had known of the plan all along and that her son had told her all about it from the first, although Guise denied any knowledge of the plot. She was appalled when Ambassador Chantonnay came to speak to her on behalf of Philip, who had not been party to the abduction plan. He said that the King of Spain thought it wise that the royal children should be taken to a place of safety in view of the trouble that would surely descend upon the kingdom. Her reply came quickly: if she must part with her sons for their own safety then she would rather place them in the hands of the King of Spain than anyone else. Catherine then tried to have Nemours arrested, but he fled to Savoy, sending an emissary to explain that the plan was no more than a fantasy. Eventually, for *raisons d'état*, Catherine decided to let the matter drop and by 9 June 1562 Nemours had returned to Court. As was her habit, however, Catherine did not forget this iniquity.

During the late autumn of 1561 monks were being killed and churches pillaged in the south-west of France where the Huguenots held sway. In revenge, Parisian Catholics rose up and attacked Huguenot gatherings. In an attempt to keep the warring parties separate, Protestants were banned from worshipping within city walls and not at all on Sundays or Catholic feast days.[28] De Bèze wrote to Calvin that he had secret permission for the Protestants to meet in safety and awaited an edict that 'gives us better and more secure terms'.[29] Catherine was making a final brave attempt to unite the two faiths. Holding back French churchmen from setting out to attend the Council of Trent, she struggled heroically to find an accommodation. She chased her dream of unity throughout the last days of 1561, but it could only be a chimera; her pragmatism and, in this case, lack of imagination fatally blinded her to the passion with which men and women clung to their spiritual beliefs.

Catherine's last effort at producing a peaceful solution came with the Edict of January. In de L'Hôpital's opening speech before the meeting to discuss it, he put forward the view he shared with the Queen Mother. Affirming that the assembly had not been called to decide which was the best religion but only the best way to restore the state, he said it was possible to be a citizen without being a Christian; indeed, it was even possible for an excommunicate to be a citizen. The debate and resulting vote took place on 15 January 1562. The edict effectively recognised and legalised the Protestant religion in France, which had hitherto been outlawed. By giving the Protestants even minimal recognition Catherine now allowed them the right of citizenship, albeit a very much second-class one. Henceforth they would be permitted to practise their religion, but only outside town walls. Closing the council with an eloquent speech in which she explained her vision and her hopes, she reaffirmed that 'she and her children and the King's Council wished to live in the Catholic faith and obedience to Rome'.[30] Catholics were furious with the edict and Parlement refused to ratify it. Even Elisabeth wrote from Spain saying bluntly that her mother must either declare unambiguously for the Catholics and receive support from Spain, or side with the Protestants in which case she could expect Spain's enmity. Finally Catherine sent her delegates to attend the Council of Trent and argued that the edict must be seen as a stopgap until the council had deliberated.

Antoine de Bourbon, who with his usual infirmity of purpose had been attending both Mass and the Protestant services during the past months, finally renounced the new religion and came over to the Triumvirs. He had been offered a mirage of thrones, territories and even the hand of Mary Stuart by the Spanish and other Catholic forces. These blandishments were without substance but they made the muddle-headed weakling into a champion of Catholicism, and he boldly denounced the recent edict and declared his intention to 'live in closest friendship with the Guises'. His wife Jeanne d'Albret, Queen of Navarre, though a long-time sympathiser, had only just officially embraced the Protestant religion. Jeanne was in despair as her husband, whom she had loved passionately, heaped this public humiliation upon her. When Catherine asked her to induce her co-religionists to adopt more moderate behaviour, the Queen of Navarre – whose eight-year-old son would succeed Catherine's sons should they die without issue – replied, 'Madame, if I had my son and all the kingdoms in the world within my hands, I would rather cast them to the bottom of the sea than lose my salvation.'[31] Calvin flew into a rage at Bourbon's behaviour: 'This wretch is completely lost and is determined that all should be lost with him.'[32] As both Protestants and Catholics continued to agitate, the edict having achieved nothing but to annoy both parties, Louis de Condé firmly stepped into his brother's much-neglected place as official leader of the Huguenots. Meanwhile Catherine finally managed to force Parlement to register the edict, even though most Catholics still demanded it be revoked.

Deciding it was time to present a spotless face upon her own religious intentions, Catherine aimed to silence her critics and parade her unshakeable Catholicism. The hope that she would convert had even been fostered by some Protestants. Although she had unwisely allowed it to appear that she was open to hearing the new teachings, she naively assumed that she would be considered above suspicion. Changing her faith, such as it was, an amalgam of superstition, habit and a genuine love of the Catholic rites and rituals, was unthinkable and held no attraction for her. When Chantonnay criticised the Queen Mother for the '*nourriture*' (in this case he meant education, not food) that she allowed the King and his brothers to receive, and the latitude she permitted them to 'say whatever pleased them on matters of religion', Catherine was stung into replying, 'This does not regard you but me alone.' The Queen Mother added that she knew well that the ambassador had been told lies about her and her actions, and that if she discovered who had spoken the untruths she would 'make them understand that it was most unwise to speak with so little reverence for their Queen'. Nevertheless, her weak position – which had in some instances been undermined by her naively ambiguous behaviour – obliged her to write a placatory letter to Philip. Her explanations were the same as ever: 'the season in which we live' constrained her from acting as she would ideally like. Catherine now ostentatiously appeared with her children at Mass, in every religious procession and observed every rule as laid down by her Church. Furthermore, she commanded her ladies to behave above reproach with regard to religion and warned that they would be banished from Court if they did not. The Constable's nephews, Coligny and d'Andelot, left Fontainebleau on 22 February after a furious quarrel with their uncle Montmorency who remarked that he wished he had not 'raised them so high'.

The Duke of Guise had been visiting his family estates in the Champagne region during early 1562 and on Sunday, 1 March rode with an armed escort to hear Mass. As he passed through the small town of Vassy belonging to his niece Mary Stuart, he heard singing coming from a barn within the town walls. A Protestant service was being held which, according to the terms of the new edict, was clearly illegal. The duke attended Mass in a church not far from the barn. To his mounting wrath the voices of the psalm singers could be clearly heard as they filtered through the church walls. Whoever provoked the subsequent fight is unclear – the duke's official version gave it out to be 'a regrettable accident' – but tempers boiled over into a violent struggle between the Huguenots and Guise's men, which left seventy-four Protestants dead and over one hundred wounded. Among the casualties were women and children. Guise himself received a cut to the face and some of his men were also hurt. The incident became known as the 'Massacre of Vassy' and it immediately lit the fuse that sparked off what came to be known as the French wars of religion.

EIGHT

The First Religious War

My courage is as great as yours

1562–64

News of the Massacre of Vassy reverberated across the kingdom, not least because it was hailed as a 'great victory' by many Catholics. François, Duke of Guise, carefully avoiding armed Huguenot contingents sent to intercept and kill him, made for Paris at the head of 3000 men. Greeted outside the city by the Constable, they rode triumphantly into the capital together. Cheered in the streets as a hero, the duke was offered help by an *infini pouple* (countless people) including the powerful Provost of Merchants, to take the fight to the Huguenots. Tactfully he replied that he would leave matters to the Queen Mother and Antoine de Bourbon, as Lieutenant-General of France, and would be content to serve them honourably in whatever capacity they saw fit. When the duke arrived in Paris, Condé was already in the city with 1000 armed Huguenots.

At Saint-Germain when she heard the news of the Massacre at Vassy, Catherine made an eleventh-hour attempt to stop open warfare breaking out in the capital. She commanded Condé's brother, the Cardinal de Bourbon, governor of Paris, to order both Guise and Condé to quit the city at once, taking their men with them. Knowing he was secure, Guise did not move, but Condé rightly feared for his life and left Paris on 23 March 1562. The Queen Mother sent four emotional letters to him in the last two weeks of March begging him not to abandon either her or the peace of France. In one she wrote, 'I see so much that pains me, that were it not for the confidence I have in God and the certainty that you will help me preserve this kingdom and serve the King, my son, I would feel even worse. I hope that we shall remedy all with your good counsel and help.' Even at the best of times Condé rarely allowed himself to be taken in by Catherine's flattery; the prince now considered it time to arm and fight for what he believed to be right. Her appeals were made in vain.

Catherine and the Court had moved to Fontainebleau when Guise arrived there on 26 March with 1000 cavalrymen. Claiming to be anxious that the Huguenots might take the royal family hostage, he said he had come to escort them back to Paris where they would be safe. Catherine refused, but when the duke insisted that the King and her children were in grave danger she tearfully capitulated and left the chateau the following day. Catherine understood all too well that once they were in possession of the King, the Catholic faction led by Guise were de facto also in possession of the law. On 2 April Condé, having earlier joined forces with Coligny and his men, took Orléans where they raised the Huguenot standard. In a local uprising Rouen fell a few days later. This was a particular blow to Guise pride since it lay in the heart of the family's Norman territories. On 8 April Condé issued a manifesto stating his aims and those of his Huguenot followers. Proclaiming their loyalty to the King and the royal family, they stated that they only wished to free them from the Guises, whom they accused of breaking the law. They also asked for their recently won freedom of conscience to be guaranteed in law beyond doubt.

Catherine – stubbornly determined not to give up her contact with Condé – travelled to Toury on 9 June where she met the rebel leader. Disarming and friendly, she kissed him on the mouth as was the proper greeting between members of the royal family. Each of the principals was accompanied by his or her own escort of one hundred men. Catherine's troops, in royal purple, contrasted strongly beside Condé and his men in white, henceforth to become the colour adopted by the Huguenot armies. Catherine, astonished at their choice, since white was for mourning but it also implied poverty and simplicity, asked Condé, 'Monsieur, why do your men dress like millers?' He replied, 'To show, Madame, that they can beat your donkeys.'[2] As the two talked, their escorts waited and one Huguenot cavalryman wrote afterwards, 'I had a dozen friends from the other side, of whom each one was as dear to me as a brother, so much so that they asked permission from their officer [to speak to us]. Soon the two separate lines of those in purple and those in white were mixed, and when the time came to separate, many of us had tears in our eyes.'[3]

Despite her efforts Catherine gained nothing more from the encounter than the promise of a further meeting. This took place a few weeks later when she met other Huguenot leaders. While these futile talks were held and Catherine tried to maintain an ultimately untenable position above the dispute, both sides appealed abroad for aid. The Huguenots turned to Geneva, the German Protestant princes and to Queen Elizabeth of England. Originally Elizabeth had offered to act as a mediator between the two sides, but the ineluctable slide towards chaos in France tempted her to closer involvement, not for any pious motives but for the spoils. With Mary on the throne of Scotland, she also had no wish to see the Guise dominate France again. Condé's delegates arrived in England and on 20 September 1562 signed the Treaty of Hampton Court. In exchange for Le Havre, which would later be substituted for Calais – the Queen's true goal – she sent 6000 men to Le Havre where they started work on improving the fortifications.

Catherine and the Triumvirs had meanwhile sent out their own appeals for help. In the first instance French nobles were heavily taxed, raising 300,000 écus. Philip of Spain rejoiced that France was at last undertaking a holy war against the Huguenots, and despatched 10,000 foot soldiers and 3000 cavalrymen. Similarly, Catherine raised money from the papacy, Florence and Venice. Swiss mercenaries and other foreign troops were hired to boost the royal army well organised by Guise. The early days of what became known as the First War of Religion were characterised by the particular viciousness of localised atrocities, committed by both sides settling old scores. In Sens monks had their throats cut; 200 Protestants were drowned at Tours, and in Angers the Duke de Montpensier decapitated those unfortunate Huguenots he managed to capture. Hot-heads from both parties committed outrages that exacerbated already deep hatreds. Francis II's heart was taken from its urn at Saint-Denis and burned; other royal tombs also suffered desecration. The intense fighting in the south of France left the area ravaged. After initially spectacular results in Guyenne by the Protestants, Blaise de Monluc, one of Henry II's most renowned soldiers, enjoyed a considerable victory there, though the Languedoc was almost entirely in Huguenot hands.

The Royalists took Poitiers and Bourges, after which they moved further into Normandy with the aim of recapturing Rouen, the defence of which was led by Gabriel de Montgomery, the young nobleman whose lance had been the unwitting cause of Henry II's death. Catherine execrated Montgomery, although Henry had personally exculpated him and one of his dying wishes had been that he should not be pursued or prosecuted for what had obviously been an accident. None of this carried any weight with the Queen Mother; Montgomery had to be punished. She believed him responsible for the kingdom's present troubles, for had Henry lived France would not have suffered such torturous ordeals. Filled with hatred for the man who had 'killed' her husband, it became her obsession that he should be brought to justice for his 'regicide'. Despite her undeserved reputation in history for vengefulness, this is one of the very few instances when Catherine did indeed pursue a personal vendetta.

In mid-October, during the bombardment of Rouen, the Queen Mother came to Fort Sainte-Catherine, above the city, to discuss the progress of her son's armies. She had brought the King with her to hearten the troops, but kept him sheltered and safe. Listening to the military experts put forward their strategies, she seemed more a campaigning king than a forty-three-year-old queen. Animated and involved, she walked the ramparts watching her guns fire upon the rebels. Both

Guise and Montmorency warned her not to expose herself to danger but she laughed at their fears, saying, 'My courage is as great as yours.' They did not exaggerate the risks she ran. When Antoine de Bourbon, occupying one of the forward royalist positions, needed to relieve himself, he wandered into the bushes a little way off from his men and was hit in the left shoulder by the shot of an arquebus. Guise, who found Bourbon knocked to the ground, picked him up and had him carried to the surgeons. At first sight the wound did not look mortal but despite what must have been excruciating exploratory surgery as the physicians poked and dug about, the bullet could not be found. Ambroise Paré, who had attended Henry II on his deathbed, became alarmed. He wrote afterwards, 'Monsieur de la Roche-sur-Yon, who loved the King of Navarre greatly, took me to one side and asked me if the wound was fatal. I answered that it was ... He asked the other [surgeons] ... who replied that they had high hopes that the King, his master, would recover, and this gave the prince much joy.'[4]

Catherine arrived at Bourbon's sickbed, bringing with her Guise and Antoine's brother, the Cardinal de Bourbon, as the host of doctors and surgeons surrounding him maintained their optimism. Ambroise Paré continued to be privately pessimistic, however, and wrote later, 'Until I saw signs of a good recovery I would not change my opinion.' While the medical consultation was in full flow, much to the royalists' delight so was the recapture of Rouen. Bourbon asked to be carried into the city through a breach in the Porte Saint-Hilaire so the walls of his room were knocked down and the victorious troops carried him into the town. Once installed there, Paré's diagnosis proved correct as the wound became gangrenous. The surgeon recalled Bourbon's suffering: 'It was necessary to open his arm, from which came a smell so foul that many people, unable to bear the stench, were forced to leave the room.' Unfortunately no pus accompanied the putrid odour and the patient grew delirious as his fever rose. He asked to be removed from the unhealthy air of Rouen and taken up the Seine on a galley. With his end approaching, Bourbon behaved as indecisively in death as he had done in life. Both Catholics and Protestants, eager to claim the salvation of this high prince, surrounded him, arguing over his soul. On 9 November he confessed to a Catholic priest, but the following day, regaining consciousness, he declared, 'I wish to live and die "en l'opinion d'Auguste"' (i.e. as a Lutheran). On the night of 17 November, one month after receiving his wound – death, the one thing Bourbon could be certain of – finally claimed him. His last words were to his Italian valet of whom he was fond; grabbing the man's beard, he gasped, 'Serve my son well and make sure he serves the King.'

Antoine's demise made his eight-year-old son, Henri, First Prince of the Blood and heir to the throne of France after Catherine's sons. Henri left Court to join his mother, Jeanne d'Albret, Queen of Navarre, where under her fanatical influence he became a follower of Calvin. If Antoine de Bourbon had been an unreliable but malleable irritant for the Queen Mother, his son Henri later grew to present a far cannier foe when provoked. More than anything else Catherine feared what the boy represented; prophesied by her soothsayers as the eventual ruler of France after her sons, Henri incarnated her very worst nightmare.

One of the joys Catherine had anticipated upon the recapture of Rouen evaded her. Gabriel de Montgomery, with a handful of men, escaped on board a ship before the town fell. In a vengeful frenzy 4000 rebel captives were put to the sword by royalist soldiers, though Guise tried to put a stop to the worst excesses and keep some of the more valuable prisoners for ransom. More pressing problems now occupied the Queen Mother, however. Despite the royalists regaining the momentum, there was a sudden and real danger posed when Condé and his army left Orléans marching towards Paris. Guise, who had planned to take Le Havre, abandoned his project and set out with his army in a headlong rush to reach the capital before the Huguenots. Guise won the race and Condé turned towards the English troops in Normandy, planning to join forces with them before any major engagement took place. He was foiled by Montmorency's army blocking the route northwards and the Battle of Dreux was fought on 19 December 1562.

Describing the opening moments of this, the first major battle in the war, François de la Noue, a Huguenot gentleman and soldier, wrote, 'Each one of us thought to himself that the men coming towards him were either his companions, his relatives or friends and within the next hour they would be killing each other. The thought filled us with horror, but we maintained our courage.' A dazzling cavalry charge led by Coligny almost won this decisive battle, but Guise, with more men, had managed to keep troops in reserve and carried the day. Saint-André, one of the Triumvirs and bosom friend of Henry II, was killed in action, and Montmorency found himself once more a prisoner of war, as did Condé. This left Guise in charge of the royalist army and the only Triumvir still in circulation. Coligny meanwhile took command of the Huguenot forces. Catherine saw the victory at Dreux as a chance to start peace talks, but with public opinion against her Guise set off for Orléans, to which he laid siege.

On the evening of 18 February 1563 the Duke of Guise inspected the progress of the siege and made an assessment of his troop dispositions at Orléans. Returning to camp as evening fell, he was preceded by a young man named Poltrot de Méré and one of his pages. Poltrot was a twenty-year-old youth, 'short in stature and yellow skinned'. It later transpired that La Renaudie, author of the Amboise Conspiracy, was a distant relation of his. De Méré, originally a spy for the Huguenots, had been turned by Guise into a counter-spy. Now, some claimed, he had been given the order to murder François of Guise by his original master, Admiral de Coligny. That evening he noticed that the duke was not wearing his usual coat of chain mail. Keeping to one side near a sentry, the would-be assassin hid behind some bushes as the duke passed him on horseback. Guise did not see his attacker as he emerged from the brush and fired an arquebus at the warlord's back. Hit by the shot, the duke fell to the ground and by the time a search began for the culprit, Poltrot de Méré had left the camp on a fast horse.

Catherine was at Blois when she heard the news. Her emotions, apart from shock, could best be described as a mixture of despair at losing 'the ablest and worthiest minister [her son] could ever have' yet delight that she might shortly be freed from the powerful duke's yoke. Knowing that Guise's death would damage the chances of a true and lasting peace almost irreparably, the Queen Mother decided that the crime must be properly examined and its perpetrator punished in an exemplary fashion. Genuinely appalled that Guise should have been struck down in this cowardly manner, she wrote to Anne d'Este, the duke's wife, 'Even though I have been assured that the wound is not fatal, I am so troubled I know not what to do. But I wish to avail myself of every favour and all the power that I possess in the world to avenge this crime and I am sure that God will forgive all that I will do to this end.'[6] As soon as she could, Catherine left Blois for the duke's camp, where she sat by his bedside.

Poltrot de Méré had, meanwhile, been caught and brought back to camp. One look at the half-witted creature satisfied everyone that this was not the work of a clever man, but a fool possibly operating under orders from others, or striking out to make his own mark on history. The gibbering youth quickly confessed that he had been working under orders from Coligny, who had offered him one hundred écus to kill the duke. Catherine wrote to her sister-in-law, Marguerite of Savoy, that Coligny and de Bèze had

> persuaded him that if he carried out their plan he would go straight to heaven ... he also told me that he had orders to keep my children and myself under surveillance and warned me of the infinite hatred that the Admiral has for me and that I must take the greatest care. There, Madame, this man of good (Coligny), who says he does nothing but for religion, but tries to have us all killed. I hear that during this war, he will eventually kill my children and get rid of my best men.[7]

Questioned by the Queen Mother, Poltrot later contradicted himself and

Catherine's husband, King Henry II, in 1547, the year
he ascended the throne of France.

Previous page Catherine de Medici during her long widowhood.

Catherine as a young woman, from a portrait in the Uffizi Gallery, Florence.

Pope Clement VII, c.1526, by Sebastiano del Piombo.

King Henry II later in his reign.

The bedroom at the Château d'Anet that Henry II shared with his lifelong mistress Diane de Poitiers.

Diane de Poitiers, the legendary beauty —
the crescent moon in her hair an allusion
to the chaste goddess of the hunt.

Diane de Poitiers as she was more accurately
depicted by the court painter François Clouet.

The ubiquitous device adopted by Henry and Diane intertwining
their initials in a way that could nonetheless also be interpreted to
include two back-to-back 'C's, as a sop to Catherine's pride. From a
panelled door originally in the Château d'Anet.

Giorgio Vasari's allegorical portrayal of Catherine and Henry's wedding in 1533. Pope Clement VII is marrying the couple.

The tournament at which Henry II was mortally wounded by a splintered jousting lance to the eye.

Catherine with other members of the royal family and senior courtiers attend the deathbed of Henry II.
Note the surgeons' futile and grisly experiments on a nearby table.

withdrew the accusation against Coligny's involvement in the attack. Nevertheless, the military man famed even more for his severe morals than his courage and military expertise found himself stained by the original accusation, one which the Guises certainly believed to be the truth. Catherine, on the other hand, had no objection to Coligny losing the moral high ground, but ultimately desired peace between France's most influential families. For the moment, the ambiguity suited her well; a tarnished and compromised Coligny would be easier to keep in check.

As was almost invariably the case, the cheery prognostications of the surgeons proved wildly optimistic and François of Guise – war hero, military genius and charismatic Catholic leader – died on 24 February 1563. On 19 March the state accorded him an almost royal funeral; the cortège, composed of twenty-two town criers ringing bells, important citizens carrying burning torches, and representatives of the Church and nobility, all processed through Paris. A large troop of armed militiamen accompanied them. Thousands of mourners lined the streets. The assassination of François of Guise set off a blood feud between his family and Coligny's – the Châtillons – that would culminate in the death of tens of thousands of people nine years later.

Coligny answered the accusations from afar, and he did so with such frankness and so contrary to the flowery usage of the day that his honesty almost incriminated him. Admitting that he had heard of several plots to kill Guise or members of his family even before Vassy, and claiming that he had warned the duke via the Duchess of Guise, he went on to say that since the Massacre he regarded Guise and his family as enemies of the King and kingdom. He added that several plots had been uncovered, instigated by the duke, to murder both Condé and himself. Furthermore, under the present situation where the two men were fighting in the war on opposite sides, he did not feel himself obliged to warn Guise of any threats to his life. Coligny went on to say that although he had never actively instigated any plans to murder the duke, he had indeed taken Poltrot de Méré into his pay as a spy. He continued that the latter was the last person to whom he would entrust such a delicate task as killing the leader of the opposition, though at their last meeting de Méré had commented upon how easy it would be to kill the duke. Coligny finished by begging that Poltrot be kept alive to testify in any legal investigation, as he was the only man who could clear his name.

Since it was not in Catherine's interests to have matters clarified by a trial, Poltrot de Méré was duly executed and dismembered before a huge crowd at the Place de Grève in Paris on 18 March. The people, inflamed at the loss of their hero, tore the flesh from Poltrot's body and dragged it round the streets of Paris. The truth, probably complicated and unlikely to have directly involved Coligny, died with him. In a letter to Catherine accompanying his statement, Coligny's 'injudicious candour' sealed the Châtillon–Guise enmity for ever. In his explanation the Admiral concluded, 'Although he was entirely innocent, he nevertheless regarded the duke's death as the greatest benefit which could have befallen the kingdom, God's Church, and in particular, his whole House.'[8]

Almost inevitably, Catherine's long and turbulent relationship with the Guises left a cloud of suspicion over her too. She is supposed to have remarked to her trusty confidant the Marshal de Tavannes, 'The Guises wished to make themselves kings, but I stopped them outside Orléans.'[9] She is also alleged to have told Condé, 'Guise's death released her from prison as she herself had freed the prince; just as he had been the duke's prisoner, so she had been his captive given the forces with which Guise had surrounded her and the King.'[10] The Venetian ambassador noted the Queen Mother's remark that 'if M. de Guise had perished sooner, peace would have been achieved more quickly'.[11] It is relatively safe to say that Catherine had nothing to do with the death of the Duke of Guise, though for the moment chance served her well in freeing her from the man who most opposed settlement with the Huguenots. She was now, by default, chief of the Catholic party, while Coligny with Condé, also by default, became the leaders of the Huguenots. It was clear to her that the majority of her people were faithful Catholics and that she must seek a peace agreement that would prevent the spread of the reform religion.

Using the two captives Condé and Montmorency as *pourparleurs* for their respective parties, their talks resulted in the Edict of Amboise on 19 March 1563. Its terms reflected the growth of Protestantism within the nobility and the concessions to noble Protestants were far greater than to the lowlier believer. Freedom of conscience was granted to all Huguenots, though their places and rights of worship favoured the nobles. Broadly speaking, a nobleman could hold services on his estates, while those further down the social scale were restricted to worshipping in their homes. Paris and its environs were banned, though Huguenots were allowed to hold services in any town they held before 7 March. Neither the two parties nor the people received the edict well, and those who subscribed to the blame-the-messenger principle threw mud at the town criers whose job it was to shout out its terms. Adding to the general tone of dissatisfaction on both sides, Calvin condemned Condé as a 'wretch who, in his vanity, had betrayed his God'.

The recapture of Le Havre now became Catherine's next objective. This would serve the added purpose of bringing the two opposing sides together against the English. Queen Elizabeth received a message from Condé and Coligny asking her to give up the town. She replied that it was her right as compensation for the loss of Calais and that she would hold Le Havre 'despite all of France'.[12] Catherine called upon Huguenot and Catholic troops to join together beneath the royal banner and remove the foreigner from French soil. With a common cause once more, Montmorency and Condé besieged Le Havre and to Elizabeth's fury succeeded in ejecting the English on 23 July 1563. Elizabeth's troops – even more afraid of the plague epidemic raging inside the town than the cannon fire to which they were subjected – made it an easy victory. Understandably, Elizabeth never viewed the Huguenots with anything other than bitterness following what she saw as their betrayal. After Catherine also arrested Sir Nicholas Throckmorton, the English ambassador, for treating with the Huguenots, Catherine and the English Queen eventually agreed peace terms under the Treaty of Troyes (12 April 1564), which officially recognised French ownership of Calais in exchange for 120,000 crowns.

Despite the Peace of Amboise, neither side in the French civil war completely disarmed. Undaunted, Catherine promoted peace at Court, hoping that it would filter down throughout the realm. Condé was reconciled with the Queen Mother in Paris as she and the King became the prince's guests for the feast of Corpus Christi. As they appeared in public together there seemed little reaction from the people, though the following day a mob attacked the Princess de Condé in her carriage while travelling to Vincennes, and one of her men, a Huguenot named Couppe, was killed in the struggle. Condé immediately accused the Guise family of seeking vengeance but Catherine soothed the prince and tried to use sedative measures upon the principal nobles at Court. She decided to employ the same principles for keeping nobles at peace that were once used by her revered father-in-law, Francis I, whose dictum had been: 'Two things are vital for the French: to love their King and to live in peace; amuse them and keep them physically active.'

Catherine resolved that her Court would be filled with glorious pleasures, balls, masques and the scintillating attractions that would bring the feudal lords, both Huguenot and Catholic, together. By keeping the *grands seigneurs* busy enjoying themselves, she hoped they would be distracted from killing each other or plotting to overthrow her son. To this end, and in a departure from her previous policy regarding her household, the Queen Mother now happily availed herself of the charms of the loveliest maidens of high birth. These young beauties became known as her 'flying squadron', numbered (according to different sources and various periods) between eighty and three hundred. Catherine insisted that they be dressed 'like goddesses' in silk and gold cloth at all times. Brantôme described the women, probably exaggerating their virtuous conduct, as 'very beautiful and very polite maidens, with whom one conversed each day in the Queen's antechamber'. He went on to add that the women provided only the most innocent and chaste diversions for the gentlemen and anyone 'who ignored this would be banished'.

Jeanne d'Albret, Queen of Navarre, scandalised by the loose living at Court, summed matters up far more accurately: 'It is not the men who invite the women but the women who invite the men.' Catherine cared only that her flying squadron should appear to behave decorously in public but privately they were free to do as they wished 'provided they had the wisdom, ability and knowledge to prevent a swelling of the stomach'. One such, Isabelle de Limeuil, *dame d'honneur* to the Queen Mother, started a passionate love affair with Condé. Unused to the refinements of Court life and the temptations it offered, the soldier prince fell completely under her sway. One pleasing result for the Queen Mother was that Condé was so influenced by Isabelle that he stopped attending Protestant worship at Court. Some time later the careless young woman became pregnant and eventually gave birth to her baby. She sent the infant to Condé in a little basket and Catherine, who quickly discovered the truth, flew into a rage and had Isabelle locked in a convent until she regained her good sense and the Queen's pleasure.

The ingenious spectacles, lavish entertainments and the flying squadron's physical attractions were henceforth to mark Catherine's rule and made her Court famous for its brilliance. Brantôme called it 'a true paradise on earth'. The Queen Mother, always in her black mourning, stood in stark but regal contrast amid the pomp and colour of her surroundings. She cleverly played to her strengths, particularly using the 'mature charms' she had acquired over the years of her long apprenticeship for power. Catherine could be witty and strangely alluring; even her sternest critics at Court could be momentarily seduced into appreciating her qualities. Yet just as they felt they had grasped her essence it would disappear, and she remained as chimerical and puzzling to them as ever. One observer of the Queen Mother during these years remarked upon her 'humanity', 'goodwill' and 'patience in meeting everyone on his own level'.[13] He also praised her 'indefatigable constancy in receiving all manner of people, listening to their speeches, and treating them with so much courtesy that it would be impossible to ask for more consideration'.[14]

Notwithstanding her efforts, Catherine's days still seemed to be spent answering complaints from both sides of the First War of Religion, each accusing the other of not observing the Peace of Amboise. To every complaint she applied herself with calm determination to settle the disputes tactfully and above all expediently. She grew so exasperated by the continual protests from Coligny that she finally wrote to him stating that if the Protestants continued to agitate and break the law, she would retaliate 'without respect to persons, religion, or any other consideration but the peace of this state'. Catherine the arbitrator was indomitable in her thankless task. The desire for vengeance, the inevitable fruit of civil war, seemed endemic, contract murders became commonplace and acquired the nickname 'vengeance in the Italian manner'. Finally, recognising that drastic measures were required, the Queen Mother took a course of inspired and audacious political bravery. She decided to have the thirteen-year-old King declared to be of age.

Although the legal age of majority for a king of France had been laid down as fourteen by Charles V of France, Catherine decided that the boy should be declared of age in his fourteenth year. She knew that the loyalty commanded by a monarch was far greater than that of a regent. The move hinged upon the gamble that although the King was still a boy, the nobles' traditional feelings of allegiance and obedience to their monarch would assert themselves, and order might thus be restored. Catherine herself would effectively continue to rule, but the essentially cosmetic change might just bring about the peace she so urgently desired. On 17 August 1563, therefore, in a great ceremony at the Parlement of Rouen – the Parlement of Paris had been rejected as the venue because they were furious at what they considered a sleight of hand by Catherine – Charles was declared of majority. Despite the Paris Parlement's argument against the declaration, Catherine insisted upon it, answering that there had been various exceptions to the age of majority 'when the situation in the kingdom required it'.

Present at the ceremony were Montmorency, the Princes of the Blood, royal councillors, many powerful nobles and the Marshals of France. Both François of Guise's brother, the Cardinal of Lorraine, and Coligny's brother, the Cardinal of Châtillon, were also in attendance. Despite the mutual hatred between the two families they appeared united for the King. The boy, tall for his age but of a puny physique and generally poor health, solemnly declared that he would no longer tolerate 'the disobedience that has, until now, been shown me'. Catherine then officially placed the governance of France in Charles's hands. Having had his powers proclaimed, he descended to where Catherine stood. As the Queen Mother approached the King he got up from the throne and made a gesture which left no doubt as to who would really be ruling France. After Catherine had curtsied deeply to him as her sovereign, the boy gave his mother a filial kiss, holding his velvet cap, and announced that he gave her 'the power to command' and stated 'that she would continue to govern and command as much and more than before'. The great nobles followed one after the other to pay homage, kissing the King's hand and bowing deeply.

In a document that she drafted for her son at this time the Queen Mother set out the four points that she believed essential to his successful rule. The King must provide leadership and be accessible and central to all that happened at Court. The key to harmony and to maintaining a grip on affairs was to 'restore the proper function of the Court'.[15] It must be the central attraction of French life and revolve around the King. She stressed the importance of a regular routine that ought to be kept by the King. Within this, priority must be given to public affairs and the 'expectations' of the nobles must be fulfilled; she also stressed her determination that the corruption of Court officials should be stamped out and business dealt with properly and quickly. Officials often left urgent affairs untended for weeks or months, adding to the impression that the King was a distant and uncaring figure. She insisted that Charles be personally available to all the people who came to present their grievances: 'Take care to speak to them whenever they present themselves in your chamber. I saw this done in the day of your grandfather and your father, and when they had finished speaking about their business, they were encouraged to converse about their families and their personal matters.'[16]

She also advised the King to keep a close hand on all questions of patronage. If he had a firm grasp of affairs relating to available offices, vacancies and everything within his gift, he would control not only the Court but also the provinces, stamp out the corruption against the Crown and win the people's loyalty at the same time. Here she cited the story that Louis XII had carried a list of vacant offices on him everywhere he went. Francis I paid key provincial figures to keep him abreast of vacancies and developments, down to the last detail. The provincial garrisons whose importance Francis had constantly stressed were not just for local defence, but also provided a useful 'chivalric centre for local magnates dissipating ... their *esprit de pis faire*' (desire to make trouble).[17] She also commended to Charles 'the care of merchants and the urban bourgeoisie'.[18] This political testament does not address many important elements required for a successful ruler, such as advice on finance or military matters, but it is believed that the original document had two parts of which only one remains.

Catherine had cleverly tied the ratification of the Peace of Amboise to the proclamation of the King's coming of age. This was greatly resented by the ultra-Catholic party whose tempers continued to run high. Almost immediately after the declaration of his majority, Charles was faced with the Guise clan's demands that the duke's murderer be brought to justice. Attempting to accentuate their cause, they made a dramatic reappearance at Court dressed in the deepest mourning. In January 1564 the King, with unusual maturity, made an official pronouncement that the case would be held over for three years in the interests of peace. In the meantime neither party was to pursue its own personal vendettas. Catherine, most probably the true author of this sage decision, trilled ecstatically at her son's great wisdom, calling him 'the new Solomon' and saying, 'The King my son of his own volition without anyone's prompting has issued a decree that is so beneficial that all the council said that God had spoken through his mouth.' Yet of course nothing changed, and the murders and assassination attempts continued. One of Catherine's bravest and most loyal captains, Captain Chaury, was killed by a Huguenot mob in Paris, but the Queen Mother decided not to pursue the killers for fear of stirring yet greater passions. An attempt on Catherine's own life was also rumoured at the same time. There were certainly two attempts to kill d'Andelot, Coligny's brother, which can be traced to the Duke d'Aumale, the late Duke of Guise's brother. D'Andelot managed to thwart the assassins, but only just escaped with his life each time.

Although Catherine hoped that Charles would command obedience as a major, his anaemic features, frail body and a disfiguring birthmark between his nose and upper lip suggested little of the majesty that his father and grandfather had possessed in abundance. He later grew a moustache which covered the birthmark, but he was known by many as 'le roi morveux' (the snotty or brat king). The Venetian ambassador, Giovanni Michiel, described the boy a little more kindly as 'an admirable child, with fine eyes, gracious movements, though he is not robust. He favours physical exercise that is too violent for his health, for he suffers from shortness of breath.'[19] Catherine undertook the unenviable task of creating a king out of Charles; fortunately a sense of majesty was one thing she understood perfectly. Though the raw material could hardly have been less promising, she nevertheless approached her project with absolute determination. Charles 'ate and drank very sparingly' – in the late Renaissance world of masculine excesses this frugality might generally be regarded as unmanly. He showed little interest in balls, Court entertainments or women, though he drove himself to excel in martial activities. Above all, he enjoyed hunting in all its forms.

Like his late brother, Francis II, Charles seemed to lose himself in the frenzy of the chase. Although weak and of ailing health, he would push himself as hard as he could. It was noticed by all that he had difficulty in catching his breath and as the years passed he grew weaker with each debilitating crisis, slowly becoming maddened in both body and mind by his infirmities. As time progressed his rages became so violent that courtiers genuinely feared for their lives. Eventually attacks of complete dementia would seize the King, but even now, at thirteen years of age, the essentially kind and generous-hearted boy found himself prey to occasional ungovernable outbursts of temper. Charles delighted in the chase but showed an abnormal and morbid interest in the 'kill', which excited and transfixed him. On occasion he eviscerated his gory prey with his own hands. All this belied the surprisingly charming poetry he wrote when the mood took him and the fact that he also enjoyed music, especially the horn, which he played well.

Catherine, eager to instil a keen appreciation of the arts so beloved by their grandfather Francis I and their Medici ancestors, in Charles and all her children, had them taught to paint, sketch, write verse and carve wood. The young King showed genuine talent in his artistic endeavours. Two of his *épîtres* were addressed to Pierre de Ronsard, the great French poet, and were published in the distinguished man's works.* Catherine ensured that her sons received an education befitting kings under the supervision of some of the most learned men of the day. Jacques Amyot, the famed translator of Plutarch, supervised the boys' intellectual formation. Among other subjects they were taught Latin, Greek, history and all the children spoke fluent Italian. Charles showed great filial respect and affection for his mother, though her evident preference for Monsieur, his brother Edouard-Alexandre, caused much rivalry and jealousy between the two.

Thirteen-year-old Edouard-Alexandre bore the title Duke of Orléans as the eldest brother of the King, but is best known to history before he ascended the throne as the Duke of Anjou (a duchy awarded to him by his brother in 1564). As he would have his name changed to Henri at his confirmation I shall henceforth refer to him as Henri, Duke of Anjou. He was a delicate though spirited child with a pallid complexion and, as so many of the Valois, a keen practical joker. He did not lack courage, yet Henri showed little of his family's traditional passion for the hunt, though he did enjoy fencing, a sport at which he showed a notable elegance. His marked interest in clothes, rich cloths and fabrics, jewels, lapdogs and toys, however, did give rise to some concern. Elegant and sophisticated beyond his years in matters of taste, he had an eye for beauty that became an obsession as he grew older. His stylish dress and long, elegant hands with tapering fingers were quite Medicean, as were his faultless manners and ability to charm and seduce whomever he met – when he wished. Henri was handsome and had a well-shaped body but a supurating fistula between his right eye and nose spoiled an otherwise

---

* Pierre de Ronsard (1524–85) served at Court and accompanied Mary of Guise to Scotland, where he stayed for three years. As well as his poetry, he wrote political reflections on the early wars of religion and the Massacre of Saint Bartholomew. He is particularly remembered for his attempt to promote the use of the French language in literature to replace the formal classicism of the Middle Ages. During his lifetime he enjoyed fame and success for his work and was honoured by Francis I, Henry II and Charles IX. A reversion to the classical form after his death meant he was forgotten and discredited until the Romantic movement of the nineteenth century rediscovered him and gave his works the recognition they still enjoy today.

beautiful face. The fistula was probably an early sign of tuberculosis, one of Catherine's lethal legacies to her sons.

Margot, dark-haired with a pretty face and tall for her age, was a studious and sweet child. Physically she continued to enjoy blooming health and had a strong enquiring mind; she enjoyed learning and received a fine education, which included learning Latin. Margot loved riding and even as a young girl excelled at the elaborate dances then so integral a part of Court ritual. Dancing was not just for amusement or flirtation; some of the more energetic steps and leaps also provided a subtle method of checking a partner's stamina, physique and general potential as a future bride and bearer of children. Yet she continued to be her mother's least favoured child; Catherine seems to have resented the good health of her daughter as though this had somehow cheated her sons of stronger constitutions. The youngest, Hercules, could truly be called the runt of the Valois litter. He had been born an attractive and loving child but at the age of eight a severe bout of smallpox left him hideously altered. 'His face was deeply pitted all over, his nose swollen and deformed, and his eyes bloodshot, so that from being pleasing and handsome he became one of the ugliest men imaginable.'[20] As though that were not enough, his legs and back were twisted, and as he grew up he became swarthy, dark and only a little taller than the Court dwarves. Often he wore the expression of a halfwit, his mouth hanging open, but with a devious look in his eyes. After his illness the boy born with a sunny nature became embittered by the curse of his looks and a name which only made him seem all the more ridiculous. He grew into a cunning schemer and was to cause Catherine continual trouble. From an early age Margot took a protective interest in her little brother, which only further annoyed her mother. Fortunately for Hercules, at the same time that his brother had his name changed at confirmation to Henri, he received the name François after his late brother and his grandfather. (I shall henceforth therefore refer to Hercules as François, Duke of Alençon.)

The royal children were surrounded by all the sumptuous splendour demanded by Catherine's atavistic desire to return to the days of Francis I's brilliant Court. No matter what the state of the royal finances and in defiance of her occasional budgetary 'cutbacks', the backdrop for Catherine and the royal children's *mise-en-scène* had to be superb. Besides, when it came to royal display, profligacy came quite naturally to the French monarchy. Catherine, a spendthrift by nature, struggled continuously to pay for the upkeep of the grandeur she insisted upon. During the reign of Francis I the people of all classes at Court numbered approximately 10,000 – only twenty-five French towns could boast a population of that size at the time – and it did not drop significantly during Catherine's tenure.[21] With approximately sixty different types of officials – from bread carriers, coopers, spit-turners, ushers, carvers and chaplains to librarians – there remained many medieval posts that were no longer relevant but were nonetheless maintained for reasons of tradition.[22] She revelled in ceremony and maintained the ancient Court customs, however anachronistic or expensive they had become. Legions of servants were required to maintain Catherine and her children.

As King, Charles had a separate household from the Queen Mother's, whose own establishment consisted of hundreds of people from nobles down to simple servants, and the number ran into thousands if all the royal residences throughout France were included. Porters, valets, lackeys, footmen and Swiss guards were of a higher grade. Armies of secretaries, almoners, physicians, tutors and *gouvernantes* for the children were employed, and the kitchens alone required vast numbers of staff to feed the host of people staying or living at Court. Here there existed a whole grading system, as in every other area of royal life: the King was fed by the *cuisine de bouche* and everybody else by the *cuisine commun*. The purveyors to the royal kitchens were kept busy finding enough for the thousands of dependants to eat. Food was divided into three sections, *panéterie*, *échansonnerie* and *fruiterie* (bread, wine and fruit).[23] One of the principal reasons that the Court had to move, frequently after only a month or two, from one château to another was the lack of food available after a stay in one particular area. Sanitation prompted another compelling reason for leaving. After weeks in the same place, especially during the summer, the stench and filth became dreadful, and the risks of disease grew proportionately. The Court also moved to find new hunting grounds where fresh game could be found. When the King left one château to lodge in another of his residences, most of the furniture and hangings accompanied the caravanserai. The castle left behind was thus almost completely empty when the royal family had moved on.

Catherine had always spent prodigiously on her beloved horses, and now that she controlled the treasury she did not stint herself when it came to building stables and acquiring new horses. Some said that as she grew fatter she caused the early deaths of many of her mounts by simply riding them too hard. A large retinue was required to keep the equestrian establishment to Catherine's extremely high standards. A *gouvernant* and an abundance of grooms and stable lads were on the royal payroll. She had her own stud farm and took an active interest in the breeding programme there. Anyone presenting her with a superb stallion or brood mare found a sure route to the Queen Mother's heart. She loved animals, especially dogs and birds, though her menagerie also contained some particularly exotic creatures. Apart from the lions that she kept at Amboise, there were a large number of bears of which the Queen was fond; these were kept muzzled and led by nose rings. In the wonderland that Catherine created around herself the bears would often form part of her escort when she travelled; following her litter, closely watched by their keeper, the great beasts would lumber obediently behind the Queen Mother.[24]

Catherine also had a great fascination for dwarves. She accorded a proper household to her troupe of them; they had their own footmen, apothecaries, laundresses, housekeepers, tutors and so on. The Queen Mother kept her dwarves superbly dressed, wearing furs and precious brocades. Among her favourites were 'Catherine La Jardinière', 'The Moor', 'The Turk', 'The dwarf Marvile' and 'August Romanesque', who carried a sword and dagger. There was even a dwarf monk. Catherine had two favourite fools, both of them Polish, nicknamed 'Le grand Polacre' and 'Le petit Polacron'. They all received pocket money from her and she married off two of her favourites in a splendid miniature ceremony. Catherine La Jardinière was the Queen Mother's best-loved dwarf and this tiny companion accompanied her almost everywhere. Catherine had two other peculiar attendants constantly by her; one was a long-tailed monkey believed to bring good luck, the other a green parrot that lived to be thirty years old.[25]

As part of her plan to educate the King, Catherine had, since the declaration of Charles's majority, been planning a stunning project. If it succeeded it would be her masterstroke. In an extraordinary undertaking she declared that she would take the young King on a vast tour of his whole realm, presenting him to the people. She thereby hoped to resuscitate the mystical tie between monarch and people. She would bring the splendour of the monarchy to the drabbest corners of the kingdom, as well as to its largest cities. Francis I had shown her what it meant to the ordinary provincial people of France to meet their King. When he brought back his two hostage sons from Spain he had taken them on a triumphal tour to thank the populace for paying their enormous ransom. As a bride Catherine had witnessed the King and his Court travel north from Marseilles to Paris and understood what huge political capital could be garnered from this magnificent gesture.

The planning required to take thousands of people to the rough roads of France equalled the complexities of organising a military campaign. She intended to take the entire apparatus of government with her for, as tradition dictated, the capital of France was located with the person of the King. By making this extensive royal progress Catherine not only hoped that she would enhance Charles's standing with the people of France, but also that he might help heal the deep wounds left by the civil war. This brilliant *coup de théâtre* would comprise twenty-eight months of travelling, attending ceremonies, banquets and presentations, and ultimately, she hoped, bring peace to France by inspiring love and loyalty for the King. He would wind up knowing his country better than any other French monarch had before or since. The Queen Mother had another sound political reason that helped inspire this stupendous voyage: she had made up her mind to meet her son-in-law, Philip II, at the Franco–Spanish border. Face to face, she felt sure she could work her magic on him and, with his backing and her country at peace, she hoped France would be set fair for a brighter future.

NINE

The Grand Tour

How Spanish you have become,
my daughter

1564–66

Catherine placed the Constable in overall charge of the royal progress, which left Paris for Fontainebleau on 24 January 1564. They were not to return until May 1566, nearly two and a half years later. Several thousand members of the Court and their servants made up this great royal caravanserai. Among the essential members of the party were the King's Council, in order that government business could be conducted en route, and the foreign ambassadors. Catherine hoped that the latter would report back to their various masters describing the splendour of her train, thereby refuting the widely held view that France teetered on the brink of bankruptcy. The royal household travelled with their usual attendants, ladies and gentlemen – including the flying squadron – tutors, priests, five doctors, five kitchen officers, five sommeliers, cooks, musicians, porters, grooms, beaters for the hunt and nine essential dwarves, who of course had their own miniature coaches.

The number of horses and mules required to transport both people and luggage – particularly the gold-studded trunks of the royal family – was phenomenal. With them the party carried everything from furniture and cooking utensils to clothes and costumes for all the festivals, feasts, *joyeuses entrées* and masques that had been planned. Portable triumphal arches, which could be easily erected when needed, were also stowed and elaborate royal barges for when the royal pageant took to the water. It was a city on the move. Catherine brought with her such diverse items as silk sheets, silver washbasins, gold plate for banquets, her writing table, registers, papers, money, hats and her lute and lyre players. In bad weather or when the need arose, she chose to travel either in a horse-drawn litter or in a large cumbersome coach drawn by six horses so that she could conduct state business in transit. The seats were lined with green velvet and cushions, and the children would often sit with her in this coach so spacious that it resembled a small room. Unfortunately these vast vehicles induced attacks of travel sickness that were anything but majestic, so when weather and work permitted the Queen Mother, who had six of her finest horses with her, would ride along with the rest of the nobles. Whenever possible the royal family would travel by barge. For protection there were four companies of *gens d'armes*, a company of light horse and a unit of the French guard whose commander was Filippo Strozzi, a second cousin to the Queen Mother.

The Court made a short stop at Saint-Maur near Vincennes – a small château that Catherine planned to rebuild upon her return – before moving on to Fontainebleau where they were to spend Lent. While at Saint-Maur, the Cardinal of Lorraine returned from the Council of Trent that had finally closed. After eighteen years of spasmodic deliberations on reforming the Catholic Church, the council gave its belated response to the reform movement in a series of fundamental changes now known as the Counter-Reformation. The Cardinal brought with him the Tridentine Decrees – the rulings of the Council of Trent – ordered by the papacy. The council clarified once and for all the impossibility of reconciling Catholicism with Protestantism and made the schism of the Christian faith complete. Since Lorraine's return, Catherine knew pressure from the more extreme Catholics would mount and she accordingly gave him a cool reception.

On 31 January the party set out for Fontainebleau where Catherine had ordered that each of the most important nobles give a reception or ball. Both the Constable and the Cardinal de Bourbon gave suppers at their lodgings, and on Dimanche Gras, Catherine threw a banquet at the dairy of Fontainebleau which lay a little way out from the palace, near a meadow. The courtiers dressed as shepherds or shepherdesses for this *fête champêtre*, a precursor of the Petit Trianon parties thrown by Marie Antoinette nearly two centuries later. Everyone judged the day a huge success; the nobles having enjoyed their little afternoon of pastoral simplicity, albeit in February. Later in the early evening the guests attended a comedy in the great ballroom, followed by a ball at which 300 'beauties dressed in gold and silver cloth' performed a specially choreographed dance. Henri of Anjou gave his banquet the next day, after which a mock battle was held between twelve young knights. On Mardi Gras an enchanted castle had been built in which six maidens were held captive by devils and guarded by a giant and a dwarf. Their liberators appeared, led by the four Marshals of France. Six groups of men came to claim the captive damsels. At the sound of a bell, Condé led the defenders out of the castle to fight a superb mock battle and the scantily-clad nymphs were rescued by their gallants. The royal children also played a role in the festivities giving a performance of a pastorale written by Ronsard.

Once the feast days had finished, the Cardinal of Lorraine, determined to grasp control of the King's Council, tried to have the rulings of the Council of Trent endorsed. Essentially the Tridentine Decrees threatened the royal rights of the French Crown over the church. With Catherine's backing, de L'Hôpital strenuously opposed the decrees, enraging the cardinal, who accused him of being a crypto-Huguenot. It is clear from surviving documents that the strenuous efforts to enforce the Edict of Amboise were initiated by the Queen Mother, who meticulously followed the various cases where the edict was being ignored. Without her support de L'Hôpital would not have been able to operate since he was otherwise mistrusted by both parties.

Catherine deeply resented the papacy's attempts to enforce their rule over matters that were, in her opinion, strictly reserved to the Crown. Her attitude hardened further when Jeanne d'Albret, Queen of Navarre, received a summons from Rome on a charge of heresy. Infuriated that Pius IV dared to threaten a sovereign, and moreover one with much land and property in France, Catherine replied that he had no licence to rule over foreign princes nor to dispose of their properties. The entire concept was anathema to the Queen Mother for whom the rights of the Crown were almost a religion in itself. She protected the Queen of Navarre and Pius deemed it wise to leave the matter alone. 'I put myself wholly under the wing of your powerful protection,' Jeanne wrote gratefully, 'I will go to find you wherever you may be and shall kiss your feet more willingly than the Pope's.'[1]

On 13 March 1564 the royal progress set off in earnest. Arriving on the evening of 14 March at Sens, the scene of an appalling massacre of Protestants two years earlier, the Court made its first stop. Two days after his arrival Charles came across a sow with a litter of newborn piglets. He picked one up to caress it at which the sow attacked him. Furious, Charles brutally killed the sow. This violent and unfortunate episode was witnessed by Claude Haton, an ecclesiastic diarist at the French Court, who noted it as an example of the King's tendency to manic rages.

The Court arrived at Troyes on 23 March to an exotic greeting by people dressed as savages and satyrs riding goats, donkeys and 'unicorns'. The welcome was an allusion to the French exploration of the Americas where they had founded colonies in Florida and Brazil; indeed, Admiral de Coligny had sent three expeditions there recently. During their stay at Troyes Charles touched the feet of the scrofulous and washed those of thirteen child paupers. He then served them at dinner, which as a young boy he had seen his father do at Fontainebleau. Catherine meanwhile did the same for thirteen mendicant women.

Easter was spent with the usual displays of piety and devotion, while Protestant members of the Court celebrated Easter four leagues outside the town. A few peaceful demonstrations took place by the Huguenots, yet no real trouble arose and most of the twenty days that the Court lodged at Troyes were spent enjoyably with banquets, parades and other pleasures. It was also here that the peace with Elizabeth of England was finally signed over Calais and Le Havre. As a subtle touch, the Queen Mother had particularly chosen this town for the signature, for it was here that 140 years earlier France had capitulated to England in the ignominious Treaty of Troyes of the Hundred Years War. Sir Nicholas Throckmorton was specially released to sign the treaty for Elizabeth, and Catherine seemed particularly gracious and cheerful that day. From Troyes the Queen Mother wrote to Coligny to reassure him about the enforcement of the Peace Edict of Amboise. She claimed, 'One of the main reasons for which the King, my lord and son, has undertaken his travels is to show his intention regarding that matter so clearly wherever he passes that no one will have any pretext or occasion to contravene it.'²

At Bar-le-Duc in early May there was a family celebration to which Catherine had been eagerly looking forward. Her first grandson, Henri, the offspring of her daughter Claude and son-in-law Charles, Duke and Duchess of Lorraine, had been born and was to be baptised. The Queen Mother, Charles and Philip II stood godparents to the baby. Catherine was overjoyed to see her daughter Claude again and pleased at the name her grandson had been given. In each town or city where the royal caravan stopped the King and his mother examined local grievances, attempting to ensure the observations of the edict. The King spoke forcefully to those he found flouting his decree and threatened harsh measures for anyone who disobeyed him. The party then moved south to Dijon, where Catherine's trusty but refined soldier, Gaspard de Saulx, Seigneur de Tavannes, was governor. The spectacle he laid on for the Court's amusement lacked the usual poetic delicacy, with nymphs and fauns versifying and extolling the virtues of their King, of most cities they visited. Instead, Tavannes had arranged for a 'mock' attack upon a fortress to entertain the royal party. An expectant hush fell upon the observers awaiting the start of the celebration when deafening live fire from four huge cannon suddenly blew the fortress to atoms, shaking the ground around them. Catherine, who had been untroubled by the bombardment at Rouen, was left trembling by the Marshal's over-enthusiastic military tribute. She had time to recover on the next stage of the voyage, which included a soothing trip by barge to Mâcon.

Before the King's *entrée joyeuse* on 3 June some of Jeanne d'Albret, Queen of Navarre's, Huguenot followers abused and heckled the Corpus Christi procession taking place in the town. Catherine, incensed, ordered that the procession take place again on 8 June. This time the Huguenots removed their hats and stood respectfully watching the proceedings; the Spanish ambassador observed their restrained behaviour with much satisfaction. In Lyons on 24 June, in order to avoid further troubles of this sort, the King decreed that during his progress throughout the kingdom Protestant worship must be suspended, save for baptisms and marriages.

Lyons was a particularly important cosmopolitan city, rich in commerce and with a significant foreign population. Large numbers of Germans and Italians lived there. Lying close to Geneva, it had fallen under Protestant domination during the First War of Religion, though the expelled Catholics had now returned. As the city boasted excellent fortifications, Montmorency took the precaution of installing his soldiers at key points taking over the artillery and forts before the royal family arrived. Ignoring rumours that the Protestants planned to rise up and kill the King, Charles made his entry into the city on 13 June. Catherine cried unrestrained tears when she saw her beloved sister-in-law, Marguerite of Savoy, and her husband Emmanuel-Philibert who now joined the Court. The duke lived up to his nickname of ironhead with his tiresome and immediate importuning of the Queen Mother over the return of two strongholds, Pinerolo and Savigliano, that had been lost to France by the duchy many years before. Catherine responded by awarding him an honorary captaincy of a French company, not quite what he had hoped to cajole from her. Alfonso d'Este, Duke of Ferrara, also arrived to pay his respects to the young King and to see what he could gain for himself; indeed, throughout the tour petitioners from all ranks of society presented themselves to the King and Queen Mother.

To demonstrate the new-found religious harmony the children made a symbolic procession through the city. They walked in pairs, Protestant and Catholic side by side. Then the foreign contingents took their turn to celebrate Charles's arrival. Each wore their local costume and traditional colour. The Florentines wore purple, the Genevoise black velvet and the Germans black silk. As they processed many noted that the King looked a sad and serious child for his age, dressed in green with a white plumed hat. Next to him sat his brother Henri of Anjou looking dashing in a crimson doublet embroidered with silver, immaculately dressed as usual. Lyons had been transformed with triumphal arches and columns imitating those of antiquity, upon which adulatory verses to the King were inscribed. Catherine noted with satisfaction that the humiliating interlaced Hs and Ds, of Henri and Diane, were no longer in evidence in the city, but instead the Medici arms were conjoined with those of France. During the Court's stay, the Queen Mother visited shops filled with exotic merchandise, silks and other delights but her spending spree had to be cut short due to a sudden outbreak of plague. Fear of contagion sent the whole Court and its followers on their way; though normally slow in packing for departure, on this occasion the exit was notable for its singular despatch. The plague went on to kill over 20,000 Lyonnaise in only a few days.

During a short stop at Crémieu – east of Lyons – en route for Roussillon, where they were to stay with the Cardinal de Tournon, Catherine mischievously sent a message to Montmorency to say that there had been a massive change in the tour schedule and that she had left for Barcelona. This sent the old man into a blind panic, until he found out that it was a practical joke. Catherine wrote to her ambassador in Spain telling him she must report the story to her daughter the Queen, 'so that she may laugh over it'.³ It was here that de L'Hôpital issued an edict to curb the growing independence of the royal towns. In future two lists of candidates for municipal posts must be presented to the King who would choose between them. This provided an important step in regaining authority over provincial towns where royal control had almost been lost, allowing leagues and parties to form.

Also at Crémieu Jeanne d'Albret begged to be allowed to retire to her own territories in Béarn on the Spanish border and to take her son with her. Catherine refused the Queen of Navarre's request outright. Instead she gave her 150,000 livres and sent her to Vendôme. As for Jeanne's adored son Henri, Catherine declared she would keep him with her. She wanted the boy by her side as a hostage against the fanatical Huguenot Queen's future plans. Jeanne had become such a strict adherent to the new faith that her son, though devoted to his mother, was relieved to remain with the royal circus and his young playmates, away from the sermonising. Through the late summer months the caravan passed through Roman, Valence, Montelimar, Orange and Avignon. The train was so long and so large that often the vanguard arrived at the party's next destination before the rearguard had left the last one. To Catherine's alarm the King caught a cold, which developed into bronchitis; his sickly lungs were a constant worry but the warm southern winds and dry climate sped his recovery.

The Queen Mother then made a visit to Nostradamus at Salon in Provence. It was an interview she had probably looked forward to and dreaded at the same time. She had infinite respect for the predictions of this great soothsayer and mystic. Unfortunately, just before the royal party arrived at Salon-de-Crau there had been an outbreak of plague and most of the townspeople had fled. For Catherine there was no question of avoiding the town or cancelling the interview. Accordingly, Charles ordered that the people return to give their King a proper welcome or face punishment. The local population evidently feared royal ire more than the plague because they turned out to watch Their Majesties' entry into the town. The royal family arrived in the mid-afternoon of 17 October. Charles was 'seated on an African horse, with a harness of black velvet with large trimmings and fringes of gold. His person was robed in a cloak of Tyrian purple, adorned with silver ribbons. He wore an amethyst in one ear and a sapphire in the other.'⁴

It was arranged that the Queen Mother would meet Nostradamus with no fuss or fanfare, and he suggested he 'move about and meet Her Majesty away from the vulgar people'. Suffering from gout, the old man walked up to the chateau to meet the King and Queen Mother. Moving slowly with a malacca cane in one hand and his velvet cap in the other, he was eventually presented to the royal party. After greeting the King properly in Latin, a long conversation ensued during which the prophet pronounced that Charles would not predecease the Constable; this hardly gave cause for celebration since Montmorency was already in his seventies. Catherine gave Nostradamus 200 écus and made him a royal councillor and king's physician.

This was not their first meeting; that had taken place at Blois in 1560, where at Catherine's request she had asked Nostradamus to draw up Henri of Anjou's horoscope that predicted he would one day be King of France. This prophecy seemed to please the Queen Mother very much indeed. Less satisfactory was the interest Nostradamus had shown during his visit in a young page-boy of the French King's suite. He insisted upon seeing the boy who, when called for, bolted in terror. The page was Henri of Navarre. The following morning at Navarre's *lever* he noticed that his servants were slow in giving him his chemise. Navarre shivered, as he recalled when he repeated the story, not from cold but from fear that he was to be whipped for some misdemeanour. In fact, the servants had withheld his shirt so that Nostradamus, who had arrived in the chamber, could inspect the boy's body, particularly his moles. This was common practice, similar to palm-reading. The old man, certain that Henri (who at the time was only sixth in line to the throne) would one day be King, pronounced forcefully to the servants around Navarre, 'You will have as a master the King of France and Navarre.'

At Aix-en-Provence the King reprimanded the Parlement for refusing to register the Edict of Amboise. He also put a commission of Parisian parlementaires in their place and suspended the local magistrates. Now came the discovery of a part of Charles's realm which seemed like paradise to Catherine's brood. For the first time in their lives the royal children experienced the sunshine and beauty of the Mediterranean. The strange fruits and smells, lavender, thyme and the sea enchanted them. They saw orange trees – imported from China via Portugal as recently as 1548 – and palm trees, another new import, growing in this strange and bewitching place. For Catherine it was a return to a landscape and climate similar to the one in which she had grown up, and she happily watched her children enjoy the countryside and all its novelties. At

Brignoles local girls greeted the King wearing the traditional Provençal dress, they danced the Volta and Martingale. Their simple enthusiastic greeting cheered the Queen Mother and her children more than any of the triumphal arches and Latin declamations they had heard so many times before on the journey. Catherine judged the whole visit such a success that she decided to buy a large property near Hyères and fill the park with orange trees. For the feast of Toussaint the royal party camped by the sea. What memories did this bring back to the Queen Mother, seeing for the first time in over thirty years the stretch of coast she had passed along all those years ago, as a fourteen-year-old bride-to-be? At Toulon Charles and his brother set out to sea in galleys provided by René of Lorraine, Marquis d'Elbeuf.

On 6 November the people of Marseilles gave the royal party the warmest greeting they had yet received. Staunchly royalist and Catholic, even the Spanish ambassador found himself grudgingly impressed by the fealty of the city. Charles and his family attended a great service of thanksgiving, which his young companion Henri of Navarre could not join because of his religion. Obliged to stand at the door of the church, he patiently waited for the service to end. Charles teased Henri about not entering and, unable to provoke his friend to put his foot over the threshold, seized his cap and threw it inside. His trick had the desired effect and Navarre leapt inside chasing after his velvet hat. Expeditions by sea were arranged and a picnic organised to the Château d'If. Taking one look at the threatening swell, Catherine decided against the plan and the party took place in a sheltered cove instead. Here Charles decided that an improvised naval battle should take place. A number of courtiers, including himself, represented the Turks, and the others Christians. This drew a withering report from the Spanish ambassador. How could the King of France play the infidel? All this was duly recorded and sent off to Philip in Madrid.

After further peregrinations, there followed a stay of nearly a month in Arles due to the flooding of the River Rhône. Finally on 7 December the party set out for Montpellier where they were to spend Christmas. This was the heart of Montmorency country and the governor was the Constable's second (and by far the most able) son, Montmorency-Damville, who had ruthlessly retaken the churches seized by Protestants and re-established the Catholics in the area after the war. If Provence had been warm and welcoming, the Languedoc, with its substantial and committed contingents of Protestants, gave a far cooler and sometimes even abusive reception. During this part of the progress Catherine discovered that here certain Catholic leagues had sprung up during the troubles and were now becoming a deep-rooted and serious problem. The leagues were against the law, but under the guise of mercantile trades unions and other such 'fronts' a variety of people, including nobles, joined up and the local authorities feared they might provoke a violent reaction by suppressing them. The Queen Mother knew that these societies represented precisely the lawless fraternities that protested allegiance to the Crown while zealously preparing to serve their own intolerant ends.

To add to her troubles, soon after Christmas Catherine received news that serious problems had arisen back in Paris. Marshal de Montmorency, the Constable's eldest son, had quarrelled with the Cardinal of Lorraine for bringing a troop escort with him into the city. As armed escorts were banned, François, Marshal de Montmorency – the governor of Paris – had been forced to use his own men to split up the cardinal's troop. Hearing this, the Guise family had sent reinforcements to their brother and Coligny ordered 500 soldiers to the capital to counter the Guises' move. Finally, Coligny's men left Paris peacefully, but a renewed outbreak of the civil war was only narrowly averted. Marshal de Montmorency's swaggering and overbearing behaviour had generally irritated almost everyone who mattered, and his bravado and abuse of power in the King's absence had been bound to cause trouble. Worrying news that Condé was fortifying garrisons in Picardy also arrived to cause the Queen Mother much disquiet, but to the astonishment of the Spanish ambassador she refused to do more than send written reprimands and keep herself informed of any further developments.

As the party changed composition all the time, some of its most powerful nobles travelled to their estates to attend to business, rejoining the royal caravan when they could. This made it harder to keep an eye on the troublemakers among them. In contrast to the darker political moments, there were many touching displays of love for the King. One day shortly after Christmas, when the party passed through a small village called Leucate, an old crone 'of eighty years or more' learned, to her complete disbelief, that the splendid train passing through was that of the King. She asked to be allowed to approach, Charles bade her to come forward then 'falling to her knees and throwing her hands up in the air, she said in her local dialect these words which were translated into French: "He that I am happy to see today that which I never hoped to see, you are most welcome my King, my son; I beg of you kiss me, for it is impossible that I shall ever see you again." '[6] Kissed by the King, the by now tearful old peasant woman watched the party's departure with her simple devotion and unshakeable love for the monarch redoubled. This was precisely the type of encounter that Catherine set much store by, not just impressing nobles and townspeople but also those toiling in the fields for whom the Second Coming of Christ would have been almost as much of a surprise as the arrival of their own sovereign.

At Carcassone, scene of some of the most terrible violence during the religious troubles, heavy snowfalls delayed the party. As the children held snowball fights the Queen learned of a local executioner whose cruelty was unsurpassed even in those grisly times. While burning five people alive, he had cut the liver out of one and eaten it before the eyes of the dying victim and then had sawn the limb off another poor soul who was not-yet-dead.

During the Court's seven-week stay at Toulouse from 1 February to 18 March, the two princes, Henri of Anjou and his younger brother Alençon, were confirmed. As their education continued during the long tour across France and their stay in Toulouse was a long one, Anjou and his friend Henri de Clermont had been given a room in the same building as they lodged in which to do their lessons. Large chambers had been sectioned off to make smaller temporary ones in order to provide private space for the family members. One day they enjoyed a lesson that was certainly not on Catherine's curriculum. Hearing a noise in the neighbouring room, the two students got up and peeped through a hole in the wall. Clermont reported about what they saw to Brantôme.

> [There were] two extremely large women, with their skirts rolled up and their undergarments [*callessons*] down and one was lying on top of the other ... they rubbed against each other, pressing hard, in short their movements were very strong, their lewdness resembled a man's. After an hour or so of this activity, having become so hot and tired, they lay red-faced and quite covered in sweat, although it was extremely cold, that they could not longer continue and had to rest.[7]

Clermont went on to add that this grotesquely sensual spectacle took place regularly for the rest of the time the Court was in residence, and that both he and Anjou enjoyed watching whenever they could.

While this rather primitive initiation took place, Catherine embarked on a remarkable spending extravaganza (even by her standards) to prepare for the most exciting part of the royal progress, the meeting with her daughter Elisabeth of Spain scheduled to take place in June 1565. Catherine had borrowed over 700,000 écus, mainly from the Gondi bank, for the lavish impression with which she intended to dazzle the Spaniards. Her correspondent economies were to cut back the pensions of the unfortunate Duke of Ferrara and the Count Palatine of the Rhine. Buying jewellery, silks and other presents for her daughter and the Spanish suite, Catherine even adopted Spanish dress herself in her excitement. For six years the Queen Mother had been asking for a meeting with Philip and for six years he had been avoiding her. He believed that Catherine, whom he apparently nicknamed 'Madame La Serpente', was a woman whose words were born only from expedience; her half-measures and inability to live according to firm and unbending principles were complete anathema to him. His defence was to remain hidden. Catherine had a well-earned reputation for her elusiveness and opaque pronouncements, particularly when he wanted her to be substantial on matters of religion. Philip decided, therefore, that if he remained invisible he could not be tricked by her manipulative charms and evaporating promises. He would have agreed with the Englishman who observed of Catherine, 'She hath too much wit for a woman, and too little honesty for a queen.' Another contemporary said of her, 'She lies even when she is telling the truth.'

Catherine's Edict of Amboise disgusted Philip and some time after the grand tour had started he informed her that since it was not customary for a sovereign to leave his own borders to meet other monarchs, there could be no encounter between them. He would, however, allow his wife to make the journey to Bayonne, where a convenient place to rendezvous lay on the frontier. It was to be considered a purely family meeting. Upon hearing that Philip refused to see her, Catherine had been utterly downcast, but when the reunion with her daughter was confirmed she had burst out into peals of laughter and lost her composure to such an extent that she had ended up sobbing.

By 1 April the tour had arrived at Bordeaux, the capital of Guyenne. On 12 April Charles held a 'lit de justice' during which Chancellor de L'Hôpital spoke sternly to the local magistrates about the King's unswerving intention to enforce the Edict of Amboise. 'All this disorder stems from the contempt in which you hold the King and his ordinances,' he told them, 'which you neither fear nor obey except at your own pleasure.' Wherever there had been poor observation or non-enforcement of the edict Charles commanded that it be put into effect.

On 3 May the party left Bordeaux. The caravan headed for Catherine's personal climax of the progress, to meet her daughter at Bayonne. She had much to prepare for the elaborate reception of the Spanish party. On 8 May at Mont Marsan Catherine heard, to her dismay, rumours that Philip had decided not to send Elisabeth after all. He was particularly displeased having heard that Catherine had received an emissary from the Sultan of Turkey and he had also learned from his spies that a French expedition to Florida was being organised by Catherine to sail from Dieppe. The Spanish felt fiercely protective of their New World discoveries and disliked the threat of any other nation interfering in the lands that they were plundering so thoroughly. Any last hopes that Catherine might have fostered of Philip attending the meeting had now died, though her daughter finally received permission to meet her mother after all. Unfortunately Philip had also decided to send the severe and ferocious Duke of Alba as his personal representative, who he hoped would talk sense into the Queen Mother about her discussions with the infidel, concessions to French Protestants and land claims in Florida. Three weeks later, on 30 May, while the Court remained at Dax, Catherine set off for Bayonne incognito. She needed time to prepare for her daughter's arrival, which had been arranged for 14 June. Meanwhile Henri of Anjou left for Vitoria in Spain from where he was to fetch his sister.

In the burning summer heat on a floating pontoon in the middle of the Bidassoa river, the twenty-year-old Elisabeth of Spain affectionately embraced her brother Charles, still only a boy of fifteen. The heat was so great that six soldiers dropped dead from standing in the sun in their armour. Arriving on the French side of the river, the scene of so many emotional moments during the last fifty years, Elisabeth rode escorted by a huge contingent of the highest nobles of France, except for those known to be Huguenots. Philip had made it a precondition that his wife should not be infected by coming into contact with heretics, and Catherine's argument that this would alienate Condé and his followers and arouse unnecessary suspicions had left the Spanish King quite unmoved. Thus, without Condé, or any other supposedly contaminating influences to greet her, the French Queen of Spain rode into Saint-Jean de Luz. Catherine had been waiting there for over two hours with ill-concealed impatience. Mother and daughter kissed and cried when they first met, then Elisabeth turned quickly to Margot and François (aged twelve and ten respectively), her two youngest siblings. They had not seen each other for six years. During the family supper that night, after a fuss between the two Queens about who should sit in the place of honour which Catherine won – insisting that a blushing Elisabeth must not forget her superior station as Queen of Spain – the Queen Mother appeared extremely moved that she had her daughter close to her again. On 15 June Elisabeth made a glittering official entry into Bayonne. The city was illuminated by flaming torches and she was mounted on an exquisite grey palfrey presented to her by Charles; its gem-studded harness worth 400,000 ducats had been a gift from Philip.

Catherine found Elisabeth much changed since leaving her mother country in 1559. Her daughter had become more Spanish than French and had acquired many of the elaborate formalities of her adopted land. When she spoke it was with the words of her husband whom she loved, and years of indoctrination by the older man – who had at last found true happiness with Elisabeth, his third wife – had brought her unformed mind to think as he did. Thus after the first impulsive embraces and displays of tenderness Elisabeth became more formal and restrained. Though they tried to recapture them, the easiness of former days was gone. Elisabeth had become Philip's mouthpiece and after a long and futile effort begging her mother to see reason, she received a quick response from Catherine: 'So your husband suspects me? Do you know that his suspicions will lead us straight to war?'[8] Elisabeth replied, 'What makes you suppose, Madame, that the King suspects Your Majesty?'[9] The Queen Mother remarked coolly, 'How Spanish you have become, my daughter.' In addition to Elisabeth and Alba, Philip had taken the trouble to replace his ambassador to France, Chantonnay, for Francès, Duke of Alava. He hoped that by removing Chantonnay, whose relationship with the Queen Mother had often been less than cordial and marked by his frequent reproaches, veiled threats and support for the Triumvirs, the new man might help bring Catherine firmly into the Catholic camp.

One of the Queen Mother's principal reasons for wanting a meeting with her daughter and son-in-law was to promote further marriages between the Valois and the Habsburgs. Alba, unaccustomed to dealing with a woman, especially one who employed every device and artifice to flatter and cajole her interlocutor, found himself greatly discomfited by Catherine's complicated artfulness. Her naive belief in the power of dynastic unions, and some say a fundamentally bourgeois desire to see her younger children well married, were not what the Duke of Alba expected. The old idea of a union between Margot and Don Carlos was resurrected, then Catherine enthusiastically suggested a fresh proposal, that Henri of Anjou be married to Juana, Dowager Queen of Portugal and Philip's sister. The fact that Juana was twice Henri's age and Don Carlos was a homicidal maniac and shortly to be locked into a cell – his father stoically hammering the bolts on to the door himself – did not worry Catherine in the slightest. Off his guard and unfamiliar with matrimonial politics, Alba grew gruff and soldierly.

In the talks that ensued, the duke kept trying to steer the discussion back to the affairs that so preoccupied his master in Madrid. He denounced the Queen Mother's policy of toleration, suggesting extreme and violent measures that certainly lacked subtlety but which would, he promised, remove the knotty religious problem from her realm for ever. Executions, expulsions, torture, a reversal of the Edict of Amboise; his message was of persecution not pacification. He would soon try these solutions himself as Philip's regent in the Netherlands, but for all his brutal thoroughness his methods succeeded no better than Catherine's. Alba also made the veiled threat that if the Queen Mother could not contain the growth of Protestantism within her son's kingdom, Philip would have to deal with the menacing heretics so close to his own frontiers himself. Catherine, detesting ultimata and threats, remained regally unmoved. As Queen of France she gave him explanations and justifications for her policy of pacification, but they all fell on stone-deaf ears. Exasperated by Catherine's darting mind and flow of impassioned talk, the duke gave up, exhausted. The Queen Mother hoped with unfounded optimism that the fabulous entertainments she had organised to enchant the visitors would give new life to the talks.

Among the exchange of gifts, decorations, ballets, jousts and mock battles, the *spectacle* on the Bidassoa river is considered one of the most famous of Catherine's ephemeral works of art. After a waterside picnic, with all the participants dressed as shepherds and shepherdesses, Charles appeared on the river in a barge that had been disguised as a floating fortress. As the other participants took to their own sumptuously decorated barges, a gigantic artificial whale appeared that was then attacked by 'fishermen'. Suddenly a gargantuan man-made tortoise was seen swimming towards them, on it stood six tritons blowing cornets. The two marine gods, Neptune and Arion, surfaced; the former in his chariot was pulled by three sea horses and the latter carried by dolphins. The extravaganza ended as three mermaids glorified France and Spain with their siren songs. Catherine, more than anyone, inaugurated the fantastic entertainments for which later French monarchs also became renowned. One spectator wrote, 'Strangers of all nations were now forced to recognise that in these things France had surpassed, with these parades, bravado, glories and magnificences, all other nations and even herself.' Catherine believed that by such fabulous displays of wealth, power and unity among her Court she had finally shown the Spanish that, far from ruined, France remained a glorious power. Better still, she believed that the result of the progress would now ensure internal peace and stability, allowing her adopted country to grow strong again.

The true outcome proved rather different; the Spanish were not impressed with the sumptuous displays by the French, which left them more distrustful of Madame La Serpente than they had been when they had arrived. Their own shabby appearance had been judged offensive by Catherine's courtiers, though this was more the fault of the sad state of Spanish finances. Philip had already been bankrupt once and his treasury was perilously bare. Despite the constant talks, nothing had been promised by the Queen Mother regarding her treatment of heretics, nor would she endorse the Tridentine Decrees. She also intended to stand by the Peace Edict of Amboise (also known as the Edict of Pacification). For the Spanish the whole excursion had been largely pointless. On 2 July 1565 Catherine and the children bade a tearful farewell to Elisabeth. They were never to meet again.

For the Queen Mother and her family there had at least been the joy of seeing Elisabeth and, while no agreement was reached between the two sovereigns, since neither side could afford further war, a cordial display had been maintained and conflict thus averted. One crucial point that the Queen Mother had signally failed to realise, however, was that having banished the Huguenots from the Spanish visit, and fraternising enthusiastically with Alba, the man most feared and hated by the Protestants in Europe, they came to believe that a pact had been concluded between the pair to exterminate them. For many years this calumny was circulated and held against the Queen Mother, particularly after the Massacre of Saint Bartholomew, when the Huguenots pointed to the meeting at Bayonne as the time and place where their near-extinction had been cold-bloodedly arranged. Catherine's policy of toleration and pacification was thus coming undone, since neither Catholic nor Protestant trusted her any longer.

As for the proposed marriages between the Habsburgs and the Valois, Catherine received not one scintilla of encouragement from the Spaniards. Margot would in any event have been quickly widowed had she married the crazed Don Carlos, for he died three years later, by then completely insane. After developing an obsessive love for his gentle mother-in-law, Margot's sister Elisabeth, and giving away state secrets to anyone who would listen, he had tried to flee to Germany. At this Philip had had him incarcerated again and he died six months later in July 1568. Rumours that he was murdered by Philip are no more than romantic fiction; a more plausible explanation is that the Infante died of pneumonia as a result of his bizarre habit of sleeping totally naked on a huge block of ice in order to keep cool during the summer months.

With the climax of the royal progress over, the journey, though still a long one, was homeward bound from now on. Catherine met Jeanne d'Albret, who had been allowed to return there from Vendôme to greet the party at Nérac (capital of the Duchy of Albret). Here Catherine showed she still lacked the capacity to comprehend how deeply people held their religious beliefs when she urged Jeanne to renounce Protestantism and return to the Catholic faith. Jeanne used this opportunity to introduce Henri to the leading Huguenots and he spent time with his uncle Condé. Leaving the Queen of Navarre's son with his mother until they were both commanded to rejoin the court at Blois, the progress continued. Journeying up through western France, the party encountered some difficulties as the King and his family were often heckled and harassed by angry reformers. Blaise de Monluc ordered a larger contingent of soldiers to accompany the royal family through this hostile country.

At Jarnac, near Cognac, on 21 August Catherine had the great pleasure of meeting Guy Chabot de Jarnac, the man who had won the duel against La Châteigneraie, Diane de Poitiers' and Henry's champion, at the beginning of Henry's reign. By November the Court were at Angers, from where the royal family sailed up the Loire, stopping at Tours, Chenonceau and Blois. On 21 December 1565 they reached Moulins, the heart of Bourbon country, and moved into the château there, the former seat of the treacherous Constable de Bourbon. An Assembly of Notables

had been convoked for the purpose of completing an enormous programme of reforms to the judiciary and administration. Among the
leading men now gathered together were Montmorency's nephews and
most of the Guise family. The two clans had not met for over a year.
After Charles officially acquitted Coligny of any part in the duke's murder,
Catherine applied her usual prescription for reconciliation: she required
the two principal parties, the Cardinal of Lorraine and Admiral de Coligny,
to kiss each other. This they did, although with how much sincerity is
highly debatable.

On 6 January 1566, before the assembly had officially opened, news
of terrible atrocities arrived from Florida, where Spanish troops had
massacred the mainly Protestant French colonists. The French had
reached the virgin territory first and claimed it in the name of their King,
but they had reckoned without Philip's fury that there should be a colony
of French heretics anywhere near Spanish territory. He had sent out a
force of 26,000 men who attacked the 600 settlers and four companies
of French soldiers in a fury of bloodletting. Most of the settlers, men,
women and children, had had their throats cut. Only a handful managed
to escape. Outrage erupted at Moulins, where, according to the Spanish
ambassador Alava 'Her Majesty was growling like a lioness' over the grim
despatches. She condemned the Spaniards as being more savage than the
Turkish infidel. Yet there was little that the Queen Mother could do.
Too weak to demand reparations from Philip successfully, she had to
content herself with marble columns inscribed with the victims' names
being placed in Fort Coligny, the sole surviving French camp in Florida.

Michel de L'Hôpital opened the Assembly of Notables and, in a
brilliant speech, outlined the purpose of the meeting. The French judiciary
required both regularisation and to be brought under the more effective
control of the Crown. The present confusion over jurisdictions, contradictory laws, abuses of power and corruption due to many factors –
not least the religious conflicts, must be tackled thoroughly, he said. The
eighty-six clauses of what became the Ordinance of Moulins of February
1566 was de L'Hôpital's masterpiece, the reforms to government and the
judiciary that it demanded returned authority to the Crown. Unfortunately
the coming civil wars prevented the proper implementation of the
ordinance, but historians agree that it served 'as a launching pad for
future attempts to reform the government of France'.[10]

At last, on 1 May 1566 the royal tour arrived back in Paris after 829
days, of which a quarter had been spent travelling and three-quarters
staying at châteaux, camps by the sea, palaces, abbeys, towns, cities and
villages. The fabulous voyage dreamt up by Catherine in a magnificent
attempt to bring concord and harmony to her son's war-riven kingdom
had covered nearly 3000 miles, crossing mountains, rivers and parched

southern plains. They had encountered snowfall, floods, plagues and scorching heat. This indomitable and imaginative woman had shown her son to the people and the people to their King. She had every reason to feel a sense of personal triumph on her return to the capital, believing, as she did, that there was now a real prospect of lasting peace. Yet she reckoned without the passion that the cause of religion could stir in men's souls.

TEN

Conciliator No Longer

The greatest wickedness in the world

1566–70

In the summer of 1566 a dramatic outbreak of violence in the Spanish Netherlands – later called 'the iconoclastic fury' – caused a huge rise in tension and mistrust between the Huguenots and Catholics in France. The uprising in the Low Countries had started as a protest by the nobility against harsh new laws and restrictions imposed on them by the regent, Margaret of Parma, Philip II's half-sister. The struggle soon encompassed the Flemish Calvinists against whom Philip now decided to take extreme measures. Religious and civil unrest so close to the French border presented a sore Catherine could not afford to disregard. The Spanish were deeply unpopular in France at the time due to the massacre of the settlers in Florida and the Queen Mother arranged a mournful procession of the victims' widows throughout the streets of Paris in the early summer of 1566, feeling this would serve as an aide-mémoire to keep alive the national sense of outrage.

Catherine could not resist a dig at the failure of Philip's rigorous and uncompromising policies in the Low Countries, writing smugly to him, 'Take us as an example, for we have sufficiently shown, at our own cost, how others should govern themselves.'[1] Then, mistakenly believing that the Spanish were about to employ a more conciliatory approach, perhaps one similar to her own, she wrote to her ambassador in Spain, 'I am marvellously pleased that they now applaud and approve in their own case what they were formerly so ready to blame in ours.' This blithe self-congratulation proved premature; she did not know it at the time but Philip shortly planned to lead an army to the Netherlands specifically to increase the repression and exact a terrible retribution on Flemish Protestants.

French Calvinists were enjoying a brief spell of favour from Catherine and Charles at Court. The King had grown particularly fond of Gaspard de Coligny who was gradually becoming Charles's mentor and friend, just as Coligny's uncle Montmorency had once been to Henry II, and Condé also made a brief appearance. The Guises once again withdrew, unable to tolerate the ascendancy of their mortal enemies. They were particularly angry that Coligny's brother, the Cardinal de Châtillon, now a Protestant and a recently married man, continued to enjoy the enormous revenues from his many rich church benefices. Only the King could annul this, but Catherine restrained him from taking any action against Châtillon or the many other converted prelates who still drew huge sums from the Church. She did not wish to provoke the Huguenots while there was peace in France, however ragged; instead, she seemed unconcerned about enraging even the moderate Catholics.

The Huguenots naturally took full advantage of their moment of seeming royal favour and began to press the cause of their co-religionists in the Netherlands, whose clamour for help grew ever more urgent. Coligny, offering Huguenot military assistance, argued forcefully that French interests would be served if they helped eject Spain from the neighbouring Low Countries, even suggesting that Charles might like to add these territories to France. Catherine promptly put a stop to this discussion. The very last thing she wanted was to inflame Philip; besides, she needed help from him with yet another matrimonial project: she wished to marry the King to one of the Habsburg Emperor Maximilian's daughters. She mistakenly imagined that Philip might feel grateful for her stand against Coligny's plans and, in return, underwrite her marital project. A further bond between the two dynasties formed when word arrived that Elisabeth, after suffering several miscarriages, had on 12 August 1567 successfully given birth to a daughter, an Infanta of Spain.

Emboldened by his sound relationship with the King, Coligny and his entourage continued, meanwhile, to agitate and petition him for action in the Netherlands. Charles – urged by his mother – closed the matter with a sharp rebuke to the Admiral by finally announcing that he wished to maintain good relations with his brother-in-law King Philip. He did not know it yet, but these were now to be severely tested. Assured of this French intention not to aid the Flemish rebels, Philip then declared that he would shortly be leaving Spain at the head of a large army bound for the Netherlands. A few weeks later his ambassador, the Duke of Alava, sought an audience with the King and Queen Mother. He delivered his master's request to disembark with his forces at Fréjus in southern France. From there Philip proposed a route northwards through eastern France to Flanders. Catherine, thunderstruck at the idea of permitting approximately 20,000 Spanish troops to travel through the length of France, unequivocally refused. The relative religious calm in the country was precarious at best; the presence of such a vast number of Spanish troops on French soil 'would set fire to the kingdom'. The Spaniards' subsequent invitation that the French might like to join their campaign against Protestantism also met with a blunt refusal. Thus denied, Philip found a different though less convenient route to his northern territories via Savoy, Milan and Lorraine.

The Spanish army marched inexorably towards Flanders, though Philip had decided not to lead his troops himself but put the Duke of Alba at their head, simultaneously replacing Margaret as regent of the Netherlands. The duke had orders to repress and if need be exterminate the rebels without mercy. Such a large Spanish force on her northern borders posed a critical danger to France, so amid great anxiety on the council, Catherine and Charles set out immediately to inspect their defences in the north. As an additional precaution Charles hired 6000 Swiss mercenaries, as well as reinforcing garrisons in Piedmont, Champagne and the Three Bishoprics.* Philip found these security measures outrageously insulting. Alava protested to the Queen Mother, 'The king has no need of such an army.'² Catherine, knowing well the reputation for ferocity of the Spanish soldiers, felt equally incensed that she had not been kept fully informed about her son-in-law's own plans. She commanded the French ambassador in Madrid to explain her situation, rhetorically asking, 'Is it reasonable that among all the violent turbulence, which is everywhere, we should be at the mercy of anyone who wishes to do us harm?'³ Typically, at the same time, to keep Philip assured of her overall goodwill, she sent his army supplies of grain. Catherine had reason to fear potential foreign predators. Maximilian, the Holy Roman Emperor, enjoying a short respite in his war against the Turks, might also find this a propitious moment to attack an enfeebled France and Queen Elizabeth I had just sent Thomas Norris as special envoy to the French Court to demand the return of Calais. Catherine formulated Charles's uncompromising reply: 'Since the Queen has broken the peace herself by taking Le Havre she should renounce Calais and be content to keep to the natural boundaries of her kingdom.'

By the summer of 1567, meanwhile, the Huguenots became increasingly convinced that a secret plan existed between the Spanish and Catherine to use the hired troops against them. This was exacerbated when Charles did not release the 6000 soldiers despite the fact that the danger of invasion had passed once Alba and his army arrived in the Netherlands. Violent attacks by Protestants against Catholics were reported in the provinces. The leading Huguenots at Court felt the chill wind of Catherine's withdrawal of favour as she went out of her way to show that she was quite ready to put down the savage behaviour of the reformers who attacked Catholics. In Pamiers, near Toulouse, there had been a particularly vicious assault by the Protestants who killed monks and ejected Catholic citizens. The Queen Mother described their conduct

* Toul, Metz and Verdun.

as no better than that of the Turks. The Protestants were equally horrified at reports of Alba's atrocities that came filtering through from the Netherlands. He had set up what is today known as the Tribunal of Blood, which oversaw the killings of hundreds of rebels and Calvinists. Engravings at Hatfield House, where Elizabeth I had heard the news of her accession to the English throne in 1558, show these grisly mass executions.[4]

The arrest of two leading rebel nobles, Counts Egmont and Horne, who were executed in June 1568, proved Alba and his regime of terror planned to make no exceptions for the high nobility. Indeed, the arrests of Egmont and Horne made the senior Huguenots south of the border even more apprehensive. Was the same fate intended for them? They protested again about the presence of the Swiss soldiers, arguing that they could not guarantee peace from their own side should the mercenaries remain in France. Catherine promised Condé that she would personally see to the strict adherence to the Edict of Amboise and punish anyone who put him- or herself above the law, yet crucially she said nothing about the troops.

Dissatisfied, Coligny demanded an explanation from his uncle about the mercenaries. The Constable replied, 'The King has paid for them; he wishes to see how his money has been used.' This simple answer was the literal truth, if no more than that, and borne out when Catherine arranged a military review for her son's amusement. The court was staying at Montceaux, just to the south-east of Paris, and the Swiss entertained them there with a parade. The Protestants set little store by this, thinking it merely a show to lull them into complacency. In the growing panic a false rumour reached them that Catherine had held a secret meeting at Montceaux giving the order to arrest the Huguenot leaders whose lives were thus in imminent danger. In that nervous period of rumour and counter-rumour they began to arm and prepare for conflict. Their plan was simple; they must first capture Catherine, Charles, Anjou and the leader of the Guise faction since his brother's death, the Cardinal of Lorraine. Several large towns were to be taken as Huguenot strongholds and troops raised that could then cut the Swiss mercenaries 'to pieces'.

Nearby at Condé's Château de Vallery the Huguenot leaders carefully composed their scheme. As they did so Catherine, who had ordered no attack of any sort upon them, was instead taking pleasure in her stay at Montceaux in the beautiful early autumn weather, cheerfully imagining that all was well. Yet on 18 September she received word of the Huguenot war preparations; there had also been sightings of approximately 1500 soldiers near Châtillon. She sent Artus de Cossé, one of her military commanders, to look into the reports and wrote to Forqueveaux, the French envoy in Madrid, to say, 'It was just a small scare which has now blown over.' Determined to enjoy her stay hunting and resting at '*sa belle maison de Montceaux*', an unprotected château vulnerable to attack, she assured the King's lieutenant in the Dauphiné that 'everything is as peaceful now, thank God, as we could hope'.[5] While Catherine's wishful thinking got the better of her instincts, the Protestants finalised their plans. Further warnings arrived from the Spanish in Brussels about the impending attack, although she brushed these aside too, dismissing them as attempts to frighten her. The Constable, who still believed his intelligence network to be as good as it had been in his prime, bolstered her confidence by declaring that not even a hundred horsemen could gather 'without my knowing of it instantly'. Unfortunately, the days when Montmorency's boast would have been true had long since passed. There was even smug talk of making it 'a capital offence to spread false alarms'.[6]

As rumour piled upon rumour, confirmed sightings of soldiers and warning messages continued to arrive that troops were massed close by at Rozay-en-Brie. Catherine could no longer ignore the awful truth; her dream had evaporated. On 26 September 1567 the Court moved to the relative safety of the fortified town at nearby Meaux. She sent out an immediate summons for the Swiss soldiers quartered at Château-Thierry. News arrived that Péronne, Melun and other towns had been attacked by the Huguenots. Worse was to come when enemy troops had been spotted on most of the roads approaching Meaux. Unable to comprehend what had prompted the Huguenot uprising, Catherine declared herself 'amazed' and 'could see no reason' for what she called 'the infamous enterprise' which became known as the '*Surprise de Meaux*'.

At three o'clock in the morning of 27 September the Swiss troops arrived and, taking the advice of the Guises against that of the Constable and de L'Hôpital, Catherine decided to make a dash for Paris, preferring to risk flight to being besieged at Meaux. At the centre of a square troop formation, surrounded by 'a forest of Swiss pikes', the Queen Mother and the King, their family and the most senior nobles set out for the capital. Terrified, the rest of the Court joined the exodus as best they could. The rebel cavalrymen harried and attacked the party several times at the start of the hazardous journey but the Swiss successfully repulsed each assault. Finally it was decided that Catherine, the King and her children should dash ahead in light carriages with a small guard to Paris where they arrived at four o'clock in the morning, eventually followed by the rest of the party. The courtiers' appearance made an unedifying spectacle as they entered the city, dishevelled, terrified and exhausted, many of them having made the journey on foot. Throughout the sprint to Paris, Catherine had watched Charles weep with rage and promise that from that day onward 'he would never allow anyone to frighten him again and swore to pursue the culprits into their houses and beds. He intended henceforth to lay down the law to everyone great and small.'[7]

Frustrated by the successful flight of their royal quarry, the Huguenot rebels stopped outside Paris at Saint-Denis and prepared to besiege the city. They also blocked supplies going down the Seine. Anxious to gain time and decide upon her next move, Catherine sent de L'Hôpital to Condé. She needed to discover the rebels' aims. The prince, offered a full amnesty in exchange for disbanding and disarming his men, disdainfully responded that this was not enough and, presenting himself as a hero of the downtrodden people, demanded that the King disband his armies and disarm entirely. He insisted upon the full reinstatement of the Edict of Amboise, an immediate recalling of the Estates-General and an overall lowering of taxes. French men and women, he declared, were suffering and paying for the greed of foreigners and 'Italians' at a time when the kingdom was not even at war. This last point could only be understood as a personal and direct attack upon Catherine, the expensive splendour of her Court and the loans from the Italian bankers who propped up her empty exchequer.

At a meeting of the King's Council Catherine is reported to have turned upon her former mentor, Michel de L'Hôpital, who offered suggestions about reconciling the two sides, angrily saying, 'It is you and your advice that have brought us to this pass!' As the Parisians began to feel the effects of the blockade, there was no solution but to fight the rebels' infamous and unprovoked treason, which she called 'the greatest wickedness in the world'. The King amassed an army while his mother sent out appeals for help to her 'cousin' Cosimo, Duke of Florence. Philip of Spain and Pope Pius V also received her applications for help. With her stubborn belief in a peace that had never really existed now shattered for good, the days of Catherine the enlightened and passionate conciliator were finally over.

In a letter to Spain she lamented, 'You may imagine with what distress I see the kingdom returning to the troubles and afflictions from which I laboured to deliver it.' Talks between the two sides foundered as the Parisians endured their hunger. On 7 October 1567 the King's herald was, according to ancient tradition, sent to Saint-Denis to demand that Coligny, d'Andelot and Condé disarm and give themselves up. The three Huguenot leaders replied that they were still loyal to their King and wanted only to deliver the country from its present troubles. Time for talk had passed; on 10 November the seventy-four-year-old Constable rode out of Paris at the head of the King's 16,000-strong army. Charles had made an impetuous attempt to lead a body of troops himself but had been restrained by Montmorency. Holding the bridle of the King's horse, he said, 'Sire, this is not how Your Majesty should risk his person; it is too dear to us and we would require at least ten thousand cavalrymen to accompany you.'8 Frustrated, Charles turned back and at three o'clock in the afternoon battle was joined outside the Porte Saint-Denis.

A sweeping and courageous cavalry charge by Condé nearly won the day, but was repulsed by the royal troops and by nightfall the Huguenot army had quitted the field. During the battle the Constable received a mortal wound: having endured several blows to the face and head, an arquebus shot in the back left him dying in agony. Carried back into the city and after much suffering, the doughty old man died on 12 November. Catherine and the King ordered a funeral with such honours that it could almost have been mistaken for a royal interment. Montmorency was finally laid to rest at Saint-Denis near the tomb of Henry II, the king he had loved and served so faithfully.

Having lost the Constable, Catherine, blind to public reaction and to common sense, announced that her adored son Henri of Anjou had been made Lieutenant-General and now commanded the army. Only sixteen years old, hitherto petted and surrounded by the Queen Mother and her women, living a cosseted life to protect his health, given specially warmed rooms, kept out of drafts and generally pandered to, he hardly presented a confidence-inspiring military leader, nor were the men she picked as his military advisers. These were the Duke of Nemours (recently married to the widowed Duchess of Guise), the Duke de Montpensier, whose Catholic zealotry was directly proportionate to his lack of military experience, and Artus de Cossé, the Royal Secretary of Finance. The parlous state of the treasury provided no source of comfort if it reflected his strategic and military abilities, though by creating him a Marshal of France it was perhaps hoped that he would find the inspiration that had hitherto evaded him. To complicate matters further, the relationship between Cossé and Montpensier could, at best, be described as one of intense mutual dislike. Catherine's appointments reflected political rather than primarily military considerations. Conducting warfare by committee is always a risky undertaking, but when the committee was composed of feuding inadequates led by an effete teenager the risk seemed near-suicidal.

Condé had withdrawn towards the east and eventually joined his forces with those of a large contingent of German *Reiters* (hired troops from Protestant princes) who had come to his aid. Just before Christmas 1567 Catherine summoned Alava and asked him to join her for a walk in the gardens of the Tuileries where building had started on a new palace. Catherine excused her son's military incompetence by blaming his youth, but Alava replied uncompromisingly. Why blame her son's youth, he asked, when she had chosen idiots as his chief commanders? Cossé was a nobody, Nemours was too love-struck to think of war and Montpensier was a fool. Alava strongly advocated that the Queen Mother appoint Tavannes, a great and loyal soldier who would not flinch from doing his duty. In January 1568 Catherine set out for Anjou's headquarters at Châlons-sur-Marne. The disarray at the camp was palpable; had it not been for the arguments between two senior officers, who preferred to arrange a private quarrel between themselves before taking up arms, the German *Reiters* might have been prevented from uniting with the enemy. Furthermore, with the army chiefs unable to agree on a course of action, the Queen found her son and his commanders in hopeless chaos. She therefore placed Tavannes at the head of the vanguard of the army and it was decided they should proceed to Troyes to try to stop the Huguenots from capturing the heartlands of France.

Catherine's visit hid a secret mission, for she also planned to meet Châtillon, who represented the rebels, to attempt to seek a formula that would end the war. She returned to Paris on 15 January 1568 and Châtillon followed two days later under a secret royal safe conduct, staying at the Château of Vincennes just outside the city. Yet word had somehow leaked out that Catherine was in talks with the Huguenot rebels. The Parisians, who had been squeezed for money to help levy troops and keenly felt the effects of the rebels' blockade, were astounded that Catherine would consider anything less than the total obliteration of the enemy. Charles received offers of money by the citizens and by Philip II to continue the war. Walking with Charles one evening in the rue Saint-Denis, the Queen Mother lifted her *touret de nez* to say something to her son when an angry voice from the menacing crowd shouted, 'Sire! Do not believe her, for she never tells you the truth!' A scuffle followed, resulting in the royal guards beating the protesters. Catherine nevertheless continued her discussions with Châtillon and his advisers, under cover of night. Her efforts proved fruitless and the talks broke up without any agreement being reached.

Despite the bitterly cold winter of 1567–68 the Huguenots and the German *Reiters* made substantial advances, reaching Auxerre, and then marching onwards to take Beauce. In the face of the Protestants' spectacular progress, Anjou was forced to pull back his forces to Nogent-sur-Seine, and Paris once again lay open to the enemy. Charles, already angry at his brother's military command and his incompetence, declared that he himself would lead the royal army to victory, but Catherine refused to allow the King to expose himself to any such danger. Condé managed to reach Chartres in late February and laid siege to the city, but his campaign stopped there due to lack of money and supplies. During the war both sides had been pillaging the countryside, leaving the land ravaged and the peasants in a precarious state; now there remained nothing to live off. Condé sent out an urgent appeal to the King for talks, which he answered and which resulted in the Peace of Longjumeau, signed on 22–23 March 1568.

As usual, the peace treaty was unpopular with both sides. The King agreed to pay the German *Reiters* to get them off French soil, the Edict of Amboise was reinstated without restrictions, and in exchange the Huguenots were ordered to hand back towns they had taken during the short and chaotic Second War of Religion. The danger Condé ignored, but which alarmed Coligny, was that Charles would keep his army intact, leaving the Protestants vulnerable to a fresh attack. In the months that followed the so-called peace, the fighting and troubles continued and were considered by some to be much worse than the short war itself. Protestants refused to quit the towns they had taken; they killed priests, burned churches, destroyed religious statues and desecrated relics. Catholics immediately responded by murdering Protestants. The barbarity on both sides continued to grow; in just one of many horrific incidents a priest captured by angry Protestants was slashed, laid out and had his wounds repeatedly covered with vinegar and salt. He took eight days to die.

As the violence escalated it became clear that the Peace of Longjumeau could barely even be called a truce. One Protestant historian claimed that more Huguenots died during the period after the second civil war than during both the first two wars together.[9] By late April 1568, when Catherine called the King's Council, she no longer knew what to do. On 28 April she fell desperately ill with a high fever, suffering from agonising headaches, vomiting and pains to her right side. By 10 May, as Catherine started to bleed from her nose and mouth, the council began discussions about what to do in the event of her death. During these urgent council meetings Charles had been lost without his mother to guide him. True to form, Lorraine pressed for the most stringent measures of repression and punishment against the Huguenots. De L'Hôpital, equally true to form, advised further conciliation. Just as all hope seemed lost, Catherine's fever abated. Though the illness and sweating returned in the evening – her bedclothes had to be changed four or five times each night – she managed to do a little work during the day. By 24 May she sat propped up in bed dictating letters and sent one to Coligny about the theft of money intended to pay for the *Reiters*' departure. Charles's almost total paralysis without his mother beside him had been an alarming taste of what to expect if Catherine died.

Of the rash of political assassinations that followed the Treaty of Longjumeau, one commentator remarked,

> Since France has learned Italian fashion in murder, and the custom has grown of hiring assassins to cut throats as one might make a deal with a mason or a carpenter, it would be almost a novelty if several days were to pass without some crime of this sort, whereas formerly a man might not hear of a murder

more than ten times in his lifetime. We know that it was the ancient custom of France, and more religiously observed than anywhere else, to attack an enemy openly, never taking him unarmed or otherwise at a disadvantage, but always warning him giving him time to draw and considering it unfair to attack him two to one. Of all this I have heard the Italians make great sport.[10]

The blame for this was often laid, however unfairly, at the door of the Medici Queen and the Italian habits she had imported with her. There was a general sense that social order was disintegrating; what had begun as a religious struggle was turning into an anarchic, depraved free-for-all.

Catherine received a sombre letter from Coligny: 'I shall remind Your Majesty of what I have sometimes said before, that religious convictions cannot be removed by fire, nor by sword, and they consider themselves highly favoured who can employ their lives in the service of God.'[11] Catherine, unimpressed, replied, 'The King wishes justice to be done to all his subjects without discrimination ... I believe that his will would produce more effect if arms were not in the hands of those who should not have them rather than in his, which is why everyone resists and prevents him from being obeyed.'[12] At the same time as this exchange of letters, Condé withdrew with a large force to Picardy, allegedly swearing, 'As long as the Cardinal of Lorraine remains at Court the peace will not hold. I will fetch him and stain his gown red with his own blood.' The sullen and uneasy atmosphere meant that neither Catherine nor Charles went anywhere without a strong escort. Speaking during an audience with the Venetian ambassador, Giovanni Correro, she whispered, 'Who knows ... even in this room there may be people who would like to see deaths, and would kill us with their own hands. But God will not allow it for our cause is His and that of all Christianity.'[13] She also told him that according to astrological predictions, fortunes changed every seven years and that since her miseries had started seven years earlier she believed that her destiny might now improve with the stars.

A few weeks after this conversation French Protestant troops, led by the Sieur de Cocqueville, crossed Picardy heading for Flanders to join a force of their Dutch co-religionists. Catherine despatched Marshal de Cossé to intercept the rebels who were caught in time. Cocqueville was summarily executed and his head sent back to Paris, where it was stuck on a pike. The Dutch members of the rebel army fared little better, delivered by the French to Alba as prisoners, from whom they could expect only torture and death. Catherine was unusually sanguine – in both senses – about the fate of the rest of the captured French rebels: 'I think some of them should be punished by execution and the rest sent to the galleys.'[14] On hearing the news of the public beheading of Counts

Egmont and Horne in June (the latter a cousin of Coligny's), Catherine remarked to the Spanish ambassador that she considered it a 'holy decision' and hoped to be able to follow the same example in France with a leader of the Huguenots.[15] Accordingly, on 29 July 1568 Catherine ordered Tavannes and his men to capture Condé. She wanted, '*cette tête si chère*' (this valuable head).

A warning of the Queen Mother's intentions reached Condé and Coligny by an intercepted message which read 'The quarry is in the trap, she wishes the hunt to begin.' The pair set out at the end of August from Noyers with their families and followers for the stronghold of La Rochelle on the south-western coast of France. As they made their way across country towards their haven, the numbers of the Huguenot party of men, women and children grew until it was hailed as a modern 'Flight from Egypt of God's chosen people'. The Admiral wrote lyrically to the Queen Mother and the King on the subject, though he stressed that unarmed people fleeing to a safe haven could hardly be considered a rebellion. In early 1567 Jeanne d'Albret had fled France for her own Principality of Béarn with her son Henri of Navarre without Catherine's permission, who as a result called her 'the most shameless women in the world'. She had thus placed herself beyond the pale. On 24 September Jeanne and the fifteen-year-old Henri met the party and four days later the leaders of the Huguenot movement rode into La Rochelle at the head of their followers. Jeanne had brought with her substantial reinforcements and immediately set them to work strengthening the town against the expected royalist onslaught. She sent word to Catherine that this was a fight for 'the service of my God and of the true faith', 'the service of my King and the observance of the Edict of Pacification', and also nothing less than 'the right of blood'.[16]

As the economic situation in France deteriorated and the hatred born of the two civil wars of religion festered, the number of Huguenots grew. Calvin's efficient organisation of proselytising agents infiltrating France, combined with the Protestant printing presses, had spread the reformers' message throughout the country to increasingly receptive people of all classes. Calvin's doctrinal tenets had by now become enmeshed with the complex conflicting political agendas that sprang not only from the different powerful factions within the kingdom itself, but also from the fear that Spain might join with the French ultra-Catholics and attempt to annihilate the Protestants altogether. The Netherlands provided a salutary example as to how the Spanish suppressed religious dissidents.

Hearing the news of the escape of the Huguenot leaders and their likening themselves to Moses' followers' flight from Pharaonic tyranny, Catherine (particularly maddened by the biblical parallel) wrote that now her sole aim was to 'run them to earth, defeat them and destroy them before they can ... do something worse'.[17] Since early August she had been suffering not just the horrific spectacle of the kingdom sliding back into anarchy, but also of the King's failing health. Retiring with over 10,000 men for protection to the Château of Madrid in the Bois de Boulogne, Catherine had watched over her fever-racked son as he grew progressively weaker. Though she did not know it, he was reaching the later stages of tuberculosis and his bouts of illness would grow more frequent and more desperate. While caring for him she received word that Pius V had authorised a special levy from the French clergy to subsidise the coming war. This provoked the final schism between her and her moderate Chancellor Michel de L'Hôpital. He argued that by allowing the order to go forth Catherine could only expect to provoke the Protestants further. She was enraged by his continued policy of appeasement and the Chancellor – once Catherine's guide and even mentor – found himself isolated in the council and finally discredited. On 19 September 1568 he refused to seal the orders arising from the papal bull which allowed the alienation of church property to prepare for the war, at which the Cardinal of Lorraine entirely lost his usual composure and had to be physically prevented from assaulting de L'Hôpital. A few days later the Chancellor retired from the council, pleading old age, and withdrew to his estates, surrendering his seals of office before his departure.

By mid-August 1568 the King had made a slow recovery, returning to the council looking frail and thin. Catherine herself then fell ill with stomach problems. Throughout her life she was prey to such gastric attacks, though it is probable that these were largely self-inflicted due to simple greed. On one occasion she nearly died from eating too much *cibreo*, one of her favourite Florentine dishes, an irresistible concoction made from gizzards, testicles, offal and cockerels' coxcombs.[18] Once she and her son had recovered, the royal family left the Château of Madrid for Catherine's much-loved castle at Saint-Maur a short distance outside Paris. The atmosphere there was grim as the council prepared for war. Anjou was kicking his heels as he waited to lead the army to victory. Charles, who jealously longed to lead his armies himself, played mournful tunes on his horn, stopping only to spit the tubercular blood-flecked sputum from his mouth. Catherine, meanwhile, worked on her own opening salvo against the Huguenots in what was to be called the Declaration of Saint-Maur. This edict effectively revoked the concessions contained in the Treaty of Amboise and banned the practice of any religion in France save Catholicism.

Catherine became distracted with worry when the King fell ill again. An infection in his arm had taken hold after he had been inefficiently but routinely bled, whereupon a huge abscess developed and once again he suffered from high fevers. The physicians feared that he might not survive. Terrified that his arm would be crippled, the young King called his mother and brothers to his side at Saint-Maur. Prayers and Masses were said for his recuperation and salvation throughout Paris. Defying medical opinion – such as it was – Charles recovered sufficiently to lead the procession through the capital that traditionally preceded military expeditions. This culminated at Saint-Denis where the King symbolically placed his crown and sceptre under Divine protection until the war was won.

The Duke of Anjou, once again named Lieutenant-General, departed for Étampes where Catherine soon joined him. After soothing the usual heated discussions among the commanders, she returned to Paris where she supervised matters regarding supplies for the army. This work, once familiar to her as a kind of quartermaster-general for her husband's forces, provided a piquant reminder of a bygone era. Back then the French were fighting a foreign enemy; now they were fighting each other. No detail proved too small for the Queen Mother's attention, though she had much to distract her personally. Her daughter Elisabeth was expecting a child again and although only four and a half months pregnant she had gained an enormous amount of weight. On 18 October 1568 Catherine wrote to Philip begging him to ensure that Elisabeth 'eats but two meals each day and only bread in between meals'. She did not know it, but as she wrote that letter her daughter had already been dead for two weeks.[19]

The day after the courier left Paris for Spain with Catherine's dietary instructions there arrived another messenger bringing the grim tidings of Elisabeth's passing. She had died at midday on 3 October giving birth prematurely; the barely-formed infant girl died immediately and Elisabeth had expired a few hours later. A typically high-flown official bulletin of the news stated that the Queen had died 'in a most Christian manner ... dressed in the habit of Saint-François, preceded to heaven by the child she carried who had received the holy water of the sacred baptism'.[20] The news came first to the Cardinals of Lorraine and Bourbon who decided they would wait until the morning – the courier having arrived in the late afternoon – before telling the King and his mother. When they gave the sad communication to Charles he went immediately to Catherine to break the news to her before she heard it accidentally from a courtier, since word spread fast at Court. Those who saw the Queen Mother's shock found it agonising to witness. She withdrew from her councillors and attendants without a word, her face an impassive mask as she went alone to her private chapel.

Paradoxically, she and Elisabeth had only become intimate after her daughter had gone to Spain. Once there, Catherine had written frequently to the young Queen pouring out her joys and troubles by letter. In general Catherine had no gift for intimacy with her children unless they were far away, only then did she feel able to unfetter her emotions and express her love. To everyone's astonishment, a few hours after she had received the dreadful news, the Queen reappeared before the council, quite composed to swear that she would, despite her tragic loss, dedicate herself to the holy task of prosecuting the war against the Huguenots. She went on to amaze the council further by declaring that if the enemy believed that the death of Elisabeth would loosen French ties with Spain they would be sadly disappointed. 'King Philip will certainly remarry. I have but one wish and that is for my daughter Marguerite (Margot) to take the place of her sister.'[21] Catherine suppressed her genuine desolation at Elisabeth's death, for her duty to her late husband, his children and France always came before her own feelings. There is no doubt that she felt devastated at losing her beloved daughter with whom she enjoyed a close relationship, albeit by letter, yet this moment of self-control – denying herself the right to collapse – was to safeguard a higher cause: the future of the Valois dynasty. Catherine had almost always been mistress of her feelings.

Now liberated from the family connection with Catherine, Philip, who had loved Elisabeth and felt distraught at losing her, nonetheless made it clear that a marriage with Margot was out of the question. He held Catherine in contempt for her handling of the heretics; and he despised the French government's woolly compromises, for which he held the Queen Mother entirely responsible. He wanted to be left to grieve in peace and have nothing more said about a union with his sister-in-law. Shortly afterwards talk arose of Philip marrying the Holy Roman Emperor's eldest daughter, Anne. At the same time the Spanish suggested that Charles take the younger daughter Elisabeth as a bride, while Margot, instead, marry the King of Portugal. Appalled, Catherine wrote to her ambassador in Madrid, Fourquevaux, that only a marriage between Margot and Philip could keep the intimate union between France and Spain. All this occurred just as the Cardinal of Guise was in Madrid presenting his condolences to the grief-stricken Philip. Fortunately Catherine managed to overcome her obsession with matchmaking for her children and thought better of fighting that particular matrimonial battle now, realising how grotesquely tactless it was. At the end of her letter to Fourquevaux she enjoined him to burn it as soon as he had read it, an invocation that usually ensures the safe and careful filing of correspondence.

On 24 October a service of remembrance was held for the Spanish Queen. Charles broke with the tradition that the monarch should not attend any such ceremony and stood, dressed in violet, beside his mother in her usual black veils. The pain of the Queen Mother and the grief of the King were so evident that all those who saw them were moved. Yet time for mourning might prove an expensive luxury as the future of Catholicism in France and possibly the House of Valois itself were at stake. Catherine raised money from all possible sources, nor did she spare herself and, as so often before, she used her own personal assets for the welfare of her cause. She even pawned jewellery left to her by her illegitimate 'brother', the murdered and now long-dead Alessandro. Cosimo de Medici, Duke of Florence, eager to repatriate the gems, haggled over their value. Surrounded by feudal lords who thought only of themselves and their own interests, an army led by her inexperienced son of seventeen and a king too frail to leave for long, Catherine, unsurprisingly, felt exhausted.

A harsh winter prevented any decisive military engagements. One battle had had to be abandoned before it began because icy conditions prevented the cavalry from moving to new positions. The waiting brought talk of peace and compromise on the council, but Catherine reacted violently against any such suggestion. This time victory must be decisive. Alava found her tearful and tired when he came to Saint-Maur for an audience. She had just returned from a meeting of the council, which had gone on for far longer than was usual and had forced her to miss Mass, something she rarely did. 'I may well seem tired, as I have to carry the whole burden of government alone.' She told him, 'You would be very surprised if you knew what has just happened. I no longer know whom to trust. Those whom I believed to be wholly devoted to the service of the King, my son, have turned around and are opposing his wishes ... I am scandalised by the conduct of members of the council; they all want me to make peace.'[22] In another moment of self-pity, she later commented upon Elizabeth of England's good fortune that 'all the subjects share the Queen's religion; in France it's quite another matter'.[23] Elizabeth would have been delighted had Catherine's remark been true, but she too faced mounting problems in England where the old religion was still adhered to in large parts of the country, but it is nonetheless instructive about the Queen Mother's state of mind at the time.

Catherine continued her work, even paying off the Protestant Prince of Orange, who had brought a large force to aid the Huguenots, to leave France. This aroused furious protest from the Spanish ambassador, though for the government it had the desired effect since a substantial number of enemy troops quitted the kingdom. At Joinville, the Guise family seat, she found time to deal with family matters and asked the Dowager Duchess of Lorraine to enter into talks with the Emperor and to help obtain his consent to a marriage between Charles and his daughter Anne. She hoped for a reply from the Emperor Maximilian while at Metz on 22 February, where she inspected work on the fortifications, visited the citadel and walked the ramparts. As part of her general review she paid a call to a hospital – always a perilous business – and shortly afterwards fell ill with a high fever and pains down her right side.

Just as Catherine lay incapacitated and feverish, Anjou was about to engage in his first important battle. The night before it, Catherine lay half sleeping, half delirious. Believing their mother to be dying, Margot, Charles, François and the Duke and Duchess of Lorraine had gathered round her bed. Margot wrote in her memoirs, 'She cried out, still asleep, as though she could see the battle of Jarnac, "See how they run! My son is victorious. Ah! My God! Pick up my son he is on the ground! Look, look among the troops, the Prince de Condé is dead!" '[24] The following night the King, already asleep, awakened to receive the news of the victory at Jarnac. He went to his mother still wearing his nightgown with a robe covering his shoulders and roused Catherine to tell her of the battle. It was just as she had dreamt it. Catherine could not contain her joy; Anjou, her favourite son, was victorious and vindicated. Te Deums were sung and church bells rung throughout Metz, and the Queen Mother made a good, if slow, recovery.

The battle of Jarnac, situated near Cognac, was notable, apart from being a royalist victory against the Huguenots, for the death of their leader Louis de Condé. The royal army, though nominally led by the Duke of Anjou, was de facto commanded by Catherine's trusty Marshal de Tavannes. On 13 March 1569, after the royalists had finally succeeded in engaging Coligny and his men in battle, Condé – who had injured his leg the night before – received an urgent summons to bring help to Coligny. According to the account of his death by the Huguenot soldier and scholar Agrippa d'Aubigné, Condé mounted his horse awkwardly and broke his injured leg so badly that the bone pierced the side of his boot. Despite this he cried out, 'To face danger for Christ is a blessing,' adding, 'Brave and noble Frenchmen, this is the moment we have waited for!'[25] He then galloped off at the head of a splendid though hopeless cavalry charge.

Coligny had already countermanded his request for help but the news did not reach Condé in time. When his horse was killed from under him, the prince could not get to his feet properly, weighed down by his armour and the pain of his broken limb. As he surrendered and lifted his visor, the two soldiers to whom he gave himself up, named d'Argens and M. de Saint-Jean, recognised him. D'Argens had fought at Angoulême with Condé where the prince had saved his life. Saint-Jean also knew him by sight. They advised him to keep his visor down if he valued his safety. The approaching guard of the Duke of Anjou, led by a Captain Montesquiou, spotted the prince and shouted, 'Kill! Kill!' At this Condé turned, saying, 'You cannot save me, d'Argens.' At that instant Montesquiou shot Condé in the back of the neck, the bullet exiting from his right eye.

Anjou savoured the death of his princely relative. His men tied Condé's body to a mule and paraded it around to shouts and jeers of the engaging ditty: 'He who avoids the Mass, now is tied to an ass'. Such behaviour was worlds away from the chivalric traditions that had been so highly valued by Anjou's father. In stark contrast, when François, Duke of Guise had taken Condé prisoner after the battle of Dreux, he had invited him to stay with him and the pair dined together. Now, asked what to do with a crowd of other captives nearby, Anjou is alleged to have ordered, 'Slay them!' He left this task to the Swiss mercenaries. Such conduct on the field of battle demonstrates clearly how the usual courtesies and traditions of knightly conduct had been entirely replaced by the passion for vengeance, as a result of the appalling acts each side had committed against the other since the first religious civil war. It is a truism that civil wars and wars of religion tend to produce the worst atrocities; how much the more ghastly, therefore, were France's civil wars of religion.

Anjou paid a brief visit to his family and proudly announced his victory to Charles, who looked hot with jealousy at his brother's 'glory' in the field. Henri using a pun on the town of Meaux where Condé had tried to kidnap the royal family, announced to his brother, 'Monseigneur, you have won the battle. The Prince de Condé is dead. I have seen his body. Alas the poor man had caused us *tant de maux* [so much trouble].'

Admiral de Coligny – who had hitherto been the true strategic and military commander of the Huguenots behind Condé, the active figurehead with the lustre of royal legitimacy – now stood alone as the head of the party in matters of policy, inspiration and military strategy. He became the protector of the two fatherless Huguenot princes, Henri of Navarre, the sixteen-year-old First Prince of the Blood, and Condé's fifteen-year-old son, also named Henri. Jeanne d'Albret led the boys out before the Huguenot troops who hailed the princes as their nominal leaders, backed by their military hero, the wise, courageous and morally gleaming Gaspard de Coligny. The Catholics knew he presented a formidable enemy. Untainted by scandal, greed or any of the usual vices, he was a leader who inspired near-veneration among his Huguenot followers.

While Anjou paid his short visit to Court he took particular care to flatter Margot, Catherine's youngest daughter, who had only come to live there with her brother François the previous year. Since leaving the royal nursery at Amboise she had grown close to Charles and he worshipped her. She knew how to calm his temper tantrums and soon became his companion and friend. The lonely King had found someone with whom he could share his secrets. By contrast Catherine barely addressed a word to Margot; she still seemed to resent her evident health, lovely face and high spirits, only speaking to her daughter when issuing an order or a reprimand. In her memoirs the princess remembered trembling when summoned by her mother. Anjou decided that he must make good use of Margot – still innocent and trusting – to help him keep command of the army, as the King openly talked of leading the troops himself. He wanted her to keep him abreast of any important developments while he was away campaigning.

Margot was in raptures to have the confidence of her glamorous brother, who told her that she had always been his favourite sibling. This closeness must now be turned to their advantage: 'It was good for our childhood,' he told her, 'but we are no longer children.'[26] He added, 'I know no one as fit as you, whom I consider my second self. You have all the requisite qualities: judgement, and intelligence and fidelity.'[27] He insisted that she attend the *lever* and *coucher* of their mother whenever possible and accompany her wherever she went, knowing well that all the ultimate political decisions were made there. Anjou confided that 'he would elect a cruel death' rather than lose command of the army and he promised that she would win their mother's approval if she aided him in this way. He encouraged his sister to 'Forget your timidity and speak to her confidentially. ... It will be a great joy and honour for you to be loved by her. You will do much for yourself and for me; and I shall owe you, after God, the preservation of my good fortune.'[28] He also fostered the hope in Margot that Catherine would come to treat her daughter quite differently if she followed Anjou's instructions.

Shortly afterwards Catherine spoke to Margot about all that Anjou had said and told her, 'Your brother has told me of your conversation, he no longer considers you a child. It will be a great pleasure for me to talk to you as I would to your brother. Wait upon me, do not fear to speak to me freely, I wish it.'[29] Margot later recalled, 'Such language was new to me, for until then I had lived aimlessly, with no thought of anything but dancing or hunting ... for I was not yet old enough for such ambition and I had been brought up in such dread of my mother that not only did I not venture to speak to her, but I died when she looked at me, for fear I had done something to displease her.' Now she felt 'a happiness so unbounded that it seemed to me as if all the pleasure I had known until then had been merely the shadow of this, and I looked upon the past disdainfully'. It was the unlucky princess's initiation into political and Court intrigues, a bent for which she soon developed about as much talent as her former sister-in-law, Mary, Queen of Scots.

On 7 April 1569 the Spanish ambassador received an audience with the still bedridden Queen Mother. The conversation that took place that day provided the basis for Catherine's later reputation as 'The Black

Queen', a scheming poisoner and a murderer. The ambassador reported his suggestion to the Queen Mother that the time had come for *la sonoria*. This expression means the 'death knell', although in this context he would probably have meant the assassination of the chief rebels, Coligny, his brother d'Andelot and the leading Protestant nobleman François III de La Rochefoucauld. Allegedly Catherine replied that she had thought of the very same solution seven years earlier at the start of the troubles. She added that not a day had passed without the regret that she had not taken these extreme measures at the time. She had, however, put a considerable price on the heads – dead or alive – of Coligny, d'Andelot and La Rochefoucauld only three days earlier. The offers of 50,000 écus for Coligny, 20,000 for d'Andelot and 30,000 for La Rochefoucauld were large enough to tempt would-be assassins.

On 7 May 1569 d'Andelot died at Saintes, probably of poison since Coligny and La Rochfoucauld fell seriously ill at the same time. Coligny was so sick that word of his death abounded; too weak to walk he had himself carried about in a litter, mingling with the public to quash the rumours. When Catherine heard the news she wrote to Fourquevaux, 'We greatly rejoiced over the news of d'Andelot's death ... I hope that God will mete out to the others the treatment they deserve.'[30] Cardinal de Châtillon, Coligny's surviving brother, escaped to England where he wrote to Frederick III, the Elector-Palatine, denouncing the Queen Mother as responsible for exacting vengeance, the traditional preserve of the Almighty. He accused Catherine of poisoning his brother, d'Andelot, and explained that not only had the post-mortem borne this out but a young Florentine who claimed responsibility for these crimes had also bragged at making the Admiral and his brother drink from the same cup. Châtillon claimed that the Italian was even then petitioning the King for his reward.

A rumour now circulated about a scented apple that the Queen Mother had supposedly ordered as a gift for Condé at the start of the religious troubles. When the apple arrived from her infamous *parfumier* Maître René, the prince's surgeon, Le Cros, happened to be present. His suspicions aroused, he took the apple and held it to his nose to smell it. Immediately his nostrils became red and inflamed. Shaving a small piece of the fruit into his dog's food, he mixed it up and as soon as the dog ate a mouthful it dropped dead. Whether this particular story is true or not, we can be certain that by now Catherine had resorted to some sinister and highly unusual practices to dispatch her enemies.

Alava reported to Spain that in January Catherine had been approached by an Italian sorcerer who worked in a squalid place known as the 'Vallée de Misère' on the Quai de Mégisserie in Paris. He promised to rid the Queen Mother of her chief enemies and she decided to hire him. His instructions were to cast lethal spells on Condé, Coligny and d'Andelot that would kill them. A metal worker arrived from Strasbourg to cast three bronze effigies of the intended victims. These were the same height and size as the three men and were cast standing up, with their faces looking upwards. Each one had very long hair dressed to stand up on end. A complex set of screws implanted into the effigies allowed their limbs to move and their chests and heads be opened up. Each day, locked away in his frightful workshop, the Italian cast horoscopes for his three victims and adjusted the screws accordingly. Sure enough, when they died both Condé's and d'Andelot's bodies reportedly had strange marks upon them that did not seem to relate to their overt causes of death. At the time it was thought that the poison had caused old wounds of d'Andelot's to flare up; Condé's marks apparently left those who saw them baffled. Yet whatever supernatural powers Catherine's sorcerer might have conjured up, Coligny seemed protected and continued to trouble the kingdom. By July, after complaints from the Queen Mother, the Italian blamed his failure to kill the Admiral on his star that was now too high and powerful, adding that he would need no fewer than seventeen such effigies of Coligny to have the desired effect.

In August a report reached Philip from Alava which told of another attempt on Coligny's life. He had met a German who had recently come from Coligny's camp and after bragging about how much he knew of the Admiral's daily routine he talked of a plot to kill Coligny. When Alava spoke to the King and his mother they asked him to beg the German to keep silent and merely told the ambassador to await good news. Sir Henry Norris, the English ambassador, also wrote of a German named Hajiz who had been paid to poison the Admiral. A few weeks later French Protestants arrested a man named Dominique d'Albe. Travelling with a *laissez-passer* from Anjou, he nevertheless claimed to be a servant of Coligny's and a search of his belongings revealed a sachet of powder hidden in his clothes that turned out to be poison. D'Albe was tried and hanged on 20 September 1569.[31] There can be little doubt that Catherine was taking great pains to rid herself of Coligny by any means possible, though without success.

Anjou and the War Council now desperately needed Catherine's presence. The Huguenots had the support of various German Protestant princes and their armies. The Duke of Bavaria, the Duke of Zweibrücken and the Flemish prince Louis of Nassau were facing a royalist army of French Catholics, Swiss mercenaries, Walloons financed by Spain, Italians from Rome and Tuscany, and soldiers led by the Margrave of Baden and Count Ernst de Mansfelt. The sides were numerically fairly evenly matched by the autumn of 1569, with the royalists holding a slight advantage. Despite this the royalist troops felt that their victory at Jarnac had been wasted and were angry that the armies of the foreign Protestant princes had successfully joined forces due to blunders by Charles's commanders. Unfortunately the Duke of Zweibrücken, a corpulent bon viveur, died before he had the pleasure of seeing his troops link up with their Protestant allies. The Marshal de Tavannes said his death was due to drinking 'the wine of Avalon', wine apparently poisoned by a village doctor and captured by the duke's men. More likely, however, he died simply from drink. Catherine, always ready to see the hand of God in everything, rejoiced at her enemy's death and wrote to the King, 'You see, my son, how God helps you more than any man, and kills your enemy without even striking a blow.'[32] During the summer of 1569 Catherine travelled to the front, watched minor engagements, reviewed the troops, helped raise further men and generally stiffened the resolve and morale of the royalists' often lacklustre leadership.

In July 1569 the King passed an edict confiscating all Huguenot property and assets, and on 13 September Coligny was condemned to death *in absentia* for the crime of *lèse-majesté*. The execution would take place at the Place de Grève when finally they captured him. Stripped of his honours, titles and estates, the Admiral suffered the immediate seizure and sale of his goods and properties. For the time being, however, the crowd had to make do with an effigy that hung in the Place de Grève. The man himself was proving highly resilient and difficult to capture or kill. The Huguenots, having generally enjoyed the advantage throughout the summer, decided despite Coligny's original reservations to lay siege to Poitiers on 14 July. By clever diversionary tactics, on 5 September Anjou managed to lift the siege. Despite his age he was quickly learning the art of warfare.

On 3 October 1569, on the advice of Tavannes, Anjou engaged the enemy in battle near Moncontour, north-west of Poitiers. The Huguenots wore white surcoats – with yellow and black armbands in memory of the late Duke of Zweibrücken. The King's men fought in the traditional surcoats emblazoned with the white cross of the Crusaders and royal shoulder sashes of red. Before the action Tavannes climbed to a spot from which he could see the disposition of the enemy army. Such was his confidence that upon his return he declared to Anjou, 'Monseigneur, with the help of God, we shall have them. I will never more take up arms again if we do not fight and vanquish today. Let us march! In the name of God!'[33]

At about three o'clock in the afternoon Montpensier received the order to attack. The Swiss soldiers, by custom, kissed the ground and a blast of trumpets gave the usual signal to prepare. Alerted, the Huguenot army responded by singing psalms as they too readied themselves. During the action Tavannes skilfully outflanked Coligny and forced him to change the disposition of his troops. Despite a brave cavalry charge the Huguenot forces could not break the royalist line and the Admiral, badly wounded by a shot in the face, passed the command to Louis of Nassau. The prince rallied the Huguenot cavalry once more and made a last desperate attack on the royal troops. In the midst of the action, Anjou was knocked off his horse; his bodyguard, led by François de Carnavalet, surrounded him as he remounted and eventually the enemy horsemen were forced off the field. At dusk in the mist the screams of the many Huguenot soldiers left behind could be heard begging and protesting for their lives, shouting that they were '*bons papistes*' before they had their throats slit. It is thought that as many as 15,000 French Protestant soldiers were put to death that night. Many old scores were settled.

Coligny and the still substantial Huguenot army – his cavalry had remained virtually intact though he had lost most of his infantry – withdrew, leaving a series of strongholds that would block the approaches to La Rochelle. The first was Saint-Jean-d'Angély, south-east of the Huguenots' citadel. Coligny continued further south to recover and recruit reinforcements with which he hoped he would soon return. Tavannes had sensibly urged immediate pursuit and destruction of the Huguenots, but the arrival of the King, anxious to share and participate in Anjou's military glory, meant a change of tactics. Charles insisted that the strongholds be taken instead of being bypassed. Thus, as the second winter of the war set in, there was no prospect of an early end to the fighting.

On 9 October, shortly after the battle of Moncontour, a close friend and senior captain of Coligny's named the Seigneur de Mouy was shot in the back and killed by Charles de Louviers, Seigneur de Maurevert. This young nobleman, originally a client of the Guise family, had gained access to the Huguenot leadership by presenting himself as a victim of his former patrons and had been greatly helped by the warm welcome extended to him by de Mouy who had once been his tutor. Maurevert's goal had been to assassinate the Admiral but lacking an opportunity he had killed de Mouy instead. Maurevert presented himself proudly at the royalist camp where most regarded him with great disgust for shooting his trusting former tutor in the back, though Anjou received him with pleasure. The King ordered that the killer receive an 'honourable gift' and awarded him with nothing less than the *collier* of the Order of Saint-Michel. Maurevert would later be known to history as '*le tueur du roi*' (the King's killer).

The siege of Saint-Jean-d'Angély proved long and arduous. The royal finances were in a parlous state and morale among the men was low. By contrast the Huguenots appeared defiantly buoyant despite the defeat at Montcontour. As was her wont, Catherine opened peace talks during the siege. The discord in the royalist camp grew as the latent rivalry between the King and Anjou simmered barely under control, and Catherine had further to contend with jealousy between Monluc and Montmorency-Damville, her two southern commanders.[34] Exhausted, she wrote to her ambassador in Madrid, 'Please make the Catholic King, my good son, believe that extreme necessity has obliged us to take the path of pacification rather than that of force.'[35] Of course the news appalled Philip who threw every obstacle he could into Catherine's path.

Jeanne d'Albret featured prominently in the peace talks but she considered the royalists' approaches with caution and mistrust, writing, 'A peace made of snow this winter that would melt in next summer's heat' was not worth the bother. She rejected Catherine's offer of peace with freedom of conscience, insisting that absolute freedom of worship must form part of any lasting agreement. She appealed to the Queen Mother: 'I can scarcely persuade myself having once had the honour of knowing Your Majesty's sentiments intimately that you could wish to see us reduced to such an extremity or to profess ourselves of no religion whatever ... We have come to the determination to die, all of us, rather than abandon our God, the which we cannot maintain unless permitted to worship publicly, any more than a human body can live without meat or drink.'[36]

During talks in April 1570 between Coligny's brother-in-law, Charles de Téligny, and the council, the King became so enraged by fresh Protestant demands that with one hand on his dagger and the other clenched into a fist he lunged at the astonished emissary, who was only saved from being stabbed by the quick reaction of those around Charles IX forcibly holding him back. Coligny meanwhile continued to enjoy a military progress towards Paris. Catherine felt embattled as Jeanne d'Albret accused the 'black-hearted' Cardinal of Lorraine of sabotaging peace prospects and claimed that his spies had been caught carrying evidence that he had hired three assassins to kill her son Henri of Navarre, her nephew Henri de Condé, and Coligny. It seems highly unlikely that the cardinal would have acted without Catherine's agreement. Jeanne stopped short, however, of actually accusing the Queen Mother of complicity in the supposed plot. Philip of Spain pushed Catherine a step further towards peace and away from Spanish influence by marrying the Emperor's eldest daughter, Anne, who the Queen Mother had hoped would make a fine bride for Charles. Not content with this, Philip also brought strong pressure to bear upon the Portuguese to prevent the young King Don Sebastian from marrying Margot.

Margot's marriage featured prominently in the peace talks, but not a union with Don Sebastian. The groom now proposed for her was Henri of Navarre, the Bourbon prince. This would unite the senior and junior branches of the royal family and also act as a beacon of hope for future peace in the kingdom. After all, the marriage of Elizabeth of York to Henry Tudor had finally brought an end to the English Wars of the Roses and perhaps the same remedy would work in France. The match held the added and intriguing possibility that should Henri de Bourbon inherit the throne of France, the blood of the Valois and Medici dynasties would continue to live and rule through his offspring with Margot. The Cardinal of Lorraine had other plans, however. He had been somewhat unrealistically promoting a marriage between Margot and his young nephew, Henri, Duke of Guise; he also nursed now increasingly remote hopes of a marriage between his niece Mary, Queen of Scots and Charles or his brother Anjou. Since Mary's flight to England and effective imprisonment in 1568 this plan had suffered a considerable setback; in consequence he looked upon the young duke and Margot as his most promising matrimonial venture.

The cardinal's plans flourished thanks to the seventeen-year-old Margot's genuine attraction to Henri of Guise. The couple flirted and corresponded, but unfortunately for them their letters fell into the wrong hands. Anjou, whose almost feline sensitivity had aroused his suspicions of a growing closeness between the couple, was told of the correspondence. He felt personally betrayed, his close relationship with Margot being compromised by his friend and rival Guise. Having only recently made her his confidante at Court, his sense of affront was immense. He quickly and spitefully passed the news – probably with some elegantly embroidered additions – on to his brother who he knew felt an unusual attachment to Margot. According to Alava's cheerful report to Philip in Madrid, on 25 June at five o'clock in the morning Charles appeared in his mother's room wearing only a nightshirt and raged about his sister's clandestine romance. Some sources claim that Henri of Guise barely escaped being caught in the princess's bed, only saving himself from discovery by climbing from a window, but this is improbable as the despoliation of the King's virgin sister would have constituted high treason and Guise is unlikely to have risked a death sentence despite his enormous ambitions.

Catherine's fury was prodigious and she summoned Margot instantly to her room with her governess. When the terrified girl came into the presence of her mother and the King, the pair fell upon her, beating and punching her, and pulling out handfuls of hair. Trying desperately to defend herself, Margot's nightdress was torn to shreds. Eventually, their fury abated, Charles and Catherine left the wretched girl alone, battered and contused. Charles sent out an order for his bastard brother Angoulême to seize Guise and have him killed. Catherine, realising that Margot must not be seen in such a shocking state, gave her daughter a fresh nightgown, spending over an hour trying to comb her hair and disguise the marks of their blows. Guise received warning of what had happened and managed to save himself by making an immediate announcement of his engagement to Catherine of Clèves, the recently widowed Princesse de Porcien.

There were deep political repercussions from these family dramas. Catherine's dreams for Margot and her sons to make matches worthy of their dynasty and position were a driving element in her desire for peace. The Guise family, disgraced for having so nearly undone her daughter's reputation, wisely left Court for their estates. The chance absence of the hawkish Cardinal of Lorraine thus facilitated a conclusion to the peace talks. On 29 July Coligny brought the prospect of agreement closer by writing to Catherine, 'When Your Majesty will study all my actions since first she knew me until now, she will admit that I am quite different from the portrait that has been painted of me. I beg you, Madam, to believe that you have no more devoted servant than I have been and have wanted to be.'[37] Catherine sent out an invitation for Coligny to come to Court, which he declined. A few days later, on 5 August, the King's Council met three times, the third meeting not ending before eleven o'clock at night.

Catherine worked tirelessly to find a solution acceptable to all. The result was the Treaty of Saint-Germain of 8 August 1570. Its main terms largely mirrored the Peace of Amboise of 1563: it allowed freedom of conscience and freedom of worship with restrictions as to location. La Rochelle, Cognac, Montauban and La Charité were granted as *places de sûreté*, in addition goods and properties seized during the civil war were to be restored. There was to be no discrimination against Huguenots regarding universities, schools or hospitals to which they were to enjoy the same access as other citizens. Once again both sides greeted this enlightened treaty with little enthusiasm. The Catholics grumbled that they were giving away more than was needed, while the Protestants thought that they were not being given enough.

Charles solemnly commanded his councillors to swear adherence to the treaty's terms and Catherine wrote, 'I am glad that my son is now old enough to see that he is better obeyed than in the past,' although she was careful to add, 'I will help him with my counsels and with all my power; I will assist him in enforcing the terms which he has conceded, as I have always wanted to see the kingdom restored to the state it was in under his royal predecessors.'[38] The Queen Mother was underscoring her determination to continue holding on to the reins of power, notwithstanding Charles's increasing maturity and desire to form his opinions independently. Though physically feeble and prey to attacks of ill health, he had begun to grow in confidence as a man and a king.

The Treaty of Saint-Germain has long been the subject of controversy. It is hard to say how much faith Catherine truly placed in the peace and its concessions. It is clear from her behaviour since the '*Surprise de Meaux*' that she was ready to take whatever steps she considered necessary to rid herself of her enemies including her 'regalian right of summary execution' and going to the other extreme of resorting to the alleged powers of the black arts. After three increasingly bitter civil wars she had learned through experience that the two religions could not coexist peacefully in France. She had also learned that her truest efforts at conciliation aroused nothing but mistrust from both Catholics and Protestants.

War brought only ruin to France and peace had thus far only come as a result of exhaustion on both sides, not outright victory. It is probable that Catherine – Florentine to her core – understood that peace, however temporary, would give her time to form a policy for the future. With that in mind she would present her habitual conciliatory face as she watched carefully for future opportunities to heal the wounded kingdom and bring it back under full control of the House of Valois. Catherine had always regarded time as her ally. The Treaty of Saint-Germain proved her right.

ELEVEN

Margot's Marriage Is Arranged

I would prefer to see him become a Huguenot than
to see him endanger his life in this way

1570–72

Once the Treaty of Saint-Germain had been signed, the Queen Mother could indulge in her favourite pastime, making grand matrimonial matches for her children. Despite Philip's anger at what he considered the capitulation of Saint-Germain – which prompted the typically smug remark from him – 'The King and the Queen will finish by losing everything, but at least I shall have the satisfaction of having always assisted them with our advice' – he no longer stood in the way of the marriage between Charles and the Emperor's younger daughter Elisabeth. Now Philip blessed the proposed alliance between Margot and King Sebastian of Portugal, and encouraged the resurrection of the negotiations. Unfortunately, the Portuguese King, who had been brought up clinging to the skirts of his domineering grandmother, appeared to be more interested in reading Thomas Aquinas, a volume of which he carried attached to a belt round his slender waist.

Tall, slim and blond, the King never ventured anywhere without his two constant companions, monks of the Theatine order intent on preserving their King's innocence. If anyone tried to approach him he would run and hide with these beloved clerics until the visitor had gone. To Catherine's indignation this monk manqué declared himself unimpressed with the suppression of the Huguenots in France and preferred to wait and see how matters evolved before making any matrimonial decision. Philip hoped that two such alliances with Portugal and the Habsburgs might help keep the troublesome Catherine and her brood firmly in the ultra-Catholic camp. Unsurprisingly, these plans made the Protestants uneasy and they consequently put forward their own suggestions. A marriage between Henri of Navarre and Margot had already been briefly considered during the early stages of the recent peace negotiations; indeed, some said the union formed a secret clause in the treaty. As Margot's nuptial future was considered she charmed the gentlemen at Court with her high spirits and youthful beauty, turning not only the head of the Duke of Guise, but also, inadvertently as she later claimed, those of her own brothers.[1]

A brilliant and tempting bride was now proposed for Anjou. The Cardinal de Châtillon and the Vidame of Chartres – a senior member of the Bourbon family and a Protestant – had fled France and were then living at the English Court. They confirmed that Queen Elizabeth of England would welcome discussions of a possible marriage with Catherine's favourite son. Catherine feverishly brushed aside any talk of their age difference – Elizabeth was thirty-seven years old and Anjou nineteen at the time – and the prickly issue of religion. Marriage with a heretic (if she was the Queen of England) presented no problems that could not be easily overcome in Catherine's ambitious maternal breast. The Queen Mother's head buzzed with the possibilities the match afforded when Anjou put a rude end to his mother's daydreams. Unaccustomedly perching himself on high moral ground, he told her that he found it unacceptable to take an illegitimate heretic as a bride, sovereign or not, let alone one who had dallied with such a number of admirers. Elizabeth's relationship with the Earl of Leicester had caused no end of ribald jokes at the French Court and Anjou made it clear he would not countenance a marriage with, as he put it, a *'putain publique'* (a public whore). He also referred to what Lady Cobham, one of the Queen's women, called the 'inequality of age'; he mocked the limp he had heard Elizabeth suffered from due to a varicose vein, calling her an 'old creature with a sore leg'.[2] This and other impertinent remarks made their way back to the English Queen who, infuriated, henceforth danced with particularly athletic vigour whenever the French ambassador was present.

Elizabeth, in any case, had only ever intended to embark upon a long diplomatic courtship that would send Spain into a frenzy of worry and end with her guarding her 'stale virginity'. So she strung out the ritual exchange of portraits, letters and talks with special emissaries for a whole year. Charles, who would have been delighted to see his brother exiled to England, denounced Anjou's priggishness, saying of the huge pension secretly paid to his brother by the Church, 'You speak of your conscience, there is another motive which you do not mention – the large sum of money – to keep you here as the champion of the Catholic cause. Let me tell you that I recognise no champion but myself ... as for those who meddle in these intrigues, I shall shorten some of them by a head if necessary.'[3] Charles could not abide the reputation his brother had acquired on the battlefield as a hero for the Catholic cause, while he had had to bear the odium of concluding unpopular peace treaties loaded with concessions.

After Jarnac and Moncontour the court poets had busied themselves praising the King as the suppressor of heretics and a modern Crusader. He angrily refused their garlands, calling them 'a mass of lies and flatteries.

I have done nothing yet worth mentioning. Keep your fine phrases ... for my brother. He affords fresh themes for your Muses every day.'[4] On another occasion he was heard to say, 'My mother loves him so much that she steals the honour due to me for him. I wish that we might take it in turn to reign, or at least that I might have his place for a half-year.'[5] The King grew increasingly hostile and uncontrollable over Anjou, and Catherine became fearful lest the King should one day harm his brother. Despite his mother's pleading and weeping 'hot tears', Anjou refused to budge over the marriage with Elizabeth. Catherine, without a blush, eventually exchanged him as a bridegroom with her youngest son, the fifteen-year-old pock-marked hunchback, François, Duke d'Alençon, as a possible husband for the Queen of England. Elizabeth, equally unblushing, recommenced the marriage ritual with all its attendant diplomatic foreplay.

On 25 November 1570 Charles's bride, Elisabeth of Austria, arrived at Mézières, a small frontier town at the edge of her father's empire. The groom and his brother Anjou had already greeted the young archduchess at Sedan where she came accompanied by a huge entourage of German nobles. Catherine, determined that the wedding should be splendid, ignored her war-ravaged treasury by raising money from the clergy and levying a special tax on cloth sales throughout the kingdom. An enthusiastic throng greeted Elisabeth as she entered Mézières in a gilded pink-and-white coach. They were enraptured by the white-skinned, blonde and beautiful princess, her loveliness enhanced by her astonishing innocence and naivety. Charles mingled incognito among the crowd as he watched his bride drive past.

Unbeknown to Elisabeth, Charles had a mistress in Paris named Marie Touchet, the daughter of a bourgeois Protestant of Flemish stock. He had decided that he loved Marie from their first encounter in Orléans in 1569 and had carried on a secret love affair for many months during that summer. A portrait of her by Clouet shows a girl with strawberry-blonde hair and a pretty round face. Charles entrusted his secret to Margot and asked her to take Marie into her household as one of her ladies. As the courtiers amused themselves during the summer evenings, the King's personal guard would, at his signal, play tambourines and pipes to create a noisy commotion, allowing him to escape to meet his love. One day he gave her a piece of paper upon which he had written *'Je charme tout'*. Marie asked what it meant and Margot explained that he had created an anagram from her name. When the Court returned to Paris, Catherine discovered the relationship and, after making enquiries about the girl, approved of the liaison with this country girl who harboured no aspirations to control Charles or detach him from her. The King's mistress was a world removed from Diane de Poitiers. In fact, she proved to be a benign influence upon the King and bore him a baby son, whom they named after his father, always known as 'Petit Charles'. He became a particular favourite among Catherine's grandchildren and was later given the title Duke of Angoulême. Petit Charles was notable among Catherine's descendants for his longevity. Having clearly inherited a strong constitution from his mother, he survived well into the reign of Louis XIV. Always conscious of being the son of a king, Petit Charles was nevertheless careful not to annoy Louis, who behaved courteously towards him but understandably considered Angoulême an insignificant relic of the past.

When Charles first received a portrait of Elisabeth of Austria his laconic comment was, 'At least she won't give me a headache.' Seeing her now so fresh and unspoiled touched him. Surrounded by painted and sophisticated courtiers, he longed to preserve her sweetness. To mark the joyous occasion of her son's marriage, Catherine made the unprecedented gesture of putting aside her habitual black dress for the ceremony and wore a gown of gold brocade and lace sparkling with diamonds and pearls. When Charles watched his bride approach him for the Nuptial Mass he seemed completely struck by her beauty. She wore a gown of silver embroidered with pearls, a purple cloak covered her shoulders decorated with the fleur-de-lys and upon her head sat a crown studded with emeralds, rubies and diamonds. Even the most critical French noblewomen had to admit that this ingenue looked ravishing. The morning after the wedding the bride, who spoke little French, seemed completely smitten with her husband and from that day forward devoted herself to his happiness. Worried that the wanton ways of the Court might shock the innocent new Queen, Catherine took great pains to protect her as far as possible from seeing too much too soon.

Elisabeth was a devout and conscientious girl who had been strictly brought up in Vienna. She attended Mass twice daily and spent many hours of the day at prayer. Her first and by no means last shock was the sight of members of Catherine's flying squadron at Mass taking the Sacrament in fits of giggles. Charles found the arrival of a wife did little to spoil his routine. His affair with Marie Touchet continued with barely an interruption. Eager for his wife to feel at home he kindly and gently taught her French ways and manners. He loved both his women and they took care of his needs between them. Anjou, unable to resist teasing and annoying his brother, also took it upon himself to initiate Elisabeth in the ways of the Court and paid her much flirtatious attention in front of an infuriated Charles. Anjou had recently adopted the habit of wearing vast pendant earrings, always made up of huge precious gems or pearls, so Charles responded by piercing the ears of fifty of his hunting companions with a needle and ordering them that henceforth they were to sport gold rings in their lobes. Just as suddenly he changed his mind and commanded that they remove these ridiculous adornments. Anjou

enjoyed baiting Charles in this kind of rivalry, showing the King that he
was the superior man and that the only thing he lacked was a crown.
Neither could know that he would eventually wear two.

During the wedding celebrations Catherine and Charles held secret
talks with the papal nuncio, Fabio Frangipani. Rumours abounded that
the Queen Mother had assured the nuncio that the recently arrived
Princess de Condé had been given a warm welcome as a prelude to
tempt other Huguenots back to Court. Many believed that the ultimate
goal was to entice Coligny and the two young Bourbon princes, Condé
and Navarre, into her web and to trap them there. The Archbishop of
Sens, Nicolas de Pellevé, told the nuncio that the Edict of Saint-Germain
had only been concluded to give the King and Queen Mother a chance
to rid themselves of the foreign soldiers fighting for the rebels, lull the
fears of the Protestants and then kill their chiefs. He added that there
were men who had already infiltrated the Huguenot high command with
orders to kill the senior officers by poison or steel.

With the King away on hunting expeditions, Catherine and her
daughter-in-law received congratulatory visits from foreign ambassadors
and princes. The main theme of the visiting notables was a plan to
vanquish the infidel Turks and form an alliance to fight a holy war.
Catherine and Charles resisted the persistent efforts to join a league
against the Turks, who were traditionally pro-French, and secretly sent
an emissary to the Sultan with a gift of a dozen particularly fine falcons
that he prized enormously.

In preparation for the magnificent official entry of the new Queen
into Paris, Catherine had frantically set about raising money from whatever
source she could; again she mortgaged and pawned her own possessions
in order to ensure a spectacular event. In January 1571, shortly before
her *entrée*, Elisabeth fell ill with bronchitis at the Château of Madrid in
the Bois de Boulogne, and Catherine and the King nursed her attentively.
Desperate to amuse his ailing bride, Charles ordered clowns and dancers
to entertain her. Once she recovered the King, Elisabeth, Margot and
Catherine decided to have some fun among the Parisian crowd. Disguised
as bourgeois they set out to enjoy a fair at Saint-Germain. Charles played
the coachman and wore a large hat to hide his face. Spotting one of his
courtiers riding along the street, he lashed his friend's shoulders with the
whip. Furious, the man turned and berated the impudent driver but just
as he was about to strike him, Charles took off his hat and everyone in
the party – especially the presumably highly relieved nobleman whose
smile might have been somewhat strained – roared with approval and
laughter. It was just the sort of rough joke that kings could revel in with
impunity. Having enjoyed the incognito visit to the fair, Charles decided
that he would go again, only this time he borrowed the robes of a

Carmelite monk and led a procession of friends similarly dressed. A scandalised Alava reported the sacrilegious behaviour to Philip, making as much of it as possible.

While Charles and his companions were enjoying themselves, Catherine had been trying to tempt Jeanne d'Albret and her son from La Rochelle to Paris. In January she had written to Jeanne saying she and the King wished to 'embrace the affairs of the Prince of Navarre whom the King and I infinitely desire to see here with you'.[6] Jeanne's reply came straight to the point: 'I am not enjoying the fruits of your edict in the majority of my strongholds, Lectoure, Villemur, Pamiers ... you can judge from this how well you are obeyed.'[7] If the King of Portugal remained uninterested by an alliance through marriage with Margot, Catherine's mind returned more and more to the idea of marrying her to Henri of Navarre. The couple's consanguinity and the fact that he was the nominal leader of the Huguenot party – yesterday's enemy – left Catherine untroubled. To achieve this union, however, she would require not only Jeanne's backing, but also a special dispensation from the Pope.

For the Queen of Navarre, the obstacles against the marriage were enormous. She did not trust Catherine and her schemes; she felt disgusted by the behaviour of the Court over which Catherine presided, and fearful of how it might corrupt her son who was proving all too weak when it came to the sins of the flesh. As a committed member of the new religion, she could not contemplate her beloved Henri falling into the papists' hands and possibly one day relinquishing his faith. An ambitious mother herself, Catherine knew that her strongest suit was to play on Jeanne's own aspirations for Henri. As First Prince of the Blood, there was much to be said on his side for uniting the junior and senior branches of the family. For the moment, however, clearly neither Jeanne nor Henri would be coming to Paris in the near future, so the Queen Mother must do without their presence at the forthcoming celebrations for Elisabeth's coronation and entrée.

On 6 March 1571 Charles made his formal entry into the capital. As both the bride and groom claimed descent from Charlemagne this theme was much played upon. Francion and Pharamond – the mythical creators of the both the French and German nations – were also glorified and depicted in magnificent sculptures. Catherine had employed some of the greatest artists and craftsmen of the day to ensure the splendour she wished the people to witness. She charged Pierre de Ronsard with commemorating the marriage in verse, Primaticcio's pupil, Nicolo dell' Abbate, painted the King and Queen and Germain Pilon, the sculptor who had made the superb marble urn that contained Henry II's heart, received the commission to create sculptures, temporary triumphal arches and other structures for the festivities.[8]

Catherine was portrayed as a goddess of antiquity holding a map of France; scattered about her were symbols of peace such as the lyre, a broken sword and two hearts entwined. This was a salute to Catherine as the author of the peace. Also surrounding the statue were four others from antiquity: one of these was Catherine's personal favourite, Queen Artemisia, wife of the Carian Satrap King Mausolus. The legend of her uxoriousness, both as a wife and a widow, was the one with which the Queen Mother most liked to be associated. According to the ancient legend, upon the cremation of Mausolus Artemisia took his ashes blended with wine and drank the mixture in a formal ceremony. This symbolised her devotion and fidelity to him, her body having become a living tomb for her husband. She also built him an actual tomb at Halicarnassus, so magnificent it gave us the word 'Mausoleum', which was one of the seven wonders of the Ancient World. Drinking the King's ashes also publicly legitimised Artemisia's regency and she continued to govern in his name for three years in the mid-fourth century BC. In 1562, soon after Francis II's death when Catherine effectively became regent of France, she had commissioned Nicolas Houel to write a history of Artemisia illustrated by Antoine Caron, which formed an iconography of her reign and her right to serve as regent.*

Charles's processional cortège stopped at Notre-Dame Cathedral where an *oraison* was sung followed by a huge banquet. On 11 March Charles gave a speech to the Parlement of Paris in which he paid eloquent homage to his mother. He told his listeners,

> After God, the Queen my mother is the person to whom I am most indebted. Her tenderness for me and for my people, her tireless work, energy and wisdom have assured the running of state affairs so well during a time when, because of my age I was unable to take charge of them myself, that even the tempests of civil war have been unable to harm my kingdom.[10]

This tribute had, of course, been orchestrated, like everything else in the celebrations, by the Queen Mother herself and it also contained the veiled message that she would continue to keep charge of state affairs, if always standing politely and tactfully a few paces behind her son. Despite the King's talk of his mother's success in guarding the kingdom during the civil wars, the unsurprising but glaring absence of the Huguenot princes and many other nobles holed up at La Rochelle was duly noted.

On 25 March 1571 Elisabeth was crowned at Saint-Denis, as Catherine had herself been over twenty years before. Her official entry into Paris followed four days later. Celebrating the theme of Franco–German

---

* Artemisia became a prototype for the future female regencies of Maria de Medici (1610–20) and Anne of Austria (1643–60).

friendship, the new Queen passed below arches emblazoned with Imperial eagles and fleur-de-lys. Much of the decoration and construction for the King's entry a few weeks before had been changed and rebuilt. A statue had also been created of Catherine placing a crown of fleur-de-lys upon her daughter-in-law's head, and one arch surmounted with a statue of Henry II bore the legend 'Protector of German Liberties' that alluded to his so-called 'Promenade to the Rhine' of 1552. Elisabeth enchanted the crowd in her litter of silver cloth. She wore a cloak of royal ermine studded with precious gems and decorated with fleur-de-lys. Her fabulous golden crown, covered in vast pearls, perfectly set off her blonde beauty to the great appreciation of the people. Flanked by her brothers-in-law Anjou and Alençon, who were almost as bejewelled as she, and followed by a splendid entourage, the new Queen enthralled Paris.

As the festivities in the capital gathered pace, a sombre marriage took place at La Rochelle. Amid the singing of psalms the black-clad Coligny married Mademoiselle d'Entremonts. Notwithstanding the general lack of adornment preferred by the Calvinists at even the most merry events, the Admiral's nuptials had been hit by exceptional gloom when the news arrived of the death at Canterbury of his last surviving brother, Cardinal Ôdet de Châtillon. Coligny felt the loss deeply; he was now the last of the three Châtillon brothers and Queen Elizabeth knew enough about the loathsome methods employed by her Continental cousins to place Châtillon's household under arrest, locking the servants into the dungeons as she ordered a post-mortem. Talk of poison received further fuel when the surgeons opened the cardinal's body: 'His liver and lungs were rotten and the stomach linings so eaten away that the skin bore a livid hue.' A few months later a young man was arrested for spying at La Rochelle. Before his execution he admitted to having poisoned the cardinal. It is hard to see Catherine's hand in this crime since Châtillon provided a channel for negotiating with Elizabeth at the English Court. Besides, killing Coligny's brother would hardly further her latest project of marrying Margot to Henri of Navarre. It is more likely that if there had been an assassination it would have been carried out by a Jesuit agent working with the Pope's benediction to kill leading Protestants, or perhaps a killer hired by the Guises who were continuing their vendetta against Coligny and his family for the murder of Duke François.

For some time Charles had become restless and he now made increasingly serious attempts to free himself from his mother's domination in matters of state. He had until then shown little interest in anything but hunting and had been happy to leave Catherine to carry the burdens of government that she seemed to relish. An opportunity arose for Charles to decide French foreign policy and gain what he coveted most – military glory. Many Flemish Protestants had taken refuge from the

Spanish at La Rochelle and were using the port as a base from which they frequently attacked Spanish shipping. In early 1571 William of Orange, their rebel leader, tried to organise an invasion of the Netherlands from Germany with the aim of liberating the Low Countries. As Orange attempted to build up a coalition of enemies of Spain, his brother Louis of Nassau remained at La Rochelle where he had been since the end of the Third War of Religion. It was essential to their plans that France support any move against Spain and Charles saw a war in the Netherlands against Philip II as a scintillating chance to lead French troops into action.

Catherine knew that by paying lip service and lending some support to the plan she would stand a real chance of winning over Coligny and Jeanne d'Albret to the marriage between Henri and Margot, which now seemed her main preoccupation. Risking war with Spain put a terrifically high price on this union, but Catherine hoped to navigate around the difficulties and gain what she most desired from being seen as an ally of the Flemish rebels without an open rupture with her powerful former son-in-law. She understood that war with Spain would be a disaster, though for the moment she would use the plans to her advantage.

Charles found an unexpected ally in his hopes for the Dutch enterprise in his distant relative Cosimo de Medici. To the fury of the Emperor Maximilian and Philip II, Cosimo, formerly the Duke of Florence, had been created Grand Duke of Tuscany by Pope Pius V in 1569. The two Habsburg potentates argued that the Pope had no right to raise Cosimo to this exalted position since they held Florence to be technically under Imperial suzerainty. Such was the ensuing row – greatly enjoyed by Catherine who despite appearances and her need for his troops in the last civil war loathed her upstart relative and his pretensions – that Cosimo felt he might be attacked or deposed by the angry Habsburgs.* Searching for allies in the event of a crisis, Cosimo drew Charles into his camp. The two agreed an alliance between Tuscany and France against Spain. This brought no comfort to Catherine, who wryly watched her son's total lack of experience in foreign affairs as he bungled about noisily in the subtle art of European diplomacy. Secrecy was almost non-existent and finesse, her own greatest strength, entirely absent in Charles's dealings.

On 11 June 1571 the ungracious King wrote with great bravado to Cosimo's ambassador Petrucci, '*La reine, ma mère, est trop timide.*' In reality he hoped to advance matters to such a point that Catherine would be

---

* In a deliberate attempt to remind Cosimo that she was a Queen of France, and to create a subtle but distinct distance between herself and a man she considered a 'country bumpkin', Catherine usually wrote to her distant relative in French, addressing him as '*Mon Cousin*'. At the same time Elizabeth I of England wrote to Cosimo in Italian and even Italianised the name of her palace at Richmond to Mi Castello di Riccamonte.

Prosp. de l'Hostel de Soissons.

Two of Catherine's architectural triumphs in Paris: the Hôtel de la Reine
(featuring the Colonne de l'Horoscope, which is all that survives today), and the Tuilleries
Palace in about 1650, home to every French monarch until Napoleon III.

Prosp: deß Runden Gippels deß Pallasts des Tuilleries
Wie solcher auff der Seilen gegen der Straßen anzusehen
Prosp. rotundi Cacuminis in Palatie des Tulleries.

A 'magnificence' in Paris in 1573 in honour of the Polish ambassadors, celebrating Catherine's son Henri III's election as King of Poland. Note Catherine's black-clad figure in the centre of the tapestry.

Clockwise from top left Charles IX as King; Hercules, later Francis, Duke of Alençon; the runt of Catherine's litter; King Philip II of Spain and his wife Elisabeth, Catherine's eldest daughter; Catherine's favourite son, the Duke of Anjou, shortly before his accession as Henri III.

The rival factions: Anne de Montmorency, Constable of France, and Henry II's mentor.

François, 2nd Duke of Guise: soldier-statesman who masterminded the 1559 coup.

GID QVE LES TRAICT DV VISAGE ET DES YEVX : LV GVIZARD VALEREVX EN CE PET
EVR SON RENO SONT GRAVE DAS LESGIEVLY · ENCOR IVS AVANT QVE CE COVP

que les traicts, du visaige et des yeulx.   Sa grandeur son renom, font grauez dans les c
alereux, En ce petit espace   Encores plus auant, que ce coup sur sa face

The Catholic Paladin: Henri, 3rd Duke of Guise, '*le balafré*', later known as
'The King of Paris' (scar clearly evident in this portrait).

forced to support his strategy. Cosimo realised that Charles might prove a liability without his mother's help and advised him to seek her counsel and approval as well as that of his father-in-law. Undaunted, Charles continued to offer support to the Flemish Protestants, and two secret meetings to further their plans were held in July 1571 with Louis of Nassau, the first at Lumigny and the second at Fontainebleau, during which Nassau hid in a gatehouse to escape detection. The discussions apparently included a general carving up of the Low Countries and as Charles's reward he could expect to expand French territories. Nassau also assured him that he would be enthusiastically welcomed as a liberator if their war against the Spanish succeeded.

It is difficult to say for certain how much Catherine knew about the plans against Spanish power in the Netherlands at this point, but she must have known enough to be fearful of her son's bellicose intentions. Everything she had tried to achieve since her husband had died would suggest opposition to armed conflict against a foreign power such as Spain. Her aims had always been simple: peace and prosperity inside France, obedience to the King, glorious alliance-building marriages for her children, and a return to the days of a powerful monarchy such as it had been under her late husband and King Francis I. She was quite capable of appearing to wish for conflict using ruses to fool her neighbouring states, but an outright foreign war was not a risk Catherine would ever have taken unless forced. As one historian has written of the Queen Mother, her 'dread of war with Spain and the concomitant effort to maintain the amity of Cateau-Cambrésis was the lodestar of her political career'.[11] Using the Netherlands only as a project by which she could bring the Huguenots to trust her and to promote her marriage plans for Henri and Margot was very much more to her taste. In July 1571 she wrote to Cosimo asking for his intervention with the Pope. She wanted Pius to understand that should Coligny return to the French Court it would redound well for the internal peace of France. Knowing she would eventually require papal dispensation for a marriage between Henri and Margot, she added that she might need Cosimo's help with this later. English support for any forthcoming hostilities against Spain was also essential, so she revived the marriage talks between Anjou and Elizabeth, but they soon foundered. Had these fruitless talks come to anything it is possible that with the English as allies Catherine might have lent her fullest support to a war in the Low Countries.

Alava, who had heard enough to become suspicious of trouble in the Netherlands, lodged an official complaint that a war with Spain would be the most likely outcome of the King's machinations with the rebels. Charles replied that he refused to be bullied over what he considered Frances's best interests, or indeed, any foreign plans. Alava complained to Catherine, who may not have known the extent of the plans but nevertheless took much the same line as her son since she was angry that Alava had been writing inflammatory reports about her to Philip for months.

After many ignored invitations, on 12 September 1571 Gaspard de Coligny arrived to join the Court at Blois. He came armed with a promise of safe conduct signed by the King, Anjou and Catherine, and promises to discuss a remedy for frequent breaches of the Peace of Saint-Germain. At last Catherine saw a scintilla of hope for Margot's marriage. She had much else to hope for now, and needed to have Coligny at Court in order to attempt to dismantle the armed mini-state at La Rochelle, where Jeanne, her son and other senior Huguenots lived under their own laws. They were inside France geographically, though not part of it politically. For Charles, Coligny's presence represented a step further towards war in the Netherlands, for he could not hope to undertake such an enterprise without the fullest understanding and harmony between himself and the Admiral. Coligny had asked to come in an unofficial capacity and to be received informally. Many of his comrades at La Rochelle had begged him not to go, fearing that his life would be in danger, if not from the Queen Mother then certainly from the Guises and other ultra-Catholics. Mindful of his responsibilities as their leader and the disastrous effect his death would have, Coligny nonetheless still believed he must see the King. Blois, 'the capital of peace', had been especially chosen for the meeting rather than Paris where he would be in far greater danger.

The Admiral arrived to find Catherine in bed with a fever and so the King received him in her room. The formal informality that had been decided upon as the correct etiquette for the meeting was observed to the last detail. After watching her son and Coligny talking, Catherine asked that the Admiral approach and kiss her. Charles is then alleged to have joked, 'We have you now, mon père, we shall not let you go whenever you please.' The recent war and deep distrust created a pregnant pause that conveyed just how unfamiliar this intimacy had become to them all. Catherine talked for a few moments with the Admiral and then he visited Anjou who, though also unwell, received him courteously. During the five weeks that Coligny spent at Blois, Charles showered him with gifts, confidences and friendship. He received 100,000 livres in compensation for his personal losses during the war and one year's income of 160,000 livres, equivalent to the sum that had been his brother's income from his church benefices. All his confiscated properties and goods that could be tracked down were returned to the Admiral. He was also permitted an escort of fifty nobles wherever he went, a privilege normally reserved only for princes.

On 3 October Catherine received a letter from Cosimo announcing that he had decided to join the Holy League against the Turks. Seeing this as an opportunity to ingratiate himself with his Imperial masters he grasped it. He also made it quite clear that the French no longer enjoyed his support for their plans in the Low Countries. This was just the sort of obstacle to the enterprise that Catherine had been hoping for and it was compounded by the league's sensational naval victory of Lepanto over the Turks, won on 7 October. Catherine's reluctance to become involved in conflict against the Spanish was amply justified by these events and she quickly despatched instructions to Fourquevaux in Madrid to congratulate Philip on his holy victory against the infidel. She assured the Spanish King that she wished only for peace between them and no matter how questionable her recent behaviour might have seemed, she claimed that she had only been monitoring events to ensure that her influence and desire for peace could be brought to bear upon them.

When Charles heard of the victory against the Turks – the news did not reach France until November – he was with the Venetian ambassador, Contarini. Venice had formed part of the Holy Alliance against the Turks and Charles, in a state of feverish overexcitement, heard of the many infidel ships that had been lost in the battle. Afterwards a member of his council reminded him that since many of the Turkish vessels were in fact on loan from France, he was celebrating the loss of his own ships and the downfall of his ally in the Mediterranean. This sobering reminder dampened his earlier high spirits. In response to the losses, shipbuilding was stepped up at Marseilles where reports stated that one hundred galleys were being constructed. Despite Lepanto, the atmosphere at Court appeared ominous and strained as Charles's war party seemed intent upon proceeding with their plans to attack the Netherlands. Alava grew increasingly paranoid about his own safety, and his fears amplified to hysteria when he was accused of writing a letter to Spain in which he denounced the King for being drunk every night and alleged that Catherine had given birth seven times to babies fathered by the late Cardinal de Châtillon while also conducting a simultaneous love affair with the Cardinal of Lorraine.

When Charles sent a delegation to the ambassador with his message of congratulation on the victory at Lepanto, Alava, sure his life was in danger and that the King had actually sent an assassin to kill him, decided he must leave France immediately. It was reported that he fled to the Netherlands 'dressed as a parrot' with a mask covering his face.[12] If indeed the ambassador was attempting to appear inconspicuous it seems a curious choice of disguise. This ludicrous episode proved a tremendous tonic for Catherine, suffering from sciatica, fever and catarrh, and it became a huge joke at Court.

On 20 October Admiral Coligny's wife of less than one year, Jacqueline d'Entremonts, was received at Blois by the King and Queen Mother. They behaved very graciously towards the young woman and made much of her. Their invitation and attention to his bride pleased her fifty-year-old husband as day by day Charles grew fonder of the older man, and once again the parallels between Henry II and his relationship with Coligny's uncle Montmorency were drawn. As a gesture of goodwill Coligny accompanied the Queen Mother to Mass, though he did not remove his hat and refused to bow to the Host. Charles ordered that anyone breaching the terms of the Peace of Saint-Germain must be held strictly accountable and even ordered that the Cross of Gastines, a monument to Catholic supremacy in the rue Saint-Denis, be dismantled. Under the recent peace treaty, any symbolic reference to the religious wars must be removed but the Parisians had hitherto refused to take down the cross. As it was finally taken away by an armed escort the seething crowd erupted in fury.

Those at Court followed the King's lead – especially since the Guise family were absent and still in disgrace – most courtiers going out of their way to extend every courtesy to Coligny. But Paris and other staunchly Catholic areas refused to bow to their sovereign's policy, and their displeasure would soon prove hard to contain. The new Queen's attitude reflected the people's true feelings as well as her own inexperience in the art of diplomacy. When Coligny was formally presented to her, the grizzled warrior bowed, stepped forward, knelt down on one knee and reached to kiss the royal hand. Elisabeth, for whom the Admiral was Satan incarnate, pulled away with a gasp of horror to avoid being touched by so evil a heretic. Naturally the incident had the courtiers sniggering; for them the practice of hiding their true feelings was not only completely natural but often crucial to their survival.

One day towards the end of Coligny's stay Catherine asked him to visit her. She wished only to conclude the marriage between her daughter and Henri, she said, and she could not do this without meeting Jeanne, who refused to expose herself to danger at a Court that she in any case regarded as a sink of iniquity. The Admiral told Catherine how well he understood Jeanne's fears for her own safety. To this Catherine replied, 'We are too old, you and I, to deceive each other. ... She has less reason to be suspicious than you because she cannot believe that the King would be trying to marry his sister to her son in order to harm her.'[13] Coligny pressed the Queen Mother on pursuing the expedition against the Spanish in the Netherlands and Catherine promised that with his support for Margot's marriage she would give the matter her full attention. But only after the wedding had taken place. How much store he set by her promise is impossible to say, but his growing influence over Charles had boosted the Admiral's confidence that his plans for the Netherlands might go forward with or without the Queen Mother's approval. Yet again someone had tried to interpose himself between Catherine and one of her children. Yet again the threat would be seen off.

Before the arrival of Coligny at Blois in September 1571, Catherine had sent Marshal de Cossé with a letter for Jeanne from the King requesting that she and Henri also join them. When Cossé arrived at Béarn he found he had just missed the Queen of Navarre who had left to take the waters at Eaux-Chaudes; she had been feeling ill for some time and hoped to regain her strength there. Marshal Biron followed Cossé and found the Queen, still feeling unwell, at Nérac on 10 December. He reported to Catherine that many of her senior advisers were counselling Jeanne against the Valois marriage. Jeanne did not like the project any more than they did but found it increasingly hard to resist. Catherine could blackmail her, since she had the power to stir up the Pope, who for obvious reasons opposed the marriage and could declare Henri of Navarre illegitimate. He was the son of Jeanne's second marriage, which 'was itself of questionable validity'.[14] Should the Pope exercise this power, Henri would immediately lose his position as First Prince of the Blood and with it his rights to the throne of France should Catherine's sons die without a male heir. Jeanne therefore wearily decided to fall in with Catherine's plans, although certain stipulations had to be met. Guyenne must form part of Margot's dowry; the towns that belonged to Jeanne currently occupied by royalist troops must be returned to her and she would only come if she could negotiate alone with Catherine. In January the fortress of Lectoure – one of Jeanne's preconditions for her rendezvous with the Queen Mother – was returned to her and she set out, at last, for her fateful meeting with Catherine.

At the same time as Jeanne prepared to meet the Queen Mother, a conspiracy to assassinate Elizabeth of England had been uncovered. Known as the Ridolfi Plot, the scheme sponsored by Spain and Rome to put Mary, Queen of Scots on the English throne with the Duke of Norfolk as her consort had very nearly succeeded. Catherine told the English ambassador that two Italians had been hired by Alava and that she had sent urgent messages warning the Queen of the great peril she faced. Charles, once protective and fond of his former sister-in-law, decided that she had finally placed herself beyond the pale with her plotting. His only comment upon the desperate situation in which Mary now found herself was prescient: 'Alas, the poor fool will never cease until she loses her head. They will put her to death. It is her own fault and folly.'[15] The upshot of the plot evoked a desire for England to draw closer to the enemies of Spain, France being the most powerful of these. Elizabeth had been given to understand that although Anjou was no longer a possible matrimonial candidate, his younger brother would serve just as well. François, Duke of Alençon, the boy usually referred to by Alava as '*le petit voyou visceux*' (the vicious little blackguard), presented an unappealing potential suitor, but nevertheless talks began. These included a mutual arrangement by which each country promised to defend the other should either be attacked by a common enemy.

Charles pushed for the English alliance, anxious to rid himself of his detested youngest sibling. Anjou disliked him equally and neither had Catherine showed Alençon any particular affection. Margot was the youth's only champion within the family. The earlier dalliance with Guise, whether innocent or not, had destroyed the perhaps unnaturally deep bond between Margot and Anjou, who felt jealous of his sister's admirer and now constantly caused trouble for her. Charles had felt equally betrayed by the Guise incident and could no longer be relied upon by Margot. Sometimes he would stroke his sister but at others she feared his blows, especially after the beating she had received from him. Both brothers behaved like lovers scorned, both were capable of hurting Margot and both were jealous of the attention she paid her younger brother.

Queen Elizabeth's envoy, Sir Thomas Smith, arrived in France in December 1571. He recommended Alençon above Anjou as a husband, writing to the Queen that the former was 'not so obstinate and forward, so papistical and (if I may say so) so foolish and restive like a mule as his brother was. He is the more moderate, the more flexible and the better fellow.'[16] Smith also reported that for the 'getting of children' Alençon was by far the better choice, being 'more apt than th'other'.[17] This presumably referred obliquely to Anjou's ambiguous sexual orientation, though the idea of either of the Valois princes fathering a child by Elizabeth was faintly comical. Catherine felt it best not to ignore the obvious and pointed out the problem of her dwarfish son's height and hideous skin, but she added reassuringly that though the seventeen-year-old was 'not tall' he showed signs of growing a beard which would obscure his horrendous complexion. Smith observed that pockmarks were anyhow of little consequence in a man and cited the illustrious precedent provided by King Pepin 'le Bref' (the Short) who despite only reaching the belted waist of his wife Queen Bertha, fathered the great Charlemagne, the first Holy Roman Emperor.

Unimpressed by her envoy's recommendations, Gloriana nonetheless realised that at thirty-eight she was losing her looks almost as fast as she was losing her hair. Despite the Queen's use of hairpieces and other artifices, Smith remarked to Lord Burghley, one of Elizabeth's chief councillors, 'The more hairy she is before [at the front] the more bald she is behind.'[18] Indeed, it could not be denied that Elizabeth was losing the *fraicheur* she had once possessed. The Queen agreed for talks to continue; these resulted in a defensive and commercial pact, the Treaty of Blois, signed between England and France on 29 April 1572. As for the marriage talks, she allowed them to dawdle along unresolved for the time being.

Elizabeth's value as an ally became doubtful when the French discovered that she had also secretly opened discussions with Alba at his request only a month before the signing of the Treaty of Blois, with the aim of restoring commercial relations between England and the Spanish Netherlands. These had been suspended in 1569 and were costing both countries dear. Though the English had found other outlets in Hamburg, their traditional and commercial associations with the Netherlands were mutually profitable and much preferred. By 1572 Spanish shipping suffered severe interruptions due to the constant attacks from William of Orange's privateers. The 'Geux de Mer' as they were known, or the 'Sea Beggars', successfully roved the English Channel, capturing or sinking a large number of enemy ships with their cargoes before taking refuge at La Rochelle and various English ports. In order for her agreement with Alba to proceed, Elizabeth had already in February 1572 ordered all the rebel ships to leave English ports. Their expulsion set off an unforeseen chain of events that would inflame the already aggravated situation in the Low Countries and encourage French Protestants to believe in the ultimate possibility of a successful invasion to eject the Spaniards altogether.

The Sea Beggars had put out to sea but were forced by a storm to drop anchor at Brille in the Netherlands. By chance the Spanish garrison there had recently departed to put down a rebellion in Utrecht and the Sea Beggars – a highly organised military and naval force – captured the port. It did not take long before they controlled most of Zeeland. Large numbers of refugees in England and La Rochelle now hurried to join them, boosted by special clandestine forces from England and other sympathetic states. On 30 April, the very day after signing the Treaty of Blois, the English announced that commercial relations with Flanders would recommence. Elizabeth, wishing triumph for neither France nor Spain, followed her own strategy of keeping the Spanish tied up in the Netherlands, the French tempted to intervene and Philip unable to concentrate on invading heretical England's shores.

During the early spring of 1572 a development arose that filled Catherine with a joyful anticipation such as she had not known for a long time. The King of Poland, Sigismund-August II, had just been widowed and his health was failing. As he had no plans to remarry and no legitimate heir, the throne of Poland would fall vacant upon his death. One of Catherine's favourite dwarves, a Pole named Krassowski, is alleged to have told his mistress that the Polish King was dying, saying, 'Madam, soon there will be a throne for the Valois.' She seized upon this dream of a distant crown and decided that her adored Anjou must be elected Sigismund-August's successor. To ensure a prime position for Anjou when the King died, she sent Jean de Balagny – the natural son of her trusty Bishop of Valence, Jean de Monluc – on a reconnaissance mission to Poland to report back on the conditions there and discover who needed to be bought, bullied or seduced.

Sigismund had also just lost one of his sisters, the wife of the Vovoid of Transylvania, and vassal of the French ally the Sultan of Turkey. To ingratiate herself with Sigismund Catherine offered Anjou's recently discarded mistress, the ravishing Renée de Rieux, Demoiselle de Châteauneuf, as a bride to the mourning Vovoid in his mountain kingdom. In order to expedite the Sultan's permission for the match, Charles wrote to his ambassador in Constantinople describing his brother's ex-mistress's marvellous attributes: 'Mademoiselle de Châteauneuf is a beautiful and virtuous girl who comes from the House of Brittany and is therefore my kinswoman.'[19] How she felt having been thrown over by Anjou for Marie of Clèves, sister to the new Duchess of Guise, and then offered as a chattel to the less than polished Vovoid is not known. Having done all she could for the moment to get the Polish plan in motion, Catherine then turned her attention back to the more immediate project, the Navarre–Valois marriage.

After receiving many letters from Catherine reassuring Jeanne that if she came to Court as her guest she would be in no danger, the Queen of Navarre could not resist writing back, 'Madame, you say that you desire to see us, and not in order to harm us. Forgive me if I feel like smiling, when I read your letters. You allay fears that I have never felt. I do not suppose, as the saying is, that you eat little children.'[20] In January Jeanne set off for the French Court at Blois. She undertook her three-week journey in a carriage so huge it resembled a house. In the middle a burning stove kept the occupants warm and mattresses and cushions compensated for the awful pitching of the coach. Nearing her destination she was asked to wait at Tours. The presence, at Blois, of Pope Pius V's legate and nephew, Cardinal Alexandrini, who had come specifically to protest against the Navarre marriage, which his uncle deeply opposed, meant Jeanne had to wait at arm's length from the Court. The cardinal's first mission had been to visit King Sebastian of Portugal. After detaining his two ever-present Theatine monks in the Monastery of Coimbre, he harangued the King and almost made him a prisoner until he finally extracted a promise from Sebastian that he would marry Margot. With the Portuguese marriage offer in his pocket, Alexandrini arrived at the French Court on 7 February 1572. Hoping that Catherine and Charles would be brimming with gratitude at the proposed Portuguese marriage, he also inserted a demand that France join the Holy League of Lepanto against the Turks.

The cardinal was to be disappointed on both counts. To avoid wasting time and to sound out Jeanne on the potential stumbling blocks that might still prevent the marriage, Catherine invited her to Chenonceau nearby, where they finally met on 15 February 1572. The religious issues surrounding the marriage in general and the ceremony in particular were carefully examined, with Jeanne taking advice from the Protestant ministers she had brought with her. At last Alexandrini left; his mission had been a complete failure. Refusing all the ritual gifts upon departure, he sped away, sulking in his carriage on the journey back to Rome. By coincidence he passed Jeanne d'Albret's coach as she approached the chateau. Alexandrini diplomatically failed to see that the passenger in the vehicle was the heretical Queen of Navarre and thus avoided having to salute or even acknowledge her as they passed.

The King welcomed Jeanne at Blois on 2 March 1572. She felt ill and tired but was driven on by her determination to see the marriage talks resolved. Torn between her religious scruples and her maternal ambitions, she strove to reconcile the apparently irreconcilable. In many ways Jeanne had dreaded coming to the debauched French Court, less for safety reasons or getting caught in Catherine's Florentine toils – she felt more than a match for those – but as a senior French princess and sovereign of her own kingdom she feared she had become stale and provincial. She suspected she might even become a laughing stock in the sophisticated hothouse of the Court. Daughter of Marguerite de Valois, Francis I's sister, she had inherited Navarre from her father and had married – for love – the First Prince of the Blood, Antoine de Bourbon. The Bourbons had suffered many setbacks since the old Constable de Bourbon's treachery in 1523. Henry II had virtually ignored them during his reign, and her womanising nincompoop of a husband had allowed himself to be consistently outmanoeuvred and marginalised during his lifetime. Jeanne was a highly intelligent and courageous sovereign, upright and morally zealous, yet there was pathos in her feminine pride, and her fear of being snubbed and thought a country bumpkin.

Since she first arrived at Chenonceau, Jeanne's letters to Henri are fraught with anxiety and complaints. On 21 February she wrote,

> I urge you not to leave Béarn until you receive word from me ... it is evident that [Catherine] thinks everything I say is only my own opinion and that you hold another. ... When you next write please tell me to remember all that you have told me and especially to sound out Madame [Margot] on her religious views, emphasizing that this is the only thing holding you back, so that when I show it to her she will tend more to believe that such is your will. ... I assure you I am very uncomfortable because they oppose me strongly and I need all the patience in the world.[21]

Jeanne's first impression of Margot was encouraging, as she wrote to Henri:

> I must tell you that Madame Marguerite showed me all possible honour and hospitality and told me frankly how much she liked you. If she embraces our religions, I may say that we are the happiest persons in the world. ... On the other hand if she should remain obdurate in her faith, and they say that she is deeply devoted to it, then this marriage will be the ruin of our friends and our country. ... Therefore, my son, if ever you prayed to God – pray to Him now.[22]

Henri's ten-year-old sister had accompanied their mother to Court and she added a postscript: 'Monsieur, I have seen Madame Marguerite, I found her very beautiful, and I wish you might have seen her ... she gave me a beautiful little dog which I love.'[23]

Margot's legendary beauty is described by Brantôme shortly before her marriage during Easter 1572 when he saw her appear in a procession during the festivities:

> So beautiful was she, that one had never seen anyone lovelier in the world. Besides the beauty of her face and her well-turned body, she was superbly dressed and fantastically valuable jewellery adorned her attire. Her lovely face shone with faultless white skin and her hair was dressed with big white pearls, precious stones and extremely rare diamonds shaped like stars – one could say that her natural beauty and the shimmering of her jewels competed with a brilliant night sky full of stars, so to speak.

Even taking into consideration royal flattery and Brantôme's customary hyperbole, Margot was undoubtedly a true sixteenth-century beauty, although today her features might not please as much as they did then. Her high cheekbones, white skin and full lips are timeless attributes, but her nose was not as delicate as the rest of her features and her round face also hinted at the full cheeks and double chin that would come with the years. A glance at her mother confirmed that inheritance. She carried herself regally, danced superbly and wore an imperious air, but even a brief look at her portraits allows one to see the seductive and playful young woman as famed for beauty as for her innate sense of style. She understood exactly how to show herself off to her best advantage.

As the negotiations continued and Jeanne's 'catarrh' caused ever more frequent and tiring coughing fits, she felt increasingly concerned about the debauched Court and what it might do to her son. She also felt fearful of the provincial rather than princely figure he might cut among the dashing courtiers. She wrote, 'I beg you to bear three things in mind; cultivate grace, speak boldly, especially when you are drawn aside, for remember that you will be judged by first impressions.' She even included a fashion tip: 'Train your hair to stand up, do not wear it in the way it is worn at Nérac, I recommend the latest fashion that I prefer.'[24] She began to see Margot in a less glowing light:

> As for the beauty of Madame Marguerite, I own that she has a fine figure; as for the face, there is too much artificial aid, it annoys me, she will spoil herself, but paint is as common in this Court as in Spain. ... I would not have you live here for all the world. I wish you to marry and come out of this corruption with your wife. Great as I believed it to be, it surpasses all my expectations. Here it is not the men who solicit the women but the women the men.[25]

Jeanne went on to complain that proper access to talk to Margot had been denied her and that the only person she could speak freely to was Catherine, 'who goads me'. The Duke of Anjou was no better:

> Monsieur tries to get around me in private with a mixture of mockery and deceit. ... Perceiving that nothing is being accomplished and that they do everything possible to bring about a hasty decision instead of proceeding logically. I have remonstrated with the Queen, but all she does is mock me. ... She treats me so shamefully that you might say that the patience I manage to maintain surpasses that of Griselda herself ... [Margot] is beautiful, discreet and graceful, but she has grown up in the most vicious and corrupt atmosphere imaginable. I cannot see that anyone escapes its poison.[26]

Jeanne did not pause to consider what Margot, beneath the charming exterior she presented, really made of the proposed match with her son. After the silky charms of Henri of Guise and the lacquer of court flirtations, the thought of marriage to Navarre was hateful to her. In her eyes he lacked any refinement, barely ever washed, wore outmoded clothes and his breath smelt famously of garlic. This could hardly be a combination to turn a girl's head; the mingled odours were more likely to make her stomach churn. For Margot, however, the principal consideration was that this plan had been conceived by her mother and had the full support of her elder brothers, by whom, as ever, she felt ill used: unable to resist their wishes, however, any thought of escape would prove useless. She was as unwilling a bride as Henri was a bridegroom.

The two sides haggled on and on over the religious issues. Jeanne feared – probably with some justification – that holes had been drilled in the walls of her apartment so that she could be easily spied upon. 'I do not know how I can stand it,' she lamented, 'they scratch me, they stick pins into me, they flatter me, they tear out my fingernails.'[27] As time went by and Jeanne refused to yield on the religious points even her Protestant nobles began to despair of her obstinacy. Suddenly the King cut the matter short and though he had not yet received papal dispensation he gave Jeanne all she asked for. He agreed that Henri need not enter the Cathedral of Notre-Dame for the Nuptial Mass and that a proxy could stand in for him. He did insist, however, that Henri come to Paris in person for the wedding to Margot. On 11 April 1572 the marriage contract was duly signed. A few weeks later Jeanne, exhausted, set out for Vendôme to rest. Henri had been summoned to meet her there but he fell ill and postponed his journey. By the time he recovered his mother, who had much to prepare before the wedding, had already set out for Paris. She needed to find gifts for her daughter-in-law-to-be and fine fashionable clothes for her son.

The images that Jeanne of Navarre had witnessed while staying at Blois of the debauched French Court in general and Margot's brothers' behaviour in particular must have haunted her. The banquets and masked balls provided opportunities for every moral laxity. Charles, still more child than King, pretending to be a horse with a saddle on his back frolicking about on all fours, his face covered in soot. Anjou, scented and begemmed, dressed in the most fabulous sartorial creations, resembled a female courtier more than a male. These japes were all presided over by Catherine who seemed to ignore the excesses of her sons – whose hatred for each other remained as alive as ever – and realised it was better to see them debauch themselves than slit each other's throats.

As Jeanne set out for the capital she looked ravaged by illness; nevertheless, determined not to appear anything less than regal, observers noted that for her journey to Paris she wore more pearls than she had ever done in her life. Once there, the Queen stayed at the house of her Bourbon relation, the Vidame de Chartres. As Catherine was not in the capital she charged the Comte de Retz – Alberto Gondi – with taking care of the Navarrese Queen. During the month of May 1572 Jeanne tried bravely to ignore her failing health and look forward to the arrival of her son. On 4 June she was forced to take to her bed and two days later she rewrote her will. Coligny, who had recently arrived at Court, heard of the Queen's desperate condition and arrived at her bedside on 8 June. Here he remained with Jeanne's chaplain, Merlin, praying and reading the Scriptures to her as she slipped in and out of consciousness. Jeanne never saw her beloved son again and died on 9 June aged only forty-four. The autopsy revealed that she had died of tuberculosis and an abscess in her right breast. After the Massacre of Saint Bartholomew the rumour predictably surfaced that Catherine had done away with the tiresome Queen who had been such anathema to her. The story was spread that Maître René, the Queen Mother's Florentine *parfumier*, had been ordered to make Jeanne a pair of gloves tainted with poison. In fact, Catherine had nothing to gain from killing the Queen of Navarre; her objectives had been achieved once the marriage contract was signed, though there is no doubt that her death dealt a great blow to the Huguenots.

One murder that almost certainly must be laid at Catherine's door at this time was that of a young gentleman named Philibert Le Vayer, Sieur de Lignerolles. By 1570 Anjou was causing Catherine much disquiet with some of his more feminine pursuits and by his general lack of interest in women (with a few notable exceptions such as his sister Margot). Catherine went to great lengths to instil simple male lust into her son. She even organised bacchanalian feasts where, it was said, the serving girls were both beautiful and naked. The only noticeable effect upon him seems to have been complete indifference, if not intense boredom. Instead, he surrounded himself with a coterie of exquisite-looking young noblemen who became known as his *mignons*. They slavishly followed their prince's pursuits and passions while he protected and cosseted them. Catherine loathed her son's gang of pretty boys and as soon as a particular favourite emerged she would do all she could to undermine him. One member of this coterie was Lignerolles, who had close Spanish con- nections and had made himself indispensable to Anjou. Lignerolles, however, differed from the others. This *mignon* encouraged a side of the duke that reflected the opposite of his normally epicurean self, a side that would later grow and eventually overpower him as the years went by.

Henri had a curious attraction to religious fanaticism and Lignerolles did all he could to foster this. Anjou found himself spellbound by the unusual favourite who encouraged such extreme devotional and ascetic practices in him that he became quite ill. Praying, fasting, pilgrimages and self-flagellation replaced the usual licentiousness and a certain detachment from his mother became noticeable. Anjou's delicate constitution soon suffered from his intense devotions and one courtier overheard Catherine say in a loud voice that Henri's 'face has become quite pale and I would prefer to see him become a Huguenot than to see him endanger his life in this way'. Catherine's love for Anjou was as blind as it was visceral; anyone who she believed threatened her son's well being and his intimacy with her risked provoking a deadly reaction. When Lignerolles was found murdered in a narrow alleyway near the Louvre no one even bothered to search for the assassin; it seemed well understood by all who had ordered the killing. For the moment Anjou returned to his normal pastimes, but his latent fanaticism would revive in the future and do him much harm in the years to come.

On 13 May a new Pope, Gregory XIII, had been elected who proved to be far more amenable and moderate than his predecessor. Catherine assured him that the Navarrese union offered the only sure way to prevent the King being led into war against Spain and to keep the peace within France. She applied for a special dispensation permitting the marriage between Henri and Margot despite the religious dichotomy and their consanguinity *à troisième degré*. Catherine was undoubtedly sincere in her desire for peace with the Spanish, but France's relationship with Spain was now jeopardised by a dangerous and highly explosive incident, which bore all the hallmarks of Admiral de Coligny trying to force his agenda of military intervention in the Netherlands.

On 17 July 1572 a Huguenot military expedition of 5000 troops led by Jean de Hangest, Seigneur de Genlis, crossed the border from France into the Spanish Netherlands where they were ambushed near Mons by Spanish troops who had been alerted about the attack well in advance. Genlis and François de la Noue, a Protestant captain, were on a mission to save Louis of Nassau who had, with the support of money and men from Charles, attacked Mons and Valenciennes. Initial success had quickly turned to failure and the Spaniards now had Nassau and his men besieged in the fortress of Mons. At the same time Prince William of Orange, Nassau's brother, planned an invasion from Germany. For weeks rumours had been circulating at the French Court about the Genlis rescue plan. Parisian armourers were reportedly working throughout the night and every day since mid-June large numbers of armed men had been seen leaving Paris heading north. Some alleged that the King personally received Genlis in Paris on or about 23 June. Charles, however, claimed total ignorance of the attack, though this is hard to credit since the Spanish were well-informed enough to prevent its success. It is most likely that Genlis had the clandestine help of Coligny and the tacit support of the King.

The Huguenot force was decimated, only a few hundred men escaping. One of the survivors was Genlis himself, who unfortunately carried a highly compromising letter written by Charles in which he encouraged French Huguenots in their rebellious activities in the Netherlands. The incursion by an armed force into Spanish territory could easily constitute an act of war by the French, and Charles hastily distanced himself by congratulating Philip on his success in defeating the expedition so roundly. Catherine, furious that her son had even covertly supported so foolish a mission, demanded that he make a public declaration denouncing the Genlis expedition, stating that his aim was to live in harmony with his neighbours. Believing the immediate crisis to have been averted, she left the capital to tend to her daughter Claude of Lorraine at Châlons, where she had been taken ill en route for Paris and Margot's wedding. Catherine had failed to grasp that as far as Coligny was concerned the Genlis expedition represented little more than an advance party for the far greater French force he planned to lead, and no sooner had the Queen Mother left Paris than the Admiral redoubled his efforts in urging Charles to declare war on Spain.

Catherine soon received warning of the Admiral's bellicose activities and dashed back to Paris on the night of 4 August to try to prevent catastrophe. Incandescent with rage, she berated the King for allowing himself to be led by the very men who had once tried to kidnap him and against whom he had been at war only a matter of months before. She urged him not to fall into their trap of starting a war against Spain that would soon leave the monarchy at the mercy of the Protestants. At the same time Coligny worked hard to convince Charles that he had not a moment to lose, and that he must see their plan through and strike in the Netherlands. Charles found himself torn between his mentor and his mother. At one point she even asked his permission for her and Anjou to retire immediately to her family estates in Auvergne – some observers reported that she wished to return to her birthplace of Florence. There she would spend the remainder of her days, she declared, rather than stay and watch her tireless work for the preservation of the monarchy go to ruin.

At the emergency council meetings on 9–10 August all those present, including Anjou, the Dukes of Nevers and Montpensier, Marshals Cossé and Tavannes voted for peace, the only dissenting voice being that of Coligny. At the outcome of the vote he is said to have given a sinister warning to the victorious Queen Mother: 'Madam, if the King decides against a war, may God spare him another from which he will not be able to extricate himself. I am not able to oppose that which Your Majesty has done but I am assured that she will have occasion to regret it.' This was clearly intended as a portentous warning, but by making this barely veiled threat Coligny had just unwittingly uttered his own death sentence.

TWELVE

The Massacre

Then kill them all! Kill them all!

August 1572

Catherine now prepared to take drastic measures to protect both her son's throne and the peace of the kingdom. The ensuing tumultuous events of August 1572 have stained her name for over 430 years, creating the legend of The Black Queen. Tragically she is not remembered for her enlightened and often frequent attempts at conciliation between Protestants and Catholics but for the chaotic bloodbath known as the Saint Bartholomew's Day Massacre.

After the heated council meeting of Sunday, 10 August 1572 Catherine prepared for her journey to the Château of Montceaux where her daughter Claude had now moved and lay recovering from her illness. Charles still believed that his mother planned to leave Court, despite her victory over Coligny. Some short time before her departure, according to Tavannes' memoirs – which were actually written by his son twenty years later – the King seemed more frightened of 'the probable designs of his mother and his brother than the proceedings of the Huguenots; for His Majesty well appreciated the power they wielded over his realm'.[1] Nonetheless Charles humbly kissed Catherine's hand and begged her not to abandon him, swearing that in future he would heed her counsels faithfully. When he discovered she had indeed left Paris he refused to eat and cut a desolate figure before deciding upon the only realistic course open to him.

Charles raced to Montceaux and there he continued to press the Queen Mother to reconsider her 'retirement' from public life. With Anjou and her trusties, Tavannes and Retz, they held a meeting in which, Tavannes recalled, 'the disloyalty, the audacity, prowess, menaces and violences of the Huguenots were magnified and exaggerated by such an infinity of mingled truths and artifices that from being the friends of the King, His Majesty was led to regard them as enemies'.[2] Charles still wavered, grasping at the mirage of military glory over Spain. He 'fluctuated greatly' but they hoped 'the King's infatuation with Coligny' was now over. So thoroughly had they permeated the King with mistrust, apprehension and doubt over his mentor that Catherine and her closest advisers believed the Admiral would never be viewed by Charles in the same light again.

The whole charade had been played with the precision at which Catherine excelled. Once in possession of her eldest surviving son, she had orchestrated to perfection the reconciliation and forgiveness of the prodigal King. With scenes of 'mingled violence and tender reproach ... the matter ended as Catherine intended it should, with the Queen receiving from her son a formal prohibition forbidding her to abandon his council. The Duke of Anjou meantime, being presented by his mother, received a fraternal embrace.'[3] According to Tavannes it was then that the Queen Mother and Anjou resolved to take the next logical step in order to 'deliver themselves from all future apprehension' that Charles might recall the Admiral at any time. They decided that Coligny must die, 'though this design was not imparted to the King'.[4] Catherine's decision to rid France of Coligny sprang not from a lust for vengeance against a powerful antagonist who had caused her so much grief and helped split the nation, but as a prerequisite for a return to a sense of national well-being. There was nothing feverish about her preparations; they were urgent, but only because of the perilous risk of the war with Spain that Coligny so assiduously promoted. She went about the removal of her adversary with the same impassive practicality she had hitherto shown in all matters of state. Coligny's death had in her view now become a necessity, and she was prepared to do whatever was needed to achieve her goal.

As the drama at Montceaux ran its course, Coligny attended the wedding of Henri de Condé to Marie of Clèves. At the celebrations he was approached several times by his followers begging him not to return to Paris where they feared his life would be at risk. They urged him to take up arms instead. He replied to their entreaties simply with the sort of noble remark that had shaped his reputation: 'I would rather be dragged through the mud in Paris than see civil war in this land once more.'[5] He went from Condé's wedding to visit his estates at Châtillon before returning to the city. In Paris the number of warnings and threats multiplied, yet he waved them aside saying that he was 'surfeited with fears' and adding that 'a man would never have peace if he listened to every alarm'. Besides, he said, 'Whatever happened he had lived long enough.'[6] His place must be in Paris for the abominable wedding of his protégé, Henri, the King of Navarre.

At fifty years of age Coligny, the warlord, the statesman, the Huguenot chief and the king's confidant, had become the caricature of a biblical hero. Leading his 'chosen people' to La Rochelle where he ruled a mini-state, independent financially thanks to the loot of privateers, he needed for nothing but to expand his domain. He had come to believe that by birth and by merit he was the man to help a weak and captive King rule France. His sober dress, dour countenance and pious utterings made him loved, but not lovable. Revered by his people for his almost theatrical rejection of anything but the loftiest aims and principles, Coligny had ceased to believe that there was any way other than his own. He did not trust in discussion or debate, but stubbornly continued upon his chosen path. This was no longer dedication to his religion or country but superb arrogance. His much-vaunted integrity, the cornerstone of his reputation, was now little more than fantastic vanity driving his relentless personal ambition.

In many ways the Admiral resembled his despised and mortal enemies, the Guises. These two great feudal entities both desired power and supremacy, both were capable of ordering the deaths of hundreds of people in the name of God, and both the late François of Guise and the Admiral were outstanding military commanders. The essential difference between Coligny and the Guises was that the Lorrainers did not dissimulate when it came to their ambitions. Their princely brilliance, their glorious reputations for chivalry and their unbudging defence of Catholicism simply made them more seductive as popular leaders of the people. But when they were not held in check, both Coligny and the Guises posed just as great a threat to France.

Henri of Navarre had attended the funeral of his mother in Vendôme on 1 July and had been in Paris since 8 July. Despite Jeanne's death there was no question of postponing the wedding. Plans for the marriage of France's most senior royal Huguenot to her exalted Catholic princess were too advanced and too many interests were involved for even a nominal adjournment. The Cardinal de Bourbon and the Duke de Montpensier greeted him as he arrived at Palaiseau at the head of 800 well-armed horsemen all clad in black, although some accounts have Henri arriving with an escort of only eighty men. No matter how large his escort, however, for the first time as a grown man (he was eighteen years old) Henri no longer enjoyed the unyielding protection of his mother. He had spent many years as a boy and youth at Catherine's Court and had been taught a love of Italian poetry by the Queen Mother herself, as well as how to acquire the many other attributes expected of a young Renaissance prince. He particularly admired the troubadours' tales of romantic chivalry and martial valour. Returning to his mother, who abominated such refinements, he had been forced to lead a simpler life exchanging Dante and Tasso for the far less melodious readings of Calvin and de Bèze.

Arriving at the Valois Court and to the web of machinations and intrigues that ensnared all who lived there would have been daunting to one used to plain speaking, simple living and maternal sermonising.

Henri remembered enough of his earlier days living under Catherine's guardianship and, though much had changed, he would need a guide to get through the labyrinth before him. He had his uncle the Cardinal de Bourbon and perhaps his bride, though he held no great expectations from the latter.

Henri was certainly no tall blond Adonis to be compared with the young Duke of Guise, but he had many attractive qualities. He was about five feet eight inches in height, with a high forehead, thick dark hair, clear skin and the prominent nose that was such a feature of the Bourbons. Used to spending much of his time on horseback, he had developed a fine muscular physique and possessed a cheerful, outgoing, generous nature. The once mischievous boy had grown into an open and straightforward man. Henri had a particular charm that derived from his frankness, masculinity and magnanimity. His physical attributes were matched by his intellect; he was not, as so many of the courtiers liked to claim, an inarticulate peasant from the Pyrenees. Notwithstanding his love of garlic and distaste for bathing, he could joke and talk with those surrounding him without losing the composure required of his rank. He combined being a man and a king with surprising social finesse. Despite himself, Charles had always liked Navarre, he could not help but be attracted to him. Henri had seen military action, and made a robust and good companion. The King found him refreshing after the ludicrous affectations of his own brother Anjou.

As the days before the wedding passed, the heat in Paris grew oppressive, the streets were dusty and the sultry city filled with strangers arriving from all over the country. Most of the Huguenots stayed at inns and taverns. Many peasants from the provinces, most without proper lodging, came to take part in the festivities and watch the great spectacle of their princess marrying the King of Navarre. Due to the drought and a poor harvest in the surrounding countryside, there were also a large number of the lowliest labourers now choking the approaches to Paris hoping to find something to eat at the great feasts that would be given. Churches, convents and other buildings had been specially opened to house the unexpectedly large influx of people, but many had to manage as best they could, sleeping in huddles in the streets.

As the first Protestants arrived, the ultra-Catholic city appeared peaceful, which surprised many Huguenots who had expected to face a simmering hatred. One of them wrote, 'This populace, which has always been described as so terrible, would like nothing better than to live in peace, if only the great, in their ambition and disloyalty, did not exploit its excitability.'[7] Around the middle of the month, however, the pulpits came alive with a clamour of disapproval at the marriage. The hate-filled inflammatory preaching, directed mainly against the Protestants and the royal family, gave birth to numerous groundless rumours that flew from the congregations through the gathering crowds. Tempers flared as pickpockets and prostitutes preyed upon a rich harvest and beggars grasped at passers-by. The atmosphere grew tense in the streets of Paris, not the Paris of today with its broad boulevards, but a medieval city of narrow winding streets opening either on to large squares, or some becoming ever narrower, leading only to dead ends.

Catherine returned to this hot, ill-tempered, pullulating city on 15 August. Almost as soon as she arrived she found herself confronted with a furious demand from the Duke of Alba requiring an urgent explanation as to why no fewer than 3000 Huguenot troops were stationed close to the border near Mons. Once again she had been fooled. As she rapidly discovered, the Admiral had continued levying troops, despite the decision of the council, and at that moment was raising a force of 12,000 arquebusiers and 2000 cavalry. Nor was it a secret that the large number of Huguenot gentlemen in Paris for the wedding intended to set out for the Netherlands as soon as the celebrations had ended. The Admiral's ultimate intention to lead a mixed force of Catholics and Protestants to fight in the Netherlands against Spain would, he believed, remove any risk of civil war in France.

The King, who had for months given unparalleled access to his 'father confessor', permitting him into his chamber at any time of the day or night, sitting closeted alone with him for hours on end, now felt too confused and weak to wrest control back from Coligny. In truth, perhaps he no longer knew what he wanted. Coligny spoke to him like a man, treated him like a king, and provided a comforting counterpoint to his mother and Anjou. Catherine grew fearful that it would soon be too late to spring her trap. Perhaps Coligny had plotted to kidnap the King and have her sent into exile? Maybe she really would wind up on her estates in the Auvergne after all.

It is impossible today to know exactly when and how the plan for the murder of Admiral Coligny was arranged, but as the Guise family were in Paris for the wedding they provided the accomplices Catherine needed. Anjou's own account must be treated with some caution, though there is much in it that is undeniably true. As he sat, lonely and remorseful, in Cracow two years later, it is believed he talked to a senior member of his household, thought to be either his physician Miron or one of his gentlemen of the chamber, M. de Souve, who recorded his master's version of events. In them the duke stated,

> We were certain from the menacing conduct of the King, that the Admiral had inspired His Majesty with a bad and sinister opinion of the Queen my mother and of myself, we resolved to rid ourselves of him, and to call to our

aid Madame de Nemours, to whom we held that we might reveal our project from the mortal hate which we knew that she bore towards the said Admiral.[8]

Some reports have Anne d'Este, Duchess of Nemours, present at Montceaux and included in the plotting to kill the man she believed had murdered her first husband, François, Duke of Guise, whose memory she had kept as alive as her desire for revenge. The duchess and the Queen Mother had passed a good deal of time in each other's company since the end of July, but no one considered this noteworthy until the events of 22–24 August, since the two women enjoyed a close friendship.

Whenever the fateful meeting did take place between Catherine and the duchess, it is clear that at some point in early August the Queen Mother had secretly revoked the royal ban preventing the Guises from exacting their vengeance. In return, she received a promise of help from the matriarch of the Guise clan and its enormous clientele, many of whom were in Paris for the wedding. Total secrecy was paramount in that age of plots and rumours of plots, and of the Guise family only the duchess, her former brother-in-law the Duke d'Aumale and Henri, the young Duke of Guise, were party to the plan. The most notable absentee from Paris during those fateful days was the Cardinal of Lorraine. Since the family's disgrace over the 'romance' between Henri of Guise and Margot, he had decided to travel to Rome. Disgusted at the outcome of the last civil war, before his departure he had complained to the Duke of Alba about Catherine: 'She is so dissimulating that when she says one thing, she thinks another, her only aim being to command, as she does. As for the rest, she cares nothing.'[9] Catherine's powers of dissimulation were now to be put to the ultimate test. If her plan failed, she and her family risked being killed by the thousands of armed Huguenots present in the city.

According to Anjou's recollections, once the complicity of the Duchess of Nemours had been assured it only remained for an assassin to be found. The Queen Mother's and her son's first candidate was 'a certain Gascon captain' whom they rejected as being too 'volatile and light-headed for our purpose'. Improbably, the pair told the unsuccessful applicant that their discussions had all been in jest and he should make nothing of it. Anjou and Catherine finally decided to employ none other than Charles de Louviers de Maurevert, the nobleman who had shot Coligny's beloved comrade de Mouy during the third civil war and been rewarded by the King. They knew that he could keep a cool head and that he had felt no scruples about shooting de Mouy, his former tutor, in the back.

Anjou's account states that Maurevert provided 'an instrument more fit to achieve our designs. ... We therefore, without loss of time, summoned him, and having incontinently revealed our design to animate him the more to the enterprise, we told him that, if he had regard for his own safety, he must not refuse to become our agent.'[10] The pair thus neatly alluded to the mortal danger Maurevert would be in if he somehow fell into Coligny's hands. After much discussion they 'next took counsel on the best mode of executing the enterprise, and found no better expedient than that suggested by Madame de Nemours, who proposed that the shot should be fired from the window of the house where Villemur – a former preceptor of the Duke of Guise – lodged, a spot very conveniently placed for our enterprise'.[11]

Catherine's use of the Guises was a calculated and brilliant one. Despite the certainty that the Huguenots would clamour for vengeance after the death of the Admiral, she and the King would be above suspicion. The house from where Maurevert would fire upon the Admiral was known to belong to the Guises. The Duchess of Nemours had actually lived there herself for a while. The Protestants would blame the Guises, assuming the murder to be only a continuation of the blood feud between the Châtillon and the Lorrainers. The Guises for their part were entirely fired up by the thought of finally seeing vengeance done, and counted on Catherine's royal protection. The Queen Mother's aims were thus probably twofold; her first consideration was to kill Coligny but if the Guises fell prey to the vengeance of the Protestants she might also achieve her ultimate goal, the downfall of both of the Houses that had menaced the state by their imperious attempts to control the monarchy since the death of Henry II.

Yet before Coligny's execution – for such was it seen by Catherine – the wedding arranged to symbolise religious and national harmony must take place. On 16 August the Cardinal de Bourbon officiated at the betrothal ceremony held at the Louvre. The wedding itself was to be celebrated two days later although the papal dispensation had not yet arrived. This could largely be attributed to the robust offices of the Cardinal of Lorraine, who had done little else since his arrival in Rome but tell anyone at the Vatican who cared to listen that Catherine was a dangerous and duplicitous woman. Ignorant of his malice, the Queen Mother had asked him to intercede with the usually fair-minded Pope Gregory XIII. Lorraine's haughty reply came back that he was in Rome on 'purely private affairs' and thus unable to help. Until the cardinal's arrival the French ambassador had been on the verge of obtaining the dispensation, but as talk of Catherine's general villainy spread, negotiations were halted and the dispensation later refused.

The Cardinal de Bourbon, though longing for the match between his nephew and Margot, suffered an attack of scruples and refused to conduct the ceremony without the necessary permission. Finally Catherine grew impatient with Bourbon and decided to trick him. She showed him a bogus letter purporting to come from the French ambassador in Rome saying that the dispensation had been agreed and that the papers would arrive shortly by courier. She then ordered that the borders near Lyons be closed until after the ceremony, to ensure that no contradictory news arrived from Rome. The cardinal fell for the ruse and agreed to officiate at the nuptials.

By now the city almost shimmered with religious and political tension. Word came that Coligny wished to leave as soon as possible after the ceremony as his wife was due to give birth at any moment and he wanted to visit her briefly before he set out on his expedition to the Netherlands. The King also awaited the birth of his first child with Elisabeth of Austria, who had stayed at Fontainebleau in the peace of the countryside. Charles decided he would quit the tinderbox city as soon as possible and decreed that all official business be suspended during the festivities, which were due to end on Sunday, 24 August. The Court would then quit Paris on 26 August.

On the morning of 18 August 1572 the nineteen-year-old bride prepared for the ceremony. She had spent the night in the episcopal palace beside the Cathedral of Notre-Dame. During the period approaching the marriage she had shown little relish for what lay ahead. When Catherine had asked her daughter in April if she agreed to marry Henri of Navarre – not so much a question as a formal request requiring a formal assent – Margot later recalled her answer, 'I had no will, nor choice but her own, and I begged her to keep in mind my strong Catholic faith.' She dreaded the thought of leaving the brilliant French Court and living at Nérac, in all its Huguenot austerity. This spontaneous child of fun, flirtation and fashion feared that her husband's kingdom might bury her alive. With Jeanne dead, however, Margot's hopes grew a little that she might be able to charm Henri's austere subjects and introduce some gaiety into their lives. Understanding and fearing her mother as she did, Margot had no illusions about the perils of being Henri's wife. If there were to be further religious conflicts her husband's camp would not trust her and her own suspicious family – once she was no longer of any use to them – would soon consider her equally tainted. She would thus become an exile from them if the peace this marriage was intended to cement did not survive. However little she cared for her mother and elder brothers, she nevertheless feared being abandoned by them.

On Monday, 18 August 1572 Margot, sumptuously dressed in a robe sparkling with gems, a glittering crown trimmed with ermine on her head, and wearing a blue coat with a thirty-foot train carried by three princesses, became the Queen of Navarre. She recalled how superb she looked that day *'moi habillée à la royale'* wearing 'all the jewels of the Crown'.

Accompanied on either side by her brothers, King Charles IX and the Duke of Anjou, the bride walked to the specially erected platform outside Notre-Dame where the first part of the ceremony was to be held. Margot 'to the last persisted in her system of silent deprecation of the alliance: if she offered no resistance, she gave no assent'.[12] As she mounted the steps of the platform with her brothers, Henri of Navarre walked up to meet her from the other side, accompanied by Henri de Condé and his noblemen, including Admiral de Coligny. One account of the marriage describes Anjou, Alençon, the King and Navarre all dressed in the same pale silk covered with silver embroidery. Anjou, unable to resist further embellishing his costume, had added a feathered *toquet* studded with thirty huge pearls. As she had done for Charles's wedding, the Queen Mother discarded her usual black and wore a gown of dark-purple brocade.

Aside from the fanfare of trumpets announcing the arrival of the couple and the royal family, the crowd watched the first part of the marriage in silence. The couple knelt before the Cardinal de Bourbon. Henri, asked if he took Margot as his wife, answered with a clear yes. The cardinal then asked Margot if she agreed to take Henri as her husband, but the princess remained silent. The cardinal asked a second time, but still no answer came. Finally the King, understandably exasperated by this petty game, marched up behind his sister and brusquely pushed down her head as though she were nodding her assent. He strode back to his seat and with that she became Henri's wife. Although Margot always denied this version of events as recorded by the historian Davila and others, it later became one of the crucial factors that enabled her to have the marriage annulled on the grounds that she had not consented to it of her own free will. Navarre then led Margot to Anjou who had been chosen to act as the groom's proxy inside the cathedral to celebrate Mass with the rest of the royal family.

During the Mass Navarre and Coligny promenaded on the platform, talking together in full view of the crowd. When the service was over, Henri went to fetch his bride and led her, followed by the royal party, over to the episcopal palace for a splendid banquet to celebrate the marriage. The young nobleman and historian Jacques-Auguste de Thou made his way into the cathedral just as the party were leaving and found himself standing close to the Admiral who was talking to Henri Montmorency-Damville, the second son of the late Constable, just beneath captured Huguenot standards from the battles of Moncontour and Jarnac. De Thou recalled the Admiral's words as he pointed mournfully to the tragic mementoes of Huguenot defeats, saying, 'Very shortly these will be taken down, and in their stead other standards more agreeable to our sight shall replace them!' He doubtless alluded to his hope of capturing Spanish banners from the war he still believed would shortly begin against the Netherlands. This conversation was overheard and repeated by many.

Salviati, the papal nuncio and a relative of Catherine's, wrote that the Admiral was, in view of the council's clear rejection of the war, 'presuming too far, they will rap him on the knuckles. I perceive that they will no longer tolerate him.'[13] A magnificent ball was held in the Salle Voutée at the Louvre, followed by the banquet at the episcopal palace. Huge artificial silver-painted rocks made to look like mountains upon which sat the King and the most senior princes were carried into the *salle*. Both Henri of Guise and Coligny attended the celebration, though Guise made his excuses and asked the King for permission to retire early. Coligny followed soon afterwards. Four days of feasting and magnificent *spectacles* were to follow, with the Queen Mother's own masterpiece on the fifth day, 22 August. Catherine had decided that this would be the moment to strike.

The festivities were surprisingly good-natured considering the tension that had built up just before the wedding. On 19 August Anjou gave a luncheon and a ball, the following night the Court attended a magnificent masked ball given by the King, at which a *pantomime tournoi* was performed in honour of his sister. An observer wrote, 'On one side of the hall was shown paradise defended by three knights, the King, M. d'Anjou and M. d'Alençon. Opposite was a hell in which a great number of devils and imps were making infinite follery and noise. A great wheel turned to the said hell, hung all over with little bells. The two regions were divided from each other by a river flowing between, on which floated a boat guided by Charon, the ferryman of hell.'[14] Nymphs adorned the Elysian Fields and as the King of Navarre appeared, leading his men all dressed in armour and livery specially made for the play, the King and his brothers prevented their entrance to paradise and sent them to a sulphurous hell, while the angelic nymphs danced a ballet. The fantastic show ended in a great false battle with the King and his brothers rescuing Navarre and his comrades from their Mephistophelian gaol. The theme being, after all, reconciliation and fraternity. To rescue the prisoners from hell, lances were broken in an unconscious reminder of the King's father's death. The evening concluded with an impressive firework display which very nearly became much more impressive than had been intended when a spark fell in among the unspent rockets. The subject matter of the *pantomime* might seem very near the bone under the prevailing political circumstances, but, heaven and hell, good and evil were almost always the subject of Renaissance Court entertainments.

For the most part Admiral de Coligny, who lodged at the Hôtel de Béthizy, kept his appearances at the wedding entertainments to a minimum. He wrote to his wife on the night of 18 August:

M'amie ... today the marriage of Madame the sister of the King and the King of Navarre was celebrated. There will follow three or four days of celebrations, masques, and combats. After these the King had assured and promised me that he will give me some time to deal with several complaints about breaches in the Edict from all around the kingdom. If I thought of nothing but my own happiness I would rather come to see you than to be at this Court, for many reasons which I will tell you. But one must look after the people before one looks after oneself.

He added a postscript: 'Let me know how the little man, or the little girl, is doing. Three days ago I had an attack of colic, partly wind, partly gravel, but, thank God, it lasted only eight or ten hours, and today I feel no effect of it thanks be to God, and I promise you that I shall not be much in evidence during all these feasts and combats during the next few days.'[15]

One account of this fateful period claims that on 20 August the King – ignorant of his mother's plan – told Coligny that he had 'no confidence' in the Guises and ordered a company of 1200 arquebusiers to be brought into the city and posted at various key positions. On 21 August the last of the celebrations, a *'course à bagues'* (a tilt at the ring), took place in the great courtyard of the Louvre followed by a ball lasting well into the early morning. On the same day the Admiral received word in cypher from the wife of one of his lieutenants of a plot being hatched against 'those of the religion'. Other Huguenot officers had also approached him during the last four days warning him of some *'méchante affaire'*. He listened to these unspecific warnings, but according to his habit he carried on as usual. Some Huguenots – including his cousin Montmorency – had felt it prudent to leave the city and had done so almost immediately after the wedding, but Coligny remained, captive of his own schemes.[16]

On 21 August the Admiral, impatient and anxious for Charles to give his ultimate sanction for the expedition into the Low Countries, apparently requested an audience with the King. Charles, whose inconsistent ardour for the project had decidedly cooled with his mother's arrival, had begun to avoid Coligny. Too cowardly to face him and exhausted by the tug-of-war between the Admiral and his mother, he put off all serious business, saying, 'Mon père, I pray you grant me four or five days of pleasure, and after that I promise you, on the faith of a king, to give you and those of your religion content.'[17] The Admiral, so infuriated at being put off this time, is said to have threatened to leave Paris, also making the imprudent comment that this abrupt departure might lead to a civil war instead of a foreign one. Upon hearing this, Anjou is reported to have moved contingents of troops to various key outposts around the city with the plausible explanation that they were merely there to stop any trouble between the Guise, Châtillon and Montmorency factions.

What now follows has been the subject of speculation for over 400 years. One thing is certain: Catherine played a leading role in the setting of the chain of events that would culminate in the bloodiest massacre in French history, unequalled until the French Revolution. Late that night, as the last of the marriage revelries took place, it is believed that the Queen Mother held a meeting that included Anjou, Guise, his uncle d'Aumale, the Duke of Nemours and Marshal de Tavannes, where they examined the plan for the morrow in detail. While the conspirators talked, the assassin Maurevert was let into Villemur's house at the cloister of Saint-Germain-l'Auxerrois by M. de Chailly, the Duke d'Aumale's maître d'hôtel. The house was located on the exact route that the Admiral would be taking in the morning to and from the council meeting at the Louvre Palace.

On the morning of Friday, 22 August, the government recess for the marriage celebrations being now over, Admiral Gaspard de Coligny left his lodgings on the rue de Béthizy – today No. 144 rue de Rivoli – for a council meeting that was to start at nine o'clock. He had wished to press for French military intervention in Flanders, but to his frustration he found Anjou presiding over the meeting as the King had risen late. Anjou left the meeting early and when matters had been concluded the Admiral came across the King on his way with Téligny and the Duke of Guise to play a game of tennis. Charles begged Coligny to join him for a game but the Admiral refused. They parted at around eleven o'clock and Coligny left the Louvre for his short walk home, reading a document while he did so. As he approached the window at which Maurevert was hiding a binding on one of his shoes came loose and he bent down to fix it. Just as he did so, a shot rang out. The bullet broke his left arm and almost tore the index finger off his right hand. Had he not bent over at the critical moment he would have been mortally wounded.

A huge commotion ensued. Having first ensured that the Admiral had not been dangerously hurt, a number of his gentlemen ran into the building from which they had heard the shot. They found a smoking arquebus behind the latticed window, but the would-be killer had already made his escape through a back door where he had had a horse waiting. Two Huguenot officers, Séré and Saint-Aubin, set off after him. Two servants found in the house were arrested. Coligny, fainting with pain and shock, and fearful of further attacks, had his men carry him quickly back to the Hôtel de Béthizy. Catherine had just sat down to eat with the Duke of Anjou when word of the failed attempt on the Admiral's life reached her. Diego de Zuñiga, the Spanish ambassador, happened to be nearby and watched the Queen Mother's completely impassive face as she heard the news. Little did he realise that the words whispered in her ear confirmed that she now faced the most hazardous situation of her life. Betraying nothing, Catherine and Anjou quietly got up from the table and walked to her private chambers.

Charles stood arguing on the tennis court over a point when he heard what had happened from the two Huguenot captains, Armand de Piles and François de Monniens, whom Coligny had immediately despatched to the King. Throwing down his racquet in a rage he screamed, 'Am I never to be left in peace? More trouble! More trouble!' and stormed off to his apartments. Here his brother-in-law Navarre, as well as Condé and other senior Huguenots soon appeared and confronted him, clamouring for justice. Sending Ambroise Paré, the famous surgeon who had tried to save his father in 1559, to Coligny, the King made three important declarations to show his good faith. He promised a full investigation into the crime, saying that the guilty parties, whoever they were, would be brought to justice. He forbade the citizens of Paris to take up arms, and ordered that the area around the Admiral be cleared of Catholics so that he would be surrounded only by his own men. The Duke of Guise wisely decided to quit the Louvre and go to his family *hôtel* while the King busily issued orders.

The scene in Coligny's room was chaotic. According to a *fidèle témoin* (a reliable witness), Paré had arrived quickly and set to work on the Admiral's wounds. Operating first on the dangling digit, it took three gruesome attempts before he finally managed to cut the finger off 'as his scissors were not well sharpened' and he then attended to the injured arm.[18] Two deep incisions were made and the bullet was mercifully extracted without endless probing. Crowding round his bed, Coligny's men gasped and wept. Their leader, maintaining his characteristic heroic composure, managed not only to keep from uttering the slightest groan but could even find words of comfort for his dismayed friends. As word spread across the city of the attempted murder the number of worried and angry Huguenots arriving at the Hôtel de Béthizy grew so rapidly that it became almost impossible to pass in or out of the house.

That afternoon the King paid a visit to the convalescing Coligny. The Queen Mother and Anjou accompanied him, determined not to be left behind, and with them came Navarre, Condé, Retz, Tavannes and Nevers. All of these except the King, Navarre and Condé were jostled menacingly by the angry crowd both inside the *hôtel* and outside in the street. Once in the Admiral's chamber, bent down beside the stricken victim, the King swore vengeance for the outrageous crime: '*Mon père! Par le mort de Dieu!* You have the wound and I the pain. I will give up my own salvation if I do not avenge this crime against you.' His outrage, oaths and tears were mimicked and magnified by the Queen Mother and Anjou, who with heroic hypocrisy strove to outdo the King in his declarations of anguish and determination to see the authors of this outrage brought to justice. Charles's vehemently-spoken words can hardly have inspired cheer in Anjou or his mother, nor is it likely that the couple's 'outrage' convinced the menacing crowd of Huguenots surrounding them, least of all the victim himself.

The King ordered that the inquiry into the crime begin immediately and be led by the Premier Président de Parlement de Thou and the Admiral's friend, Councillor Cavaignes. Coligny begged the King to come closer so that he might speak to him privately, at which Charles signalled for Catherine and Anjou to retire from the bedside further away. Anjou recalled,

> We accordingly quitted the bed and stood in the middle of the chamber where we remained during this private colloquy, which gave us great suspicion and unease. Moreover, we saw ourselves surrounded by more than two hundred ... partisans of the Admiral. ... These all had melancholy coun- tenances, and showed by their gestures and signs how disaffected they were; some whispered, others did nothing but pass behind and before us, and omitted to pay us the honour and reverence which were our due, as if they suspected us of having caused the wound of the Admiral. ... The Queen my mother has since acknowledged that never had she found herself in a more critical position.[19]

Catherine, frantic to prevent any information being passed by Coligny to the King that might compromise her and Anjou, broke into their conversation to exclaim solicitously that the Admiral must be tired and that the King was fatiguing him. Charles reluctantly withdrew and offered to have the Admiral brought to the Louvre for greater safety. Coligny replied that he felt quite safe with the King's protection. Catherine and Charles both asked to look at the blood-soaked bullet extracted from the Admiral's arm at which the Queen Mother is supposed to have declared, 'Glad am I, that it has been extracted for when M. de Guise was killed the physicians declared that his life would have been safe had they been able to find the ball.' This remark smacks of *l'esprit d'escalier,* for while it would have been poetic to mention the death of François, Duke of Guise it would undoubtedly have provoked uproar – the very last thing Catherine needed at that particular moment.

As soon as the royal party had left, the Huguenots and their leader held a meeting to decide upon the best course of action. Many wanted the Admiral removed from Paris immediately, but Téligny, Navarre and Condé felt that it would be a terrible insult to the King. Charles knew nothing of his mother's plot and had evidently convinced his Huguenot audience of the sincerity of his goodwill during the visit. Coligny agreed to stay in Paris. The trusting Téligny then suggested moving the Admiral to the Louvre, but this was rejected absolutely by the others, not only for security reasons but also because Paré declared the Admiral to be in no condition to move anywhere yet. None of the Admiral's supporters knew that among their number was one of Catherine's spies, Antoine de Bouchevannes. He reported that despite forceful argument by many of Coligny's captains to remove him from the city, by fighting their way out if necessary, the Admiral had decided to remain in Paris. She knew, however, that they might change their minds at any moment. Several of the senior members of the party, including the Bourbon Vidame de Chartres and Gabriel, Comte de Montgomery – the accidental killer of Henri II at the joust – had already decided to move across the river to the faubourg Saint-Germain, from where escape would be easier should it become necessary.

Anjou later recalled that in the carriage returning to the Louvre his mother managed to bring the conversation round to the subject most troubling her: what had the Admiral said to Charles? The King, who had until then been sitting in angry silence, flared up with the reply that Coligny had warned him that his role as king had been usurped by his mother and brother. Other accounts have Coligny also telling the King that despite his enfeebled condition, he would remain in Paris to continue with the Netherlands project and to ensure the observation of the Edict of Saint-Germain. Whatever took place in the carriage, the King certainly arrived back at the Louvre in a fury, which left Catherine and Anjou in a state of complete trepidation. That same afternoon Charles sent word to his various ambassadors throughout Europe. To La Motte-Fénélon, in England, he wrote, 'Please advise the Queen of England that I intend to obtain and ensure justice is done in such a way that this will be an example to all in my kingdom. ... I also wish to tell you that this evil deed comes from the animosity between the Houses of Châtillon and Guise, and I shall command them not to involve my subjects in their private quarrels.'[20]

It was to be a restless night for Catherine and Anjou. The duke later recalled with some humbug that 'stung and outraged by the language of the Admiral and by the faith which the King seemed to put in it ... we were so bewildered that we could find no solution for the moment, and parted deferring the matter until the next day'. Knowing that it could only be a question of time before the evidence led to the Guises, Catherine could be certain that if she took no action her role in the affair would soon be disclosed by them to the King. Not only had Coligny survived but after the King's outburst in the carriage it appeared that he was more in control than ever. Anjou recalled going to his mother's apartments at dawn to find her awake; she had not slept. Searching desperately for a solution, they both understood the imperative need to 'finish the Admiral by whatever means we could find. And since we could no longer use stratagem, it had to be done openly, but for this purpose it was necessary to bring the King around to our resolution. We decided to go to him in his study, after dinner ...'[21]

By the afternoon of Saturday, 23 August the two servants arrested at Villemur's house had been questioned. This had led to the arrest of Chailly, who had let Maurevert into the house on the night before the assassination attempt. The man who had brought the getaway horse to the house had also been found and it was quickly ascertained that the animal came from the Guises' stables. The two captains who had chased the marksman immediately after the attack had traced him as far as the country estate of M. Chailly but they had lost track of him there. They claimed, however, that the would-be-killer was none other than Maurevert. Already abominable to them for the shooting of de Mouy, he was a known client of the Guises. Deciding to pre-empt any intemperate reaction by the King, and accompanied by his uncle d'Aumale, Henri of Guise presented himself to Charles and asked for permission to leave the city. The king replied, 'You can go to the Devil if you wish, but I shall know how to find you if I need to.' The duke took his leave by the Porte Saint-Antoine, before doubling back to the security of the Hôtel de Guise.[22] As a champion of the Catholic cause he knew he would be far safer in Paris than anywhere else.

Shops were closing and the populace grew restless at the impudent and threatening attitude of the Huguenots. The Parisians had not forgotten their hunger during the siege of 1567. The heat, the marriage celebrations and the mob now roused a deep and long-held resentment against the Protestants, only further fuelled by the sight of so many black-clad Huguenots all over the city. Why, they asked themselves, did their King allow himself to be surrounded by them? The priests grew bolder in their denunciation of the King's protection of the heretics, nor was Catherine immune from their insults.

The atmosphere became desperate. Since the day of the attack on the Admiral, many Catholics had been quietly arming and preparing themselves for a strike from the Huguenots, most of whom were well equipped for their intended 'crusade' into the Low Countries. Late on 23 August after a meeting at the Louvre, the Prévôt des Marchands and magistrates ordered militiamen led by their captains to congregate at the Hôtel de Ville. They were given strict instructions not to provoke trouble; they were only there to prevent pillaging and damage if the mob went on a rampage. One emissary wrote with prescience, 'Unless this great fury passes, we shall soon hear of some huge madness.' The Spanish ambassador informed Philip II, 'It is to be hoped that the rascal [Coligny] lives, for, if he lives, suspecting the King of this assassination, he will abandon his plans against Your Majesty and turn them against the man who consented to this attempt on his person. If he should die, I am afraid that those who survive will do more than the King will permit or command.'[23] He continued, referring to Catherine, 'She has sent word to me that she cannot speak to me at this time for fear that I might be seen entering the palace, and that she does not wish even to write to Your Majesty lest what she wishes to do be discovered, for letters can be intercepted, but that soon she will speak or write to me.'[24]

Just as the tension in the street was palpable, so feelings around the Louvre Palace itself ran high. Rows broke out between the Huguenot escorts, gentlemen of Condé and Navarre, and the royal guards. Téligny arrived at the palace to present to Charles Coligny's request for a detachment of the King's personal troops to protect him at his lodgings. Anjou, who happened to be present, offered a guard of fifty arquebusiers commanded by Captain de Cosseins, a client of the Guises. Téligny knew well that de Cosseins was a declared enemy of the Admiral but feared upsetting the King who seemed pleased with the suggestion and confirmed his brother's order. The traffic between the Louvre and the Hôtel de Béthizy was constant: Margot went to visit the Admiral who, although in a weakened condition, appeared to have recovered a little of his old strength. Having spent some time sending out word to his followers in the provinces that he was alive and relatively well, he allowed a group of anxious German students to pay their hero a visit. One of them recalled that he spoke to them 'affably and seemed quite assured that nothing would happen to him without the Almighty's approval'.[25] The King had sent messengers throughout the day seeking news of an improvement in the Admiral's condition and to enquire if he needed anything to make him more comfortable. The Huguenots' anxieties increased when they noted that the authorities were making a round of the inns and boarding houses where many of them had lodged, compiling lists of the Protestants' names. Perhaps it was only a precautionary measure, but the Admiral's men felt uneasy.

On the afternoon of 23 August Catherine had called together her inner circle, Retz, Tavannes, Nevers and Chancellor Birague for a desperate 'war council' on how to proceed now that the assassination attempt had failed. According to the memoirs of the Marshal de Tavannes, she decided that the meeting would take place in the Tuileries Gardens where they could discuss their pressing problems while they walked and decide whether or not to launch a pre-emptive strike on the Huguenots. They would not be overheard. As Tavannes recalled, 'Because the attempt on the Admiral would cause a war, she and the rest of us agreed that it would be advisable to bring battle in Paris.'[26] They would finish the work so badly begun by Maurevert, but this time their victims would include not only the Admiral but also his most senior Huguenot nobles and captains so conveniently either lodged with the Admiral or around him in the city. This would effectively decapitate the rebel movement and, they hoped, prevent a fourth full-scale civil war. All agreed that such an opportunity would never present itself again. There were also worrying signs that if they did not act soon the Huguenots might strike first. Even as they had been walking behind the walls of the Queen Mother's garden, Brantôme himself reported hearing violent abuse coming from Protestants on the other side, who shouted: 'We are striking back and will kill!'

Outside the Hôtels de Guise and Aumale the same scenes were unfolding, only there the Huguenots clad in armour marched back and forth as if patrolling the walls of the two Guise strongholds.[27] The most shocking evidence that the situation was getting out of control occurred at the Queen Mother's *souper* which, despite the agitation, she decided to hold in public as usual. With the utmost contempt for her royal person, the Baron de Pardaillan Ségur, a Huguenot from Gascony, approached Catherine's table proclaiming in a loud voice that those of the new religion would not rest until justice had been meted out to the criminals guilty of the assault upon the Admiral. If there had been any doubt in Catherine's mind, this public and barely veiled threat ensured that her plan must proceed without delay. In Margot's memoirs, written many years after these events, she confirms that the threats of Pardaillan 'exposed the evil intent of the Huguenots to attack both the King and herself [Catherine] that very night'.

In order to act with full legal authority and to gain the King's support, Catherine now faced the unpleasant task of informing him that she had been deceiving him all along. She had to tell her son that it was not only the Guises who had planned the killing of Coligny but that she and Anjou had also been involved from the first. The Queen Mother selected Retz for the task of breaking the news to the King for she knew him to be well liked and trusted by Charles; only once he had absorbed the shocking and dreadful truth would she speak to him herself.

At around nine o'clock on the evening of 23 August Retz went to the King in his study, where he disclosed that his mother and brother had been accomplices in the attack on Coligny. Furthermore, according to Margot's account, he warned the King that he and the royal family now faced the gravest peril. He explained that the Huguenots planned 'not only to take the Duke of Guise, but the Queen his mother, and his brother. They also believed that the King himself had consented to the attack on the Admiral and had therefore decided to rise up that very night against them and others throughout his kingdom.'[28]

Scarcely able to believe his ears, Charles struggled to absorb what had been done. Worse still, he now found himself in the most hazardous position with no idea of how to proceed to defend himself and the realm. 'Dexterously had Catherine played her role; but with still more subtle craft did she consummate the final overthrow of those who dared to brave her power,' wrote one historian, as the Queen Mother, followed by Anjou, Nevers, Tavannes and Birague, then entered the King's room to convince him of what must now be done.[29] Catherine began by going over the old grievances against the Admiral, especially the '*Surprise de Meaux*', and the killing of Captain Charry, his friend and loyal servant, murdered in a vendetta, some believed by the order of Coligny. François, Duke of Guise could also be counted among the many victims of this evil man, they said. She cited all the years of troubles in the kingdom brought upon them by the Huguenots. As for the proposed war with Spain, how dare the Admiral proceed against Philip in defiance of the full authority of the King and his council? Figures – doubtless exaggerated to alarm him – were given to Charles from Bouchevannes, their spy at the Hôtel de Béthizy, of the large number of Huguenot troops both inside Paris already and headed for the city.

At first the King cried that these were lies and 'the Admiral loves me as though I were his own son. He would never do anything to harm me.' Eventually the haranguing of his mother and the mournful affirmations of her supporters broke his spirit and drained his endurance. Feeling he had been betrayed by his trusted friend, he began to listen to Catherine as she outlined their plan to kill all the senior Huguenots in Paris, starting with the Admiral. The Bourbon Princes of the Blood were to be kept alive and forced to abjure the Protestant faith under pain of death. Finally convinced, the young, ill and unstable King is said to have uttered the immortal cry for which he is principally remembered: 'Then kill them all! Kill them all!' It is almost certain that by this he meant all those on a list drawn up by Catherine and not, as has often been claimed, all the Huguenots in France. A terrible massacre would not resolve anything, but the killing of a select few might eliminate the heretics' high command. The King prepared and approved the list of those to be executed; he desired above all that this should be a legal state undertaking. Although no such list has ever been unearthed, that is hardly surprising considering its sensitivity.

With Charles's monarchical approval won, the plan had to be put into action immediately. Urgent despatches were written and sent out. The Duke of Guise was given the task of taking his men to the Hôtel de Béthizy and there to kill the Admiral. Le Charron, the Prévôt des Marchands, was summoned and told that at that very moment Huguenot forces marched on the city. His orders were to muster his militiamen, close the city gates and guard all other possible exits from the city. Chained barges were linked up across the Seine to prevent escape downriver. To protect the houses of the militiamen each one had an armed guard wearing a white sash on his right arm, with a flaming torch, assigned to stand in their doorways. The Catholic bourgeoise were issued arms for self-protection and cannons were placed in front of the Hôtel de Ville. The King's own royal bodyguards and the personal troops of the Guises were to undertake the actual killings, led by Guise, Aumale, Nevers, Tavannes and Angoulême, Henry II's illegitimate son.

The signal for the start of the attack – the murder of Coligny – was to be the bell of the Palais de Justice which would toll at three o'clock in the morning. In fact, the tocsin of Saint-Germain-l'Auxerrois rang out about a minute earlier and so the killings commenced. Tavannes' memoirs describe a moment of doubt in Catherine just before the bell's deadly chime sounded. It is more likely that all he witnessed was a woman gripped by a moment of fear that the plan would fail. Just like the death of Coligny, the list of condemned men caused her no personal remorse and she regarded it as a practical measure that required a decisive hand and the resolve to see it through. Decisiveness and resolve were two qualities she had in full measure when it came to protecting the Valois dynasty.

Just a few minutes' walk away from the Louvre, Guise's men had already arrived at the Hôtel de Béthizy. Guise, acting on the old truth that if something needs doing properly one should do it oneself, personally led the detachment. De Cosseins, the captain of the guard posted there by the King the day before and a man devoted to the Duke of Guise, called up to say that he had a messenger from the King who urgently needed to speak to the Admiral. Coligny's faithful maître d'hôtel therefore unlocked the door, whereupon he was immediately stabbed by de Cosseins. One of the Admiral's Swiss guards managed to get upstairs and, using a chest of drawers, he barricaded the door to his chamber. As soon as he heard the commotion the Admiral understood that this was the end. He asked for his robe and bade Merlin, the chaplain, to pray with him. Ambroise Paré, also in attendance, turned to the Admiral saying, 'Monseigneur, it is God who calls you unto him, the doors have been breached, and there are no means here for our protection.'[30] The Admiral is supposed to have replied, 'For a long time now I have been preparing for death, save yourselves, for you cannot save me. I will commend my soul to God's mercy.'[31] Unafraid, the Admiral awaited the inevitable as Téligny climbed on to the rooftop, only to be shot dead from the courtyard below. Paré and the others were spared.

Pushing the obstacle aside, Anjou's Swiss guards had followed de Cosseins up the stairs where they came face to face with the Swiss guard of Navarre. They did not fire on each other. Instead, de Cosseins called on his own guards, two of Guise's men, to kick down the door to

Coligny's bedroom, their swords in their hands. One asked him, 'Are you the Admiral?' 'I am,' he replied and, with a look of disdain, added, 'I should at least be killed by a gentleman and not by this boor,' at which the boor thrust his sword into the Admiral's chest and then beat him about the head. They then threw his body out of the window. Some say he was still just alive as they noticed his fingers clinging on to the ledge for a moment, before falling into the courtyard below, landing beside the Duke of Guise and Angoulême. Guise looked at the bloody face of the corpse at his feet before uttering, 'Ma foi! It is him!' Giving the corpse a satisfying kick, he turned and set off on horseback with Angoulême.[32]

At the Louvre, where so many Huguenot nobles had lodged for the marriage, the killings also began. Earlier, on the evening of the 23rd, Margot had been in her mother's private apartments with her sister Claude, Duchess of Lorraine. She had seen for herself that there were strange preparations being made that indicated trouble, although in her memoirs she wrote, 'As for me no one told me anything about this.' She had already fallen victim to what she feared most: excluded by the Protestants who surrounded her husband, now her family treated her as suspect. It was impossible to ignore the whispering and febrile activity around her, yet she was cold-shouldered by both sides. In her memoirs she recalled that dreadful night:

> The Huguenots suspected me because I was a Catholic, and the Catholics because I had married the King of Navarre, so that no one told me anything until that evening. I was at the *coucher* of the Queen my mother, sitting on a chest with my sister [the Duchess] of Lorraine, who was very depressed, when my mother noticed me and sent me to bed. As I was making my curtsy, my sister caught me by the sleeve and detained me. She began to weep and said, 'Mon Dieu, sister, you must not go.' This frightened me greatly. My mother, noticing it, called my sister and spoke to her sharply, forbidding her to tell me anything. My sister said that it was not right to send me away like that to be sacrificed and that, if they discovered anything, no doubt they would avenge themselves on me. My mother replied that, God willing, I would come to no harm, but in any case I must go, for fear of awaking their suspicions. I could see that they were arguing, though I did not catch the words. She commanded me sharply again to retire. My sister, melting into tears, bade me goodnight, not daring to say anything further; and I left the room bewildered and dazed without knowing what it was that I feared. No sooner had I reached my closet than I said my prayers, imploring God to take me under His wing and to guard me against what or whom I knew not.[33]

For Catherine to have withheld her daughter from the Protestants' apartments that night might have alerted them to the plot. She was therefore allowed to go to what her mother well knew would very soon become a charnel house. It was a mark of the Queen Mother's utter commitment to the success of the operation that she put the prosperity of her plans before the well-being of her daughter.

Henri of Navarre had been in his apartments at the palace holding an urgent meeting with his suite of nobles about the worrying signs that an attack of some sort might be imminent. He was restless and decided that he would speak to the King early the next morning. When Margot arrived,

> The King, my husband, who was in his bed, sent word to me that I should retire which I did. I found his bed surrounded by some thirty or forty Huguenots, who were strangers to me as yet, as I had been married only a few days. All night long they talked of the accident to the Admiral, deciding to go to the King as soon as it were day and to demand justice.[34]

Margot was to get little rest that night, for as her husband rose at the first light of dawn, having been unable to sleep, he decided to play tennis while waiting for the King to rise. He had not walked more than a few paces from his apartment when he and his companions were stopped by guards on the King's orders. Separated from his gentlemen, the elite of the Protestant party, most of whom he would never see again, Henri was taken with his cousin the Prince de Condé to a chamber and ordered to remain there by the King's command for his own safety.

As he was locked in with his cousin, his comrades were being slaughtered, easy victims trapped in the heart of their enemy's citadel. Nançay, captain of the royal guard, led his men as they began their gruesome work. Most of the Huguenots were asleep when the killing started. Dragged from their beds, their throats were cut before they had a chance to fight back. As the noise of screams and terror resounded throughout the passages, staircases, and confusing catacomb of corridors that made up part of the much-altered palace, the survivors ran desperately, attempting to hide from the teams of killers. Finding nowhere to conceal themselves, many were chased into the great courtyard of the Louvre. There, awaiting them, were the King's archers who pushed the terrified men and women on to the halbards of the Swiss guards, who impaled their unarmed quarry with grim efficiency.

Margot had just fallen asleep in her husband's bed when someone was heard desperately banging and kicking against the door, crying out, 'Navarre! Navarre!' Margot's old *nourrice* (wet-nurse), thinking it was Navarre himself, hurriedly unlocked the door only to find that it was Monsieur de Leran, one of his gentlemen. Margot was aghast when she saw him:

Wounded in the elbow by a sword and by a halberd on the arm, and [he] was pursued by four archers who followed him into the room. To save himself, he flung himself on my bed, and I, with that man holding me, rolled into the passage and he after me, still hugging my body. I did not know who he was nor whether he meant to outrage me nor whether it was him or myself whom the archers were pursuing. We both screamed and were equally terrified. But at last, as God would have it, Monsieur de Nançay, the captain of the guards, came in. Seeing me in that position, though he pitied me, he could not help laughing, and ... gave me the life of that poor man who was clinging to me. I had him laid in my closet and his wounds tended and kept him there until he recovered. While I was changing my shift, which was bloody, Monsieur de Nançay told me what was happening and assured me that the King my husband was in the King's room and that no harm would come to him. Wrapping me in a bed-robe, he led me to the apartment of my sister Madame de Lorraine where I arrived more dead than alive. As I entered the antechamber, the door of which was standing wide open, a gentleman named Bourse, running from the archers who were at his heels, was struck by a halberd not three feet away from me. I fell almost fainting into the arms of Monsieur de Nançay and ... as soon as I could recover, I ran into the little room where my sister slept.[35]

According to Margot's account she then intervened for two of her husband's men, his *valet de chambre*, Jean d'Armagnac and Jean de Miossens, first gentleman to Henri of Navarre. They begged her to save them and she in turn went on her knees before the King and Queen Mother, who reluctantly agreed to spare their lives.

As the feast day of Saint Bartholomew dawned, all but a few of the most senior Huguenots had been killed in or around the Louvre, the Admiral among the first. The flower of the French Protestant movement, many of them experienced soldiers – including Pardaillan, Piles and others who had enjoyed success in battle – were eliminated, as well as great noblemen such as La Rochefoucauld, killed in his bed by the brother of the King's fool Chicot. Neither were those poor wretches who slept in humbler lodgings or in the streets shown any mercy. Easily identifiable by their black-and-white clothes, few of those Protestants who had come to Paris, some bringing their wives and children to experience the thrill of a royal wedding, escaped. Appearing on no list of those condemned to die, these innocents now fell victim to the indiscriminate massacre that followed. Their assailants, be they militiamen, troops or hate-filled Parisians, fell upon the detested heretics, men, women and children. Pregnant women were eviscerated and had their wombs cut out. Baskets filled with dead or dying small children were cast into the Seine. Most of the victims were stripped naked for any loot.

Nearly all had had their throats cut, and many of the men were mutilated and disembowelled.

Zuñiga wrote cheerfully, if to modern ears chillingly, to his master Philip II, 'As I write, they are killing them all, they are stripping them naked, dragging them through the streets, plundering the houses and sparing not even children. Blessed be God who has converted the French princes to His cause! May he inspire their hearts to continue as they have begun!'[36] Most of the diplomatic reports written at the time convey conflicting reports and often completely false information, reflecting the confusion and chaos of the situation for those in its midst. As the frenzied slaughter broadened in scope, old scores could be conveniently settled cloaked by the bloody, dusty chaos. It was later noted that a number of bourgeois Catholic Parisians had suffered the same fate as the Protestants; many financial debts were wiped clean with the death of creditors and moneylenders that night. Here was an opportunity to rob a neighbour, kill a personal enemy, or perhaps even rid oneself of a nagging wife without risk of discovery, amidst the insane, seemingly unstoppable carnage. Libraries were set ablaze and, all the time, priests and preachers encouraged the bloodshed. There was a rumour that the Almighty Himself had sent the Parisians a special sign of his approval by the miraculous flowering of a dried-out hawthorn bush beside a statue of the Holy Virgin in the Cimitière des Innocents.

The authorised 'executions' had, as far as was possible, been completed by five o'clock in the morning of Sunday 24 August. For confirmation of their deputed killers' efficiency the King and Queen Mother needed to look no further than the courtyard of their own palace to see the grotesque piles of mutilated corpses. By the afternoon, Charles, dismayed at reports of the unbridled carnage in the streets of his capital, gave the order for the killings to stop. His command went unheeded and the violence continued for a further three days. Most citizens of Paris had stayed at home, away from the violence, their houses shuttered or boarded up for safety. It was the mob that ruled the streets during those bloody days of late August 1572.

The violence soon spread to the provinces, despite the despatch from the King on the 24th announcing that there had been a bloody clash between the houses of Guise and Châtillon and that the local authorities must keep control over their localities. By 25 August the first despatch was no longer credible and the King issued a fresh declaration stating that the Huguenots had premeditated an attack against the King which had been thwarted. By his original orders the strictest control must be kept to prevent the violence from spreading, but the commands that followed from the King or his council were by no means consistent or even comprehensible.

Misunderstanding piled upon confusion. In many regions it was too late anyhow; the flames of hatred fanned out over the country and many provincial cities followed the capital with origies of killing. In October 1572 the tumult finally reached southern France, where the last of the cruelty unleashed on Saint Bartholemew's day was finally spent.

The fortunate Huguenots who had taken the precaution of moving over the river to Saint Germain – among them the Vidame of Chartres, the Comte de Montgomery and Baron de Pardaillan, father of the man who had impetuously threatened Catherine at her public *souper* on 23 August – had heard the commotion near the Louvre and assumed at first that it was just a street brawl. When they saw their comrades who had managed to escape from the palace trying to cross the river and being shot as they did so, the Protestant *seigneurs* realised what was afoot and fled the city as fast as they could. At about five o'clock in the morning Guise and Angoulême set off after them, but having been given the wrong keys to the Porte de Bussy, the few surviving Protestant leaders had time to make a good head start. After half a dozen miles in pursuit, they gave up the chase. Only a handful of senior Huguenots had escaped, yet each carried with them the spores to start a fresh civil war.

THIRTEEN

The Last Years of Charles IX

Too much malice! Too much malice!

1572–74

As the murders continued outside, the royal family stayed, anxious and frightened, inside the Louvre. For nearly three days they did not venture outside, fearing attack. There were moments of calm in the streets outside, but all too often these were followed by a sudden resurgence of violence. Had an assault been made on the palace it would have proved singularly difficult to protect it in its current condition, halfway through its transition from medieval fortress to baroque palace. Horrified at the bloody manhunt that they had witnessed in the palace itself and what they could see from the windows, the family were nonetheless weirdly isolated in the midst of the bloodbath. Catherine had so often been forced to evolve her policies as events unfolded, navigating around difficulties as they arose, but never had her will been so completely submerged and her powers of action so circumscribed as they were during those disastrous days.

The fate of Coligny's body, the Massacre of Saint Bartholomew's first and foremost victim, epitomised the fanatical hatred that had taken over the city. The corpse had been emasculated and pieces cut off it as the crowd pulled it through the streets and then threw it into the Seine. What remained of the corpse was eventually fished out and hung by its feet from the gibbet at Montfaucon, where during the last civil war it had only hung in effigy. According to Agrippa d'Aubigné and Brantôme, the decapitated head was then presented to Catherine, who had it embalmed and sent on to Rome as a gift to the Pope.* A few days after the violence had subsided – and then only under cover of darkness – François de Montmorency sent a small group of men to cut down his uncle's remains and take them to Chantilly for a Christian burial.

Catherine's first and only thought was not for the innocent dead but how to keep the King on his throne after such a calamity. Before

---

* Other sources say that Coligny's head was originally intended as a gift for the Duke of Alba.

reliable information could be gathered she could only guess at repercussions. The King's complete loss of control over what were meant to be limited and legal executions showed how slight was his authority and what terrifying power the mob possessed. The Queen Mother also understood how the Massacre, originally driven by religious passions, had quickly spun out of control and had become a popular uprising of angry despair by people who felt little or no fear of royal retribution. Some historians have even viewed it as a portent of what was to come in 1789. Although it is impossible to say with any accuracy how many people perished during what was later called the 'Season of Saint Bartholomew' in Paris and its aftermath in the provinces, most experts believe that the death toll throughout the kingdom was possibly as high as between 20,000 and 30,000. In Paris alone it is thought that 2000 to 3000 people lost their lives. The Huguenots registered in Paris had numbered only some 800, although there were many too poor to be on any list or register and therefore the number is likely to have been far higher. This still leaves around 1000 dead Parisians who were not Huguenots. Some of these died when a Protestant victim managed to fight back, though many were probably the victims of criminals motivated by greed. It might therefore be argued that a high percentage of the remaining hundreds were killed as a result of general discontent, the 'haves' killed by the 'have-nots'.

The Duke of Guise, appalled at the scale of the bloodletting he found when he returned to the city after giving chase to Montgomery and the Vidame of Chartres, tried to calm the mob. But even he, the Catholic hero of Paris, could do nothing. Guise, already considering how his role would be perceived, had taken steps to protect his reputation, let alone his immortal soul, by defending Protestants in the streets and giving them sanctuary at the Hôtel de Guise. He argued that the Admiral's death had restored his family honour and he had sought the death only of those on the King's list. Realising that the names of the authors and perpetrators of this enormity would be stained for ever, he soon began to distance himself from the King, particularly so since Catherine was already according Guise a prominent role in the massacre. He argued that Charles should make a public avowal that the original executions were by the sovereign's command. This would be at odds with the early royal declarations that the horrors sprang from the blood feud between the Houses of Guise and Châtillon, and the ensuing carnage was perpetrated by lawless thugs and criminals.

On Tuesday, 26 August, before having regained proper control of the city, Charles held a special *Lit de Justice* attended by his brothers and Henri of Navarre, at which he carefully listed the outrages and crimes committed by Coligny and his rebels against himself and the Crown over recent years. He also outlined the number of concessions he had made to the Huguenots. In return for all his goodness, patience and generosity, he claimed that the Admiral and his cohorts had plotted to kill him and his family. He added that the Duke of Guise had acted solely with his royal authority. Finally he made the declaration: 'I wish it to be known that the severe executions of the past few days have been performed by my express command in order to prevent the results of this abominable conspiracy.' When asked if the King wished his words to be entered on to the records of the Parlement he replied, 'I wish it.' The parlementaires then proceeded to heap praise upon the King for his magnificent defence of the throne against the perfidious rebels, but in reality they lauded a convenient formula that protected them all.

France required an official explanation and Charles gave them one. The historian Jacques-Auguste de Thou, whose father was the Parlement's president and had been charged by the King to investigate the original attempt on Coligny's life, wrote that it was 'deplorable to see persons who were respectable for their piety, their knowledge and their integrity ... praising, contrary to their feelings ... an act which they detested in their hearts ... but in the false conviction that present circumstances and the good of the state required that they should speak as they did'.[1] Before the session ended the King was asked to restore order over the city. He declared that he desired this above all things. On the short journey back to the Louvre a surviving Protestant, hoping to go unnoticed, joined the large number walking with the King, but one of the lawless crew jostling among the people noticed the luckless fellow and stabbed him to death. 'I wish to God that this were the last one,' Charles muttered as he continued on his way towards the palace.

Aside from the dead, Catherine soon appreciated that the real victims of the Saint Bartholomew Massacre were the monarchy and herself. Having endured the mistrust of the Protestants despite her edicts that had favoured a number of rights and some recognition for them, she knew she must now live with their undying enmity. After 24 August the Huguenots had every reason to believe what the preachers and pamphleteers told them: that the ultimate responsibility for the premeditated and terrible massacre lay at *her* door. According to them, the royal marriage had been a devious trap set by the Machiavellian Queen Mother, perhaps with the backing of Spain, to capture and exterminate their brothers and sisters. The massacre had also made it impossible for the Huguenots, who had hitherto always claimed loyalty to the throne, to maintain this line. Once Charles had officially admitted responsibility for the order to kill the leaders of their party, ordinary Protestants knew that they could no longer offer him allegiance.

As the news spread quickly throughout the Courts of Europe, Catherine found herself the cynosure of Catholic rulers. When word first reached Philip II on 7 September the French ambassador reported that a huge smile was seen to grace the royal countenance and to his observers' further astonishment Philip danced a little jig of delight, 'so contrary to his native temperament and custom'. He then hurried to the monastery of San Geronimo to render his thanks to the Almighty for ridding France of so many heretics. Catherine and Charles enjoyed the rare and short-lived beam of approval emanating from Madrid. The Pope heard the news from the Cardinal of Lorraine himself, anxious to take as much credit for his family as possible. A special medal was struck to commemorate the glorious rout of the Protestants and Te Deums were sung in Rome. The French ambassador quickly published a short version of the events of the massacre under a pseudonym, giving all credit to the King and entitling it *The Stratagem of Charles IX*.

Cardinal Flavio Orsini, the new papal nuncio about to leave for France, carried a message of fulsome praise and thanks from Pope Gregory to the French King. Unfortunately, just as Charles and Catherine had begun to bask in this unexpected upturn in events, the true and accidental nature of the massacre was transmitted to both the Pope and Philip of Spain. Not only had the massacre been an unforeseen explosion by the mob in Paris, but the killing of Coligny – though ordered by Catherine – had been motivated by political rather than spiritual reasons. This had been no national religious crusade orchestrated by the Queen Mother and her son, but a chaotic chain of events set off by a largely secular assassination. The Pope sent a messenger to stop Orsini en route and ordered him not to pass on the message of congratulation to the King and his mother after all.

Catherine, realising that she could no longer claim the laurels that had so temptingly been held out, wrote to Philip telling him that while she had not premeditated the massacre, she had been able to stymie a Huguenot plot to kill the King and the royal family. Astonishingly, she also considered the moment propitious for putting forward another of her matchmaking plans, suggesting that Philip's eldest daughter and Catherine's granddaughter, Isabella Clara Eugenia, should marry her uncle the Duke of Anjou, in order to 'increase the friendship between the two Crowns'. Philip gave his usual negative response. Closer ties with France and the Queen Mother were an odious thought to him.

For the benefit of his father-in-law the Emperor, Charles instructed his ambassador in Vienna to peddle the story that he had been forced to act having uncovered a vast Huguenot plot. However, Maximilian II preferred to subscribe to the theory that it had been a premeditated massacre. His reason for doing so was more selfish than a humble search for truth. He coveted the vacant throne of Poland for one or other of his sons, Archdukes Ernest and Albert, at the expense of the Duke of Anjou. King Sigismund-August had died on 7 July 1572 and Maximilian knew that Anjou's candidature – and the French in general – were stained with obloquy in the eyes of the many Lutheran Polish electors whose favour was pivotal for election to the throne. Maximilian, content to keep matters that way, even employed his own team of learned men to elaborate further on the iniquitous personal role played by Anjou and his family in the horrors of August 1572.

Arnaud du Ferrier, Catherine's ambassador to Venice, sent a brutally frank account of how the events had been perceived in that bastion of pragmatic capitalism:

> Madame, the truth is certain and indubitable that the massacres which have occurred throughout the whole kingdom of France, not only against the Admiral and other principal leaders of the religion, but against so many poor and innocent people, have so profoundly moved and altered the feeling of those here who are friendly to your Crown, even though they are all Catholics, that they cannot be satisfied with any excuse, attributing everything that has been done to you alone and Monsieur d'Anjou.[2]

The Queen Mother's reply on behalf of herself and her son implied scant contrition but much justification: 'We deeply regret that, in the commotion, a number of other persons belonging to their religion were killed by the Catholics who were smarting from the infinite afflictions, pillage, murder, and other wrongs which had been inflicted upon them.'[3]

Throughout the Protestant Courts of Europe the reaction to the massacre was one of shock and unfeigned disgust. There is a legend that when Elizabeth of England, after many delays, finally received the French ambassador, she and her Court wore mourning for their co-religionists. There is no evidence of this in the ambassador's subsequent correspondence, though the Queen's attitude could best be described as most forbidding when she granted an audience to La Motte-Fénélon at Woodstock, where she had been hunting until the terrible news arrived. Elizabeth feared that the Massacre represented but the first step in a grand design against Protestantism, and her theory was supported by Burghley and her spy-master Sir Francis Walsingham, who had been in Paris at the time, barely escaping with his life. Much had been hoped from the growing closeness with France, but now, as Walsingham put it, 'I think it less peril to live with them as enemies than as friends.'[4] La Motte-Fénélon made no attempt to justify the events of Saint Bartholomew, but explained to the Queen that his master had uncovered a Huguenot plot against himself and the royal family, and had taken the necessary measures to protect his kingdom and his throne. The death of so many of the King's subjects had been an unfortunate accident. Elizabeth felt relieved, if not entirely convinced, by his account. After their meeting she continued to order defensive measures against a foreign invasion, but felt more inclined to believe that this was no opening salvo in a campaign against her and other Protestant princes by the Catholic powers. The ambassador went to great lengths to assure Elizabeth that the King wanted nothing better than closer ties with England, which was indeed the truth.

After only a few months the paranoia passed; though there remained a feeling that France must be treated as an unreliable ally and Elizabeth should do what she could to keep the French and Spanish busy with troubles in their own kingdoms, subtly supporting Protestants from time to time inside the two countries. Much as this kind of covert intervention went against her fundamental beliefs, Elizabeth was seen, albeit unwillingly, as an international champion of Protestantism. Her preferred policy was to lend her support only when she believed that a real risk existed of the complete elimination of foreign Protestantism. Even then she sanctioned aid only on the merits of each case at it arose. She was certainly loath to provoke the Catholic superpowers for a cause she did not consider primarily an English one. There seemed to be no lasting damage between Elizabeth and the French royal family, as the Queen agreed to stand godmother to Charles's daughter Isabella, born on 27 October 1572. The desultory talks over her marriage to Alençon even recommenced.

The German Lutheran princes and the Swiss Calvinists were aghast when news of the massacre reached them. Catherine promptly instructed her ambassador to assure them that the killing of Coligny and his comrades had not been because of their religion, but their plot aimed at ridding themselves of the King. As for the massacre, there had been no premeditation, he claimed. Germany had long been a source of soldiers to boost French armies and provided a useful counterbalance against Spain; to risk losing their friendship would have had grave consequences. Like Elizabeth of England, the Protestant princes feared a concerted Catholic attack against those of the new religion and ordered defensive measures to be taken. Economics proved a useful salve, helping to remove obstacles to the resumption of normal diplomatic relations between the German states and France. The German *Reiters* provided an important source of revenue for their rulers who had found French support against Habsburg domination invaluable in the past.

There was even a clamour of self-righteous protest from Tsar Ivan IV of Russia, who criticised the French for their barbarism. This sounds pretty rich coming from the man who rightfully earned history's sobriquet 'The Terrible' for his savage repression of the boyars in the 1560s and only two years before Saint Bartholomew had laid waste to the free city of Novgorod. Nor did age mellow Ivan, who in a fit of ill temper accidentally killed his eldest son in 1581. The Tsar's disingenuous daintiness can probably be ascribed to the greedy eye that he too cast towards the vacant Polish throne.

Still held captive, Navarre and Condé were only safe for as long as Catherine and royal policy deemed it important for them to remain alive. In her memoirs Margot claims that one week after the massacre Catherine and her advisers 'perceived that they had missed their main aim and hating the Huguenots less than the Princes of the Blood, became impatient that the King my husband and the Prince de Condé had survived. And knowing that since he was my husband no one would dare to attack him, they contrived another scheme.' Catherine is alleged to have approached Margot at her *lever* asking her daughter to 'swear to tell her the truth and asked me whether the King my husband were a man, adding that, if he were not, she would be able to divorce me. I begged her to believe that I did not know what she meant ... but that, since she had married me, I wished to remain so; for I suspected that they wished to separate me from him in order to do him a bad turn.'

Despite their precarious position they were alive. When they had been brought to the King's rooms on 24 August he had assured them, 'My brother and my cousin, be not fearful or troubled by what you hear, if I have summoned you it is for your own safety.' Navarre and Condé had abjured the new religion and taken their first Mass the following day. Navarre showed a cool head, but Condé, like his father before him, was unable to imitate his cousin and feign a pliable spirit of co-operation. Instead he threatened Charles, saying he had 500 men coming to his aid and to avenge the atrocities. Charles, seized with fury, pulled out his dagger and menaced Condé. He then turned to Navarre, saying, 'As for you, show some goodwill and I will treat you well.' The two princes' reception back into the Catholic Church was essential to Catherine. Until this had taken place they were still, then more than ever, the legitimate leaders of the Huguenots.

On 29 September, one month after the murder of many of their closest friends and councillors, Henri of Navarre and the Prince de Condé were officially received back into the Roman Church at Notre-Dame Cathedral during a service celebrating the Order of Saint-Michel with most of the Court present, including many foreign ambassadors. Catherine wanted as many prominent witnesses to this event as possible. As the young princes bowed their heads and made the sign of the cross before the great altar, Catherine, uncharacteristically, lost her regal composure and burst into fits of laughter. Turning to the ambassadors sitting either side of her, she mocked the young princes' attempts at piety. Perhaps it was an outburst of nervous release after the tension of the previous weeks, or maybe it was a calculated attempt to draw attention to the princes' hypocrisy in embracing the faith of their enemies due to *force majeure*.

Henri's own words lend pathos to the Queen Mother's premature and imprudent gaiety. Many years later he wrote about the anguish he felt at the time:

> Those who accompanied me to Paris and who were massacred had not left their houses during the troubles. ... You can imagine the regret this caused me, seeing those who had come because I had given them my word of honour and had no other assurance but that which the King had given me ... assuring me that he would take me as his brother. My misery was such that had I been able to buy their lives by giving my own I would have done so. I saw them killed even at my bed, I was left alone, deprived of friends.[6]

Though Henri had intended no irony, in the House of Valois to be treated as a brother was to take your life in your hands.

Despite his agony, Navarre maintained a public face of astonishing detachment. His friends' killers became his closest companions; although still a prisoner at Court he was agreeable and good company, and betrayed not a scintilla of his true feelings. He made an official apology to the Pope on 3 October 1572 and a few days later, on 16 October, came the most humiliating concession of all when he restored his Principality of Béarn to Catholicism. Unlike Condé's obvious truculence, Henri was determined to survive and employed the same submission and suppleness which his Florentine mother-in-law had once had to do.

By the end of October 1572 the 'Season of Saint Bartholomew' was over, yet its historic repercussions were only just beginning. Not only did it become a byword for oppression, tyranny, cruelty and arbitrary power, but the reverberations were to haunt Catherine's reputation throughout history. Having been so completely at the mercy of the events of Saint Bartholomew, Catherine felt relieved that the kingdom seemed under relative control and relations with the foreign powers were back to normal. She did not appreciate, however, that it was but an appearance of normality. Her enduring appetite for appearances now dangerously overwhelmed her ability to comprehend that she needed to take drastic measures to prevent the massacre from becoming a weapon for her enemies to mould and use against her. For lack of a concerted effort to present a coherent and plausible account of her actions, Catherine allowed the legend of 'The Black Queen' to take hold and to predominate over the years. One nineteenth-century historian, Jules Michelet, even dubbed her 'The Maggot from Italy's Tomb'. Over the years, pamphleteers further distorted the facts about the Queen Mother, creating a patchwork of conflicting but almost universally damning accounts.

Charles IX's reign was so dominated by his mother, due to his youth, his poor health and his lack of ability, that it is almost solely remembered for the Massacre of Saint Bartholomew. The young King remains an opaque figure to history, except as the villain-victim of the massacre, son of his evil Italian mother. Machiavelli's *The Prince*, dedicated to Catherine's father, Lorenzo II de Medici, became known as the 'textbook for tyrants', and rumour held that each of Catherine's children carried a volume with them at all times.[7] The colourful legends about Catherine arose from her tragic mishandling of the crisis and its aftermath. The Huguenots believed the killings had been planned as early as the meeting at Bayonne between the Duke of Alba and '*La Nouvelle Jezebel*', as the pamphleteers called her, where the pair had coolly plotted the massacre of the French Protestants.

Although the Huguenots had lost almost all their leaders, new men stepped in to take over and reorganise their resistance. Whipped up by their pastors, the Protestants became more zealous than ever. In southern France areas of strong Huguenot control such as Nîmes, Montauban, Privas and Sancerre locked their gates and prepared to defend themselves against further Catholic aggression. Most troublesome of all was the port of La Rochelle on the western shores of France. The citizens, who had raised a force of some 1500 men, defied the regime when, not long after Saint Bartholomew, Marshal Biron – a moderate Catholic who had saved many Protestants from the massacre – arrived at La Rochelle to take over as governor, whereupon the inhabitants denied him entry to the town. The Rochellais sought the aid of Elizabeth of England, calling her 'their natural sovereign princess for all eternity'. In November 1572 Charles and Catherine were determined that this Huguenot bastion be retaken and ordered Biron to lay siege to the city. La Rochelle boasted over fifty pastors who enjoined all the citizens, including women, to mount the strongest defence possible. Anjou, who did not take up his command until early 1573, arrived to lead a strangely mixed army, whose commanders were nearly all at odds with each other.

Since the massacre, Anjou's force now comprised reconverted Catholics, a few royalist Protestants and rival feudal lords. With him he brought Navarre, Condé and his brother, Alençon, who was furious that as brother of the King he had been given no important military role, whined about it constantly. The royalist army included many senior officers who found their loyalty to the Crown strained by the events of August 1572. The most prominent of these were Coligny's cousins, the old Constable's sons, the eldest François, Marshal de Montmorency, and his brother Henri de Montmorency Damville, the governor of Languedoc. Fearful of future Guise domination, for the duke and his uncle d'Aumale had accompanied Anjou, they decided to join the force outside La Rochelle bringing with them some junior members of the family, including Charles de Montmorency-Méru (younger son of the late Constable and Marshal de Cossé's son-in-law) and François, Vicomte de Turenne (husband to the Montmorency's sister Eleanore). Turenne and Montmorency-Méru began to form part of a clique that was grouping around the whingeing Duke d'Alençon. The city meanwhile resisted the army's assaults and put up a valiant defence, repulsing attacks and bombardments. The Rochellaise women, standing on the city ramparts exposed to royalist fire, attacked the soldiers below with rocks and stones.

Anjou not only had to endure stone-throwing women, the fanatical defence of the Rochellais, constant squabbles of his disparate group of senior commanders and a particularly harsh winter in the field, but also the reality that he might shortly become King of Poland. The prospect, once distant and with a pleasant shimmer to it, now ceased to hold quite the attraction for him that it once had. Tavannes had unhelpfully described Anjou's prospective kingdom as a 'desert and worth nothing, not so large as they say and where the people are brutes'. Catherine retorted that the Marshal would prefer 'to remain on his own dunghill' and continued, unyielding in her determination to see a crown upon her adored son's head, putting as much of a gloss on the prospect as she could.[8] 'The Poles are highly civilised and intelligent,' she wrote, adding that 'it is a good and great kingdom which can always supply 150,000 livres with which to do whatever he wished'.[9] Explaining that she could not bear to be parted from him unless it were for his own good, she reminded him, 'I have shown you only too well that I love you better where you can acquire reputation and greatness than to have you beside me. ... I am not one of those mothers who love their children only for themselves. I love you because I see and wish to see you foremost in greatness and reputation and honour.'[10] This last remark was no more than the truth; no mother in history has done more to promote her children, at whatever cost to herself, themselves and their times.

Ignoring Henri's growing reluctance, Catherine did all she could to support Jean de Monluc, Bishop of Valence, her special envoy in Poland for the election, to carry the vote in Anjou's favour. A superb diplomat, Monluc had been faced with an almost insuperable problem after Saint Bartholomew, which he privately considered 'a colossal blunder'. Anjou's role in the Massacre had been amplified by his rival the Habsburg archduke; the Emperor's camp advertised Anjou not only as a murderous Catholic fanatic but also as highly effeminate, arguing that a more martial figure would be appropriate for Poland. In religious matters the Poles were singularly tolerant and would not allow a zealot monarch, be he Protestant or Catholic, to jeopardise their exemplary religious harmony.

Fortunately the other candidates for the Crown did not appear particularly appetising to the Poles either, who also feared domination by their neighbouring states. This rather dampened the prospects for Emperor Maximilian II's son, Ernest. A Habsburg king would almost certainly involve Poland in the Empire's constant wars against the Turks. Ivan the Terrible's own candidature was also predictably rejected by the Poles, who were justifiably as afraid of his ambitions as his methods of achieving them. (Rare indeed are the people who actually elect a monarch bearing the sobriquet 'The Terrible'.) The Protestant candidates were Albert-Frederick, Duke of Prussia, and King John III of Sweden's son, the nine-year-old Sigismund. The Protestant electors were in a minority, however, and these two candidates lacked enough support for victory.

Charles was as anxious to see Anjou elected King of Poland as Catherine, albeit for quite different reasons. The thought of getting his brother packed off to Poland evinced such fraternal largesse in the King that he bedazzled the Poles. Among the sweeteners were enough funds to build a Polish fleet. Charles also promised that he would negotiate a treaty between Poland and the Sultan, France's long-time friend but traditionally Poland's foe; in addition he agreed to come to their aid if they were attacked by Russia. The income from the Duchy of Anjou and the prince's other properties were promised to settle Poland's debts. Having arrived at the same time as the Massacre of Saint Bartholomew, Monluc led a brilliant campaign despite the deluge of anti-French propaganda. On 5 April 1573 40,000 nobles assembled on the plain of Kamien south of Warsaw to elect their new King. Monluc played every ruse available to him, including feigning an illness that allowed him to defer overnight his speech for Anjou to the delegates, giving him enough time to examine, dissect and undermine the Imperials' proposals for the archduke made earlier that day.

In Monluc's masterly speech he outlined Henri of Anjou's excellent and noble lineage, the ancient friendship between France and Poland, the fine qualities of the candidate, dilating upon his virtue, wisdom and valour. The French promises of monetary, military and diplomatic aid were outlined in detail. Monluc ended his long speech with a touch of genius, by adding a note of family sentiment. Henri would be leaving his home and his family in France but he would be finding a new home and family as father and King to the Poles. Wild enthusiasm greeted his oration. Monluc had also taken the precaution of having 1000 copies translated into Polish and widely disseminated. Before the proceedings could go any further, Monluc was obliged to undertake promises on Anjou's behalf to honour the *Pacta Conventa* and the *Articuli Henriciani*, which proscribed the King's powers, protected the nobles' privileges and guaranteed freedom of worship. On 11 May 1573, at the end of the lengthy campaign, to cries of '*Gallum! Gallum!*', Henri was officially elected King of Poland.

Henri received the news on 29 May as he sat outside the intractable town of La Rochelle. By now the miserable siege and the unsuccessful assaults had allegedly cost the French army 22,000 men and two of their most important commanders; both the Marshal de Tavannes and the Duke d'Aumale had been killed. Tavannes was a particularly grievous loss to the Queen Mother; he had given her long and faithful service. The soldiers were mutinous and Anjou felt that his own life might even be at risk. The Polish news neatly provided the deus ex machina that gave the Crown an excuse to seek a peaceful solution and come to terms with the stubborn Rochellais. An agreement was reached that allowed both sides to keep their arms and honour. The Edict of Boulogne permitted the Huguenots freedom of conscience throughout the kingdom and freedom of worship at La Rochelle, Nîmes and Montauban.

Catherine received the news of Anjou's election with ecstasy, apparently hearing it from her Polish dwarf Krassowski an hour before the official confirmation arrived. He presented himself before the Queen Mother, gave a deep bow and said, 'I come to salute the mother of the King of Poland.' She wept with joy and – with some justification – regarded the election of her beloved son to the Polish throne as her personal triumph. Charles shared his mother's high good humour; buying the votes for the Crown of Poland had strained his almost empty treasury, but he considered every écu well spent. Anxious to speed the new King on his way, on 1 June 1573 he gave his brother permission to leave and to compound his own happiness he gave Henri 4000 Gascon soldiers to take with him to his new kingdom. (The Gascons – who came from a strongly Huguenot part of France – were troublesome though brave troops and had been a thorn in Charles's side for their reluctance to accept his authority.)

Initially Henri received the tidings with elation; Poland might be an unknown and distant country but now he was a king in his own right. On 17 June a delegation of Polish nobles arrived at La Rochelle to salute their King. The siege was officially lifted nine days later, giving the Poles an apt and nicely timed illustration of how the French were prepared to come to terms with their rebellious Protestant subjects. Anjou's schedule now became hectic and Catherine, as ever, became the catalyst for the organisation of the magnificent receptions and *entrées* which must be accorded to her beloved as a sovereign.

On 24 July Anjou made his *entrée* into Orléans, after which he hurried to the Château de Madrid. There in the Bois de Boulogne he received the many delegations of foreign ambassadors and officials coming to congratulate him throughout early August 1573. The Spanish, Portuguese and Imperial representatives – the latter still smarting from their defeat in the election – were notable absentees from this queue of well-wishers. Catherine's happiness was complete as she watched her son – the son she felt had been born to be a king – receiving gifts, speeches and decorations from the representatives sent by his fellow sovereigns. Henri enjoyed the fuss and there was more to come. The official Polish embassy made up of twelve men including both Catholics and Protestants had embarked upon the journey to their new King. Accompanying the ambassadors were 250 Polish nobles, composed of clergy, senators and other important feudal lords representing the Polish Diet. The twelve Polish delegates not only brought with them the official declaration of Henri's election, but also the agreements undertaken by Monluc on his behalf defining the new King's powers. The electors had been promised, too, that Henri would take the hand of the late King's sister, Anna Jagellona, a prospect that held so little attraction for him that while the diversions in France lasted he decided not to think about it.

On 19 August 1573 the people of Paris were treated to a rare and extraordinary spectacle as the Polish envoys made their official entry into the city. Their arrival was announced by a deafening volley fired by 1500 arquebusiers, and their welcome party included the Duke of Guise, his brothers and other dignitaries. Fifty Polish coaches, each pulled by seven or eight horses ridden by pages, carried the visiting officials. The Parisians, usually blasé and hard to impress, were agog at the extraordinary-looking foreigners making their way to their lodgings in the quartier des Grands-Augustins. The Poles wore their traditional costumes – fur-trimmed hats or jewelled caps, wide boots with iron spikes, fabulous scimitars and swords encrusted with precious gems, and jewelled quivers filled with arrows on their backs. The horses were almost as begemmed as the Poles, their saddles and bridles glimmered with precious stones. The Parisian crowd stood unusually silent as it watched the train of strange-looking but majestic men pass before them, with their long beards flowing 'like the sea' and their heads shaved to the nape of their necks. In an unusual break with traditional hyperbole, the inscription on the triumphal arch under which the cortège passed read *Miramur cultus, Miramur Galli, Vestra Polonorum quasi semideum.*[11]

Catherine, Charles and Elisabeth received their exotic visitors at the Louvre on 21 August. Dressed in long robes of gold brocade the Poles, led by the Bishop of Poznan, presented themselves to Their Majesties. Far from the savages anticipated by Tavannes, the ambassadors were both highly cultured and multilingual. They spoke Latin, Italian, German and some French 'with a purity of accent as if they had been born on the banks of the Seine, instead of in those distant lands watered by the Vistula or the Dnieper'. Charles and Henri probably felt a twinge of regret at their own half-hearted efforts at learning Latin. After their speech to Charles, the ambassadors went to address Catherine. She stood, looking magnificently regal, and listened to their speech in Latin. Madame Gondi, La Comtesse de Retz, gave the reply, also in Latin, after which the Queen Mother took the Bishop of Poznan to one side and they spoke together in Italian. Of the royal family, Margot alone required no translator when she and Navarre received the ambassadors a few days later. She was able to converse with them 'with vivacity and grace of manner' alternating between Italian, Latin and French. Holding out her white hand to be kissed by the delegates, she made a profound impression on her visitors. One of them, the smitten Palatine of Siradia, henceforth referred to Margot as 'that divine woman'. A large number of the French courtiers reputed to be well educated were left blushing and tongue-tied when the Poles addressed questions to them in Latin, which they found incomprehensible.

The following day, 22 August, Henri received his new countrymen and subjects at the Louvre. First they processed through Paris, even more sumptuously dressed than when they had entered the city. The twelve ambassadors wore long robes of gold cloth trimmed with sable. It was precisely the sort of glittering *tenu* that would normally have guaranteed a warm reception from Anjou, famed for his fascination with jewels and rich clothes. Now, however, it served only to remind the new King that he was leaving his beloved France for a strange country with strange customs. The early joy of his elevation, the congratulations from fellow monarchs and the other delightful accoutrements of kingship were wearing off. Soon he would be leaving home for Poland.

Before the ambassadors arrived, Henri had given his official thanks to Monluc for his success in winning him the throne, but his words of gratitude were insincere. De Thou wrote,

> Monsieur was not glad, though he hid his true sentiments. Honourable as was the dignity conferred upon him, he regarded its acceptance as an exile. He was piqued at his brother's determination to banish him from the realm. This young prince, therefore, nurtured amid the luxuries and refinements of the court of France, saw himself most unwillingly doomed to inhabit such a country as Poland.

Henri could not but be aware of the joy his imminent departure also gave to Margot and her fraternal protégé, Alençon. Delighted at the prospect of 'the favourite son's' departure, they were already planning what they could appropriate when he had gone. The Bishop of Poznan came forward to kiss the King's hand and to hail him as their new sovereign. In his address to Henri there were many references to the Diet and to the King's signature on the *Articuli Henriciana* and *Pacta Conventa*. Henri found the speech tinged with an element unfamiliar to a

French royal prince; it smacked of the 'unceremonious remonstrance with which he had been told the Polish magnates regaled their sovereign'. It was most unpleasing to the Valois ear.

If the French found the Polish ambassadors and nobles extraordinary and foreign-looking, one wonders what the Poles made of their new King. The richly dressed, elegant, slender and highly effeminate young man before them was scented, pomaded and rouged. His tong-curled, backcombed hair was topped with a *toquet* of diamonds. The trembling grapes of pearls and pendant earrings that swung with the movement of his head were certainly unusual. Compared with their own robust physiques, the Poles cannot have failed to notice Henri's physical frailty. It was common knowledge that he suffered from agonising headaches and a weak stomach. The fistula on one of Henri's eyes could be clearly seen, as was the foetid seepage from the open sore below his armpit whenever he waved or lifted his arm. It is probable that at their first meeting both parties looked at each other with equal astonishment. Henri's entourage, remarkable for its number of exquisite-looking young noblemen, might also have given the ambassadors pause for thought.

While Catherine and Monluc undertook the serious business of ratifying the details of the *Articuli* and *Conventa*, Henri used every opportunity to let his mother witness his misery. They had wept together over his imminent departure, but her maternal ambitions for her favourite son required a huge sacrifice. Blinded by her hopes for him, she seemed unable to heed another great danger ahead.

Charles was visibly dying. When Henri first saw his elder brother after the eight-month siege of La Rochelle, the deterioration in Charles's health so shook him that he is alleged to have muttered 'he is dead' to one of his suite standing beside him. As heir presumptive, Henri would be leaving a great deal at stake when he finally departed for Poland. Although Alençon was plotting with Margot at his expense, the protective presence of his mother reassured him. She would never allow anyone to usurp the French throne in his place.

As a precaution against any future move for the throne by Alençon, already clamouring for the shortly to become vacant position of Lieutenant-General, Catherine had arranged for Charles formally to acknowledge 'my brother the King of Poland' as heir-presumptive at a council meeting on 22 August 1573. This cheered Henri's drooping spirits as the arguments continued over the final agreement between the Poles and their King, undertaken by Catherine and some of France's ablest ministers, each of whom had been carefully selected by her. Worried about the hostility of the Empire at Henri's election, Catherine had also to ensure safe passage for Henri and his vast entourage to reach Poland unharmed. With this in mind, talks with the German Protestants about plans to support an attack against the Spanish Netherlands commenced. Just before Henri's departure, Catherine went so far as to promise 'to embrace the affairs of the said Netherlands as much and as far as the Protestant princes may wish'.[12] Matters with the ambassadors came to a head as Henri maintained his stubborn unwillingness to sign the agreements upon which his kingship hinged. One of the envoys made the situation absolutely clear by stating firmly, *'Jurabis aut non regnanbis!'* (Swear the oath or you will not reign!) The proposed marriage to Anna Jagellona, for which Henri had no appetite, provided the other stumbling block.

The princess, as demanded by tradition, waited in Cracow with the body of her dead brother, longing impatiently for the arrival of the dashing prince she believed would become her husband. A description of her sent to Henri, that lover of perfection and beauty, made the prospect anathema to his delicate tastes. She wore a black costume covered by a cloak of rough sackcloth, apparently traditional Polish mourning attire, and she received Henri's gentleman most graciously. He reported, 'The princess is of little stature, her age is nearly fifty years, as one may read on her highness's features.' The prospective suitor finessed his way out of the problem for the moment by protesting that since the princess's consent had not been given, the matrimonial question must remain open. On 9 September 1573, after further wrangling, Henri swore the articles of the Conventa. He gave a banquet for the ambassadors that evening and the following day a ceremony took place in which Henri undertook to uphold his oaths and commitments, Charles swearing to act as a guarantor.

On the following day at the Palais de Justice, the French royal family, nobles, dignitaries and a huge crowd watched the ambassadors come to make the official presentation of the document declaring Henri's election as King of Poland.* Two canopied thrones had been placed on a platform, one bearing the fleur-de-lys of France and the other the white eagle of Poland. The ambassadors approached in pairs, until two delegates entered carrying a large silver casket upon their shoulders. In the ornate casket lay the decree which they placed before Charles. The Bishop of Poznan formally asked the King of France whether he had his royal permission to present the decree to his brother. He then asked Catherine the same question and both of them gave their assent. Henri, who was kneeling, had the long fought-over agreement handed to him, followed by a pretty speech before the document was read out loud.

On 14 September Henri made his official entry into Paris as King of

---

* Although most historians have this ceremony taking place at the Palais de Justice, Charles's despatch to his ambassador in England describes the ceremony taking place in *'la grande salle de mon palais du Louvre'*.

Poland. To celebrate the event Catherine inaugurated her new palace of the Tuileries with a ball that was to surpass all the other entertainments that had been laid on for the Poles. Having abandoned and eventually demolished the Château des Tournelles (now the Place des Vosges) as a miserable reminder of her husband's death, in 1563 she had conceived the idea of a palace close to the Louvre extending to the banks of the Seine. This was the first palace she had built entirely for herself and in which she could indulge her great love of architecture. Other substantial works on existing châteaux had taken place at, among them, Chenonceau, Montceaux and Saint-Maur-des-Fossés, but the Tuileries was entirely her own, 'where she would never have to feel as though she were a guest of the kings of France, but that they were her guests'. The name derived, rather uninspiringly, from the tile works that had once been situated there. Designed by Philibert de l'Orme, Henry II's *surrintendent* of royal buildings and preferred architect, the palace was never completed. After de l'Orme's death in 1570 Jean Bullant took over the commission but work stopped for several years in 1572, the year of the Massacre, probably for lack of funds. Pasquier recalls that Catherine received a warning from one of her seers that if she wanted to live a long life she must avoid Saint-Germain for it would presage her death. Unfortunately she had already commissioned the building of the Tuileries Palace that lay in the parish of Saint-Germain-l'Auxerrois, whose church had tolled the signal for the Massacre to begin. Nevertheless the deeply superstitious Catherine continued to visit the Tuileries. Though she never made it her Parisian home, as had originally been intended, she used it to give large banquets and magnificences there. She also enjoyed its gardens where she often walked. Instead, she made plans for a new residence outside the parish of Saint-Germain, which was supposed to augur her death.

In 1572 Catherine decided that she wanted a residence near the Louvre but within the walls of the city. In the parish of Saint-Eustache she bought a whole area that included the Hôtel Guillart and the Filles Repenties (a convent for destitute young girls to save them from life on the streets). Also on the intended site was the Hôtel d'Albret. After acquiring the various properties she had all the existing buildings of this large site, except for the chapel of the Filles Repenties, demolished. With her love for gardens she ensured that she had acquired enough space to incorporate one that would be both large and decorative into the plans for her palace known as the 'Hôtel de la Reine'. Catherine employed Jean Bullant as the architect for this most personal of projects, the most significant feature of which was a Doric column that could be seen from afar situated in the centre of the courtyard, which is the only part of the *hôtel* that remains today.

The column, called the La Colonne de l'Horoscope, covered in lovers' knots and interlaced Hs and Cs, and other emblems of conjugal love, was both a memorial to Henri II and, it is believed, an astronomers' observatory. The first tall column of its type in Paris, it was a landmark of outstanding originality in its day. The top of the column provided enough room for three people at a time to observe the skies underneath a metal-worked dome and there is thought to have been a small balcony outside that encircled the dome, with a balustrade for safety. To reach the dome a wide staircase of 147 steps had to be climbed, leading finally to a ladder, which opened up to a trapdoor on the floor of the viewing platform. Not only could the skies be scanned by the experts, but also communication by lights with the Louvre was possible. The panoramic view could be used for pleasure but it also enabled an early warning of any approaching danger. When the *hôtel* on the rue Saint-Honoré was completed, Catherine filled it with books, various collections, and covered the walls with portraits of her family and friends. Although she never completely gave up her apartments at the Louvre – which meant that the Crown had the expense of maintaining both with the enlarged household that two residences required – Catherine used her own palace increasingly as the years went by.

The accounts of the now destroyed Hôtel de La Reine are a most intriguing insight into Catherine's personality. Although there were five magnificent princely apartments and all the splendour associated with Catherine as Queen Mother, she housed many of her personal collections here and during the last decade of her life made it a home stamped with her character as a woman rather than that of a queen. More than thirty-five portraits of the French royal family, starting with Francis I, lined the gallery; at one end a large room hung with her Medici ancestors paid homage to her own origins. In the middle of the long gallery stood a large Florentine mosaic table and at the other end was a room filled with pictures of her grandchildren, nieces and nephews. A large portrait of Catherine hung over the fireplace in the centre of the main gallery. While this area was for the more official portraits, the whole palace overflowed with pictures of loved ones; few were by artists of note but it was as though Catherine lived in a vast photograph album of her favourite people.[13]

Catherine had always been an enthusiastic if eclectic collector. She had seven stuffed crocodiles hanging from the ceiling in her huge *cabinet de travail* and minerals of every kind were displayed around this salon. Games filled the cupboards that lined its walls: chess, miniature billiards and other toys could be found to help pass the time in bad weather. Beautiful collections of china, Venetian glass and enamels stood side by side with treasured old mementoes of days past, devotional objects, dolls in various types of dress and sentimental bric-à-brac. On the bookshelves were her favourites: works dedicated to her late husband, folios containing building plans, genealogies of her maternal ancestors, the Counts of Boulogne, and books giving tips on games. These were all favourites that she liked to have to hand. The library itself boasted an outstanding collection of 4500 works, including 776 manuscripts. Some of these were ancient (including a few on papyrus) and others contemporary works. Their topics were as diverse as the rest of the Queen Mother's collections but her favourite subjects were best represented including history, classical works, occultism, mathematics, philosophy, law and astronomy. At Saint-Maur-des-Fossés, Catherine created her other principal library that contained nearly 4000 books. These two collections together made up the basis for today's Bibliothèque Nationale.[14]

The ball at the Tuileries was Henri's swansong and Catherine's tour de force. After the banquet the tables were removed for a ballet, danced by her flying squadron dressed as nymphs. Catherine is generally credited with bringing the earliest form of modern ballet and opera with her from Florence and both were frequently featured favourites at her lavish *spectacles*. Brantôme wrote,

> There appeared a high rock which slowly whirled around. Upon the summit of this rock sat sixteen beautiful nymphs, representing the sixteen provinces of France. The nymphs recited melodious verses, composed by Ronsard, commemorating the glories of the King of Poland and of the realm of France. The nymphs then descended and presented gifts to the said King. Afterwards they danced together. The beautiful order of their movements, their gestures, and extraordinary loveliness of face and figure afforded great delectation to the spectators.

There followed the enchanting voices of the castrati brought by Catherine from Italy, accompanied by the first violinist ever heard in France. Charles wrote to La Motte-Fénélon in London, 'Last evening, the Queen my mother gave a banquet at her palace, where the Polish gentlemen were so well treated and had so much pleasure that they said they had never seen anything more beautiful ... and were very happy with the honour they were shown.'[15] The Poles were indeed dazzled by the magical beauty at the French Court. They proclaimed the *fêtes* and magnificence of this court 'peerless'. 'I wish', quipped one cynical courtier, 'that they might say as much of our armies.'

After the presentation of a magnificent gift from the city of Paris, a gilded and enamelled coach pulled by two grey chargers and surmounted by an effigy of Mars, god of war, as a tribute to their prince the Catholic warrior, the inevitable could be delayed no longer. The royal party set off for Fontainebleau on the first leg of their journey. Charles had become increasingly testy at the agonisingly slow pace of his brother's departure;

he had bought Henri the throne at a ruinous cost, now he wanted to see that his cash had been well spent. To ease Catherine's mind the Imperial Diet at Frankfurt, also at a considerable cost, had promised safe passage for the new King across the Empire's territories. On 10 October 1573 the party arrived at Villers-Cotterêts on the road to Lorraine and the French frontier. Here Catherine suffered a fit of panic and decided that Henri had not brought enough gifts with him to present to the various grandees and rulers through whose lands he would now be passing. Taking him with her, she hurried back to Paris, where she raised a further half million livres, also buying a large quantity of jewels for him to hand out on his way.

In late October the royal family were forced to stop for longer than intended at Vitry-en-Perthois because Charles had fallen seriously ill. His physicians believed that he had been struck down by a type of smallpox, although it is far more likely to have been the final stages of tuberculosis. Suffering from violent fevers that left him weak and debilitated, the King lay shivering and unable to move from his bed. He was covered not only by sweat but also by watery blood that seemed to seep from the pores of his body. As he lay 'vomiting a great quantity of blood', the Court lingered and waited, immobilised by the King's condition and the uncertainties it cast upon the situation. Henri himself could hardly believe his good fortune; his brother's death could not have come at a better time for him, just as he was on the verge of leaving France. Philippe de Cheverny, one of the senior counsellors making the journey as far as the frontier, wrote, 'Many people wished to prevent the King of Poland to continue any further with his journey, remonstrating that the uncertainty of the King's condition, coming as it did from the lungs, often proved fatal.' Alençon, on the other hand, felt disconsolate; his best chance to snatch the French Crown would only come if Charles died after Henri had become ensconced in his distant kingdom.

The sight of his two ambitious brothers circling his bed like buzzards over his carrion reanimated the lucid but desperately ill King for a rally of strength that defied the doctors' gloomy predictions. Calling for his mother, he sat up in his sweat-and-blood-soaked featherbed and ordered Henri's immediate departure. Catherine promised that his wishes would be carried out, but first she arranged for a proper farewell between the brothers. The Queen Mother demanded a scene of proper family devotion before Henri's departure. She either did not care or was blind to the staged and phoney theatricals that the brothers performed for her. On 12 November 1573, with his brothers and mother standing round his bed, Charles gave Henri his farewell embrace. The copious tears the two shed as they said goodbye, punctuated by a chorus of seemly background sobs from Alençon, presented a picture of fraternal harmony considered most satisfactory by their mother. Her appetite for idealising any important family or political moment was insatiable. Some onlookers, even the most cynical, wondered if perhaps, just for a moment, the two brothers had indeed felt a true and deep sense of sadness at what both must have known would be their final adieu.

The Queen Mother, Henri and his huge train moved on to Lorraine, where the christening took place of Catherine's new grandson, recently born to her daughter Claude and son-in-law Charles, Duke and Duchess of Lorraine. Catherine stood godmother and the Bishop of Poznan godfather to the baby boy. During their brief stay in Lorraine Henri caught sight of Louise de Vaudémont, a young niece of the Duke of Lorraine. Louise was nineteen years old and a blonde beauty. Unloved by her family, she had learned to keep herself out of the way. Henri found himself very taken by the sweet girl always to be found in the background. There was another reason he found her irresistible: she resembled Marie of Clèves, the lovely wife of his mortal enemy the Prince de Condé, who had completely ensorcelled him. Marie had been Henri's romantic obsession during the past year and, although the relationship was idealised and platonic, for him it had become all-consuming. It did not go unnoticed, however, that the new King of Poland rarely left Louise's side for the few days he spent at his sister's Court at Nancy.

On 29 November the royal party arrived at Blamont, frontier town between Lorraine and the Empire. Spanish spies reported that the Queen Mother met Louis of Nassau and the son of Jean Casimir, the Elector of Palatine, whose *Reiters* had wrought such damage in France during the last civil war. Catherine had already advanced 300,000 écus to Louis to help finance his fight against the regime in the Netherlands. She now promised further aid. These talks were essentially to ensure Henri's safe passage through to Poland and to maintain a cordial relationship with the Protestant powers in case of more trouble with the Huguenots in France. Catherine had not failed to notice that Alençon was being regarded as a potential rallying element to their cause, so recently and violently deprived of most of its leaders. His royal status also lent useful legitimacy to more moderate Catholic nobles who feared their fanatical co-religionists, led by the Guises.

Henri and his mother made their tearful farewells on 2 December 1573. She had helped to choose the men who were to be his closest advisers and companions in Poland. Among the intimates he took with him were the Duke of Nevers (Louis de Gonzaga of Mantua), the Abbot of Noailles and the Duke of Mayenne (one of the Guises), Guy de Pibrac, René de Villequier, Louis du Ghast and his physician, Marc Miron. These men were his most faithful followers and Catherine knew that she had placed her son's life in devoted hands. Unable to endure the heart-wrenching scene any further, she is said to have cried out to Henri, '*Partez, mon fils! Partez! Vous n'y demeurerez pas longtemps!*' (Leave my son! Leave! You will not stay there for long!) With those words he set off in the harsh winter weather towards his throne in exile, leaving behind the woman who worshipped, protected and fought for him.

By the time Catherine returned to join Charles he had made a moderate recovery and was enjoying a rare respite from his illness. During her short absence she discovered that Alençon had been fomenting trouble and that his head was filled with 'nothing but war and tempests'. This least-loved of her sons still pressed hard for the vacant post of Lieutenant-General of the kingdom. Charles, who had originally promised him the post, now clung to the seals of this important office so recently returned to him by Henri. Catherine counselled the King against giving the office to his ambitious younger brother, but he relented on 25 January 1574. This threatened the Guises and their followers who, since Henri of Valois' departure for Poland with so many good Catholic commanders, had felt exposed and threatened. They even claimed that François de Montmorency, an intimate of Alençon's, plotted to have the Duke of Guise assassinated. At the Louvre, on 16 February, Guise attacked the supposed assassin, M. de Ventabren. Montmorency pleaded his innocence of any plot against Guise and though no charges were brought, he had to leave the Court. At the same time Charles withdrew his promise to Alençon of the Lieutenant-Generalship. The Guises had thus achieved their goal. As a consolation for Alençon, Charles made his brother head of the council and Commander-General of the armies, which the duke found quite insufficient as a compromise. Charles awarded the key post to his steady brother-in-law, the Duke of Lorraine, a cousin of the Guises, and it is likely that Catherine put Lorraine's name forward because she trusted him not to abuse his new powers, something that could not be said of her youngest son.

Alençon's clique consisted of Navarre, Condé, the four Montmorency brothers and Turenne. They felt the prince had enough power to force the Lieutenant-Generalship issue, and if he failed they had all decided to take up arms and head for Sedan where they would lead an armed force of Huguenots into the Netherlands. Alençon had hoped that once in Flanders he might be able to find himself a principality of his own. The throne he coveted most, however, was that of his dying brother Charles, but Catherine stood implacably between his dream and its realisation. This runt of her sickly litter now prepared to take on his mother and determined upon a course to remove her from power. His partisans ensured the distribution of a huge number of pamphlets that directly blamed Catherine, as a foreigner and a woman, for the Massacre of Saint Bartholomew. Other pamphlets appeared questioning Catherine's right, under Salic law, to be made regent in the event of Charles's death, arguing that the regency could only go to a male.

The Calvinist writer François Hotman was the primary 'literary terrorist' in this campaign. In his treatise *Franco Gallia* he examined and reviewed the history of the French monarchy, concluding that its present absolutism was a far cry from the original form where the monarch was elected by the National Assembly or Parlement. He also denounced the rule of women in general, citing the fact that many of history's most brutal tyrants had been female. The arguments of the Calvinist thinkers struck a chord not only with the Huguenots but also with some senior nobles and important elements of French society, who were disgusted with the extremism of both religious sides. They sought a moderate way forward that would require reforms of the monarchy and society as a whole. This growing group of disaffected nobles and moderate Catholics were soon to unite, becoming a new force in the struggle ahead. The royalists hired their own writers in retaliation and there came a blizzard of pamphlets from all sides, but the essential damage had been done. The French people had begun to question some of the most basic political principles under which they lived.

Charles's health took an increasing downturn and, as it did so, he became dark and dangerous. The Venetian ambassador wrote,

> He never looks one in the face when one addresses him, he stoops as his father used to do and contracts his shoulders, and he has a habit of lowering his head and narrowing his eyes. Then he will raise them abruptly, and as if with an effort, and gaze overhead, or drop them again, hardly glancing at the person to whom he is speaking. Besides being morose and taciturn, they say that he is also vindictive and never forgives anyone who offends him, it is feared that from being merely severe he will become cruel. For some time past all his thoughts have been of war and he has nothing else in mind, being naturally inclined to it, and his mother will have the greatest difficulty in restraining him; he wishes to conduct it in person, being bold and courageous. ... And it is for this purpose that he gives himself unremittingly to exercise and labour of every sort, to harden himself, and to be fit to endure ... the hardships of war.[16]

The King hunted for days on end and when he pointed out a dark birthmark or scar below his shoulder to one of his hunting companions he remarked that this was the way to ensure that his body could be identified if he died in battle. The King's companion begged him not to be preoccupied with so morbid a thought, at which Charles retorted, 'Do you suppose I would rather die in bed than in battle?'

Martial glory remained an unattainable phantom for Charles. The only battles he fought were the daily ones against ill-health, skirmishes with his mother and the inept plotting of his brother Alençon who, though not clever enough to be dangerous by himself, was becoming the bovine instrument for more cunning minds. Having previously declared that until he reached the age of twenty-five he would allow himself to '*faire le fou*' (play the fool), Charles now decided to take personal charge of government. He began to blame Catherine for the troubles in his kingdom, saying frequently, 'Madame, you are the cause of everything! Everything!' The Venetian ambassador went on to describe the now fraught relationship between mother and son: 'Recently, they tell me that before he will do anything his mother has to repeat it three times.' After one of the King's angry outbursts at Catherine, she complained to her entourage, 'I always had to deal with a madman and that I should never make anything of him.'[7] By late February, the King was almost constantly ill; many claimed that the Massacre of Saint Bartholomew, and the murder of Coligny and his lieutenants, some of whom had been close to Charles, haunted and unhinged him. He had once written a tribute to the great poet Ronsard, employing words that now held added pathos: 'I can give death, but you give immortality.'

A peaceful end was not to be granted to this tragic young King. In February 1574 the Court stayed at Saint-Germain. Alençon and his co-conspirators judged this to be the time to push their bid to be allowed to campaign in the Netherlands. The conspirators' plan, conceived by Hyacynthe Joseph de La Molle – a courtier who had become Margot's lover – was for Alençon and Navarre to flee from the Court, where they lived under close supervision, and then make off northwards with a force of Huguenot soldiers. They chose the night of 23–24 February, that of Mardi Gras, as ideal, since the Court would be celebrating and the princes' absence might go undetected for some time. A captain called Chaumont-Guitry had been selected to come to the palace to fetch the two princes. However, he arrived earlier than had been agreed and this minor change in the plan threw the spineless Alençon into a blithering panic and gave him an excuse not to go ahead. Instead, he raced to his mother and confessed his part in the conspiracy. Furthermore, a troop of Huguenot soldiers had been spotted not far from Saint-Germain and it became imperative for the Court to decamp immediately to Paris. A scene reminiscent of the '*Surprise de Meaux*' was re-enacted as the terrified courtiers fled, and Catherine set off grimly in her coach with her unwilling passengers Navarre and Alençon. The King, in a perilous condition, feverish and haemorrhaging blood, could hardly be left behind and had to be transported back to Paris. Upon hearing of the imminent trouble he is reported to have complained, 'If they had waited at least for my

Admiral Gaspard de Coligny, leader of the Huguenots.

The exquisite Château of Chenonceau, originally a gift from Henry to Diane,
which Catherine finally appropriated.

A romanticised portrayal of the 1561 Colloquy of Poissy. Catherine,
seated beside her son Charles IX, attempts to reconcile Catholics with Protestants.

Catherine as Queen of France, the image of majesty.

Next page A nineteenth-century depiction of the wedding celebrations of Henri de Bourbon, King of Navarre (later Henri IV) and Margot, some days before the Massacre of St Bartholemew. Note Catherine standing beside King Charles IX.

Above Catherine standing over corpses after the massacre of St Bartholemew —
probably a piece of Protestant propaganda.

Opposite top The Valois dynasty ended with the assassination of Henri III in
1589, depicted in this contemporary engraving.

Opposite bottom The future: Henry IV, King of France and Navarre. 'I rule with
my arse in the saddle and my gun in my fist.'

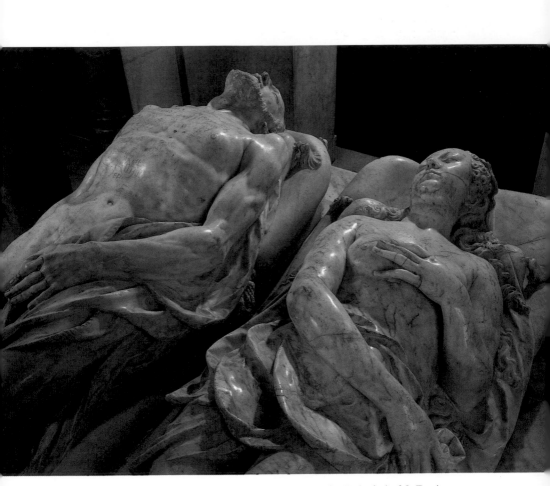

The 'gisants' of Henry II and Catherine at the Cathedral of St Denis.
Henry's agonised expression reflects the horror of his dying moments.

death' and then muttered again and again during the agonising journey, 'Too much malice. Too much malice.' It might be taken as an epitaph for his age.

On 8 March the Court moved to the Château of Vincennes, a fortress that would prove easier to defend should there be an attack. There Alençon and Navarre were questioned over the recent events by Catherine, the King and Chancellor Birague. Alençon's version changed at each recital and contained some glaring inconsistencies, though he clearly aimed to shift the blame on to the Guises. He pleaded that he had been forced to act to defend himself against the clan who seemed bent on discrediting him. He swore that the plan had been only to attack the Guises and not to harm the King or their mother. Navarre courageously compromised no one. Birague, meanwhile, urged Catherine and the King to treat Alençon and Navarre as traitors, and have them executed, but both recoiled from such an extreme measure. Their punishment was only to swear loyalty to the Crown and henceforth to live under closer guard. None of this prevented the uprising that had been planned to coincide with the escape of Alençon and Navarre. Montgomery returned to France from hiding in England and proceeded to invade Normandy. The two prisoners felt sure that they would be condemned to death once the true extent of their plans had been uncovered. They therefore decided that they must make another attempt to escape. This time they put their faith in the hands of a jumble of disaffected men, including sailors, mercenaries, horse-traders, general intriguers and Pierre de Grantrye, a former spy and magician who claimed to have discovered 'the philosopher's stone'.

The leaders of this unlikely escape team were La Molle, Margot's lover, and his friend Annibal, Comte de Coconas, the lover of the Duchess of Nevers, Margot's great friend and confidante. These two gentlemen of Alençon's band were scented Court dandies renowned for their gambling, dancing and lovemaking, but not for treacherous plotting that required discretion and dexterous planning. De Thoré (Marshal François de Montmorency's brother) and Turenne (their brother-in-law) were also linked to the conspirators. It is not surprising that Catherine soon received word that another plan to free the two royal prisoners had been cooked up, and a pre-emptive move by the King resulted in no fewer than fifty arrests from those among Alençon's closest followers. By ill luck, François de Montmorency, who was not involved in this enterprise, had just returned to Court when the plot was discovered. He found himself not only highly compromised but in immediate mortal danger.

Only weeks after their first attempted escape plan had been foiled, Alençon and Navarre were arrested again and questioned before the King and Queen Mother. Navarre nobly refrained from incriminating others and refused to direct his answers to the interrogator but addressed himself solely to Catherine. He spoke of her desire to inflame the kingdom with rumours of plots to blacken his name, and 'the insincerity and perfidy in her relations towards himself'. This brave declaration, which he had prepared with Margot, probably saved his life, as it is likely that Charles believed Navarre. When Alençon received his summons for questioning he was at his loquacious best as he abjectly gabbled out details of the utterly compromised project. To make matters worse a wax doll had been found wearing a crown with needles piercing its heart, the handiwork of Cosimo Ruggieri, the Queen Mother's own trusted necromancer and specialist in the dark arts. It was immediately assumed that the wax figure represented the King and the needles were part of an evil spell by Ruggieri. Catherine felt stunned that a man she trusted so completely could have betrayed her in such a way. Ruggieri had become close to Alençon's coterie and had befriended La Molle in particular. On 30 April the two ringleaders, Coconas and La Molle, were beheaded for treason, after which their embalmed heads were said to have been taken secretly to Margot and the Duchess of Nevers, who kept them to mourn their lost lovers. Under questioning, La Molle had revealed nothing and proved to have been made of sterner stuff than Coconas, who spilled out details of the plan to join up with Condé, Thoré, Turenne and Louis of Nassau at Sedan.

On 4 May Charles made a general move against the Montmorencys. Due to the absence of Thoré and Turenne he ordered the arrest of François de Montmorency and Marshal de Cossé, father-in-law to Montmorency's brother Méru, who were then imprisoned in the Bastille. He also revoked the absent younger brother Damville's governorship of the Languedoc. The swoop on the Montmorencys proved ruinously flawed, since Damville was at large and soon agitating among his family's vast clientele in the Languedoc. This province had been controlled by the family for almost 500 years and the people accorded them almost sovereign status there. To compound the difficulties for Catherine and Charles, Damville had a large number of troops at his disposal and it would require more than a revocation of his governorship to dislodge him. The Languedoc was a largely Protestant province and Damville soon entered into talks with its leading Huguenots. As a consequence of the attack on his family and in the absence of his elder brothers, he shortly became the new leader of the opposition. The fruit of his talks with the Huguenots, with whom he soon signed a truce, led to a union between the moderate Catholics like himself and Protestants disaffected by the massacre and the monarchy's maladministration of the kingdom. Thus emerged a new party in conflict with the Crown led by Damville, known as the 'Politiques'.

The common soldiers caught up in the scheme were hanged, while

Catherine pondered the potentially terrifying problem of what to do about Ruggieri. She dared not cross him, yet he could not go unpunished. It transpired that the wax figure wearing a crown actually represented Margot and not the King. La Molle, desperate for the Queen of Navarre to love him, had asked Ruggieri to cast a spell on her and the doll had been created for this purpose. The sinister Italian whom the Queen Mother feared and respected subsequently received a sentence to serve nine years on the galleys at Marseilles. This was merely a face-saving gesture: he did not have to serve his time but instead received permission to open a school for astrologers and was soon back serving Catherine in Paris.

Condé, in Picardy at the time of the arrests, fled to Germany and immediately abjured the Catholic faith. Ever since the Massacre of Saint Bartholomew he had been either openly difficult or mocking, unlike his cousin Navarre who had never allowed his hatred or fear to be seen, putting on the most amiable mask to survive the ordeal. Catherine had found Condé particularly tiresome because of Anjou's romantic and idealised obsession with his wife. The new King of Poland wrote to the princess every day, sometimes twice daily, from his distant kingdom, and at the end of these long and fulsome love letters Henri occasionally signed his name in his own blood. Condé – understandably vexed by the attachment – was frequently seen crossing himself at the slightest pretext. Finally Catherine snapped and demanded why, all of a sudden, did he show such piety and devotion? He replied that he must pray for the sins of his wife who loved another man. Catherine took the Princess de Condé under her protection and henceforth she spent much of her time in the Queen Mother's apartments.

Navarre and Alençon, the two principal parties in the whole plot, still feared for their lives. Once again Birague implored the King and Queen Mother to invoke the death penalty, yet the two prisoners were spared, though put under strict guard at Vincennes.

Since the beginning of May 1574 Charles had grown steadily weaker. By the middle of the month he was in a hopeless condition, though lucid throughout. His suffering was pitiful. As the end of the month of May approached he could no longer leave his bed, but lay sweating and struggling for breath between blood-soaked sheets that needed constant changing. Brantôme recounts that Charles's wife, Queen Elisabeth, became a regular figure in his chamber, as did his elderly nurse. Elisabeth, instead of sitting at her husband's bedside, sat opposite him. Although they spoke little during those last days, she gazed at her husband lovingly and he at her. Elisabeth wept 'tears so tender, and so secret, that they were hardly noticed but when she must dry her eyes frequently'.

On 29 May Catherine received word that her mortal enemy, Gabriel de Montgomery – the man whose lance had inadvertently killed her husband – had been captured at Domfront after the collapse of his invasion of Normandy. She ran into her dying son's chamber with jubilation and announced to Charles that his father's killer had been finally caught. Charles merely murmured, 'Madame, all human affairs no longer mean anything to me.' Knowing that her son might die at any moment, Catherine had to ensure that she could protect the empty throne until the arrival of the absent Henri of Poland. A formal document was drawn up on the King's orders declaring his mother's regency until the return of the new King. Navarre and Alençon witnessed this document and when the contents were announced Catherine ordered that it should be stated that it had been drawn up at their request, which was as untrue as it was unlikely.

Her legal position now secured, Catherine remained with her dying son, who was not yet twenty-four years old. He had become pathetically thin and she held his bloody body in her arms as she tried to comfort him. He had earlier made his confession and then taken some light nourishment, as he did so 'he cried over the sins he had committed out of weakness and which were the true cause of God's anger towards him and his people'. In the early afternoon of 30 May 1574 an incident is said to have occurred which is given in several accounts of the King's death, but is otherwise unverifiable. Charles allegedly asked for his brother, although Alençon was already in the room. Catherine reassured him 'he is already here'. 'No, Madame, my brother ... the King of Navarre.' Henri duly arrived at Charles's bedside who gave him a weak but affectionate embrace. 'You are losing a good friend, brother ... If I had believed all that I was told, you would not be alive. Do not trust ...' The Queen Mother apparently protested, 'Do not say it, Sire!' to which Charles replied, 'I do say it, Madame, it is the truth.' But he revealed nothing, only commending his wife and his baby daughter to Navarre.

Sorbin, his priest, had been called earlier, and read and prayed with Charles. During the afternoon he lay next to his mother who sat weeping on a chest beside him, her hand holding his as she watched him slip away, the only sound in the room the rattle of his laboured gasps for air. Shortly before four o'clock in the afternoon he tried to speak for the last time. He turned to his mother and said, '*Adieu ma mère, eh! Ma mère,*' then drifted into his final sleep, his parting words audible to all.

After the awful months of tension, attempted insurrections and Catherine's desperate attempts to keep Charles from committing fatal political blunders as he tried to wrest control from her, it was over. The Queen Mother now had much to secure and keep safe for the arrival of Henri, King of Poland, though she allowed herself a rare luxury and briefly surrendered to her genuine and terrible sorrow. Charles had been King since he was ten years old, and she had guided and protected him throughout his life; he was not her favourite but she had loved him completely, understanding his weaknesses. For all Charles's efforts at autonomy he had never been able to manage without his mother during his lifetime and the Massacre of Saint Bartholomew was to tie them together throughout history. Catherine, keeper of the Valois legend, later said, 'After God, he recognised no one but me.'[18]

FOURTEEN

Henri III, King of France

There is no country in the world
to equal this kingdom

1574–76

Once Catherine had composed herself after Charles IX's death she despatched one of her trusted officers, M. de Chemerault, with a letter to Henri in Poland telling him that he was now King of France. The next day a second courier followed de Chemerault – taking a different route – bearing a longer letter in which she expressed her sorrow at witnessing yet another of her children die: 'I beg the Almighty to send me death rather than see this again. ... Such was his love for me at the very end, not wishing to leave me and begging me to send for you without delay, he asked me to take charge of the kingdom until your arrival and to punish the prisoners whom he knew to be the cause of the troubles in the realm. After this he bade me farewell and asked me to kiss him, which almost broke my heart.'[1]

She described the scene of Charles's last few hours in which he called his senior advisers and royal bodyguards, commanding first that they obey his mother and then that they serve their new King. In her grief and with her customary ability to gloss over any unpleasant realities, she added that he spoke of the re-established loyalty expressed by Alençon and Navarre towards himself. Even more improbably, she wrote that the late King had recalled Henri's 'goodness and that you had always loved and obeyed him, serving him faithfully and had never given him any cause for grief. ... His last words were "*Eh ma mère*". My only consolation is to see you here soon in good health as your kingdom needs you, for if I were to lose you, I would have myself buried alive.'[2] She also urged him to take the safest route back to France via the Habsburg Empire and Italy.

Catherine counselled extreme caution in the manner of Henri's leaving Poland. 'As for your departure, do not allow any delays of any sort.' Warning him to beware of attempts by his northern subjects to detain him, she suggested that he leave a Frenchman to take charge of the affairs of Poland until his younger brother could be sent out, or that the Poles elect a leader from among themselves and rule their own country, supervised and aided in all things by a French commissioner. Later, perhaps, Henri could send his own second son to be their King. France had paid a hefty price for the Polish throne and Catherine felt loath simply to give it up. She imagined that the Poles would be more than content with this solution, 'for they would be kings themselves'. In fact, though his subjects would in theory have welcomed the departure of Henri himself, they were not prepared to lose a king who brought the prestige and benefits that came with close connection to a Continental superpower. Clearly some serious and prolonged negotiations would have to take place before Henri would be allowed to leave Poland.

The last part of the Queen Mother's letter was the counsel of a wise stateswoman. She implored her son to show impartiality to his entourage. Above all, she urged him not to start handing out posts and positions, favours and benefices, at least until he arrived in France. Only then could he be fully advised by her of the loyalty and good services he had received from those at home as well as those who had stayed with him during his Polish sojourn. Together, she wrote, they would go through the lists of the most deserving and able of his subjects and distribute posts, offices and rewards accordingly. She promised that nothing would be done before his arrival and that she would

> keep all benefices and offices that will fall vacant. We shall tax them, as there is not an écu left to do all the things you need to do to maintain your kingdom. ... The late King your brother charged me with the conservation of the realm and I will not fail you. I will do all that I can to hand it over to you united and at peace ... to permit you some little pleasure after all the trouble and difficulties you have endured. ... The experience you have acquired from your voyage is such that I am sure there has never been a king as wise as you ... I have had nothing but worry upon worry since you left: thus I believe that your return will bring me joy and contentment upon contentment and that I will no longer suffer from trouble or annoyance. I pray to God that it will be so and that I shall see you in good health and soon.[5]

Now the Queen Mother busied herself with a general 'house cleaning' for the new King's return. Having sent the letters to her son and, with the help of the banker Giovanni Battiste Gondi, borrowed 100,000 écus for Henri's journey to France, Catherine took the precaution of leaving Vincennes almost immediately after Charles's death. She moved into the Louvre where, for her personal security, she had all the entrances walled up except one. Some unfinished personal business of the Queen Mother's was dealt with summarily – the execution of the unfortunate regicide-turned-rebel Gabriel de Montgomery, who was decapitated and then *écartelé* (quartered). Her relentless pursuit of the man who had inadvertently killed her husband is one of the very few instances in which Catherine, despite her later reputation, sought vengeance.

Navarre and Alençon were prompt in their official ratification of Catherine's regency, published on 3 June 1574. She also ensured that the traditional forty-day lying-in-state and forthcoming funeral of her son would be every bit as splendid as that of Francis I. Catherine next focused her attention on buying a two-month truce – at a cost of 70,000 livres – with the Rochellais and the Protestant leader La Noue in Poitou, by which time she believed Henri would be back and be able to decide for himself how best to deal with the rebellious heretics. François de Montmorency and Marshal de Cossé were meanwhile left in the Bastille to await His Majesty's pleasure.

The news of his accession to the French throne reached Henri at around eleven o'clock on the morning of 15 June by a messenger from the Emperor who, despite the guards at the King's door, insisted on seeing Henri at once. After a tremendous commotion he succeeded in relaying the information to His Majesty. He arrived one hour before M. de Chemerault, despite the latter's record-breaking time covering the 800 miles from Paris to Cracow in sixteen days. During the month before Charles's death, Henri had received reports of his brother's desperate decline and imminent demise. While he expected the news, typically he had formed no real plans for action when it finally did come. The only preparation he had made had been an attempt to seduce the Poles into believing that he was finally settling in and adopting the ways of his new country. He no longer hid away in his rooms claiming ill-health, and had stopped looking obviously moody and homesick. During his time in Poland he had – in order to escape from close contact with his people – built up a barrier of etiquette that separated him from them. This had only increased their desire to see him and made him seem yet more remote and regal. Now when he appeared before his subjects he was animated and charming. He took to wearing Polish dress and even learned some of their traditional dances. Eschewing wine, he affected an enthusiastic preference for beer – though in fact he did not like alcohol at all.

By mid-April the nobles began to warm to their King. One matter which had caused great affront to the whole country since his arrival was Henri's obstinate reluctance to show any interest in his intended bride – the forty-eight-year-old spinster, Princess Anna de Jagellona. To her great disappointment he had hitherto managed to avoid her and they had only met at official functions. Knowing that his days in Poland were numbered, he felt that he would do well to pay court to the eager lady in an effort to lull his 'captors' (for this is how he viewed them) into believing in his transformation from French prince to Polish King. For Henri was Florentine to his fingertips when it came to deception.

When the news of Charles's death became public it caused great consternation in Cracow. Henri – calm and self-possessed – announced that a Diet must be called for September and that he would hand the government of France over to the Queen Mother while the Polish assembly deliberated upon how to proceed. Poland's interests must come first, cooed Henri reassuringly; France was, after all, in his mother's safe and experienced hands. The King appeared remarkably serene and though the less trusting nobles determined to keep a close eye on him, it was generally believed that he would behave honourably.

Beneath the tranquil surface, however, the King and his suite were making frantic preparations to get away as fast as possible from this detested country. They decided that the night of Friday, 18 June would be the ideal moment for escape. Three days before, Pomponne de Bellièvre, France's ambassador to Poland, took his official leave of the King since his mission had officially ended with the death of Charles IX. But Bellièvre had a secret mission: to go ahead and prepare the getaway route for Henri, supplying fresh horses at the various relays and stops, as well as other necessities for their flight. On the 18th itself, de Chemerault received a summons from the King who gave him letters for Catherine, with the urgent instruction to take them to her as soon as possible. He was given leave to depart immediately. All this took place in front of the council and seemed innocuous enough. De Chemerault was not, however, returning to France but had been instructed to meet Henri at a small ruined chapel later that same night, in a hamlet outside Cracow. He would act as a guide for the King and his suite of fellow escapees, leading them to Poland's borders with the Empire.

The whole plan suddenly risked being exposed by the incompetence of René de Villequier, Master of the King's Household, who had been spotted with a large baggage train of mules quite clearly headed away from Cracow. Now the people's suspicions were alerted, and Henri exploded with rage and berated the dunderhead Villequier. An already risky escape had just become yet more hazardous. The train contained jewels and other valuables not only belonging to Henri but also to the Crown of Poland. Much as he prized these things, he valued his life more and did not rate his chances against a mob of angry Poles if his escape plan failed. A great buzz went around that the King secretly planned to leave and Count Tenczin, his Polish Chamberlain, approached him in some dismay declaring that 'the city and senate deplored the King's intended departure'. Smoothly came the reply: 'A man of comprehension like yourself will easily perceive that it is not my intention to depart. My nobles know what I resolve upon in council in their presence. As for the populace, it is better to leave this their reverie uncontradicted! I care little for the rumour, but much for my own reputation.'[4]

Although Henri's calm had convinced Tenczin, by that evening there remained a great commotion that the King was indeed plotting his departure. The chamberlain came to tell Henri that orders had been given by the Senate to place guards around the palace. Had there been no plan the King would have manifested his outrage at this presumption; instead he remained as cool as ever and suggested that not only should the Senate have guards at the palace entrances, but that he himself would like to help 'tranquillise my good subjects and retire to bed in the presence of you all; then when you have seen me sound asleep, this panic may perhaps subside'. Supper was a merry affair that night with the King, in high spirits, at his witty best. Finally he retired to his chamber and, when left alone, as was the custom, with his Chamberlain at the foot of his bed, his curtains were drawn and Henri pretended to fall asleep. After some time Tenczin emerged from the King's room to say that His Majesty was indeed sleeping. In rooms next to Henri's those planning to leave with him had quietly been making their preparations. As soon as Henri judged it safe, he joined his companions.

The large treasure box fixed to His Majesty's bed was emptied and, aside from taking his own jewels away with him, Henri and his favourites stuffed their pockets with Polish gems, including pearls, diamonds and other jewels. These could come in handy if they needed to bribe their way through the hostile terrain ahead. To their intense consternation it transpired that all the palace doors and gates had been locked, though by chance they found that a small passage from the kitchens remained open and unguarded. After several near discoveries and various diversionary tactics, the party made their way out of the palace and arrived at the chapel beyond Cracow that served as their rendezvous.

Some of the King's suite had left the palace earlier, pretending to the guards that they were off on romantic assignations, but neither they nor de Chemerault could be found when Henri arrived at the chapel. Fortunately the horses for their flight were tethered there and after waiting for some time they all agreed that the King could tarry no longer, since his absence would not go unnoticed for long. As they set off, some of his gentlemen did indeed appear, but Villequier, Pibrac, de Chemerault and the others were still nowhere in sight. Without de Chemerault, none of the party knew the route, nor could they speak the language, but undeterred by these obstacles they rode off into the darkness. After getting lost in a forest and having their progress slowed by bog underfoot, the party managed to get to Osświecim at about midday, where to Henri's delight he found his favourites, Pibrac, Villequier, Quelus and the others, waiting anxiously for him. De Chemerault was also with them. It transpired that despite missing the rendezvous at the chapel they had managed to find their way to Osświecim with little trouble.

Meanwhile the King's flight and the missing jewels and valuables had been discovered. The alarm was raised in Cracow and a furious cry of 'Capture the perjured deserter!' rang in the ears of the Tartar cavalry troop immediately despatched to seize Henri and bring him back to face his furious subjects. Many of them had decided to join the troops and armed themselves with such basic weapons as stones, sticks and spears.

When the exhausted party spotted the pursuing troops on horseback on the distant horizon, they spurred their horses on and at last crossed the tiny bridge made of planks that spanned the Vistula, getting them safely out of Poland and into Pless, in Silesia. They destroyed the bridge by throwing the planks into the water and were thus saved from the furious soldiers and huge mob that had gathered to drag their sovereign back in shame to face justice or worse. At Pless, Bellièvre awaited Henri and although they were supposed to be travelling incognito their pretence fooled no one, especially thanks to the ecstatic greeting that Bellièvre gave his King. The governor of Pless urgently advised Henri to proceed with his journey as he had no wish to become embroiled in a war over His Majesty's person. With that the party set off again as quickly as they could and were soon in Vienna, having been met by an advance party of two of the Emperor's sons, Mathias and Maximilian.

Henri received a warm greeting from Maximilian II, the Empress Maria and a large enthusiastic crowd. His former antagonist over the election for the Polish throne, the Emperor was now the personification of a gracious host to the young King who – in the sixteenth-century manner between older and younger sovereigns – he called both son and brother. It had been a risky and narrow escape, and despite its lack of dignity, let alone majesty, Henri now found himself a free man. He wrote to his worried mother assuring her 'I am your son and have always obeyed you, and I resolve to devote myself more to you than ever before. . . . France and you are worth more than Poland. I shall always remain your devoted servant.'[5]

At the Imperial capital Henri found the money his mother had sent for his homeward journey, as well as several letters from her. Maximilian spoke to the King of the difficulties between those of the new religion and the Catholics in France, and advised his guest that when he returned he should show tolerance wherever possible and allow both religions to be practised in peace. He pointed out that this moderate approach had been a success within his own Empire and that the Lutheran princes coexisted in concord with the Catholic states. The Emperor harboured a secret hope that his widowed daughter, the Dowager Queen Elisabeth of France, might marry Henri, but the new King had his own views on the matter. He had only one bride in mind for himself and she was Marie de Clèves, the wife of his fugitive relative Condé, but this information he kept to himself.

During his stay in the Imperial capital Henri recovered from his alarming journey and appeared to be in generally good health, except for the usual trouble with the fistula on his eye and the abscess under his arm. The appearance of a new sore on his foot gave cause for concern too, especially when this stubbornly refused to heal even after applying a revolutionary new treatment to the problem. The diseased foot was placed into the throat of a newly bled bull, but despite optimistic predictions this innovative remedy proved a disappointment.

After the fugitive-like departure from Poland, Henri now showed that he could carry himself like a king and he seduced the Viennese people who were sorry to see him leave. On 11 July 1574 he arrived in the Venetian state, where he was welcomed with the gift of a golden coach and a guard of 3000 men, as cheering crowds now followed him on his route. Their number swelled as the journey progressed from village to village. They were so great that in one town, anxious to get a glimpse of the King passing in his golden carriage, the son of a senator stole the place of another man who, in the ensuing squabble, was stabbed to death.

At last Henri reached the edge of the lagoon where three gorgeously upholstered gondolas each in a different colour awaited him. Henri chose the one covered in gold brocade and the gondoliers, dressed in his livery of yellow with blue piping, helped him aboard. Setting off, he found himself surrounded by an accompanying fleet of 2000 vessels, and as a mark of honour the young nobles of the city created a half-moon of forty gondolas decorated in black velvet to sail around Henri's own. After a short while he stood up on the roof of his gondola so that the cheering crowds could catch a glimpse of him. Until late that night, Henri toured the city's canals and asked eager questions about the various Palazzi and churches they passed. On 18 July, after hearing Mass, he made his official *entrée* seated beside the Doge Mocenigo aboard the most magnificent ship he had ever seen. The purple mainsail billowed to show the emblem of the Lion of St Mark as 350 slaves rowed them across to the Lido where they dropped anchor. After hearing a Te Deum at St Nicholas, Henri took up residence at the Palazzo Foscari on the Grand Canal.

The following nine days spent in the city were probably the happiest and most carefree of Henri's life. More Italian than French by nature, the innovations and artistic beauty that he found wherever he looked enthralled him. He went to pay his respects to the eighty-seven-year-old Titian and sat for Tintoretto. Nor did he resist buying the gorgeous items thrust before him by eager merchants and craftsmen. Fortunately Catherine had sent him a sum of 30,000 écus for his enjoyment of Venice and he added to this by borrowing a further 10,000 on his own account.

His Polish treasure was for the most part squandered in an orgy of giving and spending. Like his mother, Henri was not only extravagant of nature but also extremely generous, handing diamonds, jewels and other precious items – including cash – to those who pleased and entertained him. He had never felt so happy and he wanted to show his gratitude for this rare moment of unalloyed joy. Many were able to retire for life after his visit.

Acquiring beautiful things by day, he even managed to spend 1000 écus on perfume alone. The glass blowers of Murano set up their gondolas outside his Palazzo on the Grand Canal and he watched fascinated as they fashioned their fabulous creations for him. Having visited all manner of other artisans for whom Venice is famed, by night Henri attended balls and banquets where he was fêted and adored. The twenty-two-year-old King shone in a way that he never had before, and never would again. Late at night the Duke of Ferrara, who with the Duke of Nevers had met Henri at Venice, took him out of the Palazzo by a secret passage to explore the city's other delights, and Henri would return just before dawn, in rapture. He wished his mother could have been in Venice, saying, 'If only the Queen my mother were here to take part in the honour which is paid me and which I owe to her alone.' Having uttered these worthy sentiments he did not, however, find time to write to her even once from his personal paradise.

On 27 July, when his departure could be put off no longer, Henri bade farewell to the city, inspired by the art and beauty and civilised living that he had experienced there. Indeed, he returned to France with many innovations and ideas for refining and embellishing his Court. He left, having spent a sum of 43,000 écus and incurred debts of a further 19,000, not including all the treasure and gems that he brought back from Poland and had distributed so indiscriminately around him. He had been a veritable one-man fillip to the economic life of Venice.

The Duke of Savoy had, at Catherine's request, travelled to Venice and joined her son's party there. Henri felt pleased to see his uncle and they spent much of his time in the city together. Emmanuel-Philibert's duchy formed part of the route home for the young King and that clever statesman, seeing that Henri was still untested politically, as well as in a semi-permanent state of ecstasy, decided he would press his own agenda, waiting only for a propitious moment. Their journey to France took Henri through Padua, Ferrara and on to Mantua. At each stop he received increasingly frantic letters from his mother enquiring as to her son's progress and urging him to return as the turbulent political situation in France worsened.[6] Ignoring his mother's desperate appeals, Henri stayed for twelve days in Savoy with his aunt and uncle.[7] It was now that Emmanuel-Philibert asked Henri to hand back to Savoy the last remaining towns held by France in Piedmont. Still enjoying his flush of happiness, the King declared that as a mark of friendship and goodwill he would indeed return Pinerolo, Savigliano and Peruza.[8]

Strictly speaking, this had been agreed in the 1559 Treaty of Cateau-Cambrésis, but Henri's gesture proved extremely unpopular, not only with his immediate circle of courtiers (one of whom – the Duke of Nevers – was governor of French territories in Italy) but also with the people of France generally. Although this had been precisely the sort of decision that Catherine had implored her son not to make, advising him to leave all major decisions until he had returned, she put a good face on the situation and ignored the indignant protests from the royal councillors. In return for supporting Henri's territorial promise, Catherine received 4000 troops from Savoy which she would need in her struggle to put down the rebels.

Catherine travelled from Paris to meet her son just outside Lyons. Sitting beside her in her personal coach were Alençon and Navarre. Like two naughty children, she kept them close by at all times. She had left Paris with many worries but soon forgot them when – at last – on 5 September she embraced her beloved Henri at Bourgoin, who knelt and kissed her hand. Both wept as they were finally reunited. Exhilarated, as he crossed the border into France, he had uttered the words, 'There is no country in the world to equal this kingdom.' After greeting her son she turned to his brother, Alençon, and to Henri of Navarre. Presenting the two young men to the King she said, 'Sire, deign to receive these two prisoners, whom I now resign to Your Majesty's pleasure. I have informed you of their caprices and misdemeanours. It is for Your Majesty to decree their fate.' Henri held out his hand to his brother who kissed it, then he greeted Navarre pleasantly and embraced both men. Alençon, who never knew a good thing until it was too late, could be heard trying to justify his treachery into the King's shoulder, but Henri merely smiled and said, 'Be it so, mes frères; the past is forgotten. I restore you both to liberty, and ask only in return that you will give me your love and fealty. If you cannot love me, love yourselves sufficiently to abstain from plots and intrigues which cannot but harm you and which are unworthy of the dignity of your birth.'[9] It was a noble attempt to start a reign in amity and magnanimity.

Similarly Margot approached her brother to welcome him. In her memoirs she recalls that he stared fixedly at her. He had been kept abreast of her involvement in the plots of her brother and husband. Nevertheless he enfolded her in his arms and complimented her on her beauty. Margot, having had more than her share of intimate embraces from Henri, wrote, 'When the King clasped me to him I shivered and trembled from head to foot, the which emotion I had the greatest difficulty to conceal.' The following day at Lyons he made his official entry into the city and at his special request he seated Catherine beside him; he wished to honour her for the monumental struggle she had faced keeping his kingdom intact. Later that day he called his first council meeting.

Catherine was fifty-five years old when her favourite child ascended the throne that she had so jealously guarded for her sons. In sixteenth-century terms she was already in advanced old age. She was certainly overweight, though she did not drink alcohol. Her capacity for rich foods in remarkable quantities astonished everyone, and once or twice she nearly died from the subsequent indigestion and havoc that it caused her system. Nevertheless, she remained as spry and alert as ever. She continued to ride into her sixties and still loved the chase – though she had taken several serious falls over the years – and she remained an excellent shot. Her more feminine interests and pursuits were also still in evidence. An outstanding needlewoman, as Brantôme noted, she often spent her time after dinner in her circle of ladies 'engaged on her silkwork in which she was unsurpassed'.

Catherine remained open to and intrigued by new ideas, inventions and innovations, her mind eager and enquiring. When tobacco arrived from the New World she was presented with a sample in 1560 by Jean Nicot, her ambassador to Portugal, and told that the dried leaves were to be tightly rolled in paper and smoked. It was claimed that this plant possessed all manner of healing powers. Deciding she would not smoke the tobacco, she crushed it instead into a powder, claiming to find it most efficacious against headaches. Her adoption of tobacco was naturally taken up by the Court and eventually by the people, who called it *herbe de la reine* or *nicotiane* and it is thus thanks to Catherine de Medici that the French learned to love tobacco. For all the talk of her as a poisoner, this is the only definite evidence of her use of it albeit unwittingly. Just as she had brought the side-saddle to France many years before and popularised the use of forks, her influence allowed many such novelties to flourish. Another item Catherine brought with her from Florence and made fashionable was the use of drawers for women. When dancing or dismounting from a horse, she wished to keep her modesty and instead of simply wearing the traditional linen undershirt and petticoats beneath her dress, she wore this early version of underpants to avoid accidentally exposing more than a well-shaped and beautifully stockinged leg. Her drawers were made of many different materials including gold and silver cloth, although it is hard to imagine that the latter were anything but a torture of discomfort to wear. This garment was taken up by some

Frenchwomen but generally ignored by Englishwomen, where it did not come into use until many years later.

Catherine also introduced the folding fan, which hung from a ribbon attached to the girdle and could be elaborately decorated. It became a great favourite in England. Another item she is credited with promoting, much loved by courtiers, was the handkerchief, considered an essential Renaissance fashion accessory. Handkerchiefs originated in Venice and were a luxury item only legally permitted for use by the gentry. Catherine had a huge collection of decorative ones; these had a small central cloth, which was held in the hand in order to allow the fancy edges to show. Only the simplest squares of linen were actually put to proper use, the rest were for display only.

Although fascinated by 'the new', when it came to the institution of the monarchy she maintained her atavistic reverence for the old. She had become more majestic with the passing years, and though her double chin and full but determined mouth were more accentuated than ever, she could caress her listeners with her seductive voice – appearing almost intimate with them – all the while subtly maintaining the insurmountable boundary that placed her above all others except her son the King. While introducing or encouraging many new fashions the Queen Mother ensured that her own appearance varied little, except at her children's weddings. Ever since she had been widowed she wore a wide black shirt and from her shoulders fell enormous wing sleeves; her black bodice was pointed and around the back of her white ruff stood a high black collar, and 'over all this flowed a long black mantle'. Though she presented a sombre figure, the cut and quality of the lace and work in general made her mourning anything but drab. She subtly enhanced her black dress (usually made from plain wool) by its excellent cut; sometimes she used trimmings such as fur and gems, which created a majestic effect if the occasion demanded. When it came to her undergarments she denied herself nothing: hidden beneath the black wool she wore the finest chemises and the most exquisitely embroidered petticoats. As was her intention, she stood out from the other gorgeously and colourfully dressed ladies and gentlemen, particularly during Henri III's reign. One dazzled ambassador reported of the courtiers that 'the world had never before seen anything to match them'.

Unlike her contemporary, Elizabeth of England, Catherine did not pluck her eyebrows or her forehead – a high forehead was considered a sign of great beauty – though she did wear make-up sparingly. She experimented with 'new products and formulae' and is credited with popularising their use among European noblewomen. Catherine wore rouge, over a wash of white lead to tint her skin as pale as possible, and occasionally she also used eye shadow. She did not adopt the taffeta or velvet beauty spots favoured by Elizabeth I, placed on the face to draw the eye off any imperfections (such as hideously discoloured teeth). The use of such primitive cosmetics, the layers of lead skin whitener on the face and mercury sublimate to smooth the skin, proved hazardous. As bathing was rare, these poisonous beautifiers were left on the face and added to until eventually they needed to be 'refreshed' and had to be washed off, before the process recommenced.

Catherine also promoted the use of scent. (Florence claims one of the oldest perfumeries in the modern world, set up at the convent of Santa Maria Novella.) Since personal hygiene as we know it today was practically non-existent, body odours could be quite overwhelming. Both men and women used quantities of scent to disguise their malodorousness; even pet animals were given a liberal sprinkling. At Grasse, which had become a large glove-making centre, urine was applied in the tanning process; but to remove the unpleasant stench the tanners sprinkled perfume. Thus gloves were scented and even after glove-making in Grasse collapsed in the eighteenth century, the perfume industry that had been set up there on the Florentine model continued to thrive (as it does to this day). This lack of personal hygiene and the rarely cleaned many-layered clothes also meant a constant infestation of fleas. Taffeta was used as much as possible because of the belief that it acted as a deterrent.

The colour of Catherine's naturally dark hair was from time to time lightened either by bleach or with the use of coloured hairpieces. In the sixteenth century blond hair was considered the ideal for beauty. France and Italy made the best wigs in Europe and the hair sold at public hair auctions often came from nuns. Portraits of Catherine usually show her hair parted in the middle with small sprigs of curls on either side of her face peeping out from her French hood, or later her peaked widow's cap which covered most of her hair. As she grew older these were most likely to have been hairpieces. Men were also known to wear false beards, though a small goatee beard was the fashion for the latter part of the 1500s. A century earlier the Duke of Lorraine had worn a waist-length false beard to the Duke of Burgundy's funeral.

The Queen Mother's capacity for hard work remained undiminished; indeed she thrived on the challenges she faced. She could work late into the night after an official banquet, give instructions to her secretaries on several different subjects at once and, if necessary, survive on very little sleep. Long used to the habit of power, she prepared to enter unfamiliar territory; with Henri on the throne how much real influence would she now exercise? Catherine loved Henri, but she also feared him.

Henri was a grown man, and though he was by far the most intelligent of Catherine's sons and had ideas of his own about how matters should be conducted, she knew he was capable of an indolence which as King would be dangerous were she not behind him, guiding him with her by now-unrivalled experience of ruling the country. His more eccentric personality traits also worried her; his extravagance both in material and emotional terms were troubling. He protected and loved his favourites, the handsome *mignons*, with a zealous devotion that became more marked now that he had become master of France. Nor could his passionate love for Condé's wife be considered an altogether straightforward heterosexual phenomenon; it seemed to be more an obsessive though probably platonic fascination with an idol.

Catherine could not fail to have been concerned by the two conflicting sides of her son's temperament, one the sensual lover of excess, the other a religious penitent, desperate for redemption, for whom no sacrifice to God was too great. His love of dressing in the richest clothes, later designing dresses for his wife as well as costumes for himself and his favourites, and his adoration of jewellery and other adornments would not have been tolerated by his father. As regards morals and manners, Henry II had presided over a comparatively austere Court by Renaissance standards. His code had covered clothing and he had introduced highly complex 'sumptuary laws' to curb the sartorial excesses to which courtiers often fell prone, although these regulations were frequently ignored. His cure for Henri would have been to send his son out hunting, or risking his life in some manly pursuit. The usual Valois mania for the chase and chivalrous feats were, on the whole, anathema to Henri III, who preferred to remain indoors out of the cold. Nonetheless, the obverse side to Henri's character was amply demonstrated when he made his escape from Poland. However despicable it had been, Henri had showed immense personal courage during that desperate dash for the Imperial frontier, and when his entourage of nobles begged him again and again to turn back, he had pushed on, heedless of the dangers both before and behind him.

Unfortunately, during his absence in Poland the voluptuary in Henri's nature had greatly advanced. The Venetian ambassador Giovanni Michiel wrote, 'All his old gallantry and serious ideas which were so talked about have entirely disappeared; he has given himself up to a life of such idleness, sensual pleasures dominate his existence, he takes so little exercise that everyone is astonished. He spends most of his time with the ladies, covered in scent, curling his hair, wearing large earrings and rings of all different sorts. The sums spent on his beautiful and elegant shirts alone are unimaginable.'[10] One English observer wrote to Sir Francis Walsingham, Elizabeth I's Secretary of State, about the new King but gushed compliments. He described Henri's charm and the marvellous though ephemeral *'je ne sais quoi'* that the King possessed in such large measure, but which tragically the portrait painters had never managed to capture. (Since he had once been a possible suitor for the Queen of

England's hand, this had probably prompted the favourable report.)

Zuñiga, the Spanish ambassador, wrote to Philip on 22 September 1574 that the King spent all his evenings dancing and attending banquets. To the sombre and black-clad Spanish king he continued in a vein that he knew would appall his master: 'For the last four days he has been wearing a costume of violet satin, breeches, doublet and mantlet. All the clothes are covered in pleats and long slashes strewn with buttons, and white, red and violet ribbons. He wears earrings and coral bracelets.'[11] The ambassador finished by writing, 'With all of this he shows who he really is.' This remark was surely a reference to the King's obvious effeminacy. While Zuñiga found more fault than was perhaps strictly necessary, apart from the Spanish courtiers who stuck to far more austere fashions, noblemen in the sixteenth century dressed as richly as women, wearing earrings, jewel-encrusted costumes and fantastically elaborate clothes, though Henri did favour excessive confections even by the standards of the day. At the very least his behaviour suggested a taste for transvestism.

Henri took men's fashions to new extremes. Doublets were worn over whalebone or wooden corsets – women also used the corset – which were agonising to wear and actually considered dangerous to health as they not only constricted the wearer's ribs and waist to such an extent that breathing became difficult, but they also caused sores on the skin from the friction. These seeming instruments of torture were made illegal in England, but not in Henri's France. It is often said of Catherine that she insisted her flying squadron all had 13-inch waists. While this precise measurement seems unattainable – even given that French inches were slightly bigger than English ones – a tiny waist was required and this could only have been achieved by using the unyielding wooden corsets that sometimes 'pierced the flesh with splinters'. Henri and his courtiers also wore heavily padded sleeves. A cloak was hung over the shoulders and, to balance this, the King favoured padded breeches slashed with brilliant colours. (Slashing had come into existence after the Swiss defeated the invading army of Burgundians led by Charles the Bold in 1477. In a surprise attack upon the invaders in their camp the Swiss slashed their enemy's tents and standards to shreds. To celebrate their victory they took tiny pieces of the cloth from the enemy's banners and tents, and laced them triumphantly through their clothes. This evolved into the slashing style which allowed contrasting colours and fabrics to enhance the costumes of the rich.)

In the joy of being reunited with her son, Catherine put any thoughts of his weaknesses aside. The gossips and ill-wishes might call him 'King of the Island of Hermaphrodites' but she knew that at his best Henri could rule France and be a great king. Tactfully and carefully she made some suggestions as to how he should start his reign. In her own words she summed this up: 'He can do everything but he must have the will.'[12] First she advised having a much smaller council and this he heeded, reducing its number to eight as well as the princes.

The new council was composed of Catherine's trusties and some of his own. These were René de Birague, Jean de Morvilliers (Bishop of Reims), Sebastien l'Aubespine (Bishop of Limoges), Jean de Monluc (Bishop of Valence), Guy de Pibrac, Paul de Foix, Philippe Comte de Cheverny and Pomponne de Bellièvre. Some of those who had shared the semi-exile in Poland were also rewarded with prestigious positions. Villequier and De Retz shared the post of First Gentleman of the Chamber, each rotating their duties every six months. Roger de Bellegarde became a Marshal of France and Martin Ruzé was made Secretary of State.[13] Catherine's core of loyal and experienced men were thus kept on into the new reign.

The Queen Mother had also counselled that Henri open all despatches himself and not leave matters to secretaries of state who had grown used to responding as they saw fit without consulting their master. Henri ordained that no official document be considered valid without his personal signature upon it and demanded that all correspondence be shown to him first. From the beginning his hard work is evidenced by his small neat writing on hand-drafted documents and his compact signature on official papers. The delegation of the monarch's prerogatives and powers that had been the increasing hallmark of the last reign was over; France had a King once more.

Determined to show the '*main de maître*' (hand of the master) as advised by Catherine, Henri even revoked her right to open diplomatic despatches without his seeing them first. If she was taken aback she hid her feelings; it was, after all, her own advice that he followed. She had told him to 'show that [he] was the master and not the companion'. Some time before, Catherine had also warned that the *gens de robe longue* (magistrates and office holders) were difficult, tiresome and loquacious: 'They spoil everything and try to control everything by their arguments, their verbosity, and their knowledge, which makes them so overbearing and presumptuous that they expect their opinions alone to be considered.'[14] Far better, she suggested, to have military men as his advisers who said what they meant and were brief and to the point: 'They have nothing but common sense, and are not lettered or opinionated and will at least come to terms at the discretion and according to the opinion of the King.'[15] What she meant was that military men were simpler to manipulate, more naturally loyal and their intentions far easier to read. Her long experience had taught her how to get what she wanted from them. The professionals and intellectuals were altogether too opinionated.

The names noticeably absent from the King's most important office holders were those of the great dynastics that had featured so prominently since the days of Henri's father and grandfather: the Guises and the Montmorencys had, on the whole, been left out. Catherine's advice to her son culminated in a wise discourse on the importance of keeping a regular timetable, dealing with public affairs in the morning and other matters after his *dîner* (lunch). She pressed him to make himself available to the people in the way that his grandfather, Francis I, had done. He must hear the people and receive their complaints or petitions personally. Only by doing so would it be clear that the King was the fount of all decisions in the realm, and from him emanated all honours, offices and favours. He must avoid showing too much favour to his closest friends and companions, and from making any one of them too powerful. She had certainly learned this lesson from the group of mighty nobles her husband had unintentionally bequeathed her. Henri should, she advised, implement these habits and ideas immediately, otherwise they would never get done, and only then would he be respected and obeyed as a king and not treated like a child.

Unfortunately, while Henri agreed with much of the political advice, he espoused a different view of how a monarch should comport himself and had brought back with him the habits he had acquired in Poland that were designed to keep him from the pullulating throng. These did not please the French people. He no longer took his meals surrounded by the public, but from behind a low balustrade intended to keep the crowd from coming too close. When he ate, his gentlemen attended upon him rather than his servants. The King did permit certain individuals to approach him, but they had to ask permission first and follow a strict set of rules before engaging His Majesty in conversation. *Dîner* was taken at around eleven o'clock and the more elaborate *souper* in the evening, the latter often followed by a ball or some other entertainment. Mealtimes were no longer the milling of courtiers around the person of the King while he ate.

Unlike his predecessors, Henri did not want to live as publicly, believing that overfamiliarity was the author of insolence. It offended his royal dignity to be surrounded by his most senior courtiers while he stood undressed and he ordered that henceforth they should not enter his chamber until he was clothed. Such reforms provoked a furious response, but he clung to them as far as he could, although when some nobles protested by leaving Court he was forced to relax or give up many of them, at least for the time being. In 1585 he printed a booklet of precise instructions on etiquette for his Court. This served as the foundation for the fantastically stylised manners, customs and rituals that later dictated court life at Versailles in the time of Louis XIV and his successors. Thus

Henri III could be considered the author of the bizarre and minutely ordered existence and habits of the last monarchs of the *ancien régime*. The heartily accessible yet still majestic ways of his grandfather and father were to become an abandoned relic. There was nothing hearty about Henri; he was far too dainty and aware of his position.

Catherine could not but notice within a few days of seeing her son that many of the traits that were a worry to her before he left had become yet more accentuated during his time in Poland. One observer even wondered whether, since his departure in 1573, the King had not only 'gone from Paris to Cracow but also to Sodom and Gomorrah'. She observed his intense disappointment that Condé's wife, Marie, Princess de Clèves, did not feature among the welcoming party that greeted him outside Lyons – she awaited the birth of a baby and travel would have been dangerous. Meanwhile, Condé was still at large in Germany and an enemy of the state.

Marie had abjured the Protestant religion at the same time as her husband in 1572 and had since espoused the Catholic faith with a sincere fervour. Without a blush Henri spoke quite seriously and determinedly about his forthcoming marriage to the already married and pregnant princess. He fretted about organising her divorce as quickly as possible so that their own union might take place without delay. Time spent apart from Marie had been an agony for him, as his daily letters to her had witnessed, but it would not be long now before she wore the crown of France as his wife and Queen. Catherine kept silent. She did not wish this for her son, but how could she deny him if it were to bring him happiness and, above all else, children? France needed legitimate heirs to continue the Valois line and prevent the Bourbons from taking the throne.

Rumours questioning the King's ability to produce children abounded. On 20 September 1574 Catherine's relative, the papal nuncio Salviati, wrote to Cardinal Galli saying that although the King would marry,

> it is only with difficulty that we can imagine that there will be offspring ... physicians and those who know him well say that he has an extremely weak constitution and will not live long. ... He is so feeble that if he sleeps *en compagnie* for two or three nights he is unable to get up from his bed for a whole week afterwards. When you hear that the King is suffering from an indisposition, which is presently the case, and cannot leave his bed for two or three days, you can be sure that *amour* has been the cause of his illness.[16]

It was not just *amour* that made the King ill, he also suffered from weak lungs like Charles, and drank only water as his constitution could not tolerate even so much as a glass of wine. A few days later Archbishop Frangipani wrote,

The one true and proper remedy for this kingdom would be a true king who not only wants to be a true king, but understands what it takes to be one. Then everyone would be put in their place. I do not see these qualities in this young man, neither in his spirit which is prone to indolence and sensual excess, nor in his body which is weak and prone to ill health. ... At twenty-four years old he remains indoors, and for the most part in bed. He needs to be vigorously spurred on to force him to do anything which requires action.[17]

At the time of his arrival in Lyons Henri had announced, with Damville and the rebellious Languedoc in mind, 'I have no greater desire and wish ... than to recall my subjects to me and to the natural obedience which they owe me by gentleness and clemency rather than by other means.'[18] Catherine, sure of her son's military talents – forgetting that it was the now-dead Tavannes who had usually been the actual author of her son's successes – and with men at her disposal, joined the hawks on the council. Henri, instead of following his initial inclination towards offering a general amnesty, took the uncharacteristic line pushed by his mother. For all her advice that he be the master, she had ensured that he felt there was no one else he could trust implicitly or to whom he could turn for impartial direction.

Damville, now leader of the Politiques, had made the journey to Turin (where Henri had broken his journey home to France with his aunt and uncle of Savoy) in order to explain his actions during the last days of Charles IX's reign. This presented a clear sign that he sought a peaceful solution at the start of the new one. He had also spoken of the need for concessions to pacify the reformers. If Henri had released the two 'Montmorency hostages' from the Bastille, Damville's elder brother François and his brother Méru's father-in-law Marshal de Cossé, and treated reasonably with Damville, allowing him to keep the governorship of Languedoc, then the two-month truce Catherine had bought could probably have been extended into a larger peace agreement. Yet Henri, spurred by Catherine and the warmongers on the council, rejected this peaceful option and the country prepared itself once again for renewed hostilities.

Just at this crucial moment tragedy struck for Henri: on Saturday, 30 October 1574 Marie of Clèves-Condé died of a lung infection. Rumours abounded that Condé had sprinkled poison on to a letter to his wife that would ensure a lingering but certain death, but in fact the young woman's lungs had been weak for years. A few weeks earlier all had seemed well as she had successfully given birth to a daughter who had been named Catherine after her sister, the Duchess of Guise. The news of Marie's sudden death arrived at Lyons on 1 November. The Queen Mother –

for whom this development came as a relief, since Marie had been a spirited girl who might well have proved tiresome and interfering as Henri's consort – dared not tell her son but placed the letter carrying the dread tidings under a pile of correspondence so that the King might come across it himself. When he did eventually read the report telling him that his 'Dame de Clèves ... blessed with a singular goodness and beauty' had expired, he characteristically fainted.

Henri's grief and devastation were such that Catherine feared for her son's life. Hysterical and exaggerated emotion finally exhausted the King, who suffered from a violent fever and took to his bed and would neither eat nor drink for three days. Eventually Villequier and the Duke of Guise had to force food down his throat on the Queen Mother's orders. When he did finally reappear his clothes were covered with death's heads that had been embroidered in silver thread on to his exquisitely cut black velvet costume. Tiny silk skulls even decorated his shoes. Henri cut a tragic, albeit theatrical, figure and bore his sorrow ill. The Court was ordered into full mourning, though his mother urged him not to linger overlong in his grief and resolved to look for a bride worthy of him as quickly as possible. She firmly removed all the little mementoes he carried about his person that had belonged to his beloved and began the process of finding a wife for her son. Among the possible candidates, the Queen Mother suggested a Swedish princess, Elisabeth Wasa, for she felt that only the daughter of a king provided a truly fitting bride for her son. A marriage to Elisabeth would also have helped Henri keep the Crown of Poland; and there was another unexpected bonus that recommended her to Catherine: the princess did not speak a word of French.

In his grieving lassitude, Henri appeared to agree with his mother's choice. A demand for a portrait was sent to the French ambassador in Stockholm, though all the while the King had already made up his mind to marry someone else. He had secretly decided upon Louise de Vaudémont, the princess from Lorraine whom he had met there just before leaving for Poland. Her striking resemblance to his dead Marie and her humble demeanour both charmed him. This unloved child of a minor prince of the Lorraine family, whose stepmother had treated her so cruelly, would become his bride and Queen, but for the moment Henri said nothing.

A blizzard of Protestant and Politique pamphlets attacking Catherine and the regime now deluged France, denouncing her greedy Italian financiers and ministers, the rule of women, the legitimacy of the Valois dynasty and the rights of an inherited monarchy. Published in 1576, the most notable and virulent attack upon Catherine was *Le Discours merveilleux de la vie, actions et déportements de Cathérine de Médicis, Royne-Mère*. Written by someone with an intimate knowledge of Court life cleverly blending fact with fiction, this slim volume was a huge success throughout the country and underwent several reprints. It accused the Queen Mother of every lurid and horrible crime imaginable. She had not only killed every person whose death had been convenient to her, orchestrated the Massacre of Saint Bartholomew, seduced her sons into lives of fecklessness and debauchery so that she might usurp their rights, but her whole life was also so motivated by greed, hatred and a lust for power that no crime was too vicious for her provided she kept her position as the de facto ruler of France. Catherine reacted with amused interest; the charges were so exaggerated that she laughed and encouraged her ladies to read it to her aloud. The only pity, she commented, was 'that the author had not previously applied to me for information, as by his own statement "it was impossible to fathom the depths of her Florentine deceit" ... and he evidently knew nothing of the events he pretended to discuss'. Besides, she laughed, he had left so much out!

On 13 November Damville issued a manifesto in which he promised to fight against the evil regime infected with foreigners (i.e. Italians) that bled the country to death with iniquitous taxes, and deliberately created unrest over religious matters. He demanded a meeting of the Estates-General, sectarian tolerance, freedom of conscience and a general conference to deal with religious issues.[19] On 16 November the Court left Lyons for Avignon, the royal family travelling on a well-armed ship surrounded by protecting vessels. Once at Avignon, news of Damville's military successes arrived with an alarming constancy and there was little cheer for the royalist army, despite the fact that they were well equipped and their number large. Catherine felt profound dismay; what she had hoped would be a forceful strike at the enemy bringing them to the negotiating table now turned into the same seemingly endless round of gains and losses that had bedevilled all the religious civil wars.

Henri appeared too steeped in his gloom and grief to act decisively. The loss of his adored Marie had sparked a fresh bout of religious fervour in him and he admired the procession of flagellant monks that he saw parading around the city of Avignon. The dismal sight of these dark and mysterious figures, faceless behind their enormous cowls, clad – and almost entirely covered – in blue, white or black robes, singing the 'Miserere' as they beat themselves evoked an almost mystical, perhaps even erotic thrill in Henri, who determined that he would lead a similar procession of self-mortification. This took place a week before Christmas 1574. Catherine took part to please her son, as did the rest of the Court. Some of the young courtiers whipped themselves into a frenzied state of ecstasy, led by the example of their King. Unfortunately, the cold December night grew freezing as the macabre candlelit march continued through light snowfall. The Cardinal of Lorraine, who walked barefoot for the procession, caught a chill. By 26 December this great prince of the Church, uncle of Mary, Queen of Scots, who had once ruled France in all but name with his brother François, was dead.

The cardinal had throughout the years been by turns both a scourge and a support to Catherine. His influence had been greatly reduced over the past decade, nevertheless his sudden passing at the age of forty-nine truly shocked her. Catherine heard of his death at her *souper* and seemed, for once, to be groping for words that would mark the occasion. She made a few innocuous comments, but appeared to have difficulty grasping that this man whom she had fought against, appeased, relied upon and always watched with caution, would no longer feature in her life. Almost all the 'overmighty subjects' whom she had had to put up with – and been ignored by – during her husband's reign had now gone. She had outlived nearly all of them, yet the problems for which they were responsible remained as alive as ever. She was troubled with an uneasiness over the next few days and then one evening, again at her *souper*, an incident took place, witnessed by many. She believed she saw the cardinal before her for a moment and, dropping her glass, she uttered a cry. For many nights she had terrible dreams and like Macbeth after Banquo's ghost's appearance at his feast, slept fitfully, imagining him to be nearby.

Henri, dispirited with the lack of progress in the fight against Damville, sent word to him that he wished to hear his antagonist's terms. As the noise of the rebels' cannon could be heard from Avignon he decided that he could no longer tolerate the humiliation or the risk of being in such close proximity to the enemy and made up his mind to leave the southern part of the kingdom. Having broken the news to his mother about his choice of bride and borrowed 100,000 écus to defray the expenses ahead, Henri, his mother and the Court left Avignon on 10 January 1575 and headed north on a journey that would lead him to Rheims for his coronation and marriage.

On the same day as the King's departure, Damville announced the inauguration of an independent state made up of several provinces in southern and south-central France. Once again, as with La Rochelle – which also resisted royalist assaults – France had a breakaway state within her borders; its absolute chief was the Prince de Condé (who had made an agreement with John-Casimir, son of the Elector-Palatine, for Protestant troops from Germany to aid Damville). As a Prince of the Blood, Condé lent legitimacy as the supreme figurehead, though the party ultimately hoped to make Alençon their titular head. Two secret emissaries were sent to persuade the duke to escape and join Damville, but they were arrested and summarily executed.

Catherine realised that she would not be able to change Henri's mind about the young girl that he wished to marry. Louise de Vaudémont was not a princess who could bring with her a fortune or connections to a fabulous dynasty, but Catherine concealed her frustration over this and pretended that the whole match had been her idea all along. She wished to get the ceremonies behind her and continue to Paris where the King must address the desperate state of the Treasury, the semi-insolvency in which he found himself being a fundamental cause for the Crown's inability to implement its authority.

The journey north provided a depressing reminder of the devastation left by the civil wars, never more than in the faces of the peasants. At Dijon he was unpleasantly surprised to find himself confronted with a delegation from Poland who had come to ask their King what his plans were for the throne that his mother had bought for him. With great eloquence Henri, who was perhaps one of the foremost charmers of his age, lyrically seduced his listeners, convincing them that as soon as he was married and had a son nothing would be able to prevent him from returning to his beloved Polish subjects. Once again believing their King, the Poles took their leave, assured that their union with France would remain intact.*

Further consternation en route for Rheims came when a plot was discovered to have the royal cortège attacked in Burgundy – an area with a large number of Huguenot strongholds – and for Henri's abduction. It is possible that Alençon had had a hand in this, but nothing could be proven. The King needed no added reason to hate his brother, who had already plotted to take the throne from him while Charles lay dying. Henri even told Navarre that if he should die Navarre must seize the throne and ensure that Alençon never wore the Crown of France.

The coronation itself, which took place on 13 February 1575, was replete with bad omens of all sorts. When the Cardinal of Guise (Henri, Duke of Guise's brother and nephew of the recently deceased cardinal) placed the ancient crown of Charlemagne on the King's head he felt weak and dizzy, and it slipped and nearly fell off. Henri then complained that it had injured his head. He found the constant changing of heavy robes and the five hour ceremony fatiguing to the extent that he had to lie down during it. Worse still, there was also a rumour that His Majesty had not even been able to cure those that he touched for the king's evil. To a superstitious people these signs all augured ill.

Furthermore, the preparations for the King's marriage two days later had been reduced to a farce. Henri had become so overexcited about his bride's wedding gown and other fine costumes for the festivities – all of which he had painstakingly designed himself – that he even insisted upon personally dressing her hair. The sweet-natured Louise stood patiently

* Later that same year, Etienne Bathory, Prince of Transylvania, was elected King of Poland.

for hours as the King primped and fussed over her. At one point in his creative frenzy he managed to pierce her skin with a needle while sewing yet another precious stone on to his fiancée's wedding dress; she patiently endured it all without uttering a cry. He had determined that Louise should be reinvented as his very own creation. She worshipped Henri and basked in the fuss he made over her.

Louise had been so little loved as a child that when one of Henri's *mignons*, Cheverny, had arrived in Lorraine to ask for Louise's hand in marriage on the King's behalf, the girl had been woken up in her bedchamber by her stepmother making three curtsies to her. Assuming this to be a sarcastic gesture for having overslept, Louise, who until now had been treated like a servant, only realised something serious was afoot when her father also shuffled in and made three bows. However, she had to wait a little longer before she became Queen of France. After Henri had frizzed her hair and adjusted almost every curl it was so late that the ceremony – originally due to take place in the morning – had to be postponed until the evening instead when, at last, the couple were married by the Cardinal de Bourbon.

The next embarrassment that Catherine had to endure was the royal party's lack of funds to continue to Paris. Word soon spread that 'the King had not the price of a dinner'. She made an appeal to Parlement and enough money was finally collected for the King and his Court to journey to the capital. At last, after one and a half years, Henri returned to Paris. Before him lay a truly monumental task: he must untangle years of corruption and lack of accounts, and put in place stringent measures to remedy matters, and do all this in a financial climate that was depressed all over Europe during 1575. Huge quantities of Spanish gold from the Americas had been partly responsible for destabilising the European economy. Henri applied for loans from the usual sources abroad and set about taxing the middle classes, the peasants having been squeezed for so long that they had barely enough to eat, much less to pay their King. This raised 3 million livres, 50,000 of which Henri promptly gave to his *mignon* du Ghast.

Catherine urged Henri to deal with the almost impossible task of putting the kingdom back on a financially balanced footing. Unfortunately, his former lassitude reasserted itself when he fully comprehended the magnitude of the task before him and he left his mother to do the work; soon he could no longer be bothered to attend the council meetings but engaged in frivolities with his *mignons* instead. None of this was lost on the Parisians who watched their King with scant respect. One piece of graffiti daubed on a wall near the Louvre called the King 'Henri de Valois, King of Poland and France by the grace of God and his mother, concierge of the Louvre, hairdresser-in-ordinary to his wife.' His extravagance became an act of defiance. What did it matter how much he spent on his pleasures, he seemed to be saying, since the country faced an impossible situation anyhow?

Even before arriving in Paris, Catherine had received word that her beloved daughter Claude, Duchess of Lorraine, had fallen ill again. When she reached the capital, Claude was dead. This was yet another appalling loss. One of her chief pleasures had been to visit Claude and Charles and their children for the only truly happy family reunions she had ever experienced. She often stayed with the couple in Lorraine; now this refuge where she could be a grandmother and mother without ceremony would never be the same. Catherine took to her bed with a fever and nursed her misery. Meanwhile, to everyone's astonishment, Henri briefly took to hunting (not usually his favourite sport) with his friends, riding carefree through the forests of Vincennes and the Bois de Boulogne. He conceded nothing to the loss of his sister nor to his mother's feelings; if anything the round of balls and banquets became more frenetic than ever. Catherine hid the pain that his gross callousness caused her.

Apart from abandoning himself to pleasure with his closest companions, he kept himself busy causing further strife within his family. He wanted to remove the threat of the once-cosy clique of Margot, Navarre and Alençon, and destroy their trust in each other. When it came to malicious trouble-making Henri showed himself an inspired master. Aided by his *mignons*, who liked nothing better than to run to their King and fill his head with wicked inventions, from the very first days of his reign he set about dividing his family in order to rule it. During his time in Poland he had tried to re-establish relations with Margot, but after his sense of betrayal over her romance with Henri of Guise in 1570 and the maniacal beating she had received from her mother and Charles IX as a result, Margot recalled her vow to keep 'the memory of his wrong *immortelle*'. Her love and protection for Alençon was evoked by her younger brother's neediness. Unloved by Catherine, she enjoyed her brother's 'affection and attentions', and decided to 'love and embrace all that concerned him'.[20] After Henri's departure to Poland she had made Alençon's interests her own. Unfortunately, in attempting to play at her mother's game of kingmaker, Margot found to her cost that she had backed the wrong brother.

Shortly after he first arrived at Lyons, Henri had already impugned Margot for meeting a lover while pretending to visit an abbey near her alleged admirer's house. After the visit Navarre warned Margot of Henri's accusation and had urged him to have her sent away. Margot swore that she had been falsely charged and Navarre, who had defended his wife, told her that she must go to her mother and brother who awaited her. He advised her to defend herself vigorously. Eventually it transpired that the scandal had been a malicious invention by one of the King's *mignons*, who was forced to retract his accusation. Catherine had refused to listen to Margot's explanation and berated her daughter in such a loud voice that the courtiers could overhear her shaming. Even after the truth had been uncovered, Catherine insisted that 'the King could not be mistaken' and received Margot very coldly. Without apologising, she simply told her daughter that the King wished to be reconciled with his sister. Navarre nobly supported his wife throughout the stormy ordeal, and Alençon joined the couple and embraced them both, saying that the three of them must remain united despite Henri.

Another absurd rumour now abounded that Margot had fallen under the evil and Sapphic influence of one of her ladies, Mme de Thorigny, the daughter of Marshal de Matignon. Henri insisted that the woman be sent away and not corrupt his sister further. Thus Margot lost one of her closest friends as Navarre had little choice but to obey the king. Henri's favourite, Louis du Ghast, had become a particular adversary of Margot's and, despite her brother's efforts to have her receive his favourite cordially and with courtesy, she bluntly refused, considering him her enemy and treating him with mocking disdain. This maddened du Ghast who determined upon revenge. He reported to Henri and Catherine that Margot was having a love affair with a famous and dashing courtier, Bussy d'Amboise, also a member of Alençon's set.

Catherine had by now become distracted with affairs of state and grown tired of the perpetual accusations which gave Henri an excuse to occupy his time on matters that had little to do with governing the kingdom, and she refused to react to this latest piece of gossip. The King and du Ghast decided to settle matters their own way, and organised a band of assassins to attack the young gallant as he left the Louvre late one night. Despite the surprise attack and the number of assailants, d'Amboise managed to escape. Understandably, he then decided to leave the Court immediately citing health reasons, which happened to be nothing less than the truth.

Henri next tried to create strife between Navarre and Alençon by exciting an amorous competition between them for the favours of Navarre's mistress, the lovely Charlotte de Beaunne, Baronne de Sauve. Charlotte was one of Catherine's flying squadron and just how effective these Court lovelies were in promoting the King's and Queen Mother's plans was now perfectly illustrated. Navarre had proved a canny survivor who had thus far been able to keep his judgement. When it came to beautiful women, however, the young King's common sense deserted him. Navarre and Alençon were enraptured by this young beauty and it created great friction between them. Margot recalled that Henri, and probably Catherine, had persuaded de Sauve to make herself available to the two men. 'She treated them both in such a way that they became extremely jealous of each other ... to such a point that they forgot their ambitions, their duties and their plans and thought of nothing but chasing after this woman.'[21]

The Court was no longer a place of great political machinations and manoeuvring; under Henri it became a hotbed of petty hatreds played out with knives, swords and whispered accusations. These were not only viciously fought out between the principals and their factions but also by their servants. Navarre wrote to a friend, Jean de Miossens, describing the perils he faced:

This Court is the strangest place on earth. We are nearly always ready to cut each other's throats. We carry daggers, wear coats of mail and often a cuirass beneath a cape. ... All the band you know wants my death on account of my love for Monsieur [Alençon] and they have forbidden my mistress to speak to me. They have such a hold on her that she does not dare to look at me ... they say they will kill me, and I want to be one jump ahead of them.[22]

The King, helped by Charlotte de Sauve, aroused suspicion of his wife in Navarre by warning him not to trust Margot as she would betray him for his infidelities, which in any case had probably been exaggerated by Catherine and Henri to inflame the Queen of Navarre's sense of abandonment by her husband. Margot had helped save his life on several occasions. Most recently she had prepared his brilliant defence regarding his involvement in the attempted escape and uprising during the last days of Charles IX's life. After the Saint Bartholomew Day Massacre, when the Queen Mother briefly considered having Navarre killed, Margot had stopped any question of annulment of her marriage – which would have freed Catherine's hand in ridding herself of Henri – by telling her mother that she had had sexual relations with Navarre and that he was 'in every sense' her husband.

Margot may have entered into the marriage unwillingly but she was initially loyal to Henri. Through her, he learned the ways and means to survive around the politically labyrinthine Court. His wife also helped turn Navarre into a French prince absolutely at ease at Court. She set the women's fashions, invented new dances, wrote verse and sang. She was admired by all for her beauty, wit and majesty. Since his marriage to her, Henri had become far more elegant, his manners exquisite and he always appeared to be jovial and loyal to the King who kept him cooped up in this princely prison. Margot had taught him very well to play the game that she had known since her birth.

After her beloved and adoring father's death Margot, unloved by her mother, had skilfully concealed her own emotional needs. Her marriage to Henri of Navarre was damned from its bloody beginning, but at first there existed a mutual loyalty between them on certain matters, though his constant early infidelities did much to damage her feelings for him as a husband. To keep her pride, she pretended to be more concerned for the injury his sexual adventures might do to his health, but by the end of 1575, according to Margot, the marriage showed signs of the terrible strain that external forces were putting upon it. Despite her protests that she could treat Navarre as a brother and share confidences with him, he began to keep his plans secret from her. As she recorded, 'I could not endure the pain that I felt ... and I stopped sleeping with the King my husband.' This was a real tragedy for Margot, whose life now began to take a course that would lead to her eventual disgrace and disaster.

In April 1575 the deputation of Politiques had arrived in Paris to present their terms to the King. These included a bill of rights allowing complete freedom of worship, surety towns, law courts with representatives of both religions and the prosecution of those guilty of the Massacre of Saint Bartholomew. When they were read to Henri he could hardly contain his indignation. After berating them for their impudence he drily asked, 'Well, what more do you want?' Catherine, no less astonished than the king, commented that they spoke 'as proudly' as if they had 'fifty thousand men in the field, the Admiral and their leaders all alive'. Despite their extreme reluctance, the Queen Mother and the King were unable to avoid continuing the discussions, but soon afterwards the talks broke up. Sporadic fighting continued, each side claiming victories, but none proved decisive.

Catherine's original enthusiasm and insistence that Henri fight instead of treat with the Huguenot–Politique alliance had proved a desperate error. He could have begun his reign by making peace with Damville, but the endemic conflict now once again destabilised the country. Michiel, the Venetian ambassador, described his sobering impressions of France at this time:

> Everywhere one sees ruin, the livestock for the most part destroyed ... stretches of good land uncultivated and many peasants forced to leave their homes and to become vagabonds. Everything has risen to exorbitant prices ... people are no longer loyal and courteous, either because poverty had broken their spirit and brutalized them, or because the factions and bloodshed have made them vicious and ferocious. ... The clergy and the nobility, for various reasons, are also in hard circumstances, but particularly the nobility, who are completely ruined and indebted. Those who still have some pulse of life are the bourgeois, traders ... and the class known as the *gens de robe longue* – magistrates, counsellors, treasurers, and the like – who spend little, know how to husband their resources and wait to devour the others. ...

Religion and justice have fallen into the utmost abuse ... I should say that many care very little for religion and use it for their own purposes. ... Demoralized, the people have lost their supreme reverence and obedience for the king, which was once so great that they would have given him not only their lives and their property but their souls and their honour ... as for obedience to the royal orders and edicts they seem to make sport of them.

A further and still more catastrophic blow awaited Henri and the Queen Mother when, on the night of 15 September 1575, Alençon managed to escape from Paris taking around fifteen followers with him. In the hope of reconciling her two sons, Catherine had been persuaded by Alençon that he would not flee but would always address himself to the King if he had any grievances. She in turn had counselled Henri to allow his brother some freedom of movement around Paris. Henri excoriated his mother for letting his detested sibling and heir apparent slip out of their hands, almost certainly to join the Politiques. Henri tried to gather a force of loyal officers to bring him back dead or alive, but he found the men unwilling to follow his orders regarding the most senior prince in France, knowing that the future lay with him. It is noteworthy that Alençon reached Dreux, in his apanage where he was safe, with relative ease. Those senior nobles and officers who could perhaps have stopped the duke were either deliberately tardy in taking action or would not move at all. To act against the heir apparent was dangerous, and in this case the King's mounting unpopularity was probably reflected in the demonstrable lack of effort to capture his brother.

From Dreux Alençon issued a manifesto that repeated three of the delegation's key demands. He called for the convocation of the Estates-General, the expulsion of foreigners from the council and a religious pacification until a general Church Council could be called.[23] At first Catherine simply refused to believe that Alençon had been cunning enough to fool her; normally his lies were so transparent that they were almost embarrassing. Though it was too late to catch him, she spoke to the Duke of Nevers about using five or six men to kidnap her son, though finally she decided she must deal with Alençon herself.

In Germany Condé and Jean-Casimir headed towards the Rhine and the French frontier with a large Protestant force to join up with Damville. With Alençon at liberty and possibly planning to lead the anti-royalist forces, disaster seemed imminent. Catherine's first meeting with her son took place between Chambord and Blois on 29–30 September. As he saw his mother descend from the coach, Alençon dismounted and walked towards her. He knelt before her and she raised him with an embrace. The first day was spent in tearful protestations of love between mother and son, but then Catherine tried to address the pressing business that had brought her to him. Before he would discuss his demands, Alençon insisted that as a gesture of good will François de Montmorency and Marshal de Cossé be freed immediately. On 2 October Henri reluctantly agreed to Catherine's urgent request.

As she reviewed the duke's demands, despite instructions from Henri to concede little, Catherine was anxious to conclude an agreement, even if it were only a temporary one. She needed to gain time for the forces of the Crown. She sent Alençon's demands on to Henri and begged him to agree to them but at the same time she advised him to arm himself and prepare for war. Henri, Duke of Guise alleviated matters somewhat by winning a victory at Dormans on 10 October against German *Reiters* who had invaded northern France. During the battle Guise received an horrific wound to his face that almost killed him. Henceforth he was to share his father's glorious sobriquet '*Le Balafré*' (Scarface), but the victory at Dormans bore a poisonous fruit, giving French Catholic zealots a new hero.

On 21 November a six-month truce was signed. One of the articles stipulated that the *Reiters* of Jean-Casimir would receive 50,000 livres for not crossing the border into France. Since many of the articles of the truce were not enforced, the governors of the surety towns promised to Alençon quite simply refused to give them up and, since few of the tensions had eased, it seemed almost inevitable that the conflict would soon restart. On 9 January 1576 the *Reiters* did cross into France from Lorraine, leaving ruin in their wake. Henri blamed Catherine for the failure of the truce, but she retorted that she had warned him to arm all along while she kept the talks going: 'I think I can boast of having begun, if it had not been interrupted, the greatest service a mother has ever given to her children.'[24] She also argued that she should not be held responsible if the governors of the surety towns would not give them up in accordance with the terms of the truce.

The Queen Mother returned to Paris at the end of January 1576. She had been away from her beloved Henri for four months yet her efforts on his behalf had earned her only his distrust and anger. Alençon, looking for an excuse to break with his brother, accused Chancellor Birague of trying to poison him on orders from the King and joined the Politique forces in Villefranche in south-eastern France. On 3 February, just as matters looked as if they could get no worse, the twenty-two-year-old King of Navarre – who, since Alençon's escape, had been under particularly close supervision by ultra-Catholic guards handpicked by Catherine – managed to escape his gilded gaol while out hunting. He eventually reached his own kingdom for the first time since his marriage four years earlier. On 13 June he formally abjured the Catholic religion.

Henri's fury at Navarre's escape descended upon his sister, whom he now made his prisoner. He also accused her of aiding Alençon's flight and (possibly with some cause) of having a hand in the death a few months earlier of his adored du Ghast. The *mignon* so detested by Margot, and many others besides, was murdered in his bedroom while having his toenails cut. It was hardly the glorious death the vain courtier would have chosen. He had been ill for some time and had withdrawn to his house near the Louvre. It is thought that he was suffering from a venereal disease, and had been resting and receiving treatment there. The assassin, Baron de Vitteaux, a well-known duellist on the run from justice, entered du Ghast's house by an upstairs window after climbing a rope ladder before stabbing his victim to death.

Now that Navarre had gone, Margot believed her brother would kill her. She wrote, 'If he had not been prevented by the Queen, my mother, I believe his anger was so great that he would have committed some terrible cruelty against me.'[25] Guards were placed at the doors of her apartments and 'nobody, not even those closest to me, dared to visit me in case they should ruin themselves'.[26] Margot claimed that in an act of revenge Henri had ordered the murder of her former lady-in-waiting, Gilone de Thorigny, whom he had removed from her household on the trumped-up charges of lesbianism, just after his return from Poland. The poor woman had been dragged out of her house and was being taken off to be drowned when two of Alençon's friends who happened to be passing caught up with the would-be assassins and saved her life.

With both Court and country disintegrating before her eyes, Catherine begged Henri to seek peace, at no matter what price. The King sent his mother to Sens to treat with the princes and their delegates. Catherine set out accompanied by her flying squadron and even took Margot with her. On 6 May 1576 the Peace of Beaulieu or 'La Paix de Monsieur' as it became known – since Alençon appeared to have forced it upon his brother and personally benefited the most from the terms – was proclaimed. The sixty-three-article treaty represented nothing less than a triumph for French Protestantism, which now held virtual parity with Catholicism. Alençon – among other valuable lands and titles – received the dukedom of Anjou (although I shall continue to refer to him as the Duke of Alençon). Coligny and the victims of Saint Bartholomew were posthumously rehabilitated and the Massacre was publicly condemned as a crime. Pensions were to be paid to the widows and orphans of the victims for six years. Eight surety towns were granted to the Protestants, and the *Reiters* promised a generous pay-off to leave France. Navarre received the governorship of Guyenne and monies owed to him were to be paid back with interest. Damville was confirmed as governor of the Languedoc and Jean-Casimir awarded large territories in France as well as an annuity of 40,000 livres. The King also agreed to call a meeting of the Estates-General within six months. Though the treaty represented an obvious humiliation for Henri, it allowed him to keep his throne.

Henri wept when he signed the treaty; as he struggled to raise the funds to fulfil its expensive terms he cursed his brother and, most of all, his mother. She had advised him to embark upon this ruinous war and now it was she who had forced him to sign a document that he believed dishonoured both him and France. When Catherine returned to Paris outwardly he appeared as cordial and polite as ever to her, but he did not see her in private for a full two months. From now on a definite change in the relationship between them began to manifest itself; she became cautious in all her dealings with the King and took great pains not to irritate him. The glorious opening for Henri's reign envisaged by the Queen Mother had collapsed. Now she found herself presiding over the dismal disintegration of her dreams.

FIFTEEN

Alençon's Treachery

He is my life ... Without him I wish
neither to live nor to be

1576–84

The Peace of Monsieur caused a tumult among French Catholics, who began immediately to form leagues throughout the country. Humiliated and betrayed by the treaty's terms, they no longer felt able to look to their King to protect them and their religion. The Protestants had proved what they could achieve with their effective organisation, so now the Catholic leagues employed their enemies' tactics. As the word was spread, principally by Jesuits taking the message around the kingdom, nobles and peasants alike joined the cause. Catherine, fearing the potential power of this organisation, had not forgotten those bygone days of the Triumvirate of Montmorency, Guise and Saint-André, nor the threat that they had posed to the monarchy then. The King, enraged by 'these sinister associations', sent word to his provincial officials to consider them illegal and treat any adherents to them as traitors to the Crown. Evidently he had been too young to remember the Triumvirs and their struggle against his mother, as he remarked with bitterness, 'Formerly, a Constable or a Prince of the Blood could not have formed a party in France. Now the very valets invent them.'[1]

The meeting of the Estates-General that had been stipulated in the treaty was to take place in December 1576, and as the League continued to spread through all classes it soon became obvious that they intended to hijack the assembly for their own purposes, filling it with delegates faithful to the new party. Despite their protestations of loyalty to the King, they intended to make their fealty conditional upon his agreeing to abide by the Estates' decisions. Seeing that the whole assembly was to be dominated by Catholic zealots elected through rigged ballots, the Huguenots and Politiques declared that they already regarded the coming meeting to be invalid.

The natural leader of the Leaguers was Henri, Duke of Guise, a Catholic paladin, military hero and descendant of Charlemagne. Who better to lead the fight to save Catholicism in France than this noble scion of François, Duke of Guise? The sybaritic King had proved himself wanting as a true defender of the faith, so the people turned to this young, attractive and charismatic soldier instead. Propaganda pamphlets were circulated claiming that the Valois were a corrupt and decayed dynasty, and that the Guises, virile descendants of the first Holy Roman Emperor, were more fit to occupy the French throne. It was suggested that the Duke of Guise should take control of the country, imprison the King and punish Alençon for throwing in his lot with the rebels. For the moment Guise tacitly supported the League but carefully remained aloof from becoming their acknowledged leader, though he watched their strength grow with interest. If the right circumstances prevailed he would answer the clamour and head their cause.

The only positive result to come out of the propagandists' threat that the Guises should replace the Valois was that it brought about the reconciliation, essential to the monarchy's survival, between Henri and Alençon. Henri loathed the pretentious harking back to Charlemagne that the Guises so frequently vaunted; this time it presented a real danger since it evoked feelings in the people about the role of a strong monarch that he himself could not fulfil. When the two brothers met in November 1576 at Ollainville (a country manor the King had bought for himself and the Queen), their rediscovered fraternal affection had most observers convinced that it was genuine, as 'they kissed and embraced each other'. As a particular sign of trust and affection the King insisted that his brother sleep with him in his bed on the first night of their meeting. In the morning His Majesty 'made sure that his brother had all he needed to get dressed'. Aside from sharing a common cause against the Guises, there was also a tempting overture from Catholics in the Low Countries that hinted at a throne for Alençon. The brothers agreed to put aside their differences and, without ceremony or scruple, Alençon dumped the Politique–Huguenot alliance. Later both Catherine and Henri claimed that the whole purpose of signing the treaty had not been to win over the Huguenots but to win back Monsieur, though this has more than a whiff of ex post facto rationalisation to it. On 2 November Catherine wrote that she had just had the pleasure of seeing her sons happily put aside their differences and she hoped that henceforth there would be nothing to distract them from their sole desire 'to preserve the Crown' and, in Alençon's case, to gain a new one in the Netherlands.

By the time the Estates gathered in early December, Henri, realising that he could not suppress the League, cunningly decided to place himself at the head of it. When the League was first created in Picardy the King had angrily declared that no need existed for such an association because, as the Most Christian King of France, who could be a better Catholic than he? In his address to the Estates, he held his listeners rapt with his superb oratory. *Plus Catholique que les Catholiques*, Henri agreed with the delegates that there should be religious unity in France, though this would, of course, lead to a fresh outbreak of war. He refused, however, to accede to the Estates' demand that whatever the outcome of their votes the King must be bound to accept them since this would completely vitiate his royal authority.

When it came to raising money to implement the decisions by the Estates which would effectively lead to war, the enthusiasm of the delegates cooled noticeably. To change the tone, the Queen Mother decided that her genius for entertaining might lighten the atmosphere and dazzle the niggardly deputies. Famous Italian comedians, the I Gelosi, arrived at Blois (having been captured and then ransomed by the Huguenots) and gave a performance on 24 February. In honour of the Italians' first appearance – whose ransom he had paid – the King gave a masked ball the same night, at which he appeared dressed as a woman. The self-proclaimed chief of the Catholic League wore his frizzed and refrizzed hair dressed and powdered, and his gown was cut with a low décolleté. The Most Christian King's ensemble was a breathtaking confection of brocade, lace and diamonds finished off with ten ropes of enormous pearls round his neck.

Though Catherine hoped that war might be avoided, she kept reminding Henri that he must ensure that he kept himself ready for battle should it become necessary. No money was forthcoming as the delegates sat on their hands. Meanwhile fighting broke out again in the south. In a last-ditch attempt to avoid war, Henri invited Navarre, Condé and Damville to discuss the situation with the Estates at Blois, but they refused to attend. Catherine lamented at Henri's willingness to resume hostilities and tearfully told her daughter-in-law, Queen Louise, that she no longer had any influence over her son, saying, 'He disapproves of everything I do, it is obvious I am not free to act as I wish.'[2] She regarded Damville as pre-eminent among her son's foes: 'It is him that I fear the most for he has a greater understanding, more experience and constancy. It is my opinion that we must spare nothing to win him over. For it is he who will either save us or be our downfall.'[3] Catherine also felt justifiable misgivings about Henri's ability to prosecute a war. To help her son she knew she must reduce his enemies by subtle means. First she approached Damville's wife, Antoinette de la Marck, a zealous Catholic, and managed to get to Damville himself, whom she dexterously bribed by offering him the Marquisate of Saluzzo in order to detach him from his alliance with the Huguenots and bring the Languedoc back under royal authority. He took up the offer and the removal of this formidable adversary from the Protestants greatly diminished their strength.

A short war – the Sixth War of Religion – followed, in which Alençon, nominally in command but actually under the guidance of the Duke of

Nevers, distinguished himself by capturing the Protestant stronghold of La Charité-sur-Loire on 2 May 1577. In a rush of bloodlust Alençon demanded a massacre of the Huguenot inhabitants, which the Duke of Guise managed to prevent. Unfortunately for the inhabitants of Issoire in the Auvergne, Guise was not present when the town surrendered on 12 June to the royalist army. There Alençon presided over the murder of 3000 citizens, thus earning himself the enduring hatred of the Protestants. Now his name was as stained with Protestant blood as those of his brothers Charles and Henri. Catherine and the King had the secret satisfaction of knowing that Alençon's pointless outrage meant there could be no return for him to his former Huguenot allies. That door now closed to him for ever; he was bound to his family by his crime.

To glorify the taking of La Charité-sur-Loire a huge banquet was given by Henri for his brother at Pléssis-les-Tours. In truth the King, furiously jealous of Alençon's military success, now mimicked Charles IX's hostility towards his own martial 'triumphs' at Jarnac and Montcontour. The theme of the celebration was that all should wear green, Catherine's favourite colour (coincidentally also the colour often associated at the time with insanity), and that the men were to dress as women and vice versa. On 9 June Catherine gave a superb ball at her Château of Chenonceau, with the banquet held outside on the terrace of her gardens in the glow of flaming torches. The King, or the 'Prince of Sodom' as he was frequently called behind his back, sparkled with diamonds, emeralds and pearls. His hair tinted with violet powder and wearing a dress of superb brocade, he made a definite contrast to his wife, who came simply dressed, unadorned but for her natural beauty.

The royal family, including Margot, sat at a table of their own and dinner was served by one hundred of the court's most brilliant beauties, described by Brantôme as 'half-naked with their hair loose like young brides'. Catherine had long mastered the trick of setting aside the normally draconian rules for her ladies when the occasion demanded. She would also have appeared not to notice as the evening ended in a dissolute free-for-all when many of the party drifted off into the woods together. The cost of the two 'magnificences' had been no less than 260,000 livres.[4] For Catherine it had been worth every écu as she celebrated the new entente between her sons, though had she truly wished to observe them more closely she would have seen that the brotherly spirit was nothing but a chimera. Shortly after the capture of Issoire the King recalled Alençon and gave command of the army to Nevers instead. The English began to give help to the Huguenots and Navarre remained in control of many Protestant strongholds. This and his chronic lack of money made Henri decide that the time had come to treat with the enemy.

On 17 September 1577 the Peace of Bergerac was signed, ending the

Sixth War of Religion. Commonly known as the 'Paix du Roi', this treaty went some way to removing the most odious elements of the 'Paix de Monsieur', although as usual neither the Protestants nor the Catholics were satisfied. The King could not continue paying for the war and the Huguenots, though badly mauled, were by no means completely defeated. Trouble could still be expected, particularly in the south. A huge potential source of strife had been removed by a vital clause in the treaty banning 'all leagues and confraternities'.[5] One thing was certain, however: the idle and easily enervated King would need to deploy the indefatigable Queen Mother to keep his fragile eponymous peace.

In order to regain Henri's belief in her, Catherine set off to tour the troublesome south and south-west of France, largely Huguenot country. This indomitable fifty-nine-year-old woman left Paris in the late summer of 1578 with a miniature Court (including a number of her flying squadron) to administer the peace and pour balm upon the boiling tempers, warring factions and dissatisfied people. Margot also travelled with the party, making the journey to join her husband who had demanded that his wife be returned to him. Henri, anxious to be rid of the troublemaker, hoped that his sister might even be of some use to him by Navarre's side. Margot remembered how in the weeks before her departure the King 'came to see me every morning, and declared his love for me and explained how useful this would be for me to live a happy life.'

The problems France faced were varied: most arose from the chaos of the religious wars, though there were a host of others, such as harsh taxation, social strife and individual local disputes between feuding contingents. Much of Catherine's time would be spent at considerable personal risk in what was effectively enemy territory run by the Huguenots, to whom she privately gave the sobriquet 'birds of prey' or '*les oiseaux nuisantes*' (nighthawks). Catherine endured not only open hostility at some of her stops but all the attendant discomforts and dangers of a long journey in rough terrain. She was bobbish and undeterred by plague, bandits and hazardous roads often little more than rough tracks. She remained undiscouraged when the gates to comfortable lodgings, châteaux and manor houses were frequently and unceremoniously closed to her as she arrived in a new area. Sometimes this forced her to create a makeshift home under canvas, where she hung her most cherished item, a portrait of the King.[6] No exertion was too great in the name of her *chers yeux* Henri.

The King, for his part, wrote at the outset of the journey to the Duchess d'Uzès, who accompanied Catherine, begging her, 'Above all bring back our good mother in good health, for our happiness depends upon this.' The Queen Mother's temper remained resolutely breezy in the face of the hardship and hostility she often encountered, though when the weather was clement she particularly relished the memories it evoked of her childhood in Italy. She enjoyed the 'flowering beans, hard almonds and fat cherries' that grew early in the south and complained little about the terrible pain of her gout and rheumatism, especially in the freezing cold of winter.[7] When she could she forsook her litter or vast coach and walked or rode on a mule. The sight of her astride her mule would, she wrote, 'make the King laugh'.

The only thing Catherine found hard to bear was her long separation from Henri. She wrote to the Duchess d'Uzès, who had by then returned to Court, 'I have never been so long without him since he was born. When he was in Poland it was only for eight months.' Her mission's aim to regain her place in the King's affections made the sacrifice worthwhile, as she confided to her friend: 'I hope to do far more for the service of the King and the kingdom here than I would do by staying with him and giving him ... unpalatable advice.'[8] Henri wrote to one of his ambassadors during her journey, 'The Queen, my lady and mother, is at present in Provence, where I hope that she will restore peace and unity among my subjects ... By this means will she implant in the hearts of all my subjects a memory and eternal recognition of her benefaction which will oblige them for ever to join me in praying God for her prosperity and health.'[9]

Catherine's sprightly disposition and pleasure in the adventures of her journey rarely left her. As she passed from place to place to deal with each particular difficulty – usually the implementation of the treaty and the locals' enmity either for each other or the Crown – she painstakingly dealt with their grievances. It is a tribute to her magnificent personality, her singular charm, enthusiasm and imagination that, with a few rare exceptions, she managed not only to find solutions (which she appreciated would often be all too temporary) to the deep-seated divisions France faced, but also gained the respect and grudging affection of her former opponents for her absolute commitment to maintaining the peace.

Before leaving Margot with Navarre at Nérac, Catherine told her son-in-law to turn to his wife and use her to intercede for him with the King if there were political troubles. The two adversaries had proved a match for one another. When state business required it, Navarre had become quite as gifted as Catherine herself in his use of feints, devices and legerdemain. After nearly four months of exhausting work, the Convention of Nérac was signed and Catherine moved on. On 18 May 1579 the Queen Mother wrote to the Duchess d'Uzès that she had received word about Margot and Navarre: 'My daughter is with her husband. Yesterday I had news of them. They make the best couple one could hope for. I pray God that this happiness will continue and to keep you alive until you are 147 years old and that we can dine together at the Tuileries, with hats or bonnets.'[10] Despite this jaunty tone she knew her next stop would be a perilous one.

As she had once walked without a care for her personal safety within the range of the enemy's guns overlooking the ramparts of Rouen during the First War of Religion nearly two decades earlier, she now showed the same courage at the Huguenot stronghold of Montpellier. Entering the city on 29 May 1579, she drove with cool composure between two rows of hostile Protestant arquebusiers, her carriage even touching their muzzles where the men stood menacingly, pressing close. Her pluck and dauntlessness bought her the respect of the townspeople. By the time she had completed her work there and started on the next part of her journey, she left them courteous and almost dutiful. As she wrote to the Duchess d'Uzès, 'I have seen all the Huguenots of Languedoc; God, who always backs me, has given me so much favour that I have got the better of them ... there are plenty of "nighthawks" here who would readily steal your horses ... the rest are good company who dance the Volta well.'[11]

Catherine still had to face the troubled areas of Provence and the Dauphiné. She wrote, 'I am so worried about the quarrels in Provence that my mind can only conjure up anger. ... I do not know if the people of Dauphiné will be any better ... as always I put my trust in God.'[12] Dealing firmly with the vicious fighting between the parties that was more social than religious in origin, she wrote, 'I have finished my work and, in my humble opinion, I have made many people liars and accomplished what was considered impossible. ... In ten days I shall see the dearest thing I have in this world.' At last the time drew near when she would be reunited with the King at Lyons; this one thought alone had kept her spirits unflagging. For his part, having agreed to meet his mother there, Henri, who had little inclination to bestir himself, felt that he could not refuse to make the journey after her extraordinary efforts. He wrote to a friend, 'We must resign ourselves to going to Lyons for the good woman wishes it, and she writes me too urgently to refuse. ... Adieu, I am in bed with fatigue, having just come from a game of tennis.'

Henri's 'fatigue' in fact turned out to be a near fatal ear infection, similar to the one that had killed his brother Francis II. Catherine was at least spared news of his critical condition until the worst had passed and he was recovering. Horrified when she heard of his perilous illness, she wrote to the Duchess d'Uzès,

He is my life, and without him I wish neither to live nor to be. I believe God has had pity on me, since I have had so much sorrow through the loss of my husband and my children He will not crush me by taking him also. When I think of the danger in which he has been, I do not know where I am, and I bless the good God for restoring him to me, and I pray that it may be for longer than my own life, and that as long as I live I may see no harm comes to him. Believe me it is hard to be far from one whom one loves as I love him, and to know him ill is to die by slow degrees.[13]

Catherine's longing for her cherished son was at last rewarded when they met on 9 October 1579 at Orléans. The pair then proceeded to Paris where she received a warm and enthusiastic reception as she was hailed for her untiring work to preserve the unity of France. The Venetian ambassador, Gerolamo Lippomanno, though he doubted the ultimate success of Catherine's mission, lauded her as 'an indefatigable princess born to tame and govern a people as unruly as the French. They now recognize her merits, her concern for unity and are sorry not to have appreciated her sooner.' Perhaps for some it gave a sense of security to see the familiar face of the Queen Mother again, for the King and his brother – far from being on harmonious terms during her absence – were once again engaged in a perilous internecine struggle. Thus, rather than coming home to bathe in a rare moment of national gratitude and to enjoy the tranquillity she deserved, Catherine returned to unravel her sons' hateful antics and their attendant hazards.

Even before Catherine's long journey of pacification in southern France, Alençon and Henri had fallen back into their old enmity, as ever fuelled by their respective clients and supporters. Henri had accused his brother of plotting and intriguing, particularly with a view to taking a force into the Spanish Netherlands that, once again, risked sparking a war with Philip. This culminated in a farcical scene in which the King – acting on a tip-off that he would catch Alençon plotting – had made a surprise visit to his brother during the early hours of the morning and ordered that his room be searched. As the trunks and cupboards were opened and their contents spilled out, the King himself rummaged manically through the bedclothes. To his intense satisfaction he saw Alençon attempt to hide a piece of paper. Seized and brandished without further examination as damning evidence, it was soon discovered that the paper contained nothing more incriminating than declarations of love from Madame de Sauve. The King, his brother and mother were all in their nightclothes as dawn broke upon this ludicrous and undignified scene. Catherine tried to comfort Alençon but, wisely fearing for his safety, a few days later he fled once more, this time using a silken cord hung from Margot's window.

The same old pattern reasserted itself as Catherine set out to bring Alençon back to Court with assurances from Henri regarding his safety.

Though Alençon promised his mother that he would not jeopardise peace within France, she visited him again to try to win him back. However, word soon spread that he had raised a number of fighting men to take to the Netherlands. Although he had undertaken not to engage in any fighting against the Spanish there, in July 1578 he led his 'liberating army' – actually little more than a mob of unsoldierly brigands – to Mons having declared that his nature 'abhors tyranny' and that he 'desires only to succour the afflicted'. After a few months his unpaid rabble decided to go home, and pillaged and attacked the very people and lands they were supposed to be protecting. Bussy d'Amboise, Margot's former lover and Alençon's friend, showed a particular lack of restraint during this ignominious return to France and the duke, as was his wont, reproached him for the failure of their great mission. Catherine and Henry made appropriately apologetic noises to Philip of Spain, blaming Alençon's 'youthfulness'.[14]

Prompted by the petty though murderous quarrels between Alençon's men and Henri's *mignons*, and his disastrous foray into the southern Netherlands, Catherine now attempted to find a wife for her troublesome youngest son. Apart from possibly one miscarriage in the spring of 1576, which might have damaged any further chances of becoming pregnant, Queen Louise had not shown any sign of producing the longed-for heir. She had become thin and suffered from bouts of melancholy stemming from her inability to give her adored husband a child. It was, therefore, not only to distract Alençon from making mischief that Catherine started to scout for a suitable bride but also to ensure the very continuation of the Valois dynasty itself.

Various nubile princesses were suggested, including Henri of Navarre's own sister, Catherine de Bourbon. It was, however, the now far from fecund but richly endowed Queen Elizabeth of England who in May 1578 indicated that she would welcome the reopening of the Alençon marriage talks. With Catherine's encouragement and Henri's permission these recommenced in the late summer of that year. As for the continuation of the Valois line, Henri and Louise put their faith in God. They made pilgrimages to Chartres and wore nightshirts that had been specially blessed by the Holy Virgin to overcome infertility, but to no avail. Medical treatments, special baths and embrocations were prescribed for the Queen; reminiscent of the extraordinary lengths Catherine herself had gone to for nearly a decade until she had finally produced an heir.

In 1572, during the first marriage discussions concerning Alençon and Elizabeth of England, Catherine had been effusively optimistic about the number of children the couple might have. At the time, talking to the Queen Mother the English envoy, Sir Thomas Smith, had touched upon England's usual raw nerve, saying that if only Elizabeth could produce one child then 'the troublesome titles of the Scotch Queen ... that make such gaping for her [Elizabeth's] death, would be clean choked up'.[15] Catherine had replied, 'But why stop at one child? Why not five or six?'[16] Now, seven years later, a single baby would be a near-miracle. At the age of forty-five any marriage Elizabeth entered into would be for political reasons, not for producing an heir. Alençon's enterprise in the Netherlands had caught her off guard; she did not want French troops, even ones unauthorised by the King, on Dutch soil, as they might 'wax straight [become] a greater enemy'. English interests favoured peace and trade so Elizabeth decided to distract Alençon with these marriage talks. The English Queen had also been depressed, since her favourite, the Earl of Leicester, had secretly married. Realising that this probably represented her last chance to find a husband, there was at times a hint of wistfulness in the usually cynical quality of Elizabeth's 'wooing matters'.

Alençon looked for political backing and a crown. Catherine persuaded him he could have both if he married the Queen of England. Elizabeth was rich and powerful, and the Queen Mother knew that if he succeeded in making her his bride he would stop the dangerous and inept attempts to find a state of his own in the Low Countries. After many obstacles had been cleared during the marriage talks it was decided that the duke should actually meet Elizabeth. Catherine, who at the time was still on her journey of pacification in the south, even talked of travelling to England herself, to push matters along. She wrote to the Duchess d'Uzès, 'Although our age is more suited to rest than to travel, I must go to England.'[17] Alençon eventually arrived in England on 17 August 1579, though his mother did not make the journey with him and so Elizabeth and Catherine never met.

His visit was meant to be incognito and therefore unofficial, but Elizabeth – who seemed quite charmed by the duke – whom she called 'her frog' – spent a blissful fortnight engaged in a delightful flirtation. After all she had heard from previous reports, the Queen found Alençon 'not so deformed as he was [described]'. The ostentatious showing off by Elizabeth suggested she found her mystery suitor quite irresistible, while the rest of the Court duly pretended not to have the first idea who he was. When he returned to France 'the parting was very tender on both sides'.[18] After Philip II's marriage to Mary Tudor, most English people were aghast at the idea of another foreign consort and a French Catholic prince proved a singularly unwelcome thought. One preacher denounced Alençon and his corrupt siblings, speaking of the 'marvellous licentious and dissolute youth passed by this brotherhood', adding that 'if but a fourth part of that misrule bruited should be true' the Queen must be very disturbed to consider marriage with 'this odd fellow, by birth a Frenchman, by profession a papist, an atheist by conversation, an instrument in France of uncleanness, a fly worker in England for Rome in this present affair, a sorcerer by common voice and fame ... who is not fit to look in at her great Chamber door'.[19] Evidently word had got out about the sons of Catherine de Medici.

Now returned from her long voyage in the Midi, Catherine found the peace she had fought for hard to implement. Adding to her ill-health over Christmas, during which she suffered from severe rheumatism, remaining in bed during the celebrations, she also worried about Henri's health. The King appeared exhausted, thin and generally weak. In April 1580 a surprise attack by Huguenots of Montauban started a six-month conflagration later dubbed the 'Lovers' War' since the Seventh War of Religion was wrongly blamed on sexual scandals at Navarre's Court. Margot was having a love affair with the Protestant Vicomte de Turenne, one of her husband's most senior commanders, while Navarre himself had engaged in a passionate liaison with a noted beauty known as 'La Belle Fosseuse' (at whose child's birth Margot later assisted). The goings-on in provincial Nérac had evoked bitter and contemptuous remarks from Henri, as well as causing general hilarity among the French courtiers; when his humour was high the King poked fun at the cloddish ways of the simple and distant Court. Henri knew how to turn the knife when he mocked his sister; his elegant put-downs were reported back to both Margot and her husband, though the idea that Navarre's response had been to go to war is preposterous. The Protestant offensive is far more likely to have been a reply to various Catholic attacks and to general discontent with the Convention of Nérac.

Navarre apologised to Margot, writing of his '*regret extrême* [extreme regret] that instead of bringing you contentment ... I have brought the opposite that you should see me reduced to such an unhappy situation'.[20] Catherine wrote to Navarre about the agreement that, not long before, they had so painstakingly reached together and asked him to adhere to this and remain loyal to the King. 'My son, I cannot believe that it is possible that you would wish to ruin this kingdom ... and your own, if a war starts.'[21] She appealed to him as a Prince of the Blood, writing, 'I cannot believe that coming from such a noble race you should wish to be the leader and general of brigands, thieves and criminals of this kingdom.'[22] If he did not lay down his arms he would surely be 'abandoned by God' she wrote, adding, 'You will find yourself alone accompanied by brigands and by men who deserve to hang for their crimes ... I beg you to believe me and put things back in order, in order for this poor kingdom to remain at peace. ... Please believe me, and see the difference between the advice of a mother, who loves you, and that of people who loving neither themselves nor their master, want only to pillage, ruin and lose everything.'[23] Margot tried to warn Navarre's council of the dangers that lay before them if they were to start a war. Catherine also wrote to her daughter and urged the young Queen to make her husband aware of his wrongs and to do her best to avert disaster. Had the war been caused by her daughter's loose behaviour, Catherine would hardly have been asking her to intervene with her husband to avert it. Despite their efforts the Catholic and Protestant leaders seemed powerless to prevent the short and pointless war that was brought to a close by the Peace of Fleix on 26 November 1580. The treaty, with its many 'legal rights granted to the Huguenots' that were practically unenforceable, could largely be seen as a ratification of the Paix du Roi of 1577 and also the Nérac Convention signed by Catherine and Navarre.[24] Civil war had become a lethal habit in France.

Other, natural, catastrophes also hammered the realm in 1580. In April the already devastated country was hit by an earthquake at Calais, which could be felt as far away as Paris. A few days later terrible storms caused serious flooding in the capital. Three epidemics ravaged France that same year. The first, which also reached Italy and England, struck in February, and the second – described as a disease similar to cholera – afflicted Paris in June. Catherine, Henri, the Duke of Guise and many other important figures at Court fell ill, but all survived. The symptoms were described by the historian de Thou: first the malady 'struck the base of the spine with shivering followed by a heaviness of the head and weakness in the limbs, this was accompanied by strong chest pain. If the patient had not recovered by the third or fourth day, fever would set in and in almost all cases prove fatal.'[25] The French called the illness '*la coqueluche*'. Just as this epidemic waned, the plague paid its almost annual summer visit to the capital in July. In 1580 the disease spread with unusual force and rapidity, and anyone who had the means abandoned the city. Catherine travelled to Saint-Maur and the King went to Ollainville as the epidemic claimed the lives of hundreds of people every day. In Paris, deserted but for the poorest inhabitants, the unguarded houses of the rich were looted by those who were left behind and even the Louvre itself was robbed. The estimated total number of dead from these natural disasters varies from 30,000 to 140,000 victims throughout France, far more than died by violent means in that period.

In 1580 King Henry of Portugal died. His predecessor, King Sebastien, once Margot's reluctant suitor, had died in 1578 at the battle of Alcazarquivir fighting the Moors and the throne had been briefly occupied by an elderly uncle, Cardinal Henry, who died without naming a successor. Catherine immediately pressed her own rather flimsy credentials as heir to the throne through her mother's line, as the descendant of Alfonso III (who had died in 1279) and his wife Queen Matilda of Boulogne. Nevertheless Henri III formally advanced his mother's claim. An ostentatious Requiem Mass was held at Notre-Dame for the late King, from which Henri absented himself, thus making Catherine the chief mourner.

Philip II, whose mother was the cardinal-king's sister, not only had a very much stronger claim to the throne but every intention of joining Portugal with Spain even if it meant resorting to force. He found to his exasperation that his former mother-in-law seemed quite prepared to take an equally bellicose stand to prevent him from succeeding. Catherine wrote, 'It would be no small thing if these things were to succeed and I was to have the joy of bringing this kingdom to the French by myself and on the basis of my claim (which is not a small one).'[26] It is easy to imagine how personally satisfying joining the Portuguese throne with that of France would have been to Catherine who, long ago, had endured the French nobility's cruel and snobbish sneers at her mercantile origins.

In the autumn of 1580, just as the Peace of Fleix was being signed, Alessandro Farnese, Duke of Parma, led a force of Spanish troops to besiege Cambrai. Upon hearing the news from the Netherlands, Alençon, in the Midi overseeing the tiresome and difficult terms of the treaty, could hardly wait for an excuse to get away and nobly announced that he must immediately go to the aid of the people he had pledged to protect. He had, after all, officially been named 'Defender of the liberty of the Netherlands against the tyranny of the Spaniards and their allies' (an utterly meaningless title that gave him only obligations but no accompanying powers). He now fancied himself as the protector of the Low Countries and set about raising a force to come to their aid. Catherine was in a state of 'marvellous perplexity' that the shaky peace of France should be jeopardised by her son for yet another madcap venture against the powerful Spaniards. She wrote to Alençon reminding him of his position and where his obligations lay: 'Although you have the honour of being the King's brother, you are nevertheless his subject; you owe him complete obedience and must give preference over any other consideration to the good of the kingdom which is the proper legacy of your predecessors whose heir presumptive you are.'[27]

Marriage talks with Elizabeth had taken a predictably sluggish turn and ended abruptly with the Queen arguing about the age difference between herself and the duke, his Catholicism and the danger to which he might expose her kingdom by his entanglement in the Low Countries. She suggested that a less confined alliance with France would be more desirable. The marriage commissioners from France went back home and Alençon sent troops to relieve the beleaguered city of Cambrai. Catherine caught up with him in early May 1581 in an attempt to stop her son from committing himself to so risky an enterprise. He did not heed her and set off to join his men. In July she met her wayward son again, this time realising that he would not be stopped. She therefore begged Henri to send his brother covert aid. The King, enraged at the prospect of provoking an attack on France by Spain, nonetheless agreed to lend his secret support.

Elizabeth sent a message to Henri that it would be in both French and English interests to form 'a confederation ... whereby both the King of Spain might be stayed from his overgreatness and Monsieur helped'.[28] But Henri was not about to fall into a trap where a vague promise from the Queen of England left him to face the wrath of Spain and 'fearing that [Her] Majesty might slip the collar' he pursued the talks no further. Undeterred, Elizabeth continued her attempts to form some sort of loose coalition with France. Alençon also decided to appeal for help from Elizabeth in person and arrived in England in November 1581. It was now all but certain that there would be no marriage between them; nevertheless the Queen behaved very graciously towards her 'frog'. He was given every promise of her love (and some £15,000) in private, but she would not make any firm public announcement that they were to be married. Alençon, who had arrived believing there to be no chance of marriage and had come for money, now found himself believing that the Queen might yet become his bride. The duke proved no match for this seasoned stateswoman, however, who even at her age could use her feminine guile to confuse and bewilder. She tortured him with her private promises and public evasions.

To arouse the greedy and ambitious duke, who had by now become impatient for an announcement, Elizabeth, ever mistress of the art of surprising even her closest courtiers, performed a dazzling *coup de théâtre*. On 22 November, while walking and chatting to Alençon in a gallery at Whitehall, the Queen was asked by the French ambassador for a definite answer about the marriage. Her reply silenced everyone: 'You may write to the king that the Duke of Alençon shall be my husband.' Having uttered those words, she drew Alençon to her and kissed him full on the lips, also giving him a ring from one of her fingers. She then made the same announcement to the ladies and gentlemen of her Court. The duke could hardly believe his luck and he was right not to. As her courtiers and advisers wept and groaned, Elizabeth administered the sting. She made it a condition that in order not to upset her subjects further, she could not aid him with either money or men in his venture in the Netherlands and France must guarantee to come to England's aid if she were attacked by Spain. Catherine, who had been elated at the joyous turn of events in London, now 'sat with sour countenance and manner of speaking' as she received these impossible terms from a woman just as wily as she herself.[29]

As a pay-off, the duke received the promise of a loan of £60,000 for his campaign and it is said that Elizabeth danced around her room with delight that she had found a way out of the French marriage without losing face, and that the 'frog', whom she now seemed most anxious to be rid of, was shortly to leave. Thinking that he had been bought off too cheaply and muttering at 'the lightness of women and inconstancy of islanders', Alençon decided to play the Queen at her own game and, to her horror, declared that he loved her too much to leave her and would accept her marriage terms.[30] This stopped the skip in Elizabeth's step and she turned upon him in panic, asking if he meant to 'threaten a poor old woman in her country'. Overwrought with the ups and downs of the past weeks, the duke broke down weeping but cleverly refused to leave England until the ever increasing inducements offered to him by the Queen produced a change of heart. At the beginning of February, to their mutual relief and despite a surprisingly touching farewell at Canterbury, the couple parted. Alençon set sail for Flushing and on 19 February 1582 made his official entry into Antwerp. Accompanied by William of Orange and escorted by the bourgeois militia, he was installed as Duke of Brabant. Making the Palace of Saint-Michel his new home, the Valois runt at last became a sovereign prince in his own right.

By the summer of 1582, matters in Portugal had escalated. Philip had invaded the country in 1580 and Catherine had despatched two expeditions to try to throw the Spanish out of 'her kingdom'. In June 1582 the first – much of it financed by the Queen Mother personally as Henri wished to keep a diplomatic distance – had been disastrously defeated. It had been led by Filippo Strozzi, Catherine's cousin, who was killed in the attack. The captive French soldiers had been treated as pirates and brutally executed on the orders of the Spanish commander, the pitiless hero of Lepanto, the Marquis de Santa Cruz. The Spaniard's butchery made even Henri cry out for vengeance and Catherine received some backing from him to finance a second force, bolstered by a number of ships loaned by Elizabeth of England that left a month later. This campaign also ended in tragedy and, although the leader of the expedition was allowed to treat with Santa Cruz who agreed to send the French survivors home, the Spaniard made sure the men were despatched to sea in leaky old ships without proper supplies, many of them dying before they reached France. Thus ended Catherine's dream of uniting the Portuguese Crown with that of France.

In 1582 Margot of Navarre returned to the French Court, where she came to enjoy the pleasures of sophisticated life and to get away from both the boredom of Nérac and Navarre's obsession with his mistress, La Fosseuse. At Court she continued to support Alençon whenever she could and to annoy the King at every opportunity. One of her most enjoyable pastimes was publicly to snub his two particular favourites, Jean Louis de la Valette, now raised to the dukedom of Épernon, and

Anne, Baron d'Arques (whom Henri had, in his obsessive love for this *mignon*, made his brother-in-law by marrying him to his wife's sister Marguerite de Vaudémont in September 1581, also awarding him the dukedom of Joyeuse). These men of minor provincial aristocratic families had been raised to the highest positions in the country, but Margot knew how to remind them of their inferior social origins. The Queen of Navarre had also infuriated Henri with her personal conduct, engaging in a highly public affair with Alençon's *grand écuyer*, a young gallant named Harlay de Champvallon.

Finally, in early August 1583 while he was staying at the Château de Madrid in the Bois de Boulogne during one of his frequent periods of religious retreat, the King heard rumours that his sister had borne an illegitimate child. Henri demanded that Margot leave Paris immediately and join her husband. After she had set off with two ladies in attendance, he decided to have her carriage stopped by a company of archers. When they caught up with the party they obliged the ladies to disembark while they rummaged about the vehicle looking for a baby or even a man hidden inside. Although they found nothing, Margot and her two ladies were also subjected to inspection and then taken as prisoners to a nearby abbey where the King himself questioned them.

Margot felt outraged that her brother dared subject her to a moral inquisition – in her memoirs she later accused Henri and Charles of incest – and screamed in fury, 'He complains of how I spend my time? Does he not remember that it was he who first put my foot into the stirrup!' When the King could not get the two ladies to incriminate their mistress he reluctantly allowed the three women to proceed with their journey. Champvallon had by now realised that his liaison with Margot endangered his life and escaped Paris, thus ending the affair.

By now Navarre was aware of the furore caused by the King's actions against his wife and found it gave him a perfect excuse to make further trouble. Assuming a bellicose and outraged posture, he demanded evidence of Margot's wrongdoing and furthermore stated that he could not take her back as his wife unless the King made a public declaration fully stating her innocence. Henri found himself in a difficult position. Not wishing to anger his brother-in-law and trouble the peace of the land, he sent his mother, who had only heard of the problem long after the event, to extract her son from the imbroglio. Eventually Navarre received some sort of satisfaction and the couple were reunited on 13 April 1584 at Porte-Sainte-Marie. Bellièvre carried instructions for Margot from her mother on how to protect her reputation and endear herself to her husband, citing her own experiences: 'When I was young I had the King of France as my father-in-law who did what pleased him. It was my duty to obey him and to frequent those whom he found agreeable. After he died and his son, to whom I had the honour of being married, took his place, I had to offer him the same obedience.'[31] The Queen Mother continued that neither 'one nor the other would have forced me to do something that was against my honour and my reputation'.

Catherine went on to say that she had been forced as a widow to deal with people 'de mauvais vie' (who led wicked lives) whom she would have preferred to send away, but had been obliged to keep them by her as she needed them to help her sons rule and not offend them. Most important of all, she wrote, her own good reputation enabled her to deal with anyone she needed to without being stained by them 'being who I am, known by all, having lived the way I have done all my life'. But Margot was a different creature from her mother. Catherine had loved only one man, Henry II, and she loved him still with a single-minded devotion. By contrast, Margot had never truly loved Navarre. Though they were occasionally friends and had protected each other in the past when the situation demanded, his flagrant womanising and her own compensatory and ever-growing indiscretions were destined to keep them from real intimacy. She possessed a more impulsive nature than the guarded and composed front presented by her mother and yet, despite a temperament that made her ill-suited to successful political intriguing, she wished to be at the very centre of important matters and events. Catherine fell ill due to the strains of the latest crisis, but she remained unable to blame Henri for his ill-considered actions towards Margot. She wrote to Bellièvre, who had been instrumental in sorting out the problem, 'You know his nature, which is so frank and honest that he is unable to hide his displeasure.'[32]

After his glorious acclamation as Duke of Brabant, Alençon was finding life in Antwerp difficult. He complained constantly that his brother did not give him enough money to fight off the Spaniards. When Henri did send funds, Alençon soon found out, it was never enough. His men suffered from malnutrition, lack of pay and had even resorted to begging from the inhabitants. Their numbers dwindled as they began deserting or dying. By late 1582 he wrote, 'Everything is falling apart in ruin and the worst part of it is that I was given hopes which have led me too far to back down now. ... Thus, I say, that it would be better to promise me only a little money and keep your word than to promise so much and not send anything at all.'[33] On 17 January 1583, to the hideous embarrassment of his mother and brother and the horror of the other European Courts, Alençon and his men rose up and attempted to take Antwerp in what was later called the 'French fury'. In this blackguardly episode, bearing all the hallmarks of Alençon's ignoble nature, the citizens proved more than a match for this spent and sickly rabble and they massacred the duke's men. They also killed many of his nobles, some of them from the greatest families in France. Uprisings in Bruges and Gand were also attempted, but these were put down without difficulty.

The 'French fury' had put Alençon in peril and he was branded a common criminal; furthermore his situation presented no small problem for Catherine and Henri. He tried to negotiate his way out of trouble but as ever his terms were too high for a man who had little or no support from his brother. Flying in the face of the King, Joyeuse and Épernon, Catherine did send him what aid and money she could – raised using her own assets – but Henri's *mignons* did all they could to stop help from being sent by the King, thus preventing Alençon from achieving anything in the Low Countries.

After further failed attempts fighting the Spaniards, causing yet more trouble and expense to the King, who feared Spanish reprisals, Alençon was eventually reunited with his mother at Chaulnes in mid-July 1583. His experiences over the past eighteen months had desperately undermined his health and he was described by those who saw him on his journey as appearing 'weak and debilitated ... and barely able to walk'. On 22 July 1583 Catherine wrote to the King about his brother, 'I have begged him to pull out of his enterprises that are ruining France and to stay close by me and to keep the place which is his and to live in peace with our neighbours.'[34]

Henri asked his brother to attend a large meeting of 'notables' which he had called for 15 September, but Alençon refused. Catherine believed 'his head has been filled by malicious people who have told him if he goes he will find that he is to be the subject of many restrictions against himself'.[35] The main issue for the Queen Mother was that her youngest son should retain Cambrai. He returned there in early September to negotiate with the Spanish and the Dutch. By November he crossed back again into France and decided to stay at Château-Thierry where he hoped to regain his strength, tended by Catherine. She had been appalled to hear a new rumour that he intended to sell Cambrai to the Spaniards. Writing of the shame and infamy this would bring to the country, she said, 'I am dying of misery and worry when I think of it.'[36] Catherine might have been deeply upset by the scandal of Cambrai, but she also seems to have been unaware of the gravity of Alençon's illness. He had started to cough blood and did not make the recovery he had hoped for. Assuming that both her son and his political machinations were now stabilising, Catherine left, but Alençon soon made trouble again, inflamed by his entourage who liked nothing better than to tell him how ill-used he had been by his brother.

After a short visit to Château-Thierry by Catherine on 31 December 1583 to try to solve some of Alençon's problems – he was still negotiating over Cambrai – Catherine found her son so unwilling to listen to her advice that she returned to Paris. Here she fell ill, the strain of family troubles taking their toll. At last, on 12 February 1584, Alençon came to visit his mother. Although she was in bed with a fever he begged her to take him to see his brother to thank him for confirming various promises that he had recently made regarding his apanage. Despite her high temperature, Catherine happily sacrificed her own health to watch her two surviving sons embrace each other. She wrote to Bellièvre that she had not experienced such happiness since the death of her husband and that she had wept with joy.

The two brothers celebrated Carnival together, during which Alençon is said to have debauched himself 'in erotic excess that showed up his vicious temperament'.[37] The sick young man then returned to Château-Thierry, where during March he fell desperately ill once again. Catherine hurried to his bedside to find him vomiting quantities of blood and suffering from a high fever. The symptoms of consumption should have been all too familiar to the Queen Mother but, believing her doctors who assured her that provided her son led a quiet life he would live to enjoy an old age, she took any minor abatement of the disease as a good sign. Finally, after a further visit, during which she convinced herself that he was recovering, the Queen Mother decided to rest at Saint-Maur. When she arrived she was greeted with the news that Alençon had died on 10 June 1584 shortly after they had parted.

Despite the constant trouble her youngest son had caused her, the discord with the King and his generally odious nature, her agony at his death was evident from a brief note she wrote to Bellièvre on 11 June: 'I am so wretched to live long enough to see so many people die before me, although I realise that God's will must be obeyed, that He owns everything, and that he lends us only for as long as He likes the children whom He gives us.' Her despair would have been yet more unbearable had she foreseen the effect that the heir presumptive's death would have upon Catholics in France. For unless Henri and Louise produced a Valois heir, which by then seemed extremely unlikely, the next ruler of France would be the Bourbon heretic, Henri, King of Navarre.

SIXTEEN

Hope Dies

'The Phosphorescence of Decay'

1584–88

Catherine had barely finished burying her youngest son on 25 June 1584 before the furore over the succession broke.* The Catholic leagues that had been banned since 1577 sprang once more into action with the Duke of Guise, his brothers and other senior clansmen meeting at Nancy. Broadly, their aims were to prevent Navarre's succession and to create a Holy Catholic League that would extirpate Protestantism in France and Flanders. Guise asked for the support of Philip of Spain, who agreed to give the ultra-Catholics aid under the provisions of the Treaty of Joinville, signed during the first days of 1585.

In place of the heretical Navarre's rights of succession the Holy League recognised his aged uncle, the Cardinal de Bourbon, as heir presumptive. Catholic demagogues raged and priests agitated from their pulpits as pamphlets and polemical tracts were circulated by the zealots to whip up support for the League and denounce the Valois as a 'decayed' line. Catherine's health had become increasingly poor and she had aged markedly since Alençon's death, but despite her rheumatism, gout,† colic and raging toothaches, she remained dogged in her determination that the Guises would neither supplant Henri nor become his masters, imposing their will upon him as they once had upon her.

From the moment of Alençon's death, Henri had made it clear that he viewed his brother-in-law as his legal successor, declaring, 'I recognise the King of Navarre as my sole and only heir' and adding, 'He is a prince of good birth and good parts. I have always been inclined to like him and I know that he likes me. He is a little sharp and choleric, but at bottom he is a good man. I feel certain that my disposition will please him and that we shall agree very well.'[1] He warned Navarre, 'My brother, this is to notify you that whatever resistance I have made, I have not been able to prevent the mischievous designs of the Duke of Guise. He

---

* Alençon's funeral cortège was magnificent and took over five hours to process through Paris.
† Gout was a typical Medici ailment.

is under arms. Be on your guard and make no move. ... I shall send a gentleman ... to advise you of my will. Your good brother, Henri.'² As the unmistakable signs of rebellion from the ultra-Catholics grew, Henri, in a public statement to the Provost of Merchants, supported the First Prince of the Blood: 'I am highly pleased with the conduct of my cousin of Navarre. ... There are those who are trying to supplant him, but I shall take good care to prevent them from succeeding. I find it very strange, moreover, that any dispute should arise as to who is to be my successor as if it were a question admitting of doubt or dispute.'³

The King's sentiments, however, were but brave and empty words under the circumstances. Henri supported Navarre and hoped that in due course he could persuade him to convert back to Catholicism (which would be his fifth conversion). Even Navarre's closest counsellor and friend, Philippe Duplessis-Mornay, advised him, 'Now, Your Majesty, it is time to make love to France.' But Navarre resisted, realising that the time had not yet come for a conversion as he could not afford to lose the support of the Protestants. The King also shrank from a full alliance . with his heir in order to defend his rights. Together they might have provided a buttress against the perilous menace of the Guises, but it would also have meant a coalition with the Huguenots. The idea not only repelled the King on religious grounds, as daily he grew more fanatical in his devotions, but it also guaranteed inflaming those moderate Catholics who hoped for a solution without a war, but who would not tolerate fighting alongside the Huguenots if one did break out.

As the network of the provincial leagues grew and melded with the Holy Catholic League, the Guises received arms and soldiers from Philip's forces in the Netherlands. The Duke of Guise's kinsmen, the Dukes of Elbeuf, Aumale, Mercoeur and Mayenne, incited uprisings in Normandy, Brittany, Picardy and Burgundy, and led their troops to capture several key towns including Bourges, Orléans and Lyons. The situation presented an almost complete role reversal from a decade earlier: now the Protestants, anxious to see Navarre eventually succeed the King, gave their allegiance to the Crown while many Catholics became subversive activists undermining it.

By the spring of 1585 Henri of Guise had amassed a fighting force of over 27,000 men at Châlons. France was split roughly in half, the north and centre were League territories while the south and west fell under mainly Protestant control and thus – as long as the King supported Navarre's claim – royalist.⁴ Henri responded to the Guises' imprecations by hiring Swiss mercenaries and turned to his mother for help. Ever since his return from Poland a decade earlier he had been slowly edging Catherine out of her position as his chief adviser and encouraging his *mignons* to take an increasingly prominent role in his life. Two of the

King's favourites, the Dukes of Joyeuse and d'Épernon, had become pre-eminent at Court and now wielded enormous influence. D'Épernon could often be heard speaking ill of the Queen Mother to Henri, snidely insinuating to him that she had grown senile and unreliable. Of course, Catherine knew the upstart to be her particular nemesis and she hated him, though she was powerless to harm or remove him while he held such sway over her son. In the Florentine fashion, she bided her time, believing that sooner or later he would undo himself. No one loved Henri as she did and she would wait for an opportunity to prove her devotion to him yet again. Now her time had come.

On 1 April 1585 Catherine received a letter from the King granting her full powers to negotiate with the Duke of Guise. Though she felt unwell, the message revived her spirits; filled with protestations of affection and love, it proved his trust in her. She was nonetheless still so ill with chest and ear infections and running a fever that she took to her bed whenever possible. She found breathing difficult and her teeth hurt. Pains down her side made it agonising to move or to write as she awaited the duke's arrival at Épernay in Champagne where they had agreed to meet. Catherine had also sent a request to her much-loved widowed son-in-law, the Duke of Lorraine, asking that he come to help broker a deal between the Crown and his relatives.

When Guise finally arrived on Easter Sunday, 9 April 1585, he knelt before Catherine, who had decided that her best tack would be to welcome him with all the warmth and familiarity of a grandmother. This cunning and unexpected sweetness momentarily wrong-footed the duke, who tearfully started to talk of the troubles in the kingdom, insisting that his motives had been misunderstood. She hushed him and said that it would be better if he took off his boots and ate something, after which they could speak at length. When they did meet later that same afternoon Guise, who had by now regained command of himself, seemed willing to talk about almost anything except the issue that surely burned in both their minds. All attempts by Catherine to draw the League's demands out of him were skirted by the duke or parried with questions of his own about the King's intentions.

As the days went by Catherine began to suspect that Guise had come only to play for time while preparing an attack on the King or on his Swiss mercenaries crossing into France. She wrote urgently to Henri that he must prepare for war, as peace 'would only be achieved with a stick' (*bâton porte paix* – i.e. by threat of force). On 11 April Guise left and, passing his cousin of Lorraine by chance on his route, he told him how contrite and sorry he felt that things had come to such a grave pass. When Lorraine arrived and relayed this to the Queen Mother she snorted and took it for the errant nonsense she knew it to be. If he had been serious in his desire to resolve the crisis Guise would not have left her without having made any progress whatever. Despite Henri's faith in her negotiating ability, this time she had patently failed.

Guise proceeded to Verdun while Catherine sent a message to Henri of Navarre asking him to meet her for talks. Navarre had just led his army to a victory over League forces in Bordeaux and Marseilles. This prompted Guise to hurry back to the Queen Mother, but his demands were so extortionate that even the Cardinal de Bourbon, who was also present, wrote, 'The Queen talks of peace but we ask for so much that I do not think our demands will be granted.' For as long as she could, Catherine resisted contemplating a coalition (or more realistically a capitulation) between the League and the Crown for fear that the King would become their puppet. She also worried about his safety, especially when word arrived that League forces were not far from the capital and would march on the city at the duke's command.

Paris itself was notoriously pro-League and Catherine believed that the city gates would be thrown open to welcome its army. 'Take care,' she wrote to her son, 'especially about your person, there is so much treachery around that I die of fear.' In response to the risk of capture or assassination and no longer knowing who could be counted upon to remain loyal, the King set up a special new bodyguard called *les quarante-cinq* (the forty-five) composed of that number of young noblemen, mostly Gascons famed for their martial skills and ferocity, whom Henri knew to be absolutely loyal to him. They were also, in effect, a personal force of assassins who would do their master's bidding without question. Despite his small cohort of killers, Henri nevertheless remained trapped.

By early May, the realisation finally dawned on Catherine that, for the moment at least, the King must come to some kind of terms with the League and the Guises. Hoping that he could sidestep any treaty and that it would prove as unenforceable as many of the earlier agreements with the Protestants had been, he therefore signed the Treaty of Nemours on 7 July 1585. In broad terms this revoked all previous edicts of pacification and effectively banned Protestantism in France. As a heretic Navarre was thus barred from inheriting the throne and many towns were given over to the League (or, for the most part, loyal Guise toadies) as surety. When Navarre received the terms of the treaty it is said that half of his moustache turned white overnight. Clearly he would once more have to fight for his rights and those of his co-religionists.

The new heir presumptive, the Cardinal de Bourbon, an old friend of whom Catherine was fond, paid the most florid and extravagant compliments to the Queen Mother. He lauded her for her sagacity, saying that 'without this honourable and great lady the kingdom would have been broken up and lost'. But all the phoney cooing and appropriately respectful phrases from the new pretender to the throne merely made Catherine nauseous. For the moment, though, she stayed silent. On 15 July when, after three months of struggling against, and eventually succumbing to, the overwhelming power of the chief Leaguers, she returned to Paris, the people received her at the Porte Saint-Antoine as a heroine who had saved the kingdom from heresy. The citizens rejoiced that their King would now be free to rule as he should. The reality, however, would prove very different.

At a Lit de Justice on 18 July 1585 Catherine heard her son officially remove Navarre from the succession. This went against everything that Henri, as a king, believed in. Furthermore, nothing in his coronation oath gave him the right to bar the succession of his legal heir. It also went against his personal feelings. He had hated Henri of Guise since they were teenagers when Guise had tried to seduce Margot, and had long been resentful of his rival's health, his masculinity, charisma and talents as a military commander. On the other hand, Navarre was the rightful heir to the throne of France and Henri, like his brother Charles before him, felt a sneaking admiration and fondness for the brave and honourable Bourbon soldier-prince. Navarre did not evoke any envy in the King; Guise certainly did. Now Henri's troops were joined with the League's formidable forces and he had to fight alongside his worst enemy.

In September 1585 Pope Sixtus V issued a bull excommunicating Navarre and Condé, and denied the rights of succession to the French Protestant Princes of the Blood. Navarre replied by boldly (and rather cheekily) excommunicating the Pope and had posters announcing the counter-excommunication plastered up on walls around Rome. The papal bull provoked outrage among the vast majority of Frenchmen, who jealously guarded against any encroachment by Rome on their domestic affairs. They considered it a staggering affront that the Pope dared pronounce upon who should or should not be allowed to wear the Crown of France. This had the unexpected bonus of making a David out of Navarre, facing the Goliath of Rome.

The War of the Three Henris (Valois, Guise and Navarre) should be seen as the confusing and essentially personal conflict of beliefs, ambitions and hopes for survival between the eponymous three men. At first the fighting between the Catholics and Protestants was sporadic. The King, suffering from a dire lack of funds, had promised the League that he would field three armies against the Huguenots by the following summer. The Duke of Joyeuse was sent to the Auvergne, the Duke d'Épernon to Provence and Marshal Biron to Saintonge, each at the head of an army. In July 1586 the King moved to Lyons to be near his two favourites, Joyeuse and d'Épernon.

Back in March 1585, just as the Holy League had come into being, Margot had caused a sensation by leaving Nérac, ostensibly as a protest against her husband's latest love affair with an ambitious, nobly born young widow named Diane d'Andouins (nicknamed 'La belle Corisande'). She shared not only the Christian name of Catherine's hated but now long-dead rival Diane de Poitiers, but possessed all the cool elegance of her namesake. Her stylish, remote beauty and singular determination had humiliated and effectively eclipsed Margot; now she planned to have her lover's wife repudiated and become Queen of Navarre herself. This proved too much for the dignity of the Valois princess of France who, in revenge, tried to have her seemingly bewitched husband poisoned by a secretary. When this attempt failed she took a pistol and shot at the King, but missed. With Navarre's anger fully aroused, Margot fled before he could act against her, taking refuge in her own apanage at the town of Agen. To protect herself she began to raise troops and, it is thought, secretly allied herself with the League. Margot appealed to her mother for money. For once Catherine responded sympathetically to her daughter, whom she described as 'desperately short of means' and 'in very great need, not having money even to put food on her table'.[6] Villeroy received orders to send funds to Margot. Only a short while before, the Queen Mother had optimistically described her daughter and Navarre as the happiest couple in France.

Catherine's sympathy was soon put to a severe test when she heard that Margot had written to her former brother-in-law, the widowed Duke of Lorraine, asking him to take her under his protection. This appeal and her apparent sympathy with, if not actual support for, the League, the enemy of her husband and her brother, now placed Margot entirely beyond the pale. The lovely princess's gradual loss of caste through scandalous behaviour, open love affairs and support for her late younger brother's wild schemes was now complete. Henri of Navarre regarded her as a soiled liability, as did the King. Enraged by this latest affront, Catherine referred to her daughter as an 'affliction' (mon fléau) sent to her by God 'as a punishment' for her sins.[7] Before long Margot was expelled from Agen by Marshal de Matignon acting on orders from the King and hurried on her way by the inhabitants whom she had quickly managed to alienate. She had tried to strengthen the fortifications of the city and run it as an independent fiefdom, but lack of money and tact in handling the townspeople soon proved her undoing. So she made her way to Carlat, also one of her properties, where her supporter, François de Lignerac, Lieutenant of the Haute-Auvergne, had offered her protection.

This once impregnable fortress, perched high in the mountains, might have been hard to capture, but its solitude and discomfort must also have made it even harder to endure. The castle had become a ruin but for its fortifications; Margot's medieval redoubt was a far cry from the welcoming beauty of Blois or Fontainebleau where she had once set the fashions, led the dancing and been the Court's brilliant star. Despite her daughter's absolute fall from grace, Catherine suggested that she take up residence at the manor of Iboise near Issoire, but the Queen of Navarre knew that this offer meant supervision by her mother and control from her hated brother. She declined it, writing to Catherine, 'Thanks be to God that I have no need, as I am in a very good place which belongs to me and where I am helped by decent people [*gens d'honneur*].' She added that she must protect herself from 'falling back into the hands of those that wished to take my life, my goods and my honour'. During the year that she spent at this remote eyrie Margot formed a passionate attachment with a minor nobleman, Jean de Lart de Galard, Seigneur d'Aubiac. The first time this arrestingly beautiful young gentleman set eyes upon the Queen he declared to a friend that he wished to sleep with her even if it meant that he might hang for it.

In the autumn of 1586, disgusted by the news of Margot's flagrant affair with d'Aubiac and the fact that she had now become a ruined woman, Catherine advised Henri to take 'this insufferable torment' into custody before she 'brings shame upon us again'.[8] The King needed little prompting and had in any case already issued his own orders regarding his sister. On 13 October 1586 Margot was arrested by the Marquis de Canillac, Henri's governor of the Haute-Auvergne, and taken via Ibois to the heavily fortified Château d'Usson where she was held prisoner. The château had been a favourite of Louis XI's for locking away political prisoners and the poor wretches were rarely seen again. The King also ordered that henceforth in any declarations or letters Margot should no longer be referred to as 'his well-beloved' or 'dear' sister. As he himself had predicted, Aubiac paid with his life for the love affair with the sulphurous and magnetic young woman. Although Henri wrote to Villeroy that 'the Queen my mother wishes me to hang Obyac [*sic*] in the presence of this miserable creature [Margot] in the courtyard of the Château d'Usson', mercifully for the Queen of Navarre her lover was put to death at Aigueperse without any notable spectators.

At the treble-ramparted fortress of Usson, held by Swiss guards and supervised by Canillac, Margot feared that she too would be killed. In a dramatic farewell letter to her mother she asked that her '*pauvres officiers*' (poor household) be paid their wages that were in arrears by several years and that she might be allowed a gentlewoman to keep her company in her confinement. She added the request that if she were to be put to death, to restore her honour a post-mortem be made on her body that would disprove the rumours that she carried d'Aubiac's child. Knowing her family and its methods of ridding itself of enemies, she also secretly employed a food taster.

Yet, as had long been the way in her short but tumultuous life, Margot's fortunes did not take long to turn. Canillac felt insulted at his new position as merely the goaler to the King's sister and shortly after her arrival at Usson he made a visit to Lyons. Here, in the beginning of January 1587, he joined the League. After ordering the Swiss guards away, he set Margot free. Anxious that Navarre remained married but childless, it is likely that the Guises had a hand in the plot to release his Queen.

In exchange for her liberty Margot gave Canillac all her properties in the Auvergne as well as a generous pension and other gifts. Some accounts also claim that she had seduced the marquis to win him over. Despite her new-found freedom, for the next fourteen years Margot remained in the Auvergne, far away from the political and dynastic storms ahead, living on the generosity of her sister-in-law, Charles IX's widow Elisabeth of Austria, who made half her dowry over to her. She never saw her mother or brother again.

During the months of Margot's descent into disgrace, Catherine had struggled to meet the chiefs of the factions that ranged so dangerously around her son. Ill as she was, she made several journeys to meet Navarre though he considered her to have little influence any longer. Being treated as someone of only marginal political relevance must have been a grave insult to the once all-powerful Queen Mother. Upon meeting Navarre at Saint-Brice in Cognac in December 1586, Catherine complained to him of the travails she faced in her attempts to stave off a full-scale war. His reply was acidic: 'This trouble pleases you and feeds you if you were at rest you would not know how to continue to live.' It is at Saint-Brice that the Queen Mother is believed to have made an astonishing proposal to Navarre.

The story was reported many years later both by Navarre himself and the Marshal de Retz, who had also been present at the meeting and later recounted what occurred to Claude Grouard, President of the Parlement of Normandy. It is said that Catherine offered to have Margot 'eliminated' or the marriage annulled, thus freeing her son-in-law to remarry and have children. She apparently nursed a private ambition that he should take her companion and favourite granddaughter Christina of Lorraine as his bride, thus joining all three warring dynasties by marriage. After the bloodbath following his first nuptials – which after all were also meant to bring harmony between the Huguenots and Catholics – Navarre's reaction to his mother-in-law's latest matrimonial brainwave can only be wondered at.

In whatever terms Catherine might have couched her suggestion, she had not reckoned with her son, and the King proceeded to make his position absolutely clear. He wrote to his mother in December 1586 saying Navarre must not expect us

> to treat her [Margot] inhumanely nor that he can repudiate her in order to marry another. I would like her to be kept in a place where he can see her when he wishes in order to try to have children with her. He must resolve never to marry another as long as she lives and if he should forget and do otherwise then he will place a doubt upon the legitimacy of his line for ever and have me as his *enemi capital*.[9]

If Catherine really did offer to have her daughter 'eliminated' it proves that her desire to achieve her aims overrode even her strong maternal instincts. For her, however, the disgraced Margot had virtually ceased to exist and, in Catherine's eyes, quite possibly did not even deserve to. Neither scruples nor remorse were feelings that intruded upon the Queen Mother's psyche. In order to serve her own and now Henri's interests she had proved time and again to be quite capable of doing whatever was necessary. Indeed, it is this strength that sets Catherine apart. She had placed Margot in mortal danger once before, to protect her scheme on the night of Saint Bartholomew. Yet it is difficult to believe that she would have exterminated her own child (however dishonoured), not for any sentimental reasons that might imply she loved Margot but merely because in her daughter's veins flowed the blood of her long-dead but adored husband.

While Navarre, playing for time, held futile talks with Catherine, he was also amassing a considerable army, which included Lutheran mercenaries from Jean-Casimir and the King of Denmark, to counter the threat of Spanish troops from the Low Countries. Almost immediately after the signing of the Treaty of Nemours, Navarre and Condé had met Damville and re-formed their alliance with the moderate Catholics. Navarre's plan was straightforward; he must fight for his right to the French throne and only a decisive victory over the League, crushing the Guises and their ambitions, could re-establish his proper place in the succession. He knew that the King was too weak and a virtual captive of the ultra-Catholics to be able to impose his will on events.

As for the King, once he had exerted himself by signing the Treaty of Nemours and sent his mother off on her fruitless diplomatic travels again, he returned to the life of frivolous excess and contrasting religious penitence that had marked his reign till then. Lapdogs in jewelled baskets held by ribbons hung round his neck became his latest craze, copied by the faithful *mignons*. He shocked even his more moderate and generally loyal subjects by carrying a favourite lapdog in one hand as he touched for the king's evil with the other.

Increasingly, Henri took to making long journeys by foot from Paris to Chartres Cathedral to pray to the Blessed Virgin for a son and beg the Almighty for absolution. This desperate quest for redemption took on increasingly morbid and even necromantic tones. He began wearing death's heads embroidered on his clothes and had a sinister oratory built, festooned with black crêpe, in which he placed bones and skulls that had been taken from a local cemetery. In the yellow glow of thick candles he would spend his Fridays in a trance-like state of self-mortification and prayer, attended by his most faithful monks.

Catherine fell into despair over her son; she feared for both his health and his sanity. The Pope, hearing of the extremes of the King's behaviour, wrote and reminded His Majesty that as a sovereign on the brink of a full-scale war to save France for Catholicism his duties lay elsewhere for the moment. When the reclusive Henri did bestir himself to play an active role in affairs and be seen to be the monarch of France, the people largely ignored him. Paris, the stoutest of Catholic redoubts, had created a league of its own headed by a body known as 'The Sixteen' (Les Seize) after the sixteen *quartiers* of Paris. For most of the citizens of the capital there was only one king of Paris, and that was the Duke of Guise.

To complicate matters further for Catherine, her former daughter-in-law, Mary, was about to become a Catholic martyr. At Fotheringhay Castle in October 1586 the Queen of Scots had been tried and found guilty of treason against Elizabeth I for her part in the Babington Plot that Mary had believed would place her upon the throne of England. Despite Elizabeth's long agonising over her royal prisoner's fate and her fears that in the Catholic world 'it shall be spread that for the safety of her life, a maiden Queen could be content to spill the blood even of her own kinswoman', she knew she could not spare her since this would 'cherish a sword to cut mine own throat'.[10]

Catherine, appalled at the verdict, dispatched Bellièvre to England in November 1586 to plead for clemency. Mary herself wrote to Elizabeth thanking her for her 'happy tidings', though she reminded the Queen that she would have to answer for her actions in the next world. Ignoring Mary's professed enthusiasm to 'abandon this world', Bellièvre heroically fought for, and managed to obtain, a promise from Elizabeth of a stay of execution for twelve days. Henri wrote to the Queen of England stating that he would take Mary's execution as a 'personal affront', but this only strengthened Elizabeth's resolve. Never one to bow to intimidation, she replied to the French King that this was 'the shortest way to make me dispatch the cause of so much mischief'.[11]

Catherine felt no great fondness for Mary Stuart and despised her reckless actions while on the throne of Scotland. She had been particularly outraged by the murder of Lord Darnley in 1567, that 'horrible, mischievous and strange enterprise and execution done against the King's majesty'. At the time, the Queen Mother had demanded that her former daughter-in-law show her innocence to the world and threatened that 'if she performed not her promise to have the death of the King revenged to clear herself, they [the Valois] would not only think her dishonoured but would be her enemies'.[12] Nearly twenty years later time had not changed Catherine's views; one sovereign executing another was contrary to all her beliefs. She anticipated the impact that the former Queen of France's death would have upon the Guise clan and French Catholics in general. In disgust she wrote to Bellièvre, 'I am most grieved that you have been unable to do more for the poor Queen of Scotland. It has never been the case that one queen should have jurisdiction over another having placed herself into her hands for her safety as she did when she escaped from Scotland.'[13]

Mary's execution took place on 18 February 1587. Catherine heard the news of the 'cruel death of the poor Queen of Scots' in a dispatch from Bellièvre as she made her way back to Paris from her long and hopeless peace mission in Poitou. Her initial reaction was of genuine sorrow and anger that Henri's appeals had been ignored. This turned to alarm when she arrived in Paris to find the people inflamed by the Catholic preachers ascribing Mary's death to her religion and denouncing it as an assault upon Catholicism by a heretical foreigner.

Rumours leapt through the angry mob threatening Henri, even alleging that he had had a hand in Mary's death. To be sure of his own safety he increased his personal security and, hoping to calm the furious populace, the jittery King ordered the Court into mourning. A funeral Mass was held at Notre-Dame on 13 March. Joyeuse and d'Épernon also returned to Paris at the same time and the League worried that their presence would 'put heart into the King'. Joyeuse had lost much credit with Henri since his absence, having been accused of giving tacit support to the Guises.

With Mary now dead, Philip II of Spain decided that he would carry the war to the heretical though resilient Queen of England and re-establish the One True Faith in those troublesome isles. He started to build a huge armada for a decisive invasion. The Duke of Parma, governor of the Spanish Netherlands, received instructions to acquire a vast amount of the materials required for the land and sea invasion that the Spanish King was devising. At the same time he urged Guise, now a client and ally of Spain, to push harder for ultimate victory against Navarre and the French Protestants. Planning to use some of the French Channel ports for the attack on England, Philip needed France to be subdued and under Catholic control before he undertook his 'great enterprise'. The War of the Three Henris must therefore be stepped up.

The feints, skirmishes and half-hearted battles with almost prearranged withdrawals that had thus far marked this war of confused aims and unnatural alliances now became very real. Leaving Catherine in charge of all matters of state, Henri quit the capital on 12 September at the head of an army bound for the Loire, where he hoped to intercept an army of *Reiters* coming from Germany to aid Navarre. The Queen Mother, rejuvenated by the task ahead, threw herself into providing her son's troops with supplies and arms. She was never happier than when stretched to her fullest capacities as she examined fortifications and sea defences in case of attack. Her tireless efforts achieved extraordinary results despite the meagre resources at her disposal.

On 20 October 1587, at the Battle of Coutras, Henri of Navarre routed the forces led by the Duke of Joyeuse, who was himself killed. Guise fought two successful battles against the *Reiters*, at Vimory (26 October) and Auneau (24 November), though by this time the mercenaries were already retreating, having been bribed by the King to leave French soil. Guise furiously complained to the Spanish ambassador, 'Not only has d'Épernon placed himself between the *Reiters* and me, but he has given them money ... and a thousand arquebusiers of the King's own guard and ten companies of *gens d'armes* to accompany their retreat. It is strange that Catholic forces must be employed to recompense heretics for the damage they have inflicted upon France. Every good Frenchman must feel himself outraged.'[4] Catherine saw things in quite a different light and wrote to Marshal Matignon encouraging him, 'Now we must thank God for having helped us in such a way that it is a true miracle and has showed that he loves the King and the kingdom.'[5]

When Henri returned to Paris on 23 December to honour yet another empty victory he attended the celebratory Masses sung to glorify God for delivering the Catholics. In fact, it had been winter that had closed down the campaigning for the season and not military accomplishments; underlying matters remained as unresolved as ever. Navarre still held southern France, and the people were far poorer and hungrier and more desperate than they had been before the war started. To the King's extreme irritation, Guise was acclaimed as a hero for his successes at Vimory and Auneau. As a result he expected a gesture from the King, in particular that he should receive some of the honours that had belonged to the late Duke of Joyeuse. Instead, Henri managed to infuriate Guise and the Parisians not only by giving Joyeuse a funeral fit for a royal prince but also by proceeding to heap the already overladen d'Épernon with Joyeuse's offices and honours. Guise's sister, the Duchess de Montpensier – known as the 'Fury of the League', who was as much if not a greater Catholic zealot than her brothers – denounced the King's ingratitude and took to wearing a pair of golden scissors tied to a ribbon round her waist. She announced they would give Henri his third crown;

his first being Polish, his second French and his third would come when she cut him the crown of a monk.

During January and February 1588 the Guise faction met at Nancy to review their overall position and demands. In Paris the populace grew increasingly restive and sullen. D'Épernon, Henri's remaining favourite, found himself a primary target for the League's attacks, and pamphlets denouncing him started to appear. One, entitled '*The Great Military Feats of d'Épernon*', was, when opened, a blank sheet except for the single word *rien* (nothing). The Catholic demagogues raved against him and the King for their feeble war effort, which had thus far been militarily and financially costly, and left Navarre still at large.

When the deliberations of the League were delivered to the King he resolved that he would never again allow such insolence, yet in order to avoid a clash before he was ready he refrained from replying to the rebels' conditions. These were broadly a more stringent version of their original demands. They insisted that the Treaty of Nemours be implemented in full, in addition the King must join the League unequivocally. They also required the publication of the findings of the Council of Trent and the introduction of the Holy Inquisition in France. Henceforth all senior offices of state should be barred to non-Leaguers and, as a further security, they pressed for more surety towns to be handed over to their control. This last was an entirely specious requirement and simply a method of gaining more strongholds. The goods and belongings of Protestants were to be sold and a part of the monies thus raised would go towards the war effort.

With the country effectively split into two states (the Protestants held territories in the south and the League in the north and centre) France now produced a curious and conflicting foreign policy. Though she was bound by a defensive alliance with England, the League had allied itself to Spain and the international fight against heresy, and must therefore aid the planned attack against England. The Guises, helped by Parma from the Netherlands, seized Picardy but were unable to capture Boulogne. Philip 'by whose grace he [Guise] lives' required Channel ports and their hinterland for his invasion fleet and men; he also needed to be absolutely sure that the King would not come to the aid of Elizabeth or in any way obstruct his offensive.[16] Accordingly, it had been planned that, whipped up by League preachers and the Parisian Seize, the King would be taken captive by a popular uprising led by the League and neutralised as a political force shortly before the Armada launched its attack.

Catherine had long since given up hope that Navarre would oblige everyone except the Guises by converting back to Catholicism and instead now began to cleave to the Lorrainers for the future. Her family connections to the dynasty were strong. The Duke of Lorraine was her son-in-law and she hoped to see her grandchildren well married. Ever the matchmaker, she pushed for a union between Lorraine's daughter Christina, her constant companion, and Ferdinand de Medici, the new Grand Duke of Tuscany (Grand Duke Cosimo I had died in 1574 and had been succeeded by Francesco de Medici, who died on 9 October 1587).

Despite the external pressures that might have strained most relationships, Catherine had maintained her close friendship with the Duchess of Nemours, the Duke of Guise's mother, and she generally remained on surprisingly amicable terms with Guise himself. She had known him all his life and in many ways she regarded him and his siblings as part of her extended family. She even managed to appear cordial towards the rabid League zealot, the Duchess de Montpensier, though it must be wondered what she made of the duchess's scissors that hung so menacingly from her belt. It should not be doubted, however, that the principal reason she preserved an amicable disposition with the duke was the better to protect her son. Henri was still the only person who really counted for her.

A further consideration for the Queen Mother's tendency to favour the Lorraine clan was that if the Salic law were set aside her grandson, the Duke of Lorraine's heir, the Marquis de Pont-à-Mousson, could conceivably inherit the throne of France if Henri remained childless. She had, not unreasonably, given up any hope of her bloodline being continued through Navarre and Margot. Another matter the Guises and Catherine had in common was their visceral hatred for the detested *mignon* d'Épernon. The once-powerful favourite now lived in constant danger as threats and plots to kill him were regularly uncovered. He who had so arrogantly elbowed the Queen Mother aside now begged for an audience with her.

The nuncio, Morosini, reported in a dispatch dated 15 February 1588 that the duke had 'knelt before her, with his cap in his hand. He remained thus for an hour before the Queen, without her asking him to rise or to cover himself.'[17] Begging for her help to bring about a reconciliation with the Duke of Guise, and affecting this most humble attitude, d'Épernon promised that in future he would depend entirely upon her. At the regular council meetings, where the King and Queen Mother sat together at a small desk and the councillors were seated at a long table a small distance apart, it was noticeable that Catherine and her son spoke little to each other, if at all. He no longer trusted anyone, not even her.

In April at one of these meetings the skimpy mantle covering the smouldering antipathy between Catherine and d'Épernon was cast aside and their mutual hatred flared up as they had an angry altercation, during which the duke dared to accuse the Queen Mother of being a supporter of the League. She knew that her increasingly isolated son now lived in such an advanced state of paranoia that with only very little help from d'Épernon he could easily be led to misunderstand the motives for her ties with the Guises. As she herself put it, 'Sometimes the King mistakes my meaning and supposes that I do what I do because I wish to palliate everything, or because I am fond of them, or because I am too good, as if I loved anyone more than him who will always be most dear to me, or as if I were a poor creature who is led by goodness.' The last was not an accusation often made against Catherine by anyone.

Suffering from the great infirmity of age and a raging toothache, Catherine wrote to Bellièvre on 1 April 1588 to say that the Guises were breaking every promise they had made to her that they would follow the King's commands. Henri, she wrote vainly, 'wishes to be obeyed'.[18] The King had made the same observation himself, writing to Villeroy, 'I see plainly that if I allow these people to do as they please I shall not only have them as companions but in the end they will be my masters. It is high time to put matters in order.'[19] He continued that from 'now on we must be King, for we have been the valet for too long'.[20] As Meaux, Melun and Château-Thierry fell to the League the King stayed publicly calm, but said ominously, 'Pain turns to rage when it is wounded too often. Let them not try me too far.'[21]

In May Catherine, still feeling wretched from her painful gout and a lung infection, was in Paris. She spent a large part of her days in bed at the Hôtel de la Reine with any hope of repose marred by the increasingly hostile atmosphere in the city against the King and d'Épernon. League soldiers had been smuggled into the capital over the past weeks in preparation for another Saint Bartholomew-style coup. At a signal from their master they were to rise up and kill the King's supporters, proceed to the Louvre and capture him (having first cut his hated *mignon*'s throat). Thanks to the good offices of Nicolas Poulain, a spy working for Henri who had managed to infiltrate the League, one plot to kill d'Épernon and capture the King was uncovered for the night of 24 April. Another attempt to kidnap the King proved to be the work of Guise's sister, the Duchess de Montpensier. (Guise himself disapproved of his sister's agents provocateurs, spies, assassins and revolutionary methods. They lacked the honour and essentials which he believed elevated his own actions, befitting his holy purpose and princely station.) Forewarned, Henri increased his guard and this deterred the plotters who decided to wait for another opportunity. He also ordered d'Épernon to place troops outside the city to protect it against any attacking forces.

The Parisian league decided to send an appeal to the Duke of Guise at Soissons to come to their aid. Among other excuses, they too feared another Saint Bartholomew-style massacre as the preachers had made them believe that Henri of Navarre had renewed his alliance with the King and would soon be riding to Paris at the head of an army. Henri sent Bellièvre to Guise with strict orders not to come to the capital, threatening that if he did so he would 'treat him as a criminal and author of the troubles and divisions in the kingdom'.[22] Unbeknown to Henri his mother held yet another agenda. There are strong grounds for believing that Catherine sent Bellièvre with a verbal message of her own asking the duke to come to the capital as soon as he could, judging him to be the only person who could pacify the situation. Guise received the message on 8 May and by noon the following day he rode into the capital by the Porte Saint-Martin with an escort of only ten men. He came without his usual attendants and his hat was pulled down low, his cloak wrapped high round his face and shoulders. Despite this perhaps deliberately poor attempt at appearing incognito, the crowd soon recognised their hero and many ran just to touch his cloak. Others fell to their knees and wept with joy, begging him to deliver them from their evil King and his monstrous creation the Duke d'Épernon.

Guise and his men made straight for the Hôtel de la Reine near the Louvre, where the Queen Mother lay in bed. One of her dwarves, sitting at the window, spotted the duke's unmistakable figure. He cried out that Guise was below and the Queen, who thought the dwarf was larking about to cheer her up, told someone to give him a sound beating until he learned how to tell a good joke. Hearing the commotion below, she realised that it was indeed the Duke of Guise outside, at which she was observed to 'change colour and start trembling and shaking'. She well understood that her son's place on the throne depended upon what happened next.

Catherine greeted the duke warmly, saying, 'How comforted I am to see you again, though I would rather it were in another season.' Guise then talked to the Queen Mother about the reasons for his recent actions. The King, meanwhile, fell into a murderous rage that Guise had disobeyed his command and come to Paris. It is said that when he heard of his rival's presence in the city, Henri had asked Villeroy, 'We are about to gamble everything. Is this not a question of the future of the kings of my race?' Turning to Alfonso d'Ornano, his Corsican captain, he asked, 'If you were in my place ... what would you do?' The ferociously loyal Corsican did not have to ponder over his reply; he merely said, 'Sire, there is only one important word in all of this. Do you consider M. de Guise your friend or your enemy?' Henri said nothing but made a gesture which left no doubt as to his feelings. D'Ornano is then supposed to have said, 'Let us finish with him then.'[23]

Despite her illness, Catherine, fearing her son's fury and desperate to prevent a final rupture between the two men – or worse – knew she must accompany Guise to the Louvre where the King awaited him. She dressed and then, carried in her sedan with Guise walking by her side, they headed towards the palace. As they made their short journey through the narrow streets the people cried 'Long live Guise!' and 'Long live the pillar of the Church!'. Henri awaited the duke in the Queen's apartments. Guise made a deep reverence before the King, who received him coldly and said only, 'Why are you here, my cousin?' To which, after a lengthy pause, the duke replied that he had come on the instructions of the Queen Mother. Catherine acknowledged this to be the truth and thereby made it impossible for the King to censure Guise, whether he believed them or not. Catherine then went on to explain that she had asked the duke to come in order to pacify the dangerous situation and to seek an accord between the two men.

Two days, 10 and 11 May, were spent in talks between Guise and the King. One of these meetings took place when the duke visited Catherine, where he met Henri. When Guise walked into the Queen Mother's chamber Henri saw the duke and turned his head away as though he had not spotted him. The relatively pleasant but guarded tone of the previous days then took a markedly downward turn. Guise sat beside the Queen Mother and, turning to Bellièvre, complained that much ill was being said of him. Guise did not know it yet, but Henri had heard that there was to be an uprising against him and, ignoring the ancient right of the Parisians to protect themselves in times of trouble, had called for Swiss troops and royalist soldiers to enter the city on the night of the 11 May.

The citizens were outraged when they saw the soldiers being deployed around the city. The troops had orders not to shoot though they were menaced by the angry populace, mainly consisting of bourgeois and students from the Sorbonne. During the night the citizens erected barricades of huge barrels filled with rocks and stones to block the streets. On the morning of 12 May, hearing the turmoil outside, the duke, having just risen and not yet dressed, looked out of the window of his bedchamber at the Hôtel de Guise and, affecting an air of sleepy surprise at the febrile activity below, called down to the people in a good-humoured and friendly manner, asking, 'And what is going on here?' They loved him for his easy way with them; here was a man they would follow anywhere.

As the temperature of the mob rose Henri sent Bellièvre to Guise with an assurance that the soldiers bore 'no evil design against him'. Catherine also sent a scout early on the same morning to take a friendly greeting to the duke. She arrived in person shortly afterwards and, having told him how unhappy the King was 'at all this emotion', urged him to restore order to the capital. The citizens were pelting the now-trapped soldiers with stones and a few troops had even been killed by snipers.

She feared there would be a great loss of life if he did not intervene. Guise gave a brusque reply; he was not the author of this madness, nor was he in a position to deal with it, being 'neither a colonel nor a captain'. It should, he temporised, be left to 'the authority of the city magistrates'.

At the request of the King the soldiers were brought back to safety by a number of quaking ministers. Guise himself walked the streets, unarmed, carrying only a riding crop and talking to the people. His calm reassured them and wherever he went they cried out '*Vive Guise!*', 'To Reims, we must bring Monsieur to Rheims!' Guise acknowledged the crowd but called back, 'Enough, Messieurs, it is too much. Cry *Vive le Roi!*' On the morning of the 13 May Henri was observed by Catherine's Florentine doctor Cavriani: 'The poor King, who is practically besieged here, is so sad and subdued that he is the image of death. This past night everyone was under arms, and he wept his fate bitterly, complaining of so much treachery.' The physician called it 'one of the greatest revolts and rebellions ever heard of'.

Always mistress of her emotions, especially when the situation looked bleak, the Queen Mother, carried in her sedan, ensured that she made her usual journey to hear Mass at the Saint-Chapelle. Descending from her chair, she manoeuvred her way through the barricades as if they were the most normal sight in the world. She was allowed through and greeted with respect by the barricaders who reported that the Queen Mother 'showed a smiling and assured face, without being astonished by anything'. This determined woman, ill and in complete despair over her son's future, still had the courage and ability to adapt to any situation with same sublime fortitude that she had throughout her life. Never had Catherine been more magnificent than when clambering over the rebels' barricades as they prepared to besiege her son at the Louvre. After Mass, when she had returned to her *dîner* with only her closest intimates around her, she wept silently but inconsolably.

At a council meeting that afternoon Catherine pressed her son to remain in Paris, yet hers was a lone voice among all the others who believed the King should flee while he still could. She insisted, 'Yesterday, I gathered from the words of Monsieur de Guise that he was ready to reason; I shall return to him now and I am sure that I shall make him quiet this trouble.' She had little time to lose; the Porte Neuve was the only gate to the city that still remained open, since by some amazing blunder the Leaguers had not secured it, but for how long would their mistake remain undiscovered? Guise had written with premature confidence to the Governor of Orléans, 'I have defeated the Swiss, cut to pieces a part of the guards of the King, and I am holding the Louvre so closely invested that I shall give a good account of those within it.

This victory is so great that the memory of it will live forever.'[24] Catherine hurried to Guise after the council meeting and begged him to calm the madness in the streets. He was not, he said, able to deal with the rebel mob whom he likened to 'mad bulls that were difficult to restrain'. Upon hearing this Catherine turned and whispered something to Secretary Pinart who had accompanied her. The secretary made his excuses and left the Queen Mother with Guise.

Pinart carried a message for the King that he must quit the city without delay, but Henri had not waited for his mother's signal. He had already fled, leaving word for his mother to take charge of affairs in the capital. A mob was marching towards the Louvre coming to fetch 'Brother Henri' just as the King walked casually through the Tuileries Gardens and then on to the stables. He and a group of friends had then quietly mounted their waiting horses and ridden through the Porte Neuve, close to the walls of the gardens. Cantering gently at first, the party had broken into a full gallop as it set out for Rambouillet, where they stopped for the night, then rode on to Chartres at the break of day on 14 May. About an hour after Pinart had left the Hôtel de Guise, news of the King's escape reached the duke, who still sat talking to Catherine. He cried out, 'Ah! Madame, I am killed. While Your Majesty has been holding me off here, the King has left to make me more trouble.'[25]

On the morning of the 14 May Parlement was due to meet. There still remained a strong body of men who abhorred the zealotry of the League and stayed loyal to their King no matter how weak a man he was. True to the principle that Henri had been anointed by God, they believed nobody had the right to usurp him. Guise insisted that the session begin, but Achille de Harley, the President, reproached him with the words, 'It is a great pity to see the lackey drive out the master. As for myself, my soul belongs to God, my heart to the King, and my body is in the hands of scoundrels. Do what you please.'[26]

Guise took the precaution of taking a few strategic towns around Paris to prevent any possible blockade by the royalists, then he replaced municipal officers loyal to the King with members of the League. The keys of the Bastille were sent to the duke and the League promptly filled it with their enemies. Control of the Arsenal was also handed over. Guise ensured that the frustrated mob did not go on a rampage of destruction, nor attack any royal properties, so a semblance of normality did return to the streets. Finally, though, Paris was no good to the League without the King there and he had shattered the duke's plans by escaping. As a man who believed in the honour of his rank, Guise had shrunk from killing Henri outright, but to control him in the capital as a virtual captive to the Catholic (and ultimately his own) cause would have been perfectly acceptable to his chivalrous daintiness. It is proof of his remarkable popularity with the people that he was not blamed for the monarch's escape.

The two Queens, Louise and Catherine, were well treated, save for one incident when the Queen Mother's way through a city gate to hear Mass at the Capuchins had been barred. Furious, she faced the duke and threatened to leave the city, and if necessary, she added melodramatically, she would happily die in the attempt. But this was no more than bravura; she knew that she served her son better by staying in the capital and anyhow Guise would almost certainly have prevented her from leaving had she tried to. In the end, to save face for both of them, the duke pretended that the lock to the gate had merely been broken. Semi-captive as she was, Catherine managed to keep her son informed of events by being at the centre of them, and Louise proved an asset because she was not only a Lorrainer by birth but also adored by the Parisians for her piety, beauty and sweet nature. The following month a series of deputations were sent by Guise to Henri at Chartres. They brought with them a list of demands from the League which again outlined the essentials of the Treaty of Nemours with some additions to incorporate the recent developments in Paris. These included the requirement that d'Épernon and his brother should be treated as crypto-Huguenots and banished.

The King received the delegates from the capital on 16 May. He said he would absolve the Parisians for their behaviour if they acknowledged their faults and from now on obeyed their anointed sovereign. One matter he did not fret over was the banishment of d'Épernon and his brother to Angoumois. He continued, 'The people are overburdened with taxes and as only the state can remedy the evils from which the state suffers we have resolved to summon the Estates-General at Blois so that, without injuring the rights and authority attached to the royal majesty, we may proceed freely according to the custom of the nation, to seek the means of relieving the people.'[7] But still the King and the League haggled. Catherine wrote to Bellièvre at Chartres with Henri, 'I should prefer to give away half of my kingdom and to give the Lieutenant-Generalship to Guise, and to be recognised by him and by the whole kingdom than still to tremble, as we do now, lest worse befall the King. I know this is a hard medicine for him to swallow, but it is harder yet to lose all authority and all obedience.' Then she proffered the old formula that had served her so well in the past: 'It would be much to his credit if he were to come to terms in whatever way he could for the present; for time often brings many things which one cannot foresee, and we admire those who know how to yield to time in order to preserve themselves.' Before finishing her letter she let show a rare glimpse of her inner despair at this time: 'I am preaching a sermon; excuse me, for I have never been in such trouble before, nor with less light to see my way out of it, unless God puts His Hand to it I do not know what will happen.'²⁸

At Rouen on 5 July 1588 the King finally accepted the League's demands and Parlement published the Act of Union in Paris on 21 July. In it the League received official recognition, although Henri insisted that it break all its foreign alliances immediately. He had in mind the growing peril from Spain as the Armada had set forth from Lisbon against England and was even then skirting the French coast. This stupendous flotilla, a solid evocation of Spanish naval might, provided an unsettling reminder of Guise's semi-client relationship with Philip II. Catherine in particular, stuck in Paris – now a hive of Philip's agents – had always feared an attack by Spain. She had grown restless in her isolation and fearful lest Henri's delays provoke an attack by her seemingly unstoppable former son-in-law.

The Act of Union made the Cardinal de Bourbon Henri's heir presumptive and his subjects had henceforth to give an undertaking not to allow a heretic to succeed him. Guise became Lieutenant-General and there were other rich pickings for the Lorrainers' clan and supporters. Henri also agreed to field two armies against Navarre and the Huguenots, and he extended a general amnesty to all those who had taken part in the Day of the Barricades. A special Mass held at Notre-Dame celebrated the publication of the edict, attended by the two Queens, the Cardinals de Bourbon and Vendôme. Among those also present were Guise and a host of foreign ambassadors. They were there to send reports to their masters that the new order had been officially recognised. Henri, however, remained absent from his capital and the revelry so horrid to him.

As soon as the Te Deums had been sung, Catherine and Queen Louise left Paris to meet Henri, who had moved to Mantes not far to the west of Paris. His mother begged him to return to the capital but he declined, preferring instead to go with his wife to Chartres. Catherine arrived there a few days later and Guise, anxious to pay his respects to the King whom he had recently held a virtual prisoner, accompanied her with the Cardinal de Bourbon. Guise knelt on both knees when he was brought before Henri. The King raised him gently and kissed him tenderly on both cheeks. That night he invited Guise to dine and celebrate the recent pact and reconciliation between himself and the League. Henri appeared to be enjoying the atmosphere of conviviality tinged with menace. It hung like an uninvited guest around every remark that invited a possible double entendre and every toast to empty loyalty. The King asked 'his dear cousin' to whom they should drink? 'That is for Your Majesty to determine,' came the duke's reply. 'Well, then, drink to our good friends the Huguenots,' upon which there was a roar of laughter and Guise raised his glass with the remark, 'Well said, Sire.' The laughter was strangled when Henri added, 'and to our good friends the Barricaders of Paris'. Guise did not like the association, but said nothing. Henri took great pleasure in playing this kind of game, but it was not to the duke's taste at all.

A sharp change in Spanish fortunes came at this moment of triumph for the League. Starting on 31 July and continuing until 9 August and afterwards, the Armada, the pride of Spain, was beaten by an alliance of courageous English maritime enterprise and appalling weather. The cocky Leaguers saw Spain, their cast-iron ally, desperately weakened by the brutal beating its towering fleet had taken. Philip's defeat gave new heart to the King and all the moderates in France, who felt safer now the mighty ogre had been stalled. When Mendoza, the Spanish ambassador called by Henri to give an account of the battle, arrived he claimed it a victory for his master in Madrid. As each day passed and remnants of the 'invincible' Spanish hulks washed up on the French coast, and galley slaves who had miraculously survived were brought ashore, it became harder for even the most polished diplomat to turn the truth upon its head.

Philip had fallen from his pinnacle of power. Henri could not resist introducing the Turkish galley slaves to Mendoza; they were technically men under his protection as the Sultan was France's ally. He now felt safe to ignore the League's beautifully worded but insistent entreaties to return to the capital. He claimed that his duties lay at Blois where, as stated in the Act of Union, a meeting of the Estates-General was to convene on 15 October. He had much to prepare for the coming assembly. Henri left for Blois on 1 September, taking his mother, the Queen and the Duke of Guise with him.

On 8 September at Blois, Henri made a dramatic and unexpected move by sacking all his ministers of state. This coup confounded Catherine as much as everyone else. He had not consulted her over this drastic action; indeed, when she asked for an explanation he angrily denounced the men with whom she had surrounded him. Mendoza reported to Philip that Henri accused Cheverny of lining his own pockets, Bellièvre of being a Huguenot, Villeroy was a vain glory seeker, Brulart a nobody and Pinart would not scruple to sell his own parents for cash. Henri told Catherine that they had all failed and now he made their failure his own. It was she who had counselled him to be the master when he arrived from Poland in 1574, and shortly before the debacle of the Barricades he had told Villeroy that now he must be King 'for we have been the valet for too long'. How bitter she must have felt at being cast aside with the men her son had so peremptorily dismissed, many of whom she had chosen herself and who had served her faithfully.

Bellièvre, the *surindendent des finances*, was among those to have been dispatched, along with the Chancellor Cheverny and the three Secretaries of States, Brulart, Pinart and Villeroy. The last had merely received a letter from the King with the following polite but brief instructions: 'Villeroy, I remain satisfied with your services; yet fail not to return to your home where you shall remain until I send for you. Seek not the reason for my letter, simply obey me.'[29] Catherine wrote to Bellièvre of 'the wrong that had been done me in teaching the King that one must honour and love one's mother, as God wills, but not give her so much authority and credit that she can prevent one from doing what one pleases'.[30] The men who replaced the sacked ministers were notable for three things only: they were regarded as men of integrity, they were practically unknown and they were not creatures of the Queen Mother. Catherine's days of power were over.

The Estates-General opened on 16 October with great pageantry and splendour. The ladies of the Court arrayed in their finery, dazzled from the gallery. The hall had been especially decorated and prepared for this important assembly that would decide the future of the King, the League and the country. Henri sat upon his throne with Catherine on his right-hand side and immediately below him was the Duke of Guise, his Grand Master.

The drama and tension were palpable as the delegates and courtiers sat silent with expectation. Henri opened with a fine speech paying tribute to his mother in what can only be seen as a valedictory address. In recognition for her outstanding and tireless services to France, he said she should not only be called mother of the King, but also of the kingdom. He thanked her for all she had taught him, for her efforts to resolve the nation's troubles and protecting the Catholic faith, adding that it was to her that he owed his Catholic zeal, his piety and his desire to reform France. He asked, 'Has she not sacrificed her health in the struggle? Thanks to her good example and teaching I have learned the worries that come from governing. I have called the Estates-General as the most certain remedy for the troubles that afflict my people and my mother has supported me in this decision.' After his homage to Catherine he returned to the kernel of his message, saying, 'I am your God-given King, only I can speak lawfully and truly.'

As the assembly was filled with League members the King then addressed himself to their greatest concern, the fight against heresy. He promised to pursue this with the utmost vigour, but underlined the need for money to carry the fight to Henri of Navarre and his armies. He promised to root out corruption, to stimulate commerce and to examine taxation. He called upon all his subjects to unite and follow him in his fight against the injustices and troubles that bedevilled the kingdom.

Throughout his speech the Queen Mother sat motionless and pale with a fixed gaze, still unable to grasp the finality of her removal from power. Only when Henri began an ill-disguised attack on the Guises did Catherine awake from her impassive reverie. His voice rang out replete with new-found regal authority, saying, 'Some great nobles of my kingdom have formed leagues and associations, but, as evidence of my habitual kindness, I am prepared in this regard to forget the past.' Guise, not expecting this audacious and ill-concealed assault, 'changed colour and looked discomfited'. In a fury the duke and his brother the cardinal demanded the removal of the offending references to themselves from the printed version of the King's speech. Catherine begged Henri to do as they asked and the King agreed to have the passage removed from the final version. As the sessions continued over the following weeks, Catherine became too ill to be present and for the first time in almost three decades she lacked a worthwhile reason to be there. Instead, she allowed herself to submit to her gout, persistent cough and crippling rheumatism.

On 8 December the Queen Mother managed to attend the marriage-by-proxy of her favourite grandchild, Christina of Lorraine, to Ferdinand de Medici, Grand Duke of Tuscany. It was a match she had hoped for and helped to arrange, and it gave her the last truly happy moments of her long life.* After the marriage ceremony in the chapel of the Château of Blois she gave a ball in her apartments. A week later, on 15 December she took to her bed. Her lung infection had returned and she found it difficult to breathe. The doctors fussed but offered no remedy. It was just at this moment that Henri, struggling with the Estates, heard whispers of yet another plot that he was to be kidnapped by Guise and taken to Paris. Others warned him that Guise wanted to be made Constable of France and governor of Orléans. He could no longer turn to his mother for help and his dark heart needed little encouragement to nurture his suspicions.

On 17 December the Duchess de Montpensier had been overheard at dinner with her brothers the Duke and the Cardinal of Guise and their kinsmen, to toast her elder brother as the new King of France and talk about how she would use her golden scissors on Henri. The actor and musician Venetianelli happened to be present and doubtless exaggerated what he had heard, but he nonetheless reported everything to the King. The atmosphere at the château grew fraught with rumour and counter-rumour. Finally on 19 December, with the help of a few of his trusted advisers, Henri decided that Guise, whose position was unassailable by

---

* The marriage of Catherine's granddaughter Christina of Lorraine to the Medici Grand Duke of Tuscany not only settled many vexatious issues regarding Catherine's Tuscan possessions and inheritance, but also gave the Queen Mother the great satisfaction of joining her senior branch of the family with those descended from Giovanni della Bande Nere.

normal methods, must die 'by the dagger'. He set the date for his assassination for 23 December.

Guise, who had an excellent network of spies, received several warnings of a plot against him and so he begged the nuncio, Morisini, to calm the King. The nuncio had little advice to offer, except for suggesting that the Queen Mother might be able to ease her son's temper. In the past she had provided a wall of sanity between the King and his enemies, both real and imagined. The duke visited her and she promised that she would do what she could to ease Henri's excitable mood. On 20 December the Marshal de Bassompierre and the Seigneur de Maineville, both Leaguers, urged Guise to quit Blois at once because they believed a lethal trap was being set for him.

On the morning of 21 December the King and the duke were seen having a heated discussion in the gardens of the chateau, during which Guise asked forcefully to be relieved of his position as Lieutenant-General of France. Henri believed this to be manoeuvring on the duke's part to obtain the yet greater position as Constable. Later that night he arranged to hold an urgent meeting about how to murder his increasingly threatening rival. The King could meet his co-plotters without arousing suspicion since there was a ball being held to celebrate Christina of Lorraine's marriage so the Court's attention would be elsewhere.

At the meeting, not wishing 'to be remembered as Nero', the King nevertheless stated his belief that if Guise did not die, he himself would be killed or abducted. It was decided that the Cardinal of Guise must also be executed, since he would provide too strong a rallying point for the extremists were he spared. Henri comforted himself by declaring that the two brothers were guilty of *lèse-majesté*, a crime punishable by death. Exasperated, the King asked his small circle of trusties, 'Who will kill these evil Guises for me?' His loyal '*quarante-cinq*', the special bodyguard created for him by d'Épernon, had no scruples in accepting the task. That night Morisini heard further rumours and sent his own captain of the guard to the so-called 'brains of the League', the Archbishop of Lyons, Pierre d'Epinac, with whom Guise was supping, to alert him to the plot.

The following morning as they were leaving Mass the King and the duke were reported by some observers to have had a further altercation, though this seems unlikely as they had both been invited to visit Catherine in her chamber. Henri was a picture of good humour and munificence as the pair joked and gossiped with the bedridden Queen Mother in order to cheer her up. They passed the time pleasantly, eating sweetmeats and chatting, when Catherine asked the two men to embrace each other and to forget the past. Henri is said to have taken the duke into his arms and kissed him. The two parted on what appeared to be cordial terms. The scene had particularly lifted Catherine's spirits though, as one historian noted, the words of Racine's *Britannicus* – 'I embrace my rival for then it is easier to strangle him' – would have fitted the occasion perfectly.[31]

Before the pair separated that evening the King announced to Guise that as he was to spend Christmas at a pavilion in the park he must first finish some outstanding business. He turned to the duke, saying, 'My cousin, we have difficult questions to address that must be decided before the year is out. In order to do this come tomorrow morning early to the council so that we may expedite matters.' As he was purportedly leaving for the pavilion he told the duke (who as Grand Master had charge of the keys to the château) that his carriages would be collecting his baggage at four o'clock in the morning and he therefore required the keys immediately.

Further warnings arrived for the duke that night. His mother, the Duchess of Nemours, told her son that she had heard of a royal plot to kill him in the morning. Guise is said to have replied hubristically, 'He would not dare.' At his *souper* he found a note tucked into his napkin saying that the King planned to murder him on the morrow. Guise asked for a quill and wrote, 'He would not dare,' before casting the paper aside. The fatal belief that Henri was as 'infirm of purpose' as ever blinded him to the deadly solution planned by a king who had long felt like cornered quarry. Guise was accompanied everywhere except in the King's presence by a strong and loyal escort, which tragically reinforced his feeling of security. Five further notes arrived that night, but the duke remained unruffled and even became impatient when his surgeon thrust the messages into his master's hand, angrily telling him, 'This will never happen. Let us sleep. All of you go to bed.' He had just returned from a tryst with the beautiful Madame de Sauve and went to his own bedchamber at around one o'clock in the morning.

Earlier, at 11 p.m. that night, Henri had withdrawn to his own apartments and before going to bed arranged with his valet, du Halde, to wake him at 4 a.m. He passed the night fitfully and was duly woken up – to the Queen's surprise – at that unusually early hour. He did not dress but took a candle and put on his mantle and slippers to meet the chief of his assassins, Bellegarde, and his henchmen. By five o'clock the killers of the 'forty-five' were in place. Eight among them had been selected to carry out the task; eight more were to cut off their victim's retreat and the rest were hidden about the scene in case something should go wrong at the last minute. The King heard Mass between six and seven o'clock, after which he returned to his *cabinet* (small chamber).

The duke had also risen early; the morning was dark and rain fell heavily. He dressed and went to hear Mass but found the door to the chapel locked. Instead, he made his devotions on his knees outside the chapel doors before proceeding to the council chamber. On his way an Auvergnate gentleman named Louis de Fontanges approached him, urgently begging him not to go to the council meeting, saying he would be killed there. Patiently the duke replied, 'But my friend, it is a long time since I have been cured of this fear.' Having been warned no fewer than nine times of what was about to happen, Guise's behaviour was little short of suicidal arrogance. Nevertheless, he took his leave, smiled as he turned and walked off to his fatal rendezvous.

Most of the council were already present when Guise arrived; his brother the cardinal sat beside the Archbishop of Lyons, and the members talked for a while awaiting only the arrival of Ruzé de Beaulieu who had the list of matters for discussion. The duke, who had not taken any breakfast, sent his man Péricard to fetch him something to eat. A few minutes later Captain Larchant of the King's bodyguard arrived with some of his men, ostensibly to discuss their wages. The duke agreed to their requests and, feeling cold, stood up and walked to the fire. Péricard had still not returned with anything for him to eat and he asked for a handkerchief as his nose had begun to bleed. At last, at eight o'clock and after a long wait, some of the royal plums from Brignoles were brought in for Guise and finally Secretary de Beaulieu arrived with the agenda for the meeting.

According to Miron, the King stood listening just on the other side of the wall. He seemed afraid that even outnumbered sixteen to one the duke, who he warned them was 'tall and strong', might overcome his assassins. There were two chaplains with the King who prayed for him and asked the Almighty's pardon for the frightful act he had ordered. At a given signal, Secretary of State Revol was ordered to fetch Guise, but the King took one look at Revol and said, 'For God's sake, man, you look so pale. Rub your cheeks! Rub your cheeks or you will spoil everything for me.' When Revol, presumably having reddened his cheeks to the King's satisfaction, entered the chamber and asked Guise to come into the Cabinet Vieux, the duke stood up so promptly that he knocked his chair over. Throwing the remaining plums on to the table he asked, 'Gentleman, who wants one?' He walked towards the door, turning only to say with unconscious finality, 'Gentlemen, adieu,' uttered with such lightness that he obviously had no idea what lay before him. Lining the antechamber were eight of the 'forty-five' who, to allay any fears the duke might have had, saluted him as he walked past. As they raised their right hands to their black velvet caps their left hands each held an unsheathed dagger hidden in the folds of their cloaks. Guise walked into the passage leading to the Cabinet Vieux and the eight assassins followed silently behind, cutting off his retreat.

When Guise raised the curtain to enter the passage he saw the killers standing in the *cabinet* in front of him and, realising it was a trap, tried to turn back, but the men he had just passed stood blocking his path. The *'quarante-cinq'* then fell upon him, plunging their daggers into his body. He cried out, 'Eh! Mes amis!' His cloak had prevented him from drawing his own sword before he was struck, but despite this he managed to punch two of his assailants hard in the face and knock four others to the ground. No matter how valiant his self-defence, though, there was no hope for him and he died after an heroic struggle at the foot of the King's bed. Before breathing his last he uttered the words, 'Messieurs! Messieurs!' then addressed himself to the Almighty: 'These are my offences, My God! Misericorde!'[32] Henri stood looking down at his now dead enemy and is said to have sneered, 'Look at him, the King of Paris. Not so big now!'

His Majesty then entered the council chamber with his guards and announced that Guise was dead and as their rightful King he would henceforth be obeyed by all. The guards had already sealed the room. The Cardinal of Guise was arrested along with anyone else who formed part of the Guise cabal. Elsewhere around the château at the same time eight further members of the Guise clan were also placed under arrest with other senior Leaguers.

Henri next called on his mother whose apartments lay directly beneath where the duke had been murdered. Catherine was being attended by her Italian doctor, Cavriani, who was also the Grand Duke of Tuscany's spy. He reported that the King marched into Catherine's room and, after first asking the physician about the Queen Mother's condition, said to her, 'Good morning, Madame, please excuse me but the Duke of Guise is dead and we shall speak of him no more. I have had him killed to prevent his own plans against me.' He then proceeded to talk in an animated manner of the insults and injuries committed against him by the duke, seeming almost inebriated by the murder he had just planned and witnessed. Then he said he must go to Mass and thank God for delivering him from the duke's evil plans. 'I want to be King, not a prisoner or a slave.'

Reports vary as to Catherine's reaction. Cavriani says she was too ill to speak but understood perfectly what had happened. Morisini wrote that she managed to say that instead of being King he had just lost his kingdom. This is unlikely; there would have been little point in arguing with her son when the blood had already been spilled. The deed was done and whatever she said, if anything, would probably only have been a bland murmur that she hoped Henri had done the right thing.

On the morning of Christmas Eve the Cardinal of Guise was murdered in his prison cell, and the bodies of these two Catholic princes were hacked to pieces and thrown into a fireplace at Blois to burn. The King did not want a burial site where their followers could gather and commune with their dead martyrs. On Christmas Day Catherine, though deeply depressed and in despair over her son's lunacy, spoke to a Capuchin friar begging him to pray for Henri, 'Oh! wretched man, what has he done? ... Pray for him, he needs your prayers. He is headed towards ruin and I fear he will lose his body, his soul and his kingdom.' The Guises had posed the greatest danger to her husband's dynasty ever since his death, but when they finally met their doom she was too politically acute not to understand that both their Houses would be ruined by her son's impolitic savagery.

SEVENTEEN

So Perish the Race of the Valois

What could the poor woman do ...?

1588–1615

On New Year's Eve Catherine made a supreme effort to dress, go to Mass in the chapel and then visit her old friend the Cardinal de Bourbon who was imprisoned in his apartments. She gave him her assurance that the King meant him no harm and that he would be safe. Bourbon replied ferociously to the frail old woman standing before him, shouting, 'It is on your word that we came here and you led us to this butchery!' Catherine sobbed at his angry reproach, turned and left without another word. She then stubbornly decided, against Cavriani's advice, to take a short walk although the day was extremely cold. Her fever returned.

By the morning of 5 January 1589 the Queen Mother could hardly breathe. On so many earlier occasions Catherine had, by sheer force of her personality, overcome bodily weaknesses, but not this time. Her demise was clearly imminent, 'to the great astonishment of us all,' wrote one observer. She asked to make her last testament. By now her voice had become so feeble that Henri had to dictate his mother's whispered wishes. No mention was made of Margot, the only other surviving child of the ten she had borne for her beloved husband Henry and for France. After receiving the Sacrament, Catherine de Medici, wife of one King of France and mother of three others, died at half past one in the afternoon, on the eve of the Epiphany, or what the French call 'Le Jour des Rois' (the day of the kings). She was sixty-nine.

Catherine's superstitions are not all to be scoffed at; many years earlier she had received a warning from one of her seers – to beware of 'Saint-Germain' which presaged a mortal threat. Though she had built her Hôtel de la Reine outside the parish of Saint-Germain-l'Auxerrois, and she did not often frequent the château at Saint-Germain-en-Laye, she received the last rites from her son's confessor and not her usual priest. His name was Julien de Saint-Germain.

By royal custom, Henri ordered a post-mortem that revealed pleurisy (as it is now called) as the immediate cause of death. The corpse was duly embalmed, though not all the necessary herbs and spices were available for the job to be done properly. Catherine's body was then placed in a wooden lead-lined coffin surmounted by the traditional effigy of the deceased Queen, and dressed in the robes of Anne of Brittany. Because of the desperate state of unrest that followed the murder of the Guises, and the widespread belief that the Queen Mother had had a hand in it, Parisian Leaguers threatened that her corpse would be dragged through the streets and dumped in the Seine if brought to the capital. For the time being at least, therefore, she could not be buried at Saint-Denis alongside her husband and sons in the superb Valois chapel she had especially added to inter her family. Instead, the body would have to remain at Blois until the political situation calmed down.

At the funeral, held on 4 February at the Church of Saint-Sauveur at Blois, the Archbishop of Bourges paid fine tribute to the late Queen. He spoke of her arrival in France as a splendid bride with a great dowry, the ten children she had borne Henry II, and lauded her personal courage during the many wars that had taken place during her widowhood. Whether at Rouen or Le Havre, she had been present with her armies and walked between the warring troops without fear.[1] In his peroration he asked the congregation to 'acknowledge that you have lost the most virtuous Queen, the noblest of race and generation, the most prudent in government, the sweetest in conversation, the most affable and kindly to all who wished to see her, the most humble and charitable to her children, the most obedient to her husband, but above all the most devout before God, and the most affectionate to the poor of any queen who ever reigned in France!'[2]

The chronicler Pierre l'Estoile summed up Catherine a little less reverently.

> She was seventy-one years old [in fact she was two years younger] and well preserved for such a fat woman. She ate heartily, feeding herself well and was not afraid of work although she had to face as much as any queen in the world since the death of her husband thirty years before. ... She was mourned by some of her servants and intimates and a little by her son the King. ... Those closest to her believed that the assassination of the Guises hastened her end. This was not so much due to the friendship for the victims (whom she liked in the Florentine way - that is to say in order to make use of them), but because she could see that it would benefit the King of Navarre. ... His succession was what she feared most in the world.[3]

Estoile added that in view of the Parisians' belief in her complicity in the Guises' murder her body was not welcome in the capital but 'so much for the Parisian view. In Blois where she had been adored and revered as the court's Juno, she had no sooner passed away than she was treated with as much consideration as a dead goat.'[4]

This last remark perhaps reflected the fact that the Queen Mother's ineptly embalmed corpse had begun to smell horribly and the King therefore considered it best that it be deposited at the Saint-Saveur churchyard under the cover of night in an unmarked grave. In fact, Catherine's remains were to stay in this humble plot for a further twenty-one years until Henry II's illegitimate daughter, the gentle Anne de France, had the body moved to the Valois rotunda at Saint-Denis.

The ultra-Catholics, though stricken by the loss of their leader Guise and his brother the cardinal, continued their increasingly fevered campaign against the King who had, by the summer of 1589, allied himself with Henri of Navarre. The widowed Duchess of Guise and her baby son were idolised by the Parisian crowds, who called her their 'Sainte Veuve'. But with the death of the duke the extreme Catholic movement now splintered and became chaotic. Guise's brother, the Duke of Mayenne, who did not have any of his brother's charisma, intellect or military flair, nonetheless fancied himself for the throne. He and his sister the Duchess de Montpensier even seized Catherine's Hôtel de la Reine where they lived in majestic style. Vulnerable and in a state of collapse, France once again attracted unwelcome attention from Philip II and other neighbours.

By the summer of 1589 the King and Henri of Navarre were stationed at Saint-Cloud just south-west of Paris, from where they hoped to recapture the capital. On 31 July a Dominican friar was spotted walking on the road to Saint-Cloud and was stopped by the King's Attorney-General, Jacques De La Guesle, who happened to be passing. When asked what business he had at the King's headquarters, the monk introduced himself as Jacques Clément and said that he had come from Paris with information 'of great moment' for His Majesty. He then produced a letter of introduction that appeared genuine, so De La Guesle conducted him to Saint-Cloud where he was told to wait for a possible audience. In fact, the Dominican friar was a delusional loner who believed he could hear God's voice in his head and that he had received instructions from the Almighty to kill the King.

Henri, always pleased to welcome a man of God and especially one carrying news from loyalists in Paris, agreed to see him at eight o'clock the following morning. That evening Clément dined with De La Guesle and his companions; he proved to be a jovial guest who, those present later recalled, cut his meat with his own sharp knife as he chatted about the latest news from the rebel capital.

The next morning De La Guesle fetched Clément for his audience with Henri. The guards inexplicably failed to search the assassin before he was ushered into the royal presence and after a few further questions, which seemed to satisfy everyone that he was indeed bringing vital news to the King, Clément found himself being conducted into Henri's *cabinet*. The King was only half dressed and sitting on his commode when the monk entered. He greeted him with the words, 'Mon frère, you are welcome! What news of Paris?' Ignoring protests from those present, Henri insisted that the monk draw near to impart his information. Clément kissed the King's hand and gave him his letter of introduction. Henri, asking for further news and letters, motioned the monk closer to whisper in his ear. Clément bent low as though to produce the correspondence, but instead his hand emerged from his sleeve with a knife that he plunged up to the hilt into the King's lower abdomen. Henri stood up crying, 'Ah! My God, the wretch has wounded me!' He pulled the knife out of his stomach and punched Clément twice in the face as his bodyguards fell upon the assassin, stabbing him. The guards then threw the regicide's body out of the window. Henri, bleeding profusely, was left standing with the killer's knife in one hand and his own intestines in the other.

At first the King felt little discomfort and spoke in a strong voice. The surgeons attending him seemed optimistic as they replaced the intestines protruding from the wound, though their royal patient fainted from the pain. Once they had finished they bandaged him up. Charles IX's illegitimate son, Charles of Angoulême, a young man much loved by the King, had arrived in the chamber as this gruesome operation was taking place and wept when he saw what had happened to his uncle. Regaining consciousness, Henri stroked the boy's head and comforted him, saying, 'My son, my son! Do not grieve! They have tried to kill me but, by God's mercy, they have not succeeded. This will be nothing; I shall soon be better!' With this he slipped his fingers under the bandage and prodded his wound to ensure that his intestines were indeed intact. One of the King's surgeons, unable to share his colleagues' positive prognosis, took the sixteen-year-old boy aside and whispered that he feared the injury would in fact prove fatal.

By ten o'clock the King, lying on his bed, issued orders for the news of his wounding and his hopes for recovery to be sent to the provincial governors. He also complained of cold and numbness in his feet, so 'petit Charles' tended to him by rubbing them. Mass was held by the King's bed and afterwards he dictated a letter to Queen Louise telling her about the attempt on his life. The King also issued an order to summon Navarre who, by the time he arrived at the King's bedside, could have been under no illusions as to the eventual outcome. Having slept on and off during the early afternoon, the King had become feverish and vomited a large quantity of blood. With the fever came excruciating pain.

Understanding all too well that he had not many hours left to live, the King became anxious to take the Sacrament, though he first addressed the assembled nobles. Holding out his hand to Navarre, he said, 'You see, my brother, how my subjects have treated me! ... Take good heed for your own safety.' He continued, 'It is now for you, my brother, to wear that crown which I have striven to preserve for you; justice and the principle of legitimacy demand that you should succeed me in the realm. You will experience many calamities, unless you resolve to change your religion.' Navarre, greatly moved, said nothing. The King then demanded that his officers and nobles pledge their oath of allegiance to the man who would shortly be their sovereign, stating that this sight would comfort him greatly. Kneeling at the King's bed, they duly gave their promise of loyalty to Navarre. Once this was done, Navarre, who was weeping, received the King's benediction and withdrew with the others. The King, exhausted, slept for a few hours. When he awoke he cried, 'My time has come!' After making his confession he received the last rites and died two hours later, at four o'clock on the morning of 2 August, from perforated intestines and severe internal bleeding. As Catherine's favourite son expired, so did the Valois dynasty.

The new King, Henri de Bourbon, now styled Henri IV, faced the monumental task of making himself king not only in name but also in fact. Hearing the news of the murder of Henri III, the ultra-Catholics declared the aged Cardinal Charles de Bourbon to be King Charles X, though he was shortly afterwards captured by his nephew Henri. For over four and a half years Henri fought vigorously against the powers ranged against him, including forces and aid from the Duke of Savoy, Philip II and the Pope. 'I rule with my arse in the saddle and my gun in my fist,' he declared, urging his soldiers to 'rally to my white plume'.[5]

After years of arduous campaigning during which Paris stubbornly held out, Henri finally decided that the time had come to re-convert to Catholicism. The solemn ceremony took place at Saint-Denis on 23 July 1593, witnessed by hundreds of Parisians who had slipped out of the city to watch him abjure the Protestant faith. Henri dressed simply and unadorned in the black and white of a penitent. As he walked to the church, crowds numbering between 10,000 and 30,000 people cried, '*Vive le roi!*' That summer evening after the ceremony he stood surveying the city from Monmartre, where he is said to have uttered the famous remark, 'Paris is well worth a Mass.'[6]

After long and secret negotiations, and the promise of a general amnesty, the forty-year-old king finally entered Paris just before dawn on the morning of 22 March 1594. He came into the capital by the Porte Neuve, the very gate through which Henri III had escaped after the Day of the Barricades almost six years earlier. He met no resistance. After a service of thanksgiving at Notre-Dame, he showed immense personal courage, walking unprotected through the streets, and was greeted by crowds of curious citizens who were pleasantly surprised to see that the supposed 'ogre' appeared to be a normal man. To signify their loyalty to Henri, the people tied white scarves round their arms.

The Spanish troops stationed in the capital marched out of Paris. As they saluted the King he is said to have shouted, 'Recommend me to your master, but never come back!'[7] The clemency he had promised won the respect and eventually the love of the Parisians, though the gallows he had placed near the Porte Saint-Antoine warned of his firm commitment to law and order, as he began the rebuilding of the city.

Margot had long been estranged from her husband when he became King. As early as 1592 Henri had broached the subject of having their marriage annulled; he desperately needed a legitimate heir and to free himself to marry again. Margot, still in the Auvergne, drove a fine financial bargain for herself. In addition to an excellent income and the repayment of all her outstanding debts, she would continue to be addressed as 'Your Majesty' and known as 'Queen Margot'. The couple's annulment (eventually granted in 1599) was argued on the three grounds that Margot had not consented to her marriage freely, the couple's consanguinity (as Henry II was godfather to the groom, Margot and Henri were also considered spiritual brother and sister), and that neither before nor after the wedding of August 1572 did Catherine ever receive the papal dispensation she needed to overcome these obstacles. Though canonically doubtful, Margot's supposed infertility may also have assisted the process.

After twenty-two years' absence, Margot returned to Paris in 1605 at the age of fifty-one. Daughter of a king, sister to three more and, nominally at least, Queen of France herself for a time, she came back to the scene of her youthful triumphs to find a new political order in place. Conscious of being the last of the Valois, she ensured that proper respect was accorded to her. But the Valois were a spent dynasty; the founder of the Bourbons, her former husband, now ruled and in 1600 he married, though with little enthusiasm, Maria de Medici, daughter of the late Francesco I, Grand Duke of Tuscany and thus a distant relative of Margot's.

Henri insisted on having sex with his twenty-eight-year-old bride almost immediately upon greeting her at Lyons. It is unlikely that he did this because he found her irresistibly beautiful – she was, in fact, fat and plain – but he probably wanted to ensure that there were no physical abnormalities that might prevent her from bearing an heir. The couple had already been married by proxy, but Maria tried – unsuccessfully – to insist upon waiting for the ceremony of blessing by the papal nuncio. The Medici were Henri IV's main creditors and Maria's dowry provided the principal reason for choosing her as his bride; he called her 'the fat banker' behind her back.[8] The new Queen of France promptly and obligingly ensured the continuation of the Bourbon dynasty by producing an heir, who was named Louis, the year after her marriage (he eventually became Louis XIII). Among the three further children she bore her husband was Henrietta Maria, the future wife of King Charles I of England.

Margot maintained an amicable relationship with Henri, whom she called 'my brother, my friend and my King'. She also understood that the new dynasty would benefit much from validation by the last surviving member of the Valois line and this she accorded in whatever way she could. Margot established a close bond with Queen Maria and, childless herself, doted on the royal children and in particular the Dauphin Louis who, after much debate on how to address her, called her 'Maman, ma fille'. Many of the goods and properties that should rightfully have been her inheritance were restored to her and in return she made the Dauphin her heir, once more demonstrating the joining of the two royal lines. At last living in Paris again, Margot decided she needed a residence that properly reflected her rank. Henri generously granted her a large tract of land immediately opposite her mother's palace of the Tuileries and, in what might be construed as a desire to copy Catherine but perhaps also to defy her, she built the lovely Palais des Augustins with an extensive park and gardens on the left bank of the Seine.* As well as making the left bank fashionable, she filled her palace with a bohemian mixture of musicians, writers and philosophers attracting cultured people to her salons.

Catherine's own palace, the Hôtel de la Reine, suffered an ignominious fate. One of the consequences of her last son dying seven months after her was that her debts could not now be paid off to her creditors. Though her estate was bankrupt, the vast properties she had received from her mother were legally unassailable. The Queen Mother's personal residence in Paris had no such protection, nor did Chenonceau, Montceaux or Saint-Maur-des-Fosses. Her effects were thus eventually sold off, which for all the posthumous humiliation involved, at least provides historians with plenty of information since the contents of her various homes, once the property of the woman who had for so long 'incarnated the grandeur of the French Crown', were carefully catalogued for sale and dispersal.[9]

Margot often wrote to Henri, giving her opinion of courtiers or councillors and on several occasions alerted her former husband to plots against him. Queen of nowhere and wife to no one, the last of the Valois lived the rest of her life to suit herself. She continued to take lovers, now much younger than she, and kept irregular hours; if a book pleased she would read it from cover to cover and not sleep until she had finished it. She would eat when hungry and not necessarily at appointed

---

* Margot's palace has since been destroyed. The present Académie Française stands just behind the site.

mealtimes. As the tool of her mother's and brothers' politics, she had finally earned the right to live according to her own timetable. Her health had been undermined by her adventures and exile; she suffered from appalling toothache and could only eat her food puréed. She had grown fat and jowly, physically resembling her mother more and more as she grew older. Gradually abandoning her glorious gowns, jewels and make-up, she adopted simpler clothes. Increasingly drawn to a more spiritual existence, Margot gave large sums of money to charity and religious orders and, much loved by the people, lived out the rest of her once-stormy life in relative contentment, dying in 1615.

Henri IV, the warm-hearted king famous for his love affairs and martial valour, whose natural sense of majesty did not obscure his personable traits, became one of the most popular monarchs in the whole of French history. He restored the country's economy with the aid of his trusted adviser the Duke de Sully, centralised French government and re-established a vigorous monarchy. The religious problems that had torn the country apart for forty years were settled by his Edict of Nantes of 1598, which allowed for the peaceful coexistence of Catholics and Protestants, and broadly mirrored the agreement of La Paix du Roi of 1577. Henri, with his mixture of warmth, simplicity and majesty, had the common touch necessary to make himself accessible to his people. He understood the basic requirements for their comfort, once famously remarking that a Frenchman should have a '*poule au pot*'* at least once a week. While centralising French government and administration, and re-establishing order, the founder of the Bourbon dynasty oversaw the birth of what is known by the French as the '*grande siècle*'. Tragically, Henri was assassinated in May 1610 by a Catholic zealot, François Ravaillac. By fighting to preserve the throne (albeit for her own sons) and the principle of legitimacy, Catherine de Medici – foreigner, consort and then beleaguered regent – had ensured the future of the French monarchy, at least until the revolution of 1789.

Time softened Henri's views on his long-dead former mother-in-law. Overhearing a group of courtiers blaming all the misfortunes of France upon the late Queen Mother, he is reported to have said, 'What could the poor woman do, with five children in her arms, after the death of her husband, and with two families in France – ours and the Guise – attempting to encroach on the Crown? Was she not forced to play strange parts to deceive the one and other and yet, as she did, to protect her children, who reigned in succession by the wisdom of a woman so able? I wonder that she did not do worse!'[10]

It was a valediction as wise as it was gracious.

---

* A chicken in his pot.

Conclusion

Catherine's death left people shocked and in a state of disbelief; she had been an ever-present feature in their lives since her arrival in France in 1533. Few Frenchmen could remember a time without her. The post-mortem might have shown that she died from pleurisy, but in fact her entire body had worn out. After her son's murderous attack on the Guises she was sapped of her will to continue. She had long known that only a miracle could now preserve the Valois dynasty, but she laboured on, ignoring the peril that her son seemed so wantonly to invite with each new folly, extravagantly casting away the fruits of her work both as Queen and Queen Mother.

Unbroken by the sensationally shocking death of her husband, Catherine bore her widowhood as her defining emblem; it signified that she had been wife and consort to Henry II, despite his often callous disregard for her. Their children, the Valois–Medici, were his dreadful legacy to her and to France. The thirty-year struggle since his death to preserve the kingdom for them became both her religion and her ideology. Her blinkered devotion to her sons, particularly Henri III, proved her greatest fault, but it also endowed her with her most important faculty, the fanatical determination that they must not lose their birthright. This, combined with her inability fully to appreciate their failings until it was too late, made her incapable of seeing how the odds were heaped against her. There is also a genuine sense by which Catherine wished to repay the honour that Francis I and Henry II had done her in making her – a Medici commoner – Queen of France, and she worked until her last breath to that end.

Short lives, of which the sixteenth century saw many, have intimations of tragedy, but long lives also have their own disappointments and *tristesses*. Of her ten children – her offerings to France – Catherine lived to see all but one of her sons die, and her sole surviving daughter utterly disgraced. Her courage was extraordinary, her wiliness and cunning legendary. Her optimism and energy defied the dark realities that surrounded her. Unlike her contemporary Elizabeth I, Catherine was not a sovereign in her own right and, more important, though blessed with great political talents, she lacked the gifted and great vision that the English Queen, a born stateswoman, possessed. Elizabeth's femininity was a formidable weapon, she could be cunning, but these were only part of her arsenal; she was academically Catherine's superior, and had no children to blur and blunt her judgement. As Henry VIII's daughter, Elizabeth had only one child – England.

Catherine was hampered by exceptional difficulties that the Tudor Queen did not have to face. Eight successive wars of religion that tore France apart, the last still unresolved as she died, nonetheless brought out the best in the Queen Mother. By necessity this almost constant state of stasis did not allow her the luxury of any long-term planning and her most significant attempt to do so had resulted in the Massacre of Saint Bartholomew. The best that she could do was to try to contain each conflagration as it arose; often this meant applying temporary measures to buy herself time because time, as she so often said, was her greatest ally.

Yet by 24 August 1572 time had almost run out for Catherine and the Valois. The massacre that took place that terrible night has, more than any other single action of her life, served to blacken her reputation before the bar of history. What had been intended as a relatively small-scale surgical operation designed to excise the canker in the heart of French politics, instead became a major crime against a significant number of French men, women and children, most of them innocent. Yet Catherine should be indicted primarily for a botched job, rather than judged according to twenty-first-century liberal principles of human rights and religious toleration, neither of which existed in sixteenth-century Paris. To make matters worse, Catherine's total inability to provide a convincing explanation for the Massacre, or to attempt to justify it even on *Realpolitik* grounds in a manner European opinion could understand, handed the political momentum to her enemies in the aftermath. Blunder com-pounded the crime. This was an unusual lacuna in Catherine, otherwise a skilled propagandist.

Elizabeth of England is believed to have once remarked: 'I would not open windows into men's souls.' Catherine behaved as though she would find no passionate beliefs there if she had tried. Her struggles to reconcile Protestants and Catholics were hampered by this want of imagination. The concept that deeply-held spiritual beliefs could be something men would die for was alien to her. Her overwhelming pragmatism and scepticism led her to attempt a practical solution for matters of faith; her efforts at the Colloquy of Poissy should be lauded as they spoke of an enlightened approach compared to burning people at the stake, although ultimately they proved futile. She knew also that the religious struggles served as a useful front for the political ambitions of the great houses of France, and for the over-mighty subjects who Henri II had raised so high that they threatened his own dynasty after his death.

If she did not recognize herself as a child of the Reformation, Catherine certainly thought of herself as a daughter of the Renaissance. Her love of building, probably inspired by the breathtaking châteaux built by Francis I, was often frustrated by lack of money, as a result of the endemic civil wars. La Colonne de l'Horoscope, formerly at the centre of the Hôtel de la Reine, is almost all that remains of her once ambitious and original projects, and is a poignant reminder of the fleeting nature of power. The Medici Queen's greatest Renaissance talent was, by its very nature, ephemeral. Her fabulous and unsurpassed 'magnificences' can be considered true works of art. The great painters, sculptors, poets and writers of the day played the central roles in creating these extraordinary spectacles. In them she brought together dance, song, acting and astonishingly complicated and beautiful settings. These performances were ingenious and no cost was spared in their production. They came to life for one brilliant occasion and then were dismantled forever. She carried her impresario's gift for these spectacles when making the official entries with her family into important towns around France. Their purpose was amply fulfilled; Catherine projected the glory of the monarchy both to her own people and to impress foreign visitors. The Renaissance ethos – that no matter how bad things really were, an awe-inspiring show must be put on – was one that the Queen Mother pursued, personified and perfected.

Catherine presented a powerful mixture of bold contradictions: she fought for her children yet could not be intimate with them; she did not comprehend religious passions though she held rigidly to the forms of the Roman Church and seemed baffled that anyone should feel the need to question them; she was a pragmatist racked by superstitious fears; she was majestic yet approachable, without once stepping off the high pedestal that her crown afforded her.

Catherine attracted brilliant and brave men to work for her, and inspired their loyalty. A staggering spendthrift, she found herself constantly beset by worries about the Treasury since her generosity was legendary. She could be feminine and strangely attractive though she worked, rode, hunted and faced mortal danger with the courage of a man. In an age dominated by men, she asked that no quarter be given on account of her sex. To paraphrase her Tudor contemporary, she had the heart and stomach of a king. She did not flinch from making difficult decisions, nor from executing them.

In the words of Machiavelli's *The Prince*, Catherine's epitaph should be, 'To be a great Prince one must sometimes violate the laws of humanity.'

As wife, mother, grandmother, regent and Queen of France she was a woman of action, appetites and excitement, both a great prince and a great woman.

Source Notes

Archives

Archives Nationales (Paris)
Archivio Capponi delle Rovinate (Florence) (ACRF)
Archivio di Stato di Firenzi (ASF)
Archivio Storico Italiano (ASI)
Biblioteca Nazionale Centrale di Firenzi (BNCF)
Bibliotèque Nationale (Paris)
Hatfield House Library and Archive

PROLOGUE: *Death of a King* [pp. 1–9]

1. Ralph Roederer, *Catherine de' Medici and the Lost Revolution*, London, 1937, p. 146.
2. State Papers/Elizabeth (Foreign Series) from Hugh Noel Williams, *Henry II: His Court and Times*, London, 1910, p. 430.
3. Antonia Fraser, *Mary, Queen of Scots*, London, 1969, p. 116.
4. Marguerite de Valois, *Mémoires*.
5. *Mémoires de Vieilleville* written by his secretary, Vincent Carloix.
6. Throckmorton.
7. Ibid.
8. Bishop of Troyes to Bishop of Bitonto from Williams, op. cit., p. 341.
9. Roederer, op cit., p. 164.
10. Ivan Cloulas, *Diane de Poitiers*, Paris, 1997, p. 303 and Abbé Pierre de Brantôme, *Receuil des Dames*.
11. Vincent Carloix, op. cit.
12. The accounts of Henry's accident and death are taken from several sources, though I have mainly used the letter from the Bishop of Troyes to the Bishop of Bitonto which can be found in Williams, op. cit., pp. 341–5.
13. Marguerite de Valois, *Mémoires* cited in Janine Garrison, *Marguerite de Valois*, 2000, p. 22.

ONE: *Orphan of Florence* [pp. 13–31]

1. Goro Gheri, Vol. I, 2nd ed., 1947, op. cit. ASF Minutario (15 April 1519) Vol. IV, folio 324, ACRF.
2. Edward Burman, *Italian Dynasties*, 1989, p. 146.
3. Christopher Hibbert, *The Rise and Fall of the House of Medici*, 1974, pp. 217–18.

4. Robert Knecht, *Catherine de' Medici*, 1998, p. 6.
5. Hibbert, op. cit., p. 235.
6. Archivio Capponi della Rovinate ACRF folder V, File II, doc. 76 dated 26 July 1522.
7. Ibid., ACRF II (B) folder III, docs. 146–8.
8. Bibliotecca Nazionale Centrale de Firenze, Coll. Palatino, 976, folio 77, RV.
9. Ibid.
10. Ivan Cloulas, *Catherine de Médicis*, Paris, 1979, p. 41.
11. BNCF, Coll. Palatino, 976, folio 77, RV.
12. Roederer, op. cit., p. 31.
13. BNCF, Coll. Palatino, 976, folio 77, RV.
14. Williams, op. cit., p. 68
15. Antonio Soriano, *La Diplomatie Venetienne*, Armand Baschet from Williams, op. cit., p. 68.
16. Roederer, op. cit., p. 36.
17. Ibid., p. 35.

TWO: *'The Greatest Match in the World'* [pp. 32–48]

1. Robert Knecht, *Renaissance Warrior and Patron The Reign of François Ier*, Cambridge, 1994, p. 243.
2. Ibid., p. 245 from the *Captivité de François Ier* by Champollion quoting the Frenchman President de Selve of the Parlement who was present in Madrid.
3. Williams, op. cit., p. 38.
4. Frederic Baumgartner, *Henry II King of France 1547–1599*, 1988, p. 160.
5. Knecht, op. cit., p. 256.
6. Baumgartner, op. cit., p. 18.
7. Ibid., pp. 19–22 and Williams, op. cit., from *Relations de l'Hussier Bodin*, Archives Générales de Belgique.
8. Knecht, *Catherine de' Medici*, 1998, p. 17.

THREE: *A Barren Wife* [pp. 49–69]

1. Jean Orieux, *Catherine de Médicis*, Paris, 1998, p. 117.
2. State Archive of Florence, Medici Aventi Principale (MAP), Doc. 197, folio 197, 1534.
3. Benedikt Taschen, *Châteaux of the Loire*, Cologne, Germany, 1997, p. 178.
4. Ibid., p. 180.
5. Baumgartner, op. cit., p. 133.
6. Orieux, op. cit., p. 115.
7. Edith Sichel, *Catherine de' Medici and the French Reformation*, London, 1905, pp. 37–9.
8. Orieux, op. cit., p. 155.
9. Bibliothèque Nationale Fonds Français, No. 3208, folio 13.
10. Cloulas, *Catherine de Médicis*, p. 71.
11. Williams, op. cit., p. 147 quoting Paradin.

12. Anne Somerset, *Elizabeth I*, London, 1992, p. 312.
13. Bibliothèque Nationale Fonds Français, No. 3120, folio 30.
14. Baumgartner, op. cit., p. 134.
15. Marechal de Vieilleville, *Mémoires*, as quoted in Williams, op. cit., p. 164.
16. Knecht, *Renaissance Warrior*, p. 541.
17. Williams, op. cit., p. 169.
18. Knecht, op. cit., p. 544.
19. Ibid., pp. 495–7.
20. Williams, op. cit., p. 171 quoting De Thou.
21. Ibid. quoting Saint-Mauris Imperial Ambassador despatch to Queen Dowager of Hungary, Governess of the Netherlands, May 1547.

FOUR: *The Eclipsed Consort* [pp. 70–92]

1. Roederer, op. cit., p. 70.
2. Willliams, op. cit., p. 168 quoting Baschet, *La Diplomatie Venetienne.*
3. Williams, op. cit., p. 168.
4. Ibid.
5. Roederer, op. cit., p. 60.
6. Ibid., p. 66.
7. Baumgartner, op. cit., p. 57.
8. Ibid., p. 55.
9. Williams, op. cit., p. 191.
10. Ibid., p. 192.
11. Ibid., p. 193.
12. Ibid., p. 200 quoting Vieilleville.
13. Ibid., p. 207 quoting Vieilleville.
14. Ibid., p. 209 quoting Vieilleville.
15. Mack P. Holt, *The French Wars of Religion 1562–1629*, 1995, p. 9.
16. Ibid.
17. Ibid.
18. Williams, op. cit., p. 216 quoting *La Diplomatie Venetienne.*
19. Baumgartner, op. cit., p. 56.
20. Sichel, op. cit., p. 45.
21. Williams, op. cit., p. 178.
22. Cloulas, *Catherine de Médicis*, p. 82.
23. Catherine de Medici, *Lettres*, Archives Nationales, 25 April 1584 de la Ferrière.
24. Knecht, op. cit., pp. 220–1 and 229–30.
25. Williams, op. cit., p. 222. See also Baumgartner, op. cit., pp. 134–5.
26. Cloulas, *Henri II*, 1985, pp. 229–30.
27. Ibid., p. 230.
28. Roederer, op. cit., p. 69.
29. Baumgartner, op. cit., p. 108.
30. Williams, op. cit., p. 234.

FIVE: *Catherine's Growing Importance* [pp. 93–117]

1. Baumgartner, op. cit., p. 68.
2. Fraser, op. cit., pp. 57–8.
3. Bibliothèque Nationale, *Lettres de Catherine de Medicis*, 15 May 1551.
4. Bibliothèque Nationale, Guiffrey, *Lettres de Diane de Poitiers*, p. 85.
5. Bibliothèque Nationale, Fonds Français, No. 3120, folio 79.
6. Ibid., No. 3208, folio 13, 23 August 1547.
7. Ibid., No. 3120, folio 27, 30 July 1547.
8. Ibid., folio 18, 3 May 1547.
9. Williams, op. cit., p. 241 quoting Guiffrey, *Lettres de Diane de Poitiers*.
10. Ibid.
11. Cloulas, *Henri II*, pp. 339–40 quoting from the despatches of the Ambassador Alvarotto of Ferrara; see also Cloulas, *Catherine de Médicis*, p. 89.
12. de Brantôme, op. cit.
13. Bibliothèque Nationale, *Lettres de Catherine de Medicis*; see also Williams, op. cit., p. 262, n. 2.
14. Baumgartner, op. cit., p. 143.
15. Cloulas, *Catherine de Médicis*, p. 97.
16. Bibliothèque Nationale, Fonds Français, No. 3129, folio 38.
17. Roederer, op. cit., p. 92.
18. Ibid., p. 94.
19. Knecht, *Catherine de' Medici*, p. 44 quoting Decrue, *Anne de Montmorency*, p. 115.
20. Cloulas, *Catherine de Médicis*, p. 111.
21. Roederer, op. cit., p. 5.
22. Bibliothèque Nationale, *Lettres et Mémoirs d'Estat*, t.II, p. 389, Ribier, 21, 21 April 1552.
23. Knecht, op. cit., p. 45 and Baumgartner, op. cit., p. 156.
24. Knecht, op. cit., p. 46.
25. Williams, op. cit., p. 283.
26. Baumgartner, op. cit., p. 176.
27. Ibid, p. 202.
28. Ibid., p. 200 quoting Soranzo.
29. Ibid., p. 203.
30. Fraser, op. cit., p. 101.
31. Cloulas, *Diane de Poitiers*, p. 278.
32. Baumgartner, op. cit., pp. 218–19, Michiel Venetian Ambassador.
33. Knecht, *Catherine de' Medici*, pp. 55–6.
34. Cloulas, *Henri II*, p. 582; also cited in Knecht, *Catherine de' Medici*, p. 56.
35. Roederer, op. cit., p. 137.
36. Baumgartner, op. cit., p. 227.
37. Williams, op. cit., pp. 338–9 quoting *La Place de l'Estate de la Religion et Republique*.
38. Ibid., p. 305.
39. Cloulas, *Diane de Poitiers*, p. 268.

40. Williams, op. cit., p. 310.
41. Ibid., p. 304 citing Brantôme, *Les Grandes Chasses aux XVI siècle*, La Ferrière.
42. Ibid., pp. 206–9.

SIX: *An Uneasy Partnership* [pp. 121–143]

1. Sichel, op. cit., p. 101.
2. Bibliothèque Nationale, *Lettres de Catherine de Médicis*, La Ferrière.
3. Williams, op. cit., p. 346, n 2 quoting *La Diplomatie Venetienne*.
4. Knecht, *Catherine de' Medici*, p. 232.
5. Williams, op. cit., p. 249 quoting Gabriello Simeoni, 1557.
6. Fraser, op. cit., pp. 92–3.
7. Ibid., p. 121.
8. Cloulas, *Catherine de Médicis*, p. 129.
9. Roederer, op. cit., p. 169.
10. Bibliothèque Nationale, Original, PRO, State Papers, France, 11 September 1559
11. Roederer, op. cit., p. 168.
12. Ibid., p. 169.
13. Knecht, *Catherine de' Medici*, p. 62.
14. Ibid., p. 63.
15. Ibid.
16. Ibid.
17. Fraser, op. cit., p. 129.
18. Bibliothèque Nationale, Fonds Français, No. 3294, folio 53.
19. Fraser, op. cit., p. 131.
20. Ibid.
21. Cloulas, *Catherine de' Médicis*, p. 147.
22. Knecht, *Catherine de' Medici*, p. 70.
23. Bibliothèque Nationale, Archives de Turin, end November 1560.

SEVEN. *'Gouvernante de France'* [pp. 144–162]

1. Orieux, *Catherine de Médicis ou la Reine Noire*, Paris, 1998, p 312.
2. Roederer, op. cit., p. 247.
3. Ibid.
4. Bibliothèque Nationale, Bibliothèque du Louvre original Collection Bourdin, folio 216, vol. 1, folio 194.
5. Roederer, op. cit., p. 259.
6. Sichel, op. cit., p. ?
7. Roederer, op. cit., p. 255.
8. Ibid., pp. 255–60.
9. Ibid., p. 277.
10. Ibid.
11. Fraser, op. cit., p. 149.
12. Ibid., p. 151.

13. Bibliothèque Nationale, Cinq Cents, Colbert, No. 390, folio 35.
14. Ibid.
15. Fraser, op. cit., p. 168.
16. Archives Nationales, Bibliothèque de Rouen, original Fond Leber, No. 5725.
17. Ibid.
18. Pierre Chevallier, *Henri III Roi Shakespearian*, Paris, 1985, p. 38.
19. Ibid.
20. Orieux, op. cit., p. 301.
21. Baumgartner, op. cit., p. 106.
22. Knecht, *Catherine de' Medici*, p. 76.
23. Ibid., p. 78.
24. Ibid., p. 79.
25. Ibid.
26. Ibid.
27. Chevallier, op. cit., pp. 40–1.
28. Knecht, *Catherine de' Medici*, p. 83.
29. Ibid.
30. Ibid., p. 85.
31. François de Bayrou, *Henri IV le Roi Libre*, Paris, 1994, p. 54.
32. Knecht, *Catherine de' Medici*, p. 85.

EIGHT: *The First Religious War* [pp. 163–180]

1. Cloulas, *Catherine de Médicis*, p. 171.
2. Orieux, op. cit., p. 313.
3. Ibid.
4. Bayrou, op. cit., p. 60.
5. Orieux, op. cit., p. 316.
6. Ibid., p. 319.
7. Ibid., p. 320.
8. Nicola M. Sutherland, *Princes, Politics and Religion 1547–1589*, 1984, pp. 148–9.
9. Knecht, *Catherine de' Medici*, p. 92.
10. Ibid.
11. Ibid.
12. Somerset, op. cit., p. 156.
13. Roederer, op. cit., p. 354.
14. Ibid.
15. Sutherland, op. cit., p. 38.
16. Orieux, op. cit., p. 337.
17. Sutherland, op. cit., p. 38.
18. Ibid.
19. Cloulas, *Catherine de Médicis*, p. 190.
20. Williams, op. cit., p. 296 quoting De Bouillon, *Mémoirs*.
21. Knecht, *Renaissance Warrior ...*, p. 123.
22. Ibid., p. 118.
23. Ibid.

24. Cloulas, *Catherine de Médicis*, pp. 190–1.
25. Ibid.

NINE: *The Grand Tour* [pp. 181–197]

1. Knecht, *Catherine de' Medici*, p. 99.
2. Ibid., p. 101.
3. Roederer, op. cit., p. 358.
4. Erica Cheetham, *The Final Prophecies of Nostradamus*, 1989, p. 29.
5. Ibid.
6. Michel Simonin, *Charles IX*, Paris, 1995, p. 136.
7. Cloulas, *Catherine de Médicis*, p. 207.
8. Roederer, op. cit., p. 358.
9. Ibid.
10. Knecht, *Catherine de' Medici*, p. 109.

TEN: *Conciliator No Longer* [pp. 198–223]

1. Roederer, op. cit., p. 379.
2. Cloulas, *Catherine de Médicis*, p. 224.
3. Ibid.
4. Sir Robert Cotton, *A Collection of the Most Memorable Events of the Last Hundred Years*, 1612, 2 vols, Hatfield House Archive.
5. Knecht, *Catherine de' Medici*, p. 113 quoting *Lettres* iii, pp. 58–9.
6. Roederer, op. cit., pp. 381–2.
7. Knecht, *Catherine de Medici*, p. 114 quoting BN ms.fr 3347 Bochefort to Renée of Ferrara cited by Hector de la Ferrière in *Lettres* iii.
8. Denis Crouzet, *La Nuit de Saint Barthélemy*, 1994, p. 295 cited in *Memoires de Henri de la Tour d'Auvergne dans Nouvelle collection des mémoires*, Paris, 1838.
9. Knecht, *Catherine de' Medici*, p. 118.
10. Roederer, op. cit., p. 390.
11. Ibid., p. 392.
12. Ibid.
13. Cloulas, *Catherine de Médicis*, p. 235.
14. Ibid.
15. Ibid., p. 234.
16. Knecht, *Catherine de' Medici*, p. 123.
17. Ibid. quoting *Lettres* iii, p. 178 (BN, ms.fr. 10752, 1463).
18. *Verro Libre della Cuccina Fiorentina*.
19. Cloulas, *Catherine de Médicis*, p. 240.
20. Ibid.
21. Orieux, op. cit., p. 431 and Cloulas, *Catherine de Médicis*, p. 241.
22. Knecht, *Catherine de Medici*, p. 125 cited in *Lettres* iii, pp. xxxvii-xxxviii.
23. Ibid, *Lettres*, iii, p. xl.
24. Cloulas, *Catherine de' Médicis*, p. 246.
25. Chevallier, op. cit., p. 114.

26. Roederer, op. cit., p. 413
27. Ibid.
28. Ibid.
29. Ibid., p. 414.
30. Knecht, *Catherine de' Medici*, p. 127 quoting *Lettres*, iii, p. 241.
31. Ibid., p. 129.
32. Cloulas, *Catherine de Médicis*, p. 251.
33. Chevallier, op. cit., p. 135.
34. Knecht, *Catherine de' Medici*, p. 131.
35. Ibid.
36. Ibid., p. 132 cited in N. Roelker, *Queen of Navarre*, pp. 332–5.
37. Ibid., p. 133, BN ms fr. 3193 p. 41 cited in *Lettres*, iii, p. lxv.
38. Ibid., p. 136 cited in *Lettres* iii, p. xvi.

ELEVEN: *Margot's Marriage Is Arranged* [pp. 224–247]

1. Cloulas, *Catherine de Médicis*, p. 263.
2. Alison Weir, *Elizabeth the Queen*, p. 275.
3. Roederer, op. cit., pp. 422–30.
4. Ibid., p. 423.
5. Ibid.
6. Knecht, *Catherine de' Medici*, p. 147 quoting Roelker, *Queen of Navarre*, p. 346.
7. Ibid., p. 347.
8. Cloulas, *Catherine de Médicis*, p. 268.
9. Ibid.
10. Ibid., p. 269.
11. Sutherland, op. cit., p. 178.
12. Cloulas, *Catherine de Médicis*, p. 276 and Orieux, op. cit., p. 465.
13. Knecht, *Catherine de' Medici*, p. 145 quoting Desjardins, *Negociations de la France avec la Toscane*, iii, p. 711.
14. Ibid., p. 148.
15. Weir, op. cit., p. 277.
16. Ibid., pp. 278–9.
17. Ibid., p. 279.
18. Ibid., p. 278.
19. Cloulas, *Catherine de Médicis*, p. 277.
20. Ibid., p. 278 and Roederer, op. cit., p. 432.
21. Knecht, *Catherine de Medici*, p. 148 quoting Roelker, op. cit., p. 368.
22. Roederer, op. cit., p. 432.
23. Ibid., p. 433.
24. Cloulas, *Catherine de Médicis*, p. 279.
25. Roederer, op. cit., p. 433.
26. Knecht, *Catherine de' Medici*, pp. 148–9 quoting Roelker, op. cit., pp. 372–4.
27. Ibid., p. 150 quoting Roelker, op. cit., p. 376.

TWELVE: *The Massacre* [pp. 248–272]

1. M W Freer, *Henry III King of France and Poland* Vol. 1/3, 1858, p. 131 quoting from *Mémoires de Gaspard de Tavannes, Maréchal de France*, ch. xxvii.
2. Ibid.
3. Ibid.
4. Ibid.
5. Liliane Crété, *Coligny*, Paris, 1985, p. 424.
6. Roederer, op. cit., p. 442.
7. Ibid., p. 444.
8. Freer, op. cit., p. 117 quoting from Dupuy, '*Discours de Henri III à une personne d'honneur et de qualité etant près de sa majesté à Cracovie sur les causes et motifs de la Saint Barthélemy*', MS Bib Imp, pp. 63, 68.
9. Roederer, op. cit., p. 442.
10. Freer, op. cit., p. 116 quoting from Dupuy, op. cit.
11. Ibid., pp. 116–17 quoting from Dupuy, op. cit.
12. Ibid., p. 118.
13. Roederer, op. cit., p. 447.
14. Freer, op. cit., p. 122 quoting from *Mémoires de l'Estat de France sous Charles IX*, p. 195.
15. Crété, op. cit., p. 426 citing Coligny to his wife, 18 August 1572 Bibliothèque de la Société de l'Histoire du Protestantisme Français II, pp. 4–7 and cited in Roederer, op. cit., p. 448.
16. Ibid., p. 427.
17. Freer, op. cit., p. 123 quoted in *L'Estoile Journal de Henri III Roy de France*, p. 45.
18. Crété, op. cit., p. 427.
19. Freer, op. cit., p. 134 quoting from Dupuy, op. cit., folios 63–8.
20. Cloulas, *Catherine de Médicis*, p. 286.
21. Roederer, op. cit., p. 454.
22. Cloulas, *Catherine de Médicis*, p. 286.
23. Roederer, op. cit., p. 452.
24. Ibid.
25. Crété, *Coligny*, p. 429 quoting from Memoirs of Luc Geizkoffer, translated from Latin by Edouard Fick, 1892, p. 50.
26. Cloulas, *Catherine de Médicis*, p. 289 citing from *Mémoires de Gaspard de Tavannes*.
27. Ibid.
28. Ibid., p. 290.
29. Freer, op. cit., p. 138.
30. Crété, op. cit., p. 431 quoting from *Mémoires de l'Estat de France sous Charles IX*, folio 208.
31. Ibid.
32. Account of Coligny's death from Crété, op. cit., pp. 430–3 citing from List Sources Chapter 19 note 70 and Agrippa d'Aubigné, Histoire Universelle.
33. Roederer, op. cit., p. 447 and Marguerite de Valois, *Mémoires*.
34. Ibid., p. 457 quoting from Marguerite de Valois, *Mémoires*.

35. Ibid., p. 461 quoting from Marguerite de Valois, *Mémoires.*
36. Ibid., p. 463.

THIRTEEN: *The Last Years of Charles IX* [pp. 273–301]

1. Roederer, op. cit., p. 475.
2. Ibid., p. 495.
3. Ibid., p. 496.
4. Somerset, op. cit. 274.
5. Roederer, op. cit., p. 480 quoting from Marguerite de Valois, *Mémoires.*
6. Bayrou, op. cit., pp. 154–5.
7. Knecht, *Catherine de' Medici,* p. 164.
8. Ibid., p. 168.
9. Roederer, op. cit., p. 500.
10. Ibid., pp. 500–1.
11. Chevallier, op. cit., p. 198.
12. Knecht, *Catherine de' Medici,* p. 170 quoting from Groen Van Prinstere, *Archives ou correspondance inédites de la Maison d'Orange-Nassau,* first series (Leiden 1835–96), iv, p. 279.
13. Cloulas, *Catherine de Médicis,* pp. 334–5.
14. Ibid., p. 336.
15. Freer, op. cit., p. 241.
16. Roederer, op. cit., pp. 509–10.
17. Ibid., p. 510.
18. Ibid., p. 511.

FOURTEEN: *Henri III, King of France* [pp. 302–332]

1. Cloulas, *Catherine de Médicis,* p. 315 and Knecht, *Catherine de' Medici,* pp. 172–3, cited in *Lettres,* iv, pp. 311–12.
2. Cloulas, *Catherine de Médicis,* p. 316.
3. Ibid., and Knecht, *Catherine de' Medici,* pp. 172–3 cited in *Lettres* iv, pp. 311–12.
4. Freer, op. cit., p. 334.
5. Chevallier, op. cit., p. 233.
6. Knecht, *Catherine de' Medici,* p. 175.
7. Marguérite of France, Duchess of Savoy, Catherine's friend and sister-in-law, died shortly after Henri left Turin on his journey back to France from Poland.
8. Knecht, *Catherine de' Medici,* p. 175.
9. Freer, op. cit., p. 384 quoting from Mathieu, *Histoire du Regne de Henri III* livre vii, p. 402. *L'arrivée du Roy en France et sa Réception pour sa Mère. Sommaire Discours des choses survenues,* 8 vols., Paris, 1574.
10. Chevallier, op. cit., p. 264.
11. Ibid., p. 265.
12. Knecht, *Catherine de' Medici,* p. 176 and *Lettres* v, pp. 73–5.

13. Ibid.
14. Roederer, op. cit., p. 518.
15. Ibid., p. 519.
16. Chevallier, op. cit., p. 266.
17. Ibid.
18. Knecht, *Catherine de' Medici*, p. 177.
19. Ibid.
20. Jean H. Mariéjol, *Catherine de Médicis*, Paris, 1920, p. 262.
21. Bayrou, op. cit., p. 174 quoting from Marguerite de Valois, *Mémoires*.
22. Ibid., p. 176 citing from letter from Henri de Navarre 2 January 1576 to Jean de Miossens. See also Knecht, *Catherine de' Medici*, p. 181.
23. Knecht, *Catherine de Medici*, p. 181.
24. Mariéjol, op. cit., p. 267 citing from *Lettres* v, pp. 176–7.
25. Cloulas, *Catherine de Médicis*, p. 389.
26. Garrisson, op. cit., p. 117.

FIFTEEN: *Alençon's Treachery* [pp. 333–351]

1. Roederer, op. cit., p. 539.
2. Knecht, *Catherine de' Medici*, p. 189 citing from *Lettres* v, p. 348 and Cloulas, *Catherine de Médicis*, p. 403.
3. Mariéjol, op. cit., p. 274.
4. Cloulas, *Catherine de Médicis*, p. 405–6.
5. Knecht, *Catherine de' Medici*, p. 190.
6. Roederer, op. cit., p. 247.
7. Cloulas, *Catherine de Médicis*, p. 422 and Knecht, *Catherine de' Medici*, p. 196 quoting from *Lettres* vi p. 325.
8. Knecht, *Catherine de' Medici*, p. 194 quoting *Lettres* vi, pp. 38–9.
9. Cloulas, *Catherine de Médicis*, p. 424.
10. Ibid., p. 423.
11. Cloulas, *Catherine de Médicis*, p. 424 and Knecht, *Catherine de Medici*, p. 197.
12. Ibid., and Knecht, *Catherine de' Medici*, p. 197 quoting *Lettres* vi, p. 381.
13. Ibid., p. 430 and Roederer, op. cit., p. 547 and Knecht, *Catherine de' Medici*, p. 200 quoting *Lettres* vii, p. 134.
14. Knecht, *Catherine de' Medici*, p. 193.
15. Weir, op. cit., p. 284.
16. Ibid.
17. Knecht, *Catherine de' Medici*, p. 196 quoting *Lettres* vi, p. 337.
18. Somerset, op. cit., p. 310.
19. Ibid., p. 313.
20. Mariéjol, op. cit., p. 319 citing from *Lettres* missives de Henri IV i, p. 528.
21. Cloulas, *Catherine de Médicis*, p. 440.
22. Mariéjol, op. cit., p. 319.
23. Cloulas, *Catherine de Médicis*, pp. 440–1. See also Knecht, *Catherine de' Medici*, p. 202 quoting from *Lettres* vii, pp. 252–3.
24. Holt, op. cit., p. 117.

25. Cloulas, *Catherine de Médicis*, p. 442.
26. Knecht, *Catherine de' Medici*, p. 207.
27. Ibid., p. 204 and Mariéjol, op. cit., pp. 322–3.
28. Somerset, op. cit., pp. 327–80.
29. Ibid., p. 329.
30. Ibid.
31. Cloulas, *Catherine de Médicis*, p. 471.
32. Ibid.
33. Knecht, *Catherine de' Medici*, p. 213.
34. Cloulas, *Catherine de Médicis*, p. 466.
35. Ibid., p. 469.
36. Ibid.
37. Ibid., p. 482 and Knecht, *Catherine de' Medici*, p. 217.

SIXTEEN: *Hope Dies* [pp. 352–380]

1. Roederer, op. cit., p. 553.
2. Ibid., p. 558.
3. Ibid., p. 554.
4. Knecht, *Catherine de' Medici*, p. 247.
5. Ibid., p. 250.
6. Mariéjol, op. cit., p. 386 quoting from *Lettres*, 27 April 1585, vol. viii, p. 265.
7. Ibid., quoting from *Lettres*, 15 June 1585, p. 318 and Knecht, *Catherine de' Medici*, p. 254, citing *Lettres* viii, p. 318.
8. Knecht, *Catherine de' Medici*, p. 254 citing *Lettres* ix, p. 513.
9. Cloulas, *Catherine de Médicis*, p. 527.
10. Somerset, op. cit., p. 434.
11. Ibid., p. 436.
12. Marjorie Bowen, *Mary Queen of Scots*, 1971, pp. 255–7.
13. Cloulas, *Catherine de Médicis*, p. 530.
14. Roederer, op. cit., p. 569.
15. Mariéjol, op. cit., p. 393 citing *Lettres*, 12 December 1587, ix, p. 312
16. Roederer, op. cit., p. 570, Cavriani to Florentine Court.
17. Chevallier, op. cit., p. 616.
18. Mariéjol, op. cit., p. 394 citing *Lettres* ix, p. 334.
19. Chevallier, op. cit., p. 616.
20. Ibid. and Knecht, *Catherine de' Medici*, p. 259.
21. Roederer, op. cit., p. 574 and Chevallier, op. cit., p. 628 and Mariéjol, op. cit., p. 395.
22. Chevallier, op. cit., p. 628.
23. Ibid., p. 630.
24. Roederer, op. cit., p. 581.
25. Ibid., p. 583 and Chevallier, op. cit., p. 638.
26. Roederer, op. cit., p. 584.
27. Ibid., p. 587.
28. Ibid., p. 588 and Knecht, *Catherine de' Medici*, p. 263 citing *Lettres* ix, p. 368.

29. Mariéjol, op. cit., p. 400 citing *Lettres* ix, p. 382 and Knecht, *Catherine de' Medici*, p. 264.
30. Roederer, op. cit., p. 292 and Knecht, *Catherine de' Medici*, p. 264 citing *Lettres* ix, p. 382.
31. Chevallier, op. cit., p. 670.
32. Ibid.

SEVENTEEN: *So Perish the Race of the Valois* [pp. 381–392]

1. Cloulas, *Catherine de Médicis*, p. 602.
2. Knecht, *Catherine de' Medici*, p. 268.
3. Ibid., pp. 268–9 and Cloulas, *Catherine de Médicis*, p. 603.
4. Ibid., p. 269 and Cloulas, *Catherine de Médicis*, p. 603.
5. Alistair Horne, *Seven Ages of Paris*, 2002, p. 78.
6. Ibid., p. 85.
7. Ibid., p. 87.
8. Ibid., p. 95.
9. Cloulas, *Catherine de Médicis*, p. 607.
10. Roederer, op. cit., p. 614.

Bibliography

All works are published in Paris unless otherwise stated.

Biographies of Catherine

Albèri, Eugenio, *Vita de Caterina de Medici*, Florence, 1838
Capefigue, M., *Catherine de Médicis: Mère des Rois François II, Charles IX et Henri III*, 1861
Cloulas, Ivan, *Catherine de Médicis*, 1979
De Castelnau, Jacques, *Catherine de Médicis*, 1954
De Lacombe, Bernard, *Catherine de Médicis: Entre Guise et Condé*, 1899
De Meneval, M., *Catherine de Médicis 1519–1589*, 1880
De Reumont, A., *Catherine de Médicis*, 1866
Héritier, Jean, *Catherine de Médicis*, 1940
Knecht, R. J., *Catherine de' Medici*, London, 1998
Mahoney, Irene, *Madame Catherine*, London, 1976
Mariéjol, J.H., *Catherine de Médicis 1519–1589*, 1920
Neale, J. E., *The Age of Catherine de' Medici*, London, 1943
Orieux, Jean, *Catherine de Médicis ou La Reine Noire*, 1986
Roederer, Ralph, *Catherine de' Medici and the Lost Revolution*, London, 1937
Romier, Lucien, *Le Royaume de Catherine de Médicis: La France à la Vielle des Guerres de Religion*, 2 vols, 1922
Sichel, Edith, *Catherine de' Medici and the French Reformation*, London, 1905
——*The Later Years of Catherine de' Medici*, London, 1908
Trollope, T. A., *The Girlhood of Catherine de' Medici*, 1856
Van Dyke, Paul, *Catherine de' Médicis*, 2 vols, London, 1923
Waldman, Milton, *Biography of a Family: Catherine de' Medici and her Children*, London, 1934
Watson, Francis, *The Life and Times of Catherine de' Medici*, London, 1937

Books and Articles

Acton, Harold, *The Last Medici*, London, 1958
Adamson, John, ed., *The Princely Courts of Europe 1500–1750*, London, 1999
Ariés, Phillippe and Duby, Georges, *Histoire de la Vie Privée*, 1985
Arnold, Janet, ed., *Queen Elizabeth's Wardrobe Unlock'd*, London, 1988

Baillie Cochrane, Dr. A. W. *Francis I*, 2 vols, London, 1870
Baldwin Smith, Lacey, *The Elizabethan Epic*, London 1966

Baudouin-Matuszek, M. N., ed., *Paris et Catherine de Médicis*, n.d.

Baumgartner, Frederic J., *Henri II: King of France 1547–1559*, London, 1988

Bayrou, François, *Henry IV: Le Roi Libre*, 1994

Bély, Lucien, ed., *Dictionnaire de l'Ancien Régime*, 1996

Bennassar, Bartolomé, *Histoire des Espagnols*, 1985

Bennassar, Bartolomé and Jacquart, Jean, *Le XVIe Siècle*, 1997

Bertière, Simone, *Les Reines de France au Temps des Valois*, 1994

Bostrum, Antonia, *Equestrian Statue of Henri II commissioned by Catherine de Medici 1561–65/6*, Burlington Magazine, December 1995

Bourdeille, Pierre de, Abbé de Brantôme, *The Lives of Gallant Ladies*, London, 1965

Bowen, Marjorie, *Mary, Queen of Scots*, London, 1971

Bradley, C. C., *Western World Costume*, London, 1954

Braudel, Fernand, *The Identity of France*, vol.2, London, 1990

——*Out of Italy*, 1989

Briggs, Robin, *Early Modern France 1560–1715*, Oxford, 1977

Bullard, Melissa, *Filippo Strozzi and the Medici*, Cambridge, 1980

Burman, Edward, *The Italian Dynasties*, London, 1989

Cameron, Euan, ed., *Early Modern Europe*, Oxford, 1999

Cardini, Franco (introduction), *The Medici Women*, Florence, 1993

Carroll, Stuart, *Noble Power during the French Wars of Religion: The Guise Affinity and the Catholic Cause in Normandy*, Cambridge, 1989

Castelot, André, *Marie de Médicis: Le Désordres de la Passion*, 1995

——*Diane, Henri, Catherine: Le Triangle Royal*, 1997

——*La Reine Margot*, 1993

Chastel, André, *French Art The Renaissance 1430–1562*, 1995

Cheetham, Erika, *The Final Prophecies of Nostradamus*, London, 1989

Cherubini, Giovanni and Fanelli, Giovanni, *Il Palazzo Medici Riccardi di Firenzi*, Florence, 1990

Chevalier, L'Abbé C., *Debtes et Créanciers de la Royne Mère Catherine de Médicis 1589–1606*, 1862

Chevallier, Pierre, *Henri III, Roi Shakespearian*, 1985

Cloulas, Ivan, *La Vie Quotidienne dans les Châteaux de la Loire au temps de la Renaissance*, 1983

——*Henri II*, 1985

——*Philip II*, 1992

——*Diane de Poitiers*, 1997

Codacci, L., *Caterina de' Medici: le ricette di una regina*, Lucca, 1995

Constant, Jean-Marie, *La Ligue*, 1996

Cosgrave, Bronwyn, *Costumes and Fashion: A Complete History*, London, 2000

Cotton, Sir Robert, *A Collection of the Most Memorable Events of the Last Hundred Years*, 2 vols., 1612

Crété, Liliane, *Coligny*, 1985

Crouzet, Denis, *La Nuit de la Saint-Barthélemy: Un Rêve Perdu de la Renaissance*, 1994

Darcy, Robert, *Le Duel: Le Duc de Guise contre L'Amiral de Coligny*, Dijon, 1979

Davis, Natalie Zemon, *The Gift in Sixteenth Century France*, London, 2000

De la Mar, Jensen, *Catherine de Medici and Her Florentine Friends*, Sixteenth Century *Journal*, 9 February 1978, pp. 57–79

——*French Diplomacy and the Wars of Religion*, Sixteenth Century *Journal*, 5 February 1974, pp. 23–46

De Negroni, Barbara, *Intolérances, Catholiques et Protestants en France 1560–1787*, 1996

Doran, Susan, *Elizabeth I, Gender, Power and Politics*, History Today, May 2003, pp. 29–37

Duffy, Eamon, *Saints and Sinners: A History of the Popes*, Yale, 1997

Dunn, Jane, *Elizabeth and Mary*, London, 2003

Elton, G. R., *England Under the Tudors*, London, 1974

England, Sylvia Lennie, *The Massacre of Saint Bartholemew* 1938

Erlanger, Philippe, *St Bartholemew's Night: The Massacre of Saint Bartholemew* 1962

Ferrière, de la, Hector and Baguenault de Puchesse, eds., *Lettres de Catherine de Médicis*, 10 vols., 1880–1909

Fichtner, Paula Stuter, *Emperor Maximillian II*, London, 2001

Fierro, Alfred, *Histoire et Dictionnaire de Paris*, 1996

Fraser, Antonia, *Mary, Queen of Scots*, London, 1970

Freer, Martha Walker, *Henry III, King of France and Poland: His Court and Times*, 3 vols., London, 1858

Gabel, Leonie C., *Secret Memoirs of a Renaissance Pope: The commentaries of Aeneas Sylvius Piccolomini Pius II*, 1788

Gambino, Luigi, *Regno de Francia e papato nella polemica sul Concilio di Trento (1582–1584)*, Il Pensiero Politico 8 (2), 1975, pp. 133–59

Garrisson, Janine, *Marguerite de Valois*, 1994

——*Henri IV, le Roi et la Paix (1553–1610)*, 1984

——*Tocsin pour un massacre ou la saison des Saint-Barthélemy*, 1968

Gheri, Goro, *Copialettere*, vol. iv, folio 324, ASF

Gorsline, D. W., *History of Fashion*, London, 1953

Goubert, Pierre, *Initiation à l'Histoire de la France*, 1984

Hackett, Francis, *Francis I*, London, 1934

Hale, J. R., *The Thames and Hudson Dictionary of the Italian Renaissance*, London, 1981

Hall, Peter, *Cities in Civilization*, London, 1998

Hartnell, Norman, *Royal Courts of Fashion*, London, 1971

Hibbert, Christopher, *The Rise and Fall of the House of Medici*, London, 1974

——*Florence: The Biography of a City*, London, 1993

——*The Rise and Fall of the Medici Bank*, History Today, August 1974

Holt, Mack P., *The French Wars of Religion 1562–1629*, Cambridge, 1995

Horne, Alistair, *Seven Ages of Paris – Portrait of a City*, London, 2002

Jenkins, Elizabeth, *Elizabeth the Great*, London, 1958

Johnson, Paul, *Elizabeth: a study in Power and Intellect*, London, 1998

——*The Renaissance*, London, 2000

Jouanna, Arlette, Hamon, Philippe, Biloghi, Dominique and Le Thiece, Guy, *La France de la Renaissance*, London, 2000

Kelly, Francis, M. and Schwabe, Randolph, *Historical Costume 1490–1790*, London, 1929

Kent, HRH Princess Michael of, *Cupid and the King: Five Royal Paramours*, London, 1991

Kingdon, Robert M., *Myths about the St Bartholemew's Day Massacre 1572–6* Cambridge, Mass., 1988

Koenigsberger, H. G., Mosse, George L. and Bowler, G. Q., *Europe in the Sixteenth Century*, London, 1991

Knecht, R. J., *Renaissance Warrior and Patron: The Reign of François I*, Cambridge, 1994

——*Francis I (1515–1547)* 1982

La Ferrière, Hector de, *La Saint-Barthélemy* Paris 1895

Lang, Jack, *François Ier ou le Rêve Italien*, 1997

Lebrun, François, *La Vie Conjugale sous l'Ancien Régime*, 1975

Letherington, John, ed., *Years of Renewal: European History 1470–1600*, London, 1988

LSE, *The Letters of Marcilio Ficino*, vol. vi, London, 1999

Machiavelli, Niccolò, *The Prince*, London, 1975

Martinez, Lauro, *April Blood – Florence and the plot against the Medici*, London, 2003

Melot, Michel, *Châteaux of the Loire*, Cambridge, 1997

Mignani, Daniela, *The Medicean Villas by Guisto Utens*, 1991

Milne-Tyte, Robert, *Armada*, Ware, 1998

Miquel, Pierre, *Histoire de la France*, 1976

Montaigne, Michel de, *The Complete Essays*, London, 1991

Motley, Mark, *Becoming a French Aristocrat: The Education of the Court Nobility 1580–1715*, Princeton, 1990

Murray, Linda, *The High Renaissance and Mannerism*, London, 1977

Murray, Peter and Linda, *The Art of the Renaissance*, London, 1997

Nognères, Henri, *The Massacre of Saint Bartholemew* 1962

Parker, Geoffrey, *The Grand Strategy of Philip II*, Yale, 1998

Pieraccini, Gaetano, *La stirpe dei Medici de Cafaggiolo*, Florence, 1947

Rowse, A. L., *The Elizabethan Epic: The Life of the Society*, London, 1971

Salimbeni, Gherardo Bartolini, *Chronicles of the Last Actions of Lorenzo, Duke of Urbino*, Florence, 1786

Salmon, J. H., *Marie de Médicis as Queen and Regent of France, History Today*, May 1963

Shannon, Sara, ed., *Various Styles of Clothing*, James Ford Bell Library, 2001

Simonin, Michel, *Charles IX*, 1995

Smith, Lacey Baldwin, *The Elizabethan Epic*, London, 1966

Solnon, Jean-François, *La Cour de France*, 1987

——*Henri III: Un Désir de Majesté*, 2001

Soman, Alfred, ed., *The Massacre of St Batholemew: Reappraisals and Documents* 1974

Somerset, Anne, *Elizabeth I*, London, 1992

Starkey, David, *Elizabeth: Apprenticeship*, London, 2000

Stephens, J. N., *L'Infanzia Fiorentina di Caterina de Medici regina di Francia* (ASI) 1984

Sutherland, Nicola M., *Princes, Politics and Religion*, London, 1984

Tenent, Alberto, *La Francia, Venezia, e la Sacra Lega*, pp. 398–408 in Benzoni, G., ed., *Il Mediterraneo nella seconda metà del '500 alla luce de Lepanto*, Florence, 1973

Voisin, Jean-Louis, ed., *Dictionnaire des Personnages Historiques*, 1995

Volkmann, Jean-Charles, *Les Généalogies des Rois de France*, 1996

Walsh, Michael, ed., *The Papacy*, New York, 1997

Ward, A. W. and Prothero, G. W. and Leathes, S., *The Cambridge Modern History*, vol. II, *The Reformation*, vol. III, *The Wars of Religion*, Cambridge, 1907

Weir, Alison, *Children of England: The Heirs of Henry VIII*, London, 1997

——*Elizabeth the Queen*, London, 1998

White, Henry, *The Massacre of St Bartholemew* 1868

Williams, E. N., *The Penguin Dictionary of English and European History 1485–1789*, London, 1980

Williams, Hugh Noel, *Henry II: His Court and Times*, London, 1910

Yarwood, Doreen, *Costume of the Western World*, London, 1980

Young, Colonel G. F., *The Medici*, 2 vols., London, 1909

Index